Weaving a Lexicon

Weaving a Lexicon

edited by D. Geoffrey Hall and Sandra R. Waxman

A Bradford Book

The MIT Press, Cambridge, Massachusetts, London, England

This book was set in New Baskerville on 3B2 by Asco Typesetters, Hong Kong. Printed and bound in the United States of America.

Library of Congress Cataloging-in-Publication Data

Weaving a lexicon / edited by D. Geoffrey Hall and Sandra R. Waxman.
    p.   cm.
"A Bradford Book"
Includes bibliographical references and index.
ISBN 0-262-08323-X (hc. : alk. paper) — ISBN 0-262-58249-X (pbk. : alk. paper)
    1. Language acquisition. 2. Lexicology. I. Hall, D. Geoffrey. II. Waxman, Sandra R.
P118.W367   2004
401′.93—dc22   2003060055

10 9 8 7 6 5 4 3 2 1

Contents

Contents

Contributors

Nameera Akhtar
University of California, Santa Cruz

Dare A. Baldwin
University of Oregon

Paul Bloom
Yale University

Kyle E. Chambers
University of Illinois

Barbara A. Church
S.U.N.Y. at Buffalo

Catharine H. Echols
University of Texas at Austin

Ann R. Eisenberg
University of Texas at San Antonio

Christopher Fennell
University of British Columbia

Cynthia Fisher
University of Illinois

Susan A. Gelman
University of Michigan

Dedre Gentner
Northwestern University

Henry Gleitman
University of Pennsylvania

Lila R. Gleitman
University of Pennsylvania

Susan Goldin-Meadow
University of Chicago

Roberta Michnick Golinkoff
University of Delaware

D. Geoffrey Hall
University of British Columbia

Etsuko Haryu
University of Tokyo

Elizabeth A. Hennon
Temple University

Kathy Hirsh-Pasek
Temple University

Jill M. Hohenstein
Yale University

Mutsumi Imai
Keio University

Vikram K. Jaswal
Stanford University

Contributors

Barbara Landau
Johns Hopkins University

Tracy A. Lavin
University of British Columbia

Jeffrey Lidz
Northwestern University

Mandy J. Maguire
Temple University

Ellen M. Markman
Stanford University

C. Nathan Marti
University of Texas at Austin

Letitia R. Naigles
University of Connecticut

Laura L. Namy
Emory University

Mark A. Sabbagh
Queen's University

Megan M. Saylor
University of Oregon

Jesse Snedeker
Harvard University

Sandra R. Waxman
Northwestern University

Janet F. Werker
University of British Columbia

Amanda L. Woodward
University of Chicago

Weaving an Introduction

D. Geoffrey Hall and Sandra R. Waxman

Infants and young children naturally and spontaneously acquire the lexicon of their native language. This accomplishment is a topic of central interest in the cognitive sciences, because it raises core questions in psychology, linguistics, philosophy, computer science, and related fields. The past several years have witnessed an impressive accumulation of new knowledge about the learning of words. Recent discoveries in developmental psychology have been especially noteworthy, because they have helped to illuminate a process that is inherently multidimensional and dynamic.

In this edited volume, we invoke the metaphor of weaving to consider the acquisition of a lexicon. It has become clear that, to succeed in this task, learners weave together many different threads of knowledge and skill. These strands include perceptual (visual and auditory) sensitivities, general associative-learning mechanisms, conceptual and semantic constraints, an appreciation of lexical form class, and a rich understanding of communicative intent. It has also become evident that children do not intertwine these strands in a uniform fashion over the course of infancy and childhood, resulting in a flat weave. On the contrary, the evidence reveals much more texture to the fabric of word learning, with children recruiting some abilities and understandings more heavily at some developmental points than at others.

Like infants and toddlers acquiring their native lexicon, developmental psychologists seeking to understand word learning must also become adept at weaving. For the field to progress, researchers must move beyond cataloging the isolated strands of knowledge or skill that learners use in any given act of word learning. In particular, it has become important that we abandon "either-or" approaches, in which a single thread is held to explain word learning from infancy throughout childhood. At the same time, we must progress beyond "all-inclusive" approaches, in which multiple strands are invoked in ways that fail to generate falsifiable hypotheses about lexical development. We believe that breakthroughs in theories of word learning await the discovery of precisely *which* threads of ability or understanding make *which* contributions to acquisition at *which* points during infancy and childhood.

This volume brings together chapters written by leading scholars in the field of lexical acquisition. Each contribution focuses directly on one or more of the various strands of knowledge or skill that underpin lexical development in infancy and childhood (e.g., perceptual abilities, lexical form class sensitivities, social-pragmatic understanding). Although the authors have centered their chapters primarily on the results of their own research programs, they have also considered explicitly how their work fits into the emerging picture of lexical acquisition as a multidimensional, dynamic task. As a result, the volume contains many chapters that explore the interactions among multiple threads of skill or knowledge at a specific point in development, and/or the unfolding of children's reliance on a particular thread over the course of development.

Chapter Outline

The chapters in this volume resist being divided according to simple themes. This is a testament to the authors' success in moving beyond static, one-dimensional positions. Yet the very richness of the authors' arguments presented us with an organizational dilemma. In response, we have divided the chapters into two primary sections that mirror, however imperfectly, research in the field of word learning. The breakdown reflects a rough distinction between chapters that focus on issues surrounding *initial acquisitions* (often containing research with infant participants) and those that emphasize topics surrounding *later acquisitions* (often containing research with toddler and preschooler participants). This partitioning reflects more than just subject populations. It also reflects a range of theoretical commitments within the field. Some scholars devote their primary attention to characterizing the initial state of the learner, whereas others dwell more substantively on the description and explanation of subsequent development. However, there is no doubt that the two sections contain many crosscutting themes.

Part I: Initial Acquisitions

The ten chapters in this section focus primarily on issues that arise during the earliest period of word learning.

1. How do learners represent the sound patterns of words? Fisher, Church, and Chambers defend the argument that these representations contain very fine phonetic information, contrary to traditional "abstractionist" views of lexical representation.

2. How do infants solve the fundamental problems of identifying words and their meanings? Echols and Marti point out important commonalities between children's solutions to the two problems: in both cases, children use general cues and subsequently identify and rely on language-specific cues.

3. Why is it hard for infants to use language-specific phonetic detail to map sounds to meanings? Werker and Fennell develop the argument that this difficulty reflects resource limitations, and they raise the suggestion that there is continuity between prelexical categories and the representations available for use in word learning.

4. What role does perceptual information play in grounding representations of early word meanings? Landau argues that there is a complex mapping between perception and naming in the case of both objects and object parts. She explores the implications of this proposal for the linkages between nonlinguistic and linguistic representations.

5. How is an understanding of human intentions brought to bear in early word learning? Woodward proposes that words are not merely disembodied associates for young infants. Rather, she defends the view that from the outset, infants use their developing understanding of intentional action to interpret words.

6. What underlies changes to the character of word learning during the first two years? Hirsh-Pasek, Golinkoff, Hennon, and Maguire discuss the emergentist coalition model, arguing that word learners recruit different sources of knowledge (constraints, social-pragmatic understanding, and associative abilities) as the task of acquiring a lexicon unfolds during this period of development.

7. How do young children's general cognitive abilities work together to foster word learning? Bloom presents a theory that stresses the importance of several capacities—conceptual abilities, theory of mind, and grammatical form class sensitivity—in early word learning.

8. What can the study of learners who lack a conventional model for language tell us about the nature of the early lexicon? Goldin-Meadow presents evidence that the gesture systems of these learners contain categories that function like nouns, verbs, and adjectives. The results suggest that these categories are foundational in natural languages.

9. What underlies widely observed changes in children's lexicons during the first years of life? Snedeker and Gleitman propose that these changes stem from children's growing command of the semantically relevant syntax of their language. They use their proposal to account not only for the noun dominance in early vocabularies, but also for the concreteness of children's early verbs.

10. What is the origin and evolution of the links between words and meanings? Waxman demonstrates that infants begin the task of word learning equipped with a broad expectation linking novel words to a wide range of commonalities among named objects, and that this serves as the foundation for the more finely tuned expectations linking particular types of words (e.g., nouns, adjectives) with particular types of meaning (e.g., object categories, object properties).

Part II: Later Acquisitions

The nine chapters in this section deal with questions that surface as children begin to master mappings between words from particular lexical categories and their meanings.

11. How does preschoolers' knowledge of part-of-speech to meaning mappings interact with their word-learning assumptions to promote word learning? Hall and Lavin develop the argument that these assumptions play a fundamental role in helping children acquire sensitivity to how part-of-speech categories are expressed in their language.

12. How do children recruit word-learning constraints, semantic information, and syntactic information in lexical development? Markman and Jaswal address this question by examining the learning of the distinction between proper names and count nouns. In their chapter, they focus on how lexical form class to meaning distinctions are first learned and subsequently put to use to foster lexical acquisition, and on how the ostensive learning of words compares to the indirect or inferential learning of words.

13. How can the crosslinguistic study of the acquisition of nominals (proper names and common nouns) shed light on the mechanisms that underlie word learning? Imai and Haryu review their research on word learning in Japanese-speaking preschoolers. They argue that this work helps to clarify not only the nature of proposed word-learning biases, but also the universality and flexibility of word-learning processes.

14. What types of knowledge do children recruit in the task of learning generic noun phrases (words that designate object kinds)? Gelman proposes that children draw on multiple sources of knowledge (syntactic, pragmatic, and general world knowledge) to acquire generic language, and that generic language itself supports children's acquisition of generic knowledge.

15. Why are young children so successful at acquiring words (nouns, verbs, adjectives) in a wide variety of learning contexts? Akhtar argues that young children succeed so well because they are attuned to a number of pragmatic cues to intended meaning.

16. How do word-learning constraints and pragmatic knowledge interact in lexical development? Saylor, Baldwin, and Sabbagh address this question by focusing on the relation between children's word-learning skills (their ability to acquire nouns for object parts) and the input they receive (whole- versus part-label juxtaposition).

17. What is the role of general learning mechanisms in lexical development? Gentner and Namy argue that these mechanisms play a significant role in the task of acquiring a lexicon. In particular, they focus on comparison processing—more specifically, structural alignment and mapping—in the acquisition of words.

18. What does the crosslinguistic study of the acquisition of verbs reveal about the mechanisms that underlie word learning? Hohenstein, Naigles, and Eisenberg focus on differences between English and Spanish speakers in the development of talk about motion events. Their results support the argument that, in this development, syntactic knowledge is more fundamental than knowledge of language-specific lexicalization patterns.

19. Why are verbs selective about the environments in which they appear, but at the same time understandable by children in brand-new structures? Lidz, Gleitman, and Gleitman address this apparent paradox. They argue that the choosiness of verbs reflects the fact that they project their semantics onto clause structure in fixed ways, and that the innovations stem from a certain latitude in the system, allowing verbs to be understood in new environments, as long as they are in the "neighborhood."

It is our hope that the nineteen contributions to this volume will lead to (at least) two positive outcomes for the field of lexical acquisition. First, because the chapters make significant contact with each other, we anticipate that readers will be able to discern points of convergence and divergence and thereby gain insight into the current state of theorizing in the discipline. Second, because the contributors have taken care to situate their work within the broader context (e.g., to understand the interactions among multiple types of skill and knowledge over the course of acquisition), we anticipate the emergence of new research agendas, guided by fresh theory-driven insights that will set the stage for the next generation of research in the field.

Acknowledgments

Geoffrey Hall would like to acknowledge funding from an operating grant from the Natural Sciences and Engineering Research Council

(NSERC) of Canada and from a Killam Faculty Leave Fellowship from the University of British Columbia. He thanks the University of British Columbia for ongoing support. He is indebted to Yale University (especially Paul Bloom) and New York University (especially Gary Marcus) for providing a stimulating work environment during his sabbatical. Sandra Waxman acknowledges funding from a National Institutes of Health grant (HD 28730). She is indebted to Northwestern University for ongoing support and to the Institute of Cognitive Science (Lyon, France) for providing an intellectual home during her sabbatical.

We dedicate this volume to the late Roger Brown. He is responsible for interweaving the paths of the two editors, and his pioneering work in developmental psycholinguistics continues to inspire us both.

I
Initial Acquisitions

1

Learning to Identify Spoken Words

Cynthia Fisher, Barbara A. Church, and Kyle E. Chambers

Before children can learn the meaning or syntactic privileges of a single word, they must first learn to identify its sound pattern. This achievement sets the stage for other aspects of language acquisition. Once children can identify even a few words in connected speech, they can begin to observe how those words are distributed relative to other elements in sentences and relative to real-world contexts. In every theory, these observations constitute the primary data for word and syntax learning (e.g., Fisher et al. 1994; Pinker 1984; Woodward and Markman 1998). Language acquisition begins with the perceptual analysis that reveals words and other linguistic forms in the flow of world experience.

But word perception is no simple matter. Words are not static patterns to be matched against unvarying input. Instead, their sound patterns are systematically influenced by neighboring sounds, speech rate, the idiosyncrasies of the speaker's voice and regional dialect, the prosodic structure of the utterance, and the sentence's emotional tenor (e.g., Fisher and Tokura 1996a, 1996b; Klatt 1980; Lively, Pisoni, and Goldinger 1994; Miller and Volaitis 1989; Mullennix and Pisoni 1990; Nusbaum and Goodman 1994). Despite all this variability, listeners recognize words *as such*, readily abstracting across voices and pronunciations.

The traditional approach to the problem of variability, both in linguistics and in psychology, has been to assume that the mental lexicon contains only quite abstract information about the sounds of words. In an abstractionist view, the complexities of speech perception are kept out of the lexicon, via a process of *normalization* that reveals a context-independent underlying sound pattern for each word (see, e.g., Chomsky and Halle 1968, Werker and Stager 2000, and many others in between; for a review, see Lively, Pisoni, and Goldinger 1994).

However, this segregation of speech processing and lexical representations has been questioned in recent years. While it is clear that listeners must readily abstract over variability in the sounds of words, it is not so obvious that the lexicon must discard all details in the process of abstraction. Growing evidence suggests that knowledge of spoken words includes context-sensitive acoustic-phonetic details that are difficult to incorporate into an entirely abstract, categorical model of word recognition. This evidence comes from several sources—recent research in laboratory phonology, studies of language change over time, and research on implicit memory for speech.

In this chapter, we will review some of this evidence and present our own recent work on the learning mechanisms underlying spoken-word recognition during acquisition. The picture that emerges from this evidence, though still speculative, is one in which there is no sharp division between phonological processing and the lexicon. Instead, basic properties of perceptual learning ensure that natural-language phonology and the lexicon are inextricably linked. Highly detailed lexical representations might at first seem inconsistent with the fundamentally abstract nature of word identification: the listener's goal, after all, is to determine what words were said, no matter who said them, or how. However, this is not the listener's only goal. We will argue that detailed and context-sensitive representations of spoken words are needed, both to learn the native-language phonetics and phonology, and to learn to identify and compensate for variations in dialect, accent, and social register.

1.1 Evidence for Detailed and Context-sensitive Encoding in the Lexicon

1.1.1 Small-scale Crosslinguistic Variation in Sound Systems

A recent surge of research in laboratory phonology has made it clear that languages differ in their phonetic details as well as in their phonological systems (e.g., Farnetani 1997; Keating 1985, 1990; Pierre-humbert 1990). Speech sounds are *coarticulated*—the realization of each sound is influenced by the properties of nearby sounds. Listeners readily compensate for coarticulation effects, both taking context into account in identifying each speech sound, and using anticipatory coarticulation as evidence about the identity of upcoming sounds (e.g., Dahan et al. 2001; Gow 2001; Warren and Marslen-Wilson 1987). Some context-dependent acoustic variability in speech is probably a natural result of vocal production constraints (and thus universal). Similarly, some compensation for coarticulation by listeners may follow from relatively low-level (and again universal) auditory contrast effects (e.g., Kluender, Diehl, and Wright 1988). But languages also vary in how speech sounds are influenced by neighboring sounds (e.g., Farnetani 1997; Keating 1985, 1990; Pierre-humbert 1990, 2001). Crosslinguistic variation in the vulnerability of segments to coarticulation suggests that speakers and listeners must learn how speech sounds are affected by various contexts *in their language*. Learning these facts would require quite detailed and context-sensitive representations of experience with language.

For example, speakers tend to lengthen vowels before voiced (e.g., /d, b, g/) rather than unvoiced (e.g., /t, p, k/) consonants (e.g., Chen 1970; Crystal and House 1988), and listeners use vowel length to identify both the vowel itself and the following consonant (Gordon 1989; Klatt 1976). The vowel in *mad* is longer than the vowel in *mat*, and this length difference is one of the cues listeners use to differentiate the final consonants /d/ and /t/. The usefulness of this cue is due in part to auditory contrast (Kluender, Diehl, and Wright 1988), but voicing-dependent vowel lengthening is not produced or perceived uniformly across languages. English speakers produce much longer vowels before voiced consonants, but the analogous effect is much smaller in Czech or Polish (Keating 1985). Accordingly, native speakers of different languages assign different weights to vowel length as one of the cues to the voicing of a final consonant (Crowther and Mann 1992).

Pierrehumbert (2001) reviews evidence for many such differences between languages in the minutiae of how speech sounds are affected by their contexts. The existence of such fine-grained differences between languages tells us that native speakers must develop a quantitative estimate of how each speech sound is formed in their native language, and how it is influenced by the surrounding context. This kind of learning requires the listener to encode speech with very fine acoustic-phonetic detail and to link these detailed records of linguistic experience with information about the context in which each sound is heard.

1.1.2 Sound Variability in the Lexicon: Evidence from Language Change

These considerations make clear that to conquer the contextual variability of connected speech, listeners must readily encode (even while freely abstracting over) acoustic-phonetic details and contextual information. But what tells us these details are *represented in the lexicon*, rather than purely at sublexical levels of representation? It could be that listeners collect context-sensitive and detailed representations of speech as part of the process of acquiring the phonetics and phonology of their native language, but that only abstract representations make their way into the lexicon. Such a division of labor would enable the traditional, abstractionist view of the lexicon to account for fine-grained variation in phonological patterns across languages (e.g., Werker and Stager 2000).

On the contrary, however, considerable research on phonological change over a language's history suggests that information about phonological variation is linked with particular lexical items. Languages' sound systems change over time, due at least in part to a tendency to save effort in articulation. Sounds come to be omitted or reduced in certain contexts, in turn altering the phonotactic regularities that define legal or likely sequences of phonemes. It has long been observed that these changes do not occur uniformly across words. Instead, phonological changes are diffused gradually across the lexicon (e.g., Chen and Wang 1975). Bybee (2000) reviews data on sound change in languages, and finds that changes in progress are more advanced in highly frequent words. This frequency effect suggests that words undergo phonological change as they are used, and that each word retains a separate range of variability.

For example, various dialects of Spanish delete, or reduce to [h], the /s/ before a consonant. This occurs inside words (e.g., *estilo* "style" → *ehtilo*), but also happens at the ends of words. A word-final /s/ is sometimes deleted even when the next word starts with a vowel, and therefore the context would not license application of a phonological rule such as "delete /s/ before a consonant." Bybee argues that this happens because the word itself accrues information about the change in its final sound. The more often a word is used, the more opportunities it has to lose its /s/, and the more speakers learn to utter that particular word without it. Bybee (2000; see also Dell 2000; Pierrehumbert 2001) suggests, based in part on data like these, that lexical items represent more information about phonological variation than is traditionally supposed.

Evidence that lexical items are linked with information about phonological variability does not imply that no abstract representations of phonological regularities exist. Speakers invent or borrow new words and apply the native-language phonology to those words. When we listen to foreign words we make perceptual errors that reflect the phonotactic regularities of our native language and that are not easily attributed to the influence of particular native-language words (e.g., Dupoux et al. 2001). These phenomena require representations of phonological regularities that can easily be disentangled from existing words. In addition, entirely lexical representations of phonological variation would not account well for the language-change facts described above. Representations permitting no abstraction over lexical items would not explain why language change spreads across the lexicon at all, affecting multiple words and eventually approximating a general rule (e.g., Bybee 2000; Pierrehumbert 2001). The picture suggested by these data is one of multiple levels of abstraction over the speech data listeners encounter. We learn words and keep track of the details of how each word can vary, but also develop more abstract generalizations that allow us to apply native-language sound patterns to new words.

1.1.3 Evidence from Studies of Implicit Memory for Speech

Recent research in the memory literature provides a quite distinct source of evidence for the same conclusion—that listeners routinely encode, and use in word identification, extremely detailed representations of particular words. Studies of adults' implicit memory for spoken words reveal a powerful learning mechanism that continually adapts adults' representations of words in response to listening experience (e.g., Church and Schacter 1994; Goldinger 1996; Schacter and Church 1992). Each time we attend to a word, a lasting representation is created that aids later identification of the same word.

This facilitation, known as long-term auditory word priming, depends primarily on auditory, not semantic representations of experience, happens fast (on one trial), and has very long-lasting effects (e.g., Church and Fisher 1998; Church and Schacter 1994; Fisher et al. 2001; Schacter and Church 1992). The facilitative effect of a single auditory presentation of a low-frequency word can be measured after a week's delay (Goldinger 1996).

Auditory word priming functions abstractly, facilitating word identification despite ordinary variations in the sound of the word. These include changes in speech rate, fundamental frequency, speaker's voice, pronunciation, and adjacent context (e.g., Church 1995; Church, Dell, and Kania 1996; Church and Schacter 1994; Goldinger 1996; Poldrack and Church 1997; Schacter and Church 1992; Sheffert 1998; Sommers 1999).

On the other hand, many studies find that auditory word priming can be reduced by surprisingly small changes in the sounds of words. The facilitative effect of prior exposure to a word is greatest when the items used in testing match the learning items in nearly every respect. Priming is reduced when a test word is spoken in a different voice (Church and Schacter 1994; Goldinger 1996; Schacter and Church 1992; Sheffert 1998), at a different pitch or speaking rate (Church and Schacter 1994), or when the details of the word's pronunciation change even slightly from the study episode (Church, Dell, and Kania 1996; see also our own data from children reviewed below).

For example, many English words have multiple possible pronunciations. The word *retreat* can be spoken with a full vowel in its initial unstressed syllable (/ritrit/) or with the unstressed vowel reduced to a schwa (/rətrit/). These two possibilities exist quite generally in the English lexicon: An unstressed vowel can be reduced to a schwa, but under some circumstances will emerge as a full vowel. Church, Dell, and Kania (1996) presented listeners with a set of words subject to this kind of variation; some were produced with a reduced vowel and some with a full vowel. In a later test, listeners tried to identify low-pass filtered (therefore somewhat muffled and hard-to-hear) words. Some of the test words were repeated from the study phase and some were new. Of the studied words, half were presented with the same pronunciation at study and test (e.g., /ritrit/ → /ritrit/), while half changed pronunciation from study to test (e.g., /ritrit/ → /rətrit/). Adults more accurately identified studied words than new words, even if the studied words changed pronunciation from study to test. This is an example of an abstract benefit from repetition, spanning some of the ways words ordinarily vary. However, subjects most accurately identified items that retained the same pronunciation from study to test. This result implies that listeners encoded information about whether *each word* had been pronounced with a full or a reduced vowel. Both abstract and specific priming effects are also found when words undergo even smaller changes from study to test, including changes in vowel formant frequency that are difficult for listeners to discriminate (Church 1995).

Data like these tell us that the rapidly formed and long-lasting representations created whenever we attend to speech reflect acoustic-phonetic details specific to particular instantiations of spoken words. Listeners amass fine-grained and context-sensitive information about the sounds of each word, even while they readily abstract over these details to identify familiar words in new guises. Adult implicit memory for speech seems to have exactly the properties that would account for the language-change effects reviewed above.

1.1.4 Distributional Learning at Multiple Levels of Analysis

Yet other lines of reasoning also lead to the conclusion that representations of words must be context sensitive: in the process of identifying spoken words we must locate word boundaries in connected speech. Spoken words do not arrive at the ear presegmented by unambiguous acoustic cues to their boundaries. Languages recruit probabilistic cues to the location of word boundaries, including the typical stress patterns of words in the language (e.g., Cutler and Norris 1988; Echols, Crowhurst, and Childers 1997; Jusczyk 1997), sequences of consonants that frequently occur at word boundaries (e.g., Mattys et al. 1999; Mattys and Jusczyk 2001), and allophonic (within-phonemic-category) differences between sounds at word edges and within words (Gow and Gordon 1995; Jusczyk 1997; Quené 1992). These cues are language specific, however, and even once learned, leave considerable ambiguity about the location of word boundaries. Theories of spoken-word recognition therefore typically assume that adults find word boundaries in part by identifying the sound patterns of familiar words (e.g., Dahan and Brent 1999; Klatt 1980; Marslen-Wilson 1987; McClelland and Elman 1986; McQueen et al. 1995).

Word segmentation works in infancy in much the same way. By 8 months of age, infants carve words from the flow of speech by detecting locally predictable sequences of syllables (Saffran, Aslin, and Newport 1996; Aslin, Saffran, and Newport 1998). After listening to four 3-syllable nonsense words randomly concatenated into a continuous stream, 8-month-olds listened longer to relatively novel 3-syllable "part words" that crossed the boundaries of the training words than to the now-familiar "words" from training. The stimuli were designed to offer no hints to word boundaries other than the highly predictable ordering of syllables within but not across word boundaries. Sequences of syllables that consistently repeat in connected speech become coherent, wordlike perceptual units.

To find word boundaries via distributional analysis of sound sequences, listeners must represent information about sound patterns in context. These representations must be used abstractly to identify an old pattern in a new context, while still retaining enough specific context information to detect the repeating sequences of sounds that make up words.

Furthermore, distributional patterns in speech must be detected at multiple levels of analysis. Six-month-olds do not yet reliably recognize repeating sequences of phonemes or syllables, but they do use consistent metrical or rhythmic patterns to locate wordlike units in continuous speech (Goodsitt, Morgan, and Kuhl 1993; Morgan and Saffran 1995; Morgan 1996). Two-syllable nonwords with a consistent stress pattern quickly begin to cohere as perceptual units for young infants. Just as the 8-month-olds in Saffran, Aslin, and Newport's

(1996) studies detected patterns of repeating syllables, younger infants pick up predictable metrical patterns in the speech stream.

By about 9 months, infants have begun to detect language-specific restrictions on the sequences of consonants and vowels that occur within words. These restrictions are known as *phonotactic regularities*. In English, for example, the /ŋ/ at the end of *sing* never occurs at the beginnings of words, the /h/ at the beginning of *hat* never occurs word-finally, and the sequence /tl/ never begins words. These are facts about English; other languages permit similar sounds to occur in different contexts. Nine-month-olds, like adults, use phonotactic restrictions and frequencies in speech processing: They listen longer to phonotactically legal or phonotactically frequent nonsense words (e.g., Friederici and Wessels 1993; Jusczyk, Luce, and Charles-Luce 1994), and use the probabilities of consonant sequences within words and across word boundaries to locate likely word boundaries in connected speech (Mattys et al. 1999; Mattys and Jusczyk 2001).

For present purposes, notice that similar distributional evidence is needed to achieve word segmentation and to detect the phonotactic and prosodic sequencing regularities that characterize the native-language lexicon. In each case this learning requires a mechanism that both encodes specific information about context and permits enough abstraction to detect familiar patterns across a context change. For example, to learn that /h/ cannot occur syllable-finally, a listener must abstract over many syllables containing (and not containing) an /h/.

1.1.5 Summary

The evidence reviewed here suggests some conclusions about the nature of the phonological information encoded in the mental lexicon. To learn the sound system of the native language, we must encode detailed and context-sensitive representations of language experience, so that we can generate a quantitative estimate of how sounds are affected by different contexts in our language. Evidence from quite different sources suggests that these details are not kept out of the mental lexicon. The uneven, partly lexically driven nature of sound change in languages suggests that speakers and listeners keep track of separate ranges of variability for each word (e.g., Bybee 2000). Findings of both abstract and highly specific implicit memory for spoken words lead to the same conclusion (e.g., Church and Schacter 1994; Goldinger 1996). In learning to identify spoken words, listeners collect detailed acoustic-phonetic information about how sound patterns are realized in different contexts, even as they readily abstract across contexts to identify words *as such* despite contextual variability. Similar information is compiled for units of varying scope, yielding phonotactic regularities, words, and prosodic templates.

1.2 Word Recognition in Children

Do young children represent words with anything like this level of detail? It may at first seem very unlikely that they do, simply because children are so error-prone in recognizing spoken words. Adult levels of skilled word recognition take a long time to develop. Even young school-aged children make many more errors of word recognition than adults do (for reviews, see Nittrouer and Boothroyd 1990; Gerken, Murphy, and Aslin 1995; Swingley, Pinto, and Fernald 1999). Preschoolers are much less able to judge the difference between real words and minimally different nonword foils (e.g., Gerken, Murphy, and Aslin 1995). In comprehension and word-learning tasks young children often fail to discriminate newly taught pairs of words that differ in only one speech segment, though they do better with familiar words (e.g., *bear* versus *pear*; Barton 1980). Infants and children are also slower to identify familiar words than adults are: Fernald and colleagues (1998) found that 24-month-olds took longer to shift their eyes to a picture of a named object than adults did.

Even worse difficulties with word recognition are found for infants at the very start of word learning. Stager and Werker (1997) habituated 14-month-olds to a single nonsense syllable paired with a display of a moving object, and found that infants did not recover visual attention to the moving object display when the sound changed to a different syllable (e.g., from *bih* to *dih*). Younger infants tested in the same task discriminate these two sounds with ease. Stager and Werker argued that infants failed to detect the sound change in what was—for 14-month-olds—a word-learning setting. In similar studies, 14-month-olds succeeded if the words were less confusable (e.g., *neem* and *liff*; see Werker and Stager 2000). Decades of research on speech perception have established that 14-month-olds and much younger infants discriminate syllables differing only in their initial consonant. Stager and Werker's findings suggest that using these speech-discrimination abilities in the service of word learning presents a more difficult task.

Some have suggested that infants' and toddlers' difficulties with word recognition reveal a fundamental lack of detail in their lexical representations (e.g., Hallé and de Boysson-Bardies 1996; Stager and Werker 1997; Werker and Stager 2000). This claim is derived from the traditional view of the lexicon as containing only enough information about the sounds of words to differentiate existing words. As Charles-Luce and Luce (1995) point out, each word is more distinct from its neighbors in the young child's tiny vocabulary than it would be in the more densely packed lexicon of an adult. Given a sparser lexicon, less phonetic information would be required to differentiate each of the child's words from its neighbors. If the level of phonetic detail in the lexicon is driven by the existence of minimally different pairs of words, we should expect less detailed representations of the sounds of words in young children's lexicons.

However, findings of word-recognition errors in young children do not force us to conclude that children's word representations are qualitatively different from adults' (see Fisher and Church 2001). The task of word recognition requires processing at multiple levels of analysis; each offers opportunities for error. Most word-recognition theories assume a number of distinct steps in accounting for word identification (e.g., see Jusczyk 1997). A listener must accomplish an acoustic-phonetic analysis of the speech wave, generate a phonological representation of an incoming candidate word, compare that candidate word with words in the existing lexicon, and select the best match, retrieving knowledge about the selected word. Errors could creep in at any point in this process. For example, children might tend to make more errors in initial acoustic-phonetic analysis of speech input, introducing noise into the recognition process right at the start. Children might also err in the selection of the best match in the long-term lexicon or in the inhibition of similar-sounding words. Given all these sources of error, the finding that infants and children make more errors in identifying words need not mean that children's lexical representations differ in kind from those of adults. There might be more continuity in word representation and identification across development than meets the eye.

Consistent with this possibility, recent evidence suggests that very young listeners use phonetic information to identify words much as adults do. As adults, we match incoming sounds with word candidates in the mental lexicon *incrementally* and *in parallel* (e.g., Marslen-Wilson 1987). For example, in a referential task, listeners took longer to select a word's referent when visible competitor objects had names that sounded similar at the start (e.g., *beaker* vs. *beetle*) than when all competitors' names differed from the target from the onset (e.g., *beaker* vs. *parrot*; Allopenna, Magnuson, and Tanenhaus 1998). This and many other findings tell us that adults make use of partial information to rule out inconsistent word candidates.

Swingley, Pinto, and Fernald (1999) found similar evidence of incremental use of phonetic information by 24-month-olds. In a preferential-looking comprehension task, children were quicker to move their eyes to a named target picture when the target was paired with a distractor with a dissimilar name (e.g., *dog* vs. *truck*) than when the distractor and the target words began with the same sounds (e.g., *dog* vs. *doll*). Swingley and colleagues found no evidence that children were slower to identify words in the context of distracters with rhyming names (e.g., *duck* vs. *truck*); thus it was not overall similarity in sound that slowed word recognition, but similarity at the beginning of the word. Apparently 24-month-olds, like adults, use sound information incrementally to identify words (see also Fernald, Swingley, and Pinto 2001).

Subsequent studies using the same technique suggest that young children exploit considerable phonetic detail in identifying familiar words (Swingley and Aslin 2000). Children 18 to 23 months old were instructed to look at one of two pictures; on some trials they heard correct pronunciations of the pictures' names (e.g., *baby*), and on other trials they heard mispronounced versions of them (e.g., *vaby*). In both cases children recognized the intended word and looked at the relevant picture, but they were slower and less accurate when the words were mispronounced. Finally, Jusczyk and Aslin (1995) found that 7.5-month-olds who had been familiarized with two monosyllabic words (e.g., *feet* and *bike*) later listened longer to passages in which those words were embedded than to passages not containing the familiarized words. The same effect was not found when the words were replaced in the passages with foils differing only in a single consonant (e.g., *zeet* and *gike*); infants were not fooled by these soundalike nonwords. Although infants and children make many more errors in identifying spoken words than adults do, these findings suggest that children's long-term memories of words, and the processes by which they identify words, do not differ in kind from those of adults.

1.3 Children's Memory for Spoken Words

Thus far we have argued that learners need detailed representations of experience with words in order to learn the phonological patterns of their language, and that very fine levels of detail are associated with particular words in the adult lexicon. Furthermore, as discussed in section 1.2, although children's word recognition is error-prone, recent findings suggest considerable continuity in the representations and processes underlying word recognition from late infancy to adulthood. In the remainder of this chapter we describe recent work on memory for spoken words in young children. The phenomenon of long-term auditory priming, as studied in adults, suggests that fundamental mechanisms of implicit perceptual learning create appropriately detailed and flexible representations of the sounds of words. Here we present a line of research that explores this kind of learning in toddlers and preschoolers. Our findings point toward a startling sensitivity to acoustic-phonetic detail in very young listeners, and suggest more developmental continuity in implicit memory for speech than meets the eye.

1.3.1 Effects of Experience on Word Recognition

To ask whether young children's learning about speech bears any resemblance to the adult pattern described above, the first step is simply to discover whether the same rapid and long-lasting facilitation of word identification can be found in young children at all. If a child hears a word just once, does this have any effect on later identification of that word? Several studies tell us that it does, and strongly support the developmental continuity of implicit memory for speech.

Church and Fisher (1998) found patterns of long-term auditory priming in 2-, 2.5-, and 3-year-olds that were very similar to those found in adults. In an elicited imitation task, children more accurately identified and repeated mildly low-pass filtered words that they had heard presented once several minutes before, than words that were not played previously. Thus 2-, 2.5-, and 3-year-olds, like adults, gained a significant perceptual boost for word identification from hearing a word just once. When children's and adults' baseline performance in the task was roughly equated through differential levels of low-pass filtering, we found no significant change in the magnitude of the repetition priming effect from age 2 to college age, despite the enormous change in lexical knowledge across this age range.

Auditory word priming is also qualitatively similar in preschoolers and adults. First, as found for adults (Church and Schacter 1994; Schacter and Church 1992), the advantage shown by 3-year-olds in identifying previously heard words did not depend on whether the task used in the study phase required them to retrieve the meaning of each word (choosing its referent from a set of two objects) or not (judging whether a robot said each word "really well"). This difference in encoding task did, however, affect children's ability to explicitly judge which of the test words they had heard in the study phase (Church and Fisher 1998). These results, as well as findings with nonwords presented in the next section, tell us that the facilitation in word identification due to simple repetition is largely mediated by perceptual, rather than semantic, representations of spoken words.

More recently, we have asked whether even infants show similar effects. To address this question, we adapted an object-choice and a preferential looking task to investigate the effects of repetition on 18- and 21-month-olds' identification of familiar words.

In a task developed with Caroline Hunt, 18-month-olds simply listened to a set of eight familiar object words (e.g., *bunny, candy, keys*), each presented twice in the carrier phrase "Where's the X? X!" as an experimenter entertained the infant with an unrelated stuffed toy. No referent was presented for the study words (i.e., at this point there was no bunny, candy, or keys). Following this study phase, there was a 2-minute delay during which the infant played with another set of toys. Finally the test phase began. On each trial, two objects were displayed, equidistant from the child and out of reach, and the infant heard one of the objects named twice in the same carrier phrase heard in the study phase. Half of the sixteen test items had been heard in the earlier study phase, and half were new. For studied items, the same recorded tokens of the words in their carrier phrase had been presented in the study phase. After the test words were played, the experimenter moved the two objects forward to within the infant's reach, and said "Can you get it?" All choices were applauded. The measure of interest was how often the infant chose (touched first) the named object; choices were coded offline from silent video. Infants were significantly more likely to select the named object when the test word had been studied. Hearing a familiar word just twice in a nonreferential context made infants more likely to identify that word successfully several minutes later in a comprehension task.

We found the same rapid and long-lasting facilitation for spoken-word identification in a visual preference comprehension task with 21-month-olds. The children sat on a parent's lap in front of two side-by-side video screens. All sound stimuli were played from a speaker centered between the two screens. During the initial study phase a set of words was presented twice, in the same carrier phrase used in the object-choice task described above. No referents for these words were shown; an aquarium video played on both screens as the study words were presented. A distractor phase followed, during which both video screens showed an unrelated children's video. On each trial of the final test phase, children saw different objects pictured on the two screens; the soundtrack instructed children to look at one of the pictures (e.g., "Find the truck. Truck!").

Early in each 6-second test trial the child heard an attention-getting phrase such as "Hey, look!", followed by the target words in their carrier phrase. The onset of the first presentation of the target word occurred when the pictures had been visible for 3 seconds; the onset of the second presentation occurred 1.5 seconds later. The target word was repeated to ensure that all children would eventually identify every word. The 1.5-second period between the onset of the first and second repetitions of the target word provided a test window within which to measure word-identification speed and accuracy. We coded, frame by frame from videotape, the children's visual fixations to the two screens during the test period.

Children were faster and more accurate in identifying the studied items. We analyzed the mean proportion of time spent looking at the matching picture, divided into three 500-msec segments. Children were more likely to look at the target for studied than for new items; this effect was most striking early in the test period. Further analyses revealed a significant advantage for studied items during the first 100 msec following the onset of the target word. This very early advantage for studied words is almost certainly not due to faster identification of the sound pattern of the target word itself. Since it takes time to plan and initiate an eye movement (e.g., 150–175 msec for adults with no uncertainty about target location; see Rayner 1998, for a review), the slight advantage for studied targets within 100 msec of target-word onset appears too soon to be plausibly interpreted as a response to the target word itself.

There are two likely sources for this apparent precognition on the part of the children. First, in connected speech some information about upcoming sounds can be gained from coarticulation cues (e.g., Dahan et al. 2001; Gow 2001; Warren and Marslen-Wilson 1987). The target-distractor pairs used in this study had names that were dissimilar at the onset (e.g., *candy* and *bug*), making it possible that some phonological information about the target could be detected before the word itself began. Second, 17-month-olds spend more time looking at pictured objects whose names they know well (Schafer, Plunkett, and Harris 1999). Children may have been better able to retrieve the names of target pictures on their own if they heard their names in the study phase. If so, a slight early preference for the target might appear for studied items, even before any phonological information about the target word could be detected.

To isolate the effect of the study episode on perceptual identification of the test words, we examined shifts in fixation that occurred after the onset of the target word. Following Swingley, Pinto, and Fernald (1999), we examined trials in which the child happened to be fixating the distractor at the onset of the target word. We then measured the latency of shifts in fixation from the distractor to the target picture. For this analysis, we included only shifts that occurred within the 1.5-second test window, and discarded shifts that occurred within 200 msec of target-word onset, on the assumption that these were too fast to be responses to the word. The 21-month-olds were reliably quicker to move their eyes from the distractor to the target picture for studied than for new targets. This result suggests that children were quicker to identify the sound patterns of familiar words if they had heard those words just twice in the study phase.

All of these studies show that toddlers' and preschoolers' spoken-word identification benefits incrementally from repetition. Eighteen-month-olds were more accurate in choosing a named object, 21-month-olds were quicker to look at a named object, and 2- and 3-year-olds more accurately repeated a test word, if the word had been played once or twice several minutes earlier. Just as for adults, each experience with a word adds perceptual information to the system used to identify spoken words. This information makes the system better suited to identifying the same words in the future.

1.3.2 Encoding the Details of Pronunciation

The evidence reviewed above makes it clear that early word identification benefits from each encounter with the sounds of words. In all cases so far, however, we have examined the effect of hearing the same recorded token of the word at study and test; these data therefore tell us nothing about the nature of the long-term memories added to the word-identification system each time young children listen to speech. In this section we focus on the content of these representations. How much phonetic detail is encoded in the long-term memories used for spoken-word identification, and how readily do children abstract across these details?

In two experiments, we focused on words that can be pronounced in more than one way. For example, any standard dictionary gives the following pronunciation for the word *potato*: /pəteto/, with two /t/ consonants. But every speaker of standard American English knows that this word is often pronounced with only one /t/, and with the second /t/ reduced to a tap or flap. Both pronunciations are recognizable as tokens of the same word. Many English words permit the same variation (e.g., *turtle, vegetable, daughter*). In another series of experiments, we asked whether specific information about variation in a word's pronunciation is retained in the memory representations used to identify spoken words.

Church, Fisher, and Chambers (2002) used an elicited imitation task to study memory for word variability in 2.5- and 3-year-olds. As in the experiments described in the previous section, children first simply listened to a set of words presented while they watched an unrelated children's video. After working on a puzzle for at least 2 minutes, they heard and were asked to repeat test words. The test words were presented quietly, making them hard to hear; we measured the children's accuracy in repeating the words.

In the first experiment in this series, we tested for abstract priming spanning a change in pronunciation. Children heard sixteen study words and were tested on thirty-two words. Half of the test words had been heard in the study phase and half were new. All of the studied words changed pronunciation from study to test. For example, a child who heard the /t/ version of a word in the study phase (e.g., /pəteto/) would now hear a version of the same word with a more /d/-like flap at test (/pəteɾo/). Both 2.5- and 3-year-olds identified and repeated the studied items more accurately than the new items. Since the studied words always changed pronunciation from study to test, this result shows that children's rapidly formed perceptual representations of words contain components abstract enough to support word identification across acceptable variations in pronunciation. Children profited from simply hearing a word repeated, even if that word sounded a little different the next time it was heard.

Did children also retain information about how each word was pronounced, in addition to abstracting over the change? In a second experiment using the same materials, we asked whether children's memories of spoken words included information about whether each word had been pronounced with a /t/ or a /d/-like flap. The design and materials were just as described above. The only difference was that in the second experiment, all of the test items had been heard in the study phase; thus all were studied words. In this case, however, half of the test words appeared in the *same pronunciation* at study and test (e.g., /pəteto/ → /pəteto/), while half *changed pronunciation* from study to test (e.g., /pəteɾo/ → /pəteto/). Both 2.5- and 3-year-olds more accurately identified and repeated words that were pronounced the same way at study and test, than those that changed pronunciation. Children benefited most from past experience with a word if that word was pronounced in just the same way, rather than with a legal change in pronunciation. Taken together, these two studies show that on minimal exposure, children rapidly create long-term representations of spoken words that both abstract across legal variation in word pronunciation and retain quite specific information about how each word was pronounced.

Crucially, this information had to be linked with particular words heard in the experiment: each child heard an equal number of words pronounced with a /t/ and with a flap, both at study and test. The pronunciation-specific priming effect we measured could only have been due to encoding a separate history of pronunciations for each word. This finding is strikingly reminiscent of the language-change phenomena reviewed earlier. Even 2.5- and 3-year-olds encode detailed and lexically specific information about the sound patterns of words. These lexically specific memories, as part of the system for identifying spoken words, could help explain why sound changes are not uniform across the lexicon.

1.3.3 Encoding Subphonemic Details

All of the word-priming studies described so far have examined memory representations of existing English words. Children in these studies had probably already established a robust representation for each word before they came to be in our experiments; they also had probably learned that English words can vary in whether a /t/ is released, unreleased, or produced as a flap. It might be that the patterns of abstraction and specificity we find, or even the rapid facilitation for later word identification conferred by one or two repetitions of a word's sound pattern, depend on the existence of these prior lexical representations.

Fisher et al. (2001) asked whether young children would show priming at all for entirely unknown words ·(nonwords), and if so, whether their rapidly created representations of the new words exhibited the same flexible combination of abstraction and specificity found in our studies with real words. We again used an elicited imitation task. Children simply listened to a set of nonwords, each presented twice in an initial study phase. After a 2-minute distractor task they listened to and tried to repeat nonwords. As before, the test items were presented quietly, to increase the perceptual demands of the elicited imitation test. In a first study, 2.5-year-olds more accurately identified and repeated consonant-vowel-consonant (CVC, e.g., *biss, yeeg*) nonwords that they had heard just twice in the initial study phase. This finding tells us that the kind of rapid and long-lasting facilitation we measured for toddlers and preschoolers with real words can be found with entirely novel words as well. No previously established lexical representation is required for rapid sound-pattern learning to occur.

With this result in hand, we went on to explore the contents of young children's representations of novel words. Three-year-olds heard two-syllable nonwords (CVC.CVC, e.g., *deece.gibe* /dis.gaɪb/, *tull.yave* /tʌl.jev/). Each syllable was recorded in two different contexts. For example, the component syllables of /dis.gaɪb/ were re-paired with other syllables to form /tʌl.gaɪb/ (*tull.gibe*) and /dis.jev/ (*deece.yave*). All of the nonsense-syllable pairs were recorded as coarticulated disyllables, with greater stress on the first syllable. This was done to encourage children to perceive them as possible two-syllable words. The resulting items had the phonological structure of English words like *council* or *bathtub*. We arranged these items into various study and test lists to examine how abstract, and how specific, children's representations of the nonwords were.

First, we compared test items whose component syllables had been heard in an initial study phase to test items that were entirely new. All of the studied items had changed recording context (and therefore recorded syllable token) from study to test. For example, a child who heard /tʌl.gaɪb/ and /dis.jev/ in the study phase would hear /dis.gaɪb/ and /tʌl.jev/ at test. Three-year-olds showed abstract priming for these recombined nonsense words. Children more accurately identified and repeated syllables they had heard in the study phase than syllables they had not heard, even though different tokens of the studied syllables were presented in a new wordlike context at study and test. The rapidly formed perceptual representations that aid word identification permit abstraction across acoustic and context variability, even for brand-new items.

Second, we looked for specificity effects, asking whether children encoded details relevant to the context in which they originally heard each syllable. In this study, 3-year-olds were again tested on two-syllable nonwords; all of the component syllables of the test items had been heard in the study phase. Half of the test items were presented in the same disyllabic context (and the same recorded token) at study and test, while half changed context (and recorded token) from study to test. The children more accurately identified and repeated syllables heard in the same context at study and test. This finding shows striking specificity in 3-year-olds' representations of brand-new spoken words. Based on just two exposures to a possible two-syllable word, children later more accurately identified test items if the *same tokens* of those syllables were heard in the *same context*.

What specific features of the disyllabic nonwords did the children encode? There are two classes of possibilities. Syllables that changed context from study to test differed in both the adjacent context and the recorded token. The context change itself, or changes in syllable token, or both, could have caused the reduction in priming for changed-context items. Syllables recorded in different contexts will differ in systematic coarticulatory cues at the boundary between the two syllables. We argued in the opening sections of this chapter that both context information and detailed acoustic representations are needed to support phonological learning and spoken word identification; therefore we predicted that both context and token information should be encoded in memories of syllables, and that a change in either would reduce the magnitude of priming effects.

Fisher et al. (2001) reported a final study showing that the change in syllable token from study to test was responsible for a significant part of the context-specificity effect described above. To disentangle the effects of context from changes in the syllable token itself, we spliced the second syllables out of each of the disyllabic nonwords

used in the previous experiments. Children heard the original disyllabic nonwords in an initial study phase (e.g., /dis.gaɪb/), participated in the same distractor task, and then listened to and tried to
repeat the final syllables spliced out of their disyllabic contexts and
presented in isolation (e.g., /gaɪb/). All of the test syllables were syllables the child had heard in the study phase. Half of the test syllables were the same syllable tokens, spliced out of the same-context
disyllabic items (e.g., /dis.gaɪb/ → /(dis)gaɪb/), while half were different syllable tokens, spliced out of the changed-context disyllabic
items (e.g., /dis.gaɪb/ → /(tʌl)gaɪb/). Children more accurately
identified the nonsense syllables at test if they heard the *same syllable
token* that had been presented at study, than if they heard a different
token of the same syllable.

When children attend to speech, they encode token-specific detail
about brand-new syllables. In our experiments, children benefited
a little less from repeated exposure to a syllable if the syllable was
presented in a different recorded context, or even if a different
recorded token of the same syllable, with different coarticulation
cues, was presented. At the same time, however, we measured a more
abstract facilitation—syllables that had been heard before were repeated more accurately than those that had not, even though the
studied syllables changed both recorded token and context from
study to test. Taken together, these findings tell us that young children encode even brand-new words in excruciating detail, yet readily
abstract over those details to identify a new rendition of the same
syllable.

These token-specificity effects make it clear that the level of detail
relevant for memory representations of spoken words does not
depend on the existence of minimal pairs in the lexicon: there is no
minimal pair of words that would force children to encode token-
specific information in the mental lexicon. These findings strongly
suggest that young children encode highly detailed representations
of speech, and link these detailed representations with particular
lexical items. Such representations would permit children to learn
the details of how sounds are pronounced and how individual lexical
items vary in their pronunciation.

1.3.4   Context-Sensitive Encoding

We have argued that very detailed and context-sensitive encoding of sound patterns is needed for children to learn how various sounds are affected by context in their language. Did context play any role in the context-change effect shown in Fisher et al. 2001? To isolate the influence of context from syllable-internal token changes, Chambers, Fisher, and Church (2002) tested 3-year-olds and adults with spliced-together versions of disyllabic nonword stimuli like those described in the previous section.

As in the previous context-change study, children were tested on disyllabic items all of whose component syllables had been heard in the study phase. Again, half of the test items were presented in the same disyllabic context at study and test, while half changed context from study to test. The crucial difference from the prior studies was that the same recorded syllable tokens were always presented at study and test; context-change items were simply the same syllable tokens respliced into a new disyllabic nonword. Children were tested in the elicited imitation task, and we measured the accuracy with which they repeated the novel words. Adults heard test items over headphones and tried to repeat them as quickly as possible; we measured reaction time rather than repetition accuracy.

In two studies we found small but consistent effects of a change in adjacent context for both children and adults, even though the recorded syllable token remained the same from study to test. Adults were reliably quicker, and children more accurate, in repeating same-context than changed-context items. These results suggest that listeners encoded information about adjacent context, and received slightly less facilitation from repetition if the context changed.

Interestingly, we also found variability among the items in the magnitude of the context-change effect. Using the adult reaction-time data, we examined the possibility that some consonant sequences at the syllable boundary in our CVC.CVC items might sound more like they belonged within a single word than others. Phonotactic regularities govern sound sequences within words; consonant sequences vary in how frequently they appear within versus across the boundaries of English words. For example, the sequence /ft/ is common in English words (e.g., *after*, *gift*, *lift*), while /vt/ is rare within English words but occurs across word boundaries fairly often (e.g., *love to*). Mattys and Jusczyk (2001; see also Mattys et al. 1999) found that 9-month-olds were better able to detect repeated words in connected speech if those words were edged with consonant sequences like /vt/, which are very unlikely to occur within words (and therefore good for word segmentation). Following Mattys et al. (1999), we computed both within-word and between-word transitional probabilities for the consonant sequences at the syllable boundaries of our disyllabic nonsense words, based on a phonetically transcribed online dictionary of about 20,000 English words (see Nusbaum, Pisoni, and Davis 1984).[1] In the adult reaction-time data, we found that the within-word phonotactic frequency of the consonant sequence at the syllable boundary was significantly correlated with the magnitude of the context-change reduction in priming. Adults were slower to repeat studied syllables that had been spliced into a new disyllabic context at test; this context-change effect was larger for items that had more wordlike consonant transitions at the syllable boundary.

These findings suggest that both children and adults can encode information about the adjacent context when they listen to speech, and link that context information with their representation of a particular syllable. We also found intriguing evidence that phonotactic probabilities affect the likelihood of encoding context information across a syllable boundary. Future studies will examine the possibility that language-specific cues relevant to word segmentation, including stress pattern, syllable structure, and phonotactic regularities, partly determine the effective units of memory storage in word perception.

1.3.5   Context-Sensitive Encoding at Multiple Levels of Analysis

The perceptual priming data from toddlers, preschoolers, and adults summarized above creates a picture of a very flexible lexicon full of highly detailed and context-sensitive representations of spoken words. Contrary to the traditional view of lexical-phonological representations as abstract, a considerable amount of detail, including information about the context in which each sound appears, makes its way into the mental lexicon. Preschoolers and adults readily abstract over this wealth of detail and context information, to identify words or syllables as such. We also argued in earlier sections, however, that similarly context-sensitive and flexible learning must take place at a variety of levels of analysis over the same speech data.

To learn native-language phonotactic regularities, for example, listeners must encode information about the contexts in which each speech segment (i.e., each consonant or vowel) can occur, abstracting across syllables to detect subsyllabic regularities. Even in abstracting these subsyllabic regularities, however, not all context information can be lost. Phonotactic regularities are restrictions on the context in which each sound can occur, including syllabic position (e.g., *ng* can be syllable-final but not syllable-initial in English) and adjacent sounds (e.g., only a small subset of consonants can appear syllable-finally after a long vowel; Harris 1994). Languages also have phonotactic regularities less absolute than the ban on initial *ng* in English. Vocabularies are characterized by probabilistic phonotactic patterns, and listeners (including 9-month-old infants) are sensitive to these probabilities (e.g., Jusczyk, Luce, and Charles-Luce 1994; Kessler and Treiman 1997; Mattys et al. 1999; Mattys and Jusczyk 2001).

The findings we have reviewed above suggest the operation of exactly the kind of implicit learning and memory mechanism required to learn these regularities: Information about sound patterns is encoded flexibly, both retaining fine acoustic detail and information about context, and permitting abstraction across these context-sensitive representations. If such flexible representations of speech are laid down with each listening experience, then phonotactic regularities should emerge from the accumulation of incremental changes derived from listening experience.

Dell and colleagues (2000) found that adults could learn new phonotactic regularities in a speech-production task. On each trial, adults saw a set of four nonsense syllables (e.g., *mak ghin saf hing*) and were asked to repeat them in order, in time to a metronome. The metronome encouraged a fast speech rate, increasing the likelihood of slips of the tongue. Participants repeated many such lists

over four experimental sessions on different days. All stimulus syllables complied with the phonotactic restrictions of English (e.g., *ng*
always syllable-final, *h* only initial), but the experimental stimuli also
displayed new phonotactic regularities, a subset of the English possibilities. For example, a subject might see materials in which /f/
occurred only as a coda consonant (syllable-final, e.g., *saf*), and /s/
only as an onset consonant (syllable-initial). Dell et al. examined the
speech errors the subjects made during this task. They found, as
expected, that speakers' errors respected the phonotactic regularities of English essentially 100 percent of the time. In addition,
however, participants' speech errors rapidly came to respect the
experimentally induced phonotactic regularities: errors that were
"legal" with respect to the experimental phonotactic constraints
were much more likely than errors that violated those constraints.
The experiment-wide phonotactic constraints were honored even in
errors producing syllables that were never presented in the experiment; this extension to novel syllables suggests the subjects in these
experiments learned relatively abstract, subsyllabic regularities in
sound sequences.

Dell et al. attributed their findings to implicit learning in the
language-production system. Over many trials, the production system
was given more practice with (for example) an initial /s/, and even
in error became more likely to produce this familiar pattern. Could
such rapid phonotactic learning occur based on listening alone?

Onishi, Chambers, and Fisher (2002) examined this question by
asking adults simply to listen to sets of nonsense syllables that exhibited novel phonotactic regularities, again a subset of the possibilities
of English. Subjects listened to sets of CVC syllables in which consonants were artificially restricted to syllable onset or coda position.
Onishi et al. chose constrained syllable sets that could not be differentiated based on a single phonetic feature or set of features (group
1: /b, k, m, t/, group 2: /p, g, n, ch/). Subjects heard either group 1
consonants as onsets and group 2 consonants as codas (e.g., /bæp/),
or the reverse assignment (e.g., /pæb/). Approximately twenty-five
syllables were presented during the initial study phase, presented five
times each in a simple cover task in which subjects rated clarity of
articulation. After a 2-minute distractor task subjects heard more

CVC syllables and tried to repeat them as quickly and accurately as possible. Onishi et al. measured the latency to begin speaking. The items in the test phase included two kinds of novel syllables—legal syllables, consistent with the experimental phonotactic constraints established in the study phase, and illegal syllables, violating those constraints.

The adult subjects were reliably quicker to repeat the legal than the illegal items, revealing that they had learned the novel phonotactic restrictions imposed in the study phase. Furthermore, Onishi et al. anticipated that the phonotactic learning found in this study would diminish during the test phase. The test phase included as many illegal as legal syllables, so throughout the test phase subjects were given evidence against the phonotactic restrictions established earlier in the experiment. This prediction was upheld: the advantage for legal items was significant in the first half of the test trials, and was gone in the second half. Adult listeners readily acquired restrictions on the syllable positions in which consonants could occur, simply based on listening to a set of syllables.

In a second experiment, Onishi et al. asked whether listeners could acquire phonotactic constraints involving more complex interactions between sounds. Adults heard syllables exhibiting second-order phonotactic regularities in which consonant position depended on the adjacent vowel. For example, /b/'s might be onsets and /p/'s codas for syllables containing the vowel /æ/, but these positions would be reversed for syllables containing the vowel /ɪ/. Thus each consonant appeared equally often in both onset and coda position in each study list; to pick up the phonotactic regularities embedded in these materials, subjects had to attend to the relationship between consonants and vowels. In the test phase, subjects were again faster to repeat new syllables that were legal than those that were illegal. As expected, Onishi et al. found that these second-order phonotactic restrictions waned during the test phase, as subjects heard as many illegal as legal test items.

Although the subjects in these experiments were adult native speakers of English, in only a few minutes of listening they picked up new regularities in the sequencing of segments within syllables. These findings testify further to the great flexibility of phonological representations. Listeners abstracted across syllables to learn that consonants were restricted to a subset of syllable positions. At the same time, they readily kept track of context information, thus learning that consonant position could depend on the adjacent vowel. These listening-based effects parallel the effects of speaking practice found in Dell et al.'s (2000) studies. Just as ongoing speaking practice makes it easier to produce phonotactically frequent patterns, listening practice makes it easier to identify frequently occurring sound patterns, even in new syllables.

Ongoing studies ask how abstract the phonotactic learning uncovered in these experiments was. Consonant-vowel transitions contain considerable information about phoneme identity, and useful estimates of phonotactic probabilities rely on the frequencies of pairs of phonemes as well as on position-sensitive phoneme frequencies (e.g., Bailey and Hahn 2001). Subjects in Onishi et al.'s experiments generalized the patterns they acquired in the study phase to new syllables, but may have done so by learning transitions between consonants and vowels rather than by establishing something more like the general rule "/b/'s are onsets." Preliminary data suggest, however, that adults can generalize newly learned consonant-position regularities to new vowels. Such findings would tell us that listeners establish abstract, vowel-independent knowledge of the syllable positions in which each consonant occurs, even as they detect patterns of co-occurrence between consonants and vowels.

1.4 What Good Are Detailed Lexical Representations?

We have presented many kinds of evidence that call into question traditional assumptions about how speech perception and word identification work. A common theme among diverse views of word identification has been the assumption that the lexicon contains only abstract information about the sounds of words (see Lively, Pisoni, and Goldinger 1994 for a review). This assumption is compelling in part because it seems to follow almost inevitably from the demands of the word-recognition task—we do identify words *as such*, as abstract phonological patterns, across great variability in their acoustic-phonetic details. The assumption that word representations are

abstract has held even greater sway in the developmental literature on word representations. As reviewed in section 1.2, several
researchers have invoked underspecified word representations in
children to account for their relatively poor performance in spoken-
word identification (e.g., Werker and Stager 2000; Hallé and de
Boysson-Bardies 1996).

The conclusion demanded by the data presented in this chapter,
however, is that phonological representations in the mental lexicon
are not so abstract, either for adults or for young children. On the
contrary, exceedingly fine acoustic-phonetic details make contact
with the lexicon. Our data testify to the continuity across development of the implicit learning and memory mechanisms relevant to
speech processing. Preschoolers and infants, like adults, possess a
learning mechanism that creates and updates long-term representations of the sounds of words to reflect each experience with language. One or a few exposures to a word facilitate later identification
of the same sound pattern. The representations laid down when
young children listen to speech include arbitrarily fine details about
each token. This level of detail is far beyond that required to differentiate minimal pairs of words like *bat* and *pat*. We argue that the
same perceptual learning mechanisms that permit adults to adapt
continually to new words, new speakers, new dialects, and acoustic
circumstances, play a role in the development of the auditory lexicon
from the start (see also Nusbaum and Goodman 1994).

The tendency for even infants to retain item-specific perceptual
information has been uncovered in other domains as well, including
memory for particular musical performances (Palmer, Jungers, and
Jusczyk 2001) and the identification of a colorful mobile as a cue to
carry out a previously rewarded action (e.g., Hartshorn et al. 1998).

Evidence of the great specificity of adults' memories for spoken
words, as well as the historical sound-change data reviewed above,
have persuaded some theorists to adopt episodic or instance-based
theories of spoken-word recognition (e.g., Bybee 2000; Goldinger
1998; Jusczyk 1997; Pisoni 1997), based on episodic theories of
memory and categorization (e.g., Hintzman 1986; Logan 1992;
Nosofsky 1988). In an episodic view, each encounter with a word is
retained in the memory stores used for word identification. Episodes

are context sensitive and finely detailed, and abstraction across tokens is achieved based on either the central tendency of the set of tokens activated during the recognition process, or direct similarity comparisons with individual episodes. Another class of models developed to account for the specificity of the memories that participate in word identification invokes both episodic and abstract representations (e.g., Church 1995; Church and Schacter 1994; Moscovitch 1994; Schacter 1994). Our data do not permit us to choose between such models, though we tend to prefer a hybrid model that includes both categorical and episodic representations. For now, however, we can conclude that traditional abstractionist models of the lexicon are inadequate to explain the data. Lexical representations of the sounds of words are linked with token-specific and context-sensitive details.

These details might seem to be mere obstacles to the main task of recognizing what word has been uttered. We have argued, however, that representations encoding very fine acoustic-phonetic details and permitting easy abstraction over these details are required to learn the sound system of the native language. Languages vary in the fine points of how speech sounds are produced and how they are influenced by various contexts. Thus for example, English-learning listeners come to use vowel lengthening as a powerful cue to final consonant voicing, while this cue is less relevant for Polish-learning listeners. To learn such sound-pattern regularities, learners must gather quite detailed information about speech sounds and the contexts in which they have occurred.

Finally, we should mention another set of phenomena that plainly demonstrate listeners' and speakers' ability to track the details of variability in language use. The sounds of words depend heavily on stylistic factors. Klatt (1980) gave a casual-speech transcription of the sentence "Would you hit it to Tom?" to dramatize the importance of adjacent context in ordinary word identification. As ordinarily produced, this sentence displays many contextual modifications, such as the palatalization that merges the consonants at the boundary of "would you," the deletion of one of the adjacent /t/s in "it to," and the demotion of the /t/ in the middle of "hit it" to a tap or flap. These are characteristics of *casual* American English speech. If we speak in a more formal setting, the same words can sound quite different.

More generally, language use is an inescapable part of the way speakers create a social persona, and listeners diagnose the life history, education, and affiliations of others. Particular pronunciations of words can carry social stigma or prestige, and therefore be adopted or avoided depending on the formality of the setting and on the speaker's social aspirations and group identifications (e.g., Wardaugh 1998).

For example, Labov (1972) tracked the appearance of postvocalic /r/ in the speech of New Yorkers. Pronouncing words like *fourth* and *floor* with or without an /r/ has social meaning: listeners rated speakers who included the /r/'s higher in job prospects, but rated speakers who omitted their /r/'s superior in their likely toughness in a fight. Labov collected utterances of "fourth floor" from salespeople in department stores varying in elegance, and found that salespeople in the fanciest stores were most likely to include the /r/'s. Men and women also tend to maintain separate ranges of variability in language use, and to enact different style changes as they move from one context to another (Labov 1998). Girls and boys pick up on these differences, presumably much as they pick up on gender-typed behavior in nonlinguistic domains. Though we are often unaware of it, we negotiate personal styles through the way we use language, including the details of how words are pronounced and how they are affected by their linguistic contexts.

In summary, language use is made up of more than words, characterized by their abstract phonological form. To function in a linguistic society, listeners must detect words, but also native-language phonological patterns at varying scales, changes in word pronunciation that do not apply uniformly across the lexicon, and styles of speech laden with social meaning. We have described evidence that young children's rapidly formed representations of spoken words have the right combination of abstraction and specificity to learn about speech at all these levels. By studying the implicit learning and memory mechanisms that create representations of spoken words, we can explore how languages come to be structured at so many levels.

Acknowledgments

The research described in this paper was supported by NICHD grant HD/OD34715-01 and NSF grant SBR 98-73450.

Note

1. We estimated between-word transitional probabilities for the consonant sequences based on the product of the probability that each first consonant appears at the ends of words in the same dictionary, and the probability that each second consonant appears at the beginnings of words in the dictionary.

References

Allopenna, P. D., Magnuson, J. S., and Tanenhaus, M. K. 1998. Tracking the time course of spoken word recognition using eye movements: Evidence for continuous mapping models. *Journal of Memory and Language, 38,* 419–439.

Aslin, R. N., Saffran, J. R., and Newport, E. L. 1998. Computation of conditional probability statistics by 8-month-old infants. *Psychological Science, 9,* 321–324.

Bailey, T. M., and Hahn, U. 2001. Determinants of wordlikeness: Phonotactics or lexical neighborhoods? *Journal of Memory and Language, 44,* 568–591.

Barton, D. 1980. Phonemic perception in children. In G. H. Yeni-Komshian, J. F. Kavanagh, and C. A. Ferguson, eds., *Child phonology, Vol. 2: Perception,* 97–116. New York: Academic Press.

Bybee, J. 2000. Lexicalization of sound change and alternating environments. In M. B. Broe and J. B. Pierrehumbert, eds., *Papers in Laboratory Phonology 5: Acquisition and the lexicon,* 250–268. New York: Cambridge University Press.

Carroll, J. B., Davies, P., and Richman, B. 1971. *The American Heritage word frequency book.* New York: American Heritage.

Chambers, K. E., Fisher, C., and Church, B. A. 2002. Context-specificity in preschoolers' encoding of novel spoken words. Unpublished manuscript.

Charles-Luce, J., and Luce, P. A. 1995. An examination of similarity neighborhoods in young children's receptive vocabularies. *Journal of Child Language, 22,* 727–735.

Chen, M. 1970. Vowel length variation as a function of the voicing of the consonant environment. *Phonetica, 22,* 129–159.

Chen, M. Y., and Wang, W. S.-Y. 1975. Sound change: Actuation and implementation. *Language, 51,* 255–281.

Chomsky, N., and Halle, M. 1968. *The sound pattern of English.* New York: Harper and Row.

Church, B. A. 1995. *Perceptual specificity of auditory priming: Implicit memory for acoustic information.* Unpublished doctoral dissertation, Harvard University, Cambridge, MA.

Church, B. A., Dell, G., and Kania, E. 1996, November. Representing phonological information in memory: Evidence from auditory priming. Paper presented at the meeting of the Psychonomic Society, Chicago.

Church, B. A., and Fisher, C. 1998. Long-term auditory word priming in pre-schoolers: Implicit memory support for language acquisition. *Journal of Memory and Language, 39,* 523–542.

Church, B. A., Fisher, C., and Chambers, K. E. 2002. *Abstraction and specificity in pre-schoolers' representations of familiar spoken words.* Unpublished manuscript.

Church, B. A., and Schacter, D. L. 1994. Perceptual specificity of auditory priming: Implicit memory for voice intonation and fundamental frequency. *Journal of Experimental Psychology: Learning, Memory, and Cognition, 20,* 521–533.

Crowther, C. S., and Mann, V. 1992. Native language factors affecting use of vocalic cues to final consonant voicing in English. *Journal of the Acoustical Society of America, 92,* 711–722.

Crystal, T. H., and House, A. S. 1988. Segmental durations in connected-speech signals: Current results. *Journal of the Acoustical Society of America, 83,* 1553–1573.

Cutler, A., and Norris, D. 1988. The role of strong syllables in segmentation for lexical access. *Journal of Experimental Psychology: Human Perception and Performance, 14,* 113–121.

Dahan, D., and Brent, M. 1999. On the discovery of novel word-like units from utterances: An artificial-language study with implications for native-language acquisition. *Journal of Experimental Psychology: General, 128,* 165–185.

Dahan, D., Magnuson, J. S., Tanenhaus, M. K., and Hogan, E. M. 2001. Subcategorical mismatches and the time course of lexical access: Evidence for lexical competition. *Language and Cognitive Processes, 16,* 507–534.

Dell, G. S. 2000. Commentary: Counting, connectionism, and lexical representation. In M. B. Broe and J. B. Pierrehumbert, eds., *Papers in Laboratory Phonology 5: Acquisition and the lexicon,* 335–348. New York: Cambridge University Press.

Dell, G. S., Reed, K. D., Adams, D. R., and Meyer, A. S. 2000. Speech errors, phonotactic constraints, and implicit learning: A study of the role of experience in language production. *Journal of Experimental Psychology: Learning, Memory, and Cognition, 26,* 1355–1367.

Dupoux, E., Pallier, C., Kakehi, K., and Mehler, J. 2001. New evidence for prelexical phonological processing in word recognition. *Language and Cognitive Processes, 16,* 491–505.

Echols, C. H., Crowhurst, M. J., and Childers, J. B. 1997. The perception of rhythmic units in speech by infants and adults. *Journal of Memory and Language, 36,* 202–225.

Farnetani, E. 1997. Coarticulation and connected speech processes. In W. J. Hardcastle and J. Laver, eds., *The handbook of phonetic sciences*, 371–404. Oxford: Blackwell.

Fernald, A., Pinto, J. P., Swingley, D., Weinberg, A., and McRoberts, G. W. 1998. Rapid gains in speed of verbal processing by infants in the 2nd year. *Psychological Science, 9*, 228–231.

Fernald, A., Swingley, D., and Pinto, J. P. 2001. When half a word is enough: Infants can recognize spoken words using partial phonetic information. *Child Development, 72*, 1003–1015.

Fisher, C., and Church, B. A. 2001. Implicit memory support for language acquisition. In J. Weissenborn and B. Hoehle, eds., *Approaches to bootstrapping: Phonological, syntactic, and neurophysiological aspects of early language acquisition*, 47–69. Amsterdam: Benjamins.

Fisher, C., Hall, D. G., Rakowitz, S., and Gleitman, L. 1994. When it is better to receive than to give: Syntactic and conceptual constraints on vocabulary growth. *Lingua, 92*, 333–375.

Fisher, C., Hunt, C., Chambers, K., and Church, B. A. 2001. Abstraction and specificity in preschoolers' representations of novel spoken words. *Journal of Memory and Language, 45*, 665–687.

Fisher, C., and Tokura, H. 1996a. Acoustic cues to grammatical structure in infant-directed speech: Cross-linguistic evidence. *Child Development, 67*, 3192–3218.

Fisher, C., and Tokura, H. 1996b. Prosody in speech to infants: Direct and indirect acoustic cues to syntactic structure. In J. L. Morgan and K. Demuth, eds., *Signal to syntax: Bootstrapping from speech to grammar in early acquisition*, 343–363. Mahwah, NJ: Erlbaum.

Friederici, A. D., and Wessels, J. M. 1993. Phonotactic knowledge of word boundaries and its use in infant speech perception. *Perception and Psychophysics, 54*, 287–295.

Gerken, L., Murphy, W. D., and Aslin, R. N. 1995. Three- and four-year-olds' perceptual confusions for spoken words. *Perception and Psychophysics, 57*, 475–486.

Goldinger, S. D. 1996. Words and voices: Episodic traces in spoken word identification and recognition memory. *Journal of Experimental Psychology: Learning, Memory, and Cognition, 22*, 1166–1183.

Goldinger, S. D. 1998. Echoes of echoes? An episodic theory of lexical access. *Psychological Review, 105*, 251–279.

Goodsitt, J. V., Morgan, J. L., and Kuhl, P. K. 1993. Perceptual strategies in prelingual speech segmentation. *Journal of Child Language, 20*, 229–252.

Gordon, P. C. 1989. Context effects in recognizing syllable-final /z/ and /s/ in different phrasal positions. *Journal of the Acoustical Society of America, 86*, 1698–1707.

Gow, D. W. J. 2001. Assimilation and anticipation in continuous spoken word recognition. *Journal of Memory and Language, 45*, 133–159.

Gow, D. W., and Gordon, P. C. 1995. Lexical and prelexical influences on word segmentation: Evidence from priming. *Journal of Experimental Psychology: Human Perception and Performance, 21,* 344–359.

Hallé, P. A., and de Boysson-Bardies, B. 1996. The format of representation of recognized words in infants' early receptive lexicon. *Infant Behavior and Development, 19,* 463–481.

Harris, J. 1994. *English sound structure.* Oxford: Blackwell.

Hartshorn, K., Rovee-Collier, C., Gerhardstein, P., Bhatt, R. S., Klein, P. J., Aaron, F., Wondoloski, T. L., and Wurtzel, N. 1998. Developmental changes in the specificity of memory over the first year of life. *Developmental Psychobiology, 33,* 61–78.

Hintzman, D. L. 1986. "Schema abstraction" in a multiple-trace memory model. *Psychological Review, 93,* 411–428.

Jusczyk, P. W. 1997. *The discovery of spoken language.* Cambridge, MA: MIT Press.

Jusczyk, P. W., and Aslin, R. N. 1995. Infants' detection of the sound patterns of words in fluent speech. *Cognitive Psychology, 29,* 1–23.

Jusczyk, P. W., Luce, P. A., and Charles-Luce, J. 1994. Infants' sensitivity to phonotactic patterns in the native language. *Journal of Memory and Language, 33,* 630–645.

Keating, P. A. 1985. Universal phonetics and the organization of grammars. In V. Fromkin, ed., *Phonetic linguistics: Essays in honor of Peter Ladefoged,* 115–132. New York: Academic Press.

Keating, P. A. 1990. Phonetic representations in a generative grammar. *Journal of Phonetics, 18,* 321–334.

Kessler, B., and Treiman, R. 1997. Syllable structure and the distribution of phonemes in English syllables. *Journal of Memory and Language, 37,* 295–311.

Klatt, D. H. 1976. Linguistic uses of segmental durations in English: Acoustic and perceptual evidence. *Journal of the Acoustical Society of America, 59,* 1208–1221.

Klatt, D. H. 1980. Speech perception: A model of acoustic-phonetic analysis and lexical access. In R. A. Cole, ed., *Perception and production of fluent speech,* 243–288. Hillsdale, NJ: Erlbaum.

Kluender, K. R., Diehl, R. L., and Wright, B. A. 1988. Vowel-length differences before voiced and voiceless consonants: An auditory explanation. *Journal of Phonetics, 16,* 153–169.

Labov, W. 1972. *Sociolinguistic patterns.* Philadelphia: University of Pennsylvania Press.

Labov, W. 1998. The intersection of sex and social class in the course of linguistic change. In J. Cheshire and P. Trudgill, eds., *The sociolinguistics reader, Vol. 2: Gender and discourse,* 7–52. London: Arnold.

Lively, S. E., Pisoni, D. B., and Goldinger, S. D. 1994. Spoken word recognition. In M. A. Gernsbacher, ed., *Handbook of psycholinguistics*, 265–301. New York: Academic Press.

Logan, G. D. 1992. Shapes of reaction-time distributions and shapes of learning curves: A test of the instance theory of automaticity. *Journal of Experimental Psychology: Learning, Memory, and Cognition, 18*, 883–914.

Marslen-Wilson, W. D. 1987. Functional parallelism in spoken word recognition. *Cognition, 25*, 71–102.

Mattys, S. L., and Jusczyk, P. W. 2001. Phonotactic cues for segmentation of fluent speech by infants. *Cognition, 78*, 91–121.

Mattys, S. L., Jusczyk, P. W., Luce, P. A., and Morgan, J. L. 1999. Phonotactic and prosodic effects on word segmentation in infants. *Cognitive Psychology, 38*, 465–494.

McClelland, J. L., and Elman, J. L. 1986. Interactive processes in speech recognition: The TRACE model. In J. L. McClelland and D. E. Rumelhart, eds., *Parallel distributed processing: Explorations in the microstructure of cognition*, 58–121. Cambridge, MA: MIT Press.

McQueen, J. M., Cutler, A., Briscoe, T., and Norris, D. 1995. Models of continuous speech recognition and the contents of the vocabulary. *Language and Cognitive Processes, 10*, 309–331.

Miller, J. L., and Volaitis, L. 1989. Effect of speaking rate on the perceptual structure of a phonetic category. *Perception and Psychophysics, 46*, 505–512.

Morgan, J. L. 1996. A rhythmic bias in preverbal speech segmentation. *Journal of Memory and Language, 35*, 666–688.

Morgan, J. L., and Saffran, J. R. 1995. Emerging integration of sequential and suprasegmental information in preverbal speech segmentation. *Child Development, 66*, 911–936.

Moscovitch, M. 1994. Memory and working with memory: Evaluation of a component process model and comparisons with other models. In D. L. Schacter and E. Tulving, eds., *Memory systems 1994*, 269–310. Cambridge, MA: MIT Press.

Mullennix, J. W., and Pisoni, D. B. 1990. Stimulus variability and processing dependencies in speech perception. *Perception and Psychophysics, 47*, 379–390.

Nittrouer, S., and Boothroyd, A. 1990. Context effects in phoneme and word recognition by young children and older adults. *Journal of the Acoustical Society of America, 87*, 2705–2715.

Nosofsky, R. M. 1988. Exemplar-based accounts of relations between classification, recognition, and typicality. *Journal of Experimental Psychology: Learning, Memory, and Cognition, 14*, 700–708.

Nusbaum, H. C., and Goodman, J. C. 1994. Learning to hear speech as spoken language. In J. C. Goodman and H. C. Nusbaum, eds., *The development of speech perception*, 299–338. Cambridge, MA: MIT Press.

Nusbaum, H. C., Pisoni, D. B., and Davis, C. K. 1984. Sizing up the Hoosier mental lexicon: Measuring the familiarity of 20,000 words. *Research on Speech Perception, Progress Report No. 10*. Speech Research Laboratory, Psychology Department, Indiana University, Bloomington.

Onishi, K., Chambers, K. E., and Fisher, C. 2002. Learning phonotactic constraints from brief auditory experience. *Cognition, 83*, B13–B23.

Palmer, C., Jungers, M. K., and Jusczyk, P. W. 2001. Episodic memory for musical prosody. *Journal of Memory and Language, 45*, 526–545.

Pierrehumbert, J. 1990. Phonological and phonetic representation. *Journal of Phonetics, 18*, 375–394.

Pierrehumbert, J. 2001. Exemplar dynamics: Word frequency, lenition, and contrast. In J. Bybee and P. Hopper, eds., *Frequency effects and the emergence of linguistic structure*, 137–157. Amsterdam: Benjamins.

Pinker, S. 1984. *Language learnability and language development*. Cambridge, MA: Harvard University Press.

Pisoni, D. B. 1997. Some thoughts on "normalization" in speech perception. In K. Johnson and J. W. Mullennix, eds., *Talker variability in speech processing*, 9–32. New York: Academic Press.

Poldrack, R. A., and Church, B. 1997, November. Auditory priming of new associations. Paper presented at the meeting of the Psychonomic Society, Philadelphia.

Quené, H. 1992. Durational cues for word segmentation in Dutch. *Journal of Phonetics, 20*, 331–350.

Rayner, K. 1998. Eye movements in reading and information processing: 20 years of research. *Psychological Bulletin, 124*, 372–422.

Saffran, J. R., Aslin, R. N., and Newport, E. L. 1996. Statistical learning by 8-month-old infants. *Science, 274*, 1926–1928.

Schacter, D. L. 1994. Priming and multiple memory systems: Perceptual mechanisms of implicit memory. In D. L. Schacter and E. Tulving, eds., *Memory systems 1994*, 233–268. Cambridge, MA: MIT Press.

Schacter, D. L., and Church, B. A. 1992. Auditory priming: Implicit and explicit memory for words and voices. *Journal of Experimental Psychology: Learning, Memory, and Cognition, 18*, 915–930.

Schafer, G., Plunkett, K., and Harris, P. L. 1999. What's in a name? Lexical knowledge drives infants' visual preferences in the absence of referential input. *Developmental Science, 2*, 187–194.

Sheffert, S. M. 1998. Voice-specificity effects on auditory word priming. *Memory and Cognition, 26*, 591–598.

Sommers, M. S. 1999. Perceptual specificity and implicit auditory priming in older and younger adults. *Journal of Experimental Psychology: Learning, Memory, and Cognition, 25,* 1236–1255.

Stager, C. L., and Werker, J. F. 1997. Infants listen for more phonetic detail in speech perception than in word-learning tasks. *Nature, 388,* 381–382.

Swingley, D., and Aslin, R. N. 2000. Spoken word recognition and lexical representation in very young children. *Cognition, 76,* 147–166.

Swingley, D., Pinto, J. P., and Fernald, A. 1999. Continuous processing in word recognition at 24 months. *Cognition, 71,* 73–108.

Wardaugh, R. 1998. *An introduction to sociolinguistics.* Oxford: Blackwell.

Warren, P., and Marslen-Wilson, W. 1987. Continuous uptake of acoustic cues in spoken word recognition. *Perception and Psychophysics, 41,* 262–275.

Werker, J. F., and Stager, C. L. 2000. Developmental changes in infant speech perception and early word learning: Is there a link? In M. B. Broe and J. B. Pierrehumbert, eds., *Papers in Laboratory Phonology 5: Acquisition and the lexicon,* 181–193. New York: Cambridge University Press.

Woodward, A. L., and Markman, E. M. 1998. Early word learning. In W. Damon, series ed., and D. K. Kuhn and R. S. Siegler, vol. eds., *Handbook of child psychology, Vol. 2: Cognition, perception, and language,* 5th ed., 371–420. New York: Wiley.

2

The Identification of Words and Their Meanings: From Perceptual Biases to Language-Specific Cues

Catharine H. Echols and C. Nathan Marti

The child approaching the beginnings of language learning is confronted with two fundamental problems. That child must discover how to identify words and other linguistic units in the stream of speech and must determine how to associate those words and other linguistic units with appropriate real-world referents. Neither of these problems has a simple solution. The segmentation of words is made difficult by the infrequency of pauses in spoken language and by the absence of a set of acoustic features that consistently indicates word boundaries (Cole and Jakamik 1980; Hayes and Clark 1970). The problem of linking words to referents is complicated by the virtually infinite number of possible referents that are present in any situation in which a novel word is heard (e.g., Quine 1960). A body of research, expanding rapidly over the past twenty years, provides some insight into how young children solve these two fundamental problems of language learning. Some intriguing commonalities are evident: in the initial phases of identifying both words and word meanings, children may use relatively general cues; subsequently, again for both problems, children may begin to identify language-specific cues, eventually coming to rely on these cues.

2.1 Segmentation of Word-Level Units from Speech

One possible explanation for young children's success at the difficult task of identifying words in speech is that certain perceptual or attentional processes may reduce the scope of the problem. Children may be successful at identifying words, even in the absence of an entirely consistent set of cues to boundaries between words, because they are not, in fact, seeking to identify boundaries between each of the words in a sequence of speech. Instead, properties of speech such as stress, rhythm, intonation, or position within the speech sequence may make a particular element, like a particular syllable or sequence of syllables, especially salient. Such salient elements could be readily extracted and would tend to be included in the initial representations for words. In this view, originally proposed by Gleitman and Wanner (1982; see also Echols and Newport 1992; Gleitman et al. 1988; Peters 1983), the child would extract salient elements from the stream of speech, leaving behind the remaining speech as unanalyzed sound. This would permit the child to circumvent the more difficult task of segmenting an entire speech sequence into word-level units.

Although attention to salient syllables or syllable sequences may be one important route to the identification of words in speech, it cannot be the only route. The specific cues that will be most valuable for identifying words and other linguistic units will vary across languages. For example, although stress may provide a useful cue in English, stress does not exist in some languages, or at least it functions very differently from English (see, e.g., Lehiste and Ivič 1986 on Serbo-Croatian and Pierrehumbert and Beckman 1988 on Japanese). Thus, children may be attentive to various properties of language, including stress, position, pitch patterns, or the rhythmic structure of a speech sequence. By being attentive to various aspects of prosody, or intonation, in their language, children should notice some relevant information in whatever language is being learned. Within the first year or two of life, children will need to determine which cues are relevant in the native language and will need to distinguish the specific roles those cues play. Sensitivity to language-specific configurations of cues will then become increasingly important in the identification of words and other linguistic units as the child moves through the beginning phases of language learning.

2.1.1 Evidence of Early Sensitivity to Segmentation-relevant Cues

Some of the cues that could be useful to infants in identifying words
in speech include intonation or tonal contours, rhythm, allophonic
cues (i.e., differences in the acoustic properties of a phoneme
depending on its location within a word), statistical information
regarding which syllables tend to co-occur in the input, and stressed
and final syllables. There is good evidence that infants are sensitive
to many of these cues. Infants between 1 and 4 months of age can
discriminate pitch contours in speech (Kuhl and Miller 1982), and
by 5 months of age, there is evidence that infants recognize tonal
sequences as holistic units, discriminating changes in the ordering
of tonal elements but not transpositions of the entire sequence to a
higher pitch (Chang and Trehub 1977). Evidence of rudimentary
sensitivity to rhythmic patterns is present by 2–3 months (Demany,
McKenzie, and Vurpillot 1977). By 6 months of age, infants appear
to use rhythmic cues to group syllables into units (Morgan and Saffran 1995). Infants as young as 4 days old have been shown to discriminate their native language from a nonnative language on the
basis of prosodic cues, such as intonation or rhythm (Mehler et al.
1988), though it is not clear which specific prosodic cues they use.
Moreover, newborns can discriminate speech sequences that contain
a word boundary from those that do not, probably on the basis of
stress and duration cues (Christophe et al. 1994).

Evidence of sensitivity to allophonic cues, sequential information,
and stress also is present very early. By 2 months of age, infants can
discriminate speech sequences on the basis of allophonic differences
that are relevant for segmentation (e.g., those distinguishing the two-
word sequence *night rate* from the word *nitrate*; Hohne and Jusczyk
1994). Infants between 7 and 8 months of age can attend to sequential information, noting which syllables tend to co-occur in speech to
which they have been exposed (Goodsitt, Morgan, and Kuhl 1993;
Saffran, Aslin, and Newport 1996). By 8 months of age, infants can
use their sensitivity to co-occurrence information to extract a disyllabic sequence from a continuous string of speech (Saffran, Aslin, and
Newport 1996). Infants 8 to 9 months old integrate co-occurrence

and rhythmic information, being most likely to group units when both cues are present (Morgan 1996; Morgan and Saffran 1995). Between 1 and 4 months of age, infants show evidence of being able to discriminate stress changes (Jusczyk and Thompson 1978; Spring and Dale 1977).

Although infants are capable of recognizing many of the acoustic cues that could indicate word boundaries in English from early in the first year of life, the ability to use most of these cues for segmenting words from the speech stream is likely to require substantial exposure to the native language. Languages vary greatly in the degree to which, and the specific ways in which, prosodic cues such as intonation or rhythm indicate linguistic units in speech; languages also vary with regard to the particular size of unit (e.g., word, phrase) that might be indicated by these cues. Similarly, the specific allophonic differences associated with word boundaries will vary to some degree across languages. Whereas an ability to attend to sequential regularities could be available from birth, it is likely that an infant will need to have fairly extensive exposure to the input language before the regularities that define specific words can be identified. As Saffran, Aslin, and Newport (1996) note, although the infants in their study were able to identify co-occurrence patterns with only 2 minutes of exposure, the input to which they were exposed was highly concentrated, containing only four "words" repeated over and over.

In contrast to the other cues, large amounts of exposure to the native language may not be required before infants can make use of stress and position cues. Across languages that use stress, the syllables that are stressed are perceptually highlighted in some way, typically involving one or more of the following characteristics: higher pitch, longer duration, greater amplitude, nonreduced vowel quality (Lehiste 1970). Although their sensitivity is not as great as that of adults, young infants are capable of discriminating most of the acoustic correlates of stress (Bull, Eilers, and Oller 1984; Eilers et al. 1984). Syllables in final position also may be salient independent of language exposure. Syllables that are in word-final position have the potential for being in phrase- or sentence-final positions, particularly in infant-directed speech, because parents tend to place nouns that are novel or that are the topic of discussion in sentence-final position

(Fernald and Mazzie 1991; Woodward and Aslin 1990). In sentence-final position, a syllable may benefit from a recency effect, such that it is more easily broken off and retained. In addition, phrase-, clause-, and sentence-final position is associated with acoustic highlighting, specifically lengthening (e.g., Klatt 1976; Nakatani, O'Connor, and Aston 1981), and this lengthening is particularly exaggerated in infant-directed speech (Albin and Echols 1996).

2.1.2 Evidence That Children Use Stress and Position in Word-Level Segmentation

One source of evidence for how children identify words in speech is their early productions. Young children, in the early phases of language learning, tend to omit unstressed, nonfinal syllables from their productions (e.g., Ingram 1978; Klein 1981); young children make similar omissions in languages that are from entirely distinct language families, including K'iche' Mayan (Pye 1983) and Hebrew (Berman 1977); and young children are more likely to imitate stressed and word-final syllables than unstressed, nonfinal syllables (Blasdell and Jensen 1970; Hura and Echols 1996; Oller and Rydland 1974).

In detailed analyses of early productions (Echols 1993; Echols and Newport 1992), we have shown that one-word speakers tend to omit unstressed, nonfinal syllables of the adult target (i.e., the adult word that a child is trying to produce). Indeed, in our data, children omitted more than 50 percent of unstressed, nonfinal syllables, and rarely omitted syllables that were either stressed or final. Children also tend to produce syllables that are stressed or final in the target more accurately than any unstressed, nonfinal syllables included in their productions (Echols and Newport 1992). Furthermore, effects of perceptual salience can be seen even in utterances containing more than only stressed and final syllables. In utterances including full or partial reduplications, segments that were repeated in more than one syllable of a child's production tended to originate in stressed or final syllables of the target. For example, in "nuni" for *noisy* or "bobi" for *bunny*, the /n/ and /b/, respectively, from the initial stressed syllable have spread to an unstressed (though in these examples, final) syllable. Syllables that were produced as schwa-like filler syllables tended to correspond to unstressed syllables (e.g., "uh-meh-meh" for *remember*; Echols 1993). One interpretation of these results is that even when unstressed, nonfinal syllables are incorporated into children's representations, they are incomplete (e.g., they are stored as a rhythmic placeholder, without precise sound features associated with them). At production, these incompletely represented syllables are filled in by segments spread or copied from adjacent syllables or by a default segment (e.g., a schwa).

These studies of children's productions are not conclusive evidence that the effects of stress are due to a failure to represent unstressed syllables. The stress effects are consistent with a representational account (e.g., Echols and Newport 1992), but they are also consistent with a production-based account that holds that children omit unstressed syllables that do not adhere to a trochaic (strong-weak) metrical template (Allen and Hawkins 1980; Gerken 1994). To distinguish production-based from perceptual accounts of children's omissions of unstressed syllables, it is necessary to obtain data on children's perceptions of these syllables.

2.1.3 Perceptual Evidence for the Salience of Stressed and Final Syllables

In an experiment with 9-month-olds, Childers and Echols (2002) have obtained perceptual evidence that stressed and final syllables are more salient than unstressed nonfinal syllables. Infants of this age are on the brink of language learning; accordingly, if attention to stressed and final syllables is to assist with the initial segmentation of words from speech, then 9-month-old infants should find those syllables especially salient. The logic of the study was based on the habituation procedure. Infants were exposed to trisyllabic sequences in which either the medial or final syllable was stressed. After they had an opportunity to become familiar with a given sequence, they were tested with two different variants of the sequence. One variant contained a change in the stressed syllable and the other contained a change in the unstressed syllable. For example, an infant who had been exposed during the familiarization period to *lifósa*, in which stress was on the medial syllable, would hear in alternating trials at test *livósa* and *lifóza* (changes are underlined). A second group of infants might be exposed to *lifosá*, with stress on the final syllable during familiarization, and would hear *livosá* and *lifozá* at test. If stressed and final syllables are indeed particularly salient, infants should be more likely to notice changes in those syllables than in unstressed nonfinal syllables. Because infants typically prefer novel stimuli in procedures of this type, they should prefer the sequences containing a change in a stressed or final syllable over other types of changes.

Infants' preferences were assessed by measuring the length of time they turned to listen to a particular sound sequence, using a variant of the head-turn preference procedure (Fernald 1985; Hirsh-Pasek et al. 1987; Jusczyk and Aslin 1995). This procedure makes use of infants' tendency to turn toward a sound that is interesting to them and to turn away when they lose interest. We combined this methodology with a habituation methodology by exposing infants to repeated presentations of the target stimulus before testing infants' responses to the two types of changes. To ensure that any observed differences in response to changes in medial versus final position were indeed due to position or stress level, and not to the difficulty of particular phoneme contrasts, the medial and final syllables were counterbalanced; half of the infants in each condition would hear the relevant *lifosa* variant during familiarization and half would hear a *lisafo* variant. In addition, each infant heard two different types of contrasts, one involving a voicing change in a fricative, as in the example, and another involving a place change in a stop consonant (e.g., *mobuti* to *moduti* or *mobupi*).

As can be seen in figure 2.1, a significant effect of position was obtained, $F(1, 31) = 5.28$, $p < .05$, with infants looking longer for changes in final than nonfinal syllables. However, only a trend was observed for stress $F(1, 31) = 3.20$, $p \approx .083$. Because infants would be expected to look longer when they notice changes than when they do not, these results suggest that infants more accurately represent

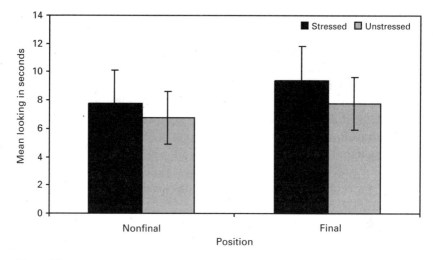

Figure 2.1
Mean looking (in seconds) for consonant changes in syllables of different stress levels and positions.

syllables in word-final than in nonfinal position. A closer examination of the data suggested that infants were performing differently on the two types of contrasts and, specifically, were showing greater evidence of discrimination for the stop/place change than the fricative/voicing change contrasts. This difference is not surprising, given the difficulty of discriminating voicing distinctions. When we analyzed separately for the two stimulus sets, the effect of stress was significant in the stop/place change set, $F(1, 30) = 5.14$, $p < .05$, but that of position was only marginally significant, $F(1, 30) = 4.08$, $p = .052$. Thus, the results provide tentative support for the proposal that stressed and final syllables are particularly salient to infants and that those salient syllables are represented more accurately than unstressed nonfinal syllables. It should be noted, however, that if attention to stressed and final syllables is to be available to infants as a segmentation strategy independent of language experience, it should be present prior to 9 months of age. Consequently, it will be important in future research to identify evidence of these tendencies in younger infants.

2.1.4   Evidence of Sensitivity to Language-Specific Segmentation Cues

In recent years, evidence of children's sensitivity to language-specific segmentation cues has exploded. There is now a large literature showing that, after about 7.5 months, infants recognize rhythmic characteristics of their native language. Specifically, English-hearing infants appear to recognize that a trochaic (strong-weak) stress pattern is dominant in their language (Jusczyk, Cutler, and Redanz 1993) and that units bearing this rhythm pattern should cohere (Echols, Crowhurst, and Childers 1997; Morgan 1996). Moreover, infants can use this knowledge to segment words from longer speech sequences (Echols, Crowhurst, and Childers 1997; Jusczyk, Houston, and Newsome 1999). In contrast, infants hearing Canadian French appear to be influenced by rhythmic properties of their native language, leading them to segment weak-strong words more readily (Polka, Sundara, and Blue 2002), though this effect has not been demonstrated in Parisian French–hearing infants (Emmanuel Dupoux, personal communication, November, 2001).

In one example of a study exploring the possibility that infants could use a language-typical rhythm pattern to extract words from a longer string of speech (Echols, Crowhurst, and Childers 1997), we exposed infants to two 4-syllable nonsense-speech sequences, one containing an embedded trochaic unit (e.g., *nud wótbun mò*) and one containing an embedded iambic unit (e.g., *bàl kusmít nur*). They were then tested with the familiar (extracted) trochaic unit, a novel trochaic unit, the familiar iambic unit, and a novel iambic unit. The prediction was that, as a result of the prior exposure, infants would find the previously heard sequences uninteresting if they recognized those sequences. Consequently, they should show a preference for the novel sequences. Thus, if they had successfully extracted the trochaic unit but failed to extract the iambic unit, they should prefer the trochaic distractor over the previously heard trochaic target but should not differentiate the iambic target and distractor. This prediction was confirmed: infants exhibited a preference for a novel trochee over the previously heard trochaic units, but they showed no differential response for the novel iamb over the previously heard iamb. In combination with research from other labs (e.g., Jusczyk, Houston, and Newsome 1999), this result suggests the trochaic stress pattern may provide a useful cue to infants in the initial identification of word-level units in speech.

During the latter half of the first year, infants also begin to exhibit evidence that they can use allophonic cues, as well as knowledge of phonotactic structure (i.e., the consonant sequences that are permissible in their native language) to segment words. By 10.5 months, infants can use allophonic cues to determine whether a speech sequence contains one or two words, and they can later recognize the appropriate sequence in fluent speech (Jusczyk, Hohne, and Bauman 1999). By 9 months, infants can distinguish English from Dutch on the basis of phonetic and phonotactic cues (Jusczyk et al. 1993), can distinguish phonotactically legal from illegal consonant clusters (Friederici and Wessels 1993), and show preferences for phonetic sequences that are more versus less frequent in their native language (Jusczyk, Luce, and Charles-Luce 1994). By the time infants have reached 10.5 months, phonetic cues appear to take precedence over prosodic cues in guiding their expectations regarding word boundaries, because their preferences for sequences containing pauses that coincide with rather than violate word boundaries disappear when speech is low-pass filtered to remove phonetic information (Myers et al. 1996). Moreover, infants of this age are successful at identifying weak-strong words in fluent speech (Jusczyk, Houston, and Newsome 1999), most likely through the use of phonetic information.

Increasing sensitivity to language-specific segmentation cues may result in the loss of some sensitivity to cues that are not relevant in the ambient language in a process similar to that which has been described for consonant and vowel discrimination (e.g., Kuhl et al. 1992; Werker and Tees 1984). Consistent with this possibility, Jusczyk (1989) found that 4.5-month-old English-hearing infants listened longer for Polish speech containing pauses consistent with linguistic units over those containing pauses that violated linguistic units. However, by 6 months, no evidence of the ability to identify linguistic units in Polish was present.

2.1.5 Use of Function Morphemes in Word-Level Segmentation

In addition to the cues mentioned above, a type of language-specific cue to word boundaries that could be quite valuable to infants is the function word (e.g., *a*, *the*). Because function words generally are unstressed in English, it is ironic, in light of our previous arguments, that we now are arguing that children not only might attend to function words, but also might use them for segmenting words from speech. However, function words are highly frequent and distinctive and, as a result, could assist word identification by indicating that a preceding or subsequent speech sequence is a possible word (Gerken, Landau, and Remez 1990; Gerken and McIntosh 1993). Moreover, as children move toward acquiring the syntactic structure of their language, function words can serve to distinguish different types of phrases (e.g., a noun phrase often will begin with *a* or *the*). Gerken, Landau, and Remez (1990) describe these two problems that function words potentially could solve, respectively, as the *segmentation* and *labeling* problems. We will discuss the apparent contradiction with our previous claims below.

The motivation for investigating prelinguistic infants' awareness of functors arose from a body of work indicating that children in the early stages of language acquisition are aware of these morphemes prior to producing them (e.g., Gerken, Landau, and Remez 1990; Gerken and McIntosh 1993; Shipley, Smith, and Gleitman 1969). For example, young 2-year-olds perform better in a picture-recognition task when nouns are preceded by the English functor *the* than when nouns are preceded by a nonsense word, an ungrammatical functor, such as *was*, or when the functor is omitted (Gerken and McIntosh 1993). Children of this age also are more likely to omit English functors from their imitations than nonsense words that resemble English functors in their stress and phonological characteristics (Gerken, Landau, and Remez 1990). By 10.5 months of age, infants listen longer to passages containing real versus nonsense function words, though it is not until 16 months that they respond differentially to passages containing misplaced function words (e.g., *is* instead of *the*; Shady 1996). In a study measuring event-related potentials (ERPs) for passages containing either English or modified function words, 11-month-olds, but not 10-month-olds, provide evidence of recognizing the function words (Shafer et al. 1998). Höhle and Weissenborn (1998) have documented recognition of German function words, after preexposure, by 7- to 15-month-old infants. The evidence indicating that these young children are aware of functors, and that their comprehension of speech is influenced by these words, gives rise to the possibility that function words also could be used to assist word-level segmentation.

To investigate 11-month-old infants' use of function morphemes for segmentation, we employed a modified head-turn preference procedure similar to that described in the previous section (Echols and Marti 1999; Marti 2001). Infants were first familiarized to two sentence-length nonsense-word utterances, then exposed to syllables extracted from those sequences. These familiarization stimuli were designed to mimic the prosody of English sentences consisting of a determiner, a noun, and a verb, in that order. The syllable in the determiner position in one sequence was an English functor (EF), and in the other sequence it was a nonsense-syllable "functor" (NF). For example, *the snook crayed* was one of the EF familiarization sequences and *kak feak pamed* was one of the NF familiarization sequences. Following the familiarization trials, four test trials were presented. These consisted of the syllables extracted from the noun positions in the EF and NF familiarization sequences and two novel syllables. During each test trial, the syllable was presented repeatedly. In the examples described above, the syllable *snook* was extracted from the EF sequence (this syllable type will be described as "the EF syllable") and *feak* was the syllable extracted from the NF sequence (hereafter "the NF syllable"). On the other two test trials, novel syllables such as *dep* and *trog* were presented. We predicted that infants would be better able to identify a novel word when it followed the familiar English function word *the* than when it followed a nonsense syllable atypical of English determiners. If infants extracted the EF syllable but failed to extract the NF syllable, they should be less attentive to the EF syllable than to either the NF syllable or the novel syllables.

When the nonsense functor was highly distinct from an English functor—that is, both stressed and phonologically heavy (consisting

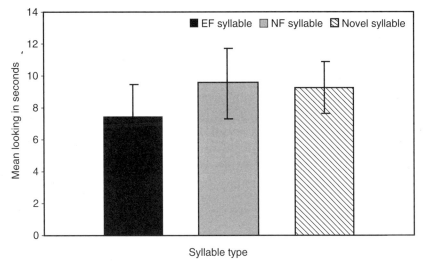

Figure 2.2
Mean looking (in seconds) for syllables following an English functor (EF), nonsense functor (NF), and novel syllables.

of a consonant-vowel-consonant sequence)—our predictions were supported. Infants looked significantly longer in the direction of novel syllables than they looked at EF syllables, $F(1, 31) = 5.77$, $p < .05$. They also looked significantly longer in the direction of NF syllables than they looked in the direction of EF syllables, $F(1, 31) = 4.26$, $p < .05$. Looking times in the direction of the NF syllables were virtually identical to the looking times in the direction of the novel syllables, indicating that they were equally interested in these syllables as they were in the novel syllables. Mean looking to each syllable type is shown in figure 2.2.

These findings were not replicated in subsequent experiments in which the nonsense functors were more similar to English functors in phonology, stress, or both (Marti 2001); clear differences in response to English and nonsense functors were observed only when the nonsense "functor" essentially was comparable to an English content word. Infants generally performed quite poorly in variants in which the nonsense functors were more similar to English, which might suggest that they were distracted by these atypical functors, even if they did not influence segmentation in the same way as the less English-like "functors." If true, that result is consistent with other work suggesting that infants of this age distinguish English from nonsense functors.

Additional evidence suggesting that infants may be capable of using function words in segmentation has been provided by Höhle and Weissenborn (2000). In a first phase of their experiment, infants were familiarized with either an unstressed determiner followed by a stressed one-syllable word or an iambic two-syllable word. At test, infants were presented with only the second syllable of each sequence embedded in a longer passage. The 10.5- to 12.5-month-old infants showed a marginally significant preference for passages containing the word from the determiner-content word sequence over those containing novel words. In contrast, infants showed no preference for passages containing the second syllable of the iambic word over passages containing only novel words.

Evidence that infants distinguish real from nonsense functors and can use function words in segmentation does not necessarily imply that infants understand the meanings of these words. It is likely that infants in our study were not using function morphemes semantically, but rather were using them solely as segmentation cues, having learned through experience with the native language that the beginning of a word follows these types of units (or at least that these syllables are words and therefore a word boundary must follow them). Indeed, it is conceivable that the use of function words in segmentation does not require experience with the native language. These syllables essentially could serve as perceptual pauses, because they are less perceptually salient than content words, and this pause could highlight the beginning of a unit such as a phrase or a word. Given evidence that infants of this age distinguish real from nonsense functors (Shady 1996; Shafer et al. 1998) and that they do not expect a word boundary after *any* unstressed syllable (e.g., Jusczyk, Houston, and Newsome 1999), we suggest that language-specific knowledge does underlie infants' use of these words in segmentation.

The growing body of evidence indicating that infants are aware of functors prior to producing them suggests that these morphemes could have a role in acquiring other aspects of language. One syntactic unit that has been difficult for perceptually based bootstrapping theories to explain is the phrase, because phrases are not consistently marked by prosodic features (Fernald and McRoberts 1996). An awareness of function morphemes would provide infants with cues that mark the beginning or endings of phrase boundaries. For example, determiners, such as *the*, consistently initiate noun phrases; function verbs, such as *was*, frequently initiate verb phrases.

2.1.6 An Integrative Account of Early Segmentation

The evidence that infants' language-specific knowledge may lead them to incorporate unstressed syllables into their productions and, indeed, may result in their making use of these syllables for segmenting additional words, leads to an expansion of an earlier account for word-level segmentation. Echols (1993) argued that infants should be prepared to attend to any of a number of potential segmentation cues and that, through experience with the ambient language, infants should become increasingly attentive to cues that are of value in the native language. More recently, we have suggested one way selective attention to language-specific segmentation cues could develop, at least in the case of children acquiring English (Echols 1996, 2001; Echols, Crowhurst, and Childers 1997). Stressed syllables and final syllables could be particularly salient at an early age because of their acoustic prominence. As a result, infants would be particularly likely to extract and store these syllables. For an infant exposed to English, this tendency frequently would result in the extraction of trochaic sequences, given the large number of trochaic disyllables in English as well as the tendency for English stress to fall in penultimate position even in words longer than two syllables. English-hearing infants may then come to recognize the stress pattern common to their multisyllabic extractions and may then begin to use that stress pattern to extract additional words. Thus, the initial perceptual tendencies would provide the basis for the development of sensitivity to language-specific cues.

This account needs to be expanded still further to incorporate evidence that infants may represent a particular class of unstressed syllables, functors, and indeed may use these syllables in tasks such as segmentation. As noted above, function words are extremely frequent. Even if infants focus primarily on stressed syllables and trochaic sequences, the very high frequency of function words should begin to attract children's attention to them. Moreover, as infants begin to recognize some words, they may turn their attention to the less salient syllables in a sentence. Infants may notice certain consistencies in the unstressed syllables contained within the short phrases that they hear. Over time, they may recognize that these syllables, too, could serve as markers indicating that a word is to follow. Shafer et al.'s (1998) data suggesting that recognition of function words is present at 11 but not 10 months accords with this possibility, because infants generally will begin recognizing some content words prior to that time. Later, infants may begin to recognize that function words tend to cue particular types of words with, for example, words like *a* and *the* cueing object words, or nouns. This possibility will be discussed in the next section.

2.2 Infants' Sensitivity to Cues That Assist in Associating Words with Referents

The identification of units in speech is only one part of the language-learning problem. The units identified will be useless for language learning unless they can be associated with a real-world referent or grammatical function.

2.2.1 Accounts of the Acquisition of Word Meaning

A number of different approaches have been taken in seeking to understand how children identify appropriate referents for words. Two that have motivated a fair amount of research in the field are constraints, or assumptions, approaches (e.g., Markman 1990; see also Golinkoff, Mervis, and Hirsh-Pasek 1994; Waxman and Kosowski 1990) and syntactic bootstrapping (e.g., Gleitman 1990). In the first of these approaches, the field of possible referents for a word is narrowed by the child's assumptions about probable relationships between words and referents. For example, children will tend to make a *whole-object assumption*, expecting words to be associated with whole objects and not with parts or properties of objects (Markman 1990). These accounts have tended to focus on the acquisition of noun meanings. Syntactic bootstrapping also addresses the problem that the extralinguistic context provides insufficient information to determine word meaning but focuses on verbs and offers the solution that children use information provided by syntactic structure to reduce the indeterminacy. Although much of the research motivated by this account has focused on verbs, the idea that syntax provides cues to word meaning has broader implications and, indeed, has been present in the literature for some time (e.g., Brown 1957; Katz, Baker, and Macnamara 1974).

Although the assumptions view, in particular has been the subject of controversy (e.g., Clark 1991; Merriman and Bowman 1989; Mervis, Golinkoff, and Bertrand 1994; Nelson 1988; Woodward and Markman 1991), we believe that an integrated account that includes different approaches will be most successful in accounting for word learning. One possible way of integrating the two accounts is analogous to that proposed for the identification of words in speech. The prelinguistic child may have certain attentional tendencies or prominent concepts that help to guide the beginnings of word-learning, but these tendencies may then be shaped and expanded by characteristics of the native language. More specifically, general tendencies assisting the identification of object labels may contribute to or at least interact with influences of syntactic cues. These language-specific syntactic cues may then assist the identification of verb meanings and various aspects of grammatical structure. The account proposed here is by no means the first effort to integrate different approaches to understanding word learning (see, e.g., Hirsh-Pasek and Golinkoff 1996), but it serves the useful function of bridging between accounts of word identification and accounts focused on the acquisition of word meaning.

2.2.2 Prelinguistic Processes: Influences of Labeling on Attention to Whole Objects

The whole-object assumption frequently is discussed as if it is a language-specific assumption. However, it also is possible that it derives from something more general. A substantial literature suggests that prelinguistic infants treat objects as coherent and substantive (e.g., Baillargeon 1993; Spelke 1991). Perhaps the whole-object assumption could derive from young children's conceptions of objects as cohesive and stable entities, a possibility suggested by Markman (1992). Speech may direct infants' attention to objects because objects have this special conceptual cohesiveness for infants. Among the youngest infants, the attentional facilitation that derives from speech may be general in the sense that infants' attention to this specific aspect of an event is increased, but they do not yet try to associate a word with the object. At this age, therefore, any speech (or at least any speech with an attention-getting intonation contour) should facilitate attention to objects, regardless of the specific content of the speech. Even if it is very general, the attentional facilitation could assist word learning by ensuring that the child's attention would be directed toward an object just as the label for that object was given. With time, then, the child may develop a more specific expectation that particular words within the speech they hear should correspond to a whole object.

One problem with this proposed account is that young children find aspects of events other than objects, such as motion, to be highly attractive. Thus, it is not clear why a general facilitation of attention that derives from speech should be directed specifically toward objects. However, not only do infants appear to perceive objects as coherent and stable but, in fact, many objects are coherent and stable. This quality of objects may give them a special status. As Gentner (1982) has proposed, objects may be more available to young children as referents in part because they are stable over time and retain their cohesiveness; in contrast, the referents of verbs are transient and may look very different across different instantiations (e.g., a person swimming versus a fish swimming). Even before infants are actively seeking to associate words with referents, these qualities of objects may make them a likely target of infants' attention.

Baldwin and Markman (1989) have shown that some aspect of labeling speech directs infants' attention to objects, at least in infants 10 to 14 months old. We have sought to extend these findings, investigating more directly the possibility that a *whole-object assumption* may derive from a tendency to attend more selectively to objects in the presence of labeling.

2.2.3 Influences of Labeling on Infants' Attention to Objects

To test the possibility that labeling selectively directs infants' attention to objects, we conducted an experiment using a variant of the habituation procedure (Echols 2002). The participants were 9-month-olds, an age at which infants are on the verge of language. The specific question was whether labeling would direct an infant's attention either to objects or to an element that is consistent across labeled events. The design was a 2 × 2 design in which half of the infants were assigned to a *labeled* and half to an *unlabeled* condition and in which half were assigned to a *consistent-object* and half to a *consistent-motion* condition. The speech stimuli for infants in the labeled condition were nonsense labels embedded in a real-word frame (e.g., "that's a *danu*"). Infants in the consistent-object condition saw a single object undergoing three different motions; those in the consistent-motion condition saw three different objects all undergoing the same motion. After four familiarization trials, infants saw two types of unlabeled test trials: a novel object in a familiar motion and a familiar object in a novel motion. Two stimulus sets were used, one consisting of brightly colored wooden objects that had some properties of animate entities (e.g., legs, heads) and the other consisting of soft felt and fur entities with eyes; this second set was more animate in appearance. Examples of one set of stimuli are shown in table 2.1. Because these are novel objects and actions, the labels shown in the table are not fully descriptive, but should be sufficient to convey the design. Test trial type and side of presentation were counterbalanced.

Three possible outcomes were considered. First, labeling might result in a general increase in attention to objects. If so, infants in both the consistent-object and the consistent-motion conditions should be more selectively focused on the objects (and less attentive to the motions) in the presence of labeling than in the absence of labeling and, as a result, should attend to the change in object at test. Second, labeling might direct infants' attention to another salient

Table 2.1
Example stimuli for object versus consistency experiment

	Consistent object condition	Consistent motion condition
Habituation	Birdlike creature—turning	Birdlike creature—turning
	Birdlike creature—bouncing	Furry creature—turning
	Birdlike creature—diagonal motion	Blue-haired creature—turning
	Birdlike creature—turning	Birdlike creature—turning
Test	Yellow-armed creature—turning	Yellow-armed creature—turning
	Birdlike creature—sideways motion	Birdlike creature—sideways motion
	Yellow-armed creature—turning	Yellow-armed creature—turning
	Birdlike creature—sideways motion	Birdlike creature—sideways motion

aspect of events—motion—when it is consistent across labeled events. Such a possibility could help to account for the presence of some nonobject words (e.g., *up*, *more*) in children's early vocabulary. In this view, objects simply may be common in early speech because objects tend to be consistent across labeled events. If labeling is directing attention to consistency, infants in the consistent-object condition should be attentive to the change in object at test, and those in the consistent-motion condition should be attentive to the change in motion. Finally, objectness and consistency may interact such that labeling speech will direct infants' attention toward objects, but only when they are consistent across repetitions of a label. In this case, labeling should result in attention to the change in object for infants in the consistent-object condition, but should have little effect in the consistent-motion condition.

The data analyzed were the times spent looking at the novel object relative to the times spent looking at both the novel object and the novel motion. Thus, scores greater than .50 reflected a preference for the change in object, whereas scores less than .50 reflected a preference for a change in motion. Combining across both stimulus sets, labeling had different effects in the consistent-object and consistent-motion conditions. Infants in the consistent-object condition who heard labeling looked relatively longer at the novel object

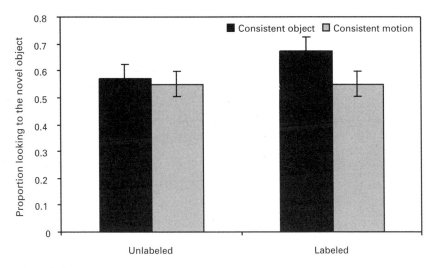

Figure 2.3
Proportion looking to the novel object as a function of labeling and consistency by 9-month-olds.

than infants in the consistent-motion condition who heard labeling, $t(14) = 2.18$, $p < .05$. Without labeling, looking behavior did not differ between the two conditions. For one of the two stimulus sets, that consisting of the more animate objects, the results were very robust, with infants in the consistent-object condition looking relatively longer at the novel object if they heard labeling than if they did not, $t(14) = 4.65$, $p < .001$, and, among all infants who heard labeling, those in the consistent-object condition looking relatively longer at the object than those in the consistent-motion condition, $t(14) = 3.59$, $p < .01$. The results across both data sets are shown in figure 2.3.

These results suggest that labeling selectively directs 9-month-olds' attention to objects that are consistent across labeled sequences. No such increase in attention is seen for consistent motion, which accords with the proposal that objects are privileged as a target of infants' attention in labeling contexts.

One issue that might be raised is whether these findings extend beyond prior evidence that labeling facilitates categorization (e.g.,

Waxman and Kosowski 1990; Waxman and Markow 1995). Some findings from our study are consistent with categorization. In that account, labeling would lead infants in the consistent-motion condition to attend to commonalities among the objects; because the novel object would appear to be another member of the category, the categorization account predicts their low level of looking toward the novel object. In contrast, because they are exposed to only one object in the consistent-object condition, infants should focus on that object, regardless of whether labeling is present, and infants should therefore treat the novel object as new. However, although categorization can account for some of the results of this study, it does not fully account for the results. In our experiment, although labeling failed to increase attention to the novel object in the consistent-motion condition, it also did not decrease attention, which should have happened if categorization entirely explained the results. A categorization account also might not predict that labeling would increase attention to the novel object for infants in the consistent-object condition. Labeling might increase attention to the object because it is the only common element, but in that case, it is puzzling that labeling failed to increase attention to the motion when it was the only common element. Consequently, these results extend beyond the evidence that labels increase categorization, by showing that labeling directs attention to an object that has been consistent over repetitions of a label, but does not do so for motion.

One final issue concerns the role of labeling speech in directing attention. It is possible that it is not labeling speech per se that is responsible for differences between unlabeled and labeled conditions, but rather an attentional facilitation that results from the association of any sound, linguistic or nonlinguistic, with an event (e.g., Roberts and Jacob 1991; although see Balaban and Waxman 1997). We do not have data that distinguishes the possible influences of labeling speech from influences of any sound. However, because the proposed attentional facilitation is very general in nature, a finding of similar facilitation by music or other interesting sounds, at least for prelinguistic infants, would be compatible with this proposed account. Nonetheless, the question of specificity is an interesting one, and is one that we are exploring in ongoing research.

2.2.4 Sensitivity to Syntactic Cues in the Identification of Word Meaning

Although evidence that young children use both syntactic and semantic information in interpreting novel words has been around for some time (e.g., Brown 1957; Katz, Baker, and Macnamara 1974), the bootstrapping proposals have given rise to a rapidly expanding body of research on young children's sensitivity to these cues (see, for example, research discussed in Gleitman 1990; Hirsh-Pasek and Golinkoff 1993). Hirsh-Pasek and Golinkoff, for instance, described sensitivity to linguistic cues to verb-object (action-patient) relations in infants 13 to 15 months old and to word-order cues to subject and object in infants 16 to 18 months old. Naigles (1990) provided evidence of sensitivity to syntactic cues to transitive versus intransitive verbs by infants between 23 and 27 months of age, and Naigles and Kako (1993) showed that when a causative syntactic frame is used to label an event, 27-month-old children override a tendency to prefer synchronous actions and instead attend to a causative event. Fisher and colleagues (1994) showed that slightly older children, 3- and 4-year-olds, distinguish between transitive and intransitive sentences and between sentences containing different types of prepositions in interpreting a novel verb.

Researchers also have linked the assumptions and bootstrapping approaches, investigating ways syntactic information may interact with word-learning assumptions to determine children's expectations concerning the meanings of novel words. Waxman and Kosowski (1990) showed that syntactic information may influence the likelihood that children will expect a novel word to refer to a category of objects. Waxman (1990, 1991) demonstrated that adjectives and nouns may exert different influences on 3- to 4-year-olds' categorization, with novel noun labels facilitating classification at the superordinate level and novel adjective labels facilitating classification at the subordinate level. In similar research with infants 12 to 13 months old, however, both nouns and adjectives facilitated categorization of objects (Waxman and Markow 1995), suggesting that very young children may be less sensitive to syntactic cues; instead, very young children may have a general bias to be directed toward categories of objects in the presence of any type of labeling. Hall, Waxman, and Hurwitz (1993) obtained evidence of interactions between word-learning assumptions and syntactic cues for 4-year-olds but not 2-years-olds. Older children's responses appeared to be influenced by adjective syntax, as well as by word-learning assumptions. In contrast, the younger children's responses appeared to be dominated by a specific word-learning assumption.

In other research assessing children's sensitivity to syntactic cues, Taylor and Gelman (1988) found modest evidence for influences of adjective versus noun syntax in an experiment with 2-year-olds that used familiar and unfamiliar objects varying in texture. Golinkoff and associates (1992) obtained evidence suggesting that 2-year-old children can attend to syntactic markers such as *a* and *one* to identify a novel word as a noun or adjective. Smith, Jones, and Landau (1992) showed that the tendency of adjectives to direct 3-year-old children to texture increased as the salience of the texture increased. In contrast, nouns resulted in same-shape extensions regardless of the salience of texture, suggesting differences in the biases that guide noun and adjective extensions. Recent studies by Hall, Lee, and Bélanger (2001), coupled with earlier studies by Katz, Baker, and Macnamara (1974) and Gelman and Taylor (1984), suggest that children can use syntax to distinguish proper from common nouns by the age of two years or slightly later.

Recent research provides evidence of more subtle influences of syntax as early as 13 to 14 months. Children as young as 14 months interpret adjective and noun syntax differently, extending words labeled with noun syntax on the basis of category information but being more flexible in their extensions of words labeled with adjective syntax (Waxman and Booth 2001). By 13 months, infants are more attentive to a change in property when familiarized using adjective than using noun syntax (Waxman 1999), suggesting that even by this age, adjective syntax and noun syntax are drawing attention to different aspects of an object.

One important distinction that can be cued by syntax is that between nouns and verbs. As noted above, the same function morphemes that can provide cues to word and phrase boundaries, also can serve as cues to the type of word or phrase. Nouns often will be preceded by *a* or *the* and the same words can mark the beginning of a noun phrase; a verb may end in *ing* and a verb phrase may begin with *is* or *was*. Even before children fully comprehend the grammatical structure of their language, they could use function words and other syntactic cues to distinguish nouns (or object words) from verbs (or action words). Indeed, arguments that children use these distributional cues to identify grammatical categories such as Noun and Verb have been in the literature for some time (e.g., Maratsos and Chalkley 1980). Golinkoff et al. (1992) obtained evidence that 24-month-olds can use syntactic cues to distinguish nouns from verbs. However, there is little evidence regarding the abilities of infants younger than 2 to make use of these cues in interpreting the meaning of a novel word. Consequently, we sought to explore that question in a study with 13- and 18-month-old infants (Echols and Marti 1999). We chose these ages because 13-month-olds generally are beginning to produce words, whereas some 18-month-olds are beginning to combine words and most understand some word combinations.

2.2.5   Infants' Ability to Use Syntactic Cues to Distinguish Nouns from Verbs

For the experiment, we used a preferential-looking procedure, modeled after that used by Golinkoff and colleagues (1987). The 13- and 18-month-old participants were familiarized with a labeled event involving a novel object and a novel action, then were tested with scenes in which the familiarized object and action were separated. More specifically, we used the procedure in the following way. Infants sat on a parent's lap facing two video monitors. During an initial familiarization period, the infants saw an animal for which they were unlikely to know a name (e.g., an anteater). The animal was doing an action for which infants also were unlikely to have a name (e.g., an opening/closing-type action with the lid of an infant cup). The infants saw this event first on one screen, then on the other, and then on both screens. An example familiarization and test sequence is shown in table 2.2. While looking at this event, infants heard one of three types of labels. Infants in a *noun-labeling condition* heard, for

Table 2.2
Example familiarization and test sequence for noun/verb study

Trial type	Left monitor	Right monitor
Familiarization	Anteater—opening	Blank
	Blank	Anteater—opening
	Anteater—opening	Anteater—opening
Change	Anteater—spinning	Manatee—opening
Test	Anteater—spinning	Manatee—opening
	Anteater—spinning	Manatee—opening

example, "that's a gep; it's a gep." Infants in a *verb-labeling condition* heard, for instance, "it's gepping; see? it geps." Finally, a third group of infants, in a *nonlabeling speech condition,* served as a control group. These infants heard speech that contained no labels (e.g., "what do you see? what's there?"). This condition assessed the possibility that speech could have some general attention-facilitating effect that might favor objects or motions. If infants use the frame in which a new word is presented to interpret the word, then infants in the noun-labeling group should expect the word *gep* to refer to the ant-eater, infants in the verb-labeling group should expect *gep* to refer to the opening action, and infants in the nonlabeling speech group should be directed neither to the object nor to the action.

After the familiarization period, during which infants had an opportunity to develop an interpretation for the new word, the scenes on the video screen changed. One screen showed the familiar animal (e.g., the anteater) engaging in a new action (e.g., a spinning action with the cup). On the other screen, infants saw a new animal for which they were unlikely to have a name (e.g., a manatee) in the familiar opening/closing action. Infants heard "Look, it changed," then, depending on the labeling condition, "Look at the gep," "Look at it gepping," or, simply, "Look! look."

If infants use syntactic frames to infer the meanings of novel words, then when asked to "look at the gep" during test trials, those infants in the noun-labeled condition should look at the previously seen animal (e.g., the anteater); when directed to "look at it gepping," infants in the verb-labeled condition should look toward the previously seen action (e.g., the manatee doing the opening/closing action); and infants in the nonlabeling speech control should show equal interest in the two changes when hearing "look! look" during the test trials.

Two different stimulus sets were used, with half of the children in each age group seeing each set. Because the more animate stimuli produced the more robust results in our previous study, both stimulus sets consisted of realistic puppets of animals that we hoped would be unfamiliar to the children. One set consisted of the manatee and anteater, and the other consisted of a sea otter and a mole. Additionally, the "verb" was transitive, involving an animate agent acting on an inanimate object, which should make it prototypically verblike (Slobin 1981).

The results were analyzed using analysis of variance, with age (13, 18 months) and labeling condition (noun, verb) as between-subjects variables and trial type (familiar object, familiar motion) as a within-subjects variable. A significant labeling condition × trial type interaction was observed, $F(1, 117) = 9.35$, $p < .005$, indicating that across both ages, infants were influenced by frame type. Results were also analyzed separately for each age group. The 18-month-olds showed a clear effect of frame type on looking behavior, as evidenced by a significant labeling condition × trial type interaction, $F(1, 57) = 6.68$, $p < .02$. Looking for infants in the nonlabeling speech trials was, as expected, relatively flat across the two trial types. These results are shown in figure 2.4. For 13-month-olds, the overall pattern was similar, but the effects were less robust, appearing only as a trend when stimulus sets were combined, $F(1, 60) = 3.10$, $p \approx .083$, and being significant for one of the two stimulus sets, $F(1, 28) = 6.15$, $p < .02$. Moreover, for that stimulus set, infants' attention also was drawn toward the object in the nonlabeling speech condition, indicating either a general tendency for speech to draw attention to the object, or that the test trials involving the familiar objects were inherently more interesting. Labeling, in the verb condition, had the effect of diminishing this tendency to focus on the familiar object, as evidenced by a significant difference in attention to the familiar

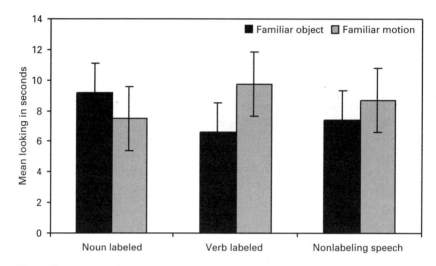

Figure 2.4
Mean looking (in seconds) by 18-month-olds for familiar objects and motions as a function of labeling frame.

object between the verb-labeled and nonlabeling speech conditions, $t(28) = 2.30$, $p < .05$. The overall pattern for 13-month-olds is shown in figure 2.5.

These results suggest that infants can use certain grammatical cues to distinguish nouns from verbs by 18 months of age, interpreting a novel word embedded in a noun frame as referring to an object and one embedded within a verb frame as referring to an action. By as early as 13 months, infants are aware of differences between noun and verb frames, though, for the younger infants, the verb frame may serve to reduce a general tendency for speech to increase attention to objects.

2.2.6 An Integrative Account of the Acquisition of Word Meaning

The attempt to develop an integrative account of early word learning may benefit from the integrative account, proposed above, for word-level segmentation. Specifically, it may be possible to apply to this domain the same general framework: in the domain of word-learning, too, prelinguistic predispositions may interact with devel-

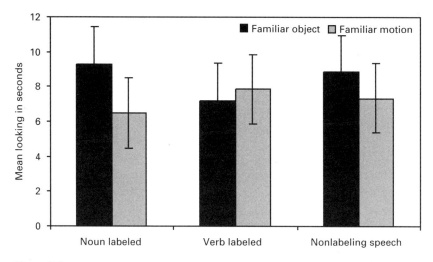

Figure 2.5
Mean looking (in seconds) by 13-month-olds for familiar objects and motions as a function of labeling frame.

oping sensitivities to cues in the native language to facilitate word learning. Our results suggest that young infants come to the task of language learning attending to labeled events in ways that may assist them in learning the meanings of words. Infants as young as 9 months of age appear to focus more selectively on an object, at least if the object is consistent, when an event is labeled. The biases that children bring to the language-learning task may be biases related to objects: objects have certain characteristics that may make them a useful early class of referents—they are solid and continuous (see, e.g., Spelke 1991). Indeed, Gentner (1982) has proposed that objects have a conceptual coherence not as readily present in other aspects of experience. Markman (1992) has proposed that the whole-object assumption may derive from this privileged status of objects in the nonlinguistic domain. Labeling speech may serve to increase infants' attention and, because of their special status, that attention may be directed specifically toward objects. However, even by 9 months, infants also appear to be sensitive to another characteristic of the context, consistency, with labeling drawing attention to objects specifically when they are consistent across labeled events.

This increased attention to consistent objects will be useful for associating words with object referents. Subsequently, it also may facilitate the identification of distributional cues to the noun category, including function words such as *a* and *the*. Once grammatical cues associated with nouns are identified, infants are likely to notice cues associated with other interesting aspects of experience, such as motion, properties of objects, and cues that distinguish specific individuals from groups of entities. Attention to each of these distinctions could build off of attention to a noun or object category. As early as 13 months of age, infants appear to be sensitive to some grammatical information, responding distinctively to different linguistic frames. Interestingly, the initial effect of a different labeling frame, in this case a verb frame, may be one of suppressing a general tendency for speech to increase attention to the object. Our 18-month-olds showed evidence that they could use both noun and verb syntax to interpret a novel word. Other research, reviewed above, suggests that sensitivity to adjective syntax may begin to appear during this period, though becoming more robust after the age of 2, and that sensitivity to syntactic cues distinguishing proper from common nouns develops around the age of 2.

2.3 Summary

In the past decade, increased attention has been directed toward understanding two fundamental problems of the beginnings of language learning, that of how the child identifies words and other linguistic units in the stream of speech and that of how the child associates the extracted language units to appropriate real-world referents. The findings suggest that a similar conceptual framework may be valuable for understanding both processes: for both tasks, children appear to start out with a set of predispositions that will assist them in solving the task. In segmentation, the predispositions may include tendencies to attend to perceptually salient syllables, rhythm, and pitch patterns. In acquiring word meaning, the predispositions may include tendencies to attend to objects and consistency. For both tasks, the initial predispositions could derive from general perceptual or attentional biases, not necessarily specific to the domain of language. For example, the initial biases guiding segmentation could be perceptual biases that result in attention to louder, longer, and higher-pitched sounds; those guiding word learning could be general expectations, either innately guided or derived from experience, that objects are cohesive and stable entities. Whatever their origins, these predispositions will be shaped and expanded on by developing sensitivities to characteristics of the native language. In segmentation, the English-learning child may begin to attend to typical stress patterns, as well as to allophonic and phonotactic cues that characterize word boundaries, the co-occurrence of particular syllables, and highly frequent words such as function words. In word meaning, children will become increasingly sensitive to the information conveyed by syntactic cues. Indeed, function words may serve to link these two tasks further. Once children have acquired sufficient experience with their native language, function words may assist segmentation by indicating a word or phrase boundary. Function morphemes also may provide cues to the grammatical category of a subsequent or, in the case of verb inflections, a preceding word. Thus, these unstressed elements that initially received less attention may, through experience with the native language, come to be important in solving these two fundamental word-learning problems.

Acknowledgments

We are deeply grateful to the following individuals for valuable contributions to research reported in this chapter: Renée Baillargeon, Jane Childers, Marlena Creusere, Megan Crowhurst, Linda Garza, Ellen Markman, Elissa Newport, Kimberley Prater Rynearson, André Thomas, Thomas Thornton, and Anthony Webb. I am thankful for the efforts of a number of undergraduate students who assisted with this research and of the children and parents who made this research possible. Stephen Piché deserves thanks for developing the timing program. This research was supported by INRSA HD07109 from NICHD, by grant 003658-368 from the Advanced Research Program of the Texas Higher Education Coordinating Board, and by NICHD grant HD30820.

References

Albin, D. D., and Echols, C. H. 1996. Stressed and word-final syllables in infant-directed speech. *Infant Behavior and Development, 19*, 401–418.

Allen, G. D., and Hawkins, S. 1980. Phonological rhythm: Definition and development. In G. Yeni-Komshian, J. F. Kavanagh, and C. A. Ferguson, eds., *Child phonology, Vol. 1: Production*, 227–256. New York: Academic Press.

Baillargeon, R. 1993. The object concept revisited: New directions in the investigation of infants' physical knowledge. In C. E. Granrud, ed., *Visual perception and cognition in infancy*, 265–315. Hillsdale, NJ: Erlbaum.

Balaban, M. T., and Waxman, S. R. 1997. Do words facilitate object categorization in 9-month-old infants? *Journal of Experimental Child Psychology, 64*, 3–26.

Baldwin, D. A., and Markman, E. M. 1989. Establishing word-object relations: A first step. *Child Development, 60*, 381–398.

Berman, R. A. 1977. Natural phonological processes at the one-word stage. *Lingua, 43*, 1–21.

Blasdell, R., and Jensen, P. 1970. Stress and word position as determinants of imitation in first language learners. *Journal of Speech and Hearing Research, 13*, 193–202.

Brown, R. 1957. Linguistic determinism and the part of speech. *Journal of Abnormal and Social Psychology, 55*, 1–5.

Bull, D., Eilers, R. E., and Oller, D. K. 1984. Infants' discrimination of intensity variation in multisyllabic stimuli. *Journal of the Acoustical Society of America, 75*, 13–17.

Chang, H. W., and Trehub, S. E. 1977. Auditory processing of relational information by young infants. *Journal of Experimental Child Psychology, 24*, 324–331.

Childers, J. B., and Echols, C. H. 2002. *Infants' attention to stressed and word-final syllables: Implications for word-level segmentation.* Unpublished manuscript, University of Texas, Austin.

Christophe, A., Dupoux, E., Bertoncini, J., and Mehler, J. 1994. Do infants perceive word boundaries? An empirical approach to the bootstrapping problem for lexical acquisition. *Journal of the Acoustical Society of America, 95*, 1570–1580.

Clark, E. V. 1991. Acquisitional principles in lexical development. In S. A. Gelman and J. P. Byrnes, eds., *Perspectives on language and thought: Interrelations in development*, 31–71. Cambridge, England: Cambridge University Press, 1991.

Cole, R. A., and Jakamik, J. 1980. A model of speech perception. In R. A. Cole, ed., *Perception and production of fluent speech*, 133–163. Hillsdale, NJ: Erlbaum.

Demany, L., McKenzie, B., and Vurpillot, E. 1977. Rhythm perception in early infancy. *Nature, 266*, 718–719.

Identification of Words and Their Meanings

Echols, C. H. 1993. A perceptually-based model of children's earliest productions. *Cognition, 46*, 245–296.

Echols, C. H. 1996. A role for stress in early speech segmentation. In J. L. Morgan and K. Demuth, eds., *Signal to syntax: Bootstrapping from speech to grammar in early acquisition*, 151–170. Hillsdale, NJ: Erlbaum.

Echols, C. H. 2001. Contributions of prosody to infants' segmentation and representation of speech. In H. Clahsen and L. White, series eds., and J. Weissenborn and B. Höhle, eds., *How to get into language: Approaches to bootstrapping in early language development*, 25–46. Amsterdam: Benjamins.

Echols, C. H. 2002. *An influence of labeling on infants' attention to objects and consistency: Implications for word-referent mappings.* Unpublished manuscript, University of Texas, Austin.

Echols, C. H., Crowhurst, M. J., and Childers, J. B. 1997. The perception of rhythmic units in speech by infants and adults. *Journal of Memory and Language, 36*, 202–225.

Echols, C. H., and Marti, C. N. 1999, April. Children's uses of syntactic cues in word learning: Successes and failures. S. R. Waxman and C. H. Echols, organizers, *Coordination of speech cues and word learning.* Symposium conducted at the biennial meeting of the Society for Research in Child Development, Albuquerque, NM.

Echols, C. H., and Newport, E. L. 1992. The role of stress and position in determining first words. *Language Acquisition, 2*, 189–220.

Eilers, R. E., Bull, D. H., Oller, D. K., and Lewis, D. C. 1984. The discrimination of vowel duration. *Journal of the Acoustical Society of America, 75*, 213–218.

Fernald, A. 1985. Four-month-old infants prefer to listen to motherese. *Infant Behavior and Development, 8*, 181–195.

Fernald, A., and Mazzie, C. 1991. Prosody and focus in speech to infants and adults. *Developmental Psychology, 27*, 209–221.

Fernald, A., and McRoberts, G. 1996. Prosodic bootstrapping: A critical analysis of the argument and the evidence. In J. L. Morgan and K. Demuth, eds., *Signal to syntax: Bootstrapping from speech to grammar in early acquisition*, 365–388. Hillsdale, NJ: Erlbaum.

Fisher, C. L., Hall, D. G., Rakowitz, S., and Gleitman, L. 1994. When it is better to receive than to give: Syntactic and conceptual constraints on vocabulary growth. *Lingua, 92*, 333–375.

Friederici, A. D., and Wessels, J. M. I. 1993. Phonotactic knowledge and its use in infant speech perception. *Perception and Psychophysics, 54*, 287–295.

Gelman, S. A., and Taylor, M. 1984. How two-year-old children interpret proper and common names for unfamiliar objects. *Child Development, 55*, 1535–1540.

Gentner, D. 1982. Why nouns are learned before verbs: Linguistic relativity versus natural partitioning. In S. Kuczaj, ed., *Language development: Language, cognition, and culture*, 301–334. Hillsdale, NJ: Erlbaum.

Gerken, L. A. 1994. A metrical template account of children's weak syllable omissions. *Journal of Child Language, 21*, 565–584.

Gerken, L. A., Landau, B., and Remez, R. 1990. Function morphemes in young children's speech perception and production. *Developmental Psychology, 26*, 204–216.

Gerken, L. A., and McIntosh, B. 1993. The interplay of function morphemes and prosody in early language. *Developmental Psychology, 29*, 448–457.

Gleitman, L. R. 1990. The structural sources of verb meanings. *Language Acquisition, 1*, 3–55.

Gleitman, L. R., Gleitman, H., Landau, B., and Wanner, E. 1988. Where learning begins: Initial representations for language learning. In F. J. Newmeyer, ed., *Linguistics: The Cambridge survey, Vol. 3: Language: Psychological and biological processes*, 150–193. Cambridge, England: Cambridge University Press.

Gleitman, L. R., and Wanner, E. 1982. Language acquisition: The state of the state of the art. In E. Wanner and L. R. Gleitman, eds., *Language acquisition: The state of the art*, 3–48. Cambridge, England: Cambridge University Press.

Golinkoff, R. M., Diznoff, J., Yasik, A., and Hirsh-Pasek, K. 1992, May. How children identify nouns versus verbs. Poster presented at the International Conference on Infancy Studies, Miami Beach, FL.

Golinkoff, R. M., Hirsh-Pasek, K., Cauley, K., and Gordon, L. 1987. The eyes have it: Lexical and syntactic comprehension in a new paradigm. *Journal of Child Language, 14*, 23–45.

Golinkoff, R. M., Mennuti, T., Lengle, C., and Hermon, G. 1992, May. Is "glorpy" a noun or an adjective? Identifying the part of speech of a novel word. Poster presented at the International Conference on Infancy Studies, Miami Beach, FL.

Golinkoff, R. M., Mervis, C. B., and Hirsh-Pasek, K. 1994. Early object labels: The case for lexical principles. *Journal of Child Language, 21*, 125–155.

Goodsitt, J. V., Morgan, P. L., and Kuhl, P. K. 1993. Perceptual strategies in prelingual speech. *Journal of Child Language, 20*, 229–252.

Hall, D. G., Lee, S. C., and Bélanger, J. 2001. Young children's use of syntactic cues to learn proper names and count nouns. *Developmental Psychology, 37*, 298–307.

Hall, D. G., Waxman, S. R., and Hurwitz, W. M. 1993. How two- and four-year-old children interpret adjectives and count nouns. *Child Development, 64*, 1651–1664.

Hayes, J. R., and Clark, H. H. 1970. Experiments on the segmentation of an artificial speech analog. In J. R. Hayes, ed., *Cognition and the development of language*, 221–234. New York: Wiley.

Hirsh-Pasek, K., and Golinkoff, R. M. 1993. Skeletal supports for grammatical learning: What infants bring to the language learning task. In C. K. Rovee-Collier and L. P. Lipsitt, eds., *Advances in infancy research, Vol. 8*, 299–338. Norwood, NJ: Ablex.

Hirsh-Pasek, K., and Golinkoff, R. M. 1996. *The origins of grammar: Evidence from early language comprehension.* Cambridge, MA: MIT Press.

Hirsh-Pasek, K., Kemler Nelson, D. G., Jusczyk, P. W., Wright-Cassidy, K., Druss, B., and Kennedy, L. 1987. Clauses are perceptual units for young infants. *Cognition, 26,* 269–286.

Höhle, B., and Weissenborn, J. 1998. Sensitivity to closed-class elements in preverbal children. In A. Greenhill, M. Hughes, H. Littlefield, and H. Walsh, eds., *Proceedings of the 22nd annual Boston University Conference on Language Development.* Somerville, MA: Cascadilla Press.

Höhle, B., and Weissenborn, J. 2000. The origins of syntactic knowledge: Recognition of determiners in one year old German children. In S. C. Howell, S. A. Fish, and T. Keith-Lucas, eds., *Proceedings of the 24th annual Boston University Conference on Language Development.* Somerville, MA: Cascadilla Press.

Hohne, E. A., and Jusczyk, P. W. 1994. Two-month-old infants' sensitivity to allophonic differences. *Perception and Psychophysics, 56,* 613–623.

Hura, S. L., and Echols, C. H. 1996. The role of stress and articulatory difficulty in children's early productions. *Developmental Psychology, 32,* 165–176.

Ingram, D. 1978. The role of the syllable in phonological development. In A. Bell and J. B. Hooper, eds., *Syllables and segments,* 143–155. Amsterdam: North-Holland.

Jusczyk, P. W. 1989, April. *Perception of cues to clausal units in native and non-native languages.* Paper presented at the biennial meeting of the Society for Research in Child Development, Kansas City, MO.

Jusczyk, P. W., and Aslin, R. N. 1995. Infants' detection of the sound patterns of words in fluent speech. *Cognitive Psychology, 29,* 1–23.

Jusczyk, P. W., Cutler, A., and Redanz, N. J. 1993. Infants' sensitivity to the predominant stress patterns of English words. *Child Development, 64,* 675–687.

Jusczyk, P. W., Friederici, A. D., Wessels, J. M. I., Svenkerud, V. Y., and Jusczyk, A. M. 1993. Infants' sensitivity to the sound patterns of native language words. *Journal of Memory and Language, 32,* 402–420.

Jusczyk, P. W., Hohne, E. A., and Bauman, A. 1999. Infants' sensitivity to allophonic cues for word-level segmentation. *Perception and Psychophysics, 61,* 1465–1476.

Jusczyk, P. W., Houston, D. M., and Newsome, M. 1999. The beginnings of word segmentation in English-learning infants. *Cognitive Psychology, 39,* 159–207.

Jusczyk, P. W., Luce, P. A., and Charles-Luce, J. 1994. Infants' sensitivity to phonotactic patterns in the native language. *Journal of Memory and Language, 33,* 630–645.

Jusczyk, P. W., and Thompson, E. 1978. Perception of phonetic contrast in multisyllabic utterances by 2-month-old infants. *Perception and Psychophysics, 23,* 105–109.

Katz, N., Baker, E., and Macnamara, J. 1974. What's in a name? A study of how children learn common and proper names. *Child Development, 45,* 469–473.

Klatt, D. H. 1976. Linguistic uses of segmental duration in English: Acoustic and perceptual evidence. *Journal of the Acoustical Society of America, 59,* 1208–1221.

Klein, H. B. 1981. Early perceptual strategies for the replication of consonants from polysyllabic lexical models. *Journal of Speech and Hearing Research, 24,* 535–551.

Kuhl, P. K., and Miller, J. D. 1982. Discrimination of auditory target dimensions in the presence or absence of variation of a second dimension by infants. *Perception and Psychophysics, 31,* 279–292.

Kuhl, P. K., Williams, K. A., Lacerda, F., Stevens, K. N., and Lindblom, B. 1992. Linguistic experience alters phonetic perception in infants by 6 months of age. *Science, 255,* 606–608.

Lehiste, I. 1970. *Suprasegmentals.* Cambridge, MA: MIT Press.

Lehiste, I., and Ivić, P. 1986. *Word and sentence prosody in Serbocroatian.* Cambridge, MA: MIT Press.

Maratsos, M., and Chalkley, M. A. 1980. The internal language of children's syntax: The ontogenesis and representation of syntactic categories. In K. Nelson, ed., *Children's language, Vol. 2,* 127–189. New York: Gardner Press.

Markman, E. M. 1990. Constraints children place on word meanings. *Cognitive Science, 14,* 57–77.

Markman, E. M. 1992. Constraints on word learning: Speculations about their nature, origins, and domain specificity. In M. R. Gunnar and M. Maratsos, eds., *The Minnesota Symposia on Child Psychology, Vol. 25: Modularity and constraints in language and cognition,* 59–101. Hillsdale, NJ: Erlbaum.

Marti, N. 2001. *11-month-old infants' use of function morphemes to identify word boundaries.* Unpublished doctoral dissertation, University of Texas, Austin.

Mehler, J., Jusczyk, P. W., Lambertz, G., Halsted, N., Bertoncini, J., and Amiel-Tison, C. 1988. A precursor of language acquisition in young infants. *Cognition, 29,* 143–178.

Merriman, W. E., and Bowman, L. L. 1989. The mutual exclusivity bias in children's word learning. *Monographs of the Society for Research in Child Development, 54*(3–4, serial no. 220).

Mervis, C. B., Golinkoff, R. M., and Bertrand, J. 1994. Two-year-olds readily learn multiple labels for the same basic-level category. *Child Development, 65,* 1163–1177.

Morgan, J. L. 1996. A rhythmic bias in preverbal speech segmentation. *Journal of Memory and Language, 35,* 666–688.

Morgan, J. L., and Saffran, J. R. 1995. Emerging integration of sequential and suprasegmental information in preverbal speech segmentation. *Child Development, 66,* 911–936.

Myers, J., Jusczyk, P. W., Kemler Nelson, D. G., Charles-Luce, J., Woodward, A. L., and Hirsh-Pasek, K. 1996. Infants' sensitivity to word boundaries in fluent speech. *Journal of Child Language, 23,* 1–30.

Naigles, L. 1990. Children use syntax to learn verb meanings. *Journal of Child Language, 17,* 357–374.

Naigles, L. G., and Kako, E. T. 1993. First contact in verb acquisition: Defining a role for syntax. *Child Development, 64,* 1665–1687.

Nakatani, L. H., O'Connor, K. D., and Aston, C. H. 1981. Prosodic aspects of American English speech rhythm. *Phonetica, 38,* 84–105.

Nelson, K. 1988. Constraints on word learning? *Cognitive Development, 3,* 221–246.

Oller, D. K., and Rydland, J. N. 1974. *Note on the stress preferences of young English-speaking children.* Unpublished manuscript, Mailman Center for Child Development, Miami.

Peters, A. M. 1983. *The units of language acquisition.* Cambridge, England: Cambridge University Press.

Pierrehumbert, J., and Beckman, M. 1988. *Japanese tone structure.* Cambridge, MA: MIT Press.

Polka, L., Sundara, M., and Blue, S. 2002, April. Native-language, cross-language, and dual-language word segmentation abilities: A comparison of English, French, and bilingual infants. Poster presented at the International Conference on Infant Studies, Toronto.

Pye, C. 1983. Mayan telegraphese: Intonational determinants of inflectional development in Quiché Mayan. *Language, 59,* 583–604.

Quine, W. 1960. *Word and object.* Cambridge, MA: MIT Press.

Roberts, K., and Jacob, M. 1991. Linguistic vs. attentional influences on nonlinguistic categorization in 15-month-old infants. *Cognitive Development, 6,* 355–375.

Saffran, J. R., Aslin, R. N., and Newport, E. L. 1996. Statistical learning in 8-month-old infants. *Science, 274,* 1926–1928.

Shady, M. E. 1996. *Infants' sensitivity to function morphemes.* Unpublished doctoral dissertation, State University of New York at Buffalo.

Shafer, V. L., Shucard, D. W., Shucard, J. L., and Gerken, L. A. 1998. An electrophysiological study of infants' sensitivity to the sound patterns of English speech. *Journal of Speech, Language, and Hearing Research, 41,* 874–886.

Shipley, E. F., Smith, C. S., and Gleitman, L. R. 1969. A study in the acquisition of language: Free responses to commands. *Language, 45,* 322–342.

Slobin, D. I. 1981. The origins of grammatical encoding of events. In W. Deutsch, ed., *The child's construction of language,* 185–199. New York: Academic Press.

Smith, L. B., Jones, S. S., and Landau, B. 1992. Count nouns, adjectives, and perceptual properties in children's novel word interpretations. *Developmental Psychology, 28,* 273–286.

Spelke, E. S. 1991. Physical knowledge in infancy: Reflections on Piaget's theory. In S. Carey and R. Gelman, eds., *The epigenesis of mind: Essays on biology and cognition,* 133–169. Hillsdale, NJ: Erlbaum.

Spring, D. R., and Dale, P. S. 1977. Discrimination of linguistic stress in early infancy. *Journal of Speech and Hearing Research, 20,* 224–232.

Taylor, M., and Gelman, S. A. 1988. Adjectives and nouns: Children's strategies for learning new words. *Child Development, 59,* 411–419.

Waxman, S. R. 1990. Linguistic biases and the establishment of conceptual hierarchies. *Cognitive Development, 5,* 123–150.

Waxman, S. R. 1991. Convergences between semantic and conceptual organization in the preschool years. In S. A. Gelman and J. P. Byrnes, eds., *Perspectives on language and thought: Interrelations in development,* 107–145. Cambridge, England: Cambridge University Press.

Waxman, S. R. 1999. Specifying the scope of 13-month-olds' expectations for novel words. *Cognition, 70,* B35–B50.

Waxman, S. R., and Booth, A. E. 2001. Seeing pink elephants: Fourteen-month-olds' interpretations of novel nouns and adjectives. *Cognitive Psychology, 43,* 217–242.

Waxman, S. R., and Kosowski, T. D. 1990. Nouns mark category relations: Toddlers' and preschoolers' word-learning biases. *Child Development, 61,* 1461–1473.

Waxman, S. R., and Markow, D. B. 1995. Words as invitations to form categories: Evidence from 12- to 13-month olds. *Cognitive Psychology, 29,* 257–302.

Werker, J. F., and Tees, R. C. 1984. Cross-language speech perception: Evidence for perceptual reorganization within the first year of life. *Infant Behavior and Development, 7,* 49–63.

Woodward, A. L., and Markman, E. M. 1991. Review: Constraints on learning as default assumptions: Comments on Merriman and Bowman's "The mutual exclusivity bias in children's word learning." *Developmental Review, 11,* 137–163.

Woodward, J. Z., and Aslin, R. N. April, 1990. Segmentation cues in maternal speech to infants. Poster presented at the International Conference on Infancy Studies, Montreal.

3

Listening to Sounds versus Listening to Words: Early Steps in Word Learning

Janet F. Werker and Christopher Fennell

Our journey into word learning began in infant speech perception. In 1984, Werker and Tees reported that infant phonetic perception becomes language specific by the end of the first year of life: infants progress from discriminating both native and nonnative consonant contrasts at 6 months of age to easily discriminating only native consonant distinctions by 10–12 months of age. In illustration, both a Hindi- and an English-learning child at 6–8 months can discriminate the differences between two "d" sounds that are used in Hindi (a retroflex /D/ vs. dental /d/), but by 10–12 months, only the Hindi-learning child continues to discriminate this difference. The English-learning child of 10–12 months, like English adults, assimilates those two "d" sounds into the single intermediate /d/ phoneme category used in English.

From these results, we assumed that the child would be able to use this language-specific sensitivity to detect just which variations in pronunciation might signal a difference in meaning and just which would not. Thus, if a Hindi-learning child at 10–12 months heard the word *dog* pronounced with a dental and retroflex /d/, she should look for two distinct mappings in the world, whereas if an English-learning child heard the same variation, she should look for only a single real-world referent. We reasoned that the establishment of language-specific phonetic categories by the end of the first year of life could serve the important role of directing information uptake, and, for example, protect the English-learning child from attempting to map two different pronunciations, of say the word *dog*, onto two different objects (see Werker 1995). We thus began a series of experiments to test whether the phonological detail used in early word learning matched the language-specific perceptual categories established during the first year of life (see Werker and Pegg 1992). Imagine our surprise when we found instead that not only was the child, at the earliest stages of word learning, collapsing nonnative distinctions, but she was actually confusing even similar-sounding words that utilized native distinctions and are discriminable in perception! Here is where our story begins.

We begin with a review of our 1997 word-learning work, which showed that infants have difficulty using even language-specific phonetic detail to map sound to meaning when they are novice word learners. We then review two contrasting theoretical perspectives that might account for this difficulty—representational discontinuity versus attentional resource limitations—and present a number of studies that attempt to disambiguate these two possible explanations. Once we identify the age and conditions under which infants can successfully learn phonetically similar words in their own language, we return to the original question and assess whether infants' learning of phonetically similar words is directed by the language-specific perceptual categories established by the end of the first year of life. We end by connecting our findings to other research in the field, and by raising a series of questions that still need to be answered in order to fully understand the link between infant speech perception and lexical use.

3.1 Initial Tests of the Phonetic Representation Used in Word Learning

To address the question of whether infants use their language-specific speech-perception categories to direct word learning, we needed to develop an appropriately sensitive procedure for testing infants in the very earliest stages of word learning (for earlier attempts with different procedures, see Werker and Pegg 1992; Stager and Werker 1998). To do this, our lab teamed up with the laboratory of Les Cohen at the University of Texas at Austin to develop a word-learning procedure. We wanted a task that would require the infant to show at least some evidence of semanticity, so it was essential that the task not just require the infant to listen to the form of a word but also require the infant to link the word to an object or event. But we wanted as well to be likely to capture infant sensitivities as close as possible to the 10–12 month age. At this age, word-comprehension knowledge likely involves only recognitory understanding rather than referential understanding (Oviatt 1982; Hirsh-Pasek and Golinkoff 1996). Recognitory comprehension involves only associative knowledge, and thus simply requires that the infant learn the link between a word and an object. Referential comprehension requires an understanding of the symbolic link between a word and an object, entailing the notion that the word can stand for the object even when the object is not present. We thus developed a word-object associative-learning task in which the infant is required to learn the arbitrary association between a particular word and a particular object, and to show recognition of that learning by differential looking to a pairing that violates, versus one that maintains, the associative link that has been learned. Even if this type of associative word-object learning does not constitute full referential word learning, there is considerable consensus that such associative learning provides a necessary step toward referential word learning.

The task we developed builds on the classic "Switch" task designed by Cohen (1992). In the word-learning variant of this procedure, infants are habituated to two word-object pairings, and tested on their ability to detect a switch in the pairing (Werker et al. 1998). The infant, seated on a parent's lap, views a video screen in which a moving object is displayed. This object is accompanied by an auditory label (e.g., on half the trials a moving toy dog is accompanied by the label "lif" delivered in infant-directed speech, and on the other trials a moving vehicle is accompanied by the label "neem"). The infant is shown these displays repeatedly until, across a set of trials, looking time declines to a criterial level, indicating that the infant has "habituated," and has learned what she can about the words and objects. To assess whether infants have learned not only about the words and objects individually, but have linked object A to word A and object B to word B, they are then tested in the switch design. This involves two test trials. On both trials a familiar object accompanied by a familiar word is presented. On the control trial (the 'same' trial), the familiar word and object are presented in a familiar combination—for example, object A with word A. On the test trial (the 'switch' trial), a familiar word and object are presented, but in a new combination—for instance, object A will now be paired with word B. If the infants have learned about the words and the objects but have not learned the associative link, the 'same' and 'switch' trials will be equally familiar, and should attract equal looking times. However, if the infant has learned the link between the specific words and objects, the 'switch' trial, as a violation of that link, should attract greater looking time than the same trial. Two other critical trials included in this procedure are the pretest and posttest. In these trials, a word-object combination that is very different, both acoustically and visually, from the habituation trials is presented to the infants. The pretest, which is the first trial of the experiment, has a dual purpose: to ensure that the infant is initially attending to the stimuli and to eliminate the variability that is often characteristic of the first trial. The posttest is present to make certain that the infant is still involved in the experiment. If the infant does not look significantly longer to the posttest than to the mean of the final block of habituation trials, it would indicate that the infant did not notice the change in the visual/audio presentation and was likely bored with the experiment. (See figure 3.1 for a diagram of the Switch procedure.)

Using this procedure, we found that infants as young as 14 months can rapidly learn to link unknown words to unknown objects and will look longer to the 'switch' than to the 'same' trials. However, infants younger than 14 months cannot learn the link. Testing of infants from 8 to 12 months of age showed that they are capable of learning about the individual objects and the individual words, but they cannot link them under these minimal-exposure conditions. We showed this by comparing the performance of infants 8–12 months in a simpler variant of the task to their performance in the full Switch procedure. In the simpler variant, infants are habituated to only a single word-object pairing and then tested in four trials, one involving a familiar word and object, one a change in the word only, one a change in the object only, and one a change in both. Infants

Listening to Sounds versus Listening to Words

Pretest

"POK"

Habituation Trials

"BIH"

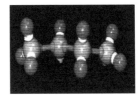

"DIH"

Same Trial   *Test Trials*   *Switch Trial*

"BIH"

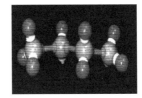

"BIH"

Posttest

"POK"

Figure 3.1
Diagram of the Switch task.

as young as 8 months noticed all changes under these testing conditions. However, when tested in the Switch design wherein the infants were required to detect not a change in the word or object, but a change in the pairing, infants 8–12 months failed (Werker et al. 1998). Other laboratories, using different procedures, have also found the youngest age at which infants can link words and objects in arbitrary associations, without considerable contextual support, to be at around this age (Schafer and Plunkett 1998 showed word learning at 15 months; Woodward, Markman, and Fitzsimmons 1994 showed it at 13 months). It is, of course, the ability to detect an arbitrary linkage between a word and its referent that makes this task directly relevant to word learning.[1]

Following the initial development of this procedure, Stager and Werker (1997) used the Switch task and subsequently, its simplified, single-object variant to directly test the question of whether infants, shortly after their first birthday, are able to use their fine phonetic discrimination capabilities in word-learning tasks. Here, infants of 14 months of age were tested on their ability to learn to associate two phonetically similar words with two different objects. Stager and Werker used a consonant distinction that is phonemic (used to distinguish meaning) in English, specifically /b/ and /d/, to ensure, first of all, that infants of this age could learn minimally different words when language-specific distinctions were used. To our consternation and surprise, the infants completely failed to even map the words to two different objects when the phonetically similar words *bih* and *dih* were used. (See figure 3.2.)

We ran a series of control studies to try to understand just why the infants aged 14 months had failed. First, we tested infants of both 14 and 8 months on their ability to detect a change in the word when tested in the single-object variant of the procedure. As we noted above, Werker et al. (1998) had shown that infants as young as 8 months can succeed in this version of the task (which does not require linking the word to the object, but can be solved as only a discrimination task) when the words are phonetically dissimilar— that is, "lif" versus "neem." In this manipulation, infants were presented with a single moving object accompanied by either the nonce word "bih" or the nonce word "dih." Following habituation, they

Listening to Sounds versus Listening to Words

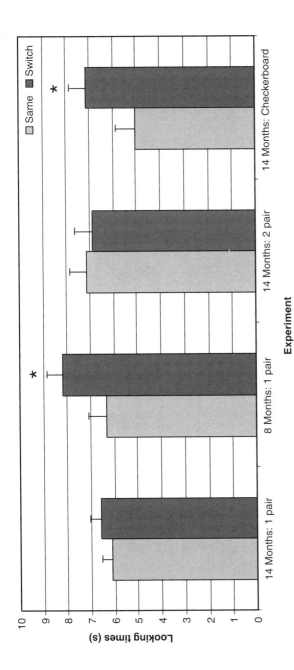

Figure 3.2
Mean looking times to test trials across four experiments from Stager and Werker 1997. The experiments are noted by the participants' age in months and experimental stimuli (1 pair = simple one word-object combination, 2 pair = two word-object combinations, checkerboard = discrimination-experiment stimulus). Significant differences in looking times are noted with an asterisk.

were presented with the same object, now accompanied by the contrasting nonce word (e.g., a change from "bih" to "dih"). Although the 8-month-olds showed unequivocal evidence of detecting the change, the infants of 14 months failed! (See figure 3.2.) The results with the 8-month-olds are similar to other work done with infants of this age showing that after familiarization with stimuli, infants of 7 and 8 months do distinguish a familiar word from a minimal pair foil (see Jusczyk and Aslin 1995). The results with the 14-month-olds suggest that the very fact of listening to words, and learning something about them, may be different for a 14-month-old than for an 8-month-old infant. It may be that infants of 8 months, who are not yet able to link words and objects under these types of conditions, treat the task as simply one of discrimination. Yet infants of 14 months—who have now become word learners—may shift into a word-learning set when conditions make word learning possible even when word learning is not required. We speculated that it was the presence of a moving, namable object that brought out word learning in the infants of 14 months, and that once word learning was evoked, attention to fine phonetic detail was no longer possible. To test this prediction, we needed to design a task that would be unlikely to evoke any word-object linking on the part of infants aged 14 months.

To design a variant of our task that would not invoke word learning, we turned to two literatures. First, we reasoned that, if the "whole-object" assumption does indeed play a central role in word learning, we would be less likely to invoke word learning on the part of the infant if we used a visual display that is not "objectlike." We then turned to the literature on object perception, and discovered that bounded, coherent, moving stimuli are most likely to be treated as whole "objects" (Spelke 1994). For this reason, we decided to pair either the nonce word "bih" or the nonce word "dih" with an unbounded, stationary object and test to see if infants could detect a change in the word under these conditions. The display we used was an unbounded, stationary checkerboard. With all other aspects of the procedure identical as before, except for the change in display, the infants of 14 months succeeded at distinguishing "bih" from "dih." (See figure 3.2.)

From these results we concluded that infants of 14 months are not able to use all of the detail in the language-specific phonetic categories they have established during infancy to discriminate possible words in a word-learning task. If the words are presented in a situation that does not entail linking them to an object, evidence of their full repertoire of phonetic discrimination abilities is obtained. But as soon as an object is presented along with the word, even if a mapping is not required (as in the single-object condition), infants of 14 months will treat the situation as one of word learning and fail to distinguish the words.

3.2 Why Do Infants of 14 Months Have Difficulty Learning Similar Words: Theoretical Positions

How does one make sense of these results? Some work in child phonology has argued that there is a discontinuity between the phonetic representations used in speech-discrimination tasks and the phonological representations required for language use (Barton 1980; Ferguson and Farwell 1979; Keating 1984, 1988, 1990; Pierrehumbert 1990). Here, it is suggested that only gradually, as they acquire words, do children come to represent the more detailed information that might distinguish one possible word from another (Brown 2000; Brown and Matthews 1997; Edwards 1974; Garnica 1973; Kay-Raining Bird and Chapman 1998; Rice and Avery 1995; Pollock 1987; Shvachkin [1948] 1973). There are different explanations for why this discontinuity might exist (see Beckman and Edwards 2000; Pierrehumbert 1990), or how deeply it might be supported (Pater, forthcoming). But all these explanations rest on the notion that one representation is built up for use in perception, and that when children start acquiring a lexicon they have to build new representations that are distinct from those used in perception. In any case, our results could be seen to support the claims that there is a discontinuity between the perceptual representations built up during the first year of life and the phonological representations that must be constructed when the child begins to learn words.

There are alternative explanations, however. The one we posited is that it is not a discontinuity in the representation that distinguishes prelexical from postlexical phonetic sensitivity; rather it is a consequence of the computational demands of word learning (see Stager and Werker 1997; Werker and Stager 2000). We suggest that the child who is only just beginning to be able to link words with objects must use most of their computational resources for the task of linking, and in so doing, has less attention available to detect and pick up the fine phonetic detail in words. This limited-resource explanation rests on the assumption that in any difficult task, something has to give (Casasola and Cohen 2000; Cohen 1998). In this case, we argue that it is the attention to fine phonetic detail that the child sacrifices. Moreover, it can be argued that this "less is more" approach is adaptive (Newport 1990). With only a small lexicon, it is likely not necessary to attend to and pick up the fine phonetic detail, because estimates of child vocabularies confirm that children have few phonetically similar words in their early lexicons (Charles-Luce and Luce 1995). This hypothesis also finds support, albeit indirectly, from other studies. As will be reviewed later, in online word-recognition tasks, infants of 14 months do seem able to use fine phonetic detail (Swingley and Aslin 2002) and infants as young as 12 months do not confuse consonants such as /b/ and /d/ in their productions (Carol Stoel-Gammon, personal communication, 2001). It would be very difficult to understand how such data patterns could be obtained if the detail were simply not there at all in the lexical representation. Instead it seems more parsimonious to suggest that the detail is available, but because of resource limitations, it is difficult to access in word-learning tasks.

The work discussed throughout the remainder of this chapter attempts to address the questions raised above. We explore the resource-limitation versus representational-discontinuity hypotheses in a number of different ways. First, we change the stimuli used to see if the results extend to different minimal-pair contrasts. Then, we make the word-learning task easier for the child and assess performance. Following this, we examine performance among more experienced word learners, including both slightly older infants and infants of 14 months who have larger vocabularies. In this work, we present the results of both behavioral and ERP studies. We examine infants being raised in bilingual environments, where the computational load of learning two languages must be even greater than that of learning only one, in order to explore the generalizability of the findings and to also provide another perspective on the viability of the resource-limitation hypothesis. And finally, with respect to our own work, we present an ongoing study in which we provide a strong test of the discontinuity hypothesis by comparing use of native and nonnative phonetic detail in slightly older infants, coming full circle and linking our word-learning work again to the perceptual-tuning findings from the first year of life. We finish by comparing our findings on word learning to those obtained in other labs that are examining online processing of already-known words.

3.3   Testing Infants on Different Sets of Minimal Pairs

In our previous work (Stager and Werker 1997), we drew the conclusion that infants of 14 months have difficulty learning minimally different words on the basis of a single pair of words, "bih" versus "dih." There are several reasons this conclusion could be problematic. Thus, in a series of studies, Pater, Stager, and Werker (1998, 2002) tested 14-month-old infants in the Switch design on phonetically similar words that differ in both word-form and phonetic-feature combinations from those used initially by Stager and Werker. The first experiment extended the findings with "bih" versus "dih" to a "bin" versus "din" comparison. This comparison is important because the "bih"-"dih" stimuli are characterized as a C (consonant) followed by a lax (short) V (vowel), but CV syllables ending in lax vowels such as "ih" are considered ill-formed words (McCarthy and Prince 1995). Thus the possibility exists that infants had difficulty mapping the "bih" and "dih" stimuli onto objects not because they could not attend to the fine phonetic features, but rather because they did not treat "bih" and "dih" as possible words. In reminder, the Stager and Werker 1997 work showed that when we used a visual display (an unbounded checkerboard) that is not a namable object, word mapping was inhibited. Similarly, word learning could be inhibited because the auditory stimulus was not a possible word. To test this, sixteen infants aged 14 months were tested on their ability to map the CVC forms "bin" and "din" onto two separate objects. Nonetheless, when infants aged 14 months were tested with these minimally contrastive syllables in valid word form, they again failed to link the words to different objects.

In the next two studies conducted by Pater, Stager, and Werker (1998, 2002), specific predictions from phonological theory were tested by varying the stimuli. In Experiment 2, infants were tested on a "bin" versus "pin" comparison. This is a phonetically similar, minimal pair where the difference in the initial consonant is one of voicing (/b/ is voiced and /p/ is voiceless), whereas the /b/-/d/ comparison involves a difference in place of articulation (bilabial vs. alveolar). If infants are filling in detail in their lexical representations in a systematic fashion, it is conceivable that a voicing distinction might be acquired earlier than a place distinction (but see Rice and Avery 1995 for the opposite prediction). Sixteen infants aged 14 months were tested and, once again, the infants failed. Finally, in Experiment 3, the stimuli were "din" versus "pin" in which both voicing and place differ (/d/ is a voiced, alveolar consonant and /p/ is a voiceless, bilabial consonant). If infants are random in precisely which detail they listen to, with some infants picking up place-of-articulation information and others picking up voicing, they should be able to succeed as long as they pay attention to one of these features. Yet, still again, infants of 14 months were unable to learn to associate the similar-sounding words with two different objects. These data are consistent with the notion that infants can simply not attend to any fine phonetic detail in the initial consonant.

3.4   Simplifying the Word-Learning Task

If the difficulty infants experience in the word-learning task were explained by a limitation in attentional resources, one would predict that, under easier word-learning conditions, infants might perform better. Thus, two experiments were conducted in which the word-learning task itself was simplified. The first study (Experiment 9 in Stager 1999) was motivated by the finding that even toddlers may assume that two objects of high similarity share a label, and that they are more likely to learn different labels for physically more distinct objects (Diesendruck and Shatz 1997). To explore this question, infants were tested on their ability to pair the stimuli "bih" and "dih" to two objects that were physically much more distinct than those used by Stager and Werker (1997). The original Stager and Werker stimuli involved two objects made out of the same material (Filo modeling clay), of the same volume, and of the same three primary colors (red, yellow, and blue). The only difference between the objects was shape, with one object comprising three half circles in the orientation of a rainbow, one of each color, sitting on a base. The other object utilized the same three half circles, but facing upward off a stem like a candelabra. The new objects we used involved one of those original objects, plus a completely different novel object made of green turquoise hard-plastic snap beads, put together in the shape of a molecule. Yet even with these objects of different colors, materials, shapes, and volumes, infants of 14 months were still unable to learn the word-object pairings.

In a follow-up study (Experiment 2 in Werker et al. 2002), 14-month-old infants were presented again with physically different objects, but this time they were also given considerably more exposure time. Again, previous research has suggested that exposure time alone can also lead to differences in word learning in these types of passive-exposure paradigms (see Hollich, Golinkoff, and Hirsh-Pasek 2000). Yet even with a nearly 50 percent longer trial time, and a stricter habituation criterion (50 percent decrement rather than the 65 percent decrement used previously), as a group, infants of 14 months failed to learn the phonetically similar words. (See figure 3.3.)

3.5 Confirming This Pattern with ERP Results

The findings presented above make it clear that under a variety of testing conditions, infants aged 14 months have difficulty learning phonetically similar words in a brief, laboratory-based habituation procedure. These results do not allow us to determine, however, whether the difficulty is one of a resource limitation or one of a lack of phonetic detail in the lexical representations that infants use at this age. Moreover, it is always uncomfortable to draw conclusions on the basis of negative results with infants. One never knows whether

Werker and Fennell

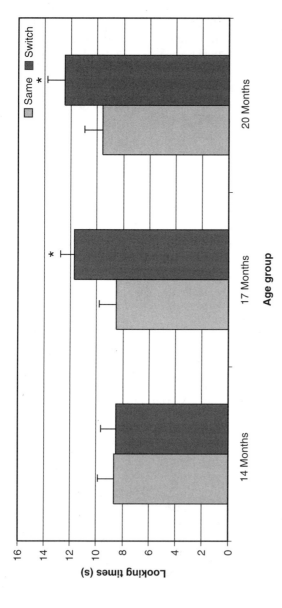

Figure 3.3
Mean looking times to test trials across three age groups in Werker et al. 2002. Significant differences in looking times are noted with an asterisk.

the continued failure of infants aged 14 months to learn phonetically similar words really reveals something about the novice status of the infants, or instead whether for any other of an infinite number of reasons, the task failed to reveal an underlying capability.

We turned to electrophysiological measures to design a study in which a positive result, rather than a negative result, would confirm (or falsify) the difficulty using fine phonetic detail we had seen at 14 months. At the same time, we used this technique to address the question of whether more expert word learners would be more likely to have more detailed phonetic information in their lexical representations. We built on previous work by Mills, Coffey-Corina, and Neville (1993; see also Mills, Coffey-Corina, and Neville 1997) revealing that infants show higher-amplitude ERP responses at 200–450 msec following presentation to known versus unknown words. At 13–17 months, this difference is detected in both hemispheres, and shows up over frontal, temporal, and parietal lobes. By 20 months, it is only observed from electrodes over the LH (left-hemisphere) temporal and parietal lobes, suggesting the emergence of specialized brain systems for processing words by that age. Moreover, the infants aged 20 months who were post (> 150 words) vocabulary spurt showed the localized LH response, whereas infants with smaller vocabularies (< 50 words) showed the more distributed response, indicating that the increasingly local nature of the differential ERP signature seen in older infants reflects greater sophistication in word knowledge rather than age per se. On the basis of these findings, Mills and colleagues hypothesized that the establishment of a specialized system for word learning makes the word spurt possible (Mills, Coffey-Corina, and Neville 1997; see also Mills, Coffey-Corina, and Neville 1993).

In collaboration with the labs of Neville and Mills, we decided to take advantage of the finding of a high-amplitude ERP response to known words, to examine the phonetic representation of words in new and more experienced word learners. We tested infants of 14 and 20 months of age in the same ERP procedure as used by Mills, Coffey-Corina, and Neville (1997). This time, however, instead of presenting the infants with randomly varying presentations of ten known and ten unknown words (as Mills and colleagues had done), we added ten unknown words that are phonetically similar to the known words. For example, as a direct replication of the previous work, we presented infants with known words such as *dog, cat, shoe, milk,* and so on, and phonetically *dis*similar nonce words such as *neem, blick, zav,* and *kobe,* but as an extension added to that a set of nonce words that are phonetically similar to the known words. This included words like *bog, gat, zue,* and *nilk.* As a replication, we predicted that infants of 14 and 20 months would show higher-amplitude ERPs to the known versus the phonetically *dis*similar unknown words, and that this would be seen across most electrode sites at 14 months but would be more localized at 20 months. As an extension, we were interested in the pattern of responses to the phonetically similar nonce words. We reasoned that if there is sufficient detail in the lexical representation, the ERP signature to these phonetically similar foils should be like that of phonetically *dis*similar unknown words. However, if the lexical representation is not detailed, these should be confused with known words.

The results were exciting. The infants aged 14 months (most of whom still had relatively small vocabularies) showed the same whole-brain pattern of high-amplitude ERP activation to known but not phonetically *dis*similar nonce words, replicating what had been previously reported by Mills, Coffey-Corina, and Neville (1997). Of interest, their ERP activation to the phonetically *similar* nonce words looked just like that to the known words. In other words, when the infants of 14 months were presented with nonce items like "bog," the ERP signature revealed recognition, indicating confusion—likely with similar-sounding known words such as "dog." At 20 months the pattern was reversed. Again, the results of Mills and colleagues were replicated such that the higher-amplitude ERP response to known words was localized to the LH temporal and parietal electrode sites, but this time the phonetically *similar* nonce words revealed an ERP signature just like the other nonce words. The brains of the infants of 20 months, all of whom were post–vocabulary spurt, did not confuse words like "bog" with the known word "dog," but instead treated it as any other unknown word such as "zav" (Mills et al., 2002).

These findings were valuable for two reasons. First, they provided confirmation that infants of 14 months do indeed have difficulty distinguishing similar-sounding words. On the basis of our behavioral work using the Switch design, we had to draw this conclusion by comparing a series of positive findings to the failures of the infants aged 14 months. In the ERP task, the infants of 14 months did not fail anything. Indeed, they showed a special "I know that one!" ERP signature to the phonetically similar words. Confirmation of our failures in the behavioral tasks with an interpretable response in the ERP task significantly strengthens the finding. Second, the ERP study made a strong prediction that by 20 months of age infants should no longer confuse phonetically similar words in a word-learning Switch design.

3.6 Testing More Expert Word Learners

The above ERP data would indicate that infants of 20 months of age, who are more expert word learners, should, unlike the 14-month-olds tested in our previous work, be able to learn phonetically similar words. To check this prediction, we tested sixteen 20-month-old infants. They were tested in the modified Switch procedure, and the MacArthur CDI was collected from their parent(s) to measure vocabulary size. First, as predicted from previous literature (e.g., Bloom 1973; Clark 1973; Nelson and Bonvillian 1973), the infants in this age group could be classified as more expert word learners because they were almost all post–vocabulary spurt, with an average productive vocabulary size of 195 words. Of most importance, they showed clear evidence of being able to learn the phonetically similar words "bih" and "dih," as indicated by significantly longer looking time to the 'switch' (12.5 seconds) than to the 'same' (9.6 seconds) trial in the test phase. These results confirm the predictions from the ERP study, and show that even with the same task at which infants of 14 months failed, infants of 20 months can learn phonetically similar words. We repeated this study with infants aged 17 months, and the pattern was intermediate between that of the 14- and 20-month infants. As a group, the infants of 17 months did learn the minimal-pair words, with significantly longer looking time to 'switch' than to 'same,' but the effect was not as robust ($p < .05$) as it was at 20 months ($p < .01$). (See figure 3.3.) This is perhaps not surprising because the average productive vocabulary size for this group was 78, indicating they were not, as a group, as proficient at word learning as were the 20-month-olds (see Werker et al. 2002, for details of the work above with infants of 14, 17, and 20 months of age).

If it is the case that infants who are more expert word learners are better able to pick up phonetic detail, and if expertise at word learning is predicted by vocabulary size (see Beckman and Edwards 2000), then infants aged 14 months who have larger vocabulary sizes should be able to learn phonetically similar words. To explore this question, we probed for a correlation between vocabulary size and minimal-pair word-learning ability in a group of sixteen infants aged 14 months who had been tested under precisely the same conditions as the infants aged 17 and 20 months discussed above. The correlation between productive vocabulary size and word learning was significant ($p = .004$). This indicates that even at 14 months, infants particularly adept at word learning are able to pick up fine phonetic detail in word-learning tasks.

3.7 Testing Bilingual Infants

Infants growing up bilingual provide another perspective on the question of whether it is a resource or representational limitation that interferes with the ability to learn minimally different words. If the resource-limitation hypothesis is correct, it would predict that bilingual infants would, like monolingual infants, have difficulty learning minimally different words at 14 months of age. Moreover, this difficulty might continue to be apparent until an older age (or level of expertise), given that bilingual infants have to acquire two lexical systems simultaneously and thus have to match multiple labels to single objects more often than monolinguals. The predictions from the resource-limitation hypothesis run counter to the dominant view that infants learning two languages should actually be better able to attend to fine phonetic detail than their monolingual peers because of heightened phonological awareness. In a variety of tasks with children aged 5–7 years, bilinguals have been shown, for example, to detect onset-time regularities (Bruck and Genesee 1995) and to perform phoneme-deletion tasks (Rubin and Turner 1989) better than age-matched monolingual children (see also Campbell and Sais 1995; Levy 1985). Moreover, it has been hypothesized that this increased metalinguistic (including phonological) awareness should be seen at the earliest stages of word learning (Lanza 1997). Given this literature, if we find that bilingual-exposed infants are not only equally poor at learning minimally different words at 14 months, but that they must be older than their monolingual peers before they reach an age at which they can succeed, additional support would be garnered for the attentional-resource explanation.

To address the question of a possible divergence from the monolingual word-learning path, we tested sixteen bilingual infants[2] of 14 months in the same object-label associative task used with the monolingual infants. All the infants had English as one of their two languages, an important point because a female native speaker of English produced the audio stimuli. They were a heterogeneous group with respect to the second language they were acquiring, as were all subsequent age groups studied. We found that the 14-month-old bilingual infants performed similarly to the monolingual infants. They did not notice a switch in the object-label pairing. There were no effects of gender or level of bilingualism. Bilingual exposure did not seem to augment the infants' phonetic awareness in this task, despite the apparent increased phonetic perceptual abilities of their older counterparts (Fennell 2000).

An alternate explanation for the findings from the 14-month-old bilingual word-learning study is that bilingual infants of this age are simply not able to discriminate "bih" and "dih," even when not pairing them with objects. Perhaps these infants, unlike their monolingual peers, have difficulties discriminating minimally different phonemes in speech perception. More specifically, their limited exposure to the English-produced /b/ versus /d/ contrast could possibly lead to a problem in perceiving this distinction. To rule out this possibility, we tested sixteen bilingual 14-month-old infants using the same discrimination study discussed earlier in the chapter, where the nonce word "bih" or the nonce word "dih" was paired with an unbounded, stationary object (i.e., a checkerboard). As with the monolingual participants, the bilingual infants of 14 months succeeded at distinguishing "bih" from "dih." This finding strengthens our position that it is the demands of the word-learning process that lead to inattention to fine phonetic detail.

The results with our bilingual 14-month-old data do not support the prediction that bilingual infants will show greater phonological awareness at a younger age. The resource-limitation hypothesis would predict not only similar performance at 14 months, but delayed onset of the age at which fine phonetic detail could be used. To investigate this possibility, sixteen 17-month-old bilingual infants participated in a study using the same procedure and stimuli as the object-label associative experiment with 14-month-old bilinguals. The 17-month-old bilinguals did look slightly longer when an object was labeled incorrectly in the 'switch' trial than in the 'same' trial, but this difference did not approach significance. Thus, unlike their monolingual peers, the 17-month-old bilinguals were unable to learn the phonetically similar-sounding labels. Preliminary results from a recently completed study indicate that by 20 months, bilingual infants can use fine phonetic detail.

Taken together, these results are entirely at odds with the prediction that bilingual-learning infants should have access to phonological detail at an earlier age than monolinguals, and are instead consistent with the attentional-resource explanation. It should be recognized, however, that although we feel that the resource-limitation hypothesis is more parsimonious, we once again cannot completely rule out the representational-limitation position. Here, the argument could be that bilingual infants take longer to build phonemic representations because of the decreased exposure time to phonemes in each of their native languages when compared to a monolingual infant.

3.8 Interlude—Resource Limitation or Representational Limitation?

A review of the evidence presented so far shows that it is difficult to disentangle the resource-limitation versus representational-discontinuity explanations. Our attempts to simplify the task for novice word learners through the use of more distinct objects and increased exposure time were not sufficient, in this case, to enable minimal-pair word learning. Nor was the use of nonce words that have a more typical word form (CVC, rather than CV). Moreover, infants of 14 months still failed when they were presented with nonce words that contrasted in a different phonetic feature (voicing rather than place) and even in two phonetic features (voicing + place, as in "din" vs. "pin"), suggesting that neither place nor voicing information is detected in this word-learning task. Yet infants just a few months older (17 and 20 months), and even infants aged 14 months with larger vocabularies, succeeded at the minimal-pair word-learning task. These results are all consistent with either a representational- or resource-limitation hypothesis.

The ERP data, on the other hand, provide relatively strong evidence that at least at the level of processing picked up by the particular electrodes used in the time course that is being measured, the lexical representation of known words does *not* contain fine phonetic detail at 14 months of age. However, even here a closer examination shows that the processing explanation is not entirely ruled out. It is possible that the context of hearing known words, like the presence of an object in the original Stager and Werker 1997 work, predisposed the infants to listen for meaning when listening to the words. Because they are still novice word learners, listening for meaning might invoke more processing demands. In this type of listening context, minimally different nonwords (as in the Switch procedure) would be confused with their real-word counterparts, which were also being presented, and only nonwords that were not at all similar to any known words would avoid being captured by the "semantic" net.

These studies all confirm the difficulty experienced by the 14-month-old word learner, but they do not provide definitive tests of the question of whether resource limitations or representational discontinuity accounts for the difficulty. All the findings are consistent with the thesis that phonetic detail is not available for a lexical representation by the infant of 14 months, but they are also consistent with the possibility that the information is available, but is simply not used, perhaps due to a limitation in attentional resources. It could be that the attempts we made to simplify the task were not the correct attempts, and that some other simplification might enable minimal-pair word learning. And it could be the case that infants pick up neither voicing nor place-of-articulation information because of resource limitations, not because of incomplete phonological representations.

This controversy is important. At a general level, it concerns the question of whether the kind of perceptual learning that takes place in infancy plays a functional role in the establishment of more complex systems. At a more specific level, it concerns the issue of whether phonological bootstrapping really does play a role in language acquisition. If it turns out that when constructing a lexicon, infants have to start anew in learning about the phonetic properties that are useful in their native language, the motivation underlying our studies of speech perception in infancy will be seriously undermined. But if there is a link between prelexical perceptual learning and postlexical phonological use, we will be able to see a way in which experience during infancy has played a significant role in propelling the child into language acquisition.

3.9 Returning to the Original Question: Do Infants Use Their Language-Specific Perceptual Categories to Map Sound onto Meaning?

Having finally found the age at which infants *can* use the phonology of their native language to learn and recognize minimally different words, and knowing more about the impact of learning two languages on phonological representations, we were finally prepared to return to the question that had originally motivated the work: Are the language-specific perceptual categories that are established at the end of infancy used when the child moves on to the task of constructing a lexicon? In other words, does the child use her perceptual knowledge to guide word learning?

As noted above, the finding that infants of 14 months cannot use all their speech-perception sensitivities in word-learning tasks raises the possibility that an entirely new set of representations must be constructed when learning words, and that infants do not have available to help them the perceptual categories established during infancy. According to this hypothesis, the successful performance of the infant at 17 and 20 months stems from the establishment of a newly formed, lexical representational structure (i.e., see Brown and Matthews 1997) rather than from the utilization of prelinguistically established perceptual categories. In the current work, we address the question of whether new representations have to be constructed when the child moves on to word learning, or, instead, whether the difficulty learning words at 14 months stems from a processing-load difficulty that interferes with access to the detail already available. We build on our previous work showing a reorganization from universal to language-specific consonant perception at the end of the first year of life. We test the thesis that the language-specific perceptual categories that the child has established provide a foundation for word learning. It is true that at 14 months the child does not use all the information in these perceptual representations in the Switch word-learning task. But if the information is nonetheless conserved, when the child reaches the age at which she can pay attention to fine phonetic detail in a word-learning task, she should have available only the detail that is in her language-specific perceptual representations.

We addressed this question in two steps. First, we tested infants of 17 months of age, who are now capable of learning native-language minimally different words, on their ability to learn two words that differ on a nonnative phonetic contrast. The prediction was that they would be unable to learn similar nonce words that differ in only a non-English contrast. This prediction was supported. Unlike their performance on the words "bih" versus "dih", 17-month-old English-learning infants were not able to learn to map the Hindi dental "dih" and the Hindi retroflex "Dih" to two different objects. We are currently testing infants learning Hindi (and other South Asian languages that have a retroflex-dental distinction). Preliminary data indicate that these infants can learn these words. These findings, if maintained, support a link in word learning to the perceptual representations established in the prelinguistic period. These data then would suggest that even though there is a temporary hiatus in access at around 14 months of age, there is a continuity between the perceptual representations built up from experience listening to speech during the prelexical period and the perceptual representations used when the child begins to establish a lexicon (see also Fennell and Werker, forthcoming; Werker and Curtin, in preparation).

3.10 How Do Our Findings Compare with Those Being Generated from Other Studies?

Other researchers have also been recently investigating infants' use of phonetic information in a word-based task. Through comparing our results to those of other researchers, we can further clarify the relevant issues to this area of research. In a study done with older infants, Swingley, Pinto, and Fernald (1999) measured infants' latency to fixate on the matching visual target (among two simultaneously presented visual displays) in response to a correct or incorrect label. The 24-month-old infants who participated in the study had delayed fixation times in the task when the label and distractor began with the same phoneme (e.g., *dog–doll*), but not when the label and distractor began with minimally different initial phonemes (e.g., *doll–ball*). Swingley and Aslin (2000) varied the above task by looking at infants' latency to look to a match when using a well-known word and a slightly mispronounced version of that word (e.g., *baby–vaby*) and by using younger infants, 18 to 23 months of age. The results followed a similar pattern to Swingley, Pinto, and Fernald 1999. The infants had a significantly delayed looking time to the match when a mispronounced version of the label was used in comparison to when the correctly pronounced label was presented. These studies demonstrate that infants aged 18 to 24 months have detailed representations of well-known words. In related work, Plunkett, Bailey, and Bryant (2000) tested whether it is recency of word learning that best predicts infants' success in distinguishing similar-sounding words. Some support was found for their hypothesis that infants aged 18–24 months represent more phonetic detail in words they have known for a long time than they do in recently learned words, but the overall pattern of results still indicated that infants of this age are sensitive to the fine phonetic detail distinguishing words. The results from these studies confirm our findings that older infants have detailed representations of word forms.

But what of younger infants? Swingley (2002) tested a group of 14-month-old participants in the "baby"–"vaby" study outlined above. Unlike our 14-month-olds, the infants in this procedure did notice the phonemic differences between the two words, as shown by their shorter looking to the object in the mispronunciation condition. There are two possible reasons for this discrepancy in the two sets of findings. One possibility is that the differences in the stimuli used in the two studies account for the difference. Perhaps at this young age, it is easier to access the detail in well-known words, whereas it is difficult with newly learned words. A study is currently underway in our lab to assess the viability of this account. In this study, 14-month-old infants are being tested in the Switch procedure; however, a familiar minimal pair ("doll" vs. "ball") is being used instead of novel word-object combinations. If infants of 14 months succeed with these already-known words, further evidence against a representational-discontinuity hypothesis will be obtained. To adhere to a representational-discontinuity hypothesis, one would have to assume the lexical representations are constructed one word at a time. Otherwise, it would be impossible to explain why a child could access the abstract phoneme /b/ with its place and voicing designations, for known words such as "ball," but not for new words such as "bin." There are accounts of phonological acquisition that build one word at a time, or one vocalic context at a time, but they become increasingly difficult to support.

The other possibility is that the procedure itself is causing this difference. The visual-latency task used by Swingley and colleagues may be easier for the infants than the task used in our studies. To succeed in the Switch procedure, the infant needs to learn two new object-label combinations and *subsequently* (thus requiring detailed memory of the combinations) notice a violation in those pairings. In the visual-latency procedure, the infant is presented with two visual choices *simultaneously*, which could significantly decrease at least part of the memory load for the infant. The more difficult nature of the Switch task may be blocking the infants' ability to notice phonetic detail. In a set of studies we are doing in collaboration with Daniel Swingley we are examining the extent to which task differences also contribute to the differences in results.

For all these reasons, although we acknowledge that it is still diffi-cult to fully disambiguate the representational- from the resource-limitation hypotheses, we would argue that the bulk of the evidence must be taken as pointing to a resource-limitation hypothesis.

3.11 Summary and Conclusions

In summary, across a series of experiments we have attempted to describe more completely the link between speech perception in infancy and the functional use of that perceptual detail in word-learning tasks. Across the first year of life, infants become rapidly attuned to many of the properties of the native language, including the language-specific phonemic categories. The question initially motivating the current series of studies was, "Do infants use those language-specific sensitivities when mapping sound onto meaning?" This is important, as noted above, because it addresses the essence of the notion of phonological bootstrapping by assessing whether infants can indeed use the surface characteristics of languages to bootstrap into language. Although our focus in this chapter has been on bootstrapping into the lexicon, we (e.g., Shi and Werker 2001) and others (see Jusczyk 1997; Morgan, Shi, and Allopena 1996) are also interested in whether the surface phonological cues can help bootstrap into grammatical acquisition as well. Across the series of experiments reviewed in this chapter we have shown that infants do not appear to be able to immediately use all the "knowledge" gained from perception when first mapping word forms onto mean-ing. We provided evidence—albeit not yet incontrovertible—to support the following argument: the difficulty more likely reflects attentional-processing limitations than a discontinuity in the under-lying representation. Moreover, our preliminary results with Hindi- and English-learning children using the Hindi retroflex versus dental categories in word-learning tasks support the notion that the pre-lexical categories established during the first year of life do set the boundaries within which lexical representations can be constructed. This body of work, then, is compatible with the hypothesis that there is indeed a continuity between the prelexical categories formed through perceptual learning in the first year of life and the functional representations available for lexical use after the onset of word learning. The challenge for future work is to characterize the relationship more precisely, and to examine the extent to which perceptual learning can help bootstrap the child into language discovery.

Notes

1. When the words and objects are linked together by some nonarbitrary feature, such as synchrony of movement, even infants as young as 7 months of age can learn the linking (Gogate and Bahrick 1998). But when synchrony is not available, infants are not successful until closer to the 14-month age we discovered. Although these nonarbitrary linkages may help ease the child into word learning, we were interested in the infants' first ability to learn the kinds of arbitrary word-object linkages that characterize word knowledge.

2. The use of the label "bilingual" during the infancy period refers to infants who are being raised in a bilingual environment, and who have been hearing two different languages in their everyday life since they were born. Utilizing the scale developed and used by Bosch and Sebastián-Gallés (1997), we measure language exposure, and, based on these data, only classify infants who have a minimum of 30 percent exposure to one language and a maximum of 70 percent exposure to the other as "bilingual." These limits are based on, but slightly more conservative than, the language-exposure limits recommended by Pearson et al. (1997).

References

Bailey, T. D., and Plunkett, K. 2002. Phonological specificity in early words. *Cognitive Development*, *17*, 1265–1282.

Barton, D. 1980. Phonemic perception in children. In G. H. Yeni-Komshian, J. F. Kavanagh, and C. A. Ferguson, eds., *Child phonology, Vol. 2: Perception.* New York: Academic Press.

Beckman, M. E., and Edwards, J. 2000. The ontogeny of phonological categories and the primacy of lexical learning in linguistic development. *Child Development*, *71*, 240–249.

Bloom, L. 1973. *One word at a time: The use of single word utterances before syntax.* The Hague: Mouton.

Bosch, L., and Sebastián-Gallés, N. 1997. Native language recognition abilities in 4-month-old infants from monolingual and bilingual environments. *Cognition*, *65*, 33–69.

Brown, C. A. 2000. The interrelation between speech perception and phonological acquisition from infant to adult. In J. Archibald, ed., *Second language acquisition and linguistic theory*, 4–63. Oxford: Blackwell.

106

Werker and Fennell

Brown, C., and Matthews, J. 1997. The role of feature geometry in the development of phonemic contrasts. In S. J. Hannahs and M. Young-Scholten, eds., *Focus on phonological acquisition*, 67–112. Amsterdam: Benjamins.

Bruck, M., and Genesee, F. 1995. Phonological awareness in young second language learners. *Journal of Child Language*, 22, 307–324.

Campbell, R., and Sais, E. 1995. Accelerated metalinguistic (phonological) awareness in bilingual children. *British Journal of Developmental Psychology*, 13, 61–68.

Casasola, M., and Cohen, L. B. 2000. Infants' association of linguistic labels with causal actions. *Developmental Psychology*, 36(2), 155–168.

Charles-Luce, J., and Luce, P. A. 1995. An examination of similarity neighbourhoods in young children's receptive vocabularies. *Journal of Child Language*, 22, 727–735.

Clark, E. 1973. What's in a word? On the child's acquisition of semantics in his first language. In T. Moore, ed., *Cognitive development and the acquisition of language*, 65–110. New York: Academic Press.

Cohen, L. B. 1992, May. The myth of differentiation. Symposium paper presented at the International Conference on Infant Studies, Providence, RI.

Cohen, L. B. 1998. An information-processing approach to infant perception and cognition. In F. Simion and G. Butterworth, eds., *The development of sensory, motor and cognitive capacities in early infancy: From perception to cognition*, 277–300. Hove, UK: Psychology Press/Erlbaum.

Diesendruck, G., and Shatz, M. 1997. The effect of perceptual similarity and linguistic input on children's acquisition of object labels. *Journal of Child Language*, 24(3), 695–717.

Edwards, M. L. 1974. Perception and production in child phonology: The testing of four hypotheses. *Journal of Child Language*, 1, 205–219.

Fennell, C. T. 2000. *Does bilingual exposure affect infants' use of phonetic detail in a word learning task?* Unpublished master's thesis, University of British Columbia, Vancouver.

Fennell, C. T., and Werker, J. F. Forthcoming. Early word learners' ability to access phonetic detail in well-known words. *Language and Speech*.

Ferguson, C. A., and Farwell, C. B. 1979. Words and sounds in early language acquisition. *Language*, 51, 419–439.

Garnica, O. K. 1973. The development of phonemic speech perception. In T. E. Moore, ed., *Cognitive development and the acquisition of language*, 215–222. New York: Academic Press.

Gogate, L. J., and Bahrick, L. E. 1998. Intersensory redundancy facilitated learning or arbitrary relations between vowel sounds and objects in seven-month-old infants. *Journal of Experimental Child Psychology*, 69, 133–149.

Hirsh-Pasek, K., and Golinkoff, R. M. 1996. *The origin of grammar*. Cambridge, MA: MIT Press.

Hollich, G. J., Golinkoff, R. M., and Hirsh-Pasek, K. 2000. Breaking the language barrier: An emergentist coalition model for the origins of word learning. *Monographs for the Society for Research in Child Development, 63*(262).

Jusczyk, P. W. 1997. *The discovery of spoken language*. Cambridge, MA: MIT Press.

Jusczyk, P. W., and Aslin, R. N. 1995. Infants' detection of sound patterns of words in fluent speech. *Cognitive Psychology, 29,* 1–23.

Kay-Raining Bird, E., and Chapman, R. S. 1998. Partial representations and phonological selectivity in the comprehension of 13- to 16-month-olds. *First Language, 18,* 105–127.

Keating, P. A. 1984. Phonetic and phonological representation of stop consonant voicing. *Language, 60,* 286–319.

Keating, P. A. 1988. Underspecification in phonetics. *Phonology, 5,* 275–292.

Keating, P. A. 1990. Phonetic representations in a generative grammar. *Journal of Phonetics, 18,* 321–334.

Lanza, E. 1997. *Language mixing in infant bilingualism: A sociolinguistic perspective.* Oxford: Clarendon Press.

Levy, Y. 1985. Theoretical gains from the study of bilingualism: A case report. *Language Learning, 35,* 541–554.

McCarthy, J., and Prince, A. 1995. Faithfulness and reduplicative identity. In J. Beckman, L. Walsh Dickey, and S. Urbanczyk, eds., *Massachusetts Occasional Papers in Linguistics [UMOP] 18: Papers in optimality theory,* 249–384. Amherst, MA: GLSA.

Mills, D. L., Coffey-Corina, S. A., and Neville, H. J. 1993. Language acquisition and cerebral specialization in 20-month-old infants. *Journal of Cognitive Neuroscience, 5,* 317–334.

Mills, D. L., Coffey-Corina, S. A., and Neville, H. J. 1997. Language comprehension and cerebral specialization from 13 to 20 months. *Developmental Neuropsychology, 13,* 397–445.

Mills, D. L., Prat, C. S., Stager, C. L., Zangl, R., Neville, H., and Werker, J. F. 2002. Language experience and the organization of brain activity to phonetically similar words: ERP evidence from 14- and 20-month-olds. Paper presented at the 13th Biennial International Conference of Infant Studies, Toronto, April 18–21.

Morgan, J. L., Shi, R., and Allopena, P. 1996. Perceptual bases of rudimentary grammatical categories: Toward a broader conceptualization of bootstrapping. In J. L. Morgan and K. Demuth, eds., *Signal to syntax: Bootstrapping from speech to grammar in early acquisition,* 263–283. Hillsdale, NJ: Erlbaum.

Nelson, K. E., and Bonvillian, J. D. 1973. Concepts and words in the 18-month-old: Acquiring concept names under controlled conditions. *Cognition, 2*(4), 435–450.

Newport, E. 1990. Maturational constraints on language learning. *Cognitive Science, 14,* 11–28.

Oviatt, S. L. 1982. Inferring what words mean: Early development in infants' comprehension of common object names. *Child Development, 53,* 274–277.

Pater, J. Forthcoming. Bridging the gap between receptive and productive development with minimally violable constraints. In R. Kager, J. Pater, and Z. Wim, eds., *Fixing priorities: Constraints in phonological acqusition.* Cambridge, England: Cambridge University Press.

Pater, J., Stager, C., and Werker, J. F. 1998. Additive effects of phonetic distinctions in word learning. *Proceedings of the 16th International Congress on Acoustics and 135th Meeting of the Acoustical Society of America,* 2049–2050. Sewickley, PA: Acoustical Society of America Publications.

Pater, J., Stager, C., and Werker, J. F. 2002. The perceptual acquisition of phonological contrasts. Unpublished manuscript.

Pearson, B. Z., Fernández, S. C., Lewedeg, V., and Oller, D. K. 1997. The relation of input factors to lexical learning by bilingual infants. *Applied Psycholinguistics, 18,* 1–58.

Pierrehumbert, J. 1990. Phonological and phonetic representation. *Journal of Phonetics, 18*(3), 375–394.

Pollock, K. E. 1987. Phonological perception of early words in young children using a visual search paradigm. *Dissertation Abstracts International, 48*(2-B), 405.

Rice, K., and Avery, P. 1995. Variability in a deterministic model of language acquisition: A theory of segmental elaboration. In J. Archibald, ed., *Phonological acquisition and phonological theory,* 23–42. Hillsdale, NJ: Erlbaum.

Rubin, H., and Turner, A. 1989. Linguistic awareness skills in grade one children in a French immersion setting. *Reading and Writing: An Interdisciplinary Journal, 1,* 73–86.

Schafer, G., and Plunkett, K. 1998. Rapid word learning by fifteen-month-olds under tightly controlled conditions. *Child Development, 69,* 309–320.

Shi, R., and Werker, J. F. 2001. Six-month-old infants' preference for lexical words. *Psychological Science, 12,* 70–75.

Shvachkin, N. K. [1948] 1973. The development of phonemic speech perception in early childhood. In C. Ferguson and D. Slobin, eds., *Studies of child language development,* 91–127. New York: Holt, Rinehart & Winston.

Spelke, E. S. 1994. Initial knowledge: Six suggestions. *Cognition, 50,* 431–445.

Stager, C. L. 1999. *A study of the phonetic detail used in lexical tasks during infancy.* Unpublished doctoral dissertation, University of British Columbia, Vancouver.

Stager, C. L., and Werker, J. F. 1997. Infants listen for more phonetic detail in speech perception than in word-learning tasks. *Nature, 388*, 381–382.

Stager, C. L., and Werker, J. F. 1998. Methodological issues in studying the link between speech perception and word learning. In C. Rovee-Collier, series ed., and L. P. Lipsitt and H. Hayne, vol. eds., *Advances in infancy research*, 237–256. Stamford, CT: Ablex.

Swingley, D., and Aslin, R. N. 2000. Spoken word recognition and lexical representation in very young children. *Cognition, 76*, 147–166.

Swingley, D., and Aslin, R. N. 2002. Lexical neighborhoods and the word-form representations of 14-month-olds. *Psychological Science, 13*, 480–484.

Swingley, D., Pinto, J. P., and Fernald, A. 1999. Continuous processing in word recognition at 24 months. *Cognition, 71*, 73–108.

Werker, J. F. 1995. Exploring developmental changes in cross-language speech perception. In D. Osherson, series ed., and L. Gleitman and M. Liberman, vol. eds., *An invitation to cognitive science, Vol. 1: Language*, 87–106. Cambridge, MA: MIT Press.

Werker, J. F., Cohen, L. B., Lloyd, V. L., Casasola, M., and Stager, C. L. 1998. Acquisition of word-object associations by 14-month-old infants. *Developmental Psychology, 34*, 1289–1309.

Werker, J. F., and Curtin, S. In preparation. The PAUSE: Mir model of infant speech processing.

Werker, J. F., Fennell, C. T., Corcoran, K. M., and Stager, C. L. 2002. Infants' ability to learn phonetically similar words: Effects of age and vocabulary size. *Infancy, 3*, 1–30.

Werker, J. F., and Pegg, J. E. 1992. Infant speech perception and phonological acquisition. In C. A. Ferguson, L. Menn, and C. Stoel-Gammon, eds., *Phonological acquisition*, 285–311. Timonium, MD: York Press.

Werker, J. F., and Stager, C. L. 2000. Developmental changes in infant speech perception and early word learning: Is there a link? In M. B. Broe and J. B. Pierre-Humbert, eds., *Papers in Laboratory Phonology 5: Acquisition and the lexicon*, 181–193. New York: Cambridge University Press.

Werker, J. F., and Tees, R. C. 1984. Cross-language speech perception: Evidence for perceptual reorganization during the first year of life. *Infant Behavior and Development, 7*, 49–63.

Woodward, A. L., Markman, E. M., and Fitzsimmons, C. M. 1994. Rapid word learning in 13- and 18-month-olds. *Developmental Psychology, 30*, 553–566.

4

Perceptual Units and Their Mapping with Language: How Children Can (Or Can't?) Use Perception to Learn Words

Barbara Landau

Our phenomenal experience of the world is one of coherence and stability—objects, motions, and events in a seamless tapestry evolving over time. Yet, as perception researchers tell us, our impression of coherence is far from a direct reflection of the physical input picked up by the perceptual systems. Rather, it is the product of rich mental representations through which we construct the world that we experience. The constancy and coherence of objects and events are part of the perceptual world of the infant. Unlike the vision of infancy articulated by Bishop Berkeley and Williams James, we now know that the infant's world is three-dimensional, populated with objects of constant shape and size that occupy specific locations in space and that travel over continuous paths through space (see Kellman and Arterberry 1998 for a review).

One of the most striking reflections of this unity is our ability to talk about what we see. Even young children talk effortlessly about objects, motions, and relationships without any apparent awareness that a conversion has taken place. This capacity to talk about what we see clearly reflects a distinctly human aspect of knowledge. But despite the apparent ease with which we do this, the mechanisms by which it is accomplished early in development are likely to be as complex as those by which our perceptual and cognitive systems first construct a unified world. This is because the mapping between perception and language demands that two systems of knowledge with quite different formats be codified in some compatible format. How is this accomplished?

The purpose of this chapter is to explore children's language of objects and object parts as case studies that can provide insight into how the mapping is accomplished. I will argue that a deeper understanding of the mechanisms underlying word acquisition requires that we understand the similarities and differences in format between the perceptual representations children might use, and the linguistic representations they must learn. As we will see, the two are never equivalent. However, in some cases, perceptual representations provide a firm ground on which language can be mapped. In other cases, perception provides a less firm ground. In either case, the mapping between perception and language is surprisingly complex. Considering both kinds of cases can serve as a starting point for understanding how learners use perception when learning words.

In what follows, I first present a general framework for thinking about language-perception mappings. Then I examine two case studies: objects and object parts. For each, I discuss the aspects of language that are firmly supported by perception, and those that are not.

4.1 Language and Perception Must Interface, But How?

Because we can talk about our spatial experience, some elements of linguistic and nonlinguistic representation must be shared. This idea has been explored extensively by cognitive scientists, psychologists, computer scientists, and linguists (H. Clark 1973; Fillmore 1997; Hayward and Tarr 1995; Herskovits 1986; Jackendoff 1983; Landau and Jackendoff 1993; Miller and Johnson-Laird 1976; Regier 1996; Talmy 1983; see Bloom et al. 1996 for recent views). In this chapter, I will focus on objects and object parts, both of which can be represented by the spatial-perceptual systems, and by language.

Let's first consider the extent to which our linguistic and nonlinguistic representations are shared. There are at least three possibilities. One is that there is complete identity between spatial representations and the language that encodes these representations. This hypothesis is easily falsified by examining object names, which typically encode an object's category (e.g., *dog, house, table*). These names encode an object's category membership, regardless of the many distinctions that can be made by the spatial-perceptual systems. For example, the same label *dog* applies to objects that vary substantially in size, color, and surface characteristics; the label is essentially "blind" to these distinctions, which are clearly made by the human perceptual system. As another example, spatial representations that guide accurate grasping must include details of object size, shape, distance, orientation, and so on (Milner and Goodale 1995). Languages, however, do not have a stock of basic spatial terms that encode absolute metric distance or orientation (Talmy 1983). Rather, spatial terms (such as *near* or *far* and equivalent terms in other languages) encode relationships that are blind to absolute distance. The encoding of metric distance is accomplished by the language's stock of metric terms (the measure terms plus number words) used in phrases. These and many other examples show that language is "blind" to many properties that are represented in our nonlinguistic systems. The design of language specifies that lexical items encode categories at a level of detail coarser than that available to perception (Landau and Jackendoff 1993); language *requires* the grouping of many perceptually distinct entities under a single term.

A second possibility is that language draws selectively on aspects of spatial representation, but that all basic spatial terms will always correspond to some unit in the nonlinguistic system. For example, the word *dog* might be linked to an abstract spatial representation of things we normally call dogs. Studying the nonlinguistic representations could shed light on the nature of named things. At the same time, study of spatial language could shed light on the nature of spatial representations. For instance, although most theories of object representation (e.g., Biederman 1987; Marr 1982) treat objects as solid volumes, the lexicon includes many names whose referents may be better represented as thickened surfaces (e.g., *record, slab, sheet, lake*), hollow containers (e.g., *cup, bowl, box, jar*), or "negative" object parts (e.g., *hole, pit, groove, slot*). The very existence of these words could provide a theoretical and empirical motivation for vision scientists to search for corresponding nonlinguistic representations (see, e.g., Willats 1992).

The third possible relationship is complete independence—that the distinctions made by spatial language emerge independently, possibly under somewhat different constraints. Kemmerer (1999) uses the example of *near/far*, as follows. Evidence from neuropsychology tells us that the brain has distinctly different mechanisms for representing "near" (peripersonal) space, which surrounds the body and extends outward to the end of the arm's reach, and "far" (extrapersonal) space, which begins at the boundary of near space and progresses outward. If spatial terms always correspond to nonlinguistic distinctions, the terms *near/far* should map directly onto the two spaces. But this is not so. Rather, these terms encode relative distance, which can be contrasted within the peripersonal space, within the extrapersonal space, or across these spaces. For example, one can refer to "the pain here" versus "the pain there," both on the lower part of the leg (hence within the peripersonal space), or to "the tree that is near" versus "the tree that is far," both within extrapersonal space. Thus whereas language makes a binary relative distinction blind to metric distance, other spatial systems do incorporate metric distance. Kemmerer concludes that such linguistic distinctions may have emerged under constraints of their own.

Of the three possible relationships, partial overlap and independence are most plausible. In either case, there will have to be means for binding spatial aspects of a word's meaning to other aspects of its representation that are more traditionally considered "linguistic." How is this accomplished? One simple scheme is to assume that a given word just "points to" a perceptual or spatial representation, with no consequences for other levels of linguistic representation pertinent to the word. The fact that there is a regular relationship between the word *dog* and the visual system's representation of dogs is not trivial (see Fodor 1998 for discussion of the necessity of this rational relationship for word learning to occur). But this scheme treats perceptual representations as just appendages to the lexical representations, and may ignore important correspondences.

A different way to do the binding is via an "interface," which captures properties shared between two or more different kinds of representation. As Jackendoff (1996) points out, every level of linguistic representation (e.g., phonology, syntax) has its own privileged vocab-

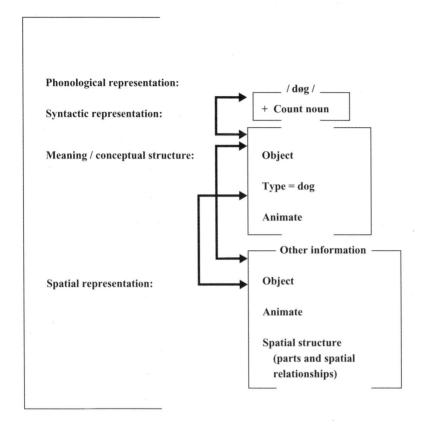

Figure 4.1
Different levels of representation for the lexical term *dog*. Each level contains information specific to itself, but commonalities across levels permit binding for a unified representation of the word.

ulary. Because of this, there is inherent incommensurability across levels. However, there are also some partial equivalences across levels, and these could bind together the different representation, as illustrated in figure 4.1. Traditionally, the lexical entry of the word *dog* will include specification of how the word sounds (its phonological representation), and the syntactic contexts in which it will occur (e.g. that it is a count noun). In Jackendoff's scheme, much of the remainder of the word's meaning is expressed in the word's "conceptual structure," which encodes, for instance, that the concept of dog represents a type of object (not just an individual token), an animate object, its taxonomic relationship to other types of objects, and possibly other information about its category or "kind."

In this scheme, words representing concrete spatial entities (such as objects or their parts) will also have a corresponding spatial representation (Jackendoff 1996; Landau and Jackendoff 1993). This spatial representation captures the fact that the entity is an object or part, the nature of its spatial structure (as described by Biederman 1987; Marr 1982), and, in the case of a word such as *dog*, perhaps its geometry over motion (Marr and Vaina 1982). Thus, syntactic, conceptual, and spatial representations would be implicated in the representation of the word *dog*. The interface captures what properties are shared across levels. In the case of *dog*, the spatial representation encodes its status as an object (along with the particulars of its spatial structure), and an animate object; conceptual structure also represents its status as object type and animate. Syntax then links to conceptual structure by formally encoding objects as count nouns. Binding the shared representations across different levels supports a unified representation for the word.

In sum, an interface might be the mechanism by which spatial representations are bound to other levels of representation pertinent to the meaning and form of a word. To the extent that spatial language—in this chapter, words for objects and object parts—engages nonlinguistic spatial representations, we would theorize that these spatial representations are a proper part of the full word's meaning. Alternatively, where spatial language does not engage nonlinguistic spatial representations, the meaning of the word would be restricted to its conceptual structure, syntax, and phonology. Importantly, it is possible that different relationships will be true of different lexical items. The evidence that follows suggests that this is the case.

4.2 Case 1: The Acquisition of Objects and Their Names

Objects are primary perceptual and cognitive units during infancy (Baillargeon 1995; Kellman and Spelke 1983; Leslie et al. 1998; Spelke, Gutheil, and Van de Walle 1995). Not surprisingly, earliest vocabulary is mostly naming of things, with 90 percent of object names applied to solid objects (Smith et al. 2002). The child's vocabulary grows slowly at first, increasing from zero to twenty-five words over a period of several months, then from twenty-five to fifty words over the next several months. During this time, it remains predominantly object oriented. Just as in perception, the object is a principal unit in early language learning.

Of course, the problem of linguistically encoding objects is much more complex than simply learning an object-name correspondence. Languages can encode the very same object at many different levels. The same dog may be referred to as *a dog, an animal, that dog,* or *Fido;* although each expression refers to the same animal, each expression points to a different concept or meaning. Thus meanings go beyond perception, and the child must learn which expressions go with which meanings, often when seeing the same object. How is this accomplished? Is perception of any use, and if so, how is it used? Let's consider several different aspects of object naming, and examine the implications for this correspondence.

4.2.1 Evidence, Part A: Where Perception Supports Language

After acquiring roughly fifty words, children begin to generalize object names to new objects, often on the basis of similarity in shape (E. Clark 1973). But the exact role of shape—and perceptual similarity more generally—is controversial (see Bloom 2000; Landau, Smith, and Jones 1998; Woodward and Markman 1998). Clearly, similar shape is not *necessary* for assigning the same name (e.g., a digital desk clock and Big Ben are both called *clock;* see Bloom 1996). The currently predominant view is that "object kind" is the basis for naming (Mandler and McDonough 1998; Markman 1989; Soja, Carey, and Spelke 1991; Waxman and Markow 1995).

Of course, the notion of "understanding kinds" does not answer the question of how the child comes to organize actual exemplars in the world into diverse kinds that he or she can name. Nor does it provide any clear mechanisms by which the child's knowledge of kinds could interface with perceptual representations of objects. Even if the child possesses categories such as animal or artifact, she will still need to determine which objects go together into each category.

This aspect of the induction problem has been largely ignored in discussions of word learning. Yet there is abundant perceptual information that can help the learner solve this problem.

Infants Are Sensitive to Rich, Subtle Kinds of Perceptual Similarity: Shape and Surface Texture

Basic-Level Categories and Shape   The three-dimensional structure of an object—its shape, as a combination of parts in a spatial structure—is critical to adults' object recognition (Biederman 1987; Marr 1982; Hoffman and Richards 1984; Singh and Hoffman 2001). These shape representations best capture objects at their basic level, an easy entry point into object naming (Brown 1958; Rosch et al. 1976; Waxman and Markow 1995; but see Mandler and Bauer 1988). The foundation for this exists in infancy.

A remarkable study by Behl-Chadha (1996) showed that even 4-month-old infants can recognize and encode complex shape-based distinctions betweeen objects in different basic-level categories—things such as chairs, couches, or tables. In Behl-Chadha's experiments, infants were habituated to a series of photographs of objects from one such category—for example, kitchen chairs, side chairs, stuffed chairs, in styles such as colonial, Victorian, and contemporary. Then they were tested for generalization to photographs of new chairs, compared to objects from a different complex category, such as dining-room tables, coffee tables that were round, oval, or rectangular, and tables with either central pedestals or four legs. Infants distinguished between the two categories of objects, suggesting that complex perceptual similarities are computed well before the child learns names for things (see related findings by Quinn and Eimas 1996 on animal categories).

Superordinate Categories and Surface Texture   Complex aspects of an object's surface structure may also support infants' categorization of superordinate categories such as natural kinds versus artifacts. Textures that characterize natural kinds (e.g., plants, animals, rock formations) are qualitatively different from those that occur in artifacts (see figure 4.2 for examples). Mandelbrot (1982) suggested that

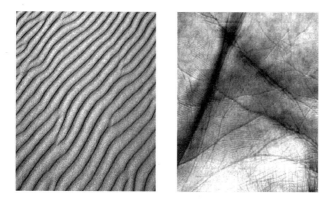

A. Natural textures

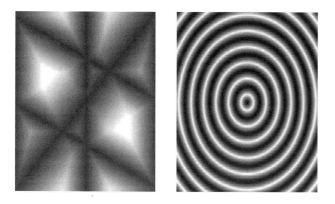

B. Artifact textures

Figure 4.2
Natural-kind objects and artifacts tend to have surface textures with unique characteristics. The surface textures in panel A are from natural entities (sand, skin) and exhibit characteristic regularities; the surface textures in panel B are from artifacts and have quite different kinds of regularities. The differences between these kinds of surface textures could support infants' categorization of natural-kind objects versus artifacts. See the text for discussion.

repeating self-similarity characterizes the surfaces of naturally occurring objects, whereas smooth, nonlayered textures characterize manufactured objects. Of course, the correlation between surface texture type and natural/artifact status is not perfect (there are leather sofas and fur coats); however, statistical regularities could allow learners to use these differing perceptual characteristics as support in forming different kinds of categories.

Smith and Heise (2000) showed that 12-month-old infants were highly sensitive to the surface textural differences of toy animals and vehicles whose shape and surface textures clearly specified their different kinds. Furthermore, they showed that surface texture—and not global shape—was sufficient for distinguishing members of these two categories. For example, infants could categorize toy animals versus vehicles that had been cut up to destroy shape information but preserve surface information, but not the reverse.

These findings suggest that infants can use both shape and the surface properties of objects during categorization. The human visual system is likely to be sensitive to important properties such as these, and hence detection of this information may play a key role in early categorization. The knowledge constructed from such activities will serve the toddler well once naming begins.

Early Object Naming May Rest on Similarities in Object Shape

Across a wide range of studies, Landau et al. found that young children show a pronounced tendency to generalize novel object names on the basis of an object's shape (Landau, Smith, and Jones 1988, 1992, 1997; Smith, Jones, and Landau 1992, 1996). For example, if shown a novel object (the "standard") and told "See this? This is a dax," children will later judge that objects having the same or similar shape also are called "dax" (see figure 4.3A). This bias in favor of object shape begins rather weakly, around age 2, and becomes quite strong by around age 3. Surprisingly, it is strong in adults in certain contexts—especially when the object is novel and no further information about its category is available (Gentner 1978; Landau, Smith, and Jones 1997; see section 2.2).

Importantly, the shape bias is reliably found in naming contexts, but not in contexts where the objects are not named (figure 4.3B).

Perceptual Units and Their Mapping with Language

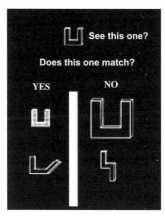

A.   B.

Figure 4.3
When young children are shown a novel object and hear it named, they tend to assume that objects with the same shape are members of the same-name category (panel A). In contrast, when children are shown the same novel object and do not hear the object named, they make similarity judgments on the basis of other properties, such as the object's size and/or texture (panel B). This pattern has been dubbed the "shape bias" (Landau, Smith, and Jones 1988).

Thus, if children are shown an object and hear only "See this?" (with no name given to the object), they will later judge objects to "go with" or "match" the standard on the basis of a variety of properties including color, texture, and size (Landau, Smith, and Jones 1988; Smith, Jones, and Landau 1992). The "shape bias" appears only in contexts of object naming (see also Baldwin 1992; Imai, Gentner, and Uchida 1994; Soja 1992; Subrahmanyam, Landau, and Gelman 1999; see Landau et al. 1998 for a review).

Note that young children *do* notice, attend to, and become engaged by other properties of objects—so it cannot simply be argued that shape is just "salient" for young children. For example, when 3-year-olds are told a novel object is "food," they generalize to new objects on the basis of color (Macario 1991). When 2-year-olds are asked to choose an object in order to "fix up" a doll's unkempt hair, they choose objects that are rigid and have prongs—objects that are functionally similar to combs—but not flimsy paper objects cut out to look exactly like a comb (Landau, Smith, and Jones 1997; see also

Brown 1990). Yet at the same time, both 2-year-olds and adults asked to find a "comb" do pick out the flimsy paper object shaped like a comb. Thus, young children know a lot about objects, and their attention can be drawn to different properties in different task contexts. The task of object naming in young children is also selective, and solution to *this* task appears to engage representations of an object's shape. We have speculated that the mechanism by which this is accomplished is quick, automatic, and encapsulated (Smith, Jones, and Landau 1996).

If object shape is privileged, then important questions follow. In what sense are the shapes of all cats or dogs similar? What level of detail is actually encoded for the purposes of object naming? Is this a different level of detail from that required for object recognition? How are such different scales of shape represented, and how are they engaged during naming? Answers to these questions provide a challenge to vision scientists, who have yet to develop complete theories of how our minds compute categories of "similar" shapes.

4.2.2 Evidence, Part B: Where More Than Perception Is Required

Although the previous discussion emphasized the strong contribution of perception to naming, other cases show the limits of perception in helping the learner acquire new names.

Named Object Categories Go Beyond the Perceptual Descriptions of Objects:
The Roles of Enriched Knowledge and Taxonomic Structure
Despite the strong role of shape in early object naming, mature object naming surely engages other kinds of distinctions and other kinds of knowledge: for adults, Big Ben and a digital clock are both definitely "clocks," and what makes all dogs members of the named category *dog* is not only (or even necessarily) their perceptual similarity (see Bloom 1996; Keil 1994; Medin and Ortony 1989; Putnam 1977; Soja, Carey, and Spelke 1991; Waxman and Markow 1995; Woodward and Markman 1998). At some point, object names become part of a hierarchy, and at some point, enriched knowledge enters into naming. These two acquisitions seem, however, to have different developmental courses.

A number of investigators have argued that children's early object naming reflects taxonomic categories (Mandler and McDonough 1998; Waxman and Markow 1995). Strong evidence for such taxonomic organization was provided by Waxman and Senghas (1992), who taught 2-year-olds different novel count nouns for each of two novel unfamiliar objects that were related to each other (e.g., a horn and a flute). When tested for their generalization of the words, toddlers sometimes generalized the word for the related items (horn, flute) to the other member of the pair, but never generalized either of these words to an unrelated item (whisk). This indicates that they set up a partition between the related items and the unrelated item. In addition, their generalization within a related pair was asymmetric. For example, a child might call both the horn and flute by the name taught to him for the horn alone, but this child never called the flute by anything except its correct (i.e., taught) name. This suggests that the children assumed that the two related objects were members of one category (horns/flutes, akin to a superordinate), and that one of the objects also had a separate name, presumably its basic-level name. Thus a single object was called by two different names, consistent with at least rudimentary hierarchical structure (see also Waxman 1990).

Enriched knowledge, however, may enter into naming later. For adults, an object's function is often more important in determining its name than its shape (Malt and Johnson 1992; Miller and Johnson-Laird 1976; Landau, Smith, and Jones 1997; Smith, Jones, and Landau 1996). If asked what makes a chair a chair, adults may say it is "something you sit on," a knife is "something you cut with," and so on. However, children initially do not seem reliant on function. Landau and colleagues presented 2-, 3-, and 5-year-olds as well as adults with novel objects, and either named the object (with a novel name) without saying more, or named the object while also describing its (fictional, but plausible) function. People then were tested for whether they would generalize the object's name to new objects that were either the same shape, but incapable of carrying out the designated function, or a different shape, but capable of carrying out the function. Subjects of all ages who were *not* told the objects' functions generalized on the basis of shape. However, for those who *were* told the objects' functions, there was a definite developmental trend: 2- and 3-year-olds still generalized on the basis of shape, but 5-year-olds and adults generalized on the basis of function. Thus, enriched knowledge about object categories—in this case, an object's function—guides naming generalization relatively late. This is consistent with the fact that so-called deeper knowledge of objects develops beyond the age of 4 or so (Gelman and Wellman 1991; Keil 1989).

As a whole, the evidence shows unequivocally that young children use a variety of kinds of evidence to decide how to call a thing. Similarity of shape is neither necessary nor sufficient for having the same name. But equally important, the evidence does not rule out a critical role of shape similarity in the early development of object naming. The most reasonable conclusion is that perceptual similarity—in particular, object shape—can serve as a rich foundation for children as they come to group objects into categories that will support early object naming. This early reliance on perceptual similarity as a guide to category membership is later enriched with additional knowledge, which may—in some cases—come to override the evidence of our perceptual systems.

Types and Tokens Are Distinguished from Each Other in Language, But Not in Perception

As we observed earlier, the very same object can be encoded by language as a type (*a dog*) or a token of the category (*that dog*). Unique tokens often have proper names: My own dog is *Fido.* Yours may look identical to mine (and may even be its identical twin), but its uniqueness is marked by a different name, *Rover.* The distinction between types and tokens can also be encoded by determiners. Both types and tokens can be encoded by count nouns (e.g., *a* dog, referring to a member of the category or to a particular dog; *the* dog, referring to any member of the category or to a particular dog). In addition, tokens can be distinguished by other determiners (*this* dog, *that* dog, both referring to a particular dog). Unique animate tokens are distinguished by proper nouns, which do not take count determiners (e.g., **The Fido*). Because the type-token distinction is encoded both conceptually and syntactically, Jackendoff (1996) has proposed that it is part of conceptual structure, which marks the item as a [TYPE] or [TOKEN]. Corresponding syntactic-morphological distinctions then appear in the syntactic representation.

Is the type-token distinction encoded by perceptual systems? If so, we might look for correspondences between the perceptual and linguistic distinctions. If not, this would appear to be a linguistic-conceptual distinction that emerges independently of perception.

A number of considerations suggest that perception encodes tokens but not types. For example, Scholl and Pylyshyn (1999) found that adults have the capacity to track the simultaneous motions of up to about four individual objects—or tokens—at a time. They suggest that a perceptual-attentional mechanism "hooks" an index to each object to be tracked. Thus, our perceptual system can track individual tokens—a particular object that could later be called "this X." A correlate of the object TYPE, however, is not apparent in perception, despite the fact that types are readily encoded by languages. That is, there is no obvious way for our perceptual system to encode the fact that a particular dog belongs to the TYPE "DOG." To do this, it must be tagged in some nonperceptual format—such as conceptual structure.

Despite this asymmetry in perception, language encodes both tokens and types. Proper nouns provide one mechanism for marking identity over time: once we give an object a proper name, it is marked as unique, and thereafter we can use its name to refer to it. Determiners also mark identity—for example, we can specify *this* dog or *that* dog. Linguistic devices such as these can be used by children as young as 18 months to make inferences about the referent of a novel noun. For instance, Katz, Baker, and Macnamara (1974) showed 18- to 24-month-olds a doll, and labeled it either "a dax" or "Dax." Children were subsequently shown the same doll plus another similar doll and asked to point out either "a dax" or "Dax." Children who heard the proper name pointed only to the original doll, whereas children who heard the count noun pointed to either (see also Gelman and Taylor 1984; Hall 1996; Liittschwager and Markman 1994). Thus types and tokens are conceptually represented by very young children and properly encoded in their early language. But it is unlikely that TYPE representations are contained in perception.

4.2.3 Evidence, Part C: Learning Affects the Perception-Naming Relationship

Even where perception serves as a foundation for object naming, there is growing evidence that learning plays an important role in modulating what is grouped together under the same name. And this appears early in development.

Infants Learn to Make New Perceptual and Category Distinctions
Eimas and Quinn (1994) found that 7-month-olds, but not 4-month-olds, could distinguish between female lions and novel cats—animals that are perceptually quite similar. How could such a distinction be learned, in the absence of language or formal tutoring? The investigators reasoned that such learning might require direct contrast of some kind. Therefore, they presented the younger infants with twelve instances of photos of cats alone, followed by six instances in which they presented pairs of familiar (just seen) cats together with (novel) female lions. They also included two pairings of familiar (just seen) cats, to highlight the difference between these completely familiar pairs and the familiar cat–novel lion pairs. Infants then were tested on their preference for novel cats relative to instances of two novel classes—either novel dogs or novel female lions. The infants preferred both the dogs and the female lions, relative to the cats, indicating that they could distinguish female lions from cats. The induction of this category (female lions) from short-lived laboratory experience suggests that, as young as 3–4 months of age, the perceptual systems of the infant are subject to modulation in response to experience—in this case, the experience stemming from direct contrast. Thus, whatever perceptually based categories the infant begins with, early nonlinguistic learning experiences can reshape these categories, at least to some degree.

Toddlers Learn That Object Shape Is Relevant for the Names of Solid Objects
Recent evidence strongly suggests that the child's tendency to name objects on the basis of shape is partly a product of learning in the context of object naming. In particular, Smith et al. (2002) found

that the shape bias in object naming is considerably strengthened during the early course of acquiring object names.

In their study, children in the early stages of vocabulary learning were brought into the laboratory over a period of several months, and were shown sets of objects in which one object (the "standard") was frequently labeled with a novel count noun. After several visits, the children were tested for their generalization of the new word to new objects, which varied from the original standard object in shape, material, or color. Results showed that only children who had productive vocabularies over fifty words generalized on the basis of shape. Children who were not exposed to the object sets but who were nevertheless tested for naming generalization did not show shape-based generalization. Nor did children who were shown the objects but did not hear them named. However, the latter group did tend to spontaneously group objects by shape as they were playing with them. This shows that the experience of seeing sets of same-shaped objects presented together heightened their attention to shape *without* connecting it to the act of naming. Clearly, shape is special. But naming by shape happened only when the children both saw the same-shaped objects and heard them named.

These findings show that shape is a prepotent organizer for young children. They also show that naming by shape depends both on this prepotence of shape *and* on the exposure to naming same-shaped objects. This helps explain why the shape bias strengthens as the child acquires vocabulary. The shape bias reflects a generalization that the child makes over his or her experiences hearing same-shaped objects named by the same name. Importantly, as the child hears the same name being applied to objects that share shape similarity, she comes to generalize that object shape, in general, is important to naming things. Now when the child hears a novel object named, she generalizes the name on the basis of the object's shape.

Learning Different Distributions of Labels Alters Naming Boundaries
Although languages show strong overlap in the kinds of objects named, there is also intriguing crosslinguistic variation in the distribution of labels across a number of domains, including color,

space, and—perhaps surprisingly—common objects (Bowerman 1996; Davidoff, Davies, and Roberson 1999; Heider and Oliver 1972; Levinson 1996; Malt et al. 1999; Munnich, Landau, and Dosher 2001). Learning one's native language thus requires changing the representational space used for naming.

A study by Landau and E. Shipley (2000) shows that even short-lived experience can alter the child's linguistic space. Two-year-olds, three-year-olds, and adults saw two quite different objects, which were either named with the Same Label, two Different Labels, or No Label at all (see figure 4.4A). In the Same Label and Different Label conditions, subjects then were asked whether objects morphed as intermediates to these standards (figure 4.4B) belonged to one of the labeled categories. In the No Label condition, they were asked whether each object was "like" one of the standards. In the Same Label condition, children and adults generalized to all inter-

A.   B.

Figure 4.4
Children and adults were shown the two objects in panel A, and heard them named with the same name (e.g., a *dax*), two different names (e.g., a *dax* and a *rif*), or no name at all. When asked to judge whether the objects in panel B were also *daxes*, children and adults in the same-name condition judged that all objects were also called *dax*. Children and adults in the different-name condition judged that only about half of the objects were also called *dax*, splitting the set of objects in half along lines of similarity to the standards. Children and adults in the no-name condition fell in between the other two groups (Landau and Shipley 2000).

mediates, whereas in the Different Label and No Label conditions, they showed division of the intermediates into two separate categories, with sharper division in the Different Labels condition. Landau and Shipley suggested that two mechanisms might underlie this shaping of the lexical space: "Boosting" the equivalence of different exemplars by naming two exemplars with the same name, even if they are perceptually quite distinctive, and "differentiating" exemplars through differences in labeling, even if the objects are quite similar. These ideas are compatible with E. J. Gibson's (1969) theory of perceptual learning: we can learn to count or discount particular object features, resulting in new equivalences or differences across objects. This also applies to learning object names.

4.2.4   Summary of Case 1

The results reviewed here suggest that infants can use rich perceptual information for naming. Representations of objects in terms of their shape and surface texture can provide an important foundation for the beginning stages of object naming. However, the relationship between perceptual representations of objects and object naming is complex. Naming spaces may be built on—but are not identical to—the perceptual spaces that support them. Perceptual foundations are modulated by early learning, both prelinguistically and during language learning. The latter can result in distinctions that are particular to naming, and not other representational domains. Finally, language encodes some aspects of object knowledge that are not transparently encoded in the perceptual systems. These include the encoding of taxonomic structure and types versus tokens.

4.3   Case 2: Object Parts and Their Names

Names for object parts appear in the child's earliest vocabulary, showing that children represent parts of objects as natural units on which language can be built. However, part names are much less frequent than names for whole objects, and are at first restricted to names for body parts—a rather limited selection from the wealth of possible object part names (Andersen 1975; Gentner 1982; Gentner and Boroditsky 2001; Nelson 1974; Smith et al. 2002). Even for 3-year-olds, learning a novel part name requires that it be introduced in the context of a known object name (Markman and Wachtel 1988). Clearly, whole objects regularly trump parts as natural units for naming during early development.

Nonetheless, the acquisition of names for parts allows us to ask how well part *naming*—by children and adults—maps onto the *visual* parsing of objects. The evidence suggests that, like objects, there are some cases where the visual theories provide natural support for language. In other cases, the naming of object parts requires more than perceptual theories currently provide.

4.3.1 Evidence, Part A: Where Perception Supports Language

In current theories, objects are assumed to be represented as parts and their spatial relationships, with mandatory early processing of parts (Biederman 1987; Hoffman and Singh 1997; Singh and Hoffman 2001). Some theorists have further suggested that mechanisms of object parsing may deliver up units appropriate for language (Hoffman and Richards 1984).

It is interesting to observe that representation of object in terms of their parts already entails rich mental structure. This is clear from comparison of the notion of part with that of piece (Cruse 1986). To generate *pieces* of an object, one need only divide it such that topological stability and spatiotemporal continuity are preserved: the pieces must come from the same whole object and each piece is a unit. However, the means for dividing the object into pieces are wholly arbitrary; I can use any scheme I wish and the result will still be a legitimate set of object pieces. Moreover, the relationship among resulting pieces is transitive. If I cut a hat into six pieces, a piece of piece A is still a piece of the hat, and a piece of the piece of piece A is still a piece of the hat, and so on.

Contrast this with an object's parts. These must also possess topological stability and spatiotemporal continuity. However, unlike pieces, objects are divided into their *parts* according to motivated boundaries (Cruse 1986)—the hat may be divided into its crown, brim, band, and feather. Each of these parts can be named. This is quite unlike the *pieces* of the hat, which hold no conceptual priority and therefore are not given names. Unlike pieces, parts do not hold the relationship of transitivity: although the spine of the feather is a part of the feather, and the feather is a part of the hat, the spine of the feather is not a part of the hat.

It is parts, not pieces, that have names, so I will focus on these, asking how "good" the results of different parsing theories are, for language. There are two main approaches to object parsing within the vision literature. In one, each object part is represented as an individual generalized cone swept along an axis; during object recognition, these units are fitted to the image so as to achieve a match, which is the basis for recognition (Marr and Nishihara 1978; Biederman 1987). In this scheme, named parts could be mapped naturally to each generalized cone. For example, the animal figures shown in figure 4.5 decompose naturally into units that are labeled by the

Figure 4.5
As discussed by Marr and Nishihara (1978), objects can be represented in terms of a hierarchically structured set of geons, with units at each level attached to units at the next level. (The figure is from Marr and Nishihara 1978, reproduced by permission of the publisher.)

Figure 4.6
The main units of the faces shown can be produced by the visual parsing algorithm
described by Hoffman and Richards (1984). Hoffman and Richards point out that
these units correspond to the main named parts of the face (e.g., lips, chin, nose,
mouth, and so on), suggesting a natural mapping between the units produced by
perception and those named by language. See the text for discussion.

English lexicon—*head*, *neck*, *tail*, *leg*, and so on. A second approach
has been taken by Hoffman and colleagues (Hoffman and Richards
1984; Hoffman and Singh 1997; see Singh and Hoffman 2001). In
this theory, part boundaries are delineated by using a general computational scheme that parses at points of local minima on the
object's surface. Using this scheme, it is easy to see how familiar
objects—such as the profile of a face—can be parsed into its main
parts (see figure 4.6; see also Hoffman and Singh 1997). Moreover,
these parts are appealingly linked to the names we use for familiar
parts—for instance, *nose*, *forehead*, *lips*, *chin*, and so on. With figure-
ground reversal, new named parts jump out from the goblet—for
example, *lip*, *bowl*, *stem*, and *base*.

How do the volumetric-unit and minima-rule approaches fare,
respectively, in mapping from the perception of parts to the naming
of object parts, and hence serving as support for the word learner?
The answer will differ, depending on the kind of named part.

Parts That Have Specific Names: Handles, Knobs, Fingers
Both approaches seem to fare reasonably well in providing units appropriate to the names for many common object parts. However, there are also limitations. The volumetric approach provides a parsing of all components of many common objects, and any one of these could in principle be named using a part term. The mimima-rule approach is more flexible, by providing the means to parse any object, and is especially useful in cases of natural-kind objects, which grow, become squashed, and move, and hence are much less likely to be appropriately characterized by combinations of geons (see, e.g., Leyton 1992).

But not all visual parts get named, even if they are very central and salient parts. For example, we have names for the handle, spout, and lid of a teapot, but no name for the central "body" portion (Cruse 1986); the same is true for the central body of cars, cups, and so forth. Similarly, several visual parts may be collapsed to yield a single named part. A striking example is found in the crosslinguistic encoding of body-part terms, which are arguably one of the earliest part terms acquired by children (Andersen 1975). Some languages, like English, use a single term (*nose*) to refer to the region from the bridge of the nose to the tip; others (like Tarascan) use a single term to include the latter plus the forehead. Whereas *leg* does not include the foot, other languages include the region of the foot ending where the toes begin, and others include the toes as well. Even common objects may have shapes that should be parsed into more parts than would naturally be named (Schyns and Murphy 1994).

Clearly, visual parsing schemes provide some support for part naming, but underdetermine the actual range of part names. The child would be safe in following two principles: (1) Part names do not violate part boundaries. This would prohibit, for example, the combination of two spatially disjunctive units (Singh and Landau 1998) without prohibiting combination of parts. (2) Part names are licensed by the existence of a visually parsed unit. That is, any visually parsed unit or combination of units could serve as a natural unit for naming. This possibility accounts for the support provided by the visual system, but does not limit naming to those units afforded by vision.

Parts That Represent Regions Located at the Ends of Axes: Tops and Bottoms

Another set of early acquired terms are those used to name spatial regions of objects. In English, these are terms such as *top, bottom, front, back,* and *side*. These terms refer to regions that lie at the ends of the three major orthogonal axes of objects. The boundaries of these regions often have no obvious perceptual discontinuity—for example, the *top* and *bottom* of a fork are the regions corresponding to some portion of the tines and some portion of the handle (and assignment varies over people).

Children acquire these terms by around age 2 or 3 (Clark 1980). What aspect of object representation is engaged when they do so? Landau and Jackendoff (1993) reviewed some possibilities. First, volumetric approaches to object parsing represent the main axis of each object part, since generalized cylinders are cross-sections swept along a central axis. For multipart objects, one would further need to designate the single part—or combination of parts—that serves to orient the object more globally. This global axis gives us the foundation for *top* and *bottom*. Further distinctions require assignment of secondary and tertiary axes to each object, which provide the region for *front/back, left/right,* and *side* (and these then apply iteratively to each object part—e.g., the *front/back* of the arm). To distinguish between the opposite ends of any single axis, we would require assignment of direction, yielding "directed" axes, and these would distinguish between, for example, *right* and *left*. The three orthogonal axes and their directional assignments thus serve as the perceptual representational basis for applying spatial-region terms.

It is likely that this aspect of object representation is foundational in the mapping between perception and language. First, the use of spatial part terms emerges in production between ages 2 and 3 (Clark 1980). Terms that engage the object's main axis (i.e., *top* and *bottom*) appear to cause less difficulty for children than terms that engage the secondary or tertiary axes. Many studies attest to the difficulties children have in sorting out *front* and *back* (Kucjaz and Maratsos 1975), and later, *right* and *left*. Apparently, children first sort out which axis is pertinent for which pairs of terms, and only later sort out the directions within the pair (Clark 1980; Landau 2002).

Second, the use of the geometric model for assignment of spatial part terms appears in languages worldwide, and most strikingly, in languages whose structure is quite different from English. Even Tzeltal, which has a large range of unusual spatial part terms, can be nicely captured within a framework quite similar to the one I have described (Levinson 1994). Thus it seems that spatial parts terms—whether in English or other languages—provide a compelling example of how representations in the visual system interface with the linguistic system, to provide the foundations for naming spatial regions. As with whole objects, visual representations provide solid support for some aspects of early word learning.

4.3.2 Evidence, Part B: Where More Than Perception Is Required

Spatial Regions Depend on Object Function as Well as Geometry
The theories of parsing just mentioned rely on object geometry, and the correspondence between parts and part names seems fairly clear. Indeed, for novel objects that may be represented solely in terms of their geometric properties, the visual representations may provide both a necessary and a sufficient means of naming regions. However, the assignment of spatial part terms for many familiar objects appears to depend very much on the object's function, as well as on other aspects of its category that are not clearly derivable from visual properties. The importance of function in assigning part terms has long been noted by linguists such as Fillmore (1997), who observed that the "front" of an animate object is typically the region having crucial functional features (such as eyes). These can be put into competition with other important properties (such as motion), and typically win, evidenced in the way we naturally express a crab's movement: it walks *sideways.*

Although these observations are often cited, there has been relatively little systematic work on how people use function in assigning spatial part terms to object regions (but see Carlson-Radvansky and Radvansky 1996). Is the visual-geometric representation primary, or does it interact with functional knowledge? Does the primacy of geometric and functional information change over development? Our lab has begun to examine these issues by investigating how people apply spatial part terms to a wide range of common objects, including glasses, cameras, pieces of furniture, common writing and measuring utensils, and so on. In one experiment, the objects are presented to people in a plastic bag; they are asked to retrieve them one at a time and to indicate the *top, bottom, front, back,* and *side.* People typically tend to retrieve objects and orient them as if in normal use—for example, retrieving the eyeglasses and orienting them for wearing, retrieving a soda can and placing it upright in front of them, or retrieving a toy dresser and placing it with the drawers facing their own body.

The patterns of labeling suggest that children and adults construct "models" of different objects, with the models following from knowledge of the objects' functions as well as geometry. The parts are labeled in accord with these models. Because the functions of different objects can vary so much, application of spatial part terms does not always follow geometric principles across different objects. For instance, for a camera and eyeglasses, spatial part terms are assigned such that *top* and *bottom* are consistent with gravitational up/down when holding the object as if to be used: *back* is assigned to the part through which the user looks, and *front* the part that faces the rest of the world. In contrast, pieces of furniture such as dressers have their *front* assigned as the part facing the user—that is, the surface with drawer knobs is labeled the *front,* and its spatial opposite the *back.* Other objects are labeled using *top* and *bottom* as their user-relevant regions. The *tops* of pencils are the region with the eraser, and the *bottom* the region with the point; the *front* is usually the surface with writing on it, and the *back* the region at the other end of the axis. In contrast, the *tops* of rulers are the surfaces with measurement indicators, the *bottoms* are the regions opposite to these (and blank); and the *front* and *back* are sometimes assigned by the same individual redundantly to these same regions (with *top* and *front* labeling the same region; *bottom* and *back* the same region).

These observations clearly indicate that the assignment of spatial part terms relies not only on geometric considerations, but also world knowledge about the object and what it is used for. Geometric representations may interact with world knowledge from the earliest points in development, or one may precede the other. At present, it seems reasonable to conclude that the acquisition of spatial part terms may depend on both geometric and functional considerations, and that their relative use may depend on familarity with the object's category.

The Relationships among Object Parts in Vision May Be Different from
Those in Language

How are part relationships specified in theories of vision? Most often, the relationships only specify *that* individual parts are attached to each other—for example, the knee bone's connected to the leg bone, the leg bone's connected to the ankle bone, and so on. These attachment relationships can be expressed linguistically by spatial prepositions and verbs (attached to the top/bottom/right/left, and so forth). In fact, Biederman's theory specifies attachment relationships that could readily be translated into the set of spatial part terms—for instance, attached end to end, side to end, and so on.

Yet our linguistic treatment of how parts are related reveals considerably more complexity than this limited set of attachment relationships. Transitivity relationships among parts adhere to certain rules that would seem to reside outside of our visual representations of objects, at least, in terms of currently available theories. For example, we might say that a house has a door, and that the door has a handle, but we would not claim that the house has a handle, even though these might be in sufficient spatial proximity that it could be merited on visual grounds.

To my knowledge, there is no current evidence on whether such "transitivity failures" are respected among young children. However, the underlying causes of them in adults are interesting. Cruse (1986) has suggested two causes. The first concerns what he calls "functional domain." Depending on context, superficially similar relationships might show transitivity in one case but not another. He gives the example of the door and handle (as above), in which transitivity fails, and contrasts it with the case in which we could say the jacket has sleeves, the sleeves have cuffs, and the jacket has cuffs. The difference, Cruse suggests, is that handles have functions that apply only to their immediately dominating node in some conceptual hierarchy—in this case, the door, but not house. In contrast, cuffs have a decorative function that applies both to sleeves and jackets—and so the function can be realized both locally (the sleeve) and more globally (the jacket).

A second kind of transitivity failure may be due to a conceptual (but not visual) distinction between units that are integral parts of an object versus parts that are "merely attached" to the rest of an object. As Cruse (1986) points out, one can describe parts that are merely attached using the predicate *attached*, but one cannot do the same with integral parts. Thus, it is fine to describe a hand as being "attached" to the arm, but clearly the hand is not "part of" the arm. In contrast, the palm is "part of" the hand, but not "attached to" the hand. Cruse further notes that the contrast can be seen in the kinds of inferences that can be made. If I am touching the elbow (which is an integral part of the arm), I am also touching the arm, but if I am touching the hand (which is only an attachment, not a part of the arm), I am not touching the arm.

These diagnostics show that the part-of relationship is conceptually different from the kinds of relationships currently available in perceptual theories. In fact, Cruse (1986) concludes that "the question of whether a finger can be said to be part of an arm cannot be settled by examining human bodies—it is a linguistic question." If he is correct, the relationship part-of will be captured most coherently by a level of representation that is distinct from our visual representation of objects.

4.3.3 Evidence, Part C: Learning Affects How We Form Parts, and Hence May Affect How We Come to Name Parts

Schyns and Murphy (1994) considered the relationship between the perceptual and conceptual representations of object parts, proposing that these representations emerge from different constraints and hence have quite different characteristics. They specifically considered the algorithm proposed by Hoffman and Richards (1984) and suggested that, although it might explain how the visual system extracts parts, it would not suffice to capture many important phenomena regarding human conceptualization of parts. Rather, Schyns and Murphy (1994, 310) argued that object parsing might also be driven by conceptual constraints, specifically, by their "functionality principle": "If a fragment of a stimulus categorizes objects (distinguishes members from nonmembers), the fragment is instantiated as a unit in the representational code of object concepts."

This principle predicts that our representation of objects parts can change radically as we undergo different learning experiences, especially those that require us to sort sets of objects into different categories. Thus, although the visual system might, in some cases, prefer to parse objects according to algorithms engaging either volumetric primitives (Biederman 1987) or contour characteristics (Hoffman and Richards 1984), these parsings will only be maintained to the extent that they serve to distinguish one set of objects from another. The implications of Schyns and Murphy's observation for part naming are enormous: an object's part structure should vary over time in accordance with different learning experiences; furthermore, the development of part naming will rest importantly on higher-level conceptual processes and so may change over development.

The evidence presented by Schyns and Murphy is compelling. In a preliminary experiment, they showed that people who divided simple pipelike objects into main parts systematically violated parsing schemes that would obtain from existing visual parsing algorithms (see figure 4.7). For example, when asked to circle the "parts" of the tube, people tended to group together several distinguishable segments as a single unit. Second, people actually created parts where

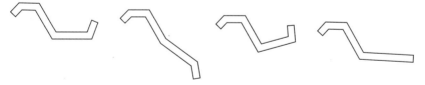

Figure 4.7
Pipelike objects used by Schyns and Murphy (1994) to test the flexibility of perceived part structure. Having parsed the tubelike object on the far left into five major parts, people often later parsed the object on the far right into five parts as well, even though no contour discontinuity marked the two parts in the "tail." Schyns and Murphy argued that our part representations of objects are flexible, susceptible to experience and learning, and guided by high-level knowledge. (The figure is reproduced from Schyns and Murphy 1994 by permission of the publisher.)

there were no clearly distinguishable parts in the image. For instance, because they observed two clear segments at the "tail" of the first figure, they later segmented the "tail" of the last figure into two parts corresponding to these segments—even though there was no evidence from the pictured object for a boundary. Because people initially saw the tube with a two-part "tail," they later assumed that a similar object also had such a two-part tail. Schyns and Murphy liken this to our tendency to mentally parse the arm into an upper and lower arm, even when the entire arm is hidden by a sleeve.

The role of experience was more closely examined in a further series of elegant experiments that demonstrated that different learning experiences could lead to different parsing of the same objects. People were presented with complex random-looking "Martian rocks," which incorporated numerous bumps and protrusions. These bump-protrusion complexes were not salient as units prior to the learning experiences. For example, when naive subjects were asked to circle "parts" of the objects, they almost never circled the parts that they later learned.

However, people were then shown a set of Martian rocks and asked to study these so that they could learn what the rocks were like in general. One group of people saw five rocks for which one complex bump-protrusion chunk—the target part—was always present. People in a second group saw five rocks for which a different complex bump-protrusion chunk was present. Also contained in each study set was a single rock from the nontarget group. After seeing each rock, people were asked to circle the target part. Over the learning trials, people came to correctly identify the target part, even though it was embedded in a highly complex configuration.

Following this learning phase, people were exposed to a new group of objects in which the target parts from both rock groups were placed adjacent to each other within the new rocks. In addition to the people who had already been tested, a third group of subjects was included—these people saw only the new rocks. After a set of learning trials with these new rocks, people from all three groups were asked to circle the "parts" of additional new rocks. The striking result was this: People who had originally seen target parts A now circled parts A and B as distinct parts. So did people who had originally seen target parts B. But people who had only seen the combination rocks (with parts A and B adjacent to each other) only circled the complex A-B part as a single unit. That is, the particular objects people had seen during the learning phase led them to form qualitatively different part units, despite the fact that they were tested with exactly the same novel rocks.

Schyns and Murphy argue that as people learned to identify parts critical to their target category, they also learned to reject units that were not important. They further argue that the process of learning can lead to the creation of novel parts, which come to have a status similar to existing familiar parts (such as wheel, handle, and so on). For Schyns and Murphy, these parts would then be a component of the representational battery that people use to categorize new objects.

4.3.4 Summary of Case 2

Just as with whole objects, the evidence on object parts suggests that the visual system has the means to parse objects into coherent parts. However, the relationship between these visually parsed units and the linguistic assignment of terms to object parts is not completely determined by such parsing algorithms. Part terms may be consistent with visually parsed parts. However, they are not identical. Some visually parsed units never receive names, others may represent complex combinations of visually parsed units, parts may be formed through learning experiences, and the application of particular part terms to an object's region engages more than the object's geometry. Finally, as with object names, part names appear to be governed by some principles not transparently available to the perceptual systems. The most obvious case of this concerns the relationships among object part terms, which often violate transitivity.

4.4 Conclusions

This chapter began with the observation that children have the remarkable capacity to talk about what they see—easily, readily, and early in development. The ease with which this aspect of language is acquired might lead us to assume that a simple theory—in which perception and language are exactly and perfectly redundant—will explain how this is accomplished. The evidence reviewed, however, indicates that even some of the simplest cases of mapping between perceptual units and language are quite complex. For example, the nonlinguistic representation of an object's shape appears to provide important support for early object naming, but the space set up by our perceptual systems is modified by input. Similarly, the nonlinguistic representations of object parts appear to provide some but not all of the distinctions children need in order to learn even the simplest part terms.

Moreover, the evidence suggests that other aspects of the early vocabulary cannot be learned by mapping onto visual representations. Some of the distinctions go beyond perception, while others are simply nowhere to be found within the perceptual systems. Examples include the encoding of object types and some conditions for tracing their identity, the encoding of object parts as they interact with functional knowledge, and the logic of how parts relate to each other. In these cases it becomes quite clear that—although perception is likely used as a bootstrapping mechanism, a grounding mechanism—the distinctions made by linguistic systems will ultimately arise in conjunction with representations and mechanisms of learning specific to language.

What does seem clear is that child learners will have to recruit all of these kinds of representations to learn even the most basic object and object part vocabulary. Learning a word—in this view—requires that the child form a mapping across levels, binding together the corresponding aspects of each representation. This binding ensures that the other aspects of the representation—which are not shared over levels—are nevertheless systematically engaged as part of the representations of the word. Thus, underlying our capacity to talk about objects and parts are sets of highly complex representations, which are bound together in the process of learning. These rich representations emerge early in development, under widely diverse learning conditions, and with no formal tutoring. This, and our naive blindness to their complexity, serves as a reminder of the ingenuity of the brain and mind in constructing for us a seamless world.

Acknowledgments

Preparation of this chapter and the results reported herein were supported in part by grants 12-0187 from the March of Dimes Foundation, 1 RO1 MH55420 from the NIMH, and 2RO1 HD28675 from the NICHD.

References

Andersen, E. 1975. Cups and glasses: Learning that boundaries are vague. *Journal of Child Language*, 2(1), 79–103.

Baillargeon, R. 1995. Physical reasoning in infancy. In M. S. Gazzaniga, ed., *The cognitive neurosciences*, 181–204. Cambridge, MA: MIT Press.

Baldwin, D. 1992. Clarifying the role of shape in children's taxonomic assumption. *Journal of Experimental Child Psychology*, 54, 392–416.

Behl-Chadha, G. 1996. Basic level and superordinate-like categorical representations in early infancy. *Cognition*, 60(2), 105–141.

Biederman, I. 1987. Recognition-by-components: A theory of human image understanding. *Psychological Review*, 94, 115–147.

Bloom, P. 1996. Intention, history, and artifact concepts. *Cognition*, 60, 1–29.

Bloom, P. 2000. *How children learn the meanings of words*. Cambridge, MA: MIT Press.

Bloom, P., Peterson, M. A., Nadel, L., and Garrett, M. F., eds. 1996. *Language and space*. Cambridge, MA: MIT Press.

Bowerman, M. 1996. Learning how to structure space for language: A cross linguistic perspective. In P. Bloom, M. A. Peterson, L. Nadel, and M. F. Garrett, eds., *Language and space*, 385–436. Cambridge, MA: MIT Press.

Brown, A. 1990. Domain-specific principles affect learning and transfer in children. *Cognitive Science*, 14, 107–133.

Brown, R. 1958. *Words and things: An introduction to language*. New York: Free Press.

Carlson-Radvansky, L., and Radvansky, G. 1996. The influence of functional relations on spatial term selection. *Psychological Science*, 7(1), 56–60.

Clark, E. 1973. What's in a word? On the child's acquisition of semantics in his first language. In T. E. Moore, ed., *Cognitive development and the acquisition of language*, 65–110. New York: Academic Press.

Clark, E. 1980. Here's the top: Nonlinguistic strategies in the acquisition of orientational terms. *Child Development* 51(2), 329–338.

Clark, H. 1973. Space, time semantics, and the child. In T. E. Moore, ed., *Cognitive development and the acquisition of language*. New York: Academic Press.

Cruse, D. A. 1986. *Lexical semantics*. Cambridge, England: Cambridge University Press.

Davidoff, J., Davies, I., and Roberson, D. 1999. Colour categories in stone-age tribe. *Nature, 398*, 203–204.

Eimas, P., and Quinn, P. 1994. Studies on the formation of perceptually based basic-level categories in young infants. *Child Development, 65*(3), 903–917.

Fillmore, C. 1997. *Lectures on deixis*. Stanford, CA: CSCI.

Fodor, J. A. 1998. *Concepts: Where cognitive science went wrong*. New York: Oxford University Press.

Gelman, S. A., and Taylor, M. 1984. How two-year-old children interpret proper and common names for unfamiliar objects. *Child Development, 55*(4), 1535–1540.

Gelman, S. A., and Wellman, H. M. 1991. Insides and essences: Early understanding of the nonobvious. *Cognition, 38*(3), 213–244.

Gentner, D. 1978. What looks like a jiggy but acts like a zimbo? A study of early word meaning using artificial objects. *Papers and Reports on Child Language Development, 15*, 1–6.

Gentner, D. 1982. Why nouns are learned before verbs: Linguistic relativity vs. natural partitioning. In S. Kuczaj, ed., *Language development, Vol. 2: Language, thought, and culture*. Hillsdale, NJ: Erlbaum.

Gentner, D., and Boroditsky, L. 2001. Individuation, relativity and early word learning. In M. Bowerman and S. Levinson, eds., *Language acquisition and conceptual development*. Cambridge, England: Cambridge University Press.

Gibson, E. J. 1969. *Principles of perceptual learning and development*. New York: Appleton-Century-Crofts.

Hall, D. G. 1996. Naming solids and nonsolids: Children's default construals. *Cognitive Development, 11*, 229–264.

Hayward, W., and Tarr, M. 1995. Spatial language and spatial representations. *Cognition, 55*, 39–84.

Heider, E. R., and Oliver, D. C. 1972. The structure of the color space in naming and memory for two languages. *Cognitve Psychology, 3*(2), 337–354.

Herskovits, A. 1986. *Language and spatial cognition: An interdisciplinary study of the prepositions in English*. Cambridge, England: Cambridge University Press.

Hoffman, D., and Richards, W. 1984. Parts of recognition. *Cognition, 18*, 65–96.

Hoffman, D., and Singh, M. 1997. Salience of visual parts. *Cogntion, 63*(1), 29–78.

Imai, M., Gentner, D., and Uchida, N. 1994. Children's theories of word meaning: The role of shape similarity in early acquisition. *Cognitive Development, 9*(1), 45–75.

Jackendoff, R. 1983. *Semantics and cognition.* Cambridge, MA: MIT Press.

Jackendoff, R. 1996. The architecture of the linguistic-spatial interface. In P. Bloom, M. A. Peterson, L. Nadel, and M. F. Garrett, eds., *Language and space,* 1–30. Cambridge, MA: MIT Press.

Katz, N., Baker, E., and Macnamara, J. 1974. What's in a name? A study of how children learn common and proper names. *Child Development, 45,* 469–473.

Keil, F. 1989. *Concepts, kinds, and cognitive development.* Cambridge, MA: Cambridge University Press.

Keil, F. 1994. Explanation, association, and the acquisition of word meaning. In L. Gleitman and B. Landau, eds., *The acquisition of the lexicon.* Cambridge, MA: MIT Press.

Kellman, P. J., and Arterberry, M. E. 1998. *The cradle of knowledge: Development of perception in infancy.* Cambridge, MA: MIT Press.

Kellman, P. J., and Spelke, E. S. 1983. Perception of partly occluded objects in infancy. *Cognitive Psychology, 15*(4), 483–524.

Kemmerer, D. 1999. "Near" and "far" in language and perception. *Cognition, 73*(1), 35–63.

Kuczaj, S. A., and Maratsos, M. P. 1975. On the acquisition of front, back, side. *Child Development, 46,* 202–210.

Landau, B. 2002. *Breakdown of reference systems in spatial language and spatial cognition.* Unpublished manuscript, Department of Cognitive Science, Johns Hopkins University.

Landau, B., and Jackendoff, R. 1993. "What" and "where" in spatial language and spatial cognition. *Behavioral and Brain Sciences, 16,* 217–265.

Landau, B., Jones, S., and Smith, L. 1992. Syntactic context and object properties in early lexical learning. *Journal of Memory and Language, 31,* 807–825.

Landau, B., and Shipley, E. 2000. Labelling patterns and object naming. *Developmental Science, 4*(1), 109–118.

Landau, B., Smith, L., and Jones, S. 1988. The importance of shape in early lexical learning. *Cognitive Development, 3,* 299–321.

Landau, B., Smith, L., and Jones, S. 1992. Syntactic context and the shape bias in children's and adults' lexical learning. *Journal of Memory and Language, 31,* 807–825.

Landau, B., Smith, L., and Jones, S. 1997. Object shape, object function, and object name. *Journal of Memory and Language, 36*(1), 1–27.

Landau, B., Smith, L., and Jones, S. 1998. Object perception and object naming in early development. *Trends in Cognitive Sciences, 2*(1), 19–24.

Leslie, A. M., Fei, X., Tremoulet, P. D., and Scholl, B. J. 1998. Indexing and the object concept: Developing "what" and "where" systems. *Trends in Cognitive Science, 2*(1), 10–18.

Levinson, S. C. 1994. Vision, shape, and linguistic description: Tzeltal body-part terminology and object description. *Linguistics, 32*(4–5), 791–855.

Levinson, S. C. 1996. Frames of reference and Molyneux's question: Crosslinguistic evidence. In P. Bloom, M. A. Peterson, L. Nadel, and M. Garrett, eds., *Language and space*. Cambridge, MA: MIT Press.

Leyton, N. 1992. *Symmetry, causality, mind*. Cambridge, MA: MIT Press.

Liittschwager, J., and Markman, E. 1994. Sixteen and 24-month-olds' use of mutual exclusivity as a default assumption in second-label learning. *Developmental Psychology, 30*(6), 955–968.

Macario, J. F. 1991. Young children's use of color in classification: Foods and canonically colored objects. *Cognitive Development, 6*(1), 17–46.

Malt, B., and Johnson, E. C. 1992. Do artifact concepts have cores? *Journal of Memory and Language, 31*, 195–217.

Malt, B. C., Sloman, S. A., Gennari, N. N. R., Shi, M. Y., and Wang, Y. 1999. Knowing versus naming: Similarity and the linguistic categorization of artifacts. *Journal of Memory and Language, 40*(2), 230–262.

Mandelbrot, B. 1982. *The fractal geometry of nature*. San Francisco: Freeman.

Mandler, J. M., and Bauer, P. J. 1988. The cradle of categorization: Is the basic level basic? *Cognitive Development, 3*(3), 247–264.

Mandler, J. M., and McDonough, L. 1998. Studies of inductive inference in infancy. *Cognitive Psychology, 37*(1), 60–96.

Markman, E. M. 1989. *Categorization in children: Problems of induction*. Cambridge, MA: Bradford/MIT Press.

Markman, E. M., and Wachtel, G. 1988. Children's use of mutual exclusivity to constrain the meanings of words. *Cognitive Psychology, 20*, 121–157.

Marr, D. 1982. *Vision*. New York: Freeman.

Marr, D., and Nishihara, H. 1978. Representation and recognition of the spatial organization of three-dimensional shapes. *Proceedings of the Royal Society of London B, 200*, 269–294.

Marr, D., and Vaina, L. 1982. Representation and recognition of the movement of shapes. *Proceedings of the Royal Society of London, 214*, 501–524.

Medin, D., and Ortony, A. 1989. Psychological essentialism. In S. Vosniadou and A. Ortony, eds., *Similarity and analogical reasoning.* New York: Cambridge University Press.

Miller, G., and Johnson-Laird, P. 1976. *Language and perception.* Cambridge, MA: Belknap Press.

Milner, A. D., and Goodale, M. A. 1995. *The visual brain in action.* Oxford: Oxford University Press.

Munnich, E., Landau, B., and Dosher, B. A. 2001. Spatial language and spatial representation: A cross-linguistic comparison. *Cognition, 81*(3), 171–207.

Nelson, K. 1974. Concept, word, and sentence: Intercorrelations in acquisition and development. *Psychological Review, 81,* 267–285.

Putnam, H. 1977. Is semantics possible? In S. P. Schwartz, ed., *Naming, necessity, and natural kinds,* 66–101. Ithaca, NY: Cornell University Press.

Quinn, P. C., and Eimas, P. D. 1996. Perceptual cues that permit categorical differentiation of animal species by infants. *Journal of Experimental Child Psychology, 63*(1), 189–211.

Regier, T. 1996. *The human semantic potential: Spatial language and constrained connectionism.* Cambridge, MA: MIT Press.

Rosch, E., Mervis, C., Gray, W., Johnson, D., and Boyes-Braem, P. 1976. Basic objects in natural categories. *Cognitive Psychology, 8,* 382–439.

Scholl, B. J., and Pylyshyn, Z. W. 1999. Tracking multiple items through occlusion: Clues to visual objecthood. *Cognitive Psychology, 38*(2), 259–290.

Schyns, P. G., and Murphy, G. L. 1994. The ontogeny of part representation in object concepts. In D. L. Medin, ed., *The psychology of learning and motivation: Advances in research and theory,* vol. 31, 305–349. New York: Academic Press.

Singh, M., and Hoffman, D. D. 2001. Part-based representations of visual shape and implications for visual cognition. In T. Shipley and P. Kellman, eds., *From fragments to objects: Segmentation and grouping in vision—Advances in Psychology 130,* 401–460. New York: Elsevier.

Singh, M., and Landau, B. 1998. Parts of visual shape as primitives for categorization. *Behavioral and Brain Sciences 21*(1), 36.

Smith, L., and Heise, D. 2000. *Infants' use of textural information to discriminate between artifacts and natural kinds.* Unpublished manuscript, Department of Psychology, Indiana University.

Smith, L., Jones, S., and Landau, B. 1992. Count nouns, adjectives, and perceptual properties in novel word interpretations. *Developmental Psychology, 28*(2), 273–286.

Smith, L., Jones, S., and Landau, B. 1996. Naming in young children: A dumb mechanism? *Cognition, 60,* 143–171.

Smith, L. B., Jones, S. S., Landau, B., Gershkoff-Stowe, L., and Samuelson, L. 2002. Object name learning provides on-the-job training for attention. *Psychological Science* *13*(1), 13–19.

Soja, N. 1992. Inferences about the meaning of nouns: The relationship between perception and syntax. *Cognitive Development, 7,* 29–46.

Soja, N., Carey, S., and Spelke, E. 1991. Ontological categories guide young children's inductions of word meanings: Object terms and substance terms. *Cognition, 38,* 179–211.

Spelke, E., Gutheil, G., and Van de Walle, G. 1995. The development of object perception. In S. M. Kosslyn and D. N. Osherson, eds., *Visual cognition,* vol. 2, 297–330. Cambridge, MA: MIT Press.

Subrahmanyam, K., Landau, B., and Gelman, R. 1999. Shape, material, and syntax: Interacting forces in child's learning in novel words for objects and substances. *Language and Cognitive Processes, 14*(3), 249–281.

Talmy, L. 1983. How language structures space. In H. Pick and L. Acredolo, eds., *Spatial orientation: Theory, research, and application.* New York: Plenum Press.

Waxman, S. R. 1990. Linguistic biases and the establishment of conceptual hierarchies: Evidence form preschool children. *Cognitive Development, 5*(2), 123–150.

Waxman, S., and Markow, D. 1995. Words as invitations to form categories: Evidence from 12-month-old infants. *Cognitive Psychology, 29,* 257–302.

Waxman, S. R., and Senghas, A. 1992. Relations among word meanings in early lexical development. *Developmental Psychology, 28*(5), 862–873.

Willats, P. 1992. Seeing lumps, sticks, and slabs in silhouettes. *Perception, 21*(4), 481–496.

Woodward, A. L., and Markman, E. M. 1998. Early word learning. In W. Damon, series ed., and D. K. Kuhn and R. S. Siegler, vol. eds., *Handbook of child psychology, Vol. 2: Cognition, perception, and language,* 5th ed., 371–420. New York: Wiley.

5

Infants' Use of Action Knowledge to Get a Grasp on Words

Amanda L. Woodward

Word learning is both an act of associative learning and an act of symbolic learning. Words are associated with their referents in the minds of language users. In addition, mature users understand the specific kind of relation between a word and the aspect of the world it goes with, namely, that the word is a symbol used to refer to that object, property, or action.[1] This aspect of linguistic knowledge rests on more general folk psychological concepts such as attention and intention—when a word is used referentially, the speaker's intention is to draw attention to a particular entity by its use, or to call to mind a particular idea in her interlocutor. Both the associative and symbolic aspects of learning are critical. Without the ability to retain and organize associations in memory, it would be impossible to build a lexicon. And, as many theorists have pointed out, the language-learning enterprise would not get far without an understanding of the referential nature of the link between words and the world (Akhtar and Tomasello 2001; Baldwin 1995; Macnamara 1982; Tomasello 1999).

There is a long-held view that one of these aspects of word learning precedes the other in ontogeny. Specifically, it has been proposed that infants begin only with the very general ability to associate stimuli that co-occur, and thus learn to associate word sounds with the perceptual impressions with which they are usually experienced. In this view, the first words are disembodied associates, learned only by virtue of their contiguity with some aspect of the environment (e.g., McShane 1979; Werker et al. 1998; Oviatt 1980). To illustrate, Werker and colleagues (1998) suggest that receptive word learning in 14-month-olds reflects the understanding that a given word "goes with" some object, but not that it "stands for" that object. These accounts further propose that at some point, this unconstrained associative learning is replaced by "truly linguistic" word learning. Some propose this change to take the form of a relatively sudden insight into the symbolic nature of words, analogous to Helen Keller's famous experience at the well (McShane 1979). Others suggest a more gradual transition, in which, over the course of successive associative-learning trials, infants become sensitive to the referential nature of words. Hollich and colleagues (Hollich, Hirsh-Pasek, and Golinkoff 2000) propose a related model. Although they believe that infants begin with a concept of reference, this concept is initially quite limited. They write,

At first ... words label what the child has in mind. That is, reference is dominated by the child's tendency to associate a word with the object, action, or event that is temporally contiguous and/or perceptually salient, much as they learn the link between any two contiguous events. Later ... the child comes to perceive the intentionality of others and can then become an apprentice to a master language user. The child comes to realize the full symbolic nature of language. (p. 27)

In this chapter, I will take issue with this general view. I will argue that it is unlikely that infants ever begin by treating words as disembodied associates. In the infant's world, words are actions, and infants most likely draw on their understanding of action in making sense of words from the very beginning. In his classic analysis, Macnamara (1982) proposed that in ontogeny, the concept of reference is derived from an understanding of acts of referring. I will follow this proposal, considering what infants know about acts of referring, and in particular, how this knowledge might draw from developing concepts of intentional action. I will depart from Macnamara's analysis on a critical point: Macnamara was pessimistic about the possibility that concepts of referring or intention could be learned, and therefore proposed that this knowledge is innately given. However, researchers have recently suggested mechanisms by which intentional understanding could be constructed, and empirical work has begun to lend support to these ideas (Baldwin and Baird 2001; Baldwin and Moses 1996; Barresi and Moore 1996; Gopnik and Meltzoff 1997; Woodward, Sommerville, and Guajardo 2001). These new ideas and findings bode well for the enterprise of constructing a developmental account of reference. As a first step in this enterprise, I will discuss recent findings that indicate the kinds of action knowledge that could contribute to infants' word learning, and the ways this knowledge might provide the basis for a developing understanding of acts of referring.

5.1 Two Ways That Adults' Actions Could Impact Infants' Word Learning

In investigating the development of word learning, it is important to consider the social context in which this learning occurs. Infants learn words from social partners who have strong effects on their attention, and, therefore, potentially strong effects on what they learn. At one level, adult actions direct infants' attention to particular parts of the world at particular points in time, and these shifts in attention could set the conditions for infants' learning to associate words with referents. For example, parents sometimes manipulate infants' attention by holding up or moving objects as they say the name for the object (Gogate, Bahrick, and Watson 2000), or pointing toward the object, thus setting up strong contiguity between hearing the word and seeing the referent. In addition, infants are sensitive to gaze direction from early in life (Butterworth and Cochran 1980), orienting their own eyes toward the objects others look at. Therefore, parents' patterns of gaze could highlight certain objects at the moment the relevant labels were uttered. If infants began only with very general associative-learning tools, these parental behaviors could ensure that they learned the right associations at least some of the time.

At another level, intelligent word learners do more than shift attention in response to the behaviors of their interlocutors. They interpret these actions as directed at, or related to, particular entities. For example, they understand that a person who looks at an object is likely to be attending to that object, and a person who points at an object both attends to it and intends for someone else to attend to it. A learner with this level of knowledge would be much more successful at acquiring the correct word-world associations, not being fooled, for example, by the coincidence of staring at the cat at the moment her mother says "Time for your nap." More critically, an intelligent learner would be much further along in getting the right kind of mapping. She would be closer to interpreting the word not as a disembodied associate of the referent object, but instead, as a symbolic tool for referring to the object.

The work of Akhtar, Baldwin, Tomasello, and others has provided compelling evidence that by 18 to 24 months of age infants are intelligent word learners of this sort (see Akhtar and Tomasello 2001; Baldwin 1995; Baldwin and Tomasello 1998; Tomasello 1999 for reviews). Across many experiments, children at these ages respond in ways that suggest they are tracking the experimenter's intentions, and using this information to interpret the words she uses. They link words with referents when the speaker is linked to these referents by gaze and pointing, but not when these links are absent, and when the speaker appears to act purposefully but not when he or she acts apparently accidentally. Moreover, 18- to 24-month-old children can use behavioral evidence of attention and purposefulness to determine which of several potential referents was the intended referent, even in the absence of contiguity between the word and its referent.

Word learning, both productive and receptive, begins well before 18 to 24 months—half a lifetime or more earlier, by 9 to 12 months (Benedict 1979; Fenson et al. 1994; Huttenlocher 1974). Moreover, by 14 months infants are such expert word learners that they can acquire a new word-object mapping in the laboratory under conditions that are somewhat to extremely artificial (Schafer and Plunkett 1998; Waxman and Booth 2001; Werker et al. 1998; Woodward, Markman, and Fitzsimmons 1994). One possibility is that at this early point, infants learn words as disembodied associates, influenced, perhaps, by the attentional shifts induced by adult actions. Another possibility, however, is that even at this early point, infants draw on an analysis of the speaker's actions in order to interpret words.

5.2 A Test of Infants' Sensitivity to Referential Actions in Word Learning

If words are initially learned as unconstrained associates, the main determiners of word learning should be the contiguity between the experience of the word and the experience of the referent. To test whether this model is accurate, I borrowed a page from Baldwin's book, adapting her procedures for use with younger infants (Woodward 2003b). In prior work, I had had success in teaching 13-month-old infants new words in a brief laboratory session, using a specially designed multiple-choice paradigm as a measure of receptive learning (Woodward, Markman, and Fitzsimmons 1994). I used this paradigm in the current study. The goal was to equate the extent to which infants had their attention drawn to an object at just the moment a label was uttered, while varying whether or not the speaker was linked to the object by referential behaviors such as looking and pointing.

Two groups of 13-month-old infants were introduced to a novel word and a novel object. Infants in both groups encountered very similar situations. They sat at a table, across from two researchers. The first researcher established joint attention on the object with the child, calling her attention to it, and directing gaze and points toward the object. For both groups of infants, just as the infant looked at the toy, the second researcher uttered a nonce word, saying for example "Look Alice, it's the gombie." The procedure for the two groups differed only in terms of the second researcher's referential actions. For infants in the "object-reference" condition, the second researcher looked at and pointed toward the object of the infant's own attention. For infants in the "ambiguous-reference" condition, the second researcher looked at a video monitor, never looking or pointing toward the objects, and never looking at the infant during the procedure. In this case, the second researcher watched the camera feed on the monitor, so that she could time her utterances to coincide with the infant's attention to the object. Infants heard the new label a total of nine times during the training phase. They were also introduced to a second novel object, which was not labeled. This second object served as the distractor on the comprehension test. To control for preferences for one particular object over another, every infant saw the same two objects. Half the infants had one of them paired with the label and the other half had the other one paired with the label. After training, a third experimenter entered the testing room and administered a multiple-choice test to assess the infant's comprehension of the new label. As in our prior studies, so that she could not influence infants' choices, this experimenter did not know which of the two objects had been paired with the label or whether the infant was in the object-reference condition or in the ambiguous-reference condition. She put both objects in a tray and asked the infant to "Get the gombie."

To test whether the manipulation played out as intended, we first coded infants' attention to the object and the experimenters during training. Our goal was to hold constant the attention-directing effects of the interaction, while varying the behavioral connection between the speaker and the object. First, we investigated the overall effects on infants' attention in the two conditions. Infants in the two conditions showed nearly identical patterns, attending most of the time to the object, then to the labeler, then to the experimenter who established joint attention. Next, we assessed the contiguity between infants' hearing the label and seeing the object. For each of the nine label utterances, we coded where the infant was looking at the time the label was uttered. Again, infants in the two conditions showed nearly identical patterns—both groups looked at the toy on average for three trials, the labeler five trials, and elsewhere on the remaining trial. Thus, infants in the two conditions had their attention directed in similar ways, and experienced the same degree of contiguity between hearing the word and seeing the referent object.

Nevertheless, infants in the two conditions performed quite differently on the comprehension test. Infants in the object-reference condition systematically chose the previously labeled object. In contrast, infants in the ambiguous-reference condition performed randomly on the comprehension test. Despite the fact that these infants had the object highlighted in attention and reliably paired with the word in the course of joint engagement with an adult, they did not form a mapping between word and object. Even early in the second year, then, infants seem to require behavioral evidence for a referential connection between a person who utters a new word and the potential referent. In fact, a couple of infants gave us tantalizing evidence that they were trying to interpret the ambiguous labels as referring to some thing. When asked to "Get the gombie" they walked over to the video monitor, looking around as if searching for some object in that vicinity.

It is easy to see how the infants in the ambiguous-reference condition might have been fooled by our manipulation. After all, they were engaged in joint attention on the object at just the moment the word was uttered. But the infants were not fooled. They closely monitored the actions of each of the experimenters, and used this information to inform their word learning. From the earliest point that we can measure word learning in the laboratory, then, infants do not respond to words as sounds from nowhere. Neither are they blindly pushed about by the attention-directing behaviors of adults. These findings are inconsistent with the view that infants begin as general-purpose associators, linking in memory any experiences that reliably co-occur. They indicate that from very early on, infants filter their word learning through their understanding of action. These findings are consistent with other recent reports suggesting that early in the second year, infants are sensitive to referential actions in the context of hearing a new word (Baldwin and Tomasello 1998; Hollich, Hirsh-Pasek, and Golinkoff 2000).

These findings make sense when we consider that words, as first encountered by infants, are actions. Mature language users understand words as symbols with a life of their own—interpretable when heard on the radio, typed on a page, or scrawled on a wall. But for babies, words are first encountered as human behaviors. This leads to the question of the kinds of action knowledge infants have at their disposal to recruit in word learning.

5.3 Infants' Sensitivity to the Relational Structure of Action

In recent work, my students and I have investigated aspects of early action knowledge that might scaffold infants' initial interpretation of words. We have found that prelinguistic infants understand that certain actions center on the relation between an agent and some object in the world. From an adult standpoint, this "object directedness" is a property of many intentional actions (Barresi and Moore 1996; Wellman and Phillips 2001; Woodward 1998; Woodward, Sommerville, and Guajardo 2001). As Barresi and Moore (1996, 107) described, adult folk psychology "represents the activities of agents that are directed at objects. Such activities include simple purposive actions or psychological orientations that are directed at real objects, such as seeing, fearing, or poking them, as well as more complex mental activities ... that may be directed at imaginary objects." Infants' sensitivity to this aspect of action seems to be limited at first. Before 9 months, infants seem to be sensitive to the agent-object relation for events involving grasping (Woodward 1998, 1999, 2003a; Woodward, Sommerville, and Guajardo 2001), and perhaps other instrumental actions (Jovanovic et al. 2002). It makes sense that infants would start here: grasping is ubiquitous in the environment, and is also one of the first instrumental actions that infants can produce themselves. Even at this early point, infants distinguish between grasping and apparently purposeless manual contact, construing the former but not the latter in terms of agent-object relations (Woodward 1999). From early in life, then, infants do not simply attend to physical contact between people and things, but instead focus more precisely on meaningful actions.

Between 9 and 12 months, infants' understanding of object-directed action is elaborated a way that may be particularly important for word learning—they begin to construe attentional behaviors, in particular looking and pointing, as being object directed. The actor-object relation is less concrete for gaze and pointing than for instrumental actions: these actions occur at a distance from the referent object, and, unlike grasping, do not generally have a visible impact on the object. Despite this lack of a concrete connection, for adults, these two actions are readily conceived of as indicating a relation between a person and the object of her gaze or point. Imagine a woman seated behind two toys, a ball and a bear, who turns to one side, directing her eyes toward the bear. Adults would probably describe this event in terms of the relation between the person and the object of her gaze—for example, "The woman looks at the bear." Notice, however, that this event could be described in ways that make no reference to this relation (e.g., "She turned her head down and to the right"). If infants did not understand the object-directed nature of looking, they might focus on these aspects of the event.

In a recent series of studies (Woodward 2003a), I used the visual-habituation paradigm to investigate infants' sensitivity to the relational structure of looking events. Infants were habituated to an event such as the one described above. A woman, seated behind two toys, made eye contact with the infant, said "Hi. Look!", and then turned to look at one of the two toys. She then remained still, looking at the toy, until the infant looked away to end the trial. This was repeated until the infant's attention had declined to half its initial level. Then the toys were reversed, and infants saw two kinds of test events in alternation. In one, the woman turned to the same side as during habituation, this time looking at the other toy (new-toy events). This event preserved many of the features of the original event, but disrupted the relation between the woman and the object of her gaze. In the other test event, the woman turned to the other side, this time looking at the same toy as during habituation (new-side events). This event preserved the relational structure of the habituation event, but disrupted other features of the event. If infants, like adults, focus on the relation between looker and object, they should find the new-toy event more novel, and therefore watch it longer, than the new-side event. The findings differed as a function of age. Seven- and 9-month-old infants did not distinguish between the two kinds of test events, and, in fact, did not recover from habituation on test trials. It was as if these infants coded the objects in the display as being the same (the woman, the bear, and the ball again), and did not consider the relations between them. Twelve-month-olds, in contrast, looked longer on new-toy trials than on new-side trials, recovering on the former but not the latter. These infants, like adults, focused on the relation between the woman and the object of her gaze.

Notably, infants at all three ages responded to the woman's shift in gaze by orienting their own eyes toward the toy she looked at. During the very same test trials on which they failed to respond to the change in actor-object relation, 7- and 9-month-old infants looked nearly twice as long at the object of the woman's gaze than at the other toy, and they followed the woman's gaze at levels indistinguishable from those of 12-month-olds. Thus, the younger infants were attentive to the woman's shift in gaze and were motivated to respond to it. At the same time, they seemed unaware of the looker-object relation—that is, of the fact that the woman was looking at the toy. This finding highlights the distinction, discussed earlier, between responsiveness to actions and knowledge about actions. Infants may respond to an action by orienting to some aspect of the environment, but this does not necessarily indicate that they understand the action in question as implying a connection between the agent and that entity. More generally, across several studies, we have found that infants' propensity to orient in response to an action does not always travel with their construal of that action as object directed (Woodward 1998, 1999, forthcoming).

In another recent study, Guajardo and I (Woodward and Guajardo 2002) found a very similar pattern for infants' comprehension of pointing as object directed. Twelve-month-olds, but not 9-month-olds, responded selectively to a change in the relation between a person who pointed and the referent object. This was true whether infants saw only a pointing hand or saw the actor's gaze coordinated with the point. In both cases the person who pointed touched the object with her index finger, thus eliminating the need to follow the point through space to the referent. Infants at both ages responded to this physical contact by orienting toward the pointing hand and the toy it indicated—that is, the point was a strong director of infants' attention. Nevertheless, 9-month-old infants seemed to be insensitive to the relational structure of the pointing event.

Between 9 and 12 months, then, infants begin to understand two actions, one done with the hands and the other with the eyes, as involving a connection between the person who performs them and some object. This co-occurrence in time suggests that at this age infants may attain a general insight about attentional connections between people and things. This conclusion converges with observations of infants' behavior in naturally occurring social interactions—

Infants' Use of Action Knowledge to Grasp Words

observers have long noted that between 9 and 12 months infants begin to "tune in" to their social partners, engaging in more shared attention and producing as well as responding to communicative gestures. The current findings provide evidence that this change in social responsiveness is accompanied by a change in infants' action knowledge, specifically, an emerging sensitivity to the relational structure of attentional behaviors.

To draw on this knowledge to inform word learning, infants must be able to relate utterances to the speaker's other object-directed actions. This ability would most likely rest on the more general ability to integrate separate actions and relate them to a common object. As yet, little is known about the development of this ability, except that it seems to be present by the end of the first year of life. To illustrate, 12-month-old infants, and some 10-month-olds, can relate the elements of a means-end sequence to an ultimate goal, for example interpreting a person's grasp of a box lid as directed at the toy within the box rather than at the box itself, so long as this analysis is consistent with the causal constraints in the situation (Sommerville 2002; Woodward and Sommerville 2000). In addition, 12- to 14-month-old infants expect that a person's gaze and manual actions will be directed toward the same target (Phillips, Wellman, and Spelke 2002; Spelke, Phillips, and Woodward 1995; Sodian et al. 2002).

To summarize, infants analyze certain actions in terms of their relational structure. This analysis goes beyond the surface level of motions and contact, and indicates that infants have begun to extract meaningful components of behavior. This analysis is first evident in 6- to 9-month-old infants' propensity to relate actors to goals for actions that appear purposeful, in particular, grasping, but not for manual contact that appears purposeless. Between 9 and 12 months, infants begin to relate actors to the objects of their attention, and also begin to relate actions in a sequence to one another in situations in which these relations are likely to be meaningful. These later developments seem to set the stage for language, providing support for infants' acquiring the right mappings between words and world, and also for their acquiring the right kind of mappings. I turn now to each of these issues.

5.4   Getting the Right Mappings

As discussed earlier, gaze and pointing are critical sources of information for word learners. Awareness of the relational nature of gaze and pointing would have a profound impact on infants' ability to learn words. For one, it would set the conditions for acquiring the right mappings. If infants are able to integrate information about the simultaneous actions a person produces, then the co-occurrence of utterances with actions such as gaze and pointing would lead them to relate words to aspects of the world to which the speaker is behaviorally connected. Infants would be able to respond to words not as disembodied sounds, but as actions that can be meaningfully related to other actions and to the environment. That is, they would be intelligent learners in the sense described earlier.

Besides making word learning accurate, knowledge about the relational structure of action may make word learning possible in the first place. Parents report the beginnings of word comprehension at 9 to 12 months (Benedict 1979; Fenson et al. 1994), just the time period during which infants become sensitive to the relational structure of gaze and pointing. Infants can form associations well before this age, and likely have heard thousands of uttered words, but before 9 to 12 months, they do not seem to form many word-world associations. Why would this be? Perhaps it is because infants younger than 9 to 12 months, lacking knowledge about attentional relations, must rely mainly on unconstrained associative learning, and this mechanism is an ineffective tool for interpreting linguistic input. By their very nature, words provide a medium for referring to absent entities, and speakers exploit this aspect of language routinely, even when talking to children. Thus, words may not covary with their referents reliably enough to support unconstrained learning. Without a lens to focus attention on particular potential mappings, infants would have little success at associating words with the correct aspects of the environment. I suggest that knowledge about attentional relations provides just such a lens, and thereby enables the first acts of word learning.

This suggestion assumes that gaze and pointing provide a useful lens—that is, that they reliably co-occur with utterances naming the entity gazed and pointed at. This seems like a reasonable assumption, though more research is required to test it thoroughly. Most studies of parental labeling behavior have focused on episodes of joint attention, and during these episodes, gaze and pointing are directed at the objects that are labeled (see Carpenter, Nagell, and Tomasello 1998 for a review). But relational-action knowledge would be useful outside of joint-attention episodes as well, and little is known about covariation between gaze, pointing, and labeling in other contexts. If gaze and pointing were regularly related to spoken words more generally, action knowledge would enable infants to interpret words based on observing the actions and interactions of adults, even when the infants themselves were not participants in the interaction. This is an important point, because although joint-attention episodes are relevant for all kinds of social learning, they do not comprise the bulk of an infant's social and linguistic experience. In a review of studies with American families, Hoff and Naigles (2002) report that parents and infants engaged in joint attention only 11 to 29 percent of the time, even in conditions designed to maximize joint attention. Joint-attention episodes are likely to be even less frequent in cultures that allot children the role of observer more than the role of equal participant in conversational exchanges (Ochs and Schieffelin 1995; Rogoff et al. 1993). Infants' success at amassing vocabularies despite the relative infrequency of joint attention indicates that at least some of the time, infants are able to interpret words by analyzing observed behavior outside of social interactions. Indeed, a recent study has demonstrated this ability in 2-year-olds (Akhtar, Jipson, and Callanan 2001).

An open question is whether other aspects of action knowledge could support word learning. Older children draw on broad behavioral evidence—for example, 2-year-olds use behavioral cues that an action was purposeful or accidental to interpret new verbs (Tomasello and Barton 1994). As discussed above, by 6 to 7 months, infants represent grasping as a relational action, and distinguish between purposeful and apparently purposeless manual contact. It is possible that this aspect of action knowledge could highlight the link between words and the objects held by the speaker, as soon as infants are able to integrate information about distinct actions. Some researchers report that, especially early on, parents are likely to manually manipulate objects while gazing at and labeling them (Gogate, Walker-Andrews, and Bahrick 2001), and this might reinforce infants' ability to relate words to referents. In addition, it might enable infants younger than 9–12 months to acquire some word-object mappings. In this case, the limiting factor on word learning would not be understanding of attentional actions per se, but rather the ability to relate distinct actions to a common object.

5.5   Getting the Right Kind of Mappings

Beyond allowing infants to focus on the right potential associations, action knowledge may set the conditions for infants acquiring the right *kind* of association between word and world—that is, an understanding of reference. The account I have sketched puts word learning in the right neighborhood, alongside of and connected to *developing* concepts of intentionality. I emphasize "developing" here because I believe it is unlikely that 9- to 12-month-old infants have an adultlike understanding of intentionality. Mature concepts of intention are embedded in rich webs of knowledge about psychological life and action. Infants lack much of this knowledge. Nevertheless, as the findings summarized so far suggest, even in the first year of life infants comprehend some aspects of intentional action. The challenge is to characterize the nature of infants' action knowledge and, by extension, the nature of their understanding of acts of referring.

Adults understand the relational structure of action in both psychological and behavioral terms. To illustrate, on observing a woman gazing at a set of keys on the sidewalk we can imagine her mental experience (her mind's-eye view of the keys), infer her likely resulting mental states (she is now aware that the keys are there, and has a belief about their location that could be false), and also predict her likely next actions (moving toward and picking up the keys). Adults also understand that different kinds of actions signal qualitatively different sorts of relations—for example, attending to an object versus having an instrumental intention toward an object. For mature language users, understanding acts of reference draws on much of this knowledge. First, an understanding of behavior-level patterns allows us to identify and interpret acts of referring. Then, from the behavioral evidence, we make inferences about the intentions, attention, and mentally represented information at play in the situation. We understand that, in referring, a speaker intends to draw someone's attention to a particular entity or to convey information from his or her own mind to the mind of another person.

We do not yet know how much of this information infants represent when they analyze the relational structure of action and use these relations to interpret words. One possibility is that infants are sensitive to the relational structure of certain actions without yet understanding their psychological correlates. That is, infants might understand actor-object relations in purely behavioral terms—for instance, knowing that a person who looks at an object is likely to remain behaviorally connected to it, or knowing that particular actions predict particular outcomes or subsequent actions. A behavior-level analysis of the relational structure of action could account for much of the intelligent behavior of 1- and 2-year-old word learners. Specifically, it would focus attention on those word-world associations that are supported by meaningful action relations between speaker and referent.

To account for the ultimate form of linguistic symbols, analysis beyond the level of behavior is needed. Insight into the inner experiences that are expressed in action, and, in particular, an understanding of attentional states as distinct from other kinds of mental relations, would contribute uniquely and critically to children's understanding of words as tools for communicating ideas from one mind to another. When does this aspect of action knowledge emerge and become recruited for language? Findings with older children indicate the existence of partial understandings of mental life in early childhood, which are enriched and elaborated in the years that follow (Flavell 1988; Wellman 1992). In turn, parts of these partial understandings may be traceable to still earlier points in ontogeny. It is noteworthy that infants' action knowledge identifies just the relations that, in mature systems, are relevant to underlying intentions and attention. It seems plausible, therefore, that infants know something about these mental states. On the other hand, even if infants are initially limited to a behavioral analysis of action, this analysis would provide a basis for subsequent discovery about the inner experiences that correlate with the observed relations. One contributor to this discovery might be word learning itself. As Baldwin and Moses (1996) have proposed, learning words and interpreting the language behavior of others may provide evidence for infants that other people have ideas.

A number of theorists have suggested another route by which infants might gain information about the inner states of others, namely, infants have access to their own inner experiences and may possess a system for relating information about the self to the actions of others (e.g., Blakemore and Decety 2001; Carpenter, Nagell, and Tomasello 1998; Gallese and Goldman 1998; Gopnik and Meltzoff 1997; Tomasello 1999). There is growing evidence that in adults, there are common neural representations for self-produced actions and the observed actions of others (see Blakemore and Decety 2001). There is not yet conclusive evidence that such representations play a role in development, but two findings from our lab are suggestive. Guajardo and I found that for infants between 9 and 12 months there was a strong relation between infants' own production of relational points and their understanding of observed points as relational (Woodward and Guajardo 2002), and Sommerville (2002) has found a similar correlation between infants' ability to produce instrumental action sequences and their understanding of others' actions.

Therefore, while infants most certainly lack aspects of action knowledge that contribute to mature language, even in infancy word learning seems to be connected to and informed by action knowledge. This sets up the conditions for the development of critical aspects of linguistic symbols, in particular, their function as tools for communicating ideas. This is not the first account to seek the origins of symbol understanding in prelinguistic social cognition. Many other accounts have done this, focusing particularly on the infants' developing participation in communicative interactions as both evidence of and a contributor to an understanding of others' communicative intentions (Bates et al. 1979; Bretherton 1991; Bruner 1978; Carpenter, Nagell, and Tomasello 1998; Tomasello 1999). The current account stresses a more general insight about intentional relations between agents and entities in the world. This aspect of action knowledge could draw from infants' experiences engaging with communicative partners, and it would contribute to infants' understanding of others' actions in these contexts. However, this knowledge could emerge from other kinds of experiences as well (e.g., observing actions of others, reflecting on one's own actions), and it would allow infants to interpret utterances outside of joint-attention episodes.

In this chapter, I have been concerned with a critical piece of symbolic understanding, which, I have argued, draws on infants' developing understanding of intentional action. I have ignored other critical aspects of symbols. In particular, it is equally important for children to discover the ways words are *not* like other actions. Words are part of a formal conventional system. This system differs from other actions, and by virtue of these differences has a different kind of expressive power than other kinds of actions do (Goldin-Meadow, McNeill, and Singleton 1996; Macnamara 1982). The system consists of a particular class of forms, which are generated by combining a circumscribed set of phonemes. Elements in this system relate arbitrarily to their referents. Thus, for these forms, similarity is a poor cue to meaning or function. Forms in this system have syntactic as well as semantic properties. To acquire these aspects of words, infants need more than knowledge about intentions—they need to be able to extract the properties of the system itself. A number of recent findings indicate that 1-year-olds have not yet completed this aspect of symbol development (Namy 2001; Namy and Waxman 1998; Stager and Werker 1997; Woodward and Hoyne 1999). Terry Regier and I have proposed that some aspects of the formal symbol system could be the result of general process learning mechanisms, so long as these mechanisms are informed and constrained by social knowledge (Regier et al. 2001).

5.6 Conclusions

There is a certain elegance to the idea that infants begin to decipher language just by remembering the sounds they have heard while attending to particular parts of the world. This model attributes to infants only the simplest and most general learning abilities. More-over, there is no doubt that associative learning is a pervasive and powerful contributor to language acquisition at every point in devel-opment. But this elegant starting position brings in its wake a host of problems.

The problems I have focused on here pertain to the future of a learner who begins in this way. Uninformed and unconstrained, a child equipped with only associative learning would be ill-prepared to make sense of words. She would likely not succeed in extracting the right mappings between word and world, and certainly miss out on getting the right kind of mappings. Our recent findings indicate a route around these problems. Infants do not treat words as sounds in the air, but rather as actions of agents. By the end of the first year of life, infants are able to analyze the relational structure of action. They encode certain actions (including attentional actions) in terms of the relation between a person and the object of her action, they distinguish between purposeful actions and apparently purposeless movements, and they can relate actions to one another and to over-arching goals. This sensitivity blossoms at just the time that infants begin to get a grasp on words' relations to the world—that is, at 9–12 months. Knowledge about the relational structure of action would impact word learning in at least two ways. First, by ruling out word-object co-occurrences that do not involve a meaningful relation be-tween speaker and object, it would lead infants to focus on the right mappings. Second, by situating word learning alongside of and con-nected to action knowledge, it would provide a starting point for infants' acquiring the right kind of mappings. Our findings indicate that by 14 months, infants use this action knowledge to interpret words. If I am right, this "intelligent" word learning should be evi-dent still younger, as soon as infants become sensitive to the rela-tional structure of action.

In addition to these problems, the general associative model belies the complexities of the learning process. It assumes that infants ac-quire stable mappings whenever they experience contiguity between two stimuli—for example, when they view a picture while hearing a recorded voice speaking a novel word. But this turns out not to be the case. Werker and colleagues (1998) found that while 14-month-olds could acquire word-picture associations under these conditions, 9-month-olds tested in the same procedure could not. They suggest that the ability to acquire word-object mappings should be viewed as a cognitive achievement because the arbitrary nature of the mapping provides few cues to support the connection between the two stimuli. More generally, based on their review of work on infants' intermodal learning, Gogate and her colleagues (2001) conclude that young infants do not readily acquire arbitrary mappings between sights and sounds, although they do readily associate stimuli that are intrinsically related, such as the visual properties of an object and the sounds it emits. These intrinsic relations involve redundant perceptual cues—for example, the visual and auditory features may share intensity shifts and commonalities in rhythm and tempo. Gogate and Bahrick (1998, 2001) hypothesized that these redundant cues would facilitate the acquisition of novel, arbitrary pairings. Consistent with this hypothesis, they found that 7-month-old infants can acquire a pairing between speech sound and object when synchrony between the object's motion and the timing of the speech sound was present, but not when it was absent. Most intriguingly for the present line of argument, in their experiments, synchrony between the speech sound and the object was achieved by showing infants a person's hands holding and moving the object as she spoke. Thus, the experiments provided just the behavioral evidence that I propose to be critical for extracting relations between words and objects.

Finally, assuming an unconstrained associative starting state can lead to problems for the other end of the theoretical spectrum as well. A number of theorists take this position as a "strawperson" to be argued against. This kind of argument sometimes leads to the impression that the only available positions are that infants learn words as disembodied associates or that they understand words as intentionally produced symbols in their fullest sense. This formulation makes it difficult to see how to bridge the gap. What would a partial understanding of reference or intention be like? By investigating infants' developing action knowledge, we may be able to formulate clearer hypotheses about the specific kinds of action knowledge that get word learning off the ground, and that, with time, develop into mature conceptions of intentions and reference.

That is, we could then make headway on the problem that Macnamara believed insoluble.

Acknowledgments

The research described in this chapter was supported by grants from the Robert R. McCormick Tribune Foundation and NIH (FIRST grant HD35707-01). I am grateful to Geoffrey Hall, Sandra Waxman, and Jennifer Sootsman for their comments on an earlier draft.

Note

1. For the purposes of this chapter, I will consider the problem of learning words that refer to observable aspects of the world, leaving aside the weighty question of how children come to understand words that do not refer in this way.

References

Akhtar, N., Jipson, J., and Callanan, M. A. 2001. Learning words through overhearing. *Child Development, 72*, 416–430.

Akhtar, N., and Tomasello, M. 2001. The social nature of words and word learning. In R. M. Golinkoff, K. Hirsh-Pasek, L. Bloom, L. B. Smith, A. L. Woodward, N. Akhtar, M. Tomasello, and G. Hollich, eds., *Becoming a word learner: A debate on lexical acquisition*, 115–135. Oxford: Oxford University Press.

Baldwin, D. A. 1995. Understanding the link between joint attention and language. In C. Moore and P. Dunham, eds., *Joint attention: Its origins and role in development*, 131–158. Hillsdale, NJ: Erlbaum.

Baldwin, D. A., and Baird, J. A. 2001. Discerning intentions in dynamic human action. *Trends in Cognitive Sciences, 5*(4), 171–178.

Baldwin, D. A., and Moses, L. M. 1996. The ontogeny of social information gathering. *Child Development, 67*, 1915–1939.

Baldwin, D. A., and Tomasello, M. 1998. Word learning: A window on early pragmatic understanding. In E. V. Clark, ed., *Proceedings of the Twenty-Ninth Annual Child Language Research Forum*, 3–23. Stanford, CA: CSLI.

Barresi, J., and Moore, C. 1996. Intentional relations and social understanding. *Behavioral and Brain Sciences, 19*, 107–154.

Bates, E., Benigni, L., Bretherton, I., Camaioni, L., and Volterra, V. 1979. *The emergence of symbols: Cognition and communication in infancy*. New York: Academic Press.

Benedict, H. 1979. Early lexical development: Comprehension and production. *Journal of Child Language, 6*, 183–200.

Blakemore, S., and Decety, J. 2001. From the perception of action to the understanding of intention. *Nature Reviews: Neuroscience, 2*, 561–567.

Bretherton, I. 1991. Intentional communication and the development of an understanding of mind. In D. Frye and C. Moore, eds., *Children's theories of mind*, 49–75. Hillsdale, NJ: Erlbaum.

Bruner, J. 1978. From communication to language: A psychological perspective. In I. Markova, ed., *The social context of language*. New York: Wiley.

Butterworth, G., and Cochran, E. 1980. Towards mechanisms of joint visual attention in human infancy. *International Journal of Behavioral Development, 3*, 253–272.

Carpenter, M., Nagell, K., and Tomasello, M. 1998. Social cognition, joint attention, and communicative competence from 9 to 15 months of age. *Monographs of the Society for Research in Child Development, 63*(4).

Fenson, L., Dale, P. S., Resnick, J. S., Bates, E., Thal, D. J., and Pethick, S. J. 1994. Variability in early communicative development. *Monographs of the Society for Research in Child Development, 59*(5).

Flavell, J. H. 1988. The development of children's knowledge about the mind: From cognitive connections to mental representations. In J. W. Astington, P. L. Harris, and D. R. Olson, eds., *Developing theories of mind*, 244–267. Cambridge, England: Cambridge University Press.

Gallese, V., and Goldman, A. 1998. Mirror neurons and the simulation theory of mind-reading. *Trends in Cognitive Sciences, 2*(12), 493–501.

Gogate, L. J., and Bahrick, L. E. 1998. Intersensory redundancy facilitates learning of arbitrary relations between vowel sounds and objects in seven-month-old infants. *Journal of Experimental Child Psychology, 69*, 133–149.

Gogate, L. J., and Bahrick, L. E. 2001. Intersensory redundancy and 7-month-old infants' memory for arbitrary syllable-object relations. *Infancy, 2*, 219–231.

Gogate, L. J., Bahrick, L. E., and Watson, J. D. 2000. A study of multimodal motherese: The role of temporal synchrony between verbal labels and gestures. *Child Development, 71*(4), 878–894.

Gogate, L. J., Walker-Andrews, A. S., and Bahrick, L. E. 2001. The intersensory origins of word comprehension: An ecological-dynamical systems view. *Developmental Science, 4*(1), 1–37.

Goldin-Meadow, S., McNeill, D., and Singleton, J. 1996. Silence is liberating: Removing the handcuffs on grammatical expression in the manual modality. *Psychological Review, 103*, 34–55.

Gopnik, A., and Meltzoff, A. 1997. *Words, thoughts, and theories*. Cambridge, MA: MIT Press.

Hoff, E., and Naigles, L. 2002. How children use input to acquire a lexicon. *Child Development, 73,* 418–433.

Hollich, G., Hirsh-Pasek, K., and Golinkoff, R. M. 2000. Breaking the language barrier: An emergentist, coalition model for the origins of word learning. *Monographs of the Society for Research in Child Development, 65*(3).

Huttenlocher, J. 1974. The origins of language comprehension. In R. Solso, ed., *Theories in cognitive psychology,* 331–368. Hillsdale, NJ: Erlbaum.

Jovanovic, B., Kiraly, I., Elsner, B., Aschersleben, G., Gergely, G., and Prinz, W. 2002. Action effects enhance the perception of action goals. Paper presented at the International Conference on Infant Studies, Toronto.

Macnamara, J. 1982. *Names for things.* Cambridge, MA: MIT Press.

McShane, J. 1979. The development of naming. *Linguistics, 17,* 879–905.

Namy, L. 2001. What's in a name when it isn't a word? *Infancy, 2,* 73–86.

Namy, L., and Waxman, S. R. 1998. Words and gestures: Infants' interpretations of different forms of symbolic reference. *Child Development, 69,* 295–308.

Ochs, E., and Schieffelin, B. 1995. The impact of language socialization on grammatical development. In P. Fletcher and B. MacWhinney, eds., *Handbook of child language,* 73–94. Oxford: Blackwell.

Oviatt, S. L. 1980. The emerging ability to comprehend language: An experimental approach. *Child Development, 51,* 97–106.

Phillips, A. T., Wellman, H. M., and Spelke, E. S. 2002. Infants' ability to connect gaze and emotional expression to intentional action. *Cognition, 85,* 53–78.

Regier, T., Corrigan, B., Cabasaan, R., Woodward, A., Gasser, M., and Smith, L. 2001. The emergence of words. In J. Moore and K. Stenning, eds., *Proceedings of the Twenty-third Annual Meeting of the Cognitive Science Society,* 815–820. Mahwah, NJ: Erlbaum.

Rogoff, B., Mistry, J., Goncu, A., and Mosier, C. 1993. Guided participation in cultural activity by toddlers and caregivers. *Monographs of the Society for Research in Child Development, 58*(8).

Schafer, G., and Plunkett, K. 1998. Rapid word learning by 15-month-olds under tightly controlled conditions. *Child Development, 69,* 309–320.

Sodian, B., Poulin-Dubois, D., Tilden, J., Metz, U., and Schoeppner, B. 2002. Implicit understanding of the seeing-knowing relation in 14- to 24-month-olds. Paper presented at the International Conference on Infant Studies, Toronto.

Sommerville, J. A. 2002. *Means-end reasoning: Infants' developing ability to interpret and perform intentional actions.* Unpublished doctoral dissertation, University of Chicago.

Spelke, E. S., Phillips, A. T., and Woodward, A. L. 1995. Infants' knowledge of object motion and human action. In A. J. Premack, D. Premack, and D. Sperber, eds., *Causal cognition: A multidisciplinary debate,* 44–77. Oxford: Clarendon Press.

Stager, C. L., and Werker, J. F. 1997. Infants listen for more phonetic detail in speech perception than in word-learning tasks. *Nature, 388*(24), 381–382.

Tomasello, M. 1999. *The cultural origins of human cognition.* Cambridge, MA: Harvard University Press.

Tomasello, M., and Barton, M. 1994. Learning words in nonostensive contexts. *Developmental Psychology, 30,* 639–650.

Waxman, S. R., and Booth, A. E. 2001. Seeing pink elephants: Fourteen-month-olds' interpretations of novel nouns and adjectives. *Cognitive Psychology, 43,* 217–242.

Wellman, H. M. 1992. *The child's theory of mind.* Cambridge, MA: MIT Press.

Wellman, H. M., and Phillips, A. T. 2001. Developing intentional understandings. In B. Malle, L. Moses, and D. Baldwin, eds., *Intentionality: A key to human understanding.* Cambridge, MA: MIT Press.

Werker, J., Cohen, L. B., Lloyd, V. L., Casasolo, M., and Stager, C. L. 1998. Acquisition of word-object associations by 14-month-olds. *Developmental Psychology, 34,* 1289–1309.

Woodward, A. L. 1998. Infants selectively encode the goal object of an actor's reach. *Cognition, 69,* 1–34.

Woodward, A. L. 1999. Infants' ability to distinguish between purposeful and non-purposeful behaviors. *Infant Behavior and Development, 22,* 145–160.

Woodward, A. L. 2003a. Infants' developing understanding of the link between looker and object. *Developmental Science, 6,* 297–311.

Woodward, A. L. 2003b. *One-year-olds' understanding of the intentional nature of words.* Unpublished manuscript.

Woodward, A. L. Forthcoming. Infants' understanding of the actions involved in joint attention. In N. Eilan, C. Hoerl, T. McCormack, and J. Roessler, eds., *Joint attention: Communication and other minds.* Oxford: Oxford University Press.

Woodward, A. L., and Guajardo, J. J. 2002. Infants' understanding of the point gesture as an object-directed action. *Cognitive Development, 17,* 1061–1084.

Woodward, A. L., and Hoyne, K. L. 1999. Infants' learning about words and sounds in relation to objects. *Child Development, 70,* 65–72.

Woodward, A. L., Markman, E. M., and Fitzsimmons, C. M. 1994. Rapid word learning in 13- and 18-month-olds. *Developmental Psychology, 30,* 553–566.

Woodward, A. L., and Sommerville, J. A. 2000. Twelve-month-old infants interpret action in context. *Psychological Science, 11,* 73–76.

Woodward, A. L., Sommerville, J. A., and Guajardo, J. J. 2001. How infants make sense of intentional action. In B. Malle, L. Moses, and D. Baldwin, eds., *Intentions and intentionality: Foundations of social cognition.* Cambridge, MA: MIT Press.

6

Hybrid Theories at the Frontier of Developmental Psychology: The Emergentist Coalition Model of Word Learning as a Case in Point

Kathy Hirsh-Pasek, Roberta Michnick Golinkoff, Elizabeth A. Hennon, and Mandy J. Maguire

There are no single effective pushes to the developing system, but rather a combination of influences that lead to observable change.
—Nelson 1996, 85

The flourishing new domain of cognitive science needs to go beyond the traditional nativist-empiricist dichotomy that permeates much of the field, in favor of an epistemology that embraces both innate predispositions and constructivism.
—Karmiloff-Smith 1992, 193

The nature of early word learning is a paradigmatic and contentious case of the nature-nurture debate. How do infants break through the language barrier with their first words at around 12 months of age? And what accounts for the transformation in word learning at around 19 months of age when a slow, laborious process turns into one in which infants learn up to nine new words a day (e.g., Carey and Bartlett 1978; but see Goldfield and Reznick 1990)? As in other areas of developmental psychology, a number of theories have sprung up to address these controversial questions. Some argue that word learning is a product of all-purpose learning mechanisms like associationism and generalization (Smith 1999, 2000). Others suggest that word learning must be accounted for through internal constraints on the learning process (Markman 1989). Still others hold that the social environment navigates word learning *for* the child (Akhtar and Tomasello 2000). In each case, theorists contend that the most parsimonious explanations of learning come from reduction to either-or theories. Either the mechanisms for learning are social and from the environment or are constraints that emanate from the child's head. The present data illustrate that word learning begins as an associative process and gradually turns into a process dependent on social cues. Between 10 and 19 months, infants come to appreciate the role that social cues play in word learning. They do not, however, start out that way. Prior research by Hollich, Hirsh-Pasek, and Golinkoff (2000) showed that 12-month-olds avoided mismapping and were sensitive to but did not recruit social cues as the 19- to 24-month-olds did. The question that remained was whether infants start out as associative animals, only later recognizing the import of the social cues that have been available all along.

Here we present a hybrid theory that pulls from both environmental and constraints approaches while at the same offering a developmental account of the word-learning process. The emergentist coalition model of word learning (Hirsh-Pasek, Golinkoff, and Hollich 2000; Hollich Hirsh-Pasek, and Golinkoff 2000; Golinkoff, Hirsh-Pasek, and Hollich 1999) suggests that infants are biased to attend to and integrate multiple pieces of information as they learn words. Current theories of word acquisition that emphasize either environmental or nativisitic approaches provide only *snapshots* of learning at different points in developmental time. In the emergentist coalition model, these snapshots are integrated in a theoretical model that takes change over time seriously. Such emergentist models are appearing throughout the developmental literature in domains of spatial development (Newcombe and Huttenlocher 2000), number theory (Gelman and Williams 1998), and language development (Hirsh-Pasek and Golinkoff 1996; MacWhinney 1999). These theories force us to reconsider the age-old link between parsimony and reductionism in favor of systems-based, dynamic models that include multiple inputs to complex processes (Thelen and Smith 1994). These newer theories occupy what Newcombe and Huttenlocher (2000) have called the "radical middle" in psychology, forcing an empirically testable balance between nature and nurture.

In this chapter, we explore the word-learning problem, review the three theories that have been proposed to address the key questions in the field, and propose an attempt at a reconciliation in the emergentist coalition model of word learning. Data on word reference and word extension will be used not only to support the theory, but to demonstrate how those working on word learning might rethink the concept of developmental change.

6.1 Three Theories of Word Learning

The Quinean conundrum (Quine 1960) provides a cornerstone for the word-learning problem. To learn a word, infants must first segment the sound stream, discover a world of objects, actions, and events, and then map the word from the sound stream (or visual stream in sign languages) onto the referent. Quine's now-famous story highlights the inherent difficulty of this so-called mapping problem: A linguist in a foreign land sees a rabbit scurrying by while hearing a native exclaim "gavagai!" Among other things, the word *gavagai* could refer to the whole rabbit, to the rabbit's ears, or to the rabbit's hopping. The world provides an infinite number of possible word-to-world mappings. How is a child to learn how the word maps onto the referent?

Theories of word learning can largely be defined by whether they embrace the Quinean conundrum as a foundational assumption or whether they reject it. Theories that posit constraints or principles adopt Quine's view of the problem space. Theories that emphasize social input or associative learning consider Quine's example largely irrelevant to the problem of word learning. These theories form the landscape for the debate about the nature of early word learning.

Constraints or principles theories take Quine seriously. Because word-to-world mapping is underdetermined, human minds must be equipped with constraints or principles that narrow the search space. According to this theory, children approach the word-learning task biased to make certain assumptions over others for what a word might mean. Domain-specific constraints theories have been posited for a number of cognitive development domains. As Gelman and Greeno (1989, 130) wrote with respect to theories of number development, "If we grant learners some domain-specific principles, we provide them with a way to define the range of relevant inputs, the ones that support learning about that domain. Because principles embody constraints on the kinds of input that can be processed as data that are relevant to that domain, they therefore can direct attention to those aspects of the environment that need to be selected and attended to." Similar statements have appeared in the literature on spatial development (Newcombe and Huttenlocher 2000) and object perception (Spelke 1990). The general thrust of the constraints or principles position is to make a daunting task manageable by restricting the number of hypotheses the learner needs to entertain to arrive at a representation of a domain.

A substantial body of evidence has accumulated to support the constraints position in word learning. Markman's (1989) principle of mutual exclusivity, for example, states that children assume that an object can have only one name. The consequence of this principle is that a novel name will not label an already-named object but rather will label an unfamiliar object. Golinkoff et al. (1992; see also Mervis and Bertrand 1994; Evey and Merriman 1998) have shown that 28-month-olds will assume that a novel label maps to an unnamed object when presented with a set of familiar and unfamiliar objects. These findings not only support Markman's mutual-exclusivity principle but also a more flexible principle ("novel name–nameless category" or N3C) posited by Golinkoff, Mervis, and Hirsh-Pasek (1994). Similarly, Clark (1983) suggested that children operate with a principle called "conventionality": Use the word that your linguistic community uses or you will not understood. Mervis (see Golinkoff, Mervis, and Hirsh-Pasek 1994) provided numerous diary entries showing that children abandon their idiosyncratic terms in favor of the standard terms (e.g., over time *pops* becomes *pacifier*).

The principles/constraints theories have flourished. Indeed, over the last 15 years, there has been a proliferation of principles, including Waxman and Kosowski's (1990) "noun-category bias," Markman's (1989) "mutual exclusivity," Markman and Hutchinson's (1984) "taxonomic assumption," and Clark's (1983) pragmatic constraint of "contrast." These principles were reviewed and placed in a developmental framework by Golinkoff, Mervis, and Hirsh-Pasek (1994), who posited a set of six principles (some new and some in the literature) that were necessary and sufficient to account both for

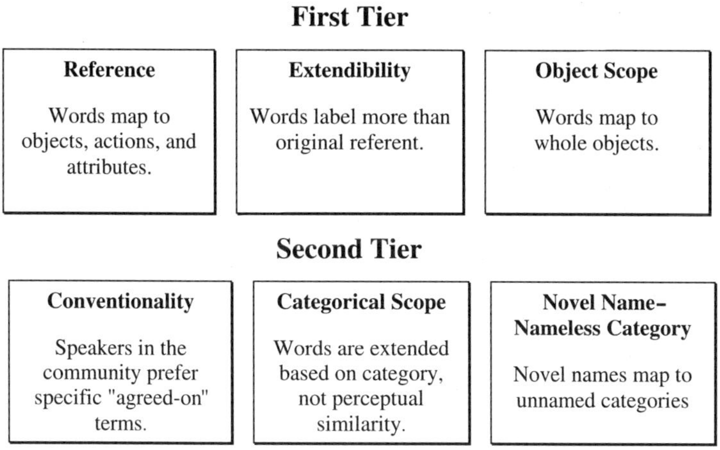

Theories at the Frontier of Developmental Psychology

First Tier

Reference	Extendibility	Object Scope
Words map to objects, actions, and attributes.	Words label more than original referent.	Words map to whole objects.

Second Tier

Conventionality	Categorical Scope	Novel Name–Nameless Category
Speakers in the community prefer specific "agreed-on" terms.	Words are extended based on category, not perceptual similarity.	Novel names map to unnamed categories

Figure 6.1
Principles of lexical learning (Hollich, Hirsh-Pasek, and Golinkoff 2000).

how children get word learning "off the ground," and for how they become "vacuum cleaners for words" (Pinker 1994) at around 19 months of age.

The Golinkoff et al. framework offered a developmental model in which the principles of word learning were organized on two tiers that captured the changing character of word learning (see figure 6.1). On the first tier, and appearing at around 12 months of age, were principles like reference (that words map to objects, actions, and events); extendibility (that words do not uniquely refer to the original referent but rather to a category of objects, actions, and events); and object scope (that words refer to whole objects rather than to object parts and to objects over actions). (See also Markman's (1989) whole-object principle.) On the second tier, the principles of N3C (that novel names label novel categories), categorical scope (that words label taxonomic categories), and conventionality (Clark 1983) (use socially agreed-on names for things) are born from the first-tier principles and help children catapult into the mature word learning characterized by the vocabulary spurt. Fundamental to the principles framework is the idea that the *principles themselves undergo change with development and are an emergent product of the combination of word-learning experience and some inborn biases.* Nested in the Golinkoff, Mervis, and Hirsh-Pasek (1994) framework is a powerful developmental solution to the Quinean dilemma.

Social-pragmatic theorists stand in stark contrast to the constraints position. Children, embedded in a social nexus, are guided by expert word learners as they embark on the word-learning task. As Nelson (1988, 240–241) has written, Quine's problem becomes irrelevant: "The typical way children acquire words ... is almost completely opposite of the Quinean paradigm. Children do not try and guess what it is that the adult intends to refer to; rather ... it is the adult who guesses what the child is focused on and then supplies the appropriate word."

Bloom (1993, 2000) similarly concludes that adults talk about objects, actions, and events that are *relevant* to children. Children do not have to wade through alternative interpretations for a word; the correct interpretation is already the focus of their attention.

There is considerable evidence that children are capable of utilizing social cues in the service of word learning. For example, Tomasello, Strosberg, and Akhtar (1996; also Tomasello and Barton 1994; Carpenter, Nagell, and Tomasello 1998; Akhtar and Tomasello 2000; Baldwin and Tomasello 1999) showed that 18- and 24-month-olds can use the intention of the experimenter to attach a label to a novel object or action. If the experimenter indicates that she erred in using a label, children will not attach a novel label to the first object or action they see but to the second. Akhtar and Tomasello (1996) showed that 24-month-old children can mine the social context to attach a novel label to a hidden object instead of to novel objects that they are shown. Furthermore, Baldwin et al. (1996) showed that 18-month-olds can evaluate whether an adult uttering a label in great excitement ("It's a toma!") while on the telephone is intending to label the object they are playing with or something else. Young children are not fooled into forming a link between a label uttered by a woman not addressing them just at the moment that they are focused on a novel toy.

Under the social-pragmatic view, children are seen as skilled apprentices to expert word learners participating in a structured social world. Children are also seen as able to read the social intent of their mentors (P. Bloom 2000) in this world. By virtue of being social animals, then, humans acquire language for free. Under this interpretation, Quine's linguist differs from real children because children are immersed in rich social contexts that naturally delimit the possible mappings between words and their referents.

The constraints/principles and the social-pragmatic theories of word learning represent the most common positions in the literature. Recently, however, a third position, outlined by Smith (1995, 1999, 2000), Samuelson and Smith (1998), and Plunkett (1997), offers a third perspective on the word-learning problem. The domain-general view of word learning rejects Quine's conundrum, suggesting that word learning can be best accounted for through "dumb attentional mechanisms" like perceptual saliency, association, and frequency. In comparing the differences in constraints theories and her own systems theory view, Smith (1995, 4) wrote: "The empirical focus [of constraints theories] becomes not the processes that enable children to interpret words in context, but whether children's biased learning has the properties needed to 'solve the induction problem.' The present thesis is that the induction problem is irrelevant to developmentalists. Learning is not necessarily hypothesis testing. Development is not induction." Children do not need constraints or principles to forge word-to-world mappings. The process of mapping a word onto an object is straightforward. Children notice objects, actions, and events that are the most salient in their environment. They associate the most frequently used label with the most salient candidate. In this way, ambiguity in the word-learning situation is removed. General cognitive mechanisms are sufficient not only to account for how young children first map words onto referents, but also can combine in ways to account for the complexity of more sophisticated word learning (Smith 2000).

This synopsis of the theoretical debate in the area of word learning parallels that seen in the developmental literature. For any given developmental problem space, theories arise that represent the domain-specific constraints alternative, a social-pragmatic or cultural alternative, and an associationist alternative. As in the area of word learning, there is mounting data to support each of the positions. There are also reasons to reject each theory. By way of example, one could argue that despite many attempts to sweep away the Quinean problem in word learning, it refuses to disappear. Any single object, action, or event presents an array of possible referents to be named. Even something as simple as a "sippy cup" has a lid, an elevated portion on the lid (mouthpiece), and possibly pink flowers on its blue plastic base. All of the parts move together when the cup is lifted and some of these parts—such as the mouthpiece—may prove more salient than the whole object. Which of these parts is graced with the name *cup*? Neither perceptually based nor socially based theories assist the child in reaching the final determination of what makes word-to-world mapping possible. Only the constraints or principles theories solve the Quinean problem. Yet they do so by default. Either they assume that principles come in full-blown and are non-developmental (Markman 1989), or they offer a developmental perspective with little emphasis on the mechanisms of change.

The debate presses on (Golinkoff et al. 2000) as scientists try to determine which theory best accounts for the data. Yet science's steadfast and historically rooted view that parsimony demands a *choice* of one theoretical explanation over the other might lie at the root of the problem. Perhaps the issue should not be cast as *which* of the particular theories is "right." Perhaps the issue should be recast as which components of which theories seem to govern children's word learning at different points in the course of development? This reframing of the question requires the creation of a hybrid approach with clear hypotheses that make the theory empirically testable. The idea that we need to consider multiple perspectives for complex problems is not new (Bloom and Lahey 1978; Bloom 1993, 2000). It was from this idea that the emergentist coalition model was born.

6.2 The Emergentist Coalition Model of Word Learning

The emergentist coalition model of word learning is a hybrid model that builds on the developmental lexical principles framework (Golinkoff, Mervis, and Hirsh-Pasek 1994). This model (Hollich, Hirsh-Pasek, and Golinkoff 1998; Golinkoff, Hirsh-Pasek, and Hollich 1999; Hollich, Hirsh-Pasek, and Golinkoff 2000) incorporates the impact of diverse factors on word learning because, as in the real world, it is likely that children avail themselves of social, attentional, cognitive, *and* linguistic cues to learn new words. The emergentist coalition model embraces this complexity. It allows for the full range of cues to word learning, rather than forcing artificial choices among them. Thus, the first defining tenet of the model is that children mine a coalition of cues on their way to word learning.

Although a range of cues are always *available*, not all cues for word learning are equally *utilized*, in the service of word learning. Younger children, just beginning to learn words, rely on only a subset of the cues in the coalition. Older, more experienced word learners rely on a wider subset of cues and on some cues more heavily then others. The model posits that social cues such as eye gaze that are subtle and may demand at least a primitive theory of mind, will be less utilized than a cue such as the salience of objects. Given a choice between attaching a novel name to a boring object that an adult is looking at versus a colorful, exciting object, the child just beginning to learn words should rely on perceptual salience (consistent with the associationist approach) before relying on the subtle social cue of eye gaze (consistent with the social-pragmatic perspectives). Thus, the second major tenet of the theory is that the cues for word learning *change their weights* over developmental time. Figure 6.2 graphically depicts how reliance on these cues shifts with development.

Because children make differential use of the available cues with development, this model holds that principles for word learning are emergent. They develop over the course of the second year of life as children gain word-learning experience. Unlike other constraints posited in the literature, the emergentist coalition model states that not all of the principles are available from the start of word learning. Lexical principles are the products and not the engines of lexical development. Children do not start word learning, for example, with the novel name–nameless category principle (N3C). Mervis and Bertrand (1994) have shown that the N3C principle is not in place until after the vocabulary spurt. The third tenet of this model, then, is that the principles for word learning are emergent and not given a priori.

Hirsh-Pasek, Golinkoff, Hennon, and Maguire

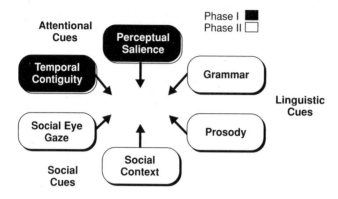

Figure 6.2
The coalition model implemented for reference. Children shift from a reliance on attentional cues like perceptual salience, to a greater dependency on social and linguistic cues.

The developmental cast of this model makes it imperative to study the origins of word learning as well as the transformation that takes place in the second year of life when the child becomes an expert word learner. Data need to be collected that demonstrate that children detect and utilize multiple cues for word learning, that their reliance on these cues changes over the course of development, and that principles for word learning emerge from word-learning experience.

Our research has assessed these claims within the context of the first-tier principles of reference (that words map onto the child's representation of objects, actions, and events) and extendibility (that words map onto more than one exemplar). First, we hypothesized that children learning their first words (at 10 or 12 months of age) would be informed by multiple cues, attentional, social, and linguistic. Second, we hypothesized that perceptual salience would be more heavily weighted than social cues for the novice than for the expert word learner. Third, we hypothesized that the word-learning principles themselves develop along a continuum from immature to mature such that children are first attracted by what is most salient to them, and only later note what is important to the speaker. As they break through the language barrier, children are guided (though not completely) by associationist laws. As they mature into veteran word learners, they are guided (though not completely) by social-pragmatic strategies. Both views are united under one theory.

6.3 Evidence for the Emergentist Coalition Model

Investigation of the hybrid model demanded experiments that could trace development of the principles of reference and extendibility from their immature to their mature states. To assess the principle of reference, we examined whether infants would attach a label to both interesting and boring objects. We reasoned that a child with an immature principle of reference might attach a novel label to the interesting object—regardless of which object an adult was labeling. The child with a mature principle, on the other hand, should over-come the salience of the object in favor of relying on the speaker's social cues to what is being labeled. To assess the principle of extendibility, we first asked whether infants would extend a label for a given object to one that differed only in color from the original exemplar. We then put infants in a very difficult task and asked whether they would use social information to extend that label to an object that bore no resemblance to the original object. After all, beanbag chairs and dining-room chairs bear little resemblance to one another, yet they are both called *chairs*. Children who fail to extend a label or who will only extend it to close perceptual relatives possess an immature principle of extendibility. Alternatively, children who trust the social mentor extending a label in the face of contrasting perceptual cues are operating with a mature principle of extendibility.

Examination of the emergentist coalition theory required a method that could be used equally effectively with children in the age range of interest (10 to 24 months) and one that would enable researchers to manipulate multiple cues (attentional, social, and linguistic) and their interactions. The interactive intermodal preferential looking paradigm (IIPLP) provided this new method (e.g., Hollich, Hirsh-Pasek, and Golinkoff 2000). Based on the intermodal preferential looking paradigm (Golinkoff et al. 1987; Hirsh-Pasek and Golinkoff 1996) used to study lexical and syntactic comprehension,

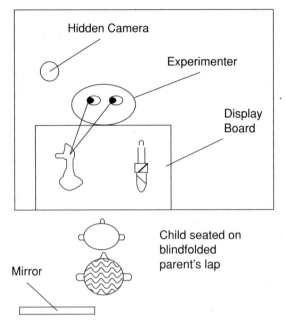

Figure 6.3
The interactive intermodal preferential-looking paradigm: A hidden camera records children's looking preferences toward two objects on a display board. The mirror allows a view of the experimenter's actions, the child's visual-fixation responses, and the objects on the board.

Baldwin's (1991, 1993) "bucket task," and Fagan's (1971; Fagan et al. 1986) infant intelligence test, the method allows for the study of multiple cues to word learning in the first two years of life. The physical setup is depicted in figure 6.3.

Infants are seated on their blindfolded mother's lap facing the experimenter and our testing apparatus. After preexposure to the toys—a pair of familiar toys on some trials and a pair of novel toys on others—the toys are fixed with Velcro onto one side of a two-sided blackboard that can be rotated so that the toys can go in and out of view for a specified period. The experimenter hides behind the board while children are inspecting the toys and during test trials. Coding is done offline from videotaped records.

Using this apparatus, it is possible to examine word learning in a controlled setting. Familiar-object trials allow us to ask whether the child can "play our game." The use of unfamiliar, novel objects permits exploration of the cues and *combinations* of cues that children use to guide word learning across development. The logic of the design (Golinkoff et al. 1987; Hirsh-Pasek and Golinkoff 1996) is that children should look more at an object that "matches" the linguistic stimulus than at an object that does not match. Thus, the dependent variable is visual fixation time to the target (named) object versus to the unnamed object.

Validation of the method comes from the familiar trials. Children at three ages were tested: 12- to 13-month-olds, just at the beginning of word learning; 19- to 20-month-olds, who may or may not have experienced a vocabulary spurt; and 24- to 25-month-olds, who typically have sizable production vocabularies. In over twenty-three experiments children demonstrated the potency of the method by looking significantly more at the target item than at the nontarget item in the familiar condition when an item was requested (Hollich, Hirsh-Pasek, and Golinkoff 2000). Evaluation of the hypotheses comes from children's responses to novel stimuli. Using this method, we were able to explore how infants move from an immature to a mature principle in reference and extendibility and to examine the hypotheses that form the foundation for the emergentist coalition model.

6.4 Evidence from the Studies on Reference

Reference, or the assumption that words refer, is the most basic of the word-learning principles. Do infants assume that a word refers to an object, action, or event? How do they choose which object, action, or event should receive the label? To investigate these questions, conditions were created in which multiple cues were available to children but were sometimes placed in conflict. In what we called the *coincident* condition, we labeled the novel toy that coincided with children's preferences—the interesting toy. In the *conflict* condition, we labeled the novel toy that did not coincide with the children's preferences—the boring toy. We reasoned that learning the word in the coincident case should be easy for children because all of the "cues," attentional, social, and linguistic, were in alignment. In contrast, learning a novel word in the conflict condition should be more difficult because the coalition of cues is not acting in concert.

The experiment was conducted in four phases. First, children were given the opportunity to explore both the interesting and the boring toy. Second, children participated in a salience trial in which they saw both toys mounted side by side. Third, in the labeling phase, the experimenter captured children's attention, displayed both toys, and labeled the target five times with a novel word (e.g., *danu*). In the coincident condition, the experimenter looked at and labeled the interesting toy; in the conflict condition, she looked at and labeled the boring toy. Finally in the test trials, the experimenter, now hiding behind the board, asked for the object labeled during training, again getting the child's attention first by asking a question like "Eve, where's the danu?" If children learned the name of the correct toy, they should look more to the target than to the nontarget (see Hollich, Hirsh-Pasek, and Golinkoff 2000 for details).

What cues do children use to determine the referent of a word? The participants were thirty-two children at each of 12, 19, and 24 months of age. At all three ages, there is evidence that children detected the range of cues available. For example, even the 12-month-olds detected the social cue of eye gaze although they could not use it when it was in conflict with perceptual salience. By way of example, they learned the name of the object only in the coincident condition, as several further studies indicated (Hollich, Hirsh-Pasek, and Golinkoff 2000). The 19-month-olds learned the names of the objects in both conditions, but were still influenced heavily by perceptual salience. Even the oldest group, who learned the names of the novel objects in both the conflict and the coincident conditions, still showed the effects of perceptual salience by looking much longer at the target object in the coincident condition than in the conflict condition. This suggests that 19-month-olds were lured by the perceptual salience of the interesting toy, but were able to overcome it when the boring toy was the focus of the experimenter's attention. In short, these data suggest that infants with an immature principle of reference are more dominated by perceptual salience

than are their counterparts with a more mature principle of reference. Nineteen- and 24-month-old children use the speaker's social
intent (as signaled by their eye gaze) when mapping word to object.
In light of these data, we are conducting studies with 10-month-old
infants to see whether children just beginning to acquire a comprehension vocabulary operate like the 12-month-olds who are starting
to produce language. Preliminary results from this group suggest
that 10-month-olds are even more bound to perceptual salience,
demonstrating a clear preference for the interesting toy even in the
conflict condition. That is, these children do not seem to be thrown
by the presence of conflicting social cues. Rather, they seem oblivi-
ous to these cues. They appear to assume that labels "go with" interesting rather than boring objects!

What we see in the data is a clear pattern that changes over time,
such that infants become increasingly less dependent on perceptual
cues and more dependent on social cues to determine reference.
Such data speak to both the associationist and the social pragmatic
theorist. The associationist position would predict that children
would form a mismapping between the *interesting* object and the label
in the conflict condition. If the 10-month-old data stand, these data
fit this prediction—but only for the very youngest children. Yet by as
early as 12 months of age, children with only three words in their
productive vocabularies are already demonstrating some sensitivity to
social information in a word-learning task. These children, at the
cusp of word learning, learned the novel labels only in the coincident condition. In the coincident condition, the experimenter labeled the object that the babies were most interested in. For these
babies, learning took place when the cues coincided. However, when
multiple cues failed to coincide in the conflict condition, infants
showed little evidence of word learning. They wanted to look at the
interesting object despite the fact that the experimenter persisted in
labeling the boring object. Though they looked at the interesting
object much more than the boring object in the conflict condition,
they did not falsely conclude that the novel label was attached to the
interesting object. Even 12-month-olds were sensitive to the fact that
the experimenter was looking elsewhere and *not* labeling the interesting object. Even 12-month-olds are able to use multiple cues for

word learning, and the cues had to *overlap* for learning to occur. While the 12-month-olds are not weighing social cues heavily yet, their performance also defies the predictions made by the associationistic camp. Only a hybrid theory that talks about attention to multiple cues and shifts in attention to these cues over time can account for the data.

6.5 Evidence from the Principle of Extendibility

Children who master reference must then learn that words generally refer to more than one exemplar. That is, most words do not refer to a single exemplar (e.g., a proper noun), but rather to groups or categories of objects. Two types of theories dominate the literature on extendibility. The "broad-to-narrow" view holds that words license attention to categories (Hall and Waxman 1993; Waxman and Markov 1995; Balaban and Waxman 1997). Children already have rich conceptual systems by the end of the first year of life (Mandler and McDonough 1996). They might assume that words map onto these categories from the outset. Note that some theorists argue that the categories need not be perceptually based. For example, Mandler and McDonough point out that airplanes are more perceptually similar to birds than they are to cars, yet infants' global categories seem to include airplanes and cars but not birds. Indeed, Hall (1991) offers evidence that even 2-year-olds will occasionally interpret proper nouns as common nouns. This position leaves open the question of how infants would ever learn that some words are more narrowly construed (for proposals of how this could occur see Hall, Quantz, and Persoage 2000; Jaswal and Markman 2001; P. Bloom 2000).

The alternative hypothesis, the "narrow-to-broad" view, holds that words label individual exemplars and only later generalize to categories, either on the basis of shared shape or on the basis of parental speech patterns that highlight perceptual similarity (Smith 2000). This view dates as far back as Locke ([1690] 1964) and the British empiricists. Under the narrow-to-broad view, perceptual similarity plays an important role in categorical extension.

To assess the development of the principle of extendibility, we asked three questions about how children would react when taught a novel label: (1) Will children label just the original object or will they be willing to extend the label to another object of similar appearance? (2) Can infants extend the label to another exemplar of similar appearance even when the original object is not present? (3) Will children use social cues to extend a novel label even in the absence of perceptual similarity? The emergentist coalition model leads us to hypothesize a narrow-to-broad progression distinct from the more perceptually dominated view presented by Smith (2000; see also Keil 1989). Children might begin with a proper-noun hypothesis, assuming that a word refers only to its original referent and cannot be extended to like objects. Later, and similar to Smith's theory, children may progress to a period in which perceptual similarity controls extension. However, Smith's view is that extension is based on perceptual similarity (in particular, the shape bias is only firmly in place at 24 months of age). Our principle of extendibility allows for early extension based on perceptual similarity (among other factors) but then gives way to a social-pragmatic one in which children rely on social and linguistic cues to determine category membership and hence word extension. Under a theory like the emergentist coalition model that allows for interaction of multiple cues and their shifting weights, noun extension that moves from being exclusively perceptually based to being more heavily based on social cues is possible. Under a theory like Smith's (2000) that emphasizes a single factor (the role of shape in extension), such a shift would not be predicted.

To distinguish between the alternative theories, two experiments were conducted: perceptual extension and social extension. The perceptual-extension study was conducted in four phases. First, the children were given the opportunity to play with three objects, two of which were identical except for color (e.g., lemon reamers in red and purple), and one that was perceptually distinct and served as the distractor item (a green travel razor holder). Second, the children participated in a salience trial in which they saw the two perceptually similar objects mounted side by side. Third, in the labeling phase, the experimenter captured the children's attention, displayed only one toy (the red lemon reamer), and labeled the target ten times with a novel word (e.g., *danu*). Fourth, the children participated in three test trials: in the novel trial, the just-labeled object (red lemon reamer) was paired with the dissimilar object (the green razor holder) to ensure that the children had learned the original label; in the proper-noun trial, the two similar objects (the red and purple lemon reamers) were placed side by side to test whether the infants would look only toward the originally labeled object; in the extend trial, the infants saw the unlabeled category member paired with the out-of-category member (the purple lemon reamer and the green razor holder) to see whether they would extend the novel word to an item in the same category in the absence of the originally labeled object.

The order of the second and third test trials was counterbalanced across children. During all testing conditions, the experimenter hid behind the board and asked for the object that was labeled during training, once again getting the child's attention first—for example, with the question "Eve, where's the danu?" If children can extend, they should learn the name for the original toy, show even looking times in the second test trial, and extend the novel name to the category member in the last test trial (Hennon et al. 2000).

Results reveal three patterns of extension depending on the age of the children. Ten- and 12-month-olds showed a proper-noun bias with no evidence of word extension. In the novel trials, the majority of the 10- and 12-month-olds did learn the original word. When they did, we examined their performance on the proper-name and extension trials. There was no evidence that these infants could extend the newly learned label. On the proper-name trials, the infants significantly preferred the originally named object. Further, the same children showed no evidence of extension when the original object was absent, distributing their looking times evenly across the like category member and the completely novel object. We interpret this result to suggest that the younger infants had a proper-name bias. Some might argue that infants looked more at the originally labeled object during the proper-name trials because it had been made more salient for them during training. We think this explanation is incorrect. Salience should have been equal across ages. As we will see, older children had no problem extending in both the proper-noun and extension trials. Thus, 10- and 12-month-old infants seemed to operate with a proper-noun bias as if the label referred only to the original object without the ability to extend to other category members.

Fourteen-month-olds showed some progress toward extension. They learned the original label in the novel trials and seemed to be in a transition phase with respect to extension. If the children saw the proper-noun trials *first* and then the extension trials, they showed no evidence of extension. They preferred to look at the originally labeled object in the proper-noun trial and demonstrated no evidence of extension in the extension trial. Yet if they saw the extension trial *first* and then the proper noun trial—they revealed an ability to extend a label to a like category member. These children looked at the like category member in the extension trial and then distributed their looking evenly across both exemplars of the category in the proper-noun trial. We interpret this to mean that these children have a fragile principle of extendibility. If they are primed to look at the original object, they will do so. If not, they can demonstrate extension (Hennon et al. 1999).

Finally, the 19- and 24-month-olds readily extended the newly learned label. These children learned the novel words, distributed their looking evenly across the two category members in the proper-name trial, and readily extended the label in the extension trial. These children had mastered the principle of extendability.

The social-extension experiment was designed to assess whether infants would extend a label based on social and linguistic cues even when there were no perceptual cues. If mature word learners recruit social information to determine category membership, they should extend a new word to an object that the speaker labels as a similar category member even if the perceptual similarity between this object and the other category members is not apparent to the child. To test for this progression, infants participated in a three-phase experiment. First, they were exposed to and played with *five* objects. Three of the objects differed only in color and were given the same name (e.g., three spaghetti measurers of different colors were each labeled a *lorbit*). Two dissimilar items were also included in the set (e.g., a coffee grinder and a stirrer) only one of which was labeled a *lorbit*. Second, the two dissimilar objects were displayed side by side on the testing board to assess salience. Third, infants participated in two test phases: (1) they saw the two dissimilar items (grinder and stirrer) displayed side by side and were asked to "find the lorbit." If they accepted the experimenter's use of the category label for this perceptually dissimilar object, they should look more to the one that had received the label; (2) the dissimilar object that was not labeled the *lorbit* (stirrer) was placed alongside one of the perceptually based category items (spaghetti measurer) while the experimenter said "Find the lorbit." This latter trial assessed whether infants had learned the category at all. If they had, they should spend more time looking at the spaghetti measurer.

Sixteen children at each of 13, 19, and 25 months of age participated in this study. All of the children were willing to learn the label for the perceptually similar items. In sharp contrast, the 18- and 24-month-olds, but not the 12-month-olds, were willing to learn the label for the perceptually dissimilar object. That is, the older children were willing to extend the label to the dissimilar object when they were taught it by an adult. The youngest children were not willing to extend the boundaries of this label to include a perceptually dissimilar object. This experiment becomes even more telling in light of a subsequent experiment in which the test objects were altered to offer some perceptual support. In the replication, children saw three like-category objects (lemon reamers in red, purple, and blue) and two test objects that shared a perceptual part with the category items (a lemon juicer that had a distinctly similar juice extractor on top, and a poker that had a perceptually similar handle with the reamers). Here, the 12-month-olds had no problem extending the name *lorbit* to the lemon juicer. These children learned a label and extended the bounds of the object category only when supplied with perceptual support. This finding also alerts us to the conditions under which 12-month-olds will extend an object label. In the perceptual-extension experiment described above, children were asked to extend a label after seeing a single exemplar of that object category. In this experiment, infants were exposed to three members of the category before they were asked to extend the label. This seemingly insignificant change in the experimental procedure had dramatic effects. When given just three instances of a category, 12-month-old infants readily extended to perceptually similar objects. This result is consistent with others in the literature (Balaban and Waxman 1997).

The results from the studies on extendibility suggest that infants are conservative word learners who start only with the principle of reference and who do not readily extend a word to a category of objects, actions, or events. Word extension does not come for free but may, as Golinkoff, Mervis, and Hirsh-Pasek (1994) and Smith (2000) argue, come about only through experience. By the beginning of the second year of life, however, children will extend words to new exemplars that share perceptual characteristics. These same children, though, will not let a social mentor guide their word extension. Indeed, it is not until 19 months of age, when most children are on the verge of the naming explosion, that infants will adopt the speaker's point of view and extend a category label to an object that does not share perceptual features with the dominant category members. It is interesting that the recruitment of social information into word learning appears at the same time for both the principles of reference and extendibility. Again, the mapping between word and referent is explained better by the associationive theory at the outset of language development and by the social-pragmatic theory by the middle of the second year of life.

The patterns that emerge in the studies of reference and extendibility allow us to evaluate the original hypotheses posed by the emergentist coalition model. They also force us to reevaluate whether the different theories of word learning really offer mutually exclusive explanations of development.

6.6 Evaluating the Hypotheses

Earlier we presented three tenets of the emergentist coalition model. After our review of some of the recent research, we are now in a position to evaluate these tenets, which are, after all, hypotheses about word learning.

6.6.1 Hypothesis 1

Is there evidence that children utilize multiple cues—both perceptual and social—in word learning? There is evidence from both the reference and the extendibility studies that very young word learners are using multiple cues to map words onto referents. In the study of word reference, for example, 12-month-olds, with an immature principle of reference, were already sensitive to both perceptual and social cues in the input. Though they were more heavily influenced by perceptual than social cues, they nonetheless did not mismap a word onto the more interesting object when social cues indicated that the boring toy was being labeled. Unlike their younger counterparts, 12-month-olds were aware of the social information even when they did not know how to recruit this information to attach a word to when the referent did not interest them.

Similarly, in the studies of social extension, the 12-month-olds could not rely on social cues for word learning in the absence of perceptual information. With some perceptual and social support, however, they could learn that a label could attach to a category member that shared only a salient part of the original object.

6.6.2 Hypothesis 2

Do the weightings of the cues shift over time? The experiments described above already give us preliminary answers to this question. For 12-month-olds, perceptual salience is dominant relative to social cues like eye gaze. For 19-month-olds, perceptual salience still predominates, but social cues have gained some prominence. Finally, for the sophisticated 24-month-olds, social information can be used to override attentional cues for word learning. This pattern was apparent in both the reference and the extendibility studies. Even when infants were sensitive to social information in our tasks, they failed to recruit this information for the purposes of word learning. This suggests that while the cues might be present for children, there is a differential reliance on these cues throughout the course of development.

6.6.3 Hypothesis 3

Does the child move from an immature to a mature principle of reference? The fact that older children use social cues to connect words with referents, and to extend the labels for words, suggests that these children are approaching word learning in a fundamentally different way. Young children are sensitive to a coalition of cues for word learning. Yet they may not know which of the many cues in the coalition can be relied on. They appear not to realize that social cues are among the most reliable for word learning. The consequence of being unsure about the merit of different cues is that the learner may at first be conservative and require converging data to form word-referent connections. Children with an immature principle of reference might need to hear a novel word more times and might need to have multiple, overlapping cues for word-referent mapping than children with a mature principle of reference (Hollich, Hirsh-Pasek, and Golinkoff 2000). We discovered that when the child is stimulated by being presented with many, converging cues, the supports are sufficiently strong to allow word learning to occur.

Similarly, children with an immature principle of extendibility need to have converging data to extend a label to a like referent. In the absence of perceptual *and* social support, younger infants—12-month-olds—refused to extend a label to a category member that did not closely resemble the original category items. Indeed, the youngest children—10-month-olds—maintained a narrow, proper-noun assumption even when presented with perceptually equivalent items. Perhaps infant conservatism can help to explain why word learning takes place so slowly in the real world outside of the laboratory. Young children may require more support to yoke a word to its referent than they generally receive. Once they are able to weight the cues more veridically, they will require less support for word learning to occur.

Even this cursory glance at the data suggests that children with an immature principle of reference differ significantly from those with a mature principle of reference. First, these children rely more heavily on their own perspective on the word-learning situation than on the speaker's perspective. They link words to referents by attending primarily to what they find interesting in the environment (perceptual salience) rather than to what the speaker is indicating. Once in possession of a more mature principle of reference, children will be able to shift their perspective to that of the speaker. When that happens, we see a fundamentally different word learner, able to serve as a socially sophisticated apprentice to the expert word learners around them. Second, immature word learners need far more support for word learning than mature word learners do. Unless there are numerous cues in alignment and frequent label exposure, they will not learn new words.

There are many more studies that reinforce this shift from immature to mature learner—from more of a salience-driven learning mechanism to a socially informed mechanism (see Hollich, Hirsh-Pasek, and Golinkoff 2000). Indeed, a computer simulation study (Hollich 1999) demonstrates clearly that neither associationist, nor social-pragmatic, nor constraints theories can alone explain the course of word learning. Although all three separate simulations provided a solution for how children might learn words, only the simulation that embraced the full complexity of word learning by offering multiple cues in interaction over time best fit the behavioral data.

These data suggest that a hybrid model can generate hypotheses about how different theories can be integrated into a unified theory of developmental change. With sensitive methods, a hybrid theory is empirically testable. One could argue, however, that even this description of development offers just a series of snapshots rather than a theory of developmental change. Creating a portrait of the immature and mature word learner is only the beginning of the story. The question that developmentalists must ask is *what motivates change?* What mechanisms, for example, cause the 12-month-old to abandon a focus on less reliable cues (such as perceptual salience) in favor of a focus on more reliable cues (such as social eye gaze)? Why does the child shift from needing multiple overlapping cues for word learning to single subtle social cues such as eye gaze? Such questions can only be addressed with hybrid theories and with methods like the IIPLP that permit the experimenter to focus on the interaction of multiple cues. Although we are just at the beginning of this enterprise, answers are probably more likely to emanate from complex, multi-faceted theories than from theories that emphasize single mechanisms. These theories offer the opportunity to ask not just *whether* children advance from one descriptive state to another but *how* they do so.

6.7 Where Does the Emergentist Coalition Model Leave Us: Theoretical Implications

For years scientists have been trying to find the crucial element in word-learning theory—endorsing one model of explanation over the others. Adopting one theory over the others, however, leaves us with theories that do part but not all of the job of accounting for word learning. Under the emergentist coalition model, the best features of these theories are combined, in a way very different from the either-or theories they incorporate. This new theoretical perspective explicitly recognizes that word learning is caused by multiple cues from the outset; single-factor models cannot do the job.

The implication of the case we have made is that the most parsimonious description will not come in the form of either-or theories that promote a single mechanism. This necessitates not only a change in our philosophy of doing research, but also a commitment to developing new methods like the IIPLP that allow for the simultaneous manipulation of multiple cues and a serious emphasis on the study of change. What have appeared to be divergent theories in our field might be different parts of the same proverbial blind man's elephant.

Though this paper concentrates on word learning, it could stand as a proxy for discussions ensuing in many domains within developmental psychology. From face perception (Nelson 1999), to the perception of number (Gelman and Williams 1998), to the perception of space (Newcombe and Huttenlocher 2000), competing theories seem always to turn on the nature-nurture dichotomy. Yet as Elman et al. (1996) and Nelson (1999) have pointed out, the brain is sculpted by experience and the emphasis on nature versus nurture is misplaced. A new concept is needed to spur the field into abandoning either-or theories and adopting theories that recognize that we live in a multivariate world where effects are caused by multiple factors. The concept of *emergentism*, with its emphasis on specifying "in mechanistic terms the interactions between biological and environmental processes" (MacWhinney 1999, x), may be the necessary antidote to this age-old and unproductive dichotomy. Emergentism seeks to account for the appearance of behaviors from the interaction of known processes without stipulating hard-wired neural circuitry.

Our version of emergentism has much in common with traditional interactionist accounts like that of Piaget (1952). However, it goes beyond interactionism since it explicitly identifies the cues that comprise the coalition influencing the emergence of new behavior and shows how reliance on those cues changes over developmental time. With its emphasis on how the organism essentially creates its own development, our version of emergentism also has much in common with dynamic systems theory (Thelen and Smith 1994). Dynamic systems theory, however, allows the organism to enter in an unbiased manner. Give the varied inputs available in the world, we join others in believing that some constraints or biases (whatever their source) are required to get developmental processes started (Gelman and Williams 1998).

What has prevented the field from focusing on the impact of multiple inputs on development in the human organism? The zeitgeist in the philosophy of science may be at fault. Human behavior is so variable and complex that to get some purchase on it we have pared down psychological problems to their bare bones. Eager for experimental control in the laboratory, we endorse theories that allow us to cleanly manipulate at most one or two factors. Despite the fact that statistical techniques such as the analysis of variance and hierarchical multiple regression allow for the measurement of interactions, our models are often fundamentally noninteractive and nondevelopmental. Truly interactive theories will isolate some description of starting points within a domain and will then ask how the behavior changes over time (Karmiloff-Smith 1992). As in the case of word learning, competing theories may not be mutually exclusive but rather are *snapshots of behavior at different points along a developmental trajectory*. Metaphorically, we must switch to a wide-angle lens attached to a movie camera to assemble the snapshots into a developmental story that is dynamic and incorporates the multiple influences that actually impinge on human organisms. It is now time to abandon traditional views of parsimony and to generate more realistic multifactor models of human development.

In sum, as hybrid, emergentist theories become more prevalent it will be clear that nativism and environmentalism can live in peaceful coexistence (Gelman and Williams 1998; Newcombe and Huttenlocher 2000). The emergentist coalition model offers only one possible picture of what this coexistence might look like. Selective attention to multiple inputs preserves a place for constraints or principles models while supporting development and change in those principles over time. Principles have some foundation at the outset but are not fully formed. They are emergent. In this emergent quality lies the potential for looking at and understanding change. If we are to understand development we must not look for a simplistic explanation. Rather, we must appreciate that the answers to our questions will come from intricate theories of the ways children process varied inputs and of the interactions among these inputs across the developmental span. We must take seriously the complexity of the factors that impact on the human organism. And we must teach the next generation of developmental psychologists to do more than pay lip service to this notion. As MacWhinney (1999, x) writes, "Students are often taught that the opposition between nativism and empiricism is the fundamental issue in developmental psychology. What they really end up learning, however, is that everything in human development depends on the interaction between nature and nurture. Unfortunately, students are given few conceptual tools to understand how this interaction occurs."

Acknowledgments

Support for the preparation of this chapter came from grants to the first two authors from the National Science Foundation (NSF grant 9601306; NSF grant 991-0842) and from a grant by the National Institute of Child Health and Human Development to the first author (grant HD25455-07).

References

Akhtar, N., and Tomasello, M. 1996. Twenty-four-month-old children learn words for absent objects and actions. *British Journal of Developmental Psychology, 14,* 79–93.

Akhtar, N., and Tomasello, M. 2000. The social nature of words and word learning. In R. M. Golinkoff, K. Hirsh-Pasek, L. Bloom, L. Smith, A. Woodward, N. Akhtar, M. Tomasello, and G. Hollich, eds., *Becoming a word learner: A debate on lexical acquisition.* New York: Oxford University Press.

Balaban, M. T., and Waxman, S. R. 1997. Do words facilitate object categorization in 9-month-old infants? *Journal of Experimental Child Psychology, 64,* 3–27.

Baldwin, D. A. 1991. Infants' contribution to the achievement of joint reference. *Child Development, 62,* 875–890.

Baldwin, D. A. 1993. Infants' ability to consult the speaker for clues to word reference. *Journal of Child Language, 20,* 394–419.

Baldwin, D. A., Markman, E. M., Bill, B., Desjardins, N., Irwin, J. M., and Tidball, G. 1996. Infants' reliance on a social criterion for establishing word-object relations. *Child Development, 67,* 3135–3153.

Baldwin, D. A., and Tomasello, M. 1999. Word learning: A window on early pragmatic understanding. In E. V. Clark, ed., *Proceedings of the Stanford Child Language Research Forum,* 3–23. Stanford, CA: Center for the Study of Language and Information.

Bloom, L. 1993. *The transition from infancy to language: Acquiring the power of expression.* New York: Cambridge University Press.

Bloom, L. 2000. The intentionality model of word learning: How to learn a word, any word. In R. M. Golinkoff, K. Hirsh-Pasek, L. Bloom, L. Smith, A. Woodward, N. Akhtar, M. Tomasello, and G. Hollich, eds., *Becoming a word learner: A debate on lexical acquisition,* 19–50. New York: Oxford University Press.

Bloom, L., and Lahey, M. 1978. *Language development and language disorders.* New York: Wiley.

Bloom, P. 2000. *How children learn the meaning of words.* Cambridge, MA: MIT Press.

Carey, S., and Bartlett, E. 1978. Acquiring a single new word. *Proceedings of the Stanford Child Language Conference, 15,* 17–29.

Carpenter, M., Nagell, K., and Tomasello, M. 1998. Social cognition, joint attention, and communicative competence from 9 to 15 months of age. *Monographs of the Society for Research in Child Development, 63*(4).

Clark, E. V. 1983. Meanings and concepts. In J. H. Flavell and E. M. Markman, eds., *Handbook of child psychology, Vol. 3: Cognitive development,* 787–840. New York: Wiley.

Elman, J. L., Bates, E. A., Johnson, M., Karmiloff-Smith, A., Parisi, D., and Plunkett, K. 1996. *Rethinking innateness: A connectionist perspective on development.* Cambridge, MA: MIT Press.

Evey, J. A., and Merriman, W. E. 1998. The prevalence and the weakness of an early naming mapping preference. *Journal of Child Language*, 25, 121–148.

Fagan, J. 1971. Infant recognition memory for a series of visual stimuli. *Journal of Experimental Child Psychology*, 11, 244–250.

Fagan, J., Singer, L., Montie, J., and Shepard, P. 1986. Selective screening device for the early detection of normal or delayed cognitive development in infants at risk for later mental retardation. *Pediatrics*, 78, 1021–1026.

Gelman, R., and Greeno, J. G. 1989. On the nature of competence: Principles for understanding in a domain. In L. B. Resnick, ed., *Knowing and learning: Essays in honor of Robert Glaser*, 125–186. Hillsdale, NJ: Erlbaum.

Gelman, R., and Williams, E. M. 1998. Enabling constraints for cognitive development and learning: Domain specificity and epigenesis. In W. Damon, series ed., and D. K. Kuhn and R. S. Siegler, vol. eds., *Handbook of child psychology, Vol. 2: Cognition, perception, and language*, 5th ed., 575–630. New York: Wiley.

Goldfield, B. A., and Reznick, S. 1990. Early lexical acquisition: Rate, content, and the vocabulary spurt. *Journal of Child Language*, 17, 171–183.

Golinkoff, R. M., Hirsh-Pasek, K., Bailey, L., and Wenger, N. 1992. Young children and adults use lexical principles to learn new nouns. *Developmental Psychology*, 28, 99–108.

Golinkoff, R. M., Hirsh-Pasek, K., Bloom, L., Smith, L., Woodward, A., Akhtar, N., Tomasello, M., and Hollich, G. 2000. *Becoming a word learner: A debate on lexical acquisition*. New York: Oxford University Press.

Golinkoff, R. M., Hirsh-Pasek, K., Cauley, K. M., and Gordon, L. 1987. The eyes have it: Lexical and syntactic comprehension in a new paradigm. *Journal of Child Language*, 14, 23–45.

Golinkoff, R. M., Hirsh-Pasek, K., and Hollich, G. 1999. Emergent cues for early word learning. In B. MacWhinney, ed., *The emergence of language*, 305–331. Mahwah, NJ: Erlbaum.

Golinkoff, R. M., Mervis, C., and Hirsh-Pasek, K. 1994. Early object labels: The case for a developmental lexical principles framework. *Journal of Child Language*, 21, 125–155.

Hall, D. G. 1991. Acquiring proper names for familiar and unfamiliar animate objects: Two-year-olds' word learning biases. *Child Development*, 62, 1442–1454.

Hall, D. G., Quantz, D. H., and Persoage, K. A. 2000. Preschoolers' use of form class cues in word learning. *Developmental Psychology*, 36, 449–462.

Hall, D. G., and Waxman, S. R. 1993. Assumptions about word learning. *Child Development*, 64, 1550.

Hennon, E. A., Hirsh-Pasek, K., Golinkoff, R. M., Rocroi, C. S., Arnold, K., Maguire, M., Baker, S., and Driscoll, K. 2000. From proper nouns to categories: Infants learn how words work. Paper presented at the International Conference on Infant Studies, Brighton, England.

Hennon, E. A., Rocroi, C., Chung, H., Hollick, G., Driscoll, K., Hirsh-Pasek, K., and Golinkoff, R. M. 1999. Testing the principle of extendibility: Are new words learned as proper nouns or category labels? Paper presented at a meeting of the Society for Research in Child Development, Alberquque, NM.

Hirsh-Pasek, K., and Golinkoff, R. M. 1996. *The origins of grammar: Evidence from early language comprehension.* Cambridge, MA: MIT Press.

Hirsh-Pasek, K., Golinkoff, R. M., and Hollich, G. 2000. An emergentist coalition model for word learning: Mapping words to objects is a product of the interaction of multiple cues. In R. M. Golinkoff, K. Hirsh-Pasek, L. Bloom, L. Smith, A. Woodward, N. Akhtar, M. Tomasello, and G. Hollich, eds., *Becoming a word learner: A debate on lexical acquisition,* 136–164. New York: Oxford University Press.

Hollich, G. 1999. *Mechanisms of word learning: A computational model.* Unpublished doctoral dissertation, Temple University, Philadelphia.

Hollich, G., Hirsh-Pasek, K., and Golinkoff, R. M. 1998. Introducing the 3-D intermodal preferential looking paradigm: A new method to answer an age-old question. In C. Rovee-Collier, ed., *Advances in infancy research,* vol. 12, 355–373. Norwood, NJ: Ablex.

Hollich, G., Hirsh-Pasek, K., and Golinkoff, R. M. 2000. Breaking the language barrier: An emergentist coalition model for the origins of word learning. *Monographs of the Society for Research in Child Development, 65*(3) (serial no. 262).

Jaswal, V. K., and Markman, E. M. 2001. Learning proper and common names in inferential versus ostensive context. *Child Development, 72,* 768–786.

Karmiloff-Smith, A. 1992. *Beyond modularity: A developmental perspective on cognitive science.* Cambridge, MA: MIT Press.

Keil, F. C. 1989. *Concepts, kinds, and cognitive development.* Cambridge, MA: MIT Press.

Locke, J. [1690] 1964. *An essay concerning human understanding.* Cleveland, OH: Meridian Books.

MacWhinney, B. 1999. *The emergence of language.* Mahwah, NJ: Erlbaum.

Mandler, J., and McDonough, L. 1996. Drinking and driving don't mix: Inductive generalization in infancy. *Cognition, 59,* 307–335.

Markman, E. M. 1989. *Categorization and naming in children: Problems of induction.* Cambridge, MA: MIT Press.

Markman, E. M., and Hutchinson, J. E. 1984. Children's sensitivity to constraints on word meaning: Taxonomic versus thematic relations. *Cognitive Psychology, 16,* 1–27.

Mervis, C. B., and Bertrand, J. 1994. Acquisition of the novel name–nameless category (N3C) principle. *Child Development, 65,* 1646–1663.

Mervis, C. B., Golinkoff, R. M., and Bertrand, J. 1994. Two-year-olds readily learn multiple labels for the same basic level category. *Child Development, 65,* 971–991.

Nelson, K. 1988. Constraints on word learning? *Cognitive Development, 3,* 221–246.

Nelson, K. 1996. *Language in cognitive development.* New York: Cambridge University Press.

Nelson, C. 1999. Neural plasticity and human development. *Current Directions in Psychological Science, 8,* 42–46.

Newcombe, N. S., and Huttenlocher, J. 2000. *Making space: The development of spatial representation and reasoning.* Cambridge, MA: MIT Press.

Piaget, J. 1952. *The origins of intelligence in children.* New York: International University Press.

Pinker, S. 1994. *The language instinct: How the mind creates language.* New York: William Morrow.

Plunkett, K. 1997. Theories of early language acquisition. *Trends in Cognitive Sciences, 1,* 146–153.

Quine, W. V. O. 1960. *Word and object.* Cambridge, England: Cambridge University Press.

Samuelson, L. K., and Smith, L. B. 1998. Memory and attention make smart word learning: An alternative account of Akhtar, Carpenter, and Tomasello. *Child Development, 69,* 94–104.

Smith, L. B. 1995. Self-organizing processes in learning to learn words: Development is not induction. In C. A. Nelson, ed., *Basic and applied perspectives on learning, cognition, and development: The Minnesota Symposia on Child Psychology,* vol. 28, 1–32. Mahwah, NJ: Erlbaum.

Smith, L. B. 1999. Children's noun learning: How general learning processes make specialized learning mechanisms. In B. MacWhinney, ed., *The emergence of language,* 227–305. Mahwah, NJ: Erlbaum.

Smith, L. B. 2000. Learning how to learn words: An associative crane. In R. M. Golinkoff, K. Hirsh-Pasek, L. Bloom, L. Smith, A. Woodward, N. Akhtar, M. Tomasello, and G. Hollich, eds., *Becoming a word learner: A debate on lexical acquisition,* 51–80. New York: Oxford University Press.

Spelke, E. S. 1990. Principles of object perception. *Cognitive Science, 14,* 29–56.

Thelen, E., and Smith, L. 1994. *A dynamic systems approach to the development of cognition and action.* Cambridge, MA: MIT Press.

Tomasello, M., and Barton, M. 1994. Learning words in non-ostensive context. *Developmental Psychology, 30,* 639–650.

Tomasello, M., Strosberg, R., and Akhtar, N. 1996. Eighteen-month-old children learn words in non-ostensive contexts. *Journal of Child Language, 23,* 157–176.

Waxman, S. R., and Kosowski, T. D. 1990. Nouns mark category relations: Toddlers' and preschoolers' word-learning biases. *Child Development, 61,* 1461–1473.

Waxman, S. R., and Markow, D. B. 1995. Words as invitations to form categories: Evidence from 12- to 13-month-old infants. *Cognitive Psychology, 29,* 257–302.

7

Myths of Word Learning

Paul Bloom

If you attend a class on language acquisition, or read any good introductory chapter on the subject, you are likely to learn the following facts about word learning. Children's first words are odd; they have funny meanings that violate certain semantic principles that hold for adult language and are learned in a slow and haphazard way. Then, at about 16 months, or after learning about fifty words, there is a sudden acceleration in the rate of word learning—a word spurt or vocabulary explosion. From this point on, children learn words at the rate of five, ten, or even fifteen new words a day.

I will suggest here that none of these claims are true. They are myths of word learning. There is no reason to believe that children's first words are learned and understood in an immature fashion— and there is considerable evidence to the contrary. There is no such thing as a word spurt, and 2-year-olds are not learning anywhere near five words per day.

To call these notions "myths" is not to say that they are silly or obviously wrong, and it certainly is not to attribute sloppiness on the part of researchers who accept them. What it does imply is that these claims about word learning exist, not because of any empirical support they have, but because they possess certain properties that hold for myths in general—they have some foundation in truth, they make for a good story, and they convey a message we want to hear (Brunvand 1981; Campbell 1972; Shermer 2000). I will critically explore each of these myths of word learning (see also Bloom 2000), suggest some reasons for their popularity, and conclude with an alternative perspective on the nature of early word learning.

7.1 Myth 1: Children's First Words Are Weird

It is often claimed that children's first words are understood and learned differently from the words that they know later. This claim of discontinuity is typically rooted in a learning or constructivist theory—children need to gradually learn, through experience, the nature of words (e.g., Nelson 1988). But it is equally consistent with a nativist view in which knowledge of language emerges through neural maturation. Chomsky (1975), for instance, suggests that "it is possible that at an early stage there is use of language-like expressions, but outside the framework imposed ... by the faculty of language—much as a dog can be trained to respond to certain commands, though we would not conclude, from this, that it is using language."

The sole source of evidence for the weird-first-words claim is anecdotal, based on observations of how children use words. And indeed, there is no shortage of reports of such odd usage. Consider the following examples:

• The word *car* used only when cars move on the street below the living-room window (L. Bloom 1973)

• The word *hot* used to describe an oven (Macnamara 1972)

• The word *flying* used to describe birds (Dromi 1987)

• The word *pee-pee* used to describe a picture of an ice-cream cone (Bloom 2000)

• The word *hat* used to describe a green pepper placed on the child's head (Bloom 2000)

• The word *moon* used to talk about a half grapefruit, the dial of a dishwasher, hangnail, and other circular entities (Bowerman 1978)

• The word *apple* used to describe a doorknob (Clark 1973)

• The word *sock* used to describe a shoe (Dromi 1987)

These are the sorts of errors typically cited, and their veracity is not in question. But what do they really tell us?

Imagine for a moment that you were to move to a foreign country, and were to have the good fortune to live with a family that includes a psychologist observing your speech habits. Your mental powers are entirely mature, but you do not know the language and you are unfamiliar with many of the objects around you.

As you begin to use words, the psychologist is likely to observe *all* of the patterns found above. You might use a word only in a certain specific context—such as *car* only when you are looking out a window—because that is the only context that inspires you to use the word. Since the oven is hot and the bird is flying, you may well point to the oven and describe it as "hot," and to the bird and describe it as "flying." (You would be particularly prone to do so if you never learned, or had forgotten, the words for oven and bird.) In a cheerful mood, hoping to impress your hosts with both your language skills and your powers of observation, you might observe that a picture of an ice-cream cone resembles a penis. What you would like to say is "Isn't it a hoot that this depiction of an ice-cream cone resembles a penis? Someone should write a nasty letter to the publisher." But since you know only a few words, you have no recourse other than to point and say *pee-pee*. For similar reasons, you use *moon* and *apple* to point out that your hangnail resembles the moon and the doorknob looks much like an apple. To amuse this family that has been so kind to you, you place a green pepper on your head and call it a *hat*. Finally, one day you wish for someone to hand you a shoe, but since you never learned the word *shoe, or* learned it and forgot it, *or* could not make sense of the puzzling footwear that these people wear, you point and say *sock*.

Imagine if you were to discover later that, on the basis of your speech patterns, the psychologist determined that you were learning words in an atypical way, without benefit of semantic constraint. Wouldn't this be unfair?

This is not a complaint about the use of anecdotal evidence to constrain theories of language acquisition. Someone once admonished, "The plural of anecdote is not data," but this seems unreasonably harsh. Properly used, anecdotes can be of considerable relevance to scientific theory, and particularly to developmental psychology. Indeed, the plural of anecdote is often a book chapter. The real worry is over the proper interpretation of this anecdotal evidence. By definition, a pattern of word usage only counts as immature if it is a different pattern of word usage than you would get from an older child or adult in the same situation. But this comparison is never done, and the sorts of examples summarized above provide not even a hint that such a difference exists.

The methodological moral here is clear enough—what one needs to do, at the very least, is compare the sorts of words spoken by young children who are picking up their first language with the sorts of words spoken by adults who are learning a second language. This might seem impractical, but one does not need to actually observe this sort of adult learning—one can mimic it in a lab, by teaching adults an artificial language, as done by Gillette et al. (1999). In fact, even without this sort of empirical contrast, one could imagine all sorts of anecdotes that really would suggest a difference between how young children learn words and how everyone else learns words. For instance, young children might generalize object names on the basis of their color, instead of overall shape and function, and so they might use *cup* to refer to all the things that are the same color of a given cup. Or they might link words to the specific people who use them, so that when Mommy says *milk* it means one thing and when Daddy says *milk* it means another. Or they might treat common nouns as picking out specific individuals, and only use *cat* to refer to their own cat. And so on. These are the sorts of patterns of language use that do not occur with older children and adults learning a second language. But they do not occur in the speech of younger children either.

Note also that when careful empirical studies are done, looking at the speech of many children, the conclusion is that early words are no different in semantic type than later words (Huttenlocher and Smiley 1987; Rescorla 1980). It is also revealing that when Nelson (1973) did her classic study of eighteen children's first fifty words, she observed that most of them were prone to point to things and ask their names, by saying something like "Wha?" or "Eh?". This suggests that they have some appreciation that words can refer to kinds of objects. Going back to Chomsky's suggestion, it certainly is not something that dogs do.

Finally, putting aside the question of how young children *understand* words, what about their ability to *learn* words? It is clear that when children start off learning language, they acquire words at a slower rate than children who already know many words. But to anticipate some of the points that will be raised below in the discussion of the word spurt, this need not be a difference in kind; it could simply be a difference in degree.

Such a difference in degree could have several sources. It might reflect the development of memory capacity. It could reflect different conceptual resources; babies learn fewer words than older children because they have a more limited conceptual structure for words to map onto. Or they might be less skilled at the phonological task of distinguishing similar-sounding words. The increase in the rate of word learning might also reflect differences in "theory of mind" capacities, corresponding to an increasing ability to discern the intentions of adults who use words. Any combinations of these factors might explain the difference in rate of learning (see Bloom 2000 for a review).

What we do know is that if you make the task easy enough, even very young children learn words quite well. In one study, 13-month-olds were told the name of a novel object several times during a five-minute session ("This is a tukey. See, it's a tukey ..."); another object was present and commented on several times, but not named ("Look at this one ..."). Even after a 24-hour delay, these children did better than chance when shown the two objects and asked to point to "the tukey" (Woodward, Markman, and Fitzsimmons 1994; see also Oviatt 1980). This poses a serious problem for any theory positing a sharp discontinuity.

7.2 Myth 2: There Is a Word Spurt, or Vocabulary Explosion

It is often said that word learning starts slowly but then, at about 16 months of age, or when a child learns about fifty words, things really start to happen. Word learning begins in earnest. This is variously called a *word burst, word spurt, vocabulary burst, naming explosion, word explosion*, and so on. There are dozens of studies that analyze children's speech, plot their vocabulary sizes at different ages, and identify the point at which the spurt takes place. Then they ask the theoretical question of what happens in the mind of the child to cause this spurt to occur. There are several possibilities. It might be the insight that language is symbolic (sometimes known as the *naming insight*) (Dore 1978; McShane 1979), the ability to categorize in a mature fashion (Gopnik and Meltzoff 1986), the onset of special word-learning constraints (Behrend 1990), or the result of the nonlinear dynamics of a connectionist learning algorithm (Plunkett et al. 1992).

But does a word spurt even exist? This might seem like an odd question. After all, I just mentioned all of the studies that *show* it does, studies that identify, for various children, the point at which the word spurt happens. So how can anyone doubt its existence?

The concern exists because these studies use an odd definition of *word spurt*. They count the child as achieving a word spurt when he or she starts to learn words at a certain rate, regardless of how rapidly the child was learning words before reaching this point. For instance, the criteria for a "word spurt" include ten or more new object names in a 3-week period (Gopnik and Meltzoff 1986); twelve or more new words in a 3-week period (Lifter and Bloom 1989); ten or more words in a 2-and-a-half-week period (Goldfield and Reznick 1990); ten or more words in a 2-week period, at least five of which are object names (Mervis and Bertrand 1995); or two new words in 2-and-a-half-week period, taken from a list of words expected to be difficult (Reznick and Goldfield 1992).

These criteria do not correspond to any *change* in rate; they correspond instead to the *attainment* of a certain rate. Because of this, they do not necessarily reflect dramatic changes in the course of word learning, and have little to do with spurts, bursts, or explosions in any normal use of the expressions. For instance, a child who learns twelve words in 3 weeks is counted as having a "word spurt" by the Lifter and Bloom 1989 criteria even if she had learned eleven words in the previous 3-week period, and ten words in the 3 weeks before that. Indeed, by these criteria, the existence of a "spurt" is a mathematical necessity. Since 17-year-olds know roughly 60,000 words (see below for discussion), then, at some point in development, they need to learn seventy words a week, which means that they must, at some point, start to learn words at the rate of over twelve in a 3-week period.

To see why this matters, consider the following example, from Bloom 2000, 41:

If Joe has eaten 40 french fries in 10 minutes, there has to be some period of time in which he eats french fries at the rate of more than 2.5 per minute. But this does not entail a "starch spurt" or "french fry explosion". One *might* occur; Joe might nibble at his fries at a leisurely rate for the first nine minutes and thirty seconds, and then gobble the rest down in the remaining half-minute. But it is also possible that Joe could eat his fries at a constant rate. Or he could eat one fry in the first minute, and then slowly speed up his rate of fry eating. There would be no spurt, just a gradual increase. To point to the moment he starts eating fries at the rate of 2.5/minute and say "aha!—that's an eating explosion" is worse than bad terminology, it leads to bad theorizing, since it gives the false impression that something special is happening at this point, something that has to be explained.

Going back to words, focusing on the point at which children learn twelve words in 3 weeks (for instance) is only interesting if this reflects a sharp increase in rate from previous word learning. If it does not, then this choice is arbitrary, and there is no rationale for trying to "explain" the cause of this point in development. One might just as well struggle to explain what happens at the point when children learn 3 words in 12 weeks, or 100 words in 3 weeks, or 45 words in 7 weeks (at least 16 of which must be verbs). It is a meaningless enterprise.

But maybe something does happen at the point of learning 12 words in 3 weeks. Perhaps this rate of word learning always coincides with a dramatic shift in development. The assumption that this is true is surely why this sort of criterion is used in the first place. If so, then this notion of a word spurt would be justified, silencing skeptics such as Bates and Carvenale (1993), Bloom (2000), and Elman et al. (1996), who suggest that there is a roughly linear increase in rate: children start learning words slowly and then gradually learn them faster and faster.

Only recently has there been data that bear on this question. Ganger and Brent (2001) analyzed the vocabulary development of several children, plotting their rate of word learning as a function of their vocabulary size. They modeled the rate with a logistic curve, and tested to see if there would be an "inflection point" at any point between thirty and sixty words—the period at which researchers claim that the spurt typically occurs. Such an inflection point would correspond to a sudden increase in the rate of word learning. Ganger and Brent also tried to model the data with a quadratic model (which includes a linear model) that does not have an inflection point. If such a model works better than the logistic model, it would suggest that the child did not have a word spurt.

They first looked at nineteen children from a large-scale study of language development in twins. (Only one child from a twin pair was sampled.) They found that five of these children had an inflection point between thirty and sixty words, and that their vocabulary development was better modeled with the logistic model than with the quadratic model. The remaining fourteen children showed no inflection point during that period; to put it differently, nothing interesting happened to their rate of word learning between thirty and sixty words.

Maybe twins are atypical. Ganger and Brent went on to analyze the published data from one of the major studies in this domain—Goldfield and Reznick 1990. The data from seventeen out of the eighteen children could be extracted from the graphs, and Ganger and Brent found that only three of these children had a word spurt in any real sense of the term—only three of the children's vocabulary rates were best modeled by logistic functions with inflection points between thirty and sixty words.

In sum, eight of the thirty-six children showed signs of a vocabulary spurt, and Ganger and Brent conclude with the following rhetorical question: "If less than a quarter of children have a spurt, do we really want to posit a substantial cognitive change, like the naming insight, to account for it?" Actually, if anything, they are being overly generous. To conclude that eight out of thirty-six children actually did go through a word spurt, one would need to do some sort of statistical analysis to determine whether the logistic patterns of these eight children may have occurred due to chance. (I am not being critical of Ganger and Brent for not doing such an analysis, because it is devilishly hard to figure out how to do so.)

Note also that when we plot changes in children's vocabulary size, we do so in a very indirect manner. We draw our graphs based on what children *say*, which is a quite imperfect measure of what they *know*. So suppose you find a sudden increase in the number of different words spoken by a given child once she has hit the fifty-word mark. This could mean that she has suddenly become better at word learning and had a word spurt. But it could also reflect a change in how talkative she is. After all, the likelihood of any given word being spoken increases as a function of the number of words that the person says. Suppose I want to estimate your vocabulary size, and had to do so by recording all the different words you used in conversation. The more you speak, the more words I am likely to find, up until the point at which you have exhausted your vocabulary.

This confound between number of words spoken and estimated vocabulary size might seem obvious, but it has some nontrivial implications. For instance, some investigators have found dips in the rate of vocabulary growth, points at which somewhat older children start learning words at a slower rate (Dromi 1987). These dips are sometimes explained as the result of children shifting resources away from word learning in order to learn syntax (van Geert 1991), but there is a simpler account. As children's vocabularies grow, any single new word is less likely to be uttered, and so, unless one moves to a different way of estimating vocabulary size, such as a comprehension measure, there will be some point at which it would appear as if they are learning words at a slower rate. Suppose two children learn 5 new words a week, but one of them starts with 20 words and the other starts with 200 words. A jump from 20 to 25 words is striking, and the investigator will observe a clear increase in vocabulary size, while a jump from 200 to 205 words is harder to notice and might look like no increase at all.

Is there any reason to reject the null hypothesis that there is no interesting change in the rate of word learning through the course of language development? Yes—but it does not come from the study of young children. Most of the words high school graduates know are not picked up through conversation; instead they are learned through reading (Sternberg 1987). By one estimate, even students who read relatively little will be exposed to about 10,000 words a year that they do not know (Nagy and Herman 1987). This suggests that there might be a spurt in the rate at which children acquire words, not when they are toddlers, but when they are in school, learning how to read.

7.3   Myth 3: Young Children Learn Ten New Words a Day

Estimates of adult vocabulary size used to be low. The linguist Max Müller suggested that highly educated people use up to 4,000 words, while other adults know about 300 words. One respected intellectual claimed that the vocabulary of peasants does not exceed 100 words; they make do with such a small number because "the same word was made to serve a multitude of purposes, and the same coarse expletives recurred with a horrible frequency in the place of every single part of speech" (as quoted by Aitchison 1994, 5). More recently, the writer Georges Simenon said that his writing style was constrained by the fact that the average Frenchman knows fewer than 600 words.

More sophisticated measures give rise to much larger estimates. One commonly accepted estimate is that a high school graduate knows 60,000 words, if one includes proper names and idiomatic expressions (e.g., Miller 1996; Nagy and Herman 1987; Pinker 1994). If we assume that children start learning words on their first birthday, this means that they have learned 60,000 words in 16 years, which equals 3,750 words per year, which equals over 10 words a day.

This is the basis for claims such as the following:

"Then the baby starts acquiring combinations of phonemes, i.e., words, at the rate of about nine new words a day" (from a popular book on language)
"... which works out roughly to nine new words a day from about eighteen months on" (from a classic review in word learning)
"... averages (after age 1) to nearly 5000 words each year, or 13 each day!" (from a best-selling introductory text in psychology)
"Since children start learning words at about their first birthday, this means that they have to learn, on average, ten new words a day, an astonishing feat" (from a 2001 article in a cognitive science journal)

The numbers differ somewhat, but given how rough the estimates of adult vocabulary size are, the lack of consensus as to what counts as a "word" and what counts as "knowing" a word, and the considerable variation of knowledge in the adult population, there is little point quarreling over a precise number (Aitchison 1994; Miller and Wakefield 1993; see Bloom 2000 for review). But what is wrong with all of these claims is the implication—made with various force in the above quotes—that the 9–13 words-per-day fact is true *early in development*, that it is true for "the baby," "from eighteen months on," "after age 1," or after "about their first birthday."

Such a claim would not be misleading if the rate of word learning were constant. If you were told how many heartbeats an average 17-year-old has had, and wanted to figure out how many heartbeats the average child has in his or her third year of life, a reasonable way of doing so would be to take the number and divide by 17. But now imagine being told how many alcoholic beverages an average 17-year-old has consumed. For the sake of illustration, I will make up a number: 160. And now consider the following claims:

"Then the baby starts drinking at the rate of ten alcoholic beverages a year"

"… which works out roughly to ten new alcoholic beverages a year, from eighteen months on"

"… averages (after age 1) to over 10 alcoholic beverages a year, or 1 every 5 weeks!"

"… this means they have to drink, on average, ten alcoholic beverages a year, an astonishing feat"

All of the above claims, like their parallels in the word-learning domain, are, in some strict sense, correct. They are also highly misleading. When you say that *babies start drinking ten beverages a year*, it strongly implies that *babies drink ten beverages a year*, which is surely not true. When the similar claims about word learning are made, their goal is to impress the reader with the astonishing power of young word learners. But if the authors really believe that 2-year-olds learn ten words a day, they are mistaken; if not, they are misleading the reader, intentionally conveying a myth of word learning.

There is only one way to figure out how many words a day children learn in a given year, and this is to look at how many words they learn during that year and to divide by 365. The answer, by the way, is that 1-year-olds learn a new word about every 2 days, and 2-year-olds learn about 2 words a day (see Fenson et al. 1994). These numbers are themselves misleading, since a child who is about to have her second birthday is learning words at a much faster rate than one who just had her first birthday, and a 2-year-old about to turn into a 3-year-old is learning at a much faster rate than one who has just turned 2. But in any case, none of these children are learning even close to ten words a day.

There is a second, subtler, problem with these numerical averages. These calculations assume that learning a word is a sudden, definitive event. It is like a heartbeat, or drinking an alcoholic beverage. And there are cases in which this is clearly true. Do you know the word *uxorious*? It means: to be excessively fond of one's spouse. There, now you know it. Some word learning really does work that way—in seconds, you can learn a new word.

But this is not necessarily how word learning works in general. Consider the following claim:

In the year before her tenure file was due, Jane wrote four empirical papers.

Does this mean that Jane wrote a paper every three months? Perhaps, but there are two problems with such an inference. The first was mentioned earlier—the rate might not be constant. Jane might have dawdled over one paper in the first six months, did the second in the next four months, the third in seven weeks, and hurried through the fourth in the final week. The second problem with this inference is that paper writing is the sort of activity that can be done in parallel. Jane might have spent the first few months writing the introductions for each of her four papers, the next six months on methods and results, and the rest of the year on the discussion, polishing the draft, and agonizing over the appropriate font. Indeed, maybe Jane is *incapable* of writing a paper in three months—she could not do it if her life depended on it. Still, this does not preclude her from writing four papers per year.

Is learning a word like drinking a beer or is it like writing a paper? Is it accurate to view an 8-year-old as learning about 20 new words a day (based on Anglin 1993), or is it better to view an 8-year-old as spending the entire year working out the meanings of 7,300 words? More generally, do children learn 10 words a day from 12 months to 17 years, or do they spend each day learning a tiny bit of each of 60,000 words?

Both extremes are unrealistic. Children plainly do learn at least some words rapidly; they do not need days, weeks, months, or years of cumulative experience to come to know their meanings. But children also learn at least some words in a drawn-out fashion, building up their meanings over the course of years. Verbs such as *pour* and *fill*, for instance, undergo semantic development that lasts until the middle years (Gropen et al. 1991). Certainly this is also the case for abstract words like *game, democracy,* and so on.

In sum, even when one is careful to allow for changes in the rate of word learning, the notion that word learning can be accurately summed up as "*x*-year-olds learn *y* words per day" is overly simple, and provides a false impression of how words are learned.

7.4 Discussion

These myths about word learning exist because they satisfy three general criteria that hold of myths in general.

First, they are rooted in truth. Someone new to the field would have no reason to doubt that 1-year-olds start off with funny non-adult-like words, then go through a dramatic change in their word-learning capacities, at which point they learn ten new words a day. When young children start to use words, they do say funny things, and we are fascinated and amused by these odd usages (consistent with myth 1). Children do start off slowly and then speed up. When one looks at the data, it turns out that the rate of growth is roughly linear, but there is a *perception* of a qualitative shift—from slow word learning to fast word learning.[1] (consistent with myth 2). And once word learning gets going, it does seem to be astonishingly fast—it really *could* be ten words per day (consistent with myth 3).

Second, they tell a good story. The child starts off poorly, undergoes a radical transition, and then comes to possess an astonishing ability. It is straight out of Dickens.

Third, it is a story that is appealing in many ways. Discontinuities of representation and of learning pose interesting research questions; they motivate scientific research programs and can lead to discoveries. And the third myth makes the entire topic of word learning appealing to a broader audience—when one announces that children learn words, on average, at the rate of ten per day, this factoid is rewarded with interest and excitement. It is, after all, quite striking, and adds spice to a colloquium or a grant proposal. If only it were true.

But the story is appealing for a deeper reason as well. Many psychologists endorse the view that word learning stands on its own as a distinct domain. It involves solving a unique induction problem; it has its own biases and constraints, its special learning principles. Word learning is special, either because it is the product of an specialized innate system, or because it become special through repeated practice and increasing understanding. These myths are entirely consistent with such a view.

This chapter has been critical, but I want to conclude on a positive note, by presenting an alternative theory, one I have defended in detail elsewhere (e.g., Bloom 2000, 2001). This is that the ability to learn words is the result of more general aspects of our mental life, including conceptual capacities, theory of mind, and grammatical knowledge. For many, this view is unappealing. It lacks the intellectual audacity of strong nativism, while at the same time missing out on the nerdy appeal of connectionism, and the down-home parsimony of associationism more generally. And it is, in some regards, pessimistic. If it is true that word learning can only be understood in terms of the interaction of more general capacities, it implies that we will only fully understand word learning once we fully understand these other capacities, which in turn implies that a complete theory of word learning will have to wait for a complete theory of psychology in general. This may be a long wait.

There is, however, considerable support for this view. Most of all, there is converging evidence from several sources that certain aspects of word learning once thought to be special to word learning actually apply more generally.

• If a child hears a word such as *koba* used to describe an object, she will remember, a month later, which object was given this name. And if she hears the fact that "this was given to me by my uncle" used to describe an object, she will also remember, a month later, which object has this property (Markson 1999; Markson and Bloom 1997). Fast mapping works for both words and facts.

• When children are given a novel name for an object and asked to extend the name, they tend to generalize on the basis of object kind, often determined on the basis of shape (e.g., Markman and Wachtel 1988; Landau, Smith, and Jones 1988; Waxman and Booth 2000). And when children are shown an object and simply asked to find another one of the same kind, they also tend to generalize on the basis of object kind, often determined on the basis of shape (e.g., Diesendruck 2001; Diesendruck and Bloom 2003). Generalizing on the basis of kind, often determined by shape, is a general cognitive practice, not one limited to words.[2]

• When children see an adult stare at an object and utter its name, they associate the name with that object, even if they themselves were attending to a different object when the word was spoken (Baldwin 1991, 1993). And if children see an adult stare at an object and look disgusted, they associate the negative emotion with that object even if they themselves were looking at a different object when the adult made that expression (Baldwin and Moses 1994). Direction of gaze is a cue that children use when learning many properties of objects, not just their names.

• When children are given a new count noun and have to interpret its meaning, they treat it as an object name, even if this is inconsistent with the grammar of the word (e.g., Macnamara 1972; Markman and Wachtel 1988). And when they are asked to count an array, they tend to count the objects, even if they are explicitly asked to do otherwise (Shipley and Shepperson 1990). The object bias holds for any cognitive process that requires individuation, not just word learning.

• When children are given one word for an object ("This is a koba") and asked about a different word ("Where is the fendle?"), they tend to seek out a second object as a referent for this different word (e.g., Markman and Wachtel 1988). And when given one fact about an object ("This is from my uncle"), and asked which object a different fact applies to ("Where is the one dogs like to play with?"), they tend to seek out a second object as corresponding to that fact (Diesendruck and Markson 2001). The "mutual-exclusivity" bias holds for communicative acts in general, not just for words.

These findings, taken together, support a very different perspective on word learning than the one that motivates—and is motivated by—ideas such as weird first words, a word spurt, and ten new words a day. The view above is not actually inconsistent with these myths. If a word spurt were to exist, for example, the above perspective might explain it as the result of a sudden increase in theory-of-mind capacities, conceptual capacities, or syntactic sensitivity. But it does not *entail* these myths—it is just as consistent with the view that children start off learning words slowly and gradually get better at it. In any case, regardless of which theory will turn out to be the right one, the study of word learning can only benefit from an accurate understanding of development—one based on facts, not myths.

Acknowledgments

Thanks to Gil Diesendruck, Geoffrey Hall, Lori Markson, and Sandra Waxman for very helpful comments on earlier drafts of this chapter.

Notes

1. It would be interesting to take adults into a lab and expose them to an abstract parallel of word learning in a child. Each day in the child's life would correspond to a second, and subjects would watch a 12-minute visual analogue of lexical development from 12 months to the child's third birthday—every time the child learned a word, a dot would appear on the screen. If subjects were shown a linear increase in the rate at which dots appeared, would they nonetheless perceive a discontinuity—a sudden shift from slow to fast? And would this perceived discontinuity correspond to the point at which developmental psychologists have identified a word spurt?

2. Of course, children do not always generalize on the basis of kind, and the theory defended here does not predict that they should (see Bloom and Markson 2001 for discussion). With regard to words, one should expect kind-based generalization only to occur for words that actually refer to kinds—which is true for count nouns, but not for proper names (which refer to specific individuals) and not for adjectives (which refer to properties). And with regard to other tasks, one would expect kind-based generalization only to occur for tasks that have to do with generalization—which is true for an instruction to "find one of the same kind," but not for a vague demand to "find another one" and not when it comes to generalizing facts that only pertain to a specific individual, as tested by Waxman and Booth (2000).

References

Aitchison, J. 1994. *Words in the mind: An introduction to the mental lexicon.* 2nd ed. Oxford: Blackwell.

Anglin, J. 1993. Vocabulary development: A morphological analysis. *Monographs of the Society for Research in Child Development*, 58 (10, serial no. 238).

Baldwin, D. A. 1991. Infants' contribution to the achievement of joint reference. *Child Development*, 62, 875–890.

Baldwin, D. A. 1993. Infants' ability to consult the speaker for clues to word reference. *Journal of Child Language*, 20, 395–418.

Baldwin, D. A., and Moses, L. M. 1994. Early understanding of referential intent and attentional focus: Evidence from language and emotion. In C. Lewis and P. Mitchell, eds., *Children's early understanding of mind: Origins and development*. Hillsdale, NJ: Erlbaum.

Bates, E., and Carnevale, G. F. 1993. New directions in research on language development. *Developmental Review*, 13, 436–470.

Behrend, D. A. 1990. Constraints and development: A reply to Nelson (1988). *Cognitive Development*, 5, 313–330.

Bloom, L. 1973. *One word at a time: The use of single word utterances before syntax*. The Hague: Mouton.

Bloom, P. 2000. *How children learn the meanings of words*. Cambridge, MA: MIT Press.

Bloom, P. 2001. Precis of *How children learn the meaning of words*. *Behavioral and Brain Sciences*, 24, 1095–1103.

Bloom, P., and Markson, L. 2001. Are there principles that apply only to the acquisition of words? A reply to Waxman and Booth. *Cognition*, 78, 89–90.

Bowerman, M. 1978. The acquisition of word meaning. In N. Waterson and C. Snow, eds., *Development of communication: Social and pragmatic factors in language acquisition*. New York: Wiley.

Brunvand, J. H. 1981. *The vanishing hitchhiker*. New York: Norton.

Campbell, J. 1972. *Myths to live by*. New York: Bantam Books.

Chomsky, N. 1975. *Reflections on language*. New York: Pantheon.

Clark, E. V. 1973. What's in a word? On the child's acquisition of semantics in his first language. In T. E. Moore, ed., *Cognitive development and the acquisition of language*. New York: Academic Press.

Diesendruck, G. 2001, April. The shape bias is not specific to naming. Paper presented at the Biennial Meeting of the Society for Research in Child Development, Minneapolis.

Diesendruck, G., and Bloom, P. 2003. How specific is the shape bias? *Child Development*, 74, 168–178.

Diesendruck, G., and Markson, L. 2001. Children's avoidance of lexical overlap: A pragmatic account. *Developmental Psychology*, 37, 630–641.

Dore, J. 1978. Conditions for the acquisition of speech acts. In L. Markova, ed., *The social context of language*, 87–111. New York: Wiley.

Dromi, E. 1987. *Early lexical development*. Cambridge, England: Cambridge University Press.

Elman, J., Bates, E., Johnson, M., Karmiloff-Smith, A., Parisi, D., and Plunkett, K. 1996. *Rethinking innateness: A connectionist perspective on development*. Cambridge, MA: MIT Press.

Fenson, L., Dale, P. S., Reznick, J. S., Bates, E., Thal, D., and Pethick, S. J. 1994. Variability in early communicative development. *Monographs of the Society for Research in Child Development, 59* (5, serial no. 242).

Ganger, J., and Brent, M. 2001. Re-examining the vocabulary spurt and its implications: Is there really a sudden change in cognitive development? In A. H.-J. Do, L. Dominguez, and A. Johansen, eds., *Proceedings of the 25th Annual Boston University Conference on Language Development*. Somerville, MA: Cascadilla Press.

Gillette, J., Gleitman, H., Gleitman, L., and Lederer, A. 1999. Human simulations of vocabulary learning. *Cognition, 7*, 135–176.

Goldfield, B. A., and Reznick, J. S. 1990. Early lexical acquisition: Rate, content, and the vocabulary spurt. *Journal of Child Language, 17*, 171–183.

Gopnik, A., and Meltzoff, A. N. 1986. Words, plans, things, and locations: Interactions between semantic and cognitive development in the one-word stage. In S. Kuczaj and M. Barrett, eds., *The development of word meaning*. New York: Springer-Verlag.

Gropen, J., Pinker, S., Hollander, M., and Goldberg, R. 1991. Syntax and semantics in the acquisition of locative verbs. *Journal of Child Language, 18*, 115–151.

Huttenlocher, J., and Smiley, P. 1987. Early word meanings: The case of object names. *Cognitive Psychology, 19*, 63–89.

Landau, B., Smith, L. B., and Jones, S. S. 1988. The importance of shape in early lexical learning. *Cognitive Development, 3*, 299–321.

Lifter, K., and Bloom, L. 1989. Object knowledge and the emergence of language. *Infant Behavior and Development, 12*, 395–423.

Macnamara, J. 1972. Cognitive basis of language learning in infants. *Psychological Review, 79*, 1–13.

Markman, E. M., and Hutchinson, J. E. 1984. Children's sensitivity to constraints on word meaning: Taxonomic versus thematic relations. *Cognitive Psychology, 16*, 1–27.

Markman, E. M., and Wachtel, G. F. 1988. Children's use of mutual exclusivity to constrain the meaning of words. *Cognitive Psychology, 20*, 121–157.

Markson, L. 1999. *Fast mapping*. Unpublished doctoral dissertation, University of Arizona.

Markson, L., and Bloom, P. 1997. Evidence against a dedicated system for word learning in children. *Nature, 385*, 813–815.

McShane, J. 1979. The development of naming. *Linguistics, 17,* 79–90.

Meltzoff, A. N. 1995. Understanding the intentions of others: Re-enactment of intended acts by 18-month-old children. *Developmental Psychology, 31*, 838–850.

Mervis, C. B., and Bertrand, J. 1995. Acquisition of the novel name–nameless category (N3C) principle. *Child Development, 65*, 1646–1663.

Miller, G. A. 1996. *The science of words*. New York: Freeman.

Miller, G. A., and Wakefield, P. C. 1993. On Anglin's analysis of vocabulary growth. *Monographs of the Society for Research in Child Development, 58* (serial no. 238), 167–175.

Nagy, W. E., and Herman, P. A. 1987. Breadth and depth of vocabulary knowledge: Implications for acquisition and instruction. In M. G. McKeown and M. E. Curtis, eds., *The nature of vocabulary acquisition*. Hillsdale, NJ: Erlbaum.

Nelson, K. 1973. Structure and strategy in learning to talk. *Monographs of the Society for Research in Child Development, 38* (serial no. 149).

Nelson, K. 1988. Constraints on word meaning? *Cognitive Development, 3*, 221–246.

Oviatt, S. L. 1980. The emerging ability to comprehend language: An experimental approach. *Child Development, 51*, 97–106.

Pinker, S. 1994. *The language instinct*. New York: HarperCollins.

Plunkett, K., Sinha, C., Møller, M. F., and Strandsby, O. 1992. Symbol grounding or the emergence of symbols? Vocabulary growth in children and a connectionist net. *Connection Science, 4*, 293–312.

Rescorla, L. A. 1980. Overextension in early language development. *Journal of Child Language, 7*, 321–335.

Reznick, J. S., and Goldfield, B. A. 1992. Rapid change in lexical development in comprehension and production. *Developmental Psychology, 28*, 406–413.

Shermer, M. 2000. How we believe. *The search for God in an age of science*. New York: Freeman.

Shipley, E. F., and Shepperson, B. 1990. Countable entities: Developmental changes. *Cognition, 34*, 109–136.

Sternberg, R. J. 1987. Most vocabulary is learned from context. In M. G. McKeown and M. E. Curtis, eds., *The nature of vocabulary acquisition*. Hillsdale, NJ: Erlbaum.

Tomasello, M., and Barton, M. 1994. Learning words in non-ostensive contexts. *Developmental Psychology, 30,* 639–650.

van Geert, P. 1991. A dynamic system model of cognitive and language growth. *Psychological Review, 98,* 3–53.

Waxman, S. R., and Booth, A. 2000. Principles that are invoked in the acquisition of words, but not facts. *Cognition, 77,* B33–B43.

Woodward, A. L., Markman, E. M., and Fitzsimmons, C. M. 1994. Rapid word learning in 13- and 18-month-olds. *Developmental Psychology, 30,* 553–566.

8

Lexical Development without a Language Model: Are Nouns, Verbs, and Adjectives Essential to the Lexicon?

Susan Goldin-Meadow

Children learn the words of the language to which they are exposed—they say *dog* if they are learning English, *chien* if they are learning French, and *perro* if they are learning Spanish. Thus, the linguistic input a child receives has an obvious impact on word learning. So too does the frequency of linguistic input. Children who are talked to a great deal experience more growth in vocabulary than children who hear less talk (Huttenlocher et al. 1991).

But young children are also particularly prepared to profit from the input they receive. Their growing sensitivity to perceptual cues within the ongoing speech stream (Jusczyk 1999a, 1999b; Morgan and Demuth 1996) allows them to begin to parse what they hear into usable units at a surprisingly young age. Their sensitivity to the pragmatic cues in the way speech is used (e.g., the eye gaze of speakers as they name objects; Baldwin and Markman 1989) allows them to begin to link words to objects and events in their worlds. Their sensitivity to the syntactic cues that their language provides (distinguishing, for example, count nouns from proper nouns and adjectives) allows them to make guesses about the meanings of a word just from hearing that word in a particular syntactic context (Brown 1957; Katz, Baker, and Macnamara 1972; Gleitman 1990; Hall, Waxman, and Hurwitz 1993; Waxman 1990).

Thus, the word-learning process is characterized by an interplay between the input children receive and the skills they bring to the language-learning task. Under typical learning conditions, it is quite difficult to tease these two influences apart and uncover the contributions children themselves make to word learning—precisely because conventional linguistic input is so rich that the child's output is overdetermined. Uncovering the child's contributions to word learning, independent of input, is most straightforward when a child is not exposed to *any* model of a conventional language whatsoever.

Such a situation cannot be engineered deliberately. However, there are naturally occurring circumstances in which children are not exposed to a usable language model. For example, deaf children born to hearing parents, at times, do not encounter conventional sign language until late adolescence. Moreover, their hearing losses are often so profound as to preclude the acquisition of any aspect of the spoken language that surrounds them. Remarkably, and despite their lack of access to usable conventional-language models in either the manual or oral modality, these deaf children invent gesture systems that they use to communicate with the hearing individuals in their worlds. Moreover, these gesture systems display many of the rudimentary properties found in conventional languages, both signed and spoken (Goldin-Meadow 2003b). As examples, these gestures are structured in their syntax (Feldman, Goldin-Meadow, and Gleitman 1978; Goldin-Meadow and Feldman 1977; Goldin-Meadow and Mylander 1984, 1998) and morphology (Goldin-Meadow, Mylander, and Butcher 1995). The question I ask in this chapter is whether the deaf children's systems also have gestural lexicons that are structured like the lexicons found in conventional languages. Specifically, do these deaf children develop gestures that work like nouns, verbs, and adjectives?

All known languages have words for describing participants (people, animals, and things), properties of participants, and activities involving participants. Typically, nouns encode the first set of meanings, adjectives the second, and verbs the third (Dixon 1994). Having distinct categories for nouns and verbs is one of the few properties that has traditionally been accepted as a linguistic universal (e.g., Givon 1979; Hawkins 1988; Hopper and Thompson 1984, 1988; Robins 1952; Sapir 1921; Schachter 1985; Thompson 1988) even across modality (i.e., in sign languages; Supalla and Newport 1978). Whereas all languages appear to have distinct categories for nouns and verbs, their treatment of adjectives is more variable (Schachter 1985). Languages can treat adjectives as a small closed class, or as an open class with grammatical properties similar to the properties of nouns, the properties of verbs, the properties of both nouns and verbs, or the properties of neither nouns nor verbs (Dixon 1994).

There is no doubt that deaf children are able to distinguish objects, actions, and properties in their nonlinguistic worlds. For example, by 18 months, both deaf and hearing children have mastered Piagetian object permanence, and thus are able to treat objects as distinct from the actions performed on them (Best and Roberts 1976). Nevertheless, it is possible that deaf children who are not exposed to a usable conventional-language model do not find it necessary to incorporate such distinctions into the lexicons of the communication systems they invent. Indeed, the lexical distinction between nouns, verbs, and adjectives may be one whose presence across natural languages has been maintained by tradition, rather than by necessity. I explore here whether the deaf child's self-styled gesture system respects such lexical divisions or, alternatively, whether lexical divisions of this sort are acquired *only* with exposure to a model of a conventional language, one that is shared within a community of users and passed down from generation to generation.

I focus on data from a single deaf child, David, whose gesture system is the most completely described. Although David had not been exposed to an accessible conventional-language model during the time of our observations, he did see the spontaneous gestures that hearing speakers typically produce as they talk (cf. Bekken 1989; Goldin-Meadow 2003a; Iverson et al. 1999; McNeill 1992; Shatz 1982). Thus, where relevant, I also describe the gestures produced by David's hearing mother.

8.1 Background on Deafness and Language Learning

Deaf children born to deaf parents and exposed from birth to a conventional sign language such as American Sign Language (ASL) acquire that language naturally—that is, these children progress through stages in acquiring sign language similar to those of hearing children acquiring a spoken language (Newport and Meier 1985).

However, 90 percent of deaf children are not born to deaf parents who could provide early exposure to a conventional sign language. Rather, they are born to hearing parents who rarely know conventional sign language and, quite naturally, expose their children to speech (Hoffmeister and Wilbur 1980). Unfortunately, it is extremely uncommon for deaf children with severe to profound hearing losses to acquire the spoken language of their hearing parents naturally— that is, without intensive and specialized instruction. Even with instruction, deaf children's acquisition of speech is markedly delayed when compared either to the acquisition of spoken language by hearing children of hearing parents, or to the acquisition of sign language by deaf children of deaf parents. By age 5 or 6, and despite intensive early training programs, the average profoundly deaf child has a very reduced oral linguistic capacity (Conrad 1979; Mayberry 1992; Meadow 1968). Moreover, although many hearing parents of deaf children send their children to schools in which one of the manually coded systems of English is taught, other hearing parents send their deaf children to "oral" schools in which sign systems are neither taught nor encouraged; thus, these deaf children are not likely to receive input in a conventional sign system, either at home or at school.

David is profoundly deaf (>90 dB bilateral hearing loss) and his hearing parents chose to educate him using an oral method. At the time of our observations, David had made little progress in oral language, occasionally producing single words but never combining those words into sentences. In addition, at the time of our observations, David had not been exposed to ASL or to a manual code of English. As a preschooler in an oral school for the deaf, David spent very little time with the older deaf children in the school who might have had some knowledge of a conventional sign system (the preschoolers only attended school a few hours a day and were not on the playground at the same time as the older children). Moreover, David's family knew no deaf adults socially and interacted only with other hearing families, typically those with hearing children. One of the primary reasons we were convinced that David had had no exposure to a conventional sign system at the time of our observations was that he did not know even the most common lexical items

Lexical Development without a Language Model

of ASL or Signed English (i.e., when a deaf native signer reviewed our tapes, she found no evidence of any conventional signs; moreover, when we informally presented to David common signs such as those for "mother," "father," "boy," "girl," "dog," we found that he did not understand any of these signs).

David was videotaped in his home during free-play sessions that lasted as long as he was cooperative, typically an hour or two. A large bag of toys, books, and puzzles served as the catalyst for communication (see Goldin-Meadow 1979). David was videotaped seven times over a period of 2 years beginning when he was 2;10 (years;months) and ending when he was 4;10.

8.2 Is the Gestural Lexicon Stable over Time?

The first question we consider is whether the gestures David created over a 2-year period were stable in form. If David created his gestures anew each time he wished to convey a particular meaning, we might expect to find some consistency of form simply because David's gesture system is iconic and iconicity constrains to some degree the set of forms that might be used to convey a meaning. However, in this event, we might also expect a great deal of variability in the set of forms he used to convey a particular meaning—variability engendered by the differences among the particular situations that each gesture was created to capture. If, on the other hand, David had a stable lexicon of gestures, we might expect to find relatively little variability in the set of forms he used for a particular meaning.

In addition to conventional emblems (nods, headshakes, hand flips, and so on) and deictic gestures (pointing at an object or holding an object up to call attention to it), David produced characterizing gestures—gestures whose iconic form captured some aspect of its referent—for example, rotating a C-shaped hand back and forth as though twisting open a jar. It is these characterizing gestures that have the potential to constitute a stable lexicon.

David's characterizing gestures can be described in terms of a simple morphology (Goldin-Meadow and Mylander 1990; Goldin-Meadow, Mylander, and Butcher 1995). Each gesture contains a handshape morpheme (e.g., an "O" form associated with the meaning "an object with a small diameter") and a motion morpheme (e.g., an "Arc To and Fro" form associated with the meaning "move back and forth"), which together create a lexical meaning ("move a small object back and forth"). We took the prototypical form for a particular lexical item to be the handshape and motion forms associated with the object and action meanings the child intended to convey (as inferred from context; see Feldman, Goldin-Meadow, and Gleitman 1978; Goldin-Meadow and Mylander 1984). For example, the meaning "twist" (as in twisting a wide jar lid—that is, rotate a large object around an axis) could be broken down into a handshape morpheme (a "C" form associated with the meaning "object with a large diameter") and a motion morpheme (a "Revolve" form associated with the meaning "rotate around an axis"). We therefore assumed that "C hand + Revolve motion" was the prototypical handshape + motion form for the lexical meaning "rotate a large object around an axis." Any gestures that David produced to mean "twist" that varied from this form we took to be incorrect.[1]

David produced 190 different lexical items (that is, 190 different form-meaning pairs) over the 2-year period.[2] Of these, 81 were used only once; thus, there was no opportunity to observe variability in these gestures. The remaining 109 lexical items were produced more than once during the period of observation and accounted for 706 gesture tokens. We found that only 73 (10%) of these 706 gestures varied from the prototype; these gestures varied either in handshape (e.g., a Fist hand was used in the gesture rather than the C hand from the prototype) or in motion (e.g., a Short Arc motion was used in the gesture rather than the Revolve motion from the prototype). For example, David conveyed the "break" meaning fifteen times over the 2-year period: fourteen times he conveyed this meaning using the form we considered to be his prototype (i.e., 2 Fist hands + Short Arc motion), and once he used an "incorrect" motion (he used a "2 Fist hands + Long Arc motion" form). David's incorrect forms were not dramatically different from his prototypical form; the forms he used did capture an aspect of the intended meaning—if not, we would not have been able to attribute any sort of meaning to the gesture in the first place. In this regard, it is important to note that we were not forced to eliminate many gestures because they were uninterpretable; only 5 percent of the characterizing gestures David produced could not be assigned a meaning and were therefore eliminated from our analyses. Thus, the database we used to assess variability in David's gestures did not come from a restricted sample of David's gestures.

In contrast, David's hearing mother showed much more variability in the gestures she produced when she talked to her child. Unlike David's characterizing gestures, only 5 percent of which could not be assigned a meaning, 25 percent of his mother's 579 characterizing gestures could not be assigned a meaning when analyzed without speech and were coded as ambiguous. Thus, a quarter of the mother's gestures had to be eliminated from our analyses, suggesting from the start that her gestures were less like a lexicon than David's. She used 159 different form-meaning pairs during the observation period, 85 of which were used only once. The remaining 74 lexical items were produced more than once during the period of observation and accounted for 290 gestures. Only 59 percent of these 290 gestures conformed to prototype in the mother's gestures, compared to 90 percent in David's 706 gestures, $x^2(1) = 131.19$, $p < .001$). In addition, the mother varied from prototype in at least one of the tokens of 65 percent of the 74 lexical items in her system, compared to 33 percent of the 109 lexical items in David's system, $x^2(1) = 18.0$, $p < .001$).

Thus, David (significantly more than his mother) used essentially the same form to convey a particular meaning throughout the 2-year period he was observed, suggesting that his gesture system adhered to standards of form—albeit standards idiosyncratic to him rather than shared by a community of language users.

8.3 Categorizing Gestures as Nouns, Verbs, and Adjectives

The next question we ask is whether David's lexicon could be divided into the grammatical categories, noun, verb, and adjective. We examined each individual gesture token that David produced and made a judgment as to whether that particular token was serving a noun function, a verb function, or an adjective function. The difficulty in making these decisions (for us and for any experimenter) is that the notions noun, verb, and adjective have to do with the way referents are construed by the speaker (or, in our case, the gesturer) rather than with the real-world referents themselves. We therefore were forced to make educated guesses at what might be in the mind of the child when he produced a gesture, guesses based on the communicative context in which that gesture was produced.

As in categorizing the early words of a hearing child (cf. Macnamara, 1982, 106), we found it easier to actually do the categorizing than to articulate how we did it. Nevertheless, as an approximate description of how we categorized gestures, we followed Sapir (1921) in considering a noun to be the focus or subject of the discourse (i.e., the something that is talked about), and verbs and adjectives to be the predicates of the discourse (i.e., what is said of this something).[3] Thus, if the child used a characterizing gesture to focus attention on an entity, it was coded as a noun, but if he used the gesture to say something about that entity (i.e., to predicate something of the entity), it was coded as either a verb or an adjective, depending on whether the gesture depicted an action or an attribute.

Not surprisingly, material entities (cf. Bloom 1990) turned out to be the most common subjects of the discourse—the nouns—and relations (actions and attributes) turned out to be the most common predicates of the discourse—the verbs and adjectives. For example, if the child used the "flap" gesture (two palms, each held at a shoulder, arced to and fro as though flapping wings) to comment on a picture of a bird riding a bicycle with its wings on the handlebars (i.e., to focus attention on the bird as an entity rather than to comment on wing flapping), the gesture would be coded as a *noun*. In contrast, if the "flap" gesture had been used to describe a toy penguin that had been wound and was flapping its wings, the gesture would be coded as a *verb* (although we do recognize that the child could have been commenting on the presence of the bird itself). As a second example, if the child used the "high" gesture (a flat palm held horizontally in the air) to comment on the fact that a cardboard chimney typically stands in the corner at Christmas time (i.e., to focus attention on the chimney as an entity rather than to comment on the chimney's height), the gesture would be coded as a *noun*. In contrast, if the "high" gesture had been used to describe the temporary height of the tower before urging his mother to hit it with a hammer and topple it, the gesture would be coded as an *adjective*.

There were, of course, occasions when it was particularly difficult to decide whether a gesture was a noun, verb, or adjective. In order not to force our intuitions into categorical decisions when none seemed just right, we classified such gestures as "unclear": 12 percent of the 915 gestures David produced could not unequivocally be assigned a grammatical category and thus were placed in this unclear category. Whatever the validity of our coding decisions, it is important to note that we were able to make these decisions reliably. Reliability was established by having a second observer independently code a randomly selected portion of the videotapes. Interrater agreement between the two coders was 94 percent for determining whether a gesture was a verb, adjective, noun, or unclear.

8.4 Nouns, Verbs, and Adjectives: Developmental Changes in How They Are Distinguished

The lexicons of all natural languages contain categories of words that are treated distinctively (Sapir 1921). David's gesture system was no exception. Moreover, over time, David altered the techniques he used to maintain distinctions between nouns, verbs, and adjectives, and his gesture system became progressively more complex with each step.

8.4.1 Distinctions Based on Form Types

During his initial observation session, David used a very small number of characterizing gestures as nouns—most of his characterizing gestures were used as verbs and adjectives (as can be inferred from figure 8.1). At first glance, this is a striking result because it suggests that nouns do not have developmental priority as they appear to have in children learning conventional languages (Gentner 1982; Waxman and Booth 2001). However, it is important to point out that David had other techniques for referring to objects, people, and places—deictic gestures (e.g., pointing at an object)—which he used early in development and often. Indeed, David's gestural

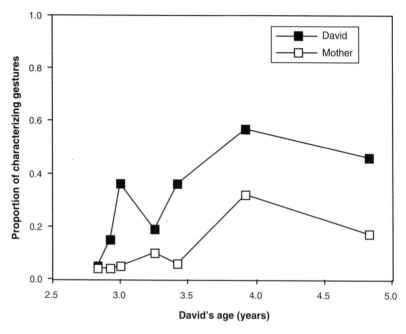

Figure 8.1
Proportion of characterizing gestures David and his hearing mother used as nouns (as opposed to verbs or adjectives) at each of the seven observation sessions.

lexicon resembles the lexicons of children learning conventional languages in breadth and extent *only if* we consider deictic gestures to be part of that lexicon (Feldman, Goldin-Meadow, and Gleitman 1978). Thus, David's first technique for distinguishing nouns from verbs and adjectives appeared to be form based—pointing gestures served nounlike functions, while characterizing gestures served predicate (i.e., verb and adjective) functions.

The pointing gesture singles out an entity that can then be commented on and, in this way, serves an important discourse function played by the noun in conventional languages. However, the pointing gesture does *not* fulfill all of the functions served by the noun, and in fact appears to function more like a pronoun (e.g., *that*) than a noun. In particular, while the pointing gesture can indicate which object is the focus of attention, it does not categorize that object as one of a type—that is, it does not classify an entity in terms of its relationship to other entities of the world (cf. Stachowiak 1976). Nouns serve this categorizing function, along with an indicating function, in conventional languages. In the deaf child's gestural lexicon, characterizing gestures can serve the categorizing function of nouns while points serve only the indicating function. The fact that a deaf child inventing his own communication system used pointing gestures (rather than characterizing gestures) to refer to objects early in development suggests that it may be the indicating function of a noun (rather than its categorizing function) that is of central importance at the earliest stages of word learning. Thus, nouns may predominate in the lexicons of young children learning many languages because of the noun's ability to single out objects for comment and not because of its ability to categorize those objects.

8.4.2 Distinctions Based on Separate Lexicons

As figure 8.1 shows, over time, David used proportionately more and more of his characterizing gestures for noun (as opposed to verb and adjective) functions. The question is whether David found a new technique for distinguishing nouns from verbs and adjectives once nounlike functions were no longer restricted to deictics. In fact, David maintained the distinction by developing a unique set of iconic gestures that referred exclusively to objects. For example, a "round" gesture might be used to refer to the jar itself (a noun function), leaving the "twist" gesture to continue to be used for opening the jar (a verb function) or the "wide" gesture to continue to be used for the width of the jar (an adjective gesture). That is, David's early noun, verb, and adjective lexicons did not overlap—he avoided inventing words like *comb*, which can be used as both a noun and a verb. David did not use the same gesture as both a noun and a verb until the fourth observation session (age 3;3), after which he used many at each session. He also did not begin to use a gesture as both a verb and an adjective until the fourth observation session, and did not use a gesture as both a noun and an adjective until the sixth observation session (age 3;11).

Interestingly, during their earliest stages of word learning, children learning English show a similar reticence to cross category lines—they either avoid using words like *comb* or use them in only one sense (i.e., as either a noun or a verb, but not both; Mcnamara 1982). Thus, like young children learning conventional languages, David did *not* violate intercategory boundaries at the earliest stages of development. His first inclination appeared to be to respect category boundaries in his self-styled gesture system and to maintain that distinction lexically (that is, by using separate lexical items as nouns, verbs, and adjectives).

Figure 8.1 also displays the characterizing gestures David's mother produced as she talked to him, categorized according to noun (as opposed to verb and adjective) functions. His mother also used few noun characterizing gestures during David's first observation session. However, she showed little increase in the proportion of gestures she used for noun functions until the sixth observation session, when approximately 40 percent of her characterizing gestures were nouns. In contrast, 40 percent of David's gestures were nouns during session 3, and by the sixth session, nouns accounted for half of his characterizing-gesture vocabulary. Thus, the mother's relatively late onset of characterizing gestures used as nouns makes it likely that her gestures did not serve as a model for using these gestures to serve noun functions.

However, the mother's gestures could well have served as a model for violating intercategory boundaries. She used a gesture as both a noun and a verb during the third observation session when David was 3;0; David did not begin until age 3;3. Moreover, she used a gesture as both a noun and an adjective during the fourth observation session when David was 3;3; David did not begin until age 3;11. Just like children learning a spoken language who presumably learn that the same word can be used as both a noun and a verb from hearing their parents use a word like *comb* in both roles, David may have acquired this type of flexibility in his gestures as a result of his mother's gestural model. Her model may, in fact, have been essential—particularly given that David's first inclination appeared to be to respect intercategory boundaries in his gestures and to use certain gestures as nouns, others as verbs, and still others as adjectives.

8.4.3 Distinctions Based on Grammatical Devices

When hearing children learn that a word can serve as both a noun and a verb, they also learn that the two functions need to be distinguished in some formal way. They hear their parents use the word as a noun in a different morphosyntactic context from the one in which they hear the word used as a verb (e.g., "Give mama the comb" vs. "Are you combing the baby's hair?"). Thus, they learn that when a word crosses intercategory boundaries, grammatical markings must be used to distinguish the two different uses. Did David attempt to grammtically mark intercategory violations in his gestures?

To determine whether David developed devices to distinguish among nouns, verbs, and adjectives, we coded the position of each characterizing gesture he produced within its sentence frame, as well as each gesture's "morphologic" markings—in particular, whether it was *abbreviated* in form (i.e., one motion rather than several repeated motions; or one hand rather than two) or *inflected* (i.e., produced near an object standing for an argument in the predicate rather than in neutral space at chest level).

Figure 8.2 displays the proportion of gestures classified as verbs, adjectives, and nouns that were marked by inflection (top left), marked by abbreviation (top right), or produced in second position of a two-gesture sentence (bottom). Focusing first on nouns and verbs, we note that David used gestures differently if they were serving noun versus verb roles. For example, if he were using a twisting motion to refer to the act of opening the jar, the gesture would not be abbreviated (that is, it would have several twisting motions), but it would be inflected (it would be produced near, but not on, the jar to be twisted) and it would occur in second position of a gesture sentence (point at jar—TWIST,[4] used to ask someone to open the jar). In contrast, if the child were using the twisting motion to refer to the jar itself, the gesture would not be inflected (it would be produced in neutral space), but it would be abbreviated (it would contain only

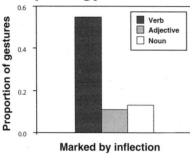
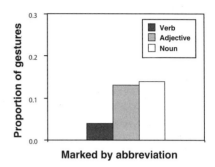

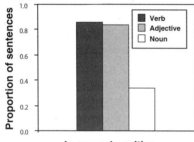

Figure 8.2
The proportion of verb, adjective, and noun gestures that David inflected (top-left graph), abbreviated (top-right graph), or placed in the second position of a two-gesture sentence (bottom graph). Nouns were abbreviated and rarely placed in second position; verbs were inflected and frequently placed in second position. Adjectives resembled nouns in terms of morphology (abbreviated rather than inflected) but verbs in terms of syntax (placed in second rather than first position).

one twisting motion) and it would occur in first position of a gesture sentence (TWIST—point at jar, used to identify the object as a jar).

The proportions in figure 8.2 are for all of the nouns and verbs David produced. However, the morphologic distinctions were equally, if not more, pronounced for the gestures that were actually used in both contexts (i.e., the gestures that violated intercategory boundaries, e.g., *twist* used as a noun in some contexts and as a verb in others): .43 of these gestures were inflected when used as verbs versus .14 when used as nouns; .22 of the gestures were abbreviated when used as nouns versus .04 when used as verbs (syntactic patterns could not be explored in these noun-verb pairs simply because too few of them occurred in two-gesture sentences).

We turn now to adjectives. As mentioned above, adjectives tend to be a less distinctive category than either nouns or verbs in languages across the globe. On the one hand, adjectives are closely aligned with nouns, being their modifiers and therefore dependent on them for their existence; indeed, in many languages (like French) adjectives assume the markings of the noun they are modifying. On the other hand, adjectives are also relational and, in this sense, are more closely aligned with verbs. Crosslinguistically, adjectives can form their own separate lexical category, or they can assume the markings of either nouns or verbs. However, there are also cases where adjectives share features with both nouns and verbs in the language (Thompson 1988; Dixon 1994). This is the pattern exhibited by David.

In terms of morphologic markings, adjectives resembled *nouns* in David's gesture system (abbreviated but not inflected). For example, if he were using the broken gesture (typically two fists held together side by side and then repeatedly broken apart) to describe the current state of a toy, that gesture would not be inflected (that is, it would be produced in neutral space at chest level) but it would be abbreviated (that is, the breaking-apart movement would be produced only once). However, in terms of syntactic structure, adjectives resembled *verbs* in David's gesture system (produced in second position rather than first). The broken gesture would be placed after the deictic gesture in a two-gesture sentence (point at toy—BROKEN).

Thus, David invented an adjective category that fits the variable pattern found in natural languages. In his system, adjectives do not form a separate lexical category but rather align themselves at times with nouns and at other times with verbs, and they do so systematically, sharing morphologic features with nouns and syntactic features with verbs. There appears to be a robust noun-verb framework within which adjectives are located, not only in conventional languages, but also in unconventional systems developed by young children.

Did David learn his grammatical marking system from his mother? In short, no. His mother produced no abbreviations at all in her gestures, and her other devices patterned differently from David's (she inflected verbs and adjectives but not nouns, and she produced both nouns and verbs in second position in her infrequent gesture strings; Goldin-Meadow et al. 1994). At best, then, his mother's gestures might have served as a starting point for the system David created. In general, David's gestures were more language-like than his mother's—having a coherent set of grammatical devices to mark gestures in their roles as nouns, verbs, or adjectives.

To summarize thus far, even without the benefit of a conventional-language model, a child can develop a stable lexicon, one that contains at least three different kinds of lexical items—nouns, verbs, and adjectives, the staple of all natural languages (Dixon 1994). Moreover, over time, the child can introduce into the communication system more and more sophisticated techniques for maintaining the distinctions among these types of lexical items, providing good evidence that the system itself contains a set (albeit a small set) of grammatical categories.

8.5 Why Did the Mother's Gestures Lack the Language-Like Features Found in Her Deaf Child's Gestures?

If the language-like properties found in David's gestures are so important to human communication, they might be expected to appear in his mother's gestures as well as his. The gestures his mother used when she communicated with David are, in fact, just like the spontaneous gestures hearing individuals typically use along with their speech (Goldin-Meadow 2003a; Goldin-Meadow and Saltzman 2000). According to McNeill (1992), the gestures hearing individuals produce along with speech are context sensitive: each gesture is created at the moment of speaking and highlights what is relevant; thus, the same referent can be—and often is—represented by gestures that change their form. This property of context sensitivity contrasts with the stability of lexical forms in a conventional linguistic system (McNeill 1992) and also with the stability of lexical form in David's self-styled gestural system.

In addition, English speakers typically produce one gesture to a clause, pausing between the gestures and relaxing the hand (McNeill 1992). Thus, the gestures of English speakers are rarely combined with one another in what we would call a gesture string (our criterion for a gesture string is that the hand cannot be relaxed at any point within the string, i.e., there can be no pauses between the gestures that comprise the string; Goldin-Meadow and Mylander 1984). David's mother's lack of gesture combinations is consequently not surprising given that almost all of her gestures were produced along with speech.

The gestures David's mother produced appeared to have been shaped by the fact that they occurred in combination with speech. Forming an integrated system with speech, these gestures were, in a sense, not "free" to take on a different, more language-like, form. Although it is likely that David made use of his mother's gestures in fashioning his own, he went well beyond the model she provided. Perhaps because David's gestures were his sole means of communication and were thus forced to assume the full burden of communication, they became more language-like than his mother's—including a stability of form and a grammatical systematicity not found in her gestures but reminiscent of natural language (see Goldin-Meadow, McNeill, and Singleton 1996 for an experimental test of this hypothesis).

8.6 Are Nouns and Verbs Grammatical Categories or Names for Objects and Actions?

We began our search for a noun-verb distinction in David's gesture system with an intuitive guess as to which of his characterizing gestures were nouns and which were verbs. Using these noun and verb categories, we found both morphologic patterns (i.e., variations within the gesture itself) and syntactic patterns (i.e., variations across a string of gestures) that distinguished between nouns and verbs in David's system. We take these formal patterns to be evidence for the noun and verb categories we coded in David's gestures since the former (the patterns) are formulated in terms of the latter (the categories). The question then arises—what are these categories that we have called "nouns" and "verbs" in David's gestures? The evidence presented thus far argues only that the categories we have isolated are categories, not that they are necessarily nouns and verbs.

To pursue this question, we explored more carefully the contextual conditions under which the categories noun and verb were coded. As a guide in determining which aspects of context ought to be coded, we used work exploring the contexts in which young English-learning children produce nouns and verbs. In their work on children's early uses of nouns and verbs in English, Huttenlocher and Smiley found that young English-learning children produced words that are verbs in the adult lexicon in contexts in which the action represented by that word is actually occurring or is being requested (Huttenlocher and Smiley 1989), and words that are nouns in the adult lexicon in contexts in which the action is not present in the immediate context (Huttenlocher and Smiley 1987).

We coded the context for each gesture in terms of the presence or absence of the action portrayed in that gesture ($\pm$A), as well as the presence or absence of the object associated with that action ($\pm$O) (see Goldin-Meadow et al. 1994 for coding details): (1) the action portrayed in the gesture occurred on an object in the immediate context (+A+O); (2) the action portrayed in the gesture did not occur in the immediate context, but an object associated with the action was present (−A+O); (3) the action portrayed in the gesture did not occur in the immediate context, and an object associated with the action was not in the context (−A−O).[5] We did this contextual coding as a separate pass through the data (i.e., independently of the noun-verb coding) for the ten most frequent gestures that David used as both nouns and verbs. David produced each of these gestures a minimum of ten times, and the average number of occurrences per gesture was 17.8. Half of the gestures whose context we explored were used as verbs ($N = 89$) and half were used as nouns ($N = 89$).

We found that David's pattern was similar to the pattern found by Huttenlocher and Smiley (1987, 1989) at the extremes. When action and object were both present (+A+O), David's gestures were always coded as verbs. When neither action nor object was present (−A −O), David's gestures were always coded as nouns. The middle category (−A+O) was where we found inconsistency between the contextual and grammatical codes—a third of the gestures in this context were coded as verbs, two-thirds were coded as nouns.

In the two instances where our contextual and grammatical codes agree (+A+O and −A−O), the predictions about how David's morphologic and syntactic devices ought to pattern are straightforward: (1) gestures coded as verbs and occurring in +A+O contexts ought to be treated like verbs (i.e., they ought to be inflected but not abbreviated, and they ought to occur in sentences in which pointing gestures precede characterizing gestures); and (2) gestures coded as nouns and occurring in −A−O contexts ought to be treated like nouns (i.e., they ought to be abbreviated but not inflected, and they ought to occur in sentences in which pointing gestures follow characterizing gestures). Figure 8.3 presents the morphologic (top-left and top-right graphs) and syntactic (bottom graph) characteristics of a gesture as a function of its grammatical code and its contextual code, and confirms these predictions (see the far-right and far-left bars in each of the three graphs).

It is, however, the middle contextual category (−A+O) that allows us to determine whether David's formal devices pattern as a function of our grammatical (N, V) or contextual (+/−A, +/−O) codes simply because both nouns and verbs were found in this context. If we are correct in arguing that David's morphologic and syntactic devices function to distinguish the grammatical categories of noun and verb, the devices ought to pattern according to the grammatical code (i.e., N and V). Thus, independent of context, nouns ought to behave like nouns with respect to both morphology and syntax, and verbs ought to behave like verbs. However, if the morphologic and syntactic devices function to distinguish objects and actions rather

Morphology

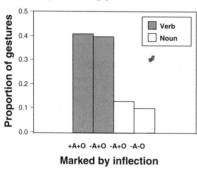

Marked by inflection

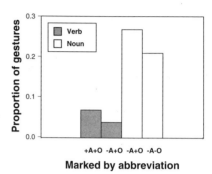

Marked by abbreviation

Syntax

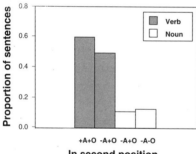

In second position

Figure 8.3
Morphologic (top graphs) and syntactic (bottom graph) properties of a set of characterizing gestures classified according to grammatical role (verb vs. noun) and the context in which they occurred (action and object both present, +A+O; action absent but object present, −A+O; action and object both absent, −A−O). Only verbs appeared in +A+O contexts and only nouns appeared in −A−O contexts; these gestures had distinct morphologic and syntactic profiles. Both nouns and verbs appeared in −A+O contexts and, although they could have taken on similar characteristics as a function of this context, they did not: nouns in −A+O contexts looked like other nouns, and verbs in −A+O contexts looked like other verbs. In other words, their morphologic and syntactic properties were governed by grammatical category, not by context.

than nouns and verbs, we might then expect the devices to pattern according to the contextual code rather than the grammatical code when the two disagree. Thus, independent of grammatical category, gestures that are produced in $-A+O$ contexts ought to behave alike, perhaps intermediate between the other two contexts (i.e., $+A+O$ and $-A-O$).

The data presented in figure 8.3 are quite clear. David's morphologic and syntactic devices pattern according to the grammatical code of a gesture rather than its contextual code. Gestures occurring in $-A+O$ contexts behave differently if they are coded as verbs versus nouns. In addition, when gestures occurring in this context are coded as nouns, they behave like other nouns; when they are coded as verbs, they behave like other verbs. Thus, David's morphologic and syntactic devices appear to distinguish between grammatical categories of noun and verb, rather than contexts that vary in the presence and absence of objects and actions.

Do the data in figure 8.3 guarantee that the categories we have isolated are truly the grammatical categories of noun and verb rather than the semantic categories of object and action? In fact, the data suggest only that the noun and verb codes we have used to describe David's gestures are not reducible to one particular set of contextual codes. Given the bootstrap nature of our coding procedure, we can never prove beyond a doubt that the categories we have isolated are indeed the grammatical categories of noun and verb. Nevertheless, the fact that the categories we have isolated pattern in three respects as do nouns and verbs in natural language provides further support that these are indeed grammatical categories rather than semantic categories.

First, there was coherence between the morphologic and syntactic devices in David's system. The morphologic devices worked together to distinguish the grammatical categories of noun and verb: inflections marked verbs, abbreviations marked nouns. Importantly, virtually *no* gestures were produced with both markings. Moreover, nouns and verbs occupied different positions in gesture sentences, verbs occurring after the pointing gesture and nouns occurring before the pointing gesture.

Second, the particular way the morphologic and syntactic devices were used to distinguish adjectives from nouns and verbs is reminiscent of patterns found in natural languages. In particular, adjectives in David's system behaved like nouns morphologically (they were abbreviated rather than inflected) but like verbs syntactically (they occurred after the pointing gesture), as do adjectives in some natural languages (cf. Thompson 1988; Dixon 1994).

Finally, in the few instances where characterizing nouns were combined with verbs within a single sentence, the gestures adhered to the syntactic rules of the system. David produced noun-characterizing gestures playing a patient role before verb-characterizing gestures (e.g., an "eat" gesture used as a noun = grape, followed by a "give" gesture), just as he produced deictic pointing gestures playing a patient role before verb-characterizing gestures (point at grape, followed by a "give" gesture). In other words, when nouns were produced in sentences with verbs, they took over the slot typically filled by deictic pronouns. Thus, the grammatical categories noun and verb were elements within David's syntactic system and, as such, were governed by the rules of that system, just as nouns and verbs are governed by the rules of syntax in natural language.

8.7 The Onset of a System

In his initial observation sessions, David used separate sets of lexical items as nouns, verbs, and adjectives. Thus, he respected intercategory boundaries in his early lexicon, as do children learning conventional languages, sign (Petitto 1992) or speech (Huttenlocher and Smiley 1987). During the fourth session (at age 3;3), David began to use some of his lexical items for more than one function, most commonly using the same gestural form as a noun and a verb. However, he continued to maintain the distinction between categories by abbreviating nouns but not verbs (akin to derivational morphology), producing verbs but not nouns in marked locations (akin to inflectional morphology), and producing verbs and nouns in distinct positions in gesture sentences (akin to syntax).

It is striking that, at this same point in development, there is also evidence that David's word stems could, for the first time, be characterized by morphologic components (Goldin-Meadow, Mylander, and Butcher 1995). Handshape and motion components combined to form word stems, which were then abbreviated when used as nouns or inflected when used as verbs and placed into distinctive positions in sentences. Thus, we see sets of units corresponding to the different levels found in conventional languages (word-stem morphology, derivational and inflectional morphology, syntax), which made up the building blocks of David's gesture system.

There were other changes that coincided with what appears to be the onset of a grammatical system in David's gestures. Prior to age 3;3, all of the gestures he produced were produced in contexts consistent with their grammatical function. Thus, during the first three observation sessions, David produced verbs only in contexts in which both the action and object were present, and nouns only in contexts in which both the action and object were absent. Thus, just as children learning English may initially distinguish between nouns and verbs on the basis of a semantic rather than a grammatical distinction (Macnamara 1982), David's first categories may also have been based on a semantic distinction rather than a grammatical distinction. It was not until age 3;3 that he began to use noun and verb gestures in intermediate contexts where the action was absent and the object present—precisely the moment when he introduced grammatical devices to keep the categories distinct. Thus, by age 3;3, David appeared to have developed a division between nouns and verbs based, not on a semantic distinction between objects and actions, but on a grammatical distinction.

Children learning conventional languages begin to use the grammatical devices provided by their languages by age 3 and use them differently for nouns and verbs from the start—they produce different inflections for their nouns than they do for their verbs (Cazden 1968; Macnamara 1982; Miller and Ervin 1964), and they produce sentences in which their nouns have different privileges of occurrence than do their verbs (Macnamara 1982). Moreover, as early as 2 to 3 years, children are able to use grammatical markings (e.g., whether a nonsense word is preceded by an article or a noun inflection) to make inferences about whether an unknown word labels an object or action (Brown 1957; Gelman and Markman 1985; Gelman

and Taylor 1984; Katz, Baker, and Macnamara 1972; Taylor and Gelman 1988). However, as is the case for the deaf child, there is no
firm evidence that children have a noun-verb distinction that is different from an object-action distinction until they begin to treat a
word referring to an action as though it were a noun in terms of
grammatical devices (e.g., the child says "dancing is fun," using the
word *dance*, which refers to an activity, in a syntactic slot reserved for
nouns). Conversely, they could treat a word referring to an object as
though it were a verb in terms of grammatical devices (e.g., the child
says "I'm going to hat you" [= put a hat on you], thus using the word
hat, which refers to an object, in a syntactic slot reserved for verbs.
Clark (1982) has found that children produce such apparent mismatches between semantic category and grammatical category as
early as age 3;0, and in this sense can be said to have developed
a noun-verb distinction that is not grounded in an object-action
distinction.

8.8 The Role of Linguistic Input

What role does linguistic input play in this developmental sequence?
Initially, children learning conventional languages maintain a semantic distinction between noun and verb categories more rigorously
than do the adults who provide the children with their linguistic
input. For example, Brown (1957) presents evidence showing that
young children's nouns are more likely to name concrete things than
are adults' nouns, and that young children's verbs are more likely
to name actions than are adults' verbs. In his analysis of early word
use in Sarah, one of the children originally studied by Brown (1973),
Macnamara (1982) found that, while Sarah rigorously maintained
the semantic integrity of the noun and verb categories in her language, the adults who spoke to her did not. The transcripts were full
of adult remarks like "Do you want a good spanking?", where the
verb *to spank* has been nominalized and, though a noun, it still refers
to an action. Moreover, the adults who spoke to Sarah used words
that can serve as both nouns and verbs in English (e.g., *brush, catch,
comb*, and so on) and routinely used those words in both of their
senses. Macnamara looked at how Sarah responded to these dual-

function words and found that she often made no response at all. Even when she herself used one of these words modeled by the adult, she did not adopt the adult's flexibility in her own word use until much later in development. Indeed, it was not until Sarah was 2.5 years old that she first used the same word for an object and an activity; nowhere in the transcripts before age 2.5 did she violate the semantic-category boundary. Thus, children's initial reliance on a semantic basis for their noun-verb distinction is not forced on them, and may not even be facilitated, by their parents' style of talking to them.

However, as noted above, children eventually do pull away from a semantic grounding for their noun and verb categories, coming to rely (as do adults) on a grammatical definition. Just as the child's linguistic input cannot adequately explain why children begin with a rigorously held semantic distinction between nouns and verbs, linguistic input is also inadequate to explain the child's transition from a semantic to a grammatical distinction between nouns and verbs. For example, Macnamara (1982) has found that the linguistic input a child receives before and during this transition does not change— adults are equally flexible in their use of words in both noun and verb contexts throughout the transition. Thus, adults do not increase their use of the same word in both a noun and verb role at a particular point in a child's development, despite the fact that such uses, with appropriate grammatical markings, might serve to highlight the grammatical distinction between nouns and verbs rather than the semantic distinction between the two.

As a result, the way adults talk to children does not appear to be able to explain when and how children take their developmental steps toward mastery of an adult noun-verb distinction. In particular, linguistic input cannot fully explain either the child's initial dependence on a semantic basis for the noun-verb distinction, or the child's eventual move to a grammatical basis for the distinction. Nevertheless, it is certainly possible that some exposure to input from a conventional-language model may be essential for children to initially come upon the idea of distinguishing between objects and actions in their communications, and for them to eventually grammaticize the division into a noun-verb distinction. After all, the input language does display a noun-verb distinction and a roughly correlated, if not exact, object-action distinction.

The data presented here do not support this hypothesis. Rather, the data suggest that it is *not* necessary for a child to be exposed to a conventional-language model to introduce noun, verb, and adjective categories into a self-styled communication system—categories initially based on a semantic distinction and later based on a more formal, grammatical distinction. Recall that, through her own spontaneous gestures, David's mother might have introduced him to the idea that the same gesture can be used in noun, verb, and adjective contexts, in a sense violating intercategory boundaries. However, his mother did not provide a model in her gestures for keeping these categories distinct. David thus invented these devices without guidance either from a conventional language or from the gestures that typically accompany that language.

Although a conventional-language model does not appear to be necessary to invent categories that function like nouns, verbs, and adjectives, it may play an important role in shaping the nature of those categories. Words draw attention to nonobvious commonalities across objects, actions, and properties (Gelman 1996; Waxman and Markow 1995)—commonalities that a child who does not have access to a conventional code might be less likely to notice. Thus, the particular categories developed by a deaf child without linguistic input might, in the end, differ from those developed by children learning their categories from conventional-language models. For example, Gentner (1982) has suggested that verb categories are more variable across languages than noun categories. Verbs might therefore be more likely than nouns to be affected by the lack of a conventional-language model, perhaps leading the deaf children to exhibit a truncated range of verbs in their gestures relative to children learning a conventional language. As a second example, it is intriguing that none of the deaf children we have studied appears to have developed gestural names for individuals—that is, they have not developed proper names.

The absence of a class of lexical items in the deaf children's gesture systems raises the possibility that that class cannot flourish without input from a conventional language—that it is a fragile property of language. Conversely, a class of lexical items that does crop up in the deaf children's gesture systems can be considered a resilient property of language (Goldin-Meadow 1982, 1991, 2003b), one whose development does not crucially depend on linguistic input. What we have seen in this chapter is that deaf children lacking linguistic input *are* able to introduce a basic distinction between nouns, verbs, and adjectives into their self-created communication systems. The noun-verb-adjective distinction consequently appears to be one whose presence across all natural languages may be maintained, not by tradition, but by its centrality to the structure and function of human language.

Acknowledgments

The work described in this chapter was supported by grant RO1 DC00491 from NIDCD. I thank my many collaborators, Lila Gleitman, Heidi Feldman, Carolyn Mylander, Cynthia Butcher, and Mark Dodge, for their help over the years in developing these ideas, and the children and their families for their continued cooperation and friendship.

Notes

1. David also produced gestures that were not composed of parts, akin to frozen forms in conventional sign language. For example, the gesture "break" (produced by holding two fists side by side and then arcing the fists away from one another in the air) appeared to be a frozen form in David's system—he used this particular handshape + motion combination for all acts of breaking (whether or not the hands were actually used to do the deed) and for all objects (whether or not the broken object could actually fit in a fist). For holistic gestures of this sort, we used frequency of occurrence to determine prototypical forms, and considered the form most frequently used to convey a meaning to be the prototypical form for that meaning (see Goldin-Meadow et al. 1994).

2. Note that 190 lexical items is a rather small lexicon for a child of David's age. However, if we consider David's pointing gestures to be part of his lexicon, his system appears to be similar in scope to a young hearing child's (see Feldman, Goldin-Meadow, and Gleitman 1978).

3. Interestingly, when we applied this discourse criterion to David's gestures, we found that he did not use his characterizing gestures as names for individuals—that is, as proper names. He did, of course, refer to people and did so either by directly pointing at a person or by pointing at an object reminiscent of the person (e.g.,

pointing at the dining-room chair where his father typically sat to refer to Dad who was not in the room at that moment; Butcher, Mylander, and Goldin-Meadow 1991). However, David did not create gestures that incorporated distinctive aspects of an individual to use as a name for that individual.

4. "Point at jar—TWIST" is a sentence consisting of two gestures. Deictic pointing gestures are displayed in lowercase letters, iconic characterizing gestures in capital letters. The boundary of a gesture sentence is determined by motoric criteria. If the hand is relaxed or returned to neutral position (chest level) prior to the onset of the next gesture, each of the two gestures is considered a separate unit. If there is no relaxation of the hand between the two gestures, the two are considered part of a single gesture sentence (see Goldin-Meadow and Mylander 1984).

5. Note that the fourth combination, +A−O, cannot occur in the real world. The action portrayed in the gesture cannot occur in the immediate context without the object also being present—for example, the act of walking cannot take place in the context without someone or something doing the walking. In other words, if the action is present in the immediate context, the object must be present as well.

References

Baldwin, D. A., and Markman, E. M. 1989. Establishing word-object relations: A first step. *Child Development, 60,* 381–398.

Bekken, K. 1989. *Is there "motherese" in gesture?* Unpublished doctoral dissertation, University of Chicago. .

Best, B., and Roberts, G. 1976. Early cognitive development in hearing impaired children. *American Annals of the Deaf, 121,* 560–564.

Bloom, P. 1990. *Semantic structure and language development.* Unpublished doctoral dissertation, Massachusetts Institute of Technology.

Brown, R. 1957. Linguistic determinism and the part of speech. *Journal of Abnormal and Social Psychology, 55,* 1–5.

Brown, R. 1973. *A first language: The early stages.* Cambridge, MA: Harvard University Press.

Butcher, C., Mylander, C., and Goldin-Meadow, S. 1991. Displaced communication in a self-styled gesture system: Pointing at the non-present. *Cognitive Development, 6,* 315–342.

Cazden, C. B. 1968. The acquisition of noun and verb inflections. *Child Development, 39,* 433–448.

Clark, E. 1982. The young word maker: A case study of innovation in the child's lexicon. In E. Wanner and L. R. Gleitman, eds., *Language acquisition: The state of the art,* 390–425. New York: Cambridge University Press.

Conrad, R. 1979. *The deaf child.* London: Harper & Row.

Lexical Development without a Language Model

Dixon, R. M. W. 1994. Adjectives. In R. E. Asher, ed., *The encyclopedia of language and linguistics*, 29–35. New York: Pergamon Press.

Feldman, H., Goldin-Meadow, S., and Gleitman, L. 1978. Beyond Herodotus: The creation of language by linguistically deprived deaf children. In A. Lock, ed., *Action, symbol, and gesture: The emergence of language*, 351–414. New York: Academic Press.

Gelman, S. A. 1996. Concepts and theories. In R. Gelman and T. Kit-Fong Au, eds., *Perceptual and cognitive development: Handbook of perception and cognition*, 2nd ed. New York: Academic Press.

Gelman, S. A., and Markman, E. 1985. Implicit contrast in adjectives vs. nouns: Implications for word-learning in preschoolers. *Journal of Child Language, 12,* 125–143.

Gelman, S. A., and Taylor, M. 1984. How two-year-old children interpret proper and common names for unfamiliar objects. *Child Development, 55,* 1535–1540.

Genter, D. 1982. Why nouns are learned before verbs: Linguistic relativity versus natural partitioning. In S. Kuczaj, ed., *Language development, Vol. 2: Language, thought, and culture*, 301–334. Hillsdale, NJ: Erlbaum.

Givon, T. 1979. *On understanding grammar.* New York: Academic Press.

Gleitman, L. 1990. The structural sources of verb meanings. *Language Acquisition, 1,* 3–55.

Goldin-Meadow, S. 1979. Structure in a manual communication system developed without a conventional language model: Language without a helping hand. In H. Whitaker and H. A. Whitaker, eds., *Studies in neurolinguistics*, vol. 4, 125–209. New York: Academic Press.

Goldin-Meadow, S. 1982. The resilience of recursion: A study of a communication system developed without a conventional language model. In E. Wanner and L. R. Gleitman, eds., *Language acquisition: The state of the art*, 51–77. New York: Cambridge University Press.

Goldin-Meadow, S. 1991. Is "innate" another name for "developmentally resilient"? *Behavioral and Brain Sciences, 14*(4), 619–620.

Goldin-Meadow, S. 2003a. *Hearing gesture: How our hands help us think.* Cambridge, MA: Harvard University Press.

Goldin-Meadow, S. 2003b. *The resilience of language: What gesture creation in deaf children can tell us about how all children learn language.* New York: Psychology Press.

Goldin-Meadow, S., Butcher, C., Mylander, C., and Dodge, M. 1994. Nouns and verbs in a self-styled gesture system: What's in a name? *Cognitive Psychology, 27,* 259–319.

Goldin-Meadow, S., and Feldman, H. 1977. The development of language-like communication without a language model. *Science, 197,* 401–403.

Goldin-Meadow, S., McNeill, D., and Singleton, J. 1996. Silence is liberating: Removing the handcuffs on grammatical expression in the manual modality. *Psychological Review, 103*, 34–55.

Goldin-Meadow, S., and Mylander, C. 1984. Gestural communication in deaf children: The effects and non-effects of parental input on early language development. *Monographs of the Society for Research in Child Development, 49*, 1–121.

Goldin-Meadow, S., and Mylander, C. 1990. The role of a language model in the development of a morphological system. *Journal of Child Language, 17*, 527–563.

Goldin-Meadow, S., and Mylander, C. 1998. Spontaneous sign systems created by deaf children in two cultures. *Nature, 391*, 279–281.

Goldin-Meadow, S., Mylander, C., and Butcher, C. 1995. The resilience of combinatorial structure at the word level: Morphology in self-styled gesture systems. *Cognition, 56*, 195–262.

Goldin-Meadow, S., and Saltzman, J. 2000. The cultural bounds of maternal accommodation: How Chinese and American mothers communicate with deaf and hearing children. *Psychological Science, 11*, 311–318.

Hall, D. G., Waxman, S. R., and Hurwitz, W. R. 1993. The development of sensitivity to syntactic cues: Evidence from preschoolers learning property terms for familiar and unfamiliar objects. *Child Development, 58*, 1021–1034.

Hawkins, J. A. 1988. Explaining language universals. In J. A. Hawkins, ed., *Explaining language universals*, 3–28. Cambridge, MA: Blackwell.

Hoffmeister, R., and Wilbur, R. 1980. Developmental: The acquisition of sign language. In H. Lane and F. Grosjean, eds., *Recent perspectives on American Sign Language*, 61–78. Hillsdale, NJ: Erlbaum.

Hopper, P. J., and Thompson, S. A. 1984. The iconicity of the universal categories "noun" and "verb." In J. Haiman, ed., *Iconicity in syntax*, 151–183. Philadelphia: Benjamins.

Hopper, P. J., and Thompson, S. A. 1988. The discourse basis for lexical categories in universal grammar. *Language, 60*(4), 703–752.

Huttenlocher, J., Haight, W., Bryk, A., Seltzer, M., and Lyons, T. 1991. Early vocabulary growth: Relation to language input and gender. *Developmental Psychology, 27*, 236–248.

Huttenlocher, J., and Smiley, P. 1987. Early word meanings: The case of object names. *Cognitive Psychology, 19*, 63–89.

Huttenlocher, J., and Smiley, P. 1989. *An emerging lexicon: Acquiring words for events.* Unpublished manuscript, University of Chicago.

Iverson, J. M., Capirci, O., Longobardi, E., and Caselli, M. C. 1999. Gesturing in mother-child interaction. *Cognitive Development, 14*, 57–75.

Jusczyk, P. W. 1999a. *The discovery of spoken language*. Cambridge, MA: MIT Press.

Jusczyk, P. W. 1999b. How infants begin to extract words from speech. *Trends in Cognitive Science, 3*, 323–328.

Katz, N., Baker, E., and Macnamara, J. 1972. What's in a name? A study of how children learn common and proper names. *Child Development, 45*, 469–473.

Macnamara, J. 1982. *Names for things*. Cambridge, MA: MIT Press.

Mayberry, R. I. 1992. The cognitive development of deaf children: Recent insights. In F. Boller and J. Graffman, series eds., and S. Segalowitz and I. Rapin, vol. eds., *Child neuropsychology, Vol. 7: Handbook of neuropsychology*, 51–68. Amsterdam: Elsevier.

McNeill, D. 1992. *Hand and mind: What gestures reveal about thought*. Chicago: University of Chicago Press.

Meadow, K. 1968. Early manual communication in relation to the deaf child's intellectual, social, and communicative functioning. *American Annals of the Deaf, 113*, 29–41.

Miller, W., and Ervin, S. 1964. The development of grammar in child language. In U. Bellugi and R. Brown, eds., The acquisition of language. *Monographs of the Society for Research in Child Development, 29* (1, serial no. 92), 9–34.

Morgan, J., and Demuth, K. 1996. *Signal to syntax: Bootstrapping from speech to grammar in early acquisition*, 389–408. Mahway, NJ: Erlbaum.

Newport, E. L., and Meier, R. P. 1985. The acquisition of American Sign Language. In D. I. Slobin, ed., *The cross-linguistic study of language acquisition, Vol. 1: The data*, 881–938. Hillsdale, NJ: Erlbaum.

Petitto, L. A. 1992. Modularity and constraints in early lexical acquisition: Evidence from children's early language and gesture. In M. Gunnar, ed., *Minnesota Symposium on Child Psychology*, vol. 25, 25–58. Hillsdale, NJ: Erlbaum.

Robins, R. H. 1952. Noun and verb in universal grammar. *Language, 28*(3), 289–298.

Sapir, E. 1921. *Language: An introduction to the study of speech*. New York: Harcourt Brace Jovanovich.

Schachter, P. 1985. Parts-of-speech systems. In T. Shopen, ed., *Language typology and syntactic description: Clause structure*, vol. 1, 3–61. Cambridge, England: Cambridge University Press.

Shatz, M. 1982. On mechanisms of language acquisition: Can features of the communicative environment account for development? In E. Wanner and L. R. Gleitman, eds., *Language acquisition: The state of the art*, 102–127. New York: Cambridge University Press.

Stachowiak, F. J. 1976. Some universal aspects of naming as a language activity. In H. Seiler, ed., *Language universals: Papers from the Conference Held at Gummersbach/Cologne, Germany*, 207–228. Tübingen: Gunter Narr Verlag.

Supalla, T., and Newport, E. L. 1978. How many seats in a chair? The derivation of nouns and verbs in American Sign Language. In P. Siple, ed., *Understanding language through sign language research*, 91–132. New York: Academic Press.

Taylor, M., and Gelman, S. A. 1988. Adjectives and nouns: Children's strategies for learning new words. *Child Development, 59*, 411–419.

Thompson, S. A. 1988. A discourse approach to the cross-linguistic category "adjective." In J. A. Hawkins, ed., *Explaining language universals*, 167–185. Cambridge, MA: Blackwell.

Waxman, S. R. 1990. Linguistic biases and the establishment of conceptual hierarchies: Evidence from preschool children. *Cognitive Development, 5*, 123–150.

Waxman, S. R., and Booth, A. 2001. Seeing pink elephants: Fourteen-month-olds' interpretations of novel nouns and adjectives. *Cognitive Psychology, 43*, 217–242.

Waxman, S. R., and Markow, D. B. 1995. Words as invitations to form categories: Evidence from 12- to 13-month-old infants. *Cognitive Psychology, 29*, 257–302.

9

Why It Is Hard to Label Our Concepts

Jesse Snedeker and Lila R. Gleitman

But if the knowledge which we acquired before birth was lost by us at birth, and afterwards by the use of the senses we recovered that which we previously knew, will not that which we call learning be a process of recovering our knowledge, and may not this be rightly termed recollection?
—Plato, *Phaedo* (c. 412 BCE)

One way to think about infants before they acquire their native tongue is as second-language (or reincarnated) learners whose task is only to find out how priorly known concepts, at the level of both words and sentences, are mapped onto linguistic forms. Life for these Platonic infants would be much easier than that faced by Quine's linguist, trapped in an exotic land where not only pronunciations but, simultaneously, the modes of thought, may be different from one's own. We ask here which of these models is closer to the real case, concentrating attention on the task of acquiring a first lexicon.

The test bed for this question as raised in this chapter concerns the changing character of child vocabularies in the first 3 years of life. Specifically, the first vocabulary (the first 100 words or so), in various languages and under marvelously varying child-rearing conditions, massively overrepresents the noun lexical class, compared to its frequency in the input corpus, and massively underrepresents the verbs. A second widely observed property is that verbs that do appear at the earliest stages of child speech and comprehension are largely limited to action terms such as *go, run,* and *throw* even though verbs like *think* and *look* are frequent in maternal speech. What accounts for such input-output disparities? Speaking broadly, we can distinguish two general kinds of explanations for these systematic asynchronies in aspects of vocabulary development. The first emphasizes children's cognitive development. The alternative, which we will try to defend in this chapter, emphasizes linguistic development. The burden in maintaining this latter stance is to understand why, all the same, the abstract words are manifestly harder to acquire than the concrete ones.

9.1 Cognitive Development and Vocabulary Learning

Plausibly enough, the changing character of vocabularies over developmental time is usually taken to reflect the changing character of the child's conceptual life. This kind of hypothesis comes in two main flavors, depending on whether the causal machinery for cognitive change is taken to be maturational or experiential. But in either case, the changes in the function over time are assigned to changes of mentality within the learner. Smiley and Huttenlocher (1995, 24) present a particularly perspicuous version of this view: "Even a very few uses may enable the child to learn words if a particular concept is accessible. Conversely, even highly frequent and salient words may not be learned if the child is not yet capable of forming the concepts they encode. These two cases, in which effects of input frequency and salience are weak, suggest that conceptual development exerts strong enabling or limiting effects, respectively, on which words are acquired." The claim is that children fail to learn certain words despite the fact that they are often uttered in their presence just because the concepts they encode are beyond their grasp. Indeed, the word-learning facts are often used as more-or-less straightforward indices of concept attainment (e.g., Huttenlocher, Smiley, and Charney 1983; Dromi 1987; Gopnik and Meltzoff 1997). Two cases in which cognitive development is posited as an explanatory mechanism are relevant to the findings we will present in this chapter.

9.1.1 Nouns Before Verbs

A first case that appears to lend itself particularly well to explanation in terms of conceptual change has to do with the temporal priority of *noun learning* over *verb learning*, a phenomenon that is apparently robust both to architectural distinctions between languages and to input differences that are correlated with linguistic distinctions (for a masterful review, see Gentner and Boroditsky 2001). Even though children hear both verbs and nouns from earliest infancy, their earliest vocabulary is overwhelmingly nominal (Goldin-Meadow, Seligman, and Gelman 1976; Bates, Dale, and Thal 1995), with only a very few true verbs.[1] Verbs are not seen in proportions similar to their proportion in the adult input until the child is about 2.5 years old, or even older in many cases. It has been conjectured that it is the typical object-labeling function of nouns versus the relational functions of verbs that accounts for these learning facts. The acquisition of concepts describing relations between objects would necessarily await acquisition of the object concepts themselves (O'Grady 1987; Caselli, Casadio, and Bates 1999).

The position, then, is that noun and verb learning occur *seriatim* as a straightforward reflex of the fact that object- and relational-type concepts become available one after the other to the infant mind. The littlest children just cannot think about relations, or at least cannot easily think about them at the level requisite to word learning, so they cannot learn the words that express such concepts.

9.1.2   Concreteness of Verbs

A second linguistic-developmental finding provides further grist for the maturational account. The earliest verbs are not an unbiased sample of those that appear frequently in the input. Children all over the world say words like *throw* and *run* well in advance of *think* and *know*. The first verbs that children produce describe actions or movement events and encode the physical motion of the agent (Bloom, Lightblown, and Hood 1975), and these verbs seem to be understood earlier or better as well (Huttenlocher, Smiley, and Charney 1983; Gentner 1978). Mental-state terms are not used as such until at least 2.5 years of age (Shatz, Wellman, and Silber 1983; Furrow et al. 1992) and are not fully distinguished from one another in comprehension until around age 4 (see, e.g., Johnson and Maratsos 1977; Moore, Gilbert, and Sapp 1995).[2] Their absence in early vocabularies is often taken as evidence that the child does not have control of the relevant concepts. As Gopnik and Meltzoff (1997, 121) put this, "The emergence of belief words like 'know' and 'think' [occurs] during the fourth year of life, after 'see' is well established. In this case … changes in the children's spontaneous extensions of these terms parallel changes in their predictions and explanations. The developing theory of mind is apparent both in semantic change and in conceptual change."

Summarizing, the position just sketched is that the word-learning function follows from, and more or less directly reflects, the concept-acquisition function. At the limit, no one could dispute the relevance of conceptual organization to word learning. One cannot acquire productive use of a term that expresses a concept that one cannot entertain. Babies could not learn *casuistry* and *transmigration* until steeped in the appropriate theological traditions, and nomads for related reasons might have trouble with *picnic*.[3] But whether these limitations are imposed by the mentality of the learner rather than ("merely") by his state of world knowledge is open to question.

9.2 Linguistic Development and the Vocabulary-Attainment Sequence

A number of influential proposals relate word learning to biases and abilities that represent stages in the development of language rather than, or in addition to, development in the general mental capacities of the learner. In particular, Markman and her colleagues (for a review, see Markman 1994) and Clark (1987) have experimentally documented biases that do not characterize learners generally, but that become operative in the specific context of word learning. Well-known examples are the whole-object bias, the principle of mutual exclusivity (or "no-synonym" constraint), and the taxonomic constraint.

Constraints of this kind provide a principled account for the noun-dominance effect in early child language. Biases such as the whole-object constraint, which assist in the acquisition of nouns, could make it more difficult to learn other types of words (Kuczaj 1990). If the child initially attempts to map every label to an object, verb learning will be delayed until enough evidence accumulates to override this default hypothesis. By positing a hierarchy of constraints which prioritize the child's hypotheses about word learning, it might be possible to extend this explanation to account for within-class sequences as well, including the order in which different types of verbs are acquired.

Gentner (1982) offers another explanation of the noun-dominance effect that is rooted in the process of language learning. She suggests that, while babies may be equally facile with object and action categorization, they may face a harder task in discovering the extensions of verbs than of nouns. According to her view, the key is in the universality, or lack of it, in the mapping relations between words and concepts from language to language. By and large, languages accomplish object description in the same way, namely with nouns, but differ in the semantic components that they characteristically encode within the verb (Talmy 1985). To the extent that this is so, one could envisage a learning procedure predisposed by nature for the object-to-nominal mapping. In contrast, acquisition of the first verbs would have to await discovery of the language-particular conflation patterns.[4]

Note, however, that this proposal leaves us in the dark about several of the gross facts about early vocabulary growth. Choi and Bowerman's work (1991) on crosscutting lexicalization patterns for motion events in English and Korean suggests that language-specific conflation patterns do not always pose a particularly difficult problem for the young language learner. Moreover, the conflation-pattern solution will not extend to the timing of "concrete" (or *action*) versus "abstract" (or *mental*) verbs since, as far as we know, there is no reason to predict that the crosslinguistic differences in conflation patterns should be more complex for more abstract verbs.

9.3 The Present Proposal

The proposal we evaluate in the present chapter also places the origin of vocabulary change in linguistic rather than conceptual development. The young child's conceptual repertoire may be rich and varied enough from the start to accommodate the commonly heard words, including *cat, throw*, and *think*. All the same, different kinds of information must be brought to bear for solving the mapping problem for these words, not all of them available from the outset. Specifically, infants must initially learn the meanings of words by inspecting the extralinguistic contexts (or situations) in which the word is used. After all, linguistic novices can glean little from the utterance in which a word occurs for the simple reason that they have not yet learned what these other words mean. This initial word-to-world pairing procedure will suffice to identify a small set of concrete nominal terms. To learn that *cat* is the English-language word for the concept "cat," the child need only note that cats are the objects most systematically present in scenes wherein the sound /kat/ is uttered (just as proposed by Augustine [398] 1992; Locke [1690] 1964; Pinker 1984; and many other commentators).[5] However, this situational evidence, taken alone, may be insufficient for the mapping of most of the vocabulary. For example, words like *think, idea, bachelor,* and *pet* seem to lack obvious and stable observational correlates (and see Plato on *virtue*). Then so long as inspection of extralinguistic context is the only learning tool available, learners should be able to acquire only a special and very limited kind of words: those that are both straightforwardly available to perception and lexically "favored," perhaps in Markman's sense.

We will demonstrate that the vocabulary could become rich and diversified owing to a succession of bootstrapping operations, *grounded in the prior acquisition of concrete nominals,* that build the words in tandem with the clause-level syntax. In this new informational state, the mapping problem is solved by the child's joint consideration of the extralinguistic and linguistic-structural contingencies for word use (a learning procedure we will be calling *structure-to-world pairing*). Acquisition of the lexicon and acquisition of the grammar, are, in these respects, parts of a single underlying process.[6]

9.4 An Experimental Analysis: The Human Simulation Paradigm

The findings we review here are from experimentation in which adult subjects try to identify words from partial information about the contexts in which they occur (see also Snedeker, Gleitman, and Brent 1999; Gillette et al. 1999; Snedeker 2000). Conceptually, these experiments are analogous to computer simulations in which a device, endowed with whatever ("innate") ideas and learning procedures its makers deem desirable to program into it, is exposed to data of the kind naturally received by the target learner it is simulating. The measure of success of the simulation is how faithfully it reproduces the learning function for that target using these authentic data.

Our test device is a population of undergraduates (hence Human Simulations). Their preprogramming includes, *inter alia*, knowledge of English. Their task is to identify words they already know when these are disguised as nonsense words, beeps, or tones. The data they receive are contextualized mother-to-child speech events, transcripts or videotapes of the situations in which a word was used. The form in which they receive information about these speech events is manipulated across conditions of the experiment.

These experiments serve two purposes. The first is to provide an estimate of the psychological potency of various cues to word meaning that are available in the real learning situation. What kinds of words can be identified by inspection of the contingencies for their use in the absence of all other cues, assuming a conceptually mature learner? The second is to estimate by reference to these outcomes something about the word- and structure-learning procedures used by children.

Restating, we attempt to reproduce in adults the learning function of the one- and two-year-old child by appropriate changes in the information structure of the input. If successful, this exercise makes plausible that the order of events in child vocabulary acquisition (here, the developmental move from nominal categories to predicate categories, and from less to more abstract verbs) is assignable to information-structure developments rather than to cognitive developments in the learner, for we have removed such possible cognitive inadequacies from the equation. When our college-age subjects fail to learn, it is not because they have some mental deficit that disbars them from attaining words like *ball* or *get*. In fact, since the test items are the most common nouns and verbs uttered by mothers in conversation with their language-learning infants, we know that these words are already in our subjects' vocabularies. All they have to do is to recover what they previously knew. Our first experimental probe asked how efficiently they can do so by using the evidence of the senses.

9.5 Simulating Word-to-World Pairing

The stimuli for these experiments were generated by Gillette et al. (1999), who videotaped mothers interacting with their 18- to 24-month-old children in an unstructured situation. The maternal speech was transcribed to find the twenty-four most frequent nouns and the twenty-four most frequent verbs that these mothers uttered during these taped sessions. To simulate a condition under which learners were presumed able only to identify recurrences of the same word (qua sound) in the speech stream and to match these with their extralinguistic contexts of use, they selected six video clips during which the mother was uttering each of these words. Each video clip started about 30 seconds before the mother uttered the word, and ended 10 seconds afterward. A pilot study indicated that this was enough to give the observer the gist of the mother-child interaction.

There were six clips for each "mystery word" these subjects were to identify. This simulates the fact that real learners are not forced to acquire meanings from a single encounter with a word and its context. Rather, by examining the use of the word in a variety of contexts, the observer can attempt to parse out those properties of the world common to all these encounters. The six video clips for the word were then spliced together with brief pauses between them. The subjects were told for each word whether it would be a noun or a verb, but *they did not hear what the mother was saying, because the audio had been removed.* Instead of the original soundtrack a single audible beep occurred at the very instant during the depicted event when the mother had actually uttered the mystery word. Subjects wrote down their guess after viewing each of the six clips for a word—that is, as cross-situational evidence accumulated. Then they were asked to make a final conjecture based on all the evidence.

Notice that this procedure cannot tell us whether a word can or cannot be acquired from extralinguistic contexts, even if word-learning mechanisms do not vary between adults and children and even if (as we suppose) the vocabulary-acquisition procedure is largely a mapping problem. This is because, though the word-learning function in children is clearly efficient and rapid (e.g., Carey 1978; Caselli et al. 1995), perhaps, for all we know, 7 or 40 or 900 exposures to new words are ordinarily required. What we can consider realistically is the *relative* efficiency of noun versus verb learning under this information condition.

The results of this procedure were very dramatic. When the subjects were limited to the information of their senses—that is, when they had to acquire the mappings of sounds (here, beeps) onto meanings solely via inspection of the extralinguistic contingencies for their use—they were able to identify 45 percent of the nouns but only 15 percent of the verbs, a difference of great magnitude and statistical reliability. Like infants learning their first words, these adult subjects "acquired" a vocabulary dominated by nouns and under-populated by verbs.

Further analyses are even more revealing of the dramatic noun-verb difference. Every noun target was correctly identified by at least one of the subjects exposed to it, whereas fully a third of the verbs were never correctly identified. In addition, the learning curve (correctness as a function of trial) is reliably steeper for nouns than for verbs. Finally, and most revealingly, subjects converge toward the correct answer for the nouns; the most frequent final guess was the correct target for over half of the nouns. In strong contrast, the most frequent final guess for the verbs was the correct target only a quarter of the time.

In sum, on the basis of accumulating cross-situational evidence, subjects identified nouns quite efficiently, and verbs very poorly. For many of the verbs the information provided by the scenes is not only inadequate, but actually misleading, leading subjects to settle on the same incorrect hypotheses.

Why should cross-situational observation have been so much more useful for noun identification than for verb identification? Gillette et al. (1999) showed that the noun-dominance effect is itself an arti-fact of another distinction, namely, one of imagability or concreteness, which is closely correlated with the noun-verb distinction in the stimulus materials. Mothers frequently say words like *think* and *like* to their toddlers but rarely say *thought* or *liking*. Both within and across lexical class, imagability ratings were highly correlated with number of subjects who identified a word. Nouns like *music* were less often identified than nouns like *drum*, and verbs like *want* were less often identified than verbs like *throw*. What these subjects' responses seem to be telling us is that, because they were limited to learning words from extralinguistic observation, they could only identify words whose real-world concomitants were stable and observable.[7]

This tautology ("only observables can be learned from observation") has to be taken very seriously in understanding the nature of infant word learning. Let us suppose that infants have adequate conceptual sophistication but are forced to deduce the meaning of terms solely by examining the world and attempting to decipher the intentions of those around them. That is, *suppose that the only problem in acquiring a mental lexicon is the mapping problem, with no concept acquisition required at all.* Then just because the verb repertoire in infant-directed speech is systematically less concrete than the noun repertoire, as was shown, it should be less amenable to acquisition by word-to-world pairing.

As we next show, changing the information structure of the input removes—in fact reverses—these effects of concreteness on the word-mapping function.

9.6   The Learning Patterns for Verbs

Smiley and Huttenlocher (1995) have shown strong timing differences in the appearance of verbs from different semantic domains in child vocabularies. For example, verbs that encode characteristic self-caused movements of an organism (e.g., *jumping*) are understood and produced earlier in life than verbs that encode change and require information about causes and goals (e.g., *opening*). And verbs that describe mental states and acts on average appear later still (Huttenlocher, Smiley, and Charney 1983; Shatz, Wellman, and Silber 1983; Gopnik and Meltzoff 1997) despite the fact that verbs from all three classes are frequent in mother-to-child speech.

As we stated in the introductory remarks, these timing effects have usually been assigned to the cognitive-representational limitations of very young children. But once again it may not be—or it may not be *only*—that these verbs are harder to acquire because the child lacks the conceptual wherewithal to represent their meanings. The same solution that applies to the acquisition differences across lexical classes (nouns before verbs) may apply within lexical class as well. It may be that the children just breaking into language lack the linguistic-learning tools for solving the mapping problem for abstract words. This seems plausible because, just as for the noun-verb learning function described earlier, the original learning machinery (word-to-world pairing) might yield adequate cues for learning which sound in English encodes *kick* and *jump*, but not for learning which sound encodes invisible mental acts like *think*. Indeed, the verbs with the highest identification scores in the Gillette study were *throw, come,* and *push,* and those with the lowest scores included all the mental-content verbs (*like, think, know, love*). Perhaps, just like our college-sophomore subjects, infant learners have the concepts encoded in these abstract terms, but insufficient tools for discovering their encoding in English.

The experiment now reported attempted to adjudicate between these two kinds of explanations via an extension of the Human Simulation paradigm. Again adult subjects were asked to solve the mapping problem. But this time we varied the information available to them.[8] In one condition, as before, they had to identify words (that is, solve the mapping problem) on the basis of observed scenes. But other subject groups were given alternative or additional information. These new information sources were attempts to simulate different ways the input might be represented at various points during language acquisition. For example, at the earliest stages we assume learners are limited to word-to-world pairing. After all, as we just showed experimentally, that assumption is sufficient to explain why they learn many concrete nouns and few verbs. But later they ought to be able to use, as well, the statistically observable facts about words' frequent local neighbors (e.g., *the* near nouns but *-ed* near verbs, food words in construction with verbs like *eat*). These auxiliary sources of evidence, increasingly available as language experience grows, might broaden the class of identifiable verbs.

Eighty-four undergraduate students participated in this new experiment, twelve in each of the experimental conditions, described below. The stimulus materials were taken from the same video-taped maternal speech as Gillette et al. 1999, but this time we focused only on the verbs, for these were the locus of difficulty in the scene-interpretation study. The twenty-four most frequent verbs in these maternal corpora were selected as the target items. As before, six instances of the use of each verb were culled from the corpora and presented to the subjects. It is important to keep in mind that while subject groups received different representations of this information (depending on which condition they were assigned to), each group was being asked to identify the *same* verbs, and based on the *same* six maternal utterances of that word.

9.7 Information Conditions for Verb Learning

The seven learning conditions were as follows:

Scenes Condition   This condition simply replicated the Gillette study. The extralinguistic contexts were presented on videotape. The original audio had been removed and a beep inserted at the point where the mother actually uttered the target word. Subjects attempted to identify the mystery word after each of the scenes and then offered their best guess in light of all of them.

Nouns Condition   Here, subjects simply saw a written list of the nouns and pronouns that had been uttered in construction with each instance of the use of the verb. For example, the maternal utterance "Did you play with the elephant?" was presented to subjects in the Nouns Condition as: "elephant, you." These subjects did not see the scene in which this utterance occurred. This condition simulates a hypothetical stage of learning that assumes the prior learning of some frequent nouns, which can now—even in the absence of knowledge of language-specific syntax—support verb learning. For example, the child who hears food names repeatedly with some novel verb might make the canny guess that it means something like *eat*. If the probabilities of this noun-verb association are stable enough, the learner could make use of such information even without knowing anything more refined about the structure of such sentences.

Frames Condition   Here, subjects were shown representations of the six maternal sentences as nonsense frames, much in the style of Lewis Carroll's "Jabberwocky" ([1865] 1989). The closed-class words (e.g., determiners or prepositions) and morphemes were left intact but all the nouns, pronouns, adjectives, and verbs appeared as nonsense forms. For example, the sentence given above ("Did you play with the elephant?") was presented as: "Did er PILK with the ramermok?" This orderly distortion of the original sentences preserved systematic clues to the syntactic category of words while removing information about their identity. Because of the strong correlations between syntactic privileges of verbs and their semantic interpretations (see Levin 1993; Fisher, Gleitman, and Gleitman 1991), it is plausible that learners once in possession of grammars could exploit this information to constrain their conjectures about verb semantics (for experimental evidence that young children do just this, see Fisher et al. 1994; Naigles, Gleitman, and Gleitman 1993; Naigles 1996).

Scenes + Nouns Condition   Subjects were presented with both the video clip in which the verb was used and the list of nouns it was used with.

Scenes + Frames Condition   Subjects in this condition were shown the video clip and the syntactic frame for each of the uses of the mystery verb.

Nouns + Frames Condition   This condition combined the two types of linguistic context, noun co-occurrence (Nouns Condition) and syntactic-frame information (Frames Condition), simply by putting the nouns and pronouns words back into the nonsense frames. Note that this manipulation converts co-occurrence information to selectional information.

Full-Information Condition   In this condition, we presented the videotaped scenes for each target, along with the sentences from the Nouns + Frames Condition.

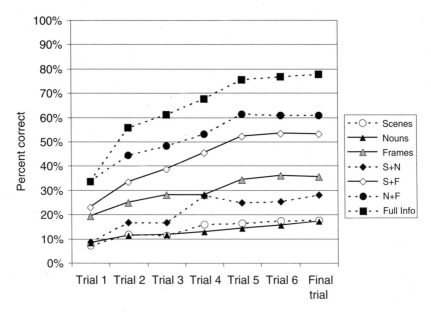

Figure 9.1
Performance across trials for each information condition (verb targets).

9.8 Results

Subjects' responses were scored as correct if they contained the same base morpheme as the target word (variation in number, tense, or voice was allowed). We begin by examining how overall performance varied across the seven information conditions, then we explore the pattern of performance for action verbs, light verbs, and mental-state verbs.

9.8.1 Information Sources for Verb Identification

Figure 9.1 presents the percent correct identification at each trial in each condition—that is, the learning curves. Figure 9.2 illustrates the percentage correct on the final trial in each condition. As the figures suggest and as verified by statistical analysis, some of the information sources we tested were more potent than others. Higher potency is

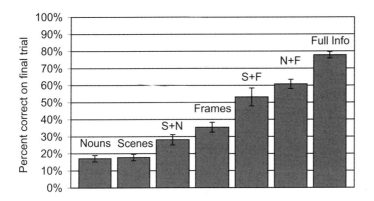

Figure 9.2
Performance on the final trial for all conditions.

manifest as an increase in correct responses on all trials, a greater improvement across trials, and a higher proportion correct on the final trial.

By comparing the three basic cue types, we can test the relative potency of each information source in isolation. By the final trial, identification of verbs is reliably higher in the Frames Condition (38% correct) than in the Nouns (17%) or Scenes (18%) Condition. Thus, we replicate Gillette et al.'s finding that scenes provide little guidance for mapping common verbs to their meanings, and confirm previous analyses of the input that showed that frames are a powerful information source for verb learning (Fisher et al. 1991; Geyer 1998; Lederer, Gleitman, and Gleitman 1995; Kako 1998). The results of comparing Final-Trial correctness scores on all cues and cue combinations yield a statistically reliable partial ordering of the potency of these different informational conditions:

$$\text{Scenes, Nouns} < S + N, \text{Frames} < S + F, N + F < \text{Full Information}$$
$$(1)$$

As we will later discuss, the rising rate of identification in our adult subjects under these different conditions of stimulus representation has the potential to support an information-based theory for why the child's verb learning is initially slow, improves somewhat in the older toddler who has amassed statistical knowledge of the co-occurrence of verbs with particular types of nouns, and then makes a dramatic move upward in the middle of the third year of life, when the phrase structure of the exposure language is well established (see also Lenneberg 1967; Caselli et al. 1995). Intriguingly, the same information-change solution that can account for the learning differences between the noun and verb lexical classes appears to hold once again when we look at the acquisition function within the verb class. Recall that the results for the verbs as a class yielded the ordering of cue-type potency given in (1). But this pattern of performance varied widely from verb to verb. This variation across items may throw light on the internal course of verb learning in young children too.

9.8.2 Different Verbs Require Different Information Sources for Identification

The maternally frequent verbs studied in these experiments fall into three classes that have been identified and discussed in the prior literature. These are the relatively concrete verbs that describe specific actions in and on the observable world (*fall, stand, turn, play, wait, hammer, push, throw, pop*), the more abstract mental-content verbs (*know, like, see, say, think, love, look, want*), and a third set, of what have been called light verbs (*come, do, get, go, have, make, put*). Light verbs are those that are relatively "bleached" of specific semantic content, but that combine with nouns in English predicate phrases to form a contentful whole (as in "make a bet" or "go skiing"). One might argue with a few of our placements of the test verbs in this trichotomy, but we have settled for following the practice of prior commentators, especially with regard to the identification of the light verbs (Clark 1996; Ninio 1996; Goldberg 1999).

Figure 9.3 presents the percent identification scores for items in these three verb classes for each of the three basic information types. As inspection of the figure reveals, while neither scenes nor nouns are very powerful cues to verb identity, they are more effective for the action verbs than for the other two classes.[9] The pattern for the Frames Condition is sharply different. First, this is the condition that

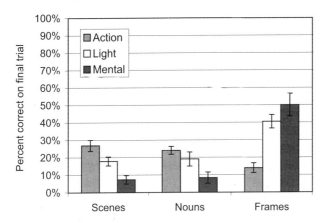

Figure 9.3
Different types of verbs require different information sources.

is overall most potent as a learning cue for verbs. Second, it is the mental and light verbs whose learning is chiefly supported by the structural information. This is hardly surprising in light of the discussion thus far. Mental events and states are hard to observe and thus are unlikely to be acquired via a stand-alone machinery of extralinguistic observation. As for light verbs, the less they mean (or the more general their meanings) the less informative their situational concomitants will be.

The third generalization that can be drawn from figure 9.3 is that frames are quite uninformative for identifying action verbs. This final result comes as something of a surprise. After all, while concrete action verbs might be readily identifiable in terms of their real-world contexts, there is no a priori reason to expect that they would not also be well differentiated by their syntactic contexts. But they are not. Action verbs were more likely to appear in intransitive or simple transitive frames. Because these frames are associated with a broad range of meanings they provide little constraint on the types of verbs that can appear in them. Mental verbs and light verbs were more likely to appear with prepositional phrases, particles, or sentence complements. These frames are more selective and thus provide more information about the verbs that occur in them. This "functional-load" or "entropy" analysis of differential frame informativeness was shown in the context of maternal-speech patterns by Lederer, Gleitman, and Gleitman (1995; see also Goldberg 1995 and Kako 1998 for experimental documentation with adult subjects).

The rationale for this distinction in the differential informativeness of frames across verb subtypes may be implicit in the needs of the learning device. Specifically, the information quality of the input is more efficient than generous. Syntactic differentiation of the verb set is provided in language design, but primarily where it is required to solve the mapping problem—that is, for the abstract component of the vocabulary for which observation fails. Notice that it is now possible to understand the course of vocabulary learning within the verb class without reference to conceptual change. Novice learners who do not yet know the language-specific syntax of the exposure language, no matter what their conceptual sophistication, cannot solve the mapping problem for abstract verbs because the information relevant to identify these items resides almost solely in their distinctive syntactic privileges.

9.8.3 Bootstrapping into Language Knowledge

Though syntactic frames appear to be a powerful source of information for verb learning, they of course do not occur in nature outside of laboratory demonstrations (e.g., Epstein 1961) and Lewis Carroll poems. By the time real children have the linguistic sophistication to identify the form that a syntactic structure takes in the exposure language, they have learned the meanings of many nouns from extralinguistic contexts (Gillette et al. 1999). This gain in syntactic knowledge clearly does not cause children to ignore the extralinguistic contexts of word use. Rather, it has the effect of enhancing the *linguistic* representations of events so that they are commensurate with the *extralinguistic* event representations that have been available from early infancy.

Several of the conditions of our simulation presented the adult learners with combinations of cues, which are by hypothesis simulations of successive states of the language learner. These were designed to support theorizing about two crucial aspects of the procedure by which novices turn into experts. The first concerns how

Why It Is Hard to Label Our Concepts

successively more complex representations of the linguistic input could be built by the learner from the resources available in the prior learning stage—that is, *how bootstrapping can be grounded*. The second pertains to the temporal succession from the concrete to the abstract in verb learning.[10]

Here, we will concentrate on the three conditions (Scenes, Scenes + Nouns, Full Information) of the simulation that are intended to model successive representational states. If the simulations mirror the vocabulary-acquisition process, these comparisons allow us to predict at which stage the child is likely to have the representational wherewithal to learn different types of verbs. The performance of subjects in these conditions, again subdivided for the three verb types (action, light, mental), is graphically presented in figure 9.4.

The First 100 Words (Word-to-World Pairing)
In previous studies we demonstrated that nouns submit most readily to the word-to-world pairing procedure simulated in the Scenes Condition, mirroring the noun-dominant children acquiring their first vocabulary items (see Gillette et al. 1999; Snedeker, Gleitman, and Brent 1999). Verbs are harder for our subjects to identify from this single evidentiary source; moreover, only for the concrete action verbs is there any substantial success in this word-to-world simulation.

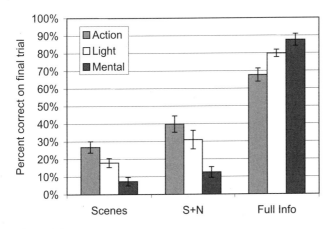

Figure 9.4
Performance for each verb class improves with increased representational resources.

First Word Combinations (Noun-to-Verb Co-occurrence)

Adding noun context information to the scene information ("S + N" in figure 9.4) raises the identification scores of our subjects in all three verb subcategories. It is easy to see why. For one thing, certain kinds of nouns tend to cluster with certain kinds of verbs. A noun like *telephone* can be a giveaway to a small class of common verbs, such as *talk, listen,* and *call.* Moreover, the number of nouns in the maternal sentence (that is, within the prosodic contour of the clause) provides an additional clue to the verb meaning. This is because in the very short sentences used to infants (and therefore in the simulated input), the number of nouns is a soft indicator of the number of arguments (Fisher et al. 1994; Fisher 1996; Gleitman 1990; Naigles 1990; Naigles, Gleitman, and Gleitman 1993). Thus *gorp* in a prosodically bounded sequence such as "... *John* ... *gorp* ..." is more likely to mean "sneeze" than "kick," even if John is in the observed scene simultaneously sneezing and kicking a ball. And "kick" is a better guess than "sneeze" for either "... *John* ... *gorp* ... *ball* ..." or "... *ball* ... *gorp* ... *John* ..." even if, because of insufficient language-specific syntactic knowledge, one cannot tell one of these last two from the other.

We have conjectured a learning device that uses this primitive quasi-structural noun-to-verb information for purposes that go beyond acquiring the specifics of verb meaning: as a bootstrap into the language-specific clause-level syntax. This is because the noun occurrences (e.g., *ball, John*) taken together with the scene information (say, John kicking a ball) allow tentative assignment of the nominals themselves to different argument positions. John is the agent, hence the subject, of the kicking event. As figure 9.4 illustrates, this combination of information is more useful for identifying action verbs and light verbs than for identifying mental verbs.[11]

Structure-to-World Pairing: Learning in the Presence of Coordinated Structural- and Semantic-Event Representations

Looking now at the rightmost columns of figure 9.4, we see the dramatic effect on verb identification of increasing representational resources. All three kinds of verbs are more efficiently identified in the presence of full information (that is, when subjects saw the scenes and were shown the mother's sentences with their nouns occurring in their original structural positions), and the presence of syntactic-frame information has a stronger impact on the identification of light and mental verbs than it does on action verbs. The result is that in the *full-information condition* the identification of light and mental verbs is as efficient as the identification of action verbs.

In this experimental condition, the adult subjects were highly efficient "learners": they correctly identified 78 percent of the target verbs, and all but three verbs were identified by more than half of them. This efficiency, accuracy, and scope of learning in the presence of full information fits well with the observed vocabulary-acquisition feats of child learners who give evidence of even rudimentary syntactic knowledge. Such children, somewhere between the third and fourth years of life, are just the ones whose vocabulary contains a complement of verbs roughly proportional to the percentage of verbs in the input (Caselli et al. 1995; Lenneberg 1967), including a substantial number of mental verbs.

9.9   The Logic of the Human Simulation Paradigm

We began this chapter with two puzzles about the course of early vocabulary growth: Why do nouns appear in much larger proportions in the earliest vocabularies compared to their proportions in the adult speech that infants hear? Why do children learn action verbs long before the equally common mental verbs? Our aim in the experimentation was to evaluate two approaches to this input-output disparity: changes in the learner's mentality versus changes in his language knowledge.

The classic method for distinguishing between internally and externally driven changes in organisms' attainments is by looking at the effects of isolation, produced either by nature (e.g., in the language-acquisition context, linguistically isolated deaf children and observationally deprived blind children; Feldman, Goldin-Meadow, and Gleitman 1978; Singleton and Newport 1994; Landau and Gleitman 1985) or by experimental artifice (e.g., Herodotus [410 BCE] 1992; for a review, see Gleitman and Newport 1995). The Human Simulation paradigm is another way of testing performance under varying conditions of external information availability. This paradigm has several critical properties that make it especially useful for our purposes: (1) it removes conceptual change as an explanation of the findings by testing adults only; (2) by the same token, it reduces the problem of vocabulary learning to mapping; (3) it therefore allows analysis of the effects of changing information on mapping success, both in rate and type of item that can be acquired; (4) it maintains control of the stimulus situation by testing the very same words in the very same sentences, differently represented across the conditions; (5) it maintains realism because the test items are the words mothers use most to novices, as they actually appeared within the mothers' own utterances.

Two important kinds of objections to the usefulness of this paradigm for theorizing have been raised in the literature. The first is a misunderstanding of what can or should be meant by "observation." To repeat a point we made earlier (see notes 5 and 8), nothing in what we say, or in the Human Simulation paradigm as instantiated here, implies that the observer, be he child or college sophomore, perceives the visible world only in terms of some low-level sensory-perceptual representation. We only ask: *Whatever* the set of interpretations that a sophisticated observer can take out of his transactions with the world, is it rich and restrictive enough to converge on the unique and specific interpretation implied by the actual lexical choice of the speaker? Can you tell from observation of, say, a book moving from Alice to John, what a speaker pertinently and saliently wants to say of it? For after all, Alice is *giving* the ball but also *handing* it and possibly *showing* it, the book itself is *moving*, and John is *getting, receiving, taking,* and maybe *snatching* it; both of them are *looking* at it, and likely one or both, or the speaker herself, is thinking about the motives behind the transfer.

Indeed, it is because of the very richness of human perception and conception that the problem of language acquisition has become so difficult to explain in the modern era. Hume did not have this problem. His babies all interpreted the scenes they saw in the same ways, those offered up by primitive sensory mechanisms. In contrast, modern babies and their simulated counterparts, while usually able to identify the referent event, are unable to assign a unique predicate interpretation to that event, a finding that should have been predicted by anyone who ever read Chomsky's (1959) review of Skinner.

A related objection that has been raised to the Human Simulation paradigm is that its observational condition either denies or fails to explore the potency of the social cues available in the ongoing interaction between the mother and child (e.g., Pinker 1994). But this is again a misunderstanding, this time of our subjects' situation. The primary cues that are available to the novice language learner are also available to the adults in these studies. During the 40-second video clip, they see the development of the ongoing interaction as well as the gestures, eye gaze, and facial expressions of both the mother and the child. And the subjects clearly use this information to restrict their hypotheses. They show a strong tendency to limit their responses to labels for the objects and events that the mother and child are focusing on. This sensitivity to social-pragmatic cues is evidenced most clearly by the target verb, *come.* In all six scenes, as it happens, each mother uses the verb to request that her child return to where she (the mother) is sitting. And in the six scenes the toddlers, true to their nature, continue to run away despite the mothers' pleas. But the lack of a direct correspondence between the depicted actions and the meaning of the word did not faze the subjects. In both studies, 75 percent of them identified the word from the video clips. The subjects' problem is not that social cues about the event in view are unavailable to them. It is that nonlinguistic social cues are often ambiguous. Children can often use eye gaze, action sequences, and gestures to learn which event or object is being referred to (Baldwin 1993; Tomasello 1995), but these cues cannot tell them what perspective the speaker is taking on that entity. Clark (1997) has pointed out that adults often provide verbal information about the perspective that a word takes in the conversation in which they introduce it. In these studies we threw out this information by erasing the audio. This was consistent with our goal of isolating the cues that are available to novice language learners.

9.10 Major Findings

Summarizing the outcomes, both very young children and their simulated adult counterparts are highly "concrete" in their vocabulary learning under the very conditions that *must* obtain in the first moments of word learning, when the only inferential tool is discovery of recurrent aspects of the extralinguistic situations in which a particular word occurs. They exhibit noun dominance, plus concreteness in their verb learning. In contrast, 3- and 4-year-olds, as well as the adult subjects when provided with coordinated structural and semantic information, seem to effortlessly acquire both abstract and concrete verbs. We conclude from the similarities between child and adult-experimental learning functions that changes in the character of early vocabularies may have less to do with the children becoming wiser over time than with their becoming experts in the semantically relevant syntax of their native tongue.

As for any experimental review, it is always possible to deny that the manipulations, limited as they are in fidelity to the real world of learners, truly model their target population. The simulations are mute about the extent to which verbs could be learned in the presence of more strenuous teaching techniques on the part of the adult community (for an important experimental demonstration and discussion, see Gropen et al. 1991), or in the presence of a massively larger input database of situational evidence. Their only interpretable finding is that adult identification is sensitive to the type of information available, in a way plausibly related to the child acquisition sequence. This is an existence proof that vocabulary acquisition in the real case may reduce mainly to a mapping problem, and does not require invocation of conceptual change to explain.

9.11 Where Did the Phrase Structure Come from? Or Why the Children of the World Oppose the Whorf-Sapir Hypothesis

Explicit in the syntactic bootstrapping approach to word and structure acquisition (and, for that matter, in the semantic bootstrapping approach of Grimshaw 1990 and Pinker 1984) are two background suppositions. The first is that infants, much like older humans, are disposed to interpret the world in terms of predicate-argument structures whose contents concern the relationships among entities, properties, states, and events. The second is that there is a mapping between these conceptual structures and the clause-level syntax of human languages that is universally the same and transparent in at least the following senses: (1) events and states are described at the level of the clause; an important corollary of this universal is that, in every language, mental-content verbs license clauselike complements; (2) by and large, there is a one-to-one relation between participants in an act (or state) and noun phrases in a clause: unary relations (e.g., John falling) will be mapped onto intransitive structures, binary relations (e.g., John carrying a suitcase) will be mapped onto transitive structures, ternary relations (John giving a ball to Horace) onto ditransitive structures (i.e., the theta criterion and the projection principle, in some form; Chomsky 1981);[12] (3) conceptual-dominance relations among actors in an event (the agent, the theme or patient, the recipient) map onto structural dominance in the sentence (the subject, the direct object, the indirect object); a thematic hierarchy. *These simplest syntax-semantics relations are unlearned, "natural," and therefore can serve as part of the presuppositional armamentarium that children bring into the language-learning situation; indeed they establish the framework within which language learning is possible at all* (see Jackendoff 1985 for detailed explication of relations between conceptual and linguistic structure, and their implications for learning).

We have invoked such unlearned principles repeatedly in the present discussion: learners can choose among the many plausible interpretations of an observed event *because* they can inspect necessary semantic implications of an observed syntactic structure. Of course, beyond these first principles, there are many syntactic-semantic correspondences that differ across languages. To pick a few at random: many languages have locative verbs where English has locative prepositions; languages differ in surface placement of subjects; not all languages have lexical causatives, and so on. So there is plenty of detailed work for a novice to carry out to achieve mature knowledge of the native tongue.

Several authors have taken a more radical position than the one defended herein. Responding to the fact that there are indubitably differences in the correspondence rules of various languages, they try to bite the bullet and claim that all such correspondences are induced via detailed environmental exposure. The results of our simulation bear on the plausibility of this claim.

9.11.1 Generalizing Syntactic-Semantic Correspondences from Meaning Correspondences

Most of these authors propose that children derive the syntactic-semantic correspondences from generalizations based on a large and diverse set of verbs whose properties the child priorly acquired one by one, by observation (e.g., Bates and MacWhinney 1987; Bowerman 1990). This view is perhaps most clearly represented in Tomasello's verb-island hypothesis (1992). Tomasello claims that each verb the child learns is initially an isolated island of meaning; the child does not recognize that verbs belong to a single class and therefore does not productively use morphology, passives, or syntactic alternations. At about 2;6 children are supposed to first notice the similarities among verbs and begin to build a syntactic class. Of course, if the children have no verb class, they have no subclasses based on refined syntactic-semantic correspondences either. For example, according to this view the correspondence between word order and thematic role assignment in caused motion events is not learned until around 3;0 (Akhtar and Tomasello 1997), by which time the child has learned hundreds of verbs. Previous spontaneous production of correct word order is attributed to the use of word-specific patterns.

The prerequisites of such generalization hypotheses are clearest in the Allen connectionist model, which essentially instantiates this process. The model "learns about verbs and their argument structures from naturalistic input" (Allen 1997, as reported in Seidenberg 1997, 1602). It is trained with a set of sentences, each paired with an interpretation. From this information the model learns a set of syntactic-semantic correspondences, as evidenced by its ability to correctly interpret novel verbs in previously encountered constructions.

The Allen model performs its learning feats only because it is given the meaning of each verb and each sentence in the training set; presumptively, in the real case that meaning must be derived by inspecting co-occurring events in the world. Our experimental child surrogates were unable to "learn about verbs and their argument structures" by comparing the situational contingencies for their occurrence—that is, by intuiting their interpretations. The subjects failed to come up with correct interpretations 85 percent of the time (figure 9.1). And when we look at their preferences at the final exposure, the choice made by the largest number of subjects is a false one for three-quarters of the items (see Snedeker 2000).

The systematicity of the errors is particularly important. Modeling work, such as Siskind 1996, shows that even a very scantily clad learning device can acquire something like an interpreted phrase-structure system by distributional analysis over highly errorful data. However, this is on the assumption, to the best of our understanding, that the errors in that data are not highly organized—that is, that they slow learning rather than causing it to converge on false solutions. What we see in the adult observational learners is hypothesis generation that is marching in two wrong directions: toward solutions that are either overly general (with accumulating evidence, many verbs come to mean "look" or "play") or overly concrete.

Our point is that all proposals requiring that verbs be learned by a procedure that gleans the intended event structure of heard sentences from extralinguistic observation alone fail to answer to the real chronology of lexical acquisition, or to its simulation in adult laboratory subjects. These proposals founder just because their rock-bottom presupposition cannot be met: the events accompanying verb use do not "naturally" and without other aids create a search space of interpretations that is at once both narrow enough to acquire verb meanings efficiently and broad enough to encompass their typology (abstract as well as concrete items). If the syntactic-semantic correspondences could be anything at all—that is, if learning had to be open-minded induction as in the more blatant forms of the Whorf-Sapir hypothesis—language knowledge would be impossible to attain.

9.11.2 The Light-Verb Hypothesis

Several researchers have suggested another possibility in the continuing search for the learning story that makes the fewest advance commitments about how language expresses reality. They propose that light verbs play a critical role and enable the acquisition of argument structure (Ninio 1996; Clark 1996; Goldberg 1999). This proposal goes something like this: Novice learners do not know about the linkages between syntactic frames (or constructions) and event semantics. They learn their first few verbs without the benefit of syntax, just as in the Allen model, by noting the extralinguistic contexts in which these verbs occur (making use, perhaps, of the nouns that occur in the utterance). Among these early-acquired verbs are the light verbs. They are learned quickly because they are so frequent. The child notices that each of these words, *in its use as a light verb*, has a fairly minimal meaning and appears most frequently in a single syntactic frame. The child associates the meaning of the verb with that frame and begins to attribute that meaning to other verbs that appear in that frame (adding for each verb the other bits of meaning suggested by the unique extralinguistic contexts in which it appears). Notice then, that this approach potentially does away with the need to posit not only a god-given ability in the infant to interpret the world but a just-as-god-given disposition to map that world only in certain ways onto linguistic structures.

But again this story critically depends on the child being able to learn verbs from extralinguistic and nominal contexts, prior to syntax. Particularly—and this alone will beg the question that the hypothesis was designed to resolve—such a learner must recognize just when this verb is being used in its *light-verb* context. How is that to be done? Consider, for example, the frequent item *bring*. How is a presyntactic infant to disentangle its standard interpretations, its "light" interpretations, and its "idiomatic" interpretations (as in, e.g., *John brought up his suitcase, his dinner, his baby, his objections; brought down his suitcase, the government, the house*). Moreover, as the Human Simulation demonstrated, the commonly used verbs that can be assigned to the light-verb class are not the sort most easily acquired by observation or by attention to their nominal contexts, even by sophisticated adults (figures 9.3 and 9.4). Close inspection of our results suggests that the only light verbs for which there was some successful identification in the *Scenes Condition* were *come*, *go*, and *put* (whose status as light verbs is least clear), and only in cases where these could be interpreted in their standard rather than light interpretation—that is, when somebody in the scene was saliently going or putting away objects.

In any case, though learned young, light verbs appear to be a feature of early word combinations rather than single-word speech (see the examples provided by Clark 1996; Goldberg 1999). Work on early comprehension and word learning indicates that children at this level of development also have the ability to use syntactic context as a cue for interpreting an ambiguous or novel verb (Naigles 1990; Naigles, Hirsh-Pasek, and Golinkoff 1996; Fisher 1999). We suspect that the acquisition of light verbs may be one of the first products of structure-guided word learning, rather than the engine that makes it possible.

9.12   Final Thoughts

We began this chapter by asking about the extent to which vocabulary learning reduces largely to mapping: Plato's problem purged of the error of reincarnation. Is the child's task merely to recover the conventional pronunciations for preexisting concepts? Usually, the vocabulary-acquisition task is taken to involve more than this, to be a problem of concept acquisition as well as a problem of mapping. This position, as we saw, is rendered plausible by noticing that concrete object terms and concrete verbs are learned earlier in life, on average, than abstract terms. The experimental work presented herein was designed to show that a closer analysis of evolving mapping strategies adequately explains these sequential aspects of word learning, without invoking conceptual change at all.

What makes the mapping problem a hard one, we have argued, is that observation offers up myriad salient and relevant representations for any single scene. The enormous breadth of the available hypothesis space for interpreting the world therefore poses real obstacles for word learning. Not only are there many possibilities for just how a heard word matches up with a single observed scene, but the next use of this same word often occurs in circumstances quite different from the first. Thus any learning device limited to inspection of external conditions for word learning faces a many-to-many sorting task of unknown complexity. The more sophisticated the learner in analyzing the social, pragmatic, conceptual, and perceptual concomitants of the scene in view, the larger the problem space becomes. As we tried to show, the best and most efficient solution is for the learner to construct a more sophisticated representation of the linguistic stimulus, one that exposes its semantically informative syntactic structure. Structure-to-world matching procedures are highly efficient, as we saw, to rein in interpretation of the novel word.

More generally, the work reported here fits into an emerging picture of language acquisition that explains the child's semantic and syntactic accomplishments in terms of layers of information that become available in sequence as a consequence of solving prior parts of the learning problem. In their current form, these bootstrapping approaches leave open almost all questions about the particulars of the lexical and grammatical representations that are finally attained. They are incompatible only with proposed learning procedures for language that assert that vocabulary attainment is prior to and independent of grammar attainment.

Acknowledgments

We thank Jane Gillette and Anne Lederer for their advice and their stimuli. We also gratefully acknowledge Tova Rosman, who collected the data for the verb-learning experiment. This work was supported by National Institutes of Health grant 1-R01-HD3750707-01 and a National Science Foundation Center Grant to the University of Pennsylvania Institute for Research in Cognitive Science.

Notes

1. In further detail, the finding is that nouns occupy a much larger proportion of the vocabulary than verbs than can be predicted from the input facts. When English-speaking children's production vocabularies are between twenty and fifty words, 45 percent of these words are common nouns and only 3 percent are verbs (for Italian the corresponding percentages are 37% and 4%) (Caselli et al. 1995). This is so even though the incidence of each word (that is, the token frequency) is higher for the verbs than for the nouns in the common set used by mothers (Sandhofer, Smith, and Luo 2000). These proportions both of types and of tokens are of course influenced by several crosscutting factors having to do with the languages themselves and even with child-rearing practices that differ cross-culturally (see Choi and Gopnik 1995; Tardif, Shatz, and Naigles 1997). Still, early noun dominance is visible crosslinguistically despite the countervailing influence of these additional variables.

2. There is some disagreement about the timing of situationally appropriate production of mental-state terms, with some investigators seeing evidence of this development well before age 3 (Shatz, Wellman, and Silber 1983; Bretherton and Beeghly 1982). There are also substantial differences within the class of mental-state predicates. In spontaneous production, predicates encoding desire, perception, and affect begin appearing around 2;0, about a year before predicates for cognition (Bartsch and Wellman 1995; Bretherton and Beeghly 1982). But there is little disagreement that concrete action verbs are spoken and understood in advance of the mental-state verbs.

3. Thanks to Daniel Reisberg for this example.

4. This story is complicated by the fact that even within a language the conflation patterns for individual words vary considerably. While many common English motion verbs encode manner (*walk* or *run*), the most common ones encode deixis instead (*go*, *come*), and a rare few encode path (*enter*, *climb*). A contact event can be described by a verb encoding manner of action (*pound*), instrument (*hammer*), or result (*hit*). Of course, this kind of componential analysis does not necessarily enter into the learning process in the first place (for discussion, see Carey 1978; Fodor 1998).

5. We presuppose here the lesson from Baldwin 1993 that all such generalizations are modulo the child's determination that, in using a novel word in a particular setting, the adult means to refer to that setting by that word use. For example a child playing with a new toy and hearing his mother say "Wow, look at the blitso!" will learn that *blitso* names that toy only if the mother was attending to it while so saying. For the moment, we leave aside the usual skeptical objections à la Quine.

6. This general position has been explored under the title *syntactic bootstrapping*. For earlier statements see Landau and Gleitman 1985 and Gleitman 1990. For analyses that emphasize the incremental nature of this procedure, see Fisher et al. 1994 and Gillette et al. 1999.

7. What can be "perceived" is among the most vexed of questions, which we do not pretend here to engage. There is considerable evidence that infants can, *pace* Hume, extract properties such as "cause," "animate agent," and "intentionality" from their observations of ongoing events (e.g., Woodward 1998; and see Kellman and Arterberry 1998 for an important general discussion and review). Moreover, young children do acquire terms like *look* and *see* despite the fact that their conversationally targeted objects are often occluded; even blind children rapidly become proficient with these terms (Landau and Gleitman 1985). Yet we suppose no one will doubt that the conditions of applicability of the terms *think* and *know* are harder to extract from inspection of ongoing scenes than are *plane* and *elephant*.

8. Some of these manipulations were also performed in Lederer, Gleitman, and Gleitman 1991, and reported in Gillette et al. 1999. However, in the current experiment, the procedural properties of the several information-condition manipulations were precisely matched, and all possible combinations of the information sources were tested. This allows us to make better-motivated comparisons of the potency of various information sources, and to directly test for interactions between information type and verb subtype. In addition, the current experiment provides a more complete representation of the extralinguistic contexts of word use (longer color video clips, shot with a more mobile camera).

9. Assigning *come* and *go* to the action class (as seems intuitively correct to us) rather than to the light-verb class (following Clark 1996 and Goldberg 1999) magnifies the difference between the verb classes still further. With this reclassification, the identification of action verbs increases from 27 to 29 percent while the identification of light verbs in the Scenes Condition drops from 18 to 8 percent.

10. We have discussed some of these issues elsewhere (see particularly Gleitman and Gleitman 2001; Gillette et al. 1999).

11. This difference across verb types is a presumptive consequence of two factors. First, the *Scenes* do not become more informative than they were before by addition of the nouns—the mental acts and states are still hidden in the nontransparent brain, opaque to the device that scans the ongoing scene. Second, some of the nouns that co-occur with the mental verbs are in the embedded rather than the matrix clause and thus play no role in the selectional privileges of the matrix verbs. We should also note that the noun-verb comparison machinery we describe here is distinct from the *semantic bootstrapping proposal* of Grimshaw 1990 and Pinker 1984, which acquires nouns and verbs alike from observation of their situational concomitants, and as a prerequisite to the construction of phrase structure. In contrast, the procedure outlined here is necessarily and crucially sequential, with asyntactic noun learning forming the required scaffold for acquisition of specific verbs, and of the phrase structure.

12. "By and large" hedges for certain architectural commitments of languages that complicate this picture—for example, the requirement for a surface subject in English such that zero-argument predicates have one too many associated noun phrases ("It rains"); symmetrically, the broad licensing of denominal verbs means that some will have too few (e.g., *butter*); in addition, each language exhibits various unsystematic quirks in these mappings. As we have discussed elsewhere, implicit arguments (and the massive argument dropping of various languages, e.g., Mandarin Chinese) are easily encompassed within our theoretical approach, just because we hold that the learner is attentive to the full *range* of structures associated with a verb, and their semantic implications. Thus one can say "I gave at the office," "I gave my life," and "I gave Jay a good idea," all these privileges consistent with and informative of the argument-level semantics of *give*. Such verbs as *go, fall, happen*, and even *rain* are licensed for the first of these three structures but crucially never could appear ditransitively because they are incompatible with the notion of transfer.

References

Akhtar, N., and Tomasello, M. 1997. Young children's productivity with word order and verb morphology. *Developmental Psychology, 33*, 952–965.

Augustine. [398] 1992. *Confessions*, commentary by J. J. O'Donnell. New York: Oxford University Press.

Baldwin, D. A. 1993. Early referential understanding: Infants' ability to recognize referential acts for what they are. *Developmental Psychology, 29*, 832–843.

Bartsch, K., and Wellman, H. 1995. *Children talk about the mind.* New York: Oxford University Press.

Bates, E., Dale, P. S., and Thal, D. 1995. Individual differences and their implications for theories of language development. In P. Fletcher and B. MacWhinney, eds., *The handbook of child language*, 96–151. Oxford: Blackwell.

Bates, E., and MacWhinney, B. 1987. Competition, variation, and language learning. In B. MacWhinney, ed., *Mechanisms of language acquisition*, 157–193. Hillsdale, NJ: Erlbaum.

Bloom, L., Lightblown, P., and Hood, L. 1975. Structure and variation in child language. *Monographs of the Society for Research in Child Development, 40*, 1–97.

Bowerman, M. 1990. Mapping thematic roles onto syntactic functions: Are children helped by innate linking rules? *Linguistics, 28*, 1253–1289.

Bretherton, I., and Beeghly, M. 1982. Talking about internal states: The acquisition of an explicit theory of mind. *Developmental Psychology, 18*(6), 906–921.

Carey, S. 1978. The child as a word learner. In M. Halle, J. Bresnan, and G. A. Miller, eds., *Linguistic theory and psychological reality*, 264–293. Cambridge, MA: MIT Press.

Carroll, L. [1865] 1989. *Alice's adventures in wonderland*. New York: Bantam Books.

Caselli, M. C., Bates, E., Casadio, P., Fenson, J., Fenson, L., Sanderl, L., and Weir, J. 1995. A cross-linguistic study of early lexical development. *Cognitive Development, 10*, 159–199.

Caselli, M. C., Casadio, P., and Bates, E. 1999. A comparison of the transition from first words to grammar in English and Italian. *Journal of Child Language, 26*, 69–111.

Choi, S., and Bowerman, M. 1991. Learning to express motion events in English and Korean: The influence of language-specific lexicalization patterns. *Cognition, 41*, 83–121.

Choi, S., and Gopnik, A. 1995. Early acquisition of verbs in Korean: A cross-linguistic study. *Journal of Child Language, 22*, 497–529.

Chomsky, N. 1959. *Verbal behavior*, by B. F. Skinner. *Language, 35*, 26–58.

Chomsky, N. 1981. *Lectures on the theory of government and binding*. Dordrectht: Foris.

Clark, E. V. 1987. The principle of contrast: a constraint in language acquisition. In B. MacWhinney, ed., *Mechanisms of language acquisition*, 1–33. Hillsdale, NJ: Erlbaum.

Clark, E. V. 1996. Early verbs, event types, and inflections. In C. E. Johnson and J. Gilbert, eds., *Children's language*, vol. 9, 61–73. Mahwah, NJ: Erlbaum.

Clark, E. V. 1997. Conceptual perspective and lexical choice in acquisition. *Cognition, 64*, 1–37.

Dromi, E. 1987. *Early lexical development*. Cambridge, England: Cambridge University Press.

Epstein, W. 1961. The influence of syntactical structure on learning. *American Journal of Psychology*, *74*, 80–85.

Feldman, H., Goldin-Meadow, S., and Gleitman, L. 1978. Beyond Herodotus: The creation of language by linguistically deprived deaf children. In A. Lock, ed., *Action, symbol, and gesture*. New York: Academic Press.

Fisher, C. 1996. Structural limits on verb mapping: The role of analogy in children's interpretations of sentences. *Cognitive Psychology*, *31*, 41–81.

Fisher, C. 1999, April. Transitivity and verb arguments in acquisition. Paper presented at the Thirtieth Annual Child Language Research Forum, Stanford University.

Fisher, C., Gleitman, H., and Gleitman, L. R. 1991. On the semantic content of subcategorization frames. *Cognitive Psychology*, *23*, 331–392.

Fisher, C., Hall, G., Rakowitz, S., and Gleitman, L. 1994. When it is better to receive than to give: Syntactic and conceptual constraints on vocabulary growth. *Lingua*, *92*, 333–375.

Fodor, J. A. 1998. *Concepts: Where cognitive science went wrong*. New York: Clarendon Press.

Furrow, D., Moore, C., Davidge, J., and Chiasson, L. 1992. Mental terms in mothers' and children's speech: Similarities and relationships. *Journal of Child Language*, *19*, 617–631.

Gentner, D. 1978. On relational meaning: The acquisition of verb meaning. *Child Development*, *49*, 988–998.

Gentner, D. 1982. Why nouns are learned before verbs: Linguistic relativity versus natural partitioning. In S. A. Kuczaj II, ed., *Language development, Vol. 2: Language, thought, and culture*, 31–53. Hillsdale, NJ: Erlbaum.

Gentner, D., and Boroditsky, L. 2001. Individuation, relativity, and early word learning. In M. Bowerman and S. Levinson, eds., *Language acquisition and conceptual development*. Cambridge, England: Cambridge University Press.

Geyer, H. 1998. *Subcategorization as a predictor of verb meaning: Evidence from Hebrew*. Unpublished manuscript, University of Pennsylvania.

Gillette, J., Gleitman, H., Gleitman, L., and Lederer, A. 1999. Human simulation of vocabulary learning. *Cognition*, *73*, 135–176.

Gleitman, L. 1990. The structural sources of word meaning. *Language Acquisition*, *1*, 3–55.

Gleitman, L., and Gleitman, H. 2001. Bootstrapping a first vocabulary. In J. Weissenborn and B. Hohle, eds., *Approaches to bootstrapping: Phonological, lexical, syntactic and neurophysiological aspects of early language acqusition*, vol. 1, 79–96. Amsterdam: John Benjamins.

Gleitman, L. R., and Newport, E. L. 1995. The invention of language by children: Environmental and biological influences on the acquisition of language. In L. Gleitman and M. Liberman, eds., *An invitation to cognitive science, Vol. 1: Language*, 1–24. Cambridge, MA: MIT Press.

Goldberg, A. 1995. *Constructions: A construction grammar approach to argument structure*. Chicago: University of Chicago Press.

Goldberg, A. 1999. The emergence of the semantics of argument structure constructions. In B. MacWhinney, ed., *The emergence of language*, 197–212. Mahwah, NJ: Erlbaum.

Goldin-Meadow, S., Seligman, M. E., and Gelman, R. 1976. Language in the two-year-old. *Cognition, 4*, 189–202.

Gopnik, A., and Meltzoff, A. N. 1997. *Words, thoughts, and theories*. Cambridge, MA: MIT Press.

Grimshaw, J. 1990. *Argument structure*. Cambridge, MA: MIT Press.

Gropen, J., Pinker, S., Hollander, M., and Goldberg, R. 1991. Affectedness and direct objects: The role of lexical semantics in the acquisition of verb argument structure. *Cognition, 41*, 153–195.

Herodotus. [410 BCE] 1992. *The histories*, trans. W. Blanco, ed. W. Blanco and J. T. Roberts. New York: Norton.

Huttenlocher, J., Smiley, P., and Charney, R. 1983. Emergence of action categories in the child: Evidence from verb meanings. *Psychological Review, 90*, 72–93.

Jackendoff, R. 1985. *Semantics and cognition*. Cambridge, MA: MIT Press.

Johnson, C. N., and Maratsos, M. P. 1977. Early comprehension of mental verbs: Think and know. *Child Development, 48*, 1743–1747.

Kako, E. 1998. *The event semantics of syntactic structures*. Unpublished doctoral dissertation, University of Pennsylvania.

Kellman, P. J., and Arterberry, M. E. 1998. *The cradle of knowledge: Development of perception in infancy*. Cambridge, MA: MIT Press.

Kelly, M. H. 1992. Using sound to solve syntactic problems: The role of phonology in grammatical category assignments. *Psychological Review, 99*, 349–364.

Kuczaj, S. A. 1990. Constraining constraint theories. *Cognitive Development, 5*, 341–344.

Landau, B., and Gleitman, L. R. 1985. *Language and experience: Evidence from the blind child*. Cambridge, MA: Harvard University Press.

Lederer, A., Gleitman, H., and Gleitman, L. 1991. The informativeness of cross-situational and cross-sentential evidence for learning the meaning of verbs. Paper presented at the Boston University Conference on Language Development.

Lederer, A., Gleitman, H., and Gleitman, L. 1995. Verbs of a feather flock together: Semantic information in the structure of maternal speech. In M. Tomasello and W. E. Merriman, eds., *Beyond names for things: Young children's acquisition of verbs*, 277–297. Hillsdale, NJ: Erlbaum.

Lenneberg, E. H. 1967. *Biological foundations of language*. New York: Wiley.

Levin, B. 1993. *English verb classes and alternations*. Chicago: University of Chicago Press.

Locke, J. [1690] 1964. An essay concerning human understanding, 259–298. Cleveland, OH: Meridian Books.

Markman, E. M. 1994. Constraints on word meaning in early language acquisition. In L. Gleitman and B. Landau, eds., *The acquisition of the lexicon*, 199–227. Cambridge, MA: MIT Press.

Moore, C., Gilbert, C., and Sapp, F. 1995. Children's comprehension of the distinction between want and need. *Journal of Child Language, 22*, 687–701.

Naigles, L. 1990. Children use syntax to learn verb meanings. *Journal of Child Language, 17*, 357–374.

Naigles, L. R. 1996. The use of multiple frames in verb learning via syntactic bootstrapping. *Cognition, 58*, 221–251.

Naigles, L. R., Gleitman, H., and Gleitman, L. R. 1993. Children acquire word meaning components from syntactic evidence. In E. Dromi, ed., *Language and cognition: a developmental perspective*, 87–102. Norwood, NJ: Ablex.

Naigles, L. R., Hirsh-Pasek, K., and Golinkoff, R. M. 1996. Young children's ability to use syntactic frames to derive meaning. In K. Hirsh-Pasek and R. M. Golinkoff, *The origins of grammar: Evidence from early language comprehension*. Cambridge, MA: MIT Press.

Ninio, A. 1996, July. Pathbreaking verbs in syntactic development. Paper presented at the Seventh International Congress for the Study of Child Language, Istanbul.

O'Grady, W. 1987. *Principles of grammar and learning*. Chicago: University of Chicago Press.

Pinker, S. 1984. *Language learnability and language development*. Cambridge, MA: Harvard University Press.

Pinker, S. 1994. How could a child use verb syntax to learn verb semantics? In L. Gleitman and B. Landau, eds., *The acquisition of the lexicon*, 377–410. Cambridge, MA: MIT Press.

Plato. [412 BCE] 1990. *Phaedo*, trans. D. Gallop. New York: Clarendon Press, 1990.

Sandhoffer, C., Smith, L., and Luo, J. 2000. Counting nouns and verbs in the input: Differential frequencies, different kinds of learning? *Journal of Child Language, 27*, 561–585.

Seidenberg, M. S. 1997. Language acquisition and use: Learning and applying probabilistic constraints. *Science, 275,* 1599–1603.

Shatz, M., Wellman, H. M., and Silber, S. 1983. The acquisition of mental verbs: A systematic investigation of the first reference to mental state. *Cognition, 14,* 301–321.

Singleton, J., and Newport, E. 1994. *When learners surpass their models: The acquisition of American Sign Language from impoverished input.* Unpublished manuscript, University of Rochester.

Siskind, J. 1996. A computational study of cross-situational techniques for learning word-to meaning mappings. *Cognition, 61,* 39–91.

Smiley, P., and Huttenlocher, J. 1995. Conceptual development and the child's early words for events, objects, and persons. In M. Tomasello and W. E. Merriman, eds., *Beyond names for things: Young children's acquisition of verbs,* 21–62. Hillsdale, NJ: Erlbaum.

Snedeker, J. 2000. Cross-situational observation and the semantic bootstrapping hypothesis. In E. Clark, ed., *Proceedings of the Thirtieth Annual Child Language Research Forum.* Stanford, CA: Center for the Study of Language and Information.

Snedeker, J., Gleitman, L., and Brent, M. 1999. The successes and failures of word-to-world mapping. In A. Greenhill, M. Hughes, H. Littlefield, and H. Walsh, eds., *Proceedings of the Twenty-Third Boston University Conference on Language Development.* Somerville, MA: Cascadilla Press.

Talmy, L. 1985. Semantics and syntax of motion. In J. Kimball, ed., *Syntax and semantics,* vol. 4, 181–238. New York: Academic Press.

Tardif, T., Shatz, M., and Naigles, L. 1997. Caregiver speech and children's use of nouns versus verbs: A comparison of English, Italian, and Mandarin. *Journal of Child Language, 24,* 535–565.

Tomasello, M. 1992. *First verbs: A case study of early grammatical development.* Cambridge, England: Cambridge University Press.

Tomasello, M. 1995. Pragmatic contexts for early verb learning. In M. Tomasello and W. E. Merriman, eds., *Beyond names for things: Young children's acquisition of verbs,* 115–146. Hillsdale, NJ: Erlbaum.

Woodward, A. L. 1998. Infants selectively encode the goal object of an actor's reach. *Cognition, 69,* 1–34.

10

Everything Had a Name, and Each Name Gave Birth to a New Thought: Links between Early Word Learning and Conceptual Organization

Sandra R. Waxman

That living word awakened my soul, gave it light, hope, joy, and set it free! ... Everything had a name, and each name gave birth to a new thought.
—Keller 1904, 22

Word learning, more than any other development achievement, stands at the very center of the crossroad of human cognition and language. Even before they can tie their own shoes, human infants spontaneously form concepts[1] to capture various relations among the objects and events they encounter, and they learn words to express them. I have argued that these two advances do not proceed independently. Rather, from the onset of word learning, human infants' conceptual and linguistic advances are powerfully linked.

This chapter is devoted to examining the origin and unfolding of these links. In recent work, I have proposed that infants approach the task of word learning equipped with a broad, universally shared expectation. This initially broad expectation permits infants to link novel words (that are applied to objects) to commonalities among those named objects. This broad initial link, which is available to infants at the very onset of word learning, serves at least three essential functions. First, it supports the formation of a stable repertoire of concepts. Second, it supports infants' first efforts to establish reference, and in this way promotes infants' earliest lexicons. Third, and perhaps most radically, this initially broad, universal link sets the stage for the discovery of the more specific links between particular types of words (e.g., nouns, adjectives, verbs) and particular types of relations that they mark (e.g., object categories, object properties, actions) (Waxman 1999b). These more specific links, which are shaped by the structure of the particular language under acquisition, do not emerge all of a piece. Instead, infants first tease apart the nouns (from among the other grammatical forms, including adjectives, verbs, prepositions, and so on) and map these specifically to object categories (from among the other candidate types of conceptual relations, including properties of objects and the actions in which they are engaged). In infants acquiring English, we have evidence that by 14 months of age, infants have begun to tease the nouns and to map them specifically to categories. Once this noun-to-object category link is in place, other specific links for other grammatical forms will follow, and these will be sensitive to the correlations between the grammatical forms that are represented in the native language and their associated meanings.

This is a distinctly developmental proposal, one that examines seriously the relative contributions of any initial expectations that learners bring to the task of acquisition, and any influence of the environment in shaping the initial system. This type of integrative approach has guided elegant developmental work in a wide range of domains, including the acquisition of physical knowledge (Baillargeon 1993; Spelke 1993), number concepts (Gelman 1991), syntax (Fisher and Gleitman 2002; Gleitman 1990; Gleitman and Gleitman 1992; Gleitman and Newport 1995; Goldin-Meadow 1997; Johnson and Newport 1991), and speech perception (Jusczyk 2002; Jusczyk and Luce 2002; Mehler, Christophe, and Ramus 2000; Morgan and Demuth 1996; Pallier et al. 1998; Werker and Fennell, chapter 3, this volume) in human infants. It is also apparent in ethological investigations detailing, for example, the course of acquisition of birdsong in white-crowned sparrows (Marler 1991) and the evolution of depth perception in kittens (Held and Hein 1963). Although these investigations focus on very different domains of knowledge, and even on very different species of learners, they share a commitment to understanding the rapid acquisition of complex systems, and to embracing the contributions of expectations or constraints inherent in the learner and the shaping role of the environment.

In the case of word learning, this interplay between initial expectations inherent in the learner and the shaping role of the environment is essential. Even a cursory glance at the problems addressed in philosophy, psychology, and linguistics serves as testimony to the complexity of the word-learning task (Bloom 2000; Goodman 1955; Lyons 1977; Quine 1960). Despite this complexity, infants are wizards of word learning. They acquire new words rapidly, in a seemingly effortless fashion. How do they accomplish this? Certainly, infants cull information from the environment, for they learn precisely the words of the language community that surrounds them, and precisely the concepts to which they are exposed (e.g., telephones and squirrels in the United States; scythes and peccaries in rural Mexico). But just as certainly, infants are guided by a powerful universal expectation that links words and concepts. This is important, because human languages differ not only in their cadences and their words, but also in the ways particular grammatical forms (e.g., nouns, adjectives, verbs) are recruited to express fundamental aspects of meaning. Yet in the face of these variations, there are striking crosslinguistic universals in the rate and timing of language acquisition in general, and word learning in particular (Gentner 1982; Huttenlocher and Smiley 1987; Maratsos 1998; Ochs and Schieffelin 1984; Waxman 1999a; Woodward and Markman 1998). Any theory of word learning must be sufficiently constrained to account for these universals in the face of crosslinguistic variation. At the same time, it must be sufficiently flexible to accommodate the systematic variations that occur across languages.

To accommodate these universals and variations, my colleagues and I have proposed that infants across the world's languages begin the process of word learning equipped with an initially broad, universal expectation linking words and concepts, and that the more fine-tuned links between particular grammatical forms and their associated meanings emerge later, once the process of lexical acquisition is underway.

Two aspects of this proposal are worth mentioning. Notice first that this is not a polarized position that locates the engine of acquisition solely within the mind of the child or solely within the environment. Rather, the claim is that infants' initially broad expectation guides their attention toward precisely the sorts of information and regularities in the environment that will make possible the rapid acquisition of word meaning. (See Gelman and Williams 1998 for an excellent discussion of this theoretical approach.) Notice also that this is a dynamic proposal. Infants' initial expectation is not rigidly fixed, exerting a uniform influence throughout the course of development. On the contrary, this expectation itself evolves over the course of development, giving way to more finely tuned links between the particular grammatical forms that are represented in the language under acquisition and their associated meanings. These more finely tuned links are calibrated on the basis of regularities present in the language under acquisition.

10.1 The Puzzle of Word Learning: Three Easy Pieces?

Let us step back from this proposal for a moment and consider the task of word learning from the perspective of the infant. In the natural course of events, the young word learner is faced with something roughly like the following situation: an individual (perhaps a parent or an older sibling) points to an ongoing stream of activity (perhaps a bunny disappearing behind a hedge), and utters a novel name (saying, "Voilà, t'as vu le lapin? Où est le lapin maintenant?" in French, or "Look, did you see the bunny? Where did the bunny go?" in English). To successfully learn a word from this (indeed from any) context, the infant must solve a difficult three-part puzzle. She must (1) parse the relevant word (*lapin* or *bunny*) from the ongoing stream of speech, (2) identify the relevant entity (the bunny, not the hedge or the act of disappearing) from the ongoing stream of activity, and (3) establish a mapping, a word-to-world correspondence, between these. To put matters more formally, successful word learning rests on human infants' ability to discover the relevant linguistic units, the relevant conceptual units, and the mappings between them. Each of these puzzle pieces takes form gradually over the first year of life, and each appears to rest on fundamental perceptual, conceptual, and even psychological capacities.

10.1.1 Discovering the Relevant Linguistic Unit: Finding the Word

Over the first year of life, infants become sensitive to the cues within the speech stream that will permit them to segment the continuous speech signal into word-sized units. To begin, we know that new-borns prefer human speech (and particularly infant-directed speech) over other sources of auditory stimulation (Jusczyk and Luce 2002; Mehler, Christophe and Ramus 2000), but their ability to parse a word from the ongoing stream of speech emerges gradually. During this time, the functional significance of infant-directed speech, and the perceptual features to which infants attend, undergo dramatic change (Fernald 1992b). Initially, in the first six to nine months, the melodies of infant-directed speech serve a primarily affective and attentional function, engaging and modulating infants' attention. By approximately 9 months of age, "words begin to emerge from the melody" (Fernald 1992a, 403) as infants become increasingly sensi-tive to the perceptual cues (morphologic, phonetic, and prosodic) and distributional regularities (transitional probabilities) that mark the word and phrase boundaries of their native language (Jusczyk and Aslin 1995; Kemler Nelson et al. 1989; Saffran, Aslin, and New-port 1996). Infants' sensitivity to these cues also permits them to tease apart two very broad classes of words: *open-class* (or *content* words, including nouns, adjectives, verbs) and *closed-class* words (or *function* words, including determiners and prepositions) (Shi, Werker, and Morgan 1999). Infants prefer to listen to open-class words, probably because they receive greater stress and enjoy more interesting me-lodic contours than do closed-class words. This preference, though primarily perceptually based, represents an important step on the way to word learning. By the close of their first year, infants not only parse individual words reliably from the speech stream but devote special attention to just those words (the open-class, content words) that appear first in the lexicon (Jusczyk and Kemler Nelson 1996; Morgan and Demuth 1996; Werker et al. 1996).

10.1.2   Identifying the Relevant Conceptual Unit; Finding the Referent(s)

The solution to this second piece of the puzzle rests on the infants' ability to identify discrete objects in the environment and to notice the relations among these objects that will support categoriza-tion. During the first year, infants demonstrate a great deal of core knowledge about objects, events, and relations (Baillargeon 2000; Spelke 2000), and this knowledge serves to organize an impressive repertoire of concepts. Some of these prelinguistic concepts are focused around richly structured category-based relations (e.g., rabbit, bottle, animal); others are focused primarily on property-based relations (e.g., red, soft) (see Quinn and Eimas 2000). Since any of these relations is a viable candidate for a word's meaning, the infants' task is to discover which of these candidates is to be mapped to the word that they have parsed (Markman 1989; Waxman 2003; Waxman and Markow 1995).

10.1.3 Establishing Word-to-World Mappings

Neither the ability to parse a novel word from the speech stream nor the ability to identify the referent of that word guarantees that the infant will successfully map a novel word to its meaning. This ability to establish a word-to-world mapping, an ability that emerges gradually over the first year, requires a firm grasp of the symbolic, referential power of words. This, in turn, depends crucially on an emerging ability to infer the goals and intentions of others, for to succeed in word learning, infants must appreciate a speaker's *intention to refer* (for a discussion, see Woodward 2000; Woodward, chapter 5, this volume). And recent work indicates that by 9 to 10 months of age, infants spontaneously follow a speaker's line of attention to discover the object of interest in a naming episode. More generally, we know that by the close of their first year, infants take advantage of the rich social and pragmatic contexts in which novel words are introduced. They have begun to make connections between words, objects, and the intentions of others, and to recruit these connections to map words to their meaning (Baldwin and Baird 1999; Guajardo and Woodward 2000).

But even this is not sufficient, for word learning entails much more than merely mapping an individual word (e.g., *bunny*) to its intended referent (e.g., the bunny running behind the hedge). In addition, the infant must be able to extend that word, appropriately and systematically, beyond the individual(s) on which it was taught, to include other objects, even some that have neither been seen nor named (e.g., other bunnies). Solving this part of the word-learning puzzle requires an inferential leap, taking them beyond word-to-object mappings toward the establishment of word-to-concept mappings (Waxman 2002). And to establish such abstract mappings, the infant must hold some principled expectations regarding the range of possible extensions for a given novel word.

An Important Wrinkle: Different Kinds of Words Highlight Different Aspects of the Very Same Scene
This discussion raises an important wrinkle for the word learner. In any given language, many different words—indeed many different *types* of words—can be applied correctly in a naming episode. But each type of word highlights a different aspect of the same observed scene and *supports a unique pattern of extension.* This is a fundamental feature of human language. Consider, for example, a situation in which an adult points to a scene (e.g., a bunny hopping behind a hedge) and utters a novel word. For instance, for speakers of English, count nouns ("Look, it's a *bunny*") pick out the object as member of an object kind and are extended spontaneously to other members of the same object kind (other bunnies); proper nouns ("Look, it's Alice") refer to the named individual but are not extended further; and adjectives ("Look, it's *fluffy*") refer to a property of the named individual and are extended to other objects sharing that property.

Smoothing Out the Wrinkle: Evidence from Preschool-Aged Children
By the time they are 2.5 to 3 years of age, children are well on their way to smoothing out this wrinkle. Roger Brown (1957) was the first to document that children are sensitive to this fundamental feature of language. More recently, several researchers have demonstrated that children's expectations regarding the range of extension for a novel word are guided by its grammatical form (for a review of recent evidence, see Hall and Lavin, chapter 11, this volume; Waxman 1998). They extend count nouns to individuals and to categories of objects (Waxman 1999b; Waxman and Markow 1995); they extend adjectives systematically to properties of objects (Klibanoff and Waxman 2000; Mintz and Gleitman 2002; Waxman and Klibanoff 2000;

Waxman and Markow 1998); and they restrict the extension of proper nouns to the named individual (Hall 1991, 1999; Jaswal and Markman 2001). Moreover, there is now crosslinguistic evidence suggesting that the link between nouns and object categories may be universal. It has been documented in preschoolers acquiring a wide range of languages, including French, Spanish, Italian, Hebrew, and Japanese (Imai and Gentner 1997). In contrast, children's expectations regarding novel adjectives appear to vary across languages (Imai and Haryu, chapter 13, this volume; Ninio 2002; Waxman and Guasti 2002; Waxman, Senghas, and Benveniste 1997).

10.1.4 Three Easy Pieces: Summary

Thus, by the time they reach their preschool years, children have assembled the three central pieces in the puzzle of word learning. They have the *linguistic* capacity to identify novel words in the speech stream and to distinguish among words of different grammatical forms (e.g., count noun, proper noun, adjective), the *conceptual* ability to appreciate different kinds of relations among objects (e.g., category-based, property-based, event-related relations), and a clear expectation that these linguistic and conceptual pieces are linked. These finely tuned links serve as powerful tools in word learning, because any cues regarding the grammatical form of a novel word can be used to narrow the range of possible interpretations for that word.

10.2 A Developmental View

The key developmental questions, of course, concern the origin and evolution of these links between word learning and conceptual organization. Which of these links, if any, are available to infants at the very onset of lexical acquisition? And how are they shaped over the course of acquisition?

To begin to answer this question, let us take stock of the repertoire available to infants as they cross the threshold into word learning. By the end of their first year, infants are well on their way to solving several key elements in the puzzle of word learning. They successfully identify novel words in the input; they appreciate many kinds of categories and relations among objects; and they take advantage of the rich social and pragmatic cues with which novel words are introduced (Baldwin and Markman 1989; Tomasello and Olguin 1993).

These accomplishments, while impressive, cannot speak to either the origin or evolution of links between word learning and conceptual organization in infants. What remains to be seen is whether any links are evident in infants, when these become available to guide acquisition, and how they are shaped in the course of acquisition. In other words, we must begin at the beginning, tracing the origin and evolution of these links between the linguistic and conceptual systems in infants.

We have therefore developed a series of experimental tasks, each designed to pinpoint the influence of novel words on infants' conceptual organization at strategic points in development. Because infants are captivated by cadence and contours of infant-directed speech, a female experimenter produces short phrases in this preferred speech register for infants in all conditions. Our goal is to compare infants' ability to form categories in "neutral" conditions (in which the experimenter presents no novel words) with their ability to do so in the context of a novel word. If there is a link between word learning and conceptual organization, infants hearing novel words should categorize differently, and in some cases more successfully, than infants hearing no novel words. In our *No Word* control conditions, the experimenter indicates objects to the infants but provides no names, saying, for example, "Do you like this?" or "Look at this." In the remaining conditions, the experimenter introduces a novel word for the very same objects; what varies is the grammatical form of the novel word. In the *Noun* condition, she says, for instance, "This is a *blicket.*" In the *Adjective* condition, she says, for example, "This is a *blick-ish* one." (For evidence that infants are sensitive to these distinct frames, see Gerken and McIntosh 1993; Waxman and Markow 1995, 1998.) We have focused primarily on novel nouns and adjectives because although words from both of these grammatical categories can be applied ostensively to individuals and to categories of objects, each grammatical form supports a different range of extension, and this permits us to examine the specificity of infants' expectations in word learning.

The logic of this design is straightforward. Performance in the No Word control condition assesses how readily infants form the various categories presented in our tasks (e.g., dog, animal, purple things) in the absence of a novel word; performance in the remaining Word conditions assesses the role of naming in this important endeavor; and a comparison of performance in the Noun and Adjective conditions permits us to trace the evolution of the finely tuned links between particular grammatical forms (e.g., count nouns, adjectives) and their associated meaning.

To illustrate the logic of this experimental approach, in the next section I will review a series of experiments designed several years ago to uncover the influence of novel words on the conceptual organization of infants on the brink of word learning.

10.3 A (Relatively) Early Demonstration: Words Serve as Invitations to Form Categories

We began by adapting the standard novelty-preference task to examine the influence of novel words on the conceptual organization of infants at 12 to 14 months of age (see Waxman and Markow 1995 for a complete description). Table 10.1 provides a sample set of stimuli and instructions. The task involved two phases. During the *familiarization phase*, the experimenter offered the infant four different toys from a given category (e.g., four animals), one at a time, in random order. This was immediately followed by a *test phase*, in which the experimenter simultaneously presented both a new member of the now-familiar category (e.g., another animal) and an object from a novel category (e.g., a fruit). Each infant completed this task with four different sets of objects, two involving basic-level categories (e.g., horses vs. cats) and two involving superordinate-level categories (e.g., animals vs. fruit). Infants manipulated the toys freely, and we used their total accumulated manipulation time as our dependent measure.

To identify any influence of novel words, we randomly assigned infants to one of three conditions. As can be seen in table 10.1, infants in all conditions heard precisely the same phrase ("See what I

Table 10.1
A schematic presentation of introductory phrases from Waxman and Markow 1995 and an example of a single superordinate-level stimulus set

	Familiarization phase				Test phase	
	Trial 1	Trial 2	Trial 3	Trial 4		
Animal set	yellow duck	green raccoon	blue dog	orange lion	red cat	red apple
Noun	This one is a(n) X.	This one is a(n) X.	See what I have?	This one is a(n) X.	See what I have?	
Adjective	This one is X-ish.	This one is X-ish.	See what I have?	This one is X-ish.	See what I have?	
No word	Look at this.	Look at this.	See what I have?	Look at this.	See what I have?	

have?") at test. The only differences among conditions occurred during familiarization.

Following the logic of the novelty-preference task, we reasoned that if infants noticed the category-based commonalities among the familiarization objects, they would reveal a preference for the novel object at test. If infants detected the presence of the novel words, and if these directed infants' attention toward the commonalities among the familiarzation objects, then infants hearing novel words should be more likely than those hearing no novel words to reveal novelty preferences. Finally, if infants' expectation is initially general, then infants in the Noun and Adjective conditions should be more likely than those in the No Word condition to form categories.

The results were consistent with these predictions. Infants in the No Word control condition revealed no novelty preference, indicating that they had not detected the category-based commonalities among the familiarization objects. In contrast, infants in both the Noun and Adjective conditions revealed reliable novelty preferences, indicating that they successfully formed object categories.[2]

This was a striking result because it offered clear evidence for a link between word learning and conceptual organization in infants who had just begun to produce words on their own. Infants reliably detected novel words presented in fluent, infant-directed speech, and these novel words (both adjectives and nouns) promoted categorization. This outcome supports the proposal that infants begin the task of lexical acquisition equipped with a general expectation linking novel word (be they nouns or adjectives) to commonalities among objects. It also reveals the conceptual power of this initial link. Although the novel words were presented only during familiarization, their influence extended beyond the named familiarization objects, influencing infants' attention to the new—and as yet unnamed—objects presented at test.

10.3.1 Words—or Sounds—as Invitations?

In a subsequent series, we asked whether infants' successful categorization stemmed specifically from the presentation of novel words, or whether this might have been the consequence of a more general, attention-engaging function associated with novel auditory stimuli. We focused on 9-month-old infants, because this is the youngest age at which infants can reliably parse individual words from the ongoing speech stream. Our question was whether words are "special" at this early point in development. To answer this question, we compared the influence of novel words and tones on infants' categorization (Balaban and Waxman 1997). We used a novelty-preference task once again, but because infants at 9 months are not especially adept at manipulating objects, we presented two-dimensional images of objects, rather than the three-dimensional objects themselves, and used infants' looking time to the images as our dependent measure.

During the familiarization phase, infants saw a series of slides, each depicting a different member of a single category (e.g., nine different rabbits). See table 10.2. Infants were randomly assigned to either a Word or a Tone condition. For infants in the Word condition, a naming phrase (e.g., "a rabbit!") accompanied the familiarization trials. For infants in the Tone condition, a sine-wave tone accompanied the familiarization trials. This tone, which was created digitally, was matched precisely to the naming phrase in amplitude, duration, and pause length. The familiarization phase was immediately followed by a silent test trial, in which infants saw a new member of the now-familiar category (e.g., another rabbit) and an object from a novel category (e.g., a pig).

We reasoned that if novel words facilitate object categorization as early as 9 months of age, infants in the Word condition should detect the commonalities among the familiarization objects and reveal a preference for the novel object (e.g., the pig) at test. If this facilitative effect is specific to words, and not to auditory stimulation more generally, infants in the Tone condition should be less likely to notice the category-based commonalities among the familiarization slides and consequently less likely to reveal a novelty preference at test.

The results echoed these predictions precisely. Although both words and tones captured the infants' attention, infants in the Word condition revealed a novelty-preference at test, but those in the Tone condition did not. This suggests that there is indeed something special about words that supports the establishment of categories. In

Table 10.2
A schematic presentation of introductory phrases from Balaban and Waxman 1997 and an example of a single basic-level stimulus set

	Familiarization phase				Test phase	
	Trial 1	Trial 2 ...	... Trial 8	Trial 9		
	(All images were black-and-white line drawings.)					
Word	"a rabbit"	"a rabbit"	"a rabbit"	"a rabbit"	Silent	
Tone	Sine-wave tone	Sine-wave tone	Sine-wave tone	Sine-wave tone	Silent	

subsequent studies, we have replicated this phenomenon, using a wider variety of sounds, including tones and tonal sequences (Balaban and Waxman 2002).

10.3.2 Some Conceptual Consequences of Naming

We have shown, then, that naming distinct objects with the same name highlights their commonalities and promotes the formation of object categories (Balaban and Waxman 1997; Waxman and Markow 1995). Research using different experimental paradigms has documented other links between words and concepts in infants. For example, naming distinct objects with distinct names (e.g., *ball, duck*) highlights distinctions among them and promotes the process of object individuation (Wilcox and Baillargeon 1998; Xu 1999). Thus, naming not only supports the establishment of a stable repertoire of object categories, but also provides infants with a means of tracing the identity of individuals within these categories.

10.3.3 Summary

The work in this section illustrates the feasibility of investigating experimentally the links between word learning and conceptual organization, even in infants who are just on the threshold of lexical development. By 9 months of age, just as soon as infants are able to parse novel words reliably from the speech stream, words exert a powerful influence on conceptual organization. Because this link between words (be they nouns or adjectives) and conceptual organization appears so early in development, we can conclude that naming has powerful cognitive consequences, even in prelinguistic infants. Words serve as invitations to form categories. Importantly, this invitation extends beyond the named individual(s) (presented during familiarization) to include new, as yet unnamed individuals (presented at test). The invitation also extends beyond the observable properties of the named individuals, guiding the discovery of hidden, perhaps deeper, commonalities that underlie some of our most fundamental concepts (Waxman and Markow 1995; Welder and Graham 2001). Thus, words are linked to concepts, and support mental representations of individuals and kinds, in infants on the threshold of word learning.

10.4 Gaining Some Precision: The Origin and Evolution Questions

In the next series of experiments, our goal was to capture more precisely the scope of infants' early expectation for word-to-world mappings, and to trace its evolution from an initially general expectation toward a more specific set of expectations. We sought greater theoretical and methodological precision, focusing on both the word and the world side of these mappings (Waxman 1999b; Waxman and Booth 2001, 2003).

10.4.1 Advances in Theory and Methodology

On the *word* side of the mapping, we asked whether (and when and under what circumstances) infants might come to distinguish between novel words presented as nouns versus adjectives. In the previously described series, there was no evidence for such a distinction: both nouns and adjectives directed infants' attention toward commonalities underlying object categories. However, the possibility that infants might distinguish between these two grammatical forms under other circumstances remained an intriguing question.

On the *world* side of the mapping, we sought to discover the scope of infants' initial expectation. We asked whether infants embark on the process of lexical acquisition with an expectation linking novel words specifically to category-based commonalities (e.g., rabbits, animals), or whether their initial link encompasses a wider range of groupings, including, for example, property-based commonalities (e.g., color: pink things; texture: soft things) as well as category-based commonalities (e.g., animal, bunny). This step toward greater precision has implications for both theory and methodology. In previous work, the link between naming and object categories was documented with one set of materials, and the link between naming and object properties with another. For example, in experiments documenting the role of naming in infants' attention to category-based commonalities (Balaban and Waxman 1997; Fulkerson and Haaf 1998; Waxman and Markow 1995), the *only* consistent relation among the familiarization objects was category based (e.g., animals). In other experiments, we have demonstrated the effect of naming on infants' attention to property-based commonalities (Waxman 1999b; Waxman and Markow 1998). But in these experiments, the *only* consistent relation among the objects was property based (e.g., color: purple things; or texture: smooth things).

In the current series, we retained the logic and design of Waxman and Markow's (1995) original paradigm, but shifted the focus to include objects that shared both category-based commonalities (e.g., animal) and property-based commonalities (e.g., color: purple things). This permits us to ask if infants are able to construe the very same set of objects (e.g., four purple animals) either as members of an object category (e.g., animals) or as embodying an object property (e.g., color: purple), and if their construal is influenced systematically by novel words.[3] In all experiments to date, we have included color as an object property. In several cases, we have gone on to ask whether we get the same pattern of effects using a different property (texture), in an effort to establish the generalizability of the phenomena. For the sake of simplicity and balance, in this chapter, we report the results based on color, followed by those based on texture, whenever those data are available.

Another goal of this series was to assess directly the developmental proposal concerning the evolution of infants' expectations. I have proposed that infants embark on the task of word learning equipped with an initially general expectation—that content words, in general, highlight commonalities among objects, in general. I have further proposed that after the onset of lexical acquisition, this initial expectation becomes fine-tuned in accordance with the more specific links between particular grammatical forms and meaning in the native language under acquisition. Unfortunately, however, our view of this critical developmental transition has been obscured, partly as a consequence of the difficulties of accommodating the very different behavioral capacities of individuals at either end of this developmental transition.

Virtually all of the evidence gathered thus far regarding infants' initial expectations in word learning has been based on the novelty-preference task. Although this task is ideally suited for infants up to approximately 16–18 months of age, older infants lose interest in this passive task. At the other end of the developmental spectrum, virtually all of the evidence documenting the more finely tuned links between grammatical form and meaning have been based on a different kind of task, known as word-extension or forced-choice tasks. In these tasks, infants are taught a novel word for an object, and are then asked to extend that word to additional, and as yet unnamed, objects. Though highly successful with older infants and preschoolers, these more active word-extension tasks are not well suited to younger infants, who have difficulty choosing systematically among objects in such forced-choice tasks.

10.4.2 Bridging the Methodological Divide: A New Experimental Paradigm

To bridge this methodological divide, we developed a new paradigm, incorporating features of the novelty-preference task and those of the word-extension paradigms (Waxman and Booth 2001, 2003). This permits us to examine the evolution of infants' expectations in word learning using the same task throughout the proposed transition period. It also permits us to ask whether infants' early expectations, previously demonstrated with novelty-preference tasks only, are sufficiently robust to influence performance in a word-extension task. This new procedure involved three distinct phases. Each infant completed the entire procedure four times, using four different sets of objects. See table 10.3 for a schematic description of the procedure and a summary of the instructions presented in each condition.

10.4.3 Familiarization Phase

The experimenter introduced infants in all conditions to four distinct objects, all drawn from the same object category (e.g., four horses or four animals) and embodying the same object property (e.g., purple). These were presented in pairs, and infants manipulated them freely.

10.4.4 Contrast Phase

The experimenter presented a new object (e.g., an orange carrot), drawn from a contrastive object category and embodying a con-

Table 10.3
A schematic presentation of introductory phrases from Waxman and Booth 2001 and an example of a single superordinate-level stimulus set

	Familiarization		Contrast	Test	
	Trial 1	Trial 2		Category	Property
Purple animal set	purple bear and lion	purple elephant and dog	orange carrot	purple horse vs. purple plate	purple horse vs. blue horse
Noun	These are blickets. This one is a blicket and this one is a blicket.	These are blickets. This one is a blicket and this one is a blicket.	Uh-oh, this one is not a blicket!	Can you give me the blicket?	Can you give me the blicket?
Adjective	These are blickish. This one is blickish and this one is blickish.	These are blickish. This one is blickish and this one is blickish.	Uh-oh, this one is not blickish!	Can you give me the blickish one?	Can you give me the blickish one?
No word	Look at these. Look at this one and look at this one.	Look at these. Look at this one and look at this one.	Uh-oh, look at this one!	Can you give me one?	Can you give me one?

trastive object property. She shook her head solemnly, and said either, for example, "Uh oh! This one is not a *blicket*" (Noun condition), "Uh oh! This one is not *blickish*" (Adjective condition), or "Uh oh! Look at this one" (No Word condition). She then re-presented a target object drawn from the original set of familiarization objects (e.g., a purple horse), and happily exclaimed, for instance, "Yay, this one is a *blicket*" (Noun condition), "Yay, this one is *blickish*" (Adjective condition), or "Yay, look at this one" (No Word condition). She placed this target object in front of the infant and outstretched her palm, asking, for example, "Can you give me the *blicket*?" (Noun condition), "Can you give me the *blickish* one?" (Adjective condition), or "Can you give me one?" (No Word condition).

Why the Contrast Phase?
We designed this phase to help young infants surmount their well-documented difficulty making systematic choices in a word-extension task. By (happily) introducing a target object, and (unhappily) introducing a contrast object, we demonstrated that some objects are good instances of the target category, but that some are not. We then went one step further. By presenting the infant with only the target object, and extending her outstretched hand, the experimenter effectively coached young infants to place a single object in her palm. Success here was guaranteed (since the infant had only one object within reach), and was rewarded by the experimenter with a big smile and an enthusiastic "Thank you!" Importantly, the contrast object was drawn from a different object category (e.g., it was not an animal) than the target, and embodied a different object property (e.g., it was not a purple thing). This ensured that there was nothing in the contrast phase that could bias infants' construal of the relation among the familiarization objects.

10.4.5   Test Phase

Half of the infants in each condition received Category test trials (e.g., a purple horse vs. a purple plate). The remaining infants received Property test trials (e.g., a purple horse vs. a blue horse). We assessed both novelty preference and word extension for each set of objects. To begin a test trial, we permitted infants to play freely with the test pair for 20 seconds. The objects were then retrieved by the experimenter. This free-play interlude served two functions. First, we recorded infants' attention to each of the objects during this interlude to derive a novelty-preference measure. Second, we have found that when infants are permitted a brief interlude of free play, they are more likely to select one of the two objects in a forced-choice test. At this point, then, we assessed word extension. The experimenter presented a target object, drawn from the original set of familiarization objects (e.g., a purple horse), and drew attention to it by pointing and saying, for instance, "This one is a *blicket*" (Noun condition), "This one is *blickish*" (Adjective condition), or "Look at this one" (No Word condition). She then presented the two test objects, placing them easily within the infant's reach, saying, "Can you give me the *blicket*?" (Noun condition), "Can you give me the *blickish* one?" (Adjective condition), or "Can you give me one?" (No Word condition).

10.4.6   Putting the Paradigm to Test

At this point in our research program, infants at 11 and 14 months of age have participated in this task. Based on previous work, we suspected that infants at these ages would span the transition from an initially general to a more refined set of expectations. We were especially curious about the 11-month-olds because to date, only a handful of experimental studies have documented successful word learning in infants at this age (Balaban and Waxman 1997; Woodward, Markman, and Fitzsimmons 1994). We examined two different kinds of object categories (basic- and superordinate-level categories) and two different kinds of object properties (color and texture). We selected these properties because they are perceptually salient to infants and because stable groupings based on these properties (e.g., purple things) can cut across category boundaries (e.g., including perhaps a plum, a t-shirt, a butterfly, and a tricycle).[4]

Our predictions were straightforward. If infants begin the process of lexical acquisition with an initially general expectation linking novel content words (in general) to commonalities among objects (in general), then at 11 months, both nouns and adjectives should highlight both category-based (e.g., animal) and property-based (e.g., purple things) commonalities among the familiarization objects. If this initial expectation is subsequently refined, as infants discover the more precise links between particular grammatical forms and their associated meaning, then for more advanced learners, a more specific pattern should emerge.

Origins: An Initially General Link

Consider first the evidence from 11-month-old infants. If our proposal is correct, 11-month-olds who are just on the brink of producing their first words should reveal a very general expectation linking words (both nouns and adjectives) to commonalities (both category- and property-based) among objects. In the context of the current design, 11-month-old infants hearing either novel nouns or adjectives should select the familiar test object on Category test trials and on Property test trials, and they should do so at a rate that exceeds that in the No Word control condition (Waxman and Booth 2003).

We tested seventy-two infants, ranging from 11.1 to 12.3 months of age. The results, expressed in table 10.4, were fully in line with our predictions. Infants extended both novel nouns and adjectives systematically to the familiar test object (e.g., the purple horse) on both Category and Property trials. Although at this age, there was no difference between performance in the Noun and Adjective conditions, infants hearing these novel words did perform differently than their counterparts in the No Word condition.

This confirms that at the very onset of building a lexicon, novel words (independent of their grammatical form) direct infants' attention quite broadly to both category- and property-based commonalities among named objects. The results also reveal, for the first time, that this early link is sufficiently strong to support the infants' extension of novel words in a word-extension task. This clear pattern of results supports the proposal that infants on the very threshold of word learning harbor a general expectation linking novel content words (both nouns and adjectives) broadly to commonalities (both category- and property-based) among objects.

Table 10.4
Means and standard deviations of category and property test trials (for color) on which the familiar test object was chosen

	14-month-olds (Waxman and Booth 2001)		11-month-olds (Waxman and Booth 2003)	
	M	SD	M	SD
Noun				
Category trial	0.68*	0.13	0.57	0.24
Property trial	0.44	0.15	0.55	0.14
Adjective				
Category trial	0.50	0.18	0.59	0.24
Property trial	0.52	0.17	0.58	0.15
No word				
Category trial	×	×	0.46	0.15
Property trial	×	×	0.49	0.09

* $p < 0.05$ versus chance of 0.50

Evolution: The Subsequent Fine-Tuning
To examine the evolution of this initially broad expectation, we turned our attention next to infants at 14 months of age. We selected this age based on previous work suggesting that at this developmental point—once word learning was well underway and infants had established a modest lexicon—a more specific pattern of expectations begins to emerge (Waxman 1999b; Waxman and Booth 2001). Our previous work indicated that these more specific expectations do not emerge all at the same time. Instead, the evidence suggested that a specific expectation linking nouns to category-based commonalities is first to emerge from the initially general expectation. We therefore expected to find that at 14 months, infants' expectation regarding the mapping for nouns would be more finely tuned than their expectation regarding adjectives.

In the context of the current design, we predicted that infants would now map novel nouns specifically to category-based (and not property-based) commonalities, but that their expectations for novel adjectives would still be quite general: adjectives should continue to direct attention broadly to both category- and property-based commonalities. Several different experiments with 14-month-olds provide strong support for this aspect of our developmental proposal.

In the first experiment, we tested forty-eight 14-month-old infants. Their results are given in table 10.4. As predicted, these infants were more likely to extend novel nouns to the familiar object (e.g., purple horse) on Category trials (e.g., purple horse vs. purple plate) than on Property trials (e.g., purple horse vs. blue horse). This suggests that by 14 months, infants have already begun to fine-tune the initially broad expectation. Unlike 11-month-olds, they expect nouns to refer specifically to category-based, but not to property-based, commonalities among objects. At the same time, infants' expectation regarding the extension of novel adjectives remained quite general. Mirroring their 11-month-old counterparts, 14-month-olds selected the familiar object (e.g., the purple horse) on both Category and Property test trials.

In the next experiment in this series, we sought additional evidence, this time using texture, rather than color, as a target property. The results with texture-based commonalities replicated the previous pattern with color-based commonalities precisely. This is consistent with the proposal that at 14 months, novel adjectives still direct infants' attention broadly toward a range of commonalities, including both category- and property-based commonalities (Booth and Waxman, forthcoming).

In a subsequent series, we modified the procedure in two ways, hoping to test the limits of infants' abilities by providing them with what we thought would be a more stringent task. (See table 10.5.) First, we pitted a category-based construal directly against a property-based construal at test. Infants saw the same familiarization objects as in the previous experiment, but at test they were required to select either the Same Category test object (e.g., a blue horse) or the Same Property test object (e.g., a purple chair) at test. Second, we presented each test phase twice, to ascertain whether infants' expectations for novel words were sufficiently stable to support a consistent pattern of extension.

Even in this apparently more stringent task, the results were consistent with our developmental proposal. (See table 10.6.) Infants in the No Word control condition performed at chance, suggesting that

Table 10.5
A schematic presentation of introductory phrases (Waxman and Booth 2001; Booth and Waxman, forthcoming) and an example of a single superordinate-level stimulus set

	Familiarization		Contrast	Test
	Trial 1	Trial 2		
Purple animal set	purple bear and lion	purple elephant and dog	orange carrot	blue horse vs. purple chair
Noun	These are blickets. This one is a blicket and this one is a blicket.	These are blickets. This one is a blicket and this one is a blicket.	Uh-oh, this one is not a blicket!	Can you give me the blicket? Can you give me the blicket?
Adjective	These are blickish. This one is blickish and this one is blickish.	These are blickish. This one is blickish and this one is blickish.	Uh-oh, this one is not blickish!	Can you give me the blickish one? Can you give me the blickish one?
No word	Look at these. Look at this one and look at this one.	Look at these. Look at this one and look at this one.	Uh-oh, look at this one!	Can you give me one? Can you give me one?

Table 10.6
Means and standard deviations of the proportion of word-extension test trials on which the familiar object was chosen (Booth and Waxman, forthcoming)

	Color		Texture	
	M	SD	M	SD
Noun	0.65*	0.21	0.65*	0.12
Adjective	0.47	0.15	0.51	0.17
No word	0.52	0.13	0.55	0.10

* $p < 0.05$ versus chance of 0.50

neither test object was more attractive than the other. Nonetheless, infants in the Noun condition revealed a reliable and consistent preference for the Same Category test object. This suggests that by 14 months, infants expect that novel nouns are extended to category-based, rather than to property-based, commonalities.

Interestingly, there was a hint of precocity in the Adjective condition: infants in the Adjective condition revealed a preference for the Same Property test object over the Same Category test object. This is an intriguing effect, because it is consistent with the possibility that a specific expectation for the grammatical form *adjective* is beginning to emerge at this age. However, this effect must be interpreted with serious caution. It has not appeared in any other experiment, and in the current experiment, we have not yet had a chance to seek replication with properties other than color. Future work will be required to gain more insight into this fragile effect. In contrast to this fragility, the evidence for the specific expectation linking nouns to object categories is robust across several tasks and several kinds of properties.

Nouns: Privileged Grammatical Form or Privileged Phrasal Position?
In the next experiment, we submitted this (apparently) robust noun-to-category link to greater further scrutiny. A review of table 10.5 reveals that there are systematic differences in our presentation of novel words in the Noun and Adjective conditions, particularly in the test phase of the experiment. Some of these differences might have favored the infants' ability to parse out the nouns, as compared to

the adjectives. Of course, our goal in designing these experiments was to provide unambiguous evidence regarding the grammatical form class assignment of the novel words. But in the process of meeting this goal, we may have inadvertently created a set of conditions in which the nouns were more easily parsed than were the adjectives. For instance, in every experiment, the nouns appeared in the (privileged) phrase-final position during familiarization and test. This was not the case for the adjectives, which appeared in a penultimate position at test. This imbalance is especially troubling when it occurred in the test phase. Notice also that the novel adjectives all ended with the same syllable (the suffix *-ish*), while the nouns varied in their endings. This variation in the final syllable might have rendered the nouns more "interesting." If the nouns were indeed more interesting, or more easily parsed than the adjectives, this could have consequences for performance.

To ascertain whether these differences in the presentation of nouns and adjectives influenced 14-month-olds' performance, we ran a control condition, this time presenting the novel nouns in a manner that better matched the presentation of the adjectives in the previous experiments (Booth and Waxman, forthcoming). In this new Noun condition, we constructed novel nouns that ended in the same syllable for every trial, and placed them in the penultimate position in the utterance at test ("Can you give me the blicket now?"). If infants' performance in the Noun conditions in previous work is attributable to unintentional confounds (e.g., morphology, utterance position), then performance in this new Noun condition should be less clear-cut than in the previous investigations. This was not the case: the modifications did not change infants' systematic extension of novel nouns in any way. The mean proportion of word extension in the Noun (utterance medial) condition was 0.68. This value is significantly greater than chance and greater than performance in either the Adjective or No Word conditions. It is also fully comparable to the original Noun phrase final condition. We therefore conclude that 14-month-old infants' precise extension of nouns to category-based commonalities cannot be attributed to these features of morphology or utterance position.

10.4.7 Summary

This section illustrates the promise of a new experimental paradigm designed to trace the origin and unfolding of links between word learning and conceptual organization in infants. We have proposed that infants begin the task of word learning equipped with a broad initial expectation that links novel words (independent of their grammatical form) to commonalities among named objects. The performance of 11-month-old infants fully supports this aspect of our developmental proposal.

We also proposed that this initially general expectation subsequently gives way to a more specific set of expectations, linking particular grammatical forms to particular types of meaning. In the work described here, we see evidence of this emergence in infants close to 14 months of age (Booth and Waxman, forthcoming; Waxman 1999b; Waxman and Booth 2001; Waxman and Markow 1995). Infants at this age are sensitive to at least some of the relevant cues that distinguish among the grammatical forms, and they recruit these distinctions actively in the task of word learning.

This work also reveals that as infants begin to refine their expectations, they first tease apart the grammatical form *noun* from among the other grammatical forms, and map this form specifically to category-based (and not property-based) commonalities. At this same developmental moment, infants' expectation for the grammatical form *adjective* remains more general, highlighting both category- and property-based commonalities. Apparently, then, the specific expectation linking the grammatical form *adjective* to its meaning is a subsequent developmental accomplishment, one that likely builds on the noun-to-category link, and one shaped by the semantic and syntactic properties of adjectives in the language under acquisition. In other work, we have shown that for infants acquiring English, a more specific expectation for adjectives emerges just a few months later, at 21 months (Waxman and Markow 1998). At this point, infants no longer interpret adjectives broadly; they restrict their extension of novel adjectives to property-based (and not category-based) commonalities. (See Klibanoff and Waxman 2000; Mintz and Gleitman 2002; Waxman and Klibanoff 2000 for evidence that the mapping for adjectives is dependent on the noun being modified; see Waxman, Senghas, and Benveniste 1997 for evidence that the mapping for adjectives is indeed sensitive to crosslinguistic variation.)

10.5 Discussion and Implications

It is a fundamental feature of human language that different kinds of words highlight different aspects of the very same observed scene. In my research program, I have asked how these specific word-to-world links are acquired, which (if any) are available at the onset of acquisition, and how they are shaped over the course of acquisition. Now, with a clear view of the current evidence, let us examine the three logically possible classes of responses to these developmental questions.

One possibility is that early lexical acquisition is guided by an a priori set of expectations, linking each type of word (e.g., noun, adjective, verb) to a particular type of meaning (e.g., object categories, object properties, actions). The developmental evidence reported here does not support this possibility in its strongest form, for infants appear to begin the process of word learning with a link that is considerably more general than that observed in mature language users. A review of the crosslinguistic literature also casts serious doubt on this possibility, because the ways particular grammatical forms are linked to meaning are not universal. The grammatical form *noun* enjoys considerable crosslinguistic stability. Across languages, this grammatical form is universally represented (Lyons 1977; Maratsos 1991), and a core function of this form is to refer to individual objects and to categories of objects. In contrast, the other grammatical forms (including adjectives and other predicates) are much more variable both in the extent to which they are represented in various languages, and in the ways these forms are recruited to express meaning (Bowerman 1996; Haryu and Imai 1999; Imai and Gentner 1997; Lyons 1977; Maratsos 1991; Regier and Carlson 2001; Waxman, Senghas, and Benveniste 1997). This crosslinguistic variability, in the adjective system, is directly related to issues of acquisition, for it reveals that infants' expectations regarding these more variably represented grammatical forms cannot be fixed from the outset. Instead, in the process of acquisition, infants must discover *whether* a particular grammatical form is realized in their native language, and *how* that form is recruited to express meaning.

A second (and radically different) possibility is that infants begin the task of word learning as tabula rasas, equipped with no a priori expectations to guide the initial steps in acquisition. This position, which has been argued forcefully, describes early word learning as the result of "dumb attentional mechanisms" (Smith 1999; Smith, Colunga, and Yoshida 2003). In this view, infants' first (scores of) words are acquired in the absence of any guiding expectations, and it is only *after* they have already amassed a sizable lexicon that they begin to detect any links between words and concepts. However, the developmental literature casts serious doubt on this possibility. There is now more than ample evidence (much of it reviewed in this volume) that infants do not approach the initial steps of word learning as tabulae rasae, but instead harbor powerful, albeit general, expectations linking words with concepts from the start (Balaban and Waxman 1997; Waxman and Markow 1995; Xu 1999). The fact that these nascent expectations are in place in advance of word learning constitutes strong empirical evidence against the possibility that infants' expectations must emerge after the onset of word learning or must be induced from infants' existing lexicons.

My colleagues and I have argued for a third possibility, one that represents an interaction between an a priori expectation inherent in the infant and the shaping role of the environment (here, the structure of the native language). We have proposed that infants embark on the task of word learning not as tabulae rasae, but equipped with a broad, universally shared expectation that links words to commonalities among objects. This initial expectation, which guides lexical acquisition from the start, provides infants with a means to establish a stable rudimentary lexicon. Using this lexicon as a base, the broad initial expectation is subsequently fine-tuned, as infants begin to tease apart the various grammatical forms in the language under acquisition and to detect the correlations between these grammatical forms and the specific ways they are recruited to express meaning.

The evidence reviewed in this chapter provides strong support for this view. We have shown, for example, that for infants on the very threshold of producing words on their own, novel content words (independent of their grammatical form) highlight a broad range of commonalities among named objects (Balaban and Waxman 1997; Waxman and Booth 2003). This initially broad, universal expectation appears to be supported by several domain-general capabilities, including a perceptual preference for listening to words over other auditory stimuli, and a capacity to notice a range of relations among objects. However, the expectation itself—linking words to commonalities—appears to be specific to word learning, for it applies to novel words, but not to other auditory signals.

I have argued that this broad initial link serves at least three essential functions. First, because words direct attention broadly to commonalities, this link facilitates the formation of an expanding repertoire of categories and concepts. In this way, words serve as invitations to form categories, highlighting relations among objects that may otherwise have gone undetected in the absence of a novel word. Second, this broad initial link supports the establishment of a rudimentary lexicon, permitting infants to establish reference and to acquire a stable set of "word-to-world" mappings. Finally, and perhaps most radically, this initially broad expectation sets the stage for the evolution of the more precise expectations, which are calibrated in accordance with the observed correlations between particular grammatical forms and their associated meanings in the language under acquisition.

10.5.1 How Might This Evolution Come About?

In our view, infants discover the distinct grammatical forms of their language when they begin to notice the distinct patterns or grammatical frames within which words tend to appear, when they discover, for example, that some (kinds of) words tend to be stressed or inflected, that some tend to be preceded consistently by (unstressed) closed-class words, that some tend to occupy particular positions (initial, final) within phrases, and so on. This discovery converges with infants' emerging sensitivity to the correlations between the particular grammatical forms represented in their native language and their links to types of meaning.

Thus, I suggest that infants' early lexicon serves as the bedrock on which infants make two discoveries: that there are distinct kinds of words (grammatical forms) in their language, and that there are correlations between these grammatical forms and the types of meaning they convey. I suspect that these two discoveries go hand in hand, each adjusting gradually to the other, in a process akin to Quine's now-classic example of the child (or the chimneysweep), scrambling "up an intellectual chimney, supporting himself against each side by pressure against the others" (Quine 1960, 93). As infants begin to scramble up the chimney of lexical acquisition, they first tease apart the nouns (from among the other grammatical forms) and map these specifically to object categories (from among the other types of commonalities, including property-based or action-based commonalities). Any subsequent linkages will build on this fundamental referential base, and will be fine-tuned as a function of experience with the specific correlations between particular grammatical forms and their associated meanings in the native language.

10.5.2   Why Is the Noun-Category Link the First Specific Link to Emerge from the More General Expectation?

On the basis of the current evidence, we cannot be certain why this is the case. Some theorists argue that this developmental priority for the noun-object category link derives primarily from factors on the *word* side of the chimney. In brief, the claim is that early emergence of this link is attributable to the acoustic, prosodic, or syntactic features that make nouns more salient than other grammatical forms in the input to children. Others argue that this developmental priority stems primarily from factors on the *world* side of the chimney. In brief, the claim is that the early emergence of the noun-object category link is a consequence of perceptual and conceptual factors that favor the representation of objects over other kinds of relations. Still others, myself included, see this early noun advantage as a product of essential interactions between linguistic and conceptual organization.

In any case, the early emergence of a noun-category linkage accords well with most current theories of language acquisition, which, despite otherwise heated debates, converge on the assumption that the learner must first identify the nouns in the input and map them to entities in the world if they are to discover the other grammatical forms and their links to meaning (Dixon 1982; Fisher and Gleitman 2002; Gentner 1982; Gleitman 1990; Grimshaw 1994; Huttenlocher and Smiley 1987; Maratsos 1998; Pinker 1984; Talmy 1985; Waxman 1999b; Wierzbicka 1984). Indeed, the argument is that discovering the meanings associated with these other grammatical forms must be grounded in the prior acquisition of nouns and the discovery of argument structure.

10.6   Conclusions

The goal of this chapter has been to articulate a developmental account of the powerful and dynamic relation between word learning and conceptual organization. What resources do infants recruit in the process of mapping their first words to meaning? How do they establish correspondences between the words, the objects, and the events they encounter? The evidence supports the view (1) that infants begin the task of word learning equipped with a broad, initial, and universally available expectation linking novel words (independent of their grammatical form) to a wide range of commonalities among named objects, (2) that this initially general expectation sets the stage for the evolution of more finely tuned expectations, calibrated in accordance with the correlations between the grammatical forms represented in the native language under acquisition and their associated meanings, and (3) that these expectations support the rapid acquisition of increasingly sophisticated language and conceptual systems that are the hallmark of human development.

Clearly, the linguistic and conceptual capacities of infants are not on a par with those of their elders. Their grammatical form distinctions are not as well defined as those of more mature speakers, and their conceptual repertoires are not as rich. Nonetheless, even before they can tie their own shoes, infants share with their elders a deep insight—that there are different types of words and that these draw attention to different aspects of the very same observed constellation of experience.

Acknowledgments

This work has been funded by a grant from the National Institutes of Child Health and Human Development. Portions of this research have been discussed in Waxman 2002 and Waxman 2003.

Notes

1. I will use the term *concept* to refer to an abstraction, a mental representation. For the concepts considered in this chapter (e.g., *dog* or *furry*), the representation will include individual instances that the infant has encountered (e.g., her own pet dog; its furry tail). The representation is sufficiently abstract to include (at least some) instances that she has not encountered (e.g., my dog; her furry ears). Used in this way, the term *concept* refers to an abstract mental representation that includes (but is not restricted to) infants' direct experiences, and may be organized around various kinds of relations, including category-based, property-based, or action-based commonalities among objects.

2. The effects in this series of experiments were most apparent on superordinate-level trials. On basic-level trials, infants in all conditions readily detected the category-based commonalities we presented.

3. This approach is predicated on the assumption that there is, indeed, a principled psychological distinction between categories versus properties of objects. Most current theorists distinguish object categories (also known as *kinds* or *sortals*) from other types of groupings (e.g., *purple things, things to pull from a burning house*) on at least three (related) grounds: Object categories (1) are richly structured, (2) capture many commonalities, including deep, nonobvious relations among properties (as opposed to isolated properties), and (3) serve as the basis for induction (Barsalou 1983; Bhatt and Rovee-Collier 1997; Gelman and Medin 1993; Kalish and Gelman 1992; Macnamara 1994; Medin and Heit 1999; Murphy and Medin 1985; Younger and Cohen 1986). Although infants and children have less detailed knowledge about many object categories than do adults, they clearly expect named-object categories to serve these functions (Gelman 1996; Keil 1994; Waxman 1999b; Welder and Graham 2001).

4. Note that an object's shape appears to be more central to its category membership than does its color or texture, particularly for simple artifacts and for animate objects (Booth and Waxman 2002; Waxman and Braig 1996).

References

Baillargeon, R. 1993. The object concept revisited: New directions in the investigation of infants' physical knowledge. In C. Granrud, ed., *Visual perception and cognition in infancy: Carnegie Mellon Symposia on Cognition*, 265–315. Hillsdale, NJ: Erlbaum.

Baillargeon, R. 2000. How do infants learn about the physical world? In D. Muir and A. Slater, eds., *Infant development: The essential readings—Essential readings in development psychology*, 195–212. Malden, MA: Blackwell.

Balaban, M. T., and Waxman, S. R. 1997. Do words facilitate object categorization in 9-month-old infants? *Journal of Experimental Child Psychology*, *64*(1), 3–26.

Balaban, M. T., and Waxman, S. R. 2002, April. Do words and melodies facilitate infants' heart rate and looking responses in an object categorization task? Poster presented at the Thirteenth Biennial International Conference on Infant Studies, Toronto.

Baldwin, D. A., and Baird, J. A. 1999. Action analysis: A gateway to intentional inference. In P. Rochat, ed., *Early social cognition: Understanding others in the first months of life*, 215–240. Mahwah, NJ: Erlbaum.

Baldwin, D. A., and Markman, E. M. 1989. Establishing word-object relations: A first step. *Child Development*, *60*(2), 381–398.

Barsalou, L. W. 1983. Ad hoc categories. *Memory and Cognition*, *11*(3), 211–227.

Bhatt, R. S., and Rovee-Collier, C. 1997. Dissociation between features and feature relations in infant memory: Effects of memory load. *Journal of Experimental Child Psychology*, *67*(1), 69–89.

Bloom, P. 2000. *How children learn the meanings of words*. Cambridge, MA: MIT Press.

Booth, A. E., and Waxman, S. R. 2002. Word learning is "smart": Evidence that conceptual information affects preschoolers' extension of novel words. *Cognition*, *84*(1), B11–B22.

Booth, A. E., and Waxman, S. R. Forthcoming. Mapping words to the world in infancy: On the evolution of expectations for count nouns and adjectives. *Journal of Cognition and Development*.

Bowerman, M. 1996. Learning how to structure space for language: A crosslinguistic perspective. In P. Bloom and M. A. Peterson, eds., *Language and space: Language, speech, and communication*, 385–436. Cambridge, MA: MIT Press.

Brown, R. W. 1957. Linguistic determinism and the part of speech. *Journal of Abnormal and Social Psychology*, *55*, 1–5.

Dixon, R. M. W. 1982. *Where have all the adjectives gone?* Berlin: Mouton.

Fernald, A. 1992a. Human maternal vocalizations to infants as biologically relevant signals: An evolutionary perspective. In J. H. Barkow, L. Cosmides, and J. Tooby, eds., *The adapted mind: Evolutionary psychology and the generation of culture*, 391–428. New York: Oxford University Press.

Fernald, A. 1992b. Meaningful melodies in mothers' speech to infants. In H. Papousek, U. Jurgens, and M. Papousek, eds., *Nonverbal vocal communication: Comparative and developmental approaches—Studies in emotion and social interaction*, 262–282. New York: Cambridge University Press.

Fisher, C., and Gleitman, L. R. 2002. Language acquisition. In H. Pashler and R. Gallistel, eds., *Stevens' handbook of experimental psychology, Vol. 3: Learning, motivation, and emotion,* 3rd ed., 445–496. New York: Wiley.

Fulkerson, A. L., and Haaf, R. A. 1998. New words for new things: The relationship between novel labels and twelve-month-olds' categorization of novel objects. Poster presented at the International Conference on Infant Studies, Atlanta.

Gelman, R. 1991. Epigenetic foundations of knowledge structures: Initial and transcendent constructions. In S. Carey and R. Gelman, eds., *The epigenesis of mind: Essays on biology and cognition—The Jean Piaget Symposium series,* 293–322. Hillsdale, NJ: Erlbaum.

Gelman, R., and Williams, E. M. 1998. Enabling constraints for cognitive development and learning: Domain specificity and epigenesis. In W. Damon, series ed., and D. K. Kuhn and R. S. Siegler, vol. eds., *Handbook of child psychology, Vol. 2: Cognition, perception, and language,* 5th ed., 575–630. New York: Wiley.

Gelman, S. A. 1996. Concepts and theories. In R. Gelman and T. Kit-Fong, eds., *Perceptual and cognitive development: Handbook of perception and cognition,* 2nd ed., 117–150. San Diego: Academic Press.

Gelman, S. A., and Medin, D. L. 1993. What's so essential about essentialism? A different perspective on the interaction of perception, language, and conceptual knowledge. *Cognitive Development, 8*(2), 157–167.

Gentner, D. 1982. Why nouns are learned before verbs: Linguistic relativity versus natural partitioning. In S. Kuczaj, ed., *Language development: Language, thought, and culture,* vol. 2, 301–334. Hillsdale, NJ: Erlbaum.

Gerken, L., and McIntosh, B. J. 1993. Interplay of function morphemes and prosody in early language. *Developmental Psychology, 29*(3), 448–457.

Gleitman, L. 1990. The structural sources of verb meanings. *Language Acquisition: A Journal of Developmental Linguistics, 1*(1), 3–55.

Gleitman, L. R., and Gleitman, H. 1992. A picture is worth a thousand words, but that's the problem: The role of syntax in vocabulary acquisition. *Current Directions in Psychological Science, 1*(1), 31–35.

Gleitman, L. R., and Newport, E. L. 1995. The invention of language by children: Environmental and biological influences on the acquisition of language. In L. R. Gleitman and M. Liberman, eds., *Language: An invitation to cognitive science,* 2nd ed., vol. 1, 1–24. Cambridge, MA: MIT Press.

Goldin-Meadow, S. 1997. The resilience of language in humans. In C. T. Snowdon and M. Hausberger, eds., *Social influences on vocal development,* 293–311. New York: Cambridge University Press.

Goodman, N. 1955. *Fact, fiction, and forecast.* Cambridge, MA: Harvard University Press.

Grimshaw, J. 1994. Minimal projection and clause structure. In B. Lust and M. Suner, eds., *Syntactic theory and first language acquisition: Cross-linguistic perspectives,* vol. 1, 75–83. Hillsdale, NJ: Erlbaum.

Guajardo, J. J., and Woodward, A. L. 2000. Using habituation to index infants' understanding of pointing. Paper presented at the Twelfth Biennial Meeting of the International Society for Infant Studies, Brighton, UK.

Hall, D. G. 1991. Acquiring proper nouns for familiar and unfamiliar animate objects: Two-year-olds' word-learning biases. *Child Development, 62*(5), 1142–1154.

Hall, D. G. 1999. Semantics and the acquisition of proper names. In R. Jackendoff, P. Bloom, and K. Wynn, eds., *Language, logic, and concepts: Essays in memory of John Macnamara*, 337–372. Cambridge, MA: MIT Press.

Haryu, E., and Imai, M. 1999. Controlling the application of the mutual exclusivity assumption in the acquisition of lexical hierarchies. *Japanese Psychological Research, 41*(1), 21–34.

Held, R., and Hein, A. 1963. Movement-produced stimulation in the development of visually guided behavior. *Journal of Comparative and Physiological Psychology, 56*(5), 872–876.

Huttenlocher, J., and Smiley, P. 1987. Early word meanings: The case of object names. *Cognitive Psychology, 19*(1), 63–89.

Imai, M., and Gentner, D. 1997. A cross-linguistic study of early word meaning: Universal ontology and linguistic influence. *Cognition, 62*(2), 169–200.

Jaswal, V. K., and Markman, E. M. 2001. Learning proper and common names in inferential versus obstensive contexts. *Child Development, 72*(3), 768–786.

Johnson, J. S., and Newport, E. L. 1991. Critical period effects on universal properties of language: The status of subjacency in the acquisition of a second language. *Cognition, 39*(3), 215–258.

Jusczyk, P. W. 2002. How infants adapt speech-processing capacities to native language structure. *Current Directions in Psychological Science, 11*(1), 15–18.

Jusczyk, P. W., and Aslin, R. N. 1995. Infants' detection of the sound patterns of words in fluent speech. *Cognitive Psychology, 29*(1), 1–23.

Jusczyk, P. W., and Kemler Nelson, D. G. 1996. Syntactic units, prosody, and psychological reality during infancy. In J. L. Morgan and K. Demuth, eds., *Signal to syntax: Bootstrapping from speech to grammar in early acquisition*, 389–408. Mahwah, NJ: Erlbaum.

Jusczyk, P. W., and Luce, P. A. 2002. Speech perception. In H. Pashler and S. Yantis, eds., *Stevens' handbook of experimental psychology, Vol. 1: Sensation and perception*, 3rd ed., 493–536. New York: Wiley.

Kalish, C. W., and Gelman, S. A. 1992. On wooden pillows: Multiple classification and children's category-based inductions. *Child Development, 63*(6), 1536–1557.

Keil, F. C. 1994. The birth and nurturance of concepts by domains: The origins of concepts of living things. In L. A. Hirschfeld and S. A. Gelman, eds., *Mapping the mind: Domain specificity in cognition and culture*, 234–254. New York: Cambridge University Press.

Keller, H. 1904. *The story of my life.* New York: Doubleday, Page.

Kemler Nelson, D. G., Hirsh-Pasek, K., Jusczyk, P. W., and Cassidy, K. W. 1989. How the prosodic cues in motherese might assist language learning. *Journal of Child Language, 16*(1), 55–68.

Klibanoff, R. S., and Waxman, S. R. 2000. Basic level object categories support the acquisition of novel adjectives: Evidence from preschool-aged children. *Child Development, 71*(3), 649–659.

Lyons, J. 1977. *Semantics.* New York: Cambridge University Press.

Macnamara, J. 1994. Logic and cognition. In J. Macnamara and G. E. Reyes, eds., *The logical foundations of cognition: Vancouver Studies in Cognitive Science,* vol. 4, 11–34. New York: Oxford University Press.

Maratsos, M. P. 1991. How the acquisition of nouns may be different from that of verbs. In N. A. Krasnegor, D. M. Rumbaugh, R. L. Schiefelbusch, and M. Studdert-Kennedy, eds., *Biological and behavioral determinants of language development,* 67–88. Hillsdale, NJ: Erlbaum.

Maratsos, M. P. 1998. The acquisition of grammar. In D. Kuhn and R. S. Siegler, eds., *Cognition, perception, and language, Vol. 2: Handbook of child psychology,* 5th ed. New York: Wiley.

Markman, E. M. 1989. *Categorization and naming in children: Problems of induction.* Cambridge, MA: MIT Press.

Marler, P. 1991. The instinct to learn. In S. Carey and R. Gelman, eds., *The epigenesis of mind: Essays on biology and cognition.* Hillsdale, NJ: Erlbaum.

Medin, D. L., and Heit, E. 1999. Categorization. In D. E. Rumelhart and B. O. Martin, eds., *Handbook of cognition and perception,* 99–143. San Diego: Academic Press.

Mehler, J., Christophe, A., and Ramus, F. 2000. How infants acquire language: Some preliminary observations. In A. Marantz, Y. Miyashita, and W. O'Neil, eds., *Image, language, brain: Papers from the First Mind Articulation Project Symposium,* 51–75. Cambridge, MA: MIT Press.

Mintz, T. H., and Gleitman, L. R. 2002. Adjectives really do modify nouns: The incremental and restricted nature of early adjective acquisition. *Cognition, 84*(3), 267–293.

Morgan, J. L., and Demuth, K., eds. 1996. *Signal to syntax: Bootstrapping from speech to grammar in early acquisition.* Mahwah, NJ: Erlbaum.

Murphy, G. L., and Medin, D. L. 1985. The role of theories in conceptual coherence. *Psychological Review, 92*(3), 289–316.

Ninio, A. 2002, August. Young children's difficulty with adjectives modifying nouns. Paper presented at the Biennial Meeting of the International Society for the Study of Behavioural Development, Ottawa.

Ochs, E., and Schieffelin, B. 1984. Language acquisition and socialization. In R. Shweder and R. LeVine, eds., *Culture theory*. Cambridge, England: Cambridge University Press.

Pallier, C., Sebastian-Galles, N., Dupoux, E., Christophe, A., and Mehler, J. 1998. Perceptual adjustment to time-compressed speech: A cross-linguistic study. *Memory and Cognition, 26*(4), 844–851.

Pinker, S. 1984. *Language learnability and language development.* Cambridge, MA: Harvard University Press.

Quine, W. V. O. 1960. *Word and object: An inquiry into the linguistic mechanisms of objective reference.* New York: Wiley.

Quinn, P. C., and Eimas, P. D. 2000. The emergence of category representations during infancy: Are separate perceptual and conceptual processes required? *Journal of Cognition and Development, 1*, 55–62.

Regier, T., and Carlson, L. 2001. Grounding spatial language in perception: An empirical and computational investigation. *Journal of Experimental Psychology: General, 130*(2), 273–298.

Saffran, J. R., Aslin, R. N., and Newport, E. L. 1996. Statistical learning by 8-month-old infants. *Science, 274*(5294), 1926–1928.

Shi, R., Werker, J. F., and Morgan, J. L. 1999. Newborn infants' sensitivity to perceptual cues to lexical and grammatical words. *Cognition, 72*(2), B11–B21.

Smith, L. B. 1999. Children's noun learning: How general learning processes make specialized learning mechanisms. In B. MacWhinney, ed., *The emergence of language,* 277–303. Mahwah, NJ: Erlbaum.

Smith, L. B., Colunga, E., and Yoshida, H. 2003. Making an ontology: Cross-linguistic evidence. In D. H. Rakison and L. M. Oakes, eds., *Early category and concept development: Making sense of the blooming, buzzing confusion,* 275–302. New York: Oxford University Press.

Spelke, E. S. 1993. Object perception. In A. I. Goldman, ed., *Readings in philosophy and cognitive science,* 447–460. Cambridge, MA: MIT Press.

Spelke, E. S. 2000. Core knowledge. *American Psychologist, 55*(11), 1233–1243.

Talmy, L. 1985. Lexicalization patterns: Semantic structure in lexical forms. In T. Shopen, ed., *Language typology and syntactic description,* vol. 3, 249–291. San Diego: Academic Press.

Tomasello, M., and Olguin, R. 1993. Twenty-three-month-old children have a grammatical category of noun. *Cognitive Development, 8*(4), 451–464.

Waxman, S. R. 1998. Linking object categorization and naming: Early expectations and the shaping role of language. In D. L. Medin, ed., *The psychology of learning and motivation,* vol. 38, 249–291. San Diego: Academic Press.

Waxman, S. R. 1999a. The dubbing ceremony revisited: Object naming and categorization in infancy and early childhood. In D. L. Medin and S. Atran, eds., *Folkbiology*, 233–284. Cambridge, MA: MIT Press.

Waxman, S. R. 1999b. Specifying the scope of 13-month-olds' expectations for novel words. *Cognition*, *70*(3), B35–B50.

Waxman, S. R. 2002. Early word learning and conceptual development: Everything had a name, and each name gave birth to a new thought. In U. Goswami, ed., *Blackwell handbook of childhood cognitive development*, 102–126. Oxford: Blackwell.

Waxman, S. R. 2003. Links between object categorization and naming: Origins and emergence in human infants. In D. H. Rakison and L. M. Oakes, eds., *Early category and concept development: Making sense of the blooming, buzzing confusion*. New York: Oxford University Press.

Waxman, S. R., and Booth, A. E. 2001. Seeing pink elephants: Fourteen-month-olds' interpretations of novel nouns and adjectives. *Cognitive Psychology*, *43*, 217–242.

Waxman, S. R., and Booth, A. E. 2003. The origins and evolution of links between word learning and conceptual organization: New evidence from 11-month-olds. *Developmental Science*, *6*(2), 130–137.

Waxman, S. R., and Braig, B. 1996. Stars and starfish: How far can shape take us? Paper presented at the International Conference on Infancy Studies, Providence, RI.

Waxman, S. R., and Guasti, M. T. 2002. *Cross-linguistic differences in children's extensions of novel count nouns and adjectives: Evidence from Italian.* Unpublished manuscript, Department of Psychology, Northwestern University.

Waxman, S. R., and Klibanoff, R. S. 2000. The role of comparison in the extension of novel adjectives. *Developmental Psychology*, *36*(5), 571–581.

Waxman, S. R., and Markow, D. B. 1995. Words as invitations to form categories: Evidence from 12- to 13-month-old infants. *Cognitive Psychology*, *29*(3), 257–302.

Waxman, S. R., and Markow, D. B. 1998. Object properties and object kind: Twenty-one-month-old infants' extension of novel adjectives. *Child Development*, *69*(5), 1313–1329.

Waxman, S. R., Senghas, A., and Benveniste, S. 1997. A cross-linguistic examination of the noun-category bias: Its existence and specificity in French- and Spanish-speaking preschool-aged children. *Cognitive Psychology*, *32*(3), 183–218.

Welder, A. N., and Graham, S. A. 2001. The influences of shape similarity and shared labels on infants' inductive inferences about nonobvious object properties. *Child Development*, *72*(6), 1653–1673.

Werker, J. F., Lloyd, V. L., Pegg, J. E., and Polka, L. 1996. Putting the baby in the bootstraps: Toward a more complete understanding of the role of the input in infant speech processing. In J. L. Morgan and K. Demuth, eds., *Signal to syntax: Bootstrapping from speech to grammar in early acquisition*, 427–447. Mahwah, NJ: Erlbaum.

Wierzbicka, A. 1984. Apples are not a "kind of fruit": The semantics of human categorization. *American Ethnologist, 11*, 313–328.

Wilcox, T., and Baillargeon, R. 1998. Object individuation in infancy: The use of featural information in reasoning about occlusion events. *Cognitive Psychology, 37*(2), 97–155.

Woodward, A. L. 2000. Constraining the problem space in early word learning. In R. M. Golinkoff, K. Hirsh-Pasek, L. Bloom, L. B. Smith, A. L. Woodward, M. Tomasello, and G. Hollich, eds., *Becoming a word learner: A debate on lexical acquisition.* Oxford: Oxford University Press.

Woodward, A. L., and Markman, E. M. 1998. Early word learning. In W. Damon, D. Kuhn, and R. Siegler, eds., *Handbook of child psychology, Vol. 2: Cognition, perception, and language*, 371–420. New York: Wiley.

Woodward, A. L., Markman, E. M., and Fitzsimmons, C. M. 1994. Rapid word learning in 13- and 18-month-olds. *Developmental Psychology, 30*(4), 553–566.

Xu, F. 1999. Object individuation and object identity in infancy: The role of spatio-temporal information, object property information, and language. *Acta Psychologica, 102*(2–3), 113–136.

Younger, B. A., and Cohen, L. B. 1986. Developmental change in infants' perception of correlations among attributes. *Child Development, 57*(3), 803–815.

II

Later Acquisitions

11

Preschoolers' Use and Misuse of Part-of-Speech Information in Word Learning: Implications for Lexical Development

D. Geoffrey Hall and Tracy A. Lavin

Researchers who study word learning in preschool children generally stress its efficiency and accuracy, and for good reason. Given only limited exposure to a novel word, preschoolers are remarkably skilled at determining its intended meaning (e.g., Carey 1978; Heibeck and Markman 1987). One often-cited example of this proficiency is preschoolers' ability to use knowledge of links between particular part-of-speech categories and corresponding types of meanings to learn new words (for reviews of the experimental literature, see Bloom 2000; Woodward and Markman 1998). In the adult language, these form-meaning connections are highly, perhaps perfectly, reliable (Bloom 1994a; Macnamara 1986; Pinker 1996). As a result, once children learn the syntactic and morphological cues that signal a word's part-of-speech category, they have a powerful learning tool at their disposal.

Yet surprisingly, even after they have learned to assign novel words to appropriate part-of-speech categories, preschoolers do not rely consistently on these form-meaning correspondences to learn words. In ostensive learning situations in which they hear a word for a specified material entity, preschoolers frequently do use part-of-speech information to constrain the meaning appropriately. But sometimes they fail to do so, making systematic misinterpretations. In nonostensive learning situations in which they hear a word and must map it to one of several material entities, preschoolers show no systematic mapping preferences when the word belongs to certain part-of-speech categories. Yet they do make consistent mappings when the word comes from other part-of-speech categories.

The first of two main objectives in this chapter is to document children's patterns of use (and misuse) of part-of-speech information in word learning; the second is to consider how these patterns might inform the study of lexical development. To accomplish the first goal, we will review the experimental literature on preschoolers' use of part-of-speech information to learn words for material entities. We will consider children's use of part-of-speech information to constrain a word's meaning in ostensive learning situations, and to choose one particular entity from multiple possibilities as the referent of a nonostensively presented word. The review will show that preschoolers' word learning is indeed guided by sensitivity to part-of-speech information, but it will also reveal that this learning is guided by several default assumptions. The role of these assumptions is to lead children to interpret words used under specified conditions as having certain types of meanings and—because of the links between meanings and forms—as belonging (or not belonging) to particular part-of-speech categories. We will argue that part-of-speech sensitivity often fails to foster word learning when it conflicts with a default assumption or when a relevant default assumption cannot be invoked.

What do the preceding findings reveal about lexical development? On a general level, they indicate that part-of-speech knowledge and default assumptions both play a role in preschoolers' word learning. More specifically, we will argue that the potency of children's default assumptions reflects their central role in helping children learn how part-of-speech categories are expressed in their language—in discovering the syntactic and morphological cues marking particular lexical categories. This argument might sound contradictory, in light of our discussion indicating that these default assumptions often lead preschoolers to disregard part-of-speech information in word-learning experiments. However, we will argue that this proposal gains plausibility in light of research examining how caregivers—not experimental psychologists—label material entities for preschool children. Although experimental psychologists' labeling practices and children's default assumptions are often at odds, we will review evidence indicating that caregivers' labeling practices are in striking harmony with these assumptions. This fact supports the proposal that preschoolers' default assumptions may actually assist them in learning the language-specific properties of words from different part-of-speech categories.

11.1 Sensitivity to Part-of-Speech Information

As a preliminary, we offer a brief discussion of links between part-of-speech categories and their corresponding meanings. In reference to any material entity, speakers may use words from (at least) four different part-of-speech categories: count nouns, proper names, adjectives, and mass nouns. These parts of speech appear to be perfectly associated with specific types of meaning in the adult language (e.g., Bloom 1994a, 2000; Macnamara 1986; Pinker 1996). Count nouns designate categories of individuals, including categories of objects (e.g., DOG); proper names designate individuals, including individual objects (e.g., FIDO); adjectives designate properties, including properties of objects (e.g., SPOTTED); and mass nouns designate categories of nonindividuated stuff, including substance categories (e.g., FUR).

In experimental studies of word learning, information signaling a word's part-of-speech category is usually conveyed through simple syntactic and/or morphological cues. For example, words in English may be marked as count nouns (e.g., *dog*) by appearing in contexts such as "*an* X." They may be given as proper names (e.g., *Fido*) by occurring in phrases such as "*named* X" or as adjectives (e.g., *spotted*) by appearing in locutions such as "*very* X." And words may be marked as mass nouns (e.g., *fur*) by occurring in phrases such as "*some* X."

Knowing a word's part-of-speech category sometimes allows us to specify its meaning fully. For example, knowing that a word applied to a dog is a proper name makes us aware that the word designates that individual dog (e.g., FIDO). In other cases, however, knowledge of a word's part-of-speech category only partially restricts its meaning. For instance, knowing that a word for a dog is a count noun tells us that the word names a category of individuals, but it does not indicate which of many possible categories is the appropriate one.

The word could pick out the object category DOG, but it could also mark the object categories POODLE or ANIMAL.

Some scholars have argued that these form-meaning correspondences (e.g., between count nouns and categories of individuals) are innate (see Bloom 1994a, 2000; Pinker 1996; but see also Markman 1994; Woodward and Markman 1998). Yet even if the links are unlearned, different languages mark membership in particular part-of-speech classes in different ways. Thus, there can be no doubt that children must learn the syntactic and morphological cues that indicate the parts of speech to which words belong in their own language. How children learn these cues is an important question in the study of language development. It is important not only because these cues provide reliable information about a novel word's meaning, but also because they indicate a word's lexical-category membership—crucial information since the rules and principles of grammar are expressed in terms of these categories. We will argue that insight into this question can be gained by examining how children use part-of-speech information to acquire words *after* they have gained sensitivity to the relevant form-meaning correspondences. But before presenting that argument, we offer a preliminary discussion of a competing force driving preschoolers' word learning—default assumptions.

11.2 Default Assumptions

Preschoolers' word learning also appears guided by several default assumptions that direct them to interpret words used in certain circumstances as having particular types of meanings—and, therefore, as belonging (or not belonging) to particular part-of-speech categories. These assumptions function as probabilistic biases that must eventually be overridden in the course of acquiring a lexicon, but that nevertheless may play an important role in getting language development off the ground (see Woodward and Markman 1991). Although the existence of these assumptions has been the subject of debate (for different perspectives, see Bloom 2000; Woodward and Markman 1998), we believe that they are needed in a complete explanation of lexical development.

Two assumptions that appear to be involved in acquiring words for material entities may be called the *object-category assumption* and the *substance-category assumption* (for different formulations of these assumptions, see Golinkoff, Mervis, and Hirsh-Pasek 1994; Hall and Waxman 1993; Imai and Gentner 1997; Lavin and Hall 2002; Markman 1989; Soja, Carey, and Spelke 1991; Subrahmanyam, Landau, and Gelman 1999; Waxman 1990). These assumptions help children acquire count nouns and mass nouns. The object-category assumption leads learners to assume that a word for an unfamiliar solid entity designates an object category (i.e., is a count noun). The term *unfamiliar* here refers to children's lack of knowledge of a count noun for an entity, usually a basic-level count noun (e.g., the word *dog* for a dog or *chair* for a chair; Rosch et al. 1976). The rationale for this assumption is that children commonly interpret words for unfamiliar solid entities as designating entire object categories. Moreover, additional evidence suggests that this assumption is a bias to treat words as basic-level object-category terms (e.g., DOG rather than SPANIEL or ANIMAL; see Hall 1993; Hall and Waxman 1993). A similar rationale motivates the proposal that children make a substance-category assumption: they typically treat a word applied to an unfamiliar nonsolid entity as designating a substance category (i.e., as a mass noun). In this case, *unfamiliar* pertains to the lack of prior knowledge of a mass noun for the entity.

It has been proposed that the preceding assumptions are not necessary to explain lexical development, because they can be subsumed by knowledge of the part-of-speech to meaning links described earlier, and by a general bias toward construing solid entities as individuals and nonsolids as substances (e.g., Bloom 1994a). We are sympathetic to the goal of minimizing the word-learning apparatus attributed to children, but we are not convinced that this proposal accounts for certain details about word learning. For example, suppose children hear a word for an unfamiliar animate entity. Even if they are biased toward construing this entity as an individual, how do they know whether to interpret the word as picking out a category of individuals (invoking the link for a count noun) or the individual itself (invoking the link for a proper name)? Children could use their understanding of form-meaning links to distinguish between these two possibilities, but they appear to ignore part-of-speech information in this type of situation. Preschoolers tend to interpret the word as designating a category of individuals, even when part-of-speech information indicates that the word is a proper name (Hall 1991). Moreover, they make a category-of-individual interpretation even in a language (e.g., Japanese) in which part-of-speech information does not normally distinguish between proper names and count nouns (Imai and Haryu 2001). As a result, we suggest that preschoolers' word learning is directed by the object-category assumption described earlier—a word for an unfamiliar solid entity designates an object category (i.e., is a count noun).

Several other default assumptions also appear to guide preschoolers' word learning. For example, preschoolers seem guided by an *inanimate-object assumption* that leads them to expect that a word for a familiar inanimate object does not designate the individual object (i.e., is not a proper name; e.g., Gelman and Taylor 1984; Hall 1994b; Katz, Baker, and Macnamara 1974). This assumption may derive from children's understanding that proper names are words that designate individuals, and so they should not pick out entities seen to be unimportant as individuals (see Sorrentino 2001). Preschoolers also seem directed by a *range-of-reference assumption* that guides them to expect that a word applied to two or more familiar animate objects is not a term for the individual objects (i.e., is not a proper name). This assumption may stem from children's understanding that proper names are words that designate individuals, and so they should not be extended to more than one object (e.g., Hall 1996b; Hall and Bélanger 2003).

Finally, preschoolers appear to be guided by a *mutual-exclusivity assumption* that directs them to expect that a word should not be an object-category term (i.e., a count noun) for an object, if they already know a count noun for that object. One role of this assumption is to motivate children to acquire count nouns for unfamiliar objects in their environment. Some have argued that this assumption pertains specifically to word meaning (e.g., Woodward and Markman 1998), but others have suggested that it is pragmatic in nature (i.e., related to children's understanding of speakers' communicative intentions). One reason for suggesting that the assumption is pragmatic is that it guides children's inferences about object labels, specifically count nouns, as well as object facts (Diesendruck and Markson 2001). We agree that this assumption may reflect pragmatic knowledge in at least some circumstances. However, we also suspect that it sometimes reflects semantic knowledge, because children distinguish between situations in which more than one word can be applied to a given object and situations in which only one can be applied. For example, as with count nouns, children avoid mapping a second proper name onto an object, but they allow a second adjective to be applied to a single object (Hall and Graham 1999).

Having described several default assumptions that guide preschoolers' word learning, we now review how children use part-of-speech information to acquire words *after* they have gained sensitivity to the relevant form-meaning mappings. We will examine two different types of learning situations, ostensive and nonostensive, in which children use part-of-speech information. In this review, it will become clear that the default assumptions play an ongoing role in word learning—even after preschoolers have acquired sensitivity to the relevant form-meaning correspondences. We will later propose that the potency of the default assumptions reflects their pivotal role in helping children acquire sensitivity to part-of-speech information.

11.3 Part-of-Speech Information in Ostensive Word Learning

Preschoolers are highly adept at using part-of-speech information to constrain the meanings of words in simple ostensive contexts. Suppose, for instance, a caregiver points to a novel object and labels it with a novel word (e.g., "X"). Preschoolers readily use the part-of-speech information accompanying the word to restrict its possible meaning. Hearing "It's *an* X!", they are able to infer that the word is a count noun labeling a category of individuals (e.g., DOG). But if children hear "It's *named* X!", they instead are able to conclude that the word is a proper name marking that specific individual (e.g., FIDO). In a similar way, children who hear "It's *very* X!" or "It's *some* X!" are able to judge that the word is, respectively, an adjective indicating a property (e.g., SPOTTED) or a mass noun marking a category of stuff (e.g., FUR). The evidence to support these claims comes from a number of experimental investigations of preschoolers' patterns of extension of novel words from different part-of-speech categories (for reviews, see Bloom 2000; Woodward and Markman 1998). The results of these studies indicate that sensitivity to these form-meaning mappings is present in 2- to 4-year-olds. In fact, some of the most recent results indicate that the ability to use part-of-speech information to constrain word meanings may be present before the second birthday (e.g., Hall, Lee, and Bélanger 2001; Waxman 1999; Waxman and Booth 2001; Waxman and Markow 1995).

Even though part-of-speech information offers a highly reliable cue to a word's meaning, preschoolers do not use it consistently in ostensive learning situations. Although they often do exploit this information to constrain word interpretations, they sometimes disregard it when it conflicts with their default assumptions. Children's tendency to invoke these assumptions often depends on a labeled entity's familiarity, animacy, and solidity.

11.3.1 Familiarity

A number of researchers have compared preschoolers' interpretation of words for familiar (e.g., a dog) and unfamiliar (e.g., a wombat) objects. In several studies, the familiarity of an object has significantly affected preschoolers' use of part-of-speech information to learn a word for it. If preschool children hear a novel word applied ostensively to a *familiar* object (e.g., a dog), they often use part-of-speech information to restrict the word's meaning appropriately. Specifically, they interpret novel count nouns as object-category terms (e.g., SPANIEL; see Taylor and Gelman 1989; Waxman and Gelman 1986; Waxman and Kosowski 1990), proper names as labels for individual objects (e.g., FIDO; see Hall 1991), adjectives as object-property terms (e.g., SPOTTED; see Hall, Waxman, and Hurwitz 1993), and mass nouns as substance-category labels (e.g., FUR; see Markman and Wachtel 1988).

Yet if preschoolers hear the same novel word applied in the same way to an *unfamiliar* object (e.g., a wombat), they are less likely to use part-of-speech information effectively to constrain the word's meaning. In such a situation, there is evidence that children will interpret a novel count noun as an object-category term (e.g., WOMBAT; e.g., Gelman and Taylor 1984; Taylor and Gelman 1989). They will also, however, override the part-of-speech information in order to assign an object-category interpretation to a proper name (e.g., Hall 1991), an adjective (e.g., Hall, Waxman, and Hurwitz 1993; Landau, Smith, and Jones 1992; Smith, Jones, and Landau 1992), and a mass noun (e.g., Dickinson 1988; Markman and Wachtel 1988; Soja 1992). See the top panel of figure 11.1.

The preceding evidence suggests that preschoolers use their sensitivity to form-meaning correspondences selectively in ostensive word learning. They use it appropriately to restrict their inferences when the referent entity is familiar, but they often override it when that entity is unfamiliar. This tendency to override part-of-speech information is consistent with the operation of the object-category assumption described earlier—a word for an unfamiliar object designates an object category (i.e., is a count noun). Thus, when preschoolers hear a novel word for an unfamiliar object, their sensitivity to part-of-speech information and the object-category assumption may suggest conflicting interpretations. When this happens, preschoolers often honor the assumption.

11.3.2 Animacy

Researchers have also compared the acquisition of words for animate (generally dolls or stuffed animals) and inanimate (usually toy artifacts) objects. The animacy of an object has also been shown to influence children's use of part-of-speech information to learn a word for it. If preschool children hear a novel word for an *animate* object (e.g., a dog), there is evidence that they will use part-of-speech information appropriately to constrain the word's meaning. Specifically, they will interpret a count noun as designating an object category (although usually not a basic-level category, if they already know a basic-level count noun for it; instead, they may tend to make a subordinate-level category interpretation, e.g., SPANIEL; see Jaswal and Markman 2001; Katz, Baker, and Macnamara 1974; Macnamara

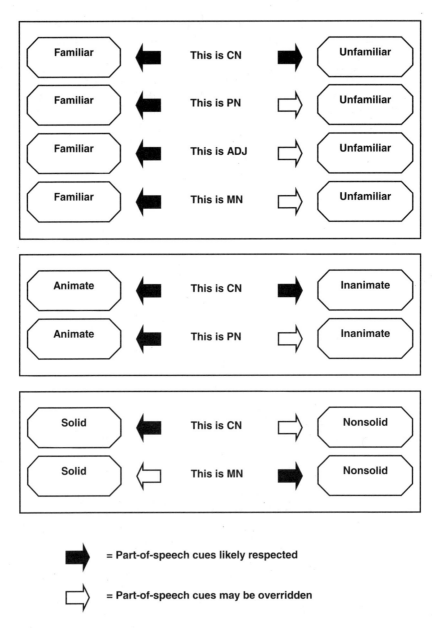

Figure 11.1
Possible word-referent mappings in ostensive learning. CN = count noun; PN = proper name; ADJ = adjective; MN = mass noun.

1982; Taylor and Gelman 1989). Similarly, preschoolers will interpret a proper name as marking an individual object (e.g., FIDO; see Jaswal and Markman 2001; Katz, Baker, and Macnamara 1974; Macnamara 1982).

In contrast, when preschoolers hear the same novel word provided for an *inanimate* object (e.g., a chair), they will often fail to exploit the form-meaning links to interpret the word. For example, they will appropriately interpret a count noun as designating an object category (e.g., ROCKER; see Jaswal and Markman 2001; Katz, Baker, and Macnamara 1974; Macnamara 1982; Taylor and Gelman 1989). However, they will tend not to interpret a proper name as marking the individual object, often instead treating it as an object-category or object-property term (e.g., Katz, Baker, and Macnamara 1974; Macnamara 1982) or as a proper name for a nondesignated animate object (e.g., Gelman and Taylor 1984; Jaswal and Markman 2001). See the middle panel of figure 11.1.

There is thus further evidence that preschoolers selectively use their sensitivity to form-meaning links to learn an ostensively defined word. They use it appropriately to limit a word's meaning when the referent is animate, but they may fail to do so when the referent is inanimate. Children's misuse of proper-name part-of-speech cues suggests the operation of the inanimate-object assumption described earlier—a word for an inanimate object should not be interpreted as designating an individual object (i.e., as a proper name). The basis for this assumption has been the subject of some discussion in the literature. There is general agreement that children typically fail to interpret words for inanimate objects as proper names, but there have been suggestions that they fail to do so not because the objects are inanimate per se, but rather because inanimate objects are generally seen to be unimportant as individuals in their own right (e.g., Hall 1994b; Hall, Veltkamp, and Turkel forthcoming; Sorrentino 2001). In either case, it is clear that when preschoolers hear a novel word for a familiar inanimate object, their sensitivity to part-of-speech information and their inanimate-object assumption may suggest conflicting interpretations. When this happens, preschoolers often give priority to the assumption.

11.3.3 Solidity

Finally, a number of scholars have compared the acquisition of words for solid entities (often simple or complex objects) and non-solid entities (portions of nonsolid substances). The solidity of a word's referent may also affect children's use of part-of-speech information to learn a word for it. If preschoolers hear a word for an unfamiliar *solid* entity (e.g., a chair), there is evidence that they will use the accompanying part-of-speech information selectively to guide their interpretation. They will appropriately interpret a count noun as marking an object category (e.g., CHAIR). However, they may also inappropriately make the same interpretation if the word is presented as a mass noun (e.g., Dickinson 1988; Prasada 1993; Soja, Carey, and Spelke 1991; Soja 1992; Subrahmanyam, Landau, and Gelman 1999). Conversely, if children encounter an unfamiliar *nonsolid* entity (e.g., a pile of sand), they will appropriately interpret a mass noun for it as labeling a substance category (e.g., SAND). They will, however, sometimes wrongly make the same interpretation if the word is a count noun (e.g., Soja 1992; Subrahmanyam, Landau, and Gelman 1999). See the bottom panel of figure 11.1.

The preceding patterns of interpretation provide still further evidence of preschoolers' selective use of knowledge of form-meaning links to constrain their interpretations of ostensively defined words. These patterns suggest the operation of the object-category assumption and the substance-category assumption described earlier—a word for an unfamiliar solid entity designates an object category (i.e., is a count noun), and a word for an unfamiliar nonsolid entity marks a substance category (i.e., is a mass noun). The nature of these assumptions has been the subject of recent debate in the literature. Specifically, some researchers have proposed that they do not pertain to the interpretation of words for solid and nonsolid entities per se, but rather to the interpretation of words for entities perceived to have structures that are nonarbitrary (e.g., purposefully created) or arbitrary (e.g., accidentally created; e.g., Prasada, Ferenz, and Haskell 2002; see also Lavin and Hall 2002; Proctor and Hall 2003). We will return to this issue later.

There is some evidence that the object-category assumption is more powerful than the substance-category assumption, because there is an asymmetry in preschoolers' misuse of part-of-speech information in the two situations just described. Specifically, the tendency to misinterpret a mass noun for a solid entity as marking an object category appears to be greater than the tendency to misinterpret a count noun for a nonsolid entity as indicating a substance category (see Soja 1992; Subrahmanyam, Landau, and Gelman 1999). This asymmetry suggests that the object-category assumption is especially potent in early lexical development, and it may play a role in explaining other phenomena surrounding children's use of part-of-speech information in nonostensive word learning, discussed later.

To summarize this section: preschool children can readily draw on part-of-speech information to constrain the meaning of an ostensively defined word—to learn a count noun, proper name, adjective, or mass noun. Clearly they have knowledge of appropriate form-meaning links for these parts of speech. Yet preschoolers often fail to use their knowledge of these links when it conflicts with their default assumptions. In the case of such conflicts, they often override their part-of-speech knowledge in order to honor the assumptions. These assumptions direct preschoolers to interpret words for unfamiliar solids as being count nouns, words for familiar inanimate objects as not being proper names, and words for unfamiliar nonsolids as being mass nouns. On a general level, these findings reveal that preschoolers' sensitivity to part-of-speech information interacts with default assumptions to direct word learning. More specifically, the potency of preschoolers' default assumptions suggests that they could play a key role in helping children acquire sensitivity to part-of-speech information in their language. Before presenting that argument in more detail, we will review the evidence concerning a second way children use part-of-speech information in word learning.

11.4 Part-of-Speech Information in Nonostensive Word Learning

On the surface, it might seem that part-of-speech information could help children learn words for material entities only in situations in which a speaker unambiguously indicates the referent. In this case, the task is simply to constrain the interpretation of the novel word—as marking an object category (if the word is a count noun), an individual object (if the word is a proper name), an object property (if the word is an adjective), or a substance category (if the word is a mass noun). This is the situation children face in acquiring words through ostensive definition: they hear a novel term as a speaker points directly toward an entity. Yet word learning often, perhaps typically, takes place in situations in which the referent entity is not singled out unambiguously (see, e.g., Akhtar, chapter 15, this volume). Frequently, more than one material entity is present in the scene at the time of labeling. In such contexts, children face a doubly complicated task. Before they can constrain the meaning of the new word, they must first locate the appropriate referent. How do children establish word-referent mappings in these nonostensive situations?

In these ambiguous contexts, it is clear that preschoolers can draw on their understanding of social cues to help them locate a word's intended referent. For example, they can use a speaker's gaze direction (Baldwin 1991) or affective reaction (Tomasello and Barton 1994) to single out the intended referent; they can also use certain cues available in the discourse context (Akhtar and Tomasello 1996; see Ahktar, chapter 15, this volume). But without disambiguating social information, how could preschoolers use part-of-speech information to establish word-referent mappings in nonostensive situations? The form-meaning links discussed earlier simply specify connections from particular part-of-speech categories to abstract types of meanings. They do not point learners to particular entities in the world. Moreover, material entities are *potentially* the bearers of words from *any* of the part-of-speech categories we have been discussing. For instance, imagine a scene containing two dogs, only one of which is the referent of a novel word. Both are equally good candidates, regardless of whether the novel word is a count noun (e.g., *dog*), a proper name (e.g., *Fido*), an adjective (e.g., *spotted*), or a mass noun (e.g., *fur*).

Yet starting with the influential work by Brown (1957), a number of studies have found that part-of-speech information *can* direct children to establish word-referent mappings in various nonostensive learning situations. However, this information appears to foster the formation of these connections only in situations in which preschoolers can also invoke relevant default assumptions. In particular, part-of-speech information seems helpful in directing the establishment of word-referent mappings in situations containing both a familiar and an unfamiliar entity, both an animate and an inanimate entity, or both a solid and a nonsolid entity.

11.4.1 Familiarity

Suppose that children must choose the referent of a novel word in a situation that contains both a familiar and an unfamiliar object. In this type of ambiguous context, there have been several demonstrations that part-of-speech information may help children map words to particular entities. Specifically, when children hear a novel count noun (e.g., "Find me one that is *an* X!"), they will map it systematically to the unfamiliar object (e.g., Au and Glusman 1990; Evey and Merriman 1998; Golinkoff et al. 1992; Graham, Poulin-Dubois, and Baker 1998; Hall, Quantz, and Persoage 2000; Hutchinson 1986; Markman and Wachtel 1988; Merriman and Bowman 1989; Merriman and Schuster 1991; Mervis and Bertrand 1994). In contrast, when children hear the same novel word presented as a proper name (e.g., "Find me one that is *named* X!") or adjective (e.g., "Find me one that is *very* X!"), they do not show a preference for mapping it systematically to either object (e.g., Hall, Quantz, and Persoage 2000). See the top panel of figure 11.2.

Why do children make systematic word-object mappings for count nouns in this situation? As discussed earlier, in addition to having part-of-speech sensitivity, preschoolers appear to make a mutual-exclusivity assumption that leads them to avoid interpreting a word for a familiar object as a second count noun. (It is also possible that children are guided by the object-category assumption, which leads them to expect that a word for an unfamiliar object will be a count noun. This assumption could lead them to seek out an unfamiliar object, if one is present, as the referent of a count noun; see the "novel-name–nameless-category" principle in Golinkoff, Mervis, and

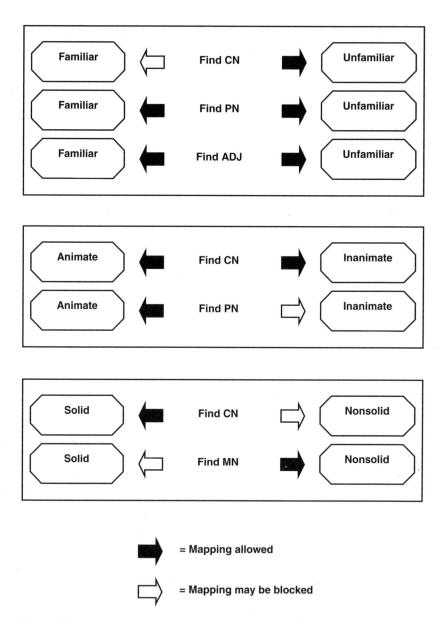

Figure 11.2
Possible word-referent mappings in nonostensive learning. CN = count noun; PN = proper name; ADJ = adjective; MN = mass noun.

Hirsh-Pasek 1994.) The mutual-exclusivity assumption would guide preschoolers to map a count noun systematically to the unfamiliar object in this situation. But mutual exclusivity would not be invoked when children are asked to locate the referent of a proper name or adjective, because it pertains specifically to learning count nouns. As a result, neither object should be favored as a referent for a proper name or an adjective. Preschoolers' understanding of part-of-speech information thus may lead to systematic word-referent mappings in nonostensive contexts, but only when it can be invoked along with a relevant default assumption.

If familiarity is defined as prior knowledge of a proper name for an object, then part-of-speech information may foster different word-object mappings in the same type of nonostensive situation. Suppose that preschoolers must choose the referent for a word in a situation involving two "count-noun familiar" objects, in which they know a proper name for one but not for the other. In this ambiguous situation, if they are asked to locate the referent of a novel proper name (e.g., "Find me one that is *named* X!"), preschoolers will systematically map the word to the object that lacks a proper name (Hall and Graham 1999). They will not show this mapping preference when asked to locate the referent of a novel adjective (e.g., "Find me one that is *very* X!"; Hall and Graham 1999).

Why do preschoolers establish consistent word-object mappings for proper names in this situation? Hall (1999; Hall and Graham 1999) has argued that children may be driven by an analogue of the mutual-exclusivity assumption—the assumption that a word applied to an object that already has a proper name attached to it will not be another proper name (e.g., one dog will not be labeled both *Fido* and *Rover*). As a result of this assumption, preschoolers may map a proper name systematically to the proper-nameless object. Yet children do not invoke this default assumption when interpreting an adjective, because it pertains specifically to learning proper names. Thus they do not favor one object over the other as a referent for an adjective. Again, then, preschoolers' understanding of part-of-speech information may promote systematic word-referent mappings, but only when it can be used along with a relevant default assumption.

11.4.2   Animacy

Suppose now that preschoolers must locate the referent of a word in a situation that contains both an animate and an inanimate object. In this ambiguous context, there have been demonstrations that part-of-speech information may lead them to map the word systematically to a particular object. Specifically, if children hear the word modeled as a proper name (e.g., "Find X!"), they will map it to the animate object. But if they hear the same novel word presented as a count noun (e.g., "Find *an* X!"), they will show no mapping preference (e.g., Liittschwager and Markman 1993; Jaswal and Markman 2001). See the middle panel of figure 11.2.

In this situation, why do preschoolers establish systematic word-object mappings for proper names? As discussed earlier, besides possessing part-of-speech sensitivity, preschoolers seem to have a default assumption that a word for an inanimate object is not a proper name. As a result, preschoolers in this situation map a proper name to the animate object. Children do not engage this assumption when interpreting a count noun, and so no systematic mappings result in this case. Again, preschoolers readily establish word-referent mappings only when their knowledge of part-of-speech information and a relevant word-meaning assumption can both be engaged.

11.4.3   Solidity

Consider one final case in which children must find the referent of a word, but now the situation contains both a solid and a nonsolid entity. In this ambiguous context, there have again been demonstrations, dating back to Brown 1957, that part-of-speech information may help the child map the word to a particular entity. Specifically, if children hear a count noun (e.g., "Show me *an* X!"), they will map it to the solid entity. If, on the other hand, children hear a mass noun (e.g., "Show me *some* X!"), they will map the word to the nonsolid entity (e.g., Brown 1957; Proctor and Hall 2003; Lavin, Proctor, and Hall 2001). See the bottom panel of figure 11.2.

Why do preschoolers make different word-referent mappings for these two part-of-speech categories? As discussed earlier, in addition to having part-of-speech knowledge, preschoolers appear to be guided by two further default assumptions: a word for an unfamiliar solid entity is a count noun, and a word for an unfamiliar nonsolid entity is a mass noun. As a result of these assumptions, preschoolers in this situation may seek out an unfamiliar solid, if one is available, as the referent of a count noun; and they may look for an unfamiliar nonsolid, if one is available, as the referent of a mass noun. Thus, when knowledge of part-of-speech information and relevant assumptions can both be invoked, preschoolers again readily form mappings between words and specific entities.

According to some researchers, these two final assumptions pertain to entities' perceptual properties: words for solid entities are object-category terms (i.e., count nouns), and words for nonsolid entities are substance-category terms (i.e., mass nouns; see Imai and Gentner 1997; Soja, Carey, and Spelke 1991; Soja 1992). According to recent work, however, these assumptions are more abstract: words for entities that are seen as nonarbitrarily structured (e.g., intentionally created) are count nouns, and words for entities that are taken as arbitrarily structured (e.g., accidentally created) are mass nouns (e.g., Prasada, Ferenz, and Haskell 2002). In either formulation, the assumptions would often promote the same word-entity mappings, because people generally think of solid entities (e.g., a chair) as being nonarbitrarily structured, whereas they typically consider nonsolid entities (e.g., a pile of sand) to be arbitrarily structured. Thus, children's word-entity mappings often fail to shed light on which of the two formulations reflects their underlying assumptions.

There is, however, some recent evidence to help adjudicate between the two formulations. This evidence comes from studies involving the manipulation of information about a creator's intent accompanying the solid and nonsolid entities in a nonostensive learning task (Proctor and Hall 2003). For one group of preschoolers, a solid entity was described as nonarbitrarily structured (made on purpose) and a nonsolid entity was described as arbitrarily structured (made by accident). In this case, children showed the mapping results predicted under both formulations of the assumptions: they had a preference for mapping a count noun to the solid and a mass noun to the nonsolid. However, for another group of preschoolers, the designations were reversed: the solid was described as arbitrarily structured (made by accident) and the nonsolid was described as nonarbitrarily structured (made intentionally). Now the two formulations of the assumptions lead to different predictions.

If children's assumptions pertain to the entities' perceptual properties, they should have mapped the count noun to the solid and the mass noun to the nonsolid, as before. On the other hand, if children's assumptions pertain to the perceived arbitrariness of the entities' structures, they should have reversed these mappings. They should have mapped the count noun to the nonsolid (with a nonarbitrary structure) and the mass noun to the solid (with an arbitrary structure). There is also a third possibility. Recall the asymmetry discussed in the previous section, suggesting that preschoolers have an especially powerful assumption that a word for a solid entity marks an object category (is a count noun; e.g., Soja 1992; Subrahmanyam, Landau, and Gelman 1999). As a result of this asymmetry, preschoolers may find it more difficult to use information about the process underlying an entity's creation to map mass nouns to solids that were created accidentally than to map count nouns to nonsolids that were intentionally created.

There was clear support for this third possibility. When the perceptual information (solid, nonsolid) and the process of creation information (accidental, intentional) were in conflict, children mapped the count noun systematically to the intentionally created nonsolid. However, they also mapped the mass noun systematically to the intentionally created nonsolid. This result suggests that children do find it more difficult to see accidentally created solids as the potential referents of mass nouns than to see intentionally created nonsolids as the potential referents of count nouns. These findings suggest that the frequently observed mapping effects in this nonostensive learning situation (count nouns to solids; mass nouns to nonsolids) reflect both conceptual and perceptual factors. Conceptual information about the process by which an entity was created affects children's use of part-of-speech information in making word-entity mappings. However, perceptual information about the solidity of the entity also has a powerful effect on these mappings: children show a strong tendency to construe solid entities as objects (the potential bearers of count nouns), regardless of the process underlying their creation (Proctor and Hall 2003).

To summarize this section: preschool children can use part-of-speech information to establish word-referent mappings in nonostensive learning situations. Yet they establish these mappings only when their knowledge of form-meaning links can be used along with relevant default assumptions. When an appropriate assumption does not apply, preschoolers fail to use part-of-speech information to make systematic word-referent mappings. Thus, preschoolers map count nouns to unfamiliar rather than familiar objects, because they can invoke the mutual-exclusivity assumption and avoid assigning a second count noun to the familiar object. They map proper names to animate rather than inanimate objects, because they engage the assumption that a word for an inanimate object should not be a proper name. They map count nouns to solids rather than nonsolids, and mass nouns to nonsolids rather than solids. In doing so, they draw on two further assumptions: a word for a solid entity is a count noun, and a word for a nonsolid entity is a mass noun. These findings offer evidence that preschoolers' sensitivity to part-of-speech information interacts with their default assumptions to direct word learning even in nonostensive learning situations.

11.5 Acquiring Sensitivity to Part-of-Speech Information

The preceding evidence indicates that preschoolers are sensitive to form-meaning connections associated with four parts of speech commonly used in reference to material entities: count nouns, proper names, adjectives, and mass nouns. Recent findings suggest that children first gain sensitivity to at least some of these connections by their second birthday (e.g., Hall, Lee, and Bélanger 2001; Waxman 1999; Waxman and Booth 2001; Waxman and Markow 1995, 1998). Moreover, preschoolers can use their understanding of part-of-speech information both to constrain the meanings of certain ostensively defined words and to establish word-referent mappings in some nonostensive learning situations. But how do children learn how different part-of-speech categories are expressed in their language?

We propose that children's sensitivity to part-of-speech information derives from the operation of some of their default assumptions. This proposal might at first sound contradictory, in light of the preceding evidence that these assumptions often lead children to override part-of-speech information in ostensive learning situations. However, the proposal gains plausibility from the fact that the input young children receive from their caregivers is very different from the input young children receive from experimenters in word-learning experiments. Specifically, in ostensive learning situations, caregivers typically label material entities for their preschool children using words from part-of-speech categories that closely match children's default assumptions. This match is no doubt only probabilistic and does not obviate the need for preschoolers to be acutely sensitive to the communicative intent of their caregivers. But because of the fit between children's default assumptions and caregivers' speech, the assumptions should typically lead children to interpret words for material entities in ways congruent with part-of-speech information. The default assumptions could thus help children learn the language-specific properties of words from different part-of-speech classes, provided that children keep track of the words (and morphemes) that co-occur with labels from each class (e.g., count nouns may be preceded by the determiner *a*; mass nouns may be preceded by the determiner *much*). These words (and morphemes) could then start to serve as cues to help children not only to learn the meanings of new words, but also to identify words' part-of-speech categories, an important precursor to mastering a grammar whose rules and principles are defined in terms of these categories.

But what is the evidence that caregivers actually do tend to label material entities with new words from part-of-speech categories that match preschoolers' default assumptions? To date this evidence comes from a handful of studies of the speech caregivers use when they provide labels in ostensive learning contexts. Caregivers typically use words from parts of speech that closely match children's assumptions pertaining to the familiarity, animacy, and solidity of the referent entity.

11.5.1 Familiarity

Preschool children appear to assume as a default that a novel word for an unfamiliar solid entity is a count noun. Consistent with this assumption, caregivers tend to label unfamiliar solid objects with (basic-level) count nouns when they offer their children ostensive definitions (e.g., Callanan 1985; Hall 1994a; Ninio 1980; Shipley, Kuhn, and Madden 1983). In this way, children's assumptions are consistent with the part-of-speech information caregivers typically provide when they label objects, and so these assumptions could help children learn count nouns.

11.5.2 Animacy

Preschoolers also seem to assume as a default that a novel word for an inanimate object (especially a familiar one) is not a proper name. Again caregiver input appears consistent with this assumption. In a recent study of parental speech to preschool children, caregivers tended to flag for their children (e.g., by referring to the usage as "odd" or "weird") those cases in which novel proper names were paired with familiar inanimate objects. This behavior appeared specific to proper names, because caregivers drew no attention to the use of novel adjectives paired with the same objects (e.g., Hall, Burns, and Pawluski, forthcoming). This finding suggests that caregivers may tend to avoid providing proper names for familiar inanimate objects, unless they also offer an explicit rationale for the usage. Thus, children's assumptions again appear consistent with the part-of-speech information caregivers provide in labeling objects, and so these assumptions could assist children in identifying proper names in speech.

Unfortunately for children, only some of the words applied to familiar animate objects are proper names. How do preschoolers determine which ones are proper names rather than, say, adjectives? Two further assumptions may help preschoolers make this determination. One of these assumptions was mentioned earlier: children appear to assume that a word applied to a familiar animate object that already has a proper name will not be a second proper name

(Hall and Graham 1999). The other is the range-of-reference as-sumption discussed earlier—a word applied to two familiar animate objects will not be a proper name (Hall 1996b). These assumptions do not constrain children's interpretations of adjectives: pre-schoolers allow any number of adjectives to apply to a given object (because objects may have many properties), and they allow adjectives to be extended across objects that bear the appropriate property. As a result, these two additional assumptions might help children determine whether words for familiar animate objects are proper names or adjectives.

Moreover, these additional assumptions are generally congruent with how caregivers label material entities. In one study, caregivers flagged for their children those situations in which two proper names were given to one familiar animate object, but not those in which two adjectives were given to the object (Hall, Burns, and Pawluski, forthcoming). Caregivers also flagged situations in which one proper name was given to two familiar animate objects, but not those in which one adjective was given to the objects (Hall, Burns, and Pawluski, forthcoming; see also Manders and Hall 2002). These results suggest that caregivers may tend to avoid providing two proper names for one familiar animate object or one proper name for two familiar animate objects, without offering some explicit ex-planation for the usage. In these two further ways, then, children's default assumptions are consistent with parental labeling practices and might help in learning the part-of-speech cues associated with proper names and adjectives.

11.5.3 Solidity

Preschool children tend to assume that a novel word for an unfamil-iar solid object is a count noun, but they tend to interpret the same novel word applied to an unfamiliar nonsolid as a mass noun. Con-sistent with the first assumption, caregivers tend to label unfamiliar solid entities with (basic-level) count nouns, as noted earlier. There have been fewer investigations of how caregivers label unfamiliar nonsolid entities, but there is some evidence to suggest that this labeling is also consistent with children's assumptions. For example, in a study in which parents were asked to label solid entities (e.g., a wooden triangle), they typically used count nouns (e.g., "a triangle"); when asked to name nonsolid entities matched for shape (e.g., a triangle made of peanut butter), they tended to provide mass nouns (e.g., "some peanut butter"; Hall 1996a). These findings suggest that children's default assumptions are again consistent with the part-of-speech information caregivers provide when they label material entities. These assumptions thus might help children learn the part-of-speech cues associated with count nouns and mass nouns.

The preceding evidence indicates that caregivers label material entities for preschoolers in ostensive situations using words from part-of-speech categories that match preschoolers' default assumptions. There is less evidence about caregivers' labeling practices in nonostensive situations. Presumably in these situations, caregivers often offer many social cues (e.g., pointing, looking, expressing positive affect) when they provide new words to guide children to the intended referent. Yet if this social information is not available to direct children to establish word-referent mappings, caregivers should ask for the referent of a novel label only when the situation allows children to invoke a relevant assumption along with part-of-speech information. For example, caregivers might request the referent of a novel count noun in situations containing one unfamiliar and one familiar object (rather than, say, two unfamiliar objects). Or they might ask for the referent of a novel proper name in a situation containing a familiar animate and a familiar inanimate object (rather than, say, two familiar animate objects).

To summarize this section: in ostensive learning situations, caregivers typically label material entities for preschoolers in ways consistent with children's default assumptions. They tend to label unfamiliar solid entities with count nouns. They avoid ostensively labeling familiar inanimate objects with proper names, without further explanation. In labeling animate objects, they use proper names and adjectives in ways that match children's further default assumptions (i.e., proper names should not apply to objects that already have a proper name, and proper names should not be extended to two different objects). And whereas they tend to label unfamiliar solids with count nouns, they label unfamiliar nonsolids with mass nouns. In all these cases, caregivers' labeling practices are in striking harmony with children's default assumptions. The results do not, of course, indicate why caregivers' labeling practices and preschoolers' assumptions are consistent with each other (for discussion, see Hall 1994a; Hall, Burns, and Pawluski, forthcoming). Regardless of their origin, however, caregivers' labeling practices could permit children to make part-of-speech-appropriate interpretations of novel words, thereby enabling them to acquire sensitivity to these words' language-specific properties.

11.6 Conclusion

This chapter began with a question: What does children's use (or misuse) of part-of-speech information in learning words reveal about lexical development? Given the dependable connection that exists between particular parts of speech and corresponding types of meaning in the adult lexicon, knowing a word's part of speech should provide children with consistent help in word learning. Yet in experiments involving ostensive learning of new words, preschoolers often use, but sometimes systematically misuse, this information. Moreover, in experiments in which preschoolers are asked to learn words nonostensively, they show no preferences when mapping words from some part-of-speech categories, but they do map words from other part-of-speech categories in systematic ways.

The proposed explanation for the preceding findings is that preschoolers possess, in addition to sensitivity to part-of-speech information, certain default assumptions that direct them to interpret words used under particular conditions as having particular types of meaning and—because of the links between meaning and lexical form class—as belonging (or not belonging) to particular part-of-speech categories. In ostensive learning, when children's knowledge of part-of-speech information and their default assumptions are in synchrony, children use the part-of-speech knowledge to constrain their interpretation, but when the two are not in harmony, children often respect the assumption and override the part-of-speech knowledge. In nonostensive learning, when children's sensitivity to part-of-speech information and a relevant assumption can both be invoked, children use part-of-speech knowledge to establish word-referent mappings; when no relevant assumption can be invoked along with the part-of-speech knowledge, preschoolers fail to establish systematic word-object mappings.

A general implication of the preceding findings is that preschoolers' word learning draws on knowledge from multiple sources, including part-of-speech sensitivity and default assumptions. More specifically, however, the potency of the default assumptions in preschoolers' word learning suggests that the assumptions could furnish robust help to children in acquiring knowledge of how part-of-speech categories are expressed in their language. Since caregivers label material entities with words that generally match the assumptions, the assumptions should typically lead preschoolers to make interpretations consistent with part-of-speech information. As a result, the assumptions should give them the opportunity to learn how different parts of speech are expressed syntactically and morphologically in their language.

Why are these probabilistic default assumptions such powerful influences for preschoolers—often more potent than knowledge of more deterministic part-of-speech to meaning links? We suspect that their potency stems from the foundational role they play in early language development, in helping children learn how part-of-speech categories are expressed in their language. Learning how these categories are expressed is of vital importance. It matters not only for learning the meanings of new words, but also for acquiring the rules and principles of grammar. Children therefore require a robust way to learn to identify words' part-of-speech categories. Moreover, acquiring sensitivity to part-of-speech information is a complex task, requiring children to learn a number of syntactic and morphological cues that signal membership in these categories. As result, the task is likely a protracted one, requiring that the default assumptions remain influential over an extended period. Consistent with this proposal, part-of-speech information appears to grow in strength as a cue to word interpretation over the course of the preschool years. In a number of experiments, the tendency to override part-of-speech information in order to respect default assumptions diminishes with age, such that older preschoolers are more likely than younger ones to respect part-of-speech information (e.g., Bloom 1994b; Dickinson 1988; Gordon 1985; Hall, Waxman, and Hurwitz 1993; Smith, Jones, and Landau 1992; Soja 1992; Subrahmanyam, Landau and Gelman 1999). In this way, the default assumptions gradually yield power to part-of-speech knowledge, as they accomplish their goal of ensuring that children succeed in learning how different parts of speech are marked in their native language.

Acknowledgments

The writing of this chapter was supported by an operating grant from the Natural Sciences and Engineering Research Council of Canada.

References

Akhtar, N., and Tomasello, M. 1996. Two-year-olds learn words for absent objects and actions. *British Journal of Developmental Psychology, 14*, 79–93.

Au, T., and Glusman, M. 1990. The principle of mutual exclusivity in word learning: To honor or not to honor? *Child Development, 61*, 1474–1490.

Baldwin, D. 1991. Infants' contribution to the achievement of joint reference. *Child Development, 62*, 875–890.

Bloom, P. 1994a. Possible names: The role of syntax-semantics mappings in the acquisition of nominals. *Lingua, 92*, 297–329.

Bloom, P. 1994b. Semantic competence as an explanation for some transitions in language development. In Y. Levy, ed., *Other children, other languages: Theoretical issues in language acquisition*, 41–75. Hillsdale, NJ: Erlbaum.

Bloom, P. 2000. *How children learn the meaning of words.* Cambridge, MA: MIT Press.

Brown, R. W. 1957. Linguistic determinism and the part of speech. *Journal of Abnormal and Social Psychology, 55*, 1–5.

Callanan, M. 1985. How parents label objects for young children: The role of input in the acquisition of category hierarchies. *Child Development, 56*, 508–523.

Carey, S. 1978. The child as word learner. In J. Bresnan, G. Miller, and M. Halle, eds., *Linguistic theory and psychological reality*, 264–293. Cambridge, MA: MIT Press.

Dickinson, D. 1988. Learning names for materials: Factors limiting and constraining hypotheses about word meaning. *Cognitive Development, 3*, 15–35.

Diesendruck, D., and Markson, L. 2001. Children's avoidance of lexical overlap: A pragmatic account. *Developmental Psychology, 37,* 630–641.

Evey, J., and Merriman, W. 1998. The prevalence and the weakness of an early name mapping preference. *Journal of Child Language, 25,* 121–147.

Gelman, S. A., and Taylor, M. 1984. How two-year-old children interpret proper and common names for unfamiliar objects. *Child Development, 55,* 1535–1540.

Golinkoff, R., Hirsh-Pasek, K., Bailey, L., and Wenger, N. 1992. Young children and adults use lexical principles to learn new nouns. *Developmental Psychology, 28,* 99–108.

Golinkoff, R., Mervis, C., and Hirsh-Pasek, K. 1994. Early object labels: The case for lexical principles. *Journal of Child Language, 21,* 125–155.

Gordon, P. 1985. Evaluating the semantic categories hypothesis: The case of the count/mass distinction. *Cognition, 20,* 209–242.

Graham, S. A., Poulin-Dubois, D., and Baker, R. K. 1998. Infants' disambiguation of novel object words. *First Language, 18,* 149–164.

Hall, D. G. 1991. Acquiring proper names for familiar and unfamiliar animate objects: Two-year-olds' word learning biases. *Child Development, 62,* 1142–1154.

Hall, D. G. 1993. Basic-level individuals. *Cognition, 48,* 199–221.

Hall, D. G. 1994a. How mothers teach basic-level and situation-restricted count nouns. *Journal of Child Language, 21,* 391–414.

Hall, D. G. 1994b. Semantic constraints on word learning: Proper names and adjectives. *Child Development, 65,* 1291–1309.

Hall, D. G. 1996a. Naming solids and nonsolids: Children's default construals. *Cognitive Development, 11,* 229–264.

Hall, D. G. 1996b. Preschoolers' default assumptions about word meaning: Proper names designate unique individuals. *Developmental Psychology, 32,* 177–186.

Hall, D. G. 1999. Semantics and the acquisition of proper names. In R. Jackendoff, P. Bloom, and K. Wynn, eds., *Language, logic, and concepts,* 337–372. Cambridge, MA: MIT Press.

Hall, D. G., and Bélanger, J. 2003. *Using a word's range of reference as a cue to its meaning: Evidence from young children.* Unpublished manuscript, University of British Columbia.

Hall, D. G., Burns, T., and Pawluski, J. Forthcoming. Caregivers' sensitivity to lexical form class distinctions. *Journal of Child Language.*

Hall, D. G., and Graham, S. A. 1999. Lexical form class information guides word-to-object mapping in preschoolers. *Child Development, 70,* 78–91.

Hall, D. G., Lee, S. C., and Bélanger, J. 2001. Young children's use of syntactic cues to learn proper names and count nouns. *Developmental Psychology, 37,* 298–307.

Hall, D. G., Quantz, D., and Persoage, K. 2000. Preschoolers' use of form class cues in word learning. *Developmental Psychology, 36,* 449–462.

Hall, D. G., Veltkamp, B., and Turkel, W. Forthcoming. Proper namable things. *First Language.*

Hall, D. G., and Waxman, S. R. 1993. Assumptions about word meaning: Individuation and basic-level kinds. *Child Development, 64,* 1550–1570.

Hall, D. G., Waxman, S. R., and Hurwitz, W. 1993. How 2- and 4-year-old children interpret adjectives and count nouns. *Child Development, 64,* 1651–1664.

Heibeck, T. H., and Markman, E. M. 1987. Word learning in children: An examination of fast mapping. *Child Development, 58,* 1021–1034.

Hutchinson, J. 1986, April. Children's sensitivity to the contrastive use of object category terms. Paper presented at the Stanford Child Language Research Forum, Palo Alto, CA.

Imai, M., and Gentner, D. 1997. A crosslinguistic study of early word meaning: Universal ontology and linguistic influence. *Cognition, 62,* 169–200.

Imai, M., and Haryu, E. 2001. Learning proper nouns and common nouns without clues from syntax. *Child Development, 72,* 787–802.

Jaswal, V., and Markman, E. 2001. Learning proper and common names in inferential versus ostensive contexts. *Child Development, 72,* 768–786.

Katz, N., Baker, E., and Macnamara, J. 1974. What's in a name? A study of how children learn common and proper names. *Child Development, 45,* 469–473.

Landau, B., Smith, L., and Jones, S. 1992. Syntactic context and the shape bias in children's and adults' lexical learning. *Journal of Memory and Language, 31,* 807–825.

Lavin, T. A., and Hall, D. G. 2002. Domain effects in lexical development: Learning words for toys and foods. *Cognitive Development, 16,* 929–950.

Lavin, T. A., Proctor, J. M., and Hall, D. G. 2001, April. Preschoolers' use of syntactic and domain cues in the inferential learning of words for objects and substances. Poster presented at the Biennial Meeting of the Society for Research in Child Development, Minneapolis.

Liittschwager, J., and Markman, E. 1993. Young children's acquisition of proper versus common nouns. Poster presented at the Biennial Meeting of the Society for Research in Child Development, New Orleans.

Macnamara, J. 1982. *Names for things.* Cambridge, MA: MIT Press.

Macnamara, J. 1986. *A border dispute.* Cambridge, MA: MIT Press.

Manders, K., and Hall, D. G. 2002. Comparison, basic-level categories, and the teaching of adjectives. *Journal of Child Language, 29,* 923–937.

Markman, E. 1989. *Categorization and naming in children.* Cambridge, MA: MIT Press.

Markman, E. 1994. Constraints on word meaning in early language acquisition. *Lingua, 92,* 199–227.

Markman, E., and Wachtel, G. 1988. Children's use of mutual exclusivity to constrain the meanings of words. *Cognitive Psychology, 20,* 121–157.

Merriman, W. E., and Bowman, L. 1989. The mutual exclusivity bias in children's word learning. *Monographs of the Society for Research in Child Development, 54* (serial no. 220).

Merriman, W. E., and Schuster, J. M. 1991. Young children's disambiguation of object name reference. *Child Development, 62,* 1288–1301.

Mervis, C. B., and Bertrand, J. 1994. Acquisition of the novel name/nameless category (N3C) principle. *Child Development, 65,* 1646–1662.

Ninio, A. 1980. Ostensive definition in vocabulary teaching. *Journal of Child Language, 7,* 565–573.

Pinker, S. 1996. *Language learnability and language development.* Rev. ed. Cambridge, MA: Harvard University Press.

Prasada, S. 1993. Learning names for solid substances: Quantifying solid entities in terms of portions. *Cognitive Development, 8,* 83–104.

Prasada, S., Ferenz, K., and Haskell, T. 2002. Conceiving of entities as objects and as stuff. *Cognition, 83,* 141–165.

Proctor, J. M., and Hall, D. G. 2003. *Preschoolers' use of syntactic and intentional cues in non-ostensive word learning.* Unpublished manuscript, University of British Columbia.

Rosch, E., Mervis, C. B., Grey, W. D., Johnson, D. M., and Boyes-Braem, P. 1976. Basic objects in natural categories. *Cognitive Psychology, 8,* 382–439.

Shipley, E., Kuhn, I., and Madden, E. 1983. Mothers' use of superordinate category terms. *Journal of Child Language, 10,* 571–588.

Smith, L., Jones, S., and Landau, B. 1992. Count nouns, adjectives, and perceptual properties in children's novel word interpretations. *Developmental Psychology, 28,* 273–286.

Soja, N. 1992. Inferences about the meanings of nouns: The relationship between perception and syntax. *Cognitive Development, 7,* 29–45.

Soja, N., Carey, S., and Spelke, E. 1991. Ontological categories guide young children's inductions of word meaning: Object terms and substance terms. *Cognition, 38,* 179–211.

Sorrentino, C. 2001. Individuation, identity, and proper names in cognitive development. *Developmental Science, 4,* 399–407.

Subrahmanyam, K., Landau, B., and Gelman, R. 1999. Shape, material, and syntax: Interacting forces in children's learning in novel words for objects and substances. *Language and Cognitive Processes, 14*, 249–281.

Taylor, M., and Gelman, S. A. 1989. Incorporating new words into the lexicon: Preliminary evidence for language hierarchies in two-year-old children. *Child Development, 60*, 625–636.

Tomasello, M., and Barton, M. E. 1994. Learning words in nonostensive contexts. *Developmental Psychology, 30*, 639–650.

Waxman, S. R. 1990. Linguistic biases and the establishment of conceptual hierarchies: Evidence from preschool children. *Cognitive Development, 5*, 123–150.

Waxman, S. R. 1999. Specifying the scope of 13-month-olds' expectations for novel words. *Cognition, 70*, B35–B50.

Waxman, S. R., and Booth, A. E. 2001. Seeing pink elephants: Fourteen-month-olds' interpretations of novel nouns and adjectives. *Cognitive Psychology, 43*, 217–242.

Waxman, S. R., and Gelman, R. 1986. Preschoolers' use of superordinate relations in classification and language. *Cognitive Development, 1*, 139–156.

Waxman, S. R., and Kosowski, T. D. 1990. Nouns mark category relations: Toddlers' and preschoolers' word-learning biases. *Child Development, 61*, 1461–1473.

Waxman, S. R., and Markow, D. B. 1995. Words as invitations to form categories: Evidence from 12- and 13-month-old infants. *Cognitive Psychology, 29*, 257–302.

Waxman, S. R., and Markow, D. B. 1998. Object properties and object kind: Twenty-one-month-old infants' extensions of novel adjectives. *Child Development, 69*, 1313–1329.

Woodward, A., and Markman, E. 1991. Constraints on learning as default assumptions: Comments on Merriman and Bowman's "The mutual exclusivity bias in children's word learning." *Developmental Review, 11*, 137–163.

Woodward, A., and Markman, E. 1998. Early word learning. In W. Damon, series ed., and D. K. Kuhn and R. S. Siegler, vol. eds., *Handbook of child psychology, Vol. 2: Cognition, perception, and language*, 5th ed., 371–420. New York: Wiley.

12

Acquiring and Using a Grammatical Form Class: Lessons from the Proper-Count Distinction

Ellen M. Markman and Vikram K. Jaswal

The distinction between individuals and kinds is crucial in the representation of knowledge. Some information is idiosyncratic and tied to the identity of a specific individual, while other information is characteristic of a kind and can be generalized to other members. As a result, whether we treat objects as individuals or as members of a kind has important implications. For example, treating objects as members of a kind allows us to make inductive inferences from one member to another (Gelman and Markman 1986), while treating objects as individuals allows us to track particular objects through space and time (Liittschwager 1995), and to enumerate sets of objects, all of which could be of like kind (Wynn 1992; Xu and Spelke 2000). Notions of kind membership and individuality may play off each other such that one can (but does not always have to) use knowledge of kind membership *in order to* individuate objects (Xu 1999; Xu and Carey 1996).

Languages have several devices for highlighting the difference between individuals and kinds. Forms of definite reference and description can be used to identify and pick out individuals, making it clear what the scope of reference should be. Another linguistic device is the distinction between proper and common names. Labels can refer to an object as a specific individual or as a member of a kind. Some ostensive contexts can be found where there is only minimal information that distinguishes these two types of reference, yet children as young as 24 months and probably younger (e.g., Katz,

Baker, and Macnamara 1974) are able to make this subtle distinction. Proper names have captured the interest of researchers for this reason. Moreover, the acquisition and use of the proper-count distinction can provide a window on a range of important issues in lexical acquisition.

In this chapter, we raise a number of questions about the acquisition of proper names versus count nouns that have implications for word learning more broadly. In particular, we address issues about how specific lexical items can be treated as proper names versus count nouns before a general proper-count contrast is learned, how the contrasting grammatical form classes might first be acquired, and how once acquired, the contrast plays a role in further lexical acquisition. We also use the acquisition of proper versus count nouns to explore issues about fast mapping, about acquiring vocabulary through indirect versus direct means, and about when a lexical item is still open to revision and when it is considered fully learned. Some of these issues are barely discussed in the literature, yet must be resolved before we have a full understanding of lexical acquisition.

12.1 Selective Review of Children's Use of the Proper-Count Distinction

Before we turn to the main focus of this chapter, we provide a brief and selective summary of issues that have been addressed in the experimental literature on the acquisition of proper names and point to other reviews for more details. It is by now well accepted that children make use of a number of sources of information when learning words, and that a theory of lexical acquisition needs to specify how children coordinate, weigh, and integrate information from these various sources (for reviews, see Hollich, Hirsh-Pasek, and Golinkoff 2000; Woodward and Markman 1998). In addition to learning words through the brute-force, associationist learning mechanisms proposed by thinkers as early as Locke ([1690] 1964), children can exploit pragmatic information (e.g., Baldwin 1991, 1993; Bloom 1993; Tomasello 2001), grammatical information (e.g., Brown 1957; Gleitman and Gillette 1999), semantic cues (e.g., Goodman, McDonough, and Brown 1998), word-learning constraints (e.g., Markman 1989,

1994; Waxman 1991), phonological cues (e.g., Kelly 1992), and distributional analyses (e.g., Cartwright and Brent 1997; Maratsos 1988; Saffran, Aslin, and Newport 1996).

A number of authors have considered how these kinds of sources of information can be integrated to facilitate the acquisition of proper names (Hall 1999; Imai and Haryu, chapter 13, this volume). Katz, Baker, and Macnamara's (1974) classic work in this area asked whether children could use grammatical cues in conjunction with the animacy of the named referent in order to decide whether a new name was proper or common. In English, proper names are not preceded by a determiner (e.g., a, the, and so on), while common names often are. Additionally, as we will discuss in detail later, animate things are more likely to be called by proper names than inanimate ones. Katz et al. found that girls as young as 17 months treated a common name (e.g., a dax) as referring to a kind, regardless of the animacy of the labeled item. A proper name (e.g., Dax), by contrast, was treated as referring to the particular item labeled—but only if the labeled item was animate; if the item was inanimate, the name was treated as referring to a kind, even though it had been provided in a proper-name frame.

Gelman and Taylor (1984) replicated and extended this work with preschoolers, and a number of researchers since then have taken up the issue. One line of inquiry has considered whether children truly make proper-name interpretations of proper names or whether they may instead make subordinate-level kind interpretations. A proper-name interpretation would mean that the name applied to a specific individual, regardless of any transformations that individual might undergo (e.g., a haircut, wardrobe change, and so on; see Liittschwager 1995). In Liittschwager and Markman 1993, preschoolers who saw a distinctive marker (e.g., a bib) removed from an animate object that had been labeled with a proper name still treated the proper name as referring to that individual only. Indeed, Sorrentino (1999) found that even when the distinctive marker was actually placed on another identical toy, preschoolers continued to treat the proper name as referring to the originally labeled object only.

Other researchers have been interested in evaluating pragmatic sources of information that children might use in deciding whether a new word is a proper name. For example, in a sentence like "This is Dax," *Dax* could be construed as a proper name or as an adjective. Hall (1996) found that preschoolers who heard *Dax* applied to a single animate object treated the word as a proper name, but those who heard it applied to two different animate objects treated it like an adjective. Thus, the number of things a speaker labels with the same word provides information about the appropriate interpretation of the word. In another study, Birch and Bloom (2002) have suggested that preschoolers may be sensitive to information indicating whether the speaker is familiar with the animate object being labeled—in a sense, evaluating the plausibility that the speaker could know its proper name.

Word-learning constraints are a further source of information available in learning proper names. Young children make preliminary assumptions, or best first guesses, on hearing new words that help them quickly narrow down the inductive space of possible referents (e.g., Golinkoff, Mervis, and Hirsh-Pasek 1994; Liittschwager and Markman 1994; Markman 1994; Markman and Wachtel 1988; Waxman and Markow 1995). Although a full discussion of word-learning constraints is beyond the scope of this chapter (but see, for example, Bloom, Tinker, and Margulis 1993; Bloom 2000; Deak 2000; Markman 1989; Nelson 1988), we believe that expectations children have about words play an integral role in the acquisition of proper names. For instance, experimental research has suggested that infants as young as 15 months abide by *mutual exclusivity*, one of the proposed constraints that holds that children expect a single object to have only one kind term (Markman 1992). Thus, children who hear a term applied to an already-named object will be motivated to seek out an interpretation of this term that avoids attributing two category labels to the same object (Markman and Wachtel 1988). Indeed, Hall (1991) found that preschoolers were more likely to make proper-name interpretations of names applied to animate objects for which they knew the kind label (e.g., cats) than for those they did not (e.g., monsters; in which case, they tended to make common-name interpretations).

Clearly, children can draw on a number of sources of information when learning proper names. All of the research on this topic to date, however, has focused on children above 17 months, and most has examined children 2 to 3 years old—children old enough to have acquired the grammatical form class distinction that distinguishes proper names from common ones in English. Very little is known about how babies or younger children learn proper names, or how they could actually use the sources of information described earlier to *learn* the grammatical form class distinction. We turn now to some speculations about how this might be achieved.

12.2 How the Proper-Count Distinction Could Be Learned

On hearing a new word applied to a new object, a word learner must first decide whether the word applies to the whole object or to some other aspect of the object—for example, a part or property. Under a constraint known as the *whole-object assumption*, word learners assume that new words name objects as wholes (e.g., Baldwin 1989; Kobayashi 1998; Markman and Wachtel 1988; Woodward 1992). Once the word learner has decided that the word applies to the whole object, he or she must decide whether it is being used to refer to an individual qua individual, or an individual as a member of a kind. P. Bloom (1994) proposes that children treat noun phrases as referring to individuals, rather than objects, and that they will treat proper names as referring to individuals and count nouns as generalizing. This assumes, however, that children can distinguish between the proper names and count nouns, which is the problem at hand.

12.2.1 The Taxonomic Assumption as Part of the Problem

Deciding that a name refers to an individual poses a challenge because of the *taxonomic assumption*, a word-learning constraint that motivates children to extend newly learned labels to other members of like kind. The taxonomic assumption was originally postulated to explain why children extend words to things of like kind rather than to things strongly associated with each other (Markman and Hutchinson 1984). This assumption, as well as other related ones such as "object scope" (Golinkoff, Mervis, and Hirsh-Pasek 1994; Golinkoff et al. 1995), suggests that children will generalize newly learned words. Using this assumption, children would run into trouble in learning proper names. How is it that children come to treat proper names as referring to individuals if, on the taxonomic assumption, they expect labels to refer to kinds?

12.2.2 Do Children First Adopt a Conservative Strategy?

One solution to this problem would be for children to begin with a much more conservative strategy of word learning where they refrain from generalizing a newly learned word beyond the first exemplar until they are given positive evidence to the contrary. Once they have reason to generalize a term, they would generalize according to like kind as the taxonomic assumption specifies. If babies first operated according to the strategy "assume this word does not extend beyond this exemplar unless given positive evidence to the contrary," they would readily find positive evidence that many count nouns generalize. On first hearing the word *spoon*, for example, a child would treat *spoon* as referring to that individual spoon, but as soon as another spoon was labeled the child would assume *spoon* generalizes to other spoons (or silverware, or teaspoons—the precise scope of the category is another issue). In everyday situations, common objects are routinely labeled. A baby starting to eat might drop his spoon and his mother might get him another one, saying "use this spoon, that one's dirty." Routine comments on artifacts, pieces of clothing, pieces of furniture, or animals in the child's everyday environment or in books would provide ample opportunity for positive generalization of a term. This conservative strategy would prevent the overgeneralization of proper names while at the same time allowing for ready generalization of count nouns on the basis of a small amount of evidence. The problem with this explanation is that, so far, there is no evidence to support it, although there are reports of some of children's earliest object labels being overly narrow and highly context dependent (Bates 1979; Bloom 1973).

In some unpublished research, Markman tested this hypothesis by teaching babies a novel count noun and then seeing if they generalized it. There is an important methodological issue here: babies may require only minimal positive evidence that an object label generalizes before overriding a conservative "proper-name" bias, if one exists. If babies need only one instance of the newly learned term being applied to a second object to generalize the term, some kinds of test trials could themselves provide that positive evidence, thus invalidating the test. Suppose, for example, you showed a baby a terrier and said it was a *dog*. In the conservative strategy view, the baby should start out assuming *dog* refers to that specific terrier and nothing else. Now suppose you gave a test trial that showed a different terrier, or a collie—some other dog—and a distractor item, say a shoe, and asked the child for a *dog*. The question itself implies that there is a dog present and yet the original item is nowhere in sight. So this form of the question provides a kind of positive evidence that at least one of these things is a dog, and, under the right circumstances, it will be easy for children to see which it is. With this kind of test, then, we could find a great deal of generalization, but it would not rule out the conservative strategy.

To avoid this problem, Markman used the following two kinds of test trials. On one, the original item was paired with a distractor. This test would reveal whether babies learned the word at all. The second kind of trial paired the original item with another similar item. The question here was whether the original was selected at above-chance levels or whether children chose both exemplars equally—a test for generalization analogous to the one Katz, Baker, and Macnamara (1974) used in their investigation of whether babies treated a word as a common or proper name. Briefly, the results were as follows: babies as young as 15 months spontaneously generalized a newly learned word without positive evidence. In other words, 15-month-olds, as well as 18-month-olds, were not using a conservative strategy. Using this procedure with 13-month-olds yielded ambiguous results because there was no clear evidence that the babies learned the word in the first place. So the question of whether they were generalizing could not be addressed.

Related findings are reported in two studies by Hennon et al. (1999). Using a preferential-looking procedure, they found that 14- and 19-month-olds extended a newly learned word to another exemplar of the same category. However, the design of their extension trial was flawed in that it paired a novel exemplar of the category with a distractor. This is exactly the design that Markman avoided because, as described earlier, the trial itself provides some evidence that the word generalizes. Thus, from Hennon et al., it is not clear that 14- or 19-month-olds generalize spontaneously, but given Markman's unpublished studies finding generalization in 15-month-olds, we assume they would. Hennon et al. also claim that 12-month-olds *fail* to generalize a newly learned label, which looks like support for the conservative strategy. However, their data do not show that these infants learned the word in the first place. In their first study, following training on a novel label, on one test trial, babies were shown the originally labeled object and a distractor and heard the novel label. On this trial, 12-month-olds showed no preference for the target object over the distractor, meaning there was no evidence that they learned the word at all. So it is not meaningful to evaluate whether babies generalized the word to another member of the category since there is no evidence that they learned the word in the first place. In a second study, Hennon et al. included only a generalization trial, again failing to provide evidence that these infants had learned the word. So it is impossible to evaluate whether 12-month-olds failed to generalize or whether they just had not learned.

Another study that, at first glance, appears to support an early conservative strategy is by Samuelson and Smith (1999). These authors argue that "young children do not generalize novel names for solid things by shape until they already know many names for solid things in shape-based categories" (p. 29). Instead, Samuelson and Smith argue that, in the process of acquiring their earliest nouns, children detect statistical regularities between object properties and category organizations—and in particular, they learn that solid objects are named by shape. In one study (Study 2) 17- to 33-month-old children watched as the experimenter named a novel solid, nonrigid, or nonsolid target object (e.g., "This is my *lom*"). The experimenter then pushed a tray with two objects toward the child: one object matched the target in shape (but not material), and the other matched it in material (but not shape). Samuelson and Smith found that children with small productive-noun vocabularies (< 150 nouns on the MacArthur Communicative Development Inventory) were no more likely to select the shape-based match for the solid target object than for the nonrigid or nonsolid target objects. Children with larger noun vocabularies were. This might suggest that those with smaller noun vocabularies were adhering to a conservative strategy—either waiting for further positive evidence, or needing to develop the expectation that solid objects are named by shape.

We do not, however, find Samuelson and Smith's (1999) study to be convincing evidence of such a conservative strategy. First, the experimenter named the novel target object just once. Given this minimal training, it is possible that these very young children (who may or may not have been paying attention at that time) failed to learn the word. What is needed is a test of learning in which the target object is actually paired with a distractor that is neither of the same shape nor of the same material as the target. As was the case in Hennon et al.'s (1999) second study, there is no way to interpret children's failure to generalize appropriately without evidence that they have learned the word in the first place. Indeed, there is good evidence that when young children have demonstrated that they have learned a new word, they do extend it to other members of like kind. For example, Woodward, Markman, and Fitzsimmons (1994) found that 18-month-olds who heard a novel object labeled nine times both learned that word and extended it to other members of like kind (differing in color). It is also noteworthy that the average productive vocabulary of these infants was 119 *words*; recall that Samuelson and Smith found that successful generalization for solid objects on the basis of shape took place only for groups with productive vocabularies of more than 150 *nouns*.

At present, then, there is no good evidence for a conservative strategy study by which babies would wait for positive evidence that a term should be generalized. Instead, the evidence shows that as soon as babies have demonstrated clear learning of a word, they also generalize that word to new exemplars. Research demonstrating clear learning of a new label by younger babies is needed to provide a definitive test of this hypothesis, but for now, we turn to other ways babies might be able to restrict the scope of proper names. If it turns out that younger babies do have a very conservative "proper-name" strategy, these other mechanisms would still serve to bolster the learning.

12.2.3 Detecting Correlational Structure

If babies start out applying the taxonomic assumption broadly, how do they then determine which labels are restricted to individuals and which refer to kinds? One way, maybe the only way, is to figure out the correlation between proper names and the kinds of referents they take. The question then becomes how babies use information from input to figure out the relevant correlations between the referents of proper names and the names themselves, and the referents of kind terms and the terms themselves.

There are several different ways to think about what kinds of correlations children need to work out in order to acquire the proper-count distinction in English. One is the range of grammatical markers that distinguish count nouns from proper names, such as use of determiners, plural markings, and other forms of quantification. The presence or absence of articles is the main issue that experimental work on the acquisition of proper names has explored, but there are many other grammatical correlates of the proper-count distinction in English. For fluent speakers, hearing a term quantified—for example, "Some candy"—should be sufficient to rule out a proper-name interpretation. Hearing quantification plus a determiner—for instance, "Those five girls"—provides even more redundant information that would rule out a proper-name interpretation of the noun.

Another source of information loosely correlated with the proper-count distinction is the more limited range of entities that accept proper names. Experimental work here has focused mostly on animate versus inanimate as the conceptual domains, the assumption being that proper names are more likely to be attributed to animate objects. Obviously there are many exceptions. All animate objects can be referred to by a large number of count nouns (e.g., *boy, person, cousin, enemy, obstacle*). And inanimate things take proper names (e.g., *Canada, Stanford*). Another relevant correlation is whether any given lexical item, such as *John* or *boy*, functions as a count noun or proper name, in terms of the range of referents it is applied to. That is, with no grammatical information at all, one might still detect that particular words are used for only one individual, while other words are used more generally. Which of these relations children work out at different ages is not yet fully documented, although we know from several studies that the presence or absence of articles and whether the object being labeled is animate have been sorted out at least to some extent by 24-month-olds (Hall, Lee, and Bélanger 2001) and maybe by 17-month-olds, or perhaps only 17-month-old girls (Katz, Baker, and Macnamara 1974). How these relations are worked out has barely been studied and is not yet well understood.

Although there are no experiments directly studying how infants establish the relevant relations to acquire the proper-count distinction, there have been striking demonstrations of infants' abilities to detect other kinds of correlations. Saffran, Aslin, and Newport (1996) discovered that 8-month-olds can use the statistical relationships between speech sounds to segment speech into words. In fluent speech there may not be pauses or acoustic cues that signal word boundaries. How then might babies hearing continuous speech segment the speech into discrete words? Suppose, for example, a baby hears "Hello Daddy." How will the baby determine that the adjacent sounds in *loda* (from "Hel*lo Da*ddy") do not form a word while the sequential sounds in *Daddy* do? One possibility is to rely on the transitional probabilities of adjacent speech sounds. Typically the transitional probabilities will be higher for adjacent speech sounds from the same word, such as *Daddy*, than for adjacent sounds that cross word boundaries, such as *loda*.

Saffran, Aslin, and Newport (1996) asked whether 8-month-old infants can compute and use these kinds of transitional probabilities. Babies were familiarized to a 2-minute tape of continuous speech made up of four 3-syllable nonsense words presented in a random order. The only information that specified word boundaries was the transitional probability between adjacent syllables. In this study, the transitional probability was set at 1.0 within words and 0.33 between words. After the babies listened to the 2 minutes of continuous speech, they were presented with test items that either were three-syllable words from the artificial language or "nonwords" composed of the same three syllables but in a different order. These 8-month-olds were capable of distinguishing the words from nonwords, listening longer to the novel nonwords.

From this and related research (e.g., Elman et al. 1996; Saffran et al. 1999), we know that babies are quickly able to calculate rough correlations between adjacent elements in speech and also in music. Could this same ability help in the acquisition of grammatical form class and, in particular, in distinguishing proper from common names? There are enough differences between the two kinds of problems that it is hard to know whether the same statistical ability could underlie both. The problem for segmentation is to use transitional probabilities between elements of a given type—for example, syllables for words. But at least some of the problem for making the proper noun–common noun distinction involves noting correlations between linguistic elements (say the presence or absence of an article) and nonlinguistic elements—the kind of referents and the scope of the reference category. There is no adjacency or segmentation at issue. The experimental paradigm also sets some limits on the generalizability to the question of distinguishing proper from common nouns. In Saffran, Aslin, and Newport 1996, the within-word boundary transitional probability was set at 1. How good would babies be at detecting weaker correlations? In addition, the statistics were computed over a steady, uninterrupted stream of repeated speech segments. But the task for the child in figuring out the proper-common contrast must be to register and compute correlations over input presented sporadically over longer periods of time. (This is probably true for word segmentation in natural contexts as well.) A child might, for example, one day hear someone comment on a cat that walked into their yard, but it could be days before another discussion about a cat takes place. Still, it is tempting to extrapolate from these demonstrations of babies' abilities to detect correlations in speech and tones to say that such abilities could help them work out the various correlations surrounding the contrast between proper and common nouns. While we are not really justified in drawing any strong conclusions about whether this statistical capacity is available for a quite different kind of problem, it remains an intriguing possibility.

12.2.4   Noticing the Nonoccurrence of Labels

Proper names must not be generalized. If babies are computing correlations about the use of proper names, an important part of the correlation is the *non*occurrence of the proper names to items similar to the one named. This poses a problem closely related to learnability arguments about the absence of negative evidence (e.g., Pinker 1989; Wexler and Culicover 1980). In those arguments about the acquisition of grammar, one important question was how children avoid postulating grammars that are overly general. And if they did postulate such a grammar, how would they be able to correct it given the lack of negative evidence? Suppose a child interprets a word to be more general than the correct use. For example, a child might think that *dog* refers to cats or even to any four-legged animal. If a child incorrectly calls a cat "a dog," then an adult can readily correct that mistake with explicit feedback. So as long as the child makes a clear, explicit error, negative feedback should be straightforward. The same would be true in the case of proper names. If a child called many boys *John*, for example, this could be explicitly corrected. The problem (and an important part of the puzzle) is that there is little evidence suggesting that babies overextend proper names. There are, of course, reports that some children call other men *Daddy*, but *Daddy* clearly is not a typical proper name. Other men are appropriately called *Daddy* by their children, children hear about Mommy and Daddy bears, they encounter stories with characters called Mom and Dad, and so on. There are not many other reports of misuses of proper names. On the contrary, Macnamara (1982) comments on the remarkable accuracy of children's ability to restrict proper names from the start. So one assumption is that, however proper names are learned, it is not by explicit correction of errors since these errors do not seem to exist. Or to be more accurate, these errors do not appear in children's productions.

Given the lack of explicit feedback because of the absence of errors, we have a situation analogous to the problem presented in learnability theory (e.g., Pinker 1989; Wexler and Culicover 1980). Suppose that in comprehension, a child assumes that *John* refers to boys or brunette boys. Because this takes place prior to production, the child's assumptions are not made apparent. How would the child, with no feedback, figure out that he or she was wrong? The child must come to realize that *John* is restricted to one individual and not generalized to others, which requires noting the failure of a speaker to label other boys or brunette boys as *John*. The problem here is that adults are failing to label most things in the child's environment most of the time. Do we take every failure to comment on the ceiling, walls, radio, furniture, every piece of clothing on every person around as evidence about the semantic restriction of a given lexical item? Such a mechanism would be computing like mad all the time and nonoccurrences of labels would swamp all other data. So how could nonoccurrences enter into the correlations babies need to compute? The answer may lie with a pragmatic ability that would drastically narrow the range of nonoccurrences of labels that would be noticed and, ironically, with children's reliance on the taxonomic assumption—the same assumption that at first seemed to pose a problem for children figuring out proper names but that now can be seen as part of the solution.

The Taxonomic Assumption as Part of the Solution
Recall that the question posed earlier was that if children tend to generalize newly learned object labels to things of like kind, how do they rein in these generalizations in the case of proper names? If children made many overextensions that were explicitly corrected by adults, that would be one way to correct the tendency to generalize, but as we just mentioned, children do not tend to use proper names erroneously but, from the start of production, appear to use proper names to refer to specific individuals. If children were very conservative learners and refused to generalize until given positive evidence that a word referred to more than a single instance, that would account for their early restriction of the scope of proper names. But, again, children seem to generalize a newly learned word, at least in comprehension, at the youngest ages tested so far. So the problem is that if children generalize a newly learned term—that is, if they honor the taxonomic assumption—how do they come to quickly limit the scope of proper names? We now think that the taxonomic assumption, coupled with some pragmatic ability described next, could provide a way for children to notice the *non*occurrence of a label, which is critical for working out the semantics of proper names. In particular, because the taxonomic assumption leads children to expect a term to extend to things of like kind, it would

lead children to expect an object similar to one given a proper name to be labeled similarly. This expectation is then violated. So, the nonoccurrence may become more salient and informative because it violates an expectation on the part of the child. There is still the problem that most objects are not being labeled most of the time, and that is where the pragmatic knowledge we describe next comes in.

Pragmatics: Indications of a Speaker's Intent to Refer
The problem of detecting the failure of a term to be used is that we are usually surrounded by objects we are not labeling. As mentioned earlier, even if it were possible to register and retain information about these failures to label, they would be misleading and largely irrelevant to figuring out the scope of reference of a term. What is needed is a mechanism for determining which failures to label are informative. Such a mechanism is likely to be found in children's understanding of some pragmatic principles, especially ones related to monitoring a speaker's intent to refer. There is ample evidence that children as young as 18 months register information about a speaker's focus of attention, such as eye gaze, and use it in determining the intended referent of a novel word (e.g., Baldwin 1991, 1993; Baldwin and Tomasello 1998; Tomasello 2001). Young children will avoid mapping a novel label to a novel object they were attending to if it turns out that the speaker was not attending to the same object.

From this work we know that when a speaker does provide a label, children attend to information relevant to determining which object the speaker intended to refer to. The argument we are now making is that children could use their sensitivity to a speaker's intent to refer to notice significant failures to label. The idea here is that if a child could be confident that a speaker in fact intended to refer to an object, say, because the speaker actually did refer to the object, maybe even labeled the object, but did not use the label the child expected based on the taxonomic assumption, then that failure would be salient, relevant, and informative and should be used by children in assessing the scope of a given term. Framed this way, this set of principles could explain how children narrow a number of kinds of overextensions, not just proper names. Imagine, for example, that a child has overextended the term *cow* to refer to horses. When an adult looks at, points to, or otherwise designates a horse, and says "Oh, look at the ...," the child who thinks horses are called *cows* will expect to hear *cow*. On hearing *horse* instead, the child's expectation is violated and the nonoccurrence of *cow* made salient. A single instance is not sufficient evidence to narrow the scope of a word. The adult could well say "Look at that" or "Look at that animal" or "What a beauty," and these alone should not restrict the scope of a noun. But at least this provides a mechanism that would furnish input into the data children could use to establish a correlation. This same principle would help in restricting subordinate terms—for example, that *poodle* applies only to some kinds of dogs— as well as helping children narrow overextended terms. Whether children lacking an understanding of grammatical form class interpret a new word as a proper name (as in *Fido*), a subordinate term (as in *poodle*), or an adjective (as in *friendly*) will be determined, in part, on what this mechanism detects on repeated exposures to the word. Over multiple occasions, some of which might confirm an expectation and some of which might violate an expectation, children could continue to refine their hypotheses about the scope of the word.

A variant on this use of pragmatic signals of an intent to refer could occur when the adult provides clear evidence of noticing an object but does not label it, while at the same time labeling another similar object. The child's expectation that the same label be extended would again be violated and the nonoccurrence of the label noted. Again, this could be used to narrow overextended count nouns as well as proper names, and to learn the narrower range of subordinate compared to basic-level terms. In the case of subordinate classification, there is some empirical evidence for this mechanism at work. Merriman et al. (1995, 1890) propose a pragmatic principle they termed *exhaustive reference* that they define as follows: "When a novel generic word is used to name something, expect it to be extended to all entities in a situation that the speaker perceives and believes to be exemplars of the name." This formulation starts out assuming that the term used is a "generic" term, which we believe is overly constraining and telescopes the propensity to generalize and the monitoring of the speaker's intent to refer into a single expectation on the part of the child. We prefer to keep these two abilities distinct. Additionally, Merriman et al. seem to suggest that exhaustive reference operates in a particular situation involving multiple potential exemplars. We suggest instead that a mechanism that notes occurrences and nonoccurrences very likely stores and analyzes this input over extended periods of time.

Despite these differences, the principle of exhaustive reference captures the kind of processes we have in mind. Merriman et al. (1995, 1891) argue that the principle of exhaustive reference entails the *nominal passover effect* that they formulate as: "If a speaker labels only one object in an array with a novel term, the addressee should construe this behavior as evidence that the other object or objects are not referents of the term." As we discussed earlier, we do not want to restrict this kind of inference to novel terms. Familiar terms that have been overextended could be corrected by this kind of reasoning. Proper names that have been originally construed as count nouns could be reassessed to be proper names by this kind of mechanism. In broad strokes, then, this is the kind of mechanism that could help with the problem of noting nonoccurrences of labels.

Merriman et al. (1995) found evidence for the nominal passover effect in two experiments with 3-year-olds. Children saw two novel objects designed to be fairly similar. The experimenter said "Look at these" and went on to label one of them with a novel label (e.g., "This one is a jegger") and comment on it (e.g., "Isn't it neat"). This object was commented on and labeled ten times, while the other similar object next to it was either ignored or referred to with a pronoun (e.g., "Look at this one"). After this training, there were two kinds of tests for how children extended the novel term. One was a forced-choice generalization task where the two objects were placed in front of the child, who was asked to perform four actions with, for example, "a jegger." The second test involved free-choice name generalization, where several objects were placed on the table and the child asked, for instance, to "put the jeggers in a bag." The sets included the two training objects plus another similar object as well as other objects. The results from the forced-choice, but not the free-choice, procedure provided evidence for the nominal passover effect: 3-year-olds asked to find a *jegger* selected the target object that had been labeled more often than the similar object that had not been labeled.

There is some evidence, then, that pragmatic assumptions about when a speaker is intending to refer to an object yet fails to label it could make nonoccurrences of labels salient. The evidence is limited in several ways. First, the results of the Merriman et al. 1995 studies were not particularly robust. On the other hand, this particular methodology may underestimate the power of the effect under more naturalistic circumstances. Second, only 3-year-olds were tested in the Merriman et al. studies, so there is no direct evidence about whether 18-month-olds or even younger babies would be sensitive to such pragmatic cues. Third, Merriman et al. tested children's use of this principle for forming subordinate categories, not proper names per se. At least in principle, however, the problem of noticing failures to label and thereby having nonoccurrences entered into the tabulations of correlations could be solved by the combination of pragmatic principles and the expectations generated by the taxonomic assumption. The evidence from Merriman et al. is encouraging, but studies with much younger children are needed to see if this account is empirically correct.

12.2.5 How These Mechanisms Explain the Acquisition of the Proper-Count Distinction in Languages without the Syntactic Distinction

To summarize, we propose several mechanisms that could account for two related problems. They could help explain how very young children who have not yet acquired the grammatical distinction between proper and common nouns determine that a given lexical item, say *Bob* or *boy*, labels a single individual or a category, and they help explain how children register the relevant data for determining the grammatical distinction. The mechanisms include a conservative strategy that limits generalization of a term to referents other than the initial one only when positive evidence is provided in input. So far there is no evidence for this conservative strategy, but it may exist in children younger than 15 months of age. Alternatively, the problem of noting nonoccurrences of labels could be solved by the taxonomic assumption that would lead children who learned a label to expect it to generalize coupled with pragmatic knowledge that a speaker had the opportunity and intent to refer to an object with the expected label but did not. Children would also need the capacity to perform some kind of statistical or distributional analysis on the input.

There is a third problem that these same mechanisms could help solve: they could explain the acquisition of proper names versus count nouns in languages that do not have as explicit a grammatical contrast as does English. Take Japanese, for example. According to Imai and Haryu (2001, 789), "In Japanese, all nouns, including count nouns, mass nouns, and proper nouns, are syntactically treated the same. That is, no syntactic marker distinguishes the names for particular individuals, object types, and substances. Nor is there any syntactic device marking the singular/plural distinction." We suspect that this is somewhat of an overstatement. Although there may be no explicit grammatical marker that occurs in *all* contexts to distinguish these types of nouns, there still are likely to be other correlated constructions that do distinguish them.

In English, for example, certain sentence frames fail to distinguish between adjectives, mass nouns, and proper names. In a sentence of the form "This is X," X could be an adjective as in "This is expensive," a mass noun as in "This is clay," or a proper name as in "This is Jim." But from this we would not conclude that there are no grammatical distinctions between these grammatical form classes; there are constructions in English that *do* distinguish between them. For example, adjectives can be preceded by *very*, while mass nouns and proper names cannot; mass nouns can be preceded by *some*, while adjectives and proper names cannot; and so on. Likewise, in Japanese, although proper and count nouns are not distinguished by articles or by a plural making, count nouns are more readily modified by adjectives, and proper names are more likely to take titles such as *Mr.* or *Honorable*. Other contexts such as number (five boys versus five Johns) and other forms of quantification (many, few) may distinguish the two. There is also the possibility that some phonological distinctions may be correlated with proper names. In English, many nicknames have a diminutive ending, as in Becky, Suzie, Connie, Bobby, Jimmy, Ricky, Larry, and so on. So although in any given sentence there may be nothing to distinguish proper names from count nouns, adjectives, or mass nouns, an analysis of the distribution of contexts in which they occur would.

Even in languages where the grammatical distinction between proper and common names is not as clear as in English, the mechanisms we have just reviewed could enable children to acquire a lexical item in exactly the same way as English-speaking children who have not yet acquired the form class distinction learn that *Bob* is a proper name. One possibility is that children learning such languages rely on a conservative strategy that does not allow for generalization until given evidence to the contrary. However, there is no evidence that this strategy exists. The second possibility, and, given the evidence, the one we favor, is that they have the ability to evaluate whether someone had the opportunity and intent to refer to a given object with an expected count noun but did not.

So far we have considered how babies and young children might acquire specific proper names versus count nouns and how they could build up a general grammatical contrast between them. We turn now to how this distinction, once learned, could facilitate lexical acquisition.

12.3 Using the Proper-Count Distinction to Acquire New Words: Importance of Animacy

One of the most robust findings in the literature on the acquisition of proper names is that, from an early age, children expect that the referent for a proper name will be animate. Katz, Baker, and Macnamara (1974) argue that the expectation that proper names refer to animate things reflects a learned semantic distinction that it is more important for us to individuate and track animate things than inanimate ones. Indeed, when we give a proper name to a person, for example, it allows us to pick that person out from the set of all other people (except for those who have the same name). Of course, at times it is important for us to individuate inanimate things, too—

for example, it is quite important that we use our own toothbrush, and yet we do not give our toothbrushes proper names. Instead, inanimate things are typically individuated by some other linguistic device, such as a possessive or prenominal adjective—for instance, "my toothbrush" or "the red shoes."

As mentioned earlier, in their classic study, Katz, Baker, and Macnamara (1974) taught young children a new label for an object, modeled in a proper-name frame (e.g., "This is Dax") or a common-name frame (e.g., "This is a dax"). Some of the participants heard the common or proper name applied to a doll and others heard it applied to a block. Subsequently, children were provided with two objects: the one the experimenter had just named and another, highly similar one. They were asked to perform several actions with an object requested by the same name used in training (e.g., "Dax" or "a dax," depending on which condition the child had been in).

Results from Katz, Baker, and Macnamara 1974 showed that, as expected, when asked to perform actions with an object requested by a common name, children tended to select the originally labeled object and the other category member about equally. This was true regardless of whether the originally labeled object had been a doll or a block. However, when asked to perform actions with an object requested by a proper name, an important sensitivity to animacy emerged. When a doll had been labeled with a proper name, girls as young as 17 months selected primarily that same doll; in contrast, when a block had been labeled with a proper name, they selected that block and the other block about equally—essentially treating the proper name as a common one. Boys tended to treat the proper name as a common one regardless of the animacy of the object. Using a different procedure and only animate stimuli, Hall, Lee, and Bélanger (2001) found evidence for a proper-count distinction at 24 months in boys and girls, but not at 20 months.

In languages that do not make a syntactic distinction between proper and common names, animacy might be particularly important, interacting with whether a basic-level count noun is already known for the object. For example, as mentioned earlier, in Japanese, the same expression ("Kore wa dax desu") could mean "This is Dax," "This is a dax," "Those are daxes," "This is some dax," or

"This is dax [e.g., *red*]." Imai and Haryu (2001) found that if a count noun is not known for the object being referred to, Japanese preschoolers treat a new word applied to it like a count noun, extending it to other members of like kind at the basic level. In contrast, in accord with the mutual-exclusivity assumption, second labels for animate things are treated like proper names and second labels for inanimate things like subordinate-level nouns. Recall that Hall (1991) found that English-speaking children were also more likely to make proper-name interpretations for proper names given to animate objects for which they already had a label than for those they did not.

Things that young children come into contact with that receive proper names do tend to be animate—that is, they possess physical features like fur or skin, a face with eyes, biological shape, and so on. Indeed, outside the experimental situation, they also possess many more cues to animacy, such as self-propelled motion and correlated limb movements. Children may be exposed to many commercial and/or storybook characters that are normally inanimate, but that receive proper names (e.g., "Thomas the Train"). In most cases, however, these characters are likely to be anthropomorphized, with faces and the ability to talk and/or move.

It is interesting to note that certain things like insects are animate, but they lack some of the more common features correlated with animacy, such as a face. Hall (1994) showed that children were unlikely to treat a proper name given to an insect as referring to that particular individual unless it was described as being owned by someone (e.g., "This is my caterpillar. This caterpillar is Daxy"). Expressing ownership of an inanimate object (e.g., a boat), however, did not lead to a proper-name interpretation. Another way to induce a proper-name interpretation for a new name given to an object that would not normally take a proper name is to describe that object as having mental states. Sorrentino (1997) found that when a toy that was neither animal-like nor a typical artifact was described as having hopes, likes, and wants, 2-year-old girls (but not boys) tended to treat a new proper name as referring to that particular toy. In another condition where the toy was described with nonmental information (e.g., location, weight, tactile qualities), they did not. Thus, animal-like perceptual features may be a sufficient cue as to whether something is a candidate referent for a proper name, but they are not necessary.

One potentially interesting line of research could consider the range of cues that might lead a child to view an otherwise ambiguous object as a candidate for a proper name. From Sorrentino 1997, we know that the use of mental-state vocabulary in describing the object is sufficient (at least for 2-year-old girls), but it might also be interesting to consider whether attributes intrinsic to the object might lead to the same interpretation. For example, if the object appeared intentional by, say, demonstrating goal-directed motion (e.g., Woodward 1998), would that make it a candidate for a proper name? If it responded contingently to the child or another object (e.g., Johnson, Slaughter, and Carey 1998), would that suffice? Clearly, there is much to be worked out with regard to what aspects of an object make it likely to take a proper name.

In all of the work just mentioned, children acquired a proper name more readily when it was used to refer to something they could construe as animate. In a serendipitous finding, Gelman and Taylor (1984) noted that children would treat a proper name as referring to an animate object even when that was not what they had been taught. Their study was designed as a replication of the original Katz, Baker, and Macnamara 1974 study, using unfamiliar stimuli and changing the procedure slightly. In their revised version (which used 2.5-year-olds), the stimulus set consisted of a labeled object and a member of like kind (as before), but also two distractors of the opposite animacy. For example, in training, an unfamiliar monsterlike creature was called *Dax*. Later, in testing, the child was asked to perform a number of actions with *Dax*, selecting from an array consisting of the same monsterlike creature, a similar creature, and two (different) blocklike toys. The results were generally in line with those of Katz et al., but the addition of the distractor category led to an unexpected result: when the experimenter labeled a blocklike toy with a proper name, half of the children ignored this training and, at test, consistently selected one of the monster toys instead. This finding is noteworthy because the blocklike toy was unambiguously labeled not just once, but *six times*, and the monster toys were also present during training and were clearly *not* labeled with the name (see Merriman et al. 1995 and above for a discussion of the effects of nonnaming). Clearly, many children were unwilling to accept an inanimate referent for a proper name despite direct, ostensive input.

Taking this expectation one step further, in a pilot study, Liittschwager and Markman (1993) simply presented preschoolers with a pair of objects, one animate and one inanimate, and asked them to "point to Dax" (proper-name condition), "point to a dax" (common-name condition), or "point to one" (baseline condition). The results were striking: even without training of any kind, children overwhelmingly selected the animate object as the referent for the proper name, but had no preference in the common-name or baseline conditions.

12.3.1 Direct vs. Indirect Instruction

In a series of studies, we have taken advantage of children's ability to infer that the referent for a proper name should be animate to investigate the functional strength of word-referent mappings following two types of learning: direct and indirect. In direct instruction, the researcher names an object (e.g., "This is *Blicket*"), while pointing to, looking at, and clearly *intending to refer* to a particular item. In indirect instruction, in contrast, the researcher requests an object (e.g., "Where is *Blicket*?"), and the child, on the basis of this linguistic information and the range of possible referents, must decide which object to select; the researcher does not indicate the referent through overt pragmatic cues.

Although ostension has sometimes been treated as the prototypical word-learning situation, we know that children learn much of their vocabulary in nonostensive contexts (Akhtar, Jipson, and Callanan 2001; Akhtar and Tomasello 1996; Bloom 1993). Several experimental studies have shown that, in the absence of ostension, children successfully integrate a number of linguistic and nonlinguistic cues to identify a referent and then to infer at least some aspects of the word's meaning—a process called *fast mapping* (Au and Markman 1987; Carey 1978; Carey and Bartlett 1978; Dockrell and Campbell 1986; Hall, Quantz, and Persoage 2000; Heibeck and

Markman 1987). For example, in Carey and Bartlett 1978, 3- and 4-year-olds were introduced to a new color word in a sentence contrasting it with another known color word. In their study, a teacher requested one of two differently colored trays, saying "You see those two trays over there? Bring me the *chromium* one, not the red one, the *chromium* one." Children readily complied with this request, bringing the nonred tray, and many children demonstrated some appropriate understanding of the word a week later.

We were interested in whether direct instruction about the referent for a new word conferred any advantage over indirect instruction in terms of the robustness of the word-referent mapping. One might reasonably expect that direct instruction, with all of its overt social-pragmatic cues, might result in a stronger mapping than a fast mapping that required the child to identify the referent. Our studies were therefore designed with the explicit goal of comparing a word-learning situation where the child had to infer the referent for a new word with an analogous situation where no such inference was required.

Accuracy of Direct vs. Indirect Learning
In the first set of studies (Jaswal and Markman 2001), 2- and 3-year-old children were presented with a pair of novel objects. One object possessed physical features common to animate things (e.g., a face, hair, biological body shape), while the other was a novel artifact. Children in the *direct-instruction* condition watched as the researcher labeled the animate object four times with either a proper or common name: "This is [a] Dax. Would you like to look at [a] Dax? Here, why don't you have a look at [a] Dax. This is [a] Dax." The children were then allowed to play with both the animate and inanimate objects. Children in the *indirect-instruction* condition heard the researcher request one of the two objects by a proper or common name: "Point to [a] Dax." After a selection had been made, the researcher provided neutral feedback (e.g., "Thank you"), and allowed the children to play with both objects. To ensure that the objects in each pair were equally attractive, either before or after the labeling or selection, we asked the children in both conditions simply to "Point to one" of the objects.

As in Liittschwager and Markman 1993, the children showed no preference for animate or inanimate objects when asked to point to one. When children in the indirect-instruction condition were asked to select the referent for a common name, they also showed no preference. However, when the same children were asked to select the referent for a proper name, they showed a clear preference, selecting the animate object 84 percent of the time.

The key extension of the Liittschwager and Markman 1993 results was the generalization trial, which was identical for children in the direct-instruction condition and those in the indirect one. We knew that children could identify the referent for a new proper name on the basis of animacy and grammatical form class, but did they also represent it as referring to a specific individual? We presented children with an array of three objects: the one that had just been labeled by the researcher or the one they had just selected as the referent for the new word (target); a second, very similar object to the target, but differing in coloring or clothing (generalization stimulus); and a third object, of the same animacy, but different kind (distractor). For example, suppose that during the first part of the trial, a child in the indirect-instruction condition was presented with a koosh-like doll (animate) and a bendable wand, and asked to "Point to Dax." Most children would select the koosh-like doll. On the second part of the trial, that child would be presented with the same koosh-like doll, another koosh-like doll with differently colored and styled hair and clothing, and a mosquito-like stuffed animal. In the direct instruction condition, the researcher always labeled the animate object, and so children in this condition always saw the originally labeled animate object, a member of like kind, and a distractor.

At this point, we asked the children to perform a series of actions with an object requested by the same name used previously. For example, we asked them to "Put *Dax* down the chute [in a bucket, in a box, etc.]." Following Katz, Baker, and Macnamara (1974) and Gelman and Taylor (1984), we predicted that, if children treated a newly learned word as a proper name, they would make selections primarily of the target object. If, on the other hand, they treated it as a common name, they would be equally likely to select the target or generalization object. In neither case, however, should they select the distractor.

Results for the 3-year-olds were directly in line with these predictions. Following both proper- and common-name requests, they selected the target more frequently than chance; however, they were *more* likely to select the target object following a proper-name request than a common-name one. This pattern of results held true regardless of whether the children had been in the direct- or indirect-instruction condition. Results for the 2-year-olds were generally very similar. In short, children who inferred that the proper name should apply to the animate object restricted its scope as much as children directly taught the proper name. Similarly, children who inferred that the common name applied to either the animate or inanimate object extended its scope as much as (or more than) children directly taught the common name.

Maintenance of Learning Over a Delay

It is possible that differences between ostensive and inferential word learning may only emerge when increased demands are placed on the child. In the next studies (Jaswal and Markman 2003), we explored how the method of word learning (indirect vs. direct) affected 3-year-olds' comprehension of novel proper and common names when testing occurred with a memory delay of at least 2 days. The procedure was basically the same as that described earlier: children were shown a pair of animate-inanimate objects, and were either trained on the referent for a new proper or common name (direct instruction), or made an inference about it (indirect instruction). As before, children had no preference in the baseline trial. Similarly, those in the indirect-instruction condition had no preference when a common-name request was made. When the request was made in a proper-name frame, however, they preferred the animate object, selecting it 81 percent of the time.

Rather than immediately proceeding to the generalization test with the target, generalization, and distractor stimuli, we inserted a delay of at least 2 days, thus providing a more challenging measure of the strength of the word-referent mappings. Results were remarkably consistent with those obtained from the immediate testing studies. Children selected the target more than the generalization stimulus following all types of requests, but they were more likely to do so following proper-name requests than common-name ones, regardless of whether the training at the earlier session had been direct or indirect. In short, even after a delay of at least 2 days, 3-year-olds who inferred the referent for a novel proper or common name performed as well on a comprehension test as those who received training on the name.

It is interesting to note that many fast-mapping studies with preschoolers suggest that the mapping resulting from a brief exposure to a new word is partial, and requires additional experience to align with an adult meaning (e.g., Carey and Bartlett 1978; Dockrell and Campbell 1986; Goodman, McDonough, and Brown 1998). For example, Carey (1978) reviews evidence suggesting that children quickly learn certain aspects of, say, color words and spatial adjectives (e.g., semantic domain, polarity), but they take much longer to work out other aspects of those words (e.g., scope, dimensionality). Dockrell and Campbell (1986) argue that there are some semantic domains (e.g., shape, animal terms) where an initial fast mapping can provide a rather complete meaning of the term, and others (e.g., pattern, color) where this is not the case.

Our studies cannot address this issue directly because there are no partial meanings of proper names. Once children have figured out that a word is a proper name (through grammatical form class and animacy cues in our studies), they do not have to work out anything further about its meaning: it refers to one particular individual under all circumstances. Children in our studies seemed to understand this, regardless of whether they learned the new proper name directly or indirectly. Nor can our studies address how complete the meanings of the common names are. Although non-basic-level terms in particular may require more experience before children produce and comprehend them appropriately (see Callanan 1989; Liu, Golinkoff, and Sak 2001; Tenenbaum and Xu 2000), in our studies, we did not vary the similarity of the generalization stimulus and the target; they were quite similar. Thus, beyond saying that children extend new common names to similar, but not extremely different, items (i.e., the distractor), our results do not address questions about the scope of generalization of common names.

Resistance to Inconsistent Information

Although we cannot use proper names to evaluate how *complete* mappings are following indirect and direct instruction, we can use them to address further the question of how *robust* the mappings are. In particular, we can ask whether direct instruction makes children more confident in their mappings, and therefore more resistant to later information that is inconsistent with that mapping. For example, from the studies described so far, we know that children will treat a proper name as referring to a particular individual and not to another member of like kind. However, what if the researcher provides social-pragmatic cues indicating that another member of like kind shares the same name as the target? How might children deal with inconsistent information about a proper name's referent? Although there is not much experimental evidence on this issue, there are logically three alternatives:

1. Ignore the inconsistency altogether. This is what adults are likely to do if a word is well known. For instance, Naigles, Gleitman, and Gleitman (1992) showed that adults and many older preschoolers tended to treat an intransitive verb in a transitive frame (e.g., *"The elephant *comes* the giraffe") as if the speaker had meant the frame to be intransitive (e.g., "The elephant *comes to* the giraffe"). In other words, they ignored the transitive frame, treating it like an error. Thus, children might simply treat inconsistent information about a proper name's referent as if it were an error.

2. Incorporate the inconsistent information into an existing representation. For example, younger preschoolers in the Naigles, Gleitman, and Gleitman 1992 study treated the ungrammatical sentence above as if it actually were transitive, which necessitated a causal action (e.g., "The elephant (pushes, carries, moves, brings) the giraffe"). The youngest preschoolers, it seems, "assume that not all structures [in which a verb can appear] have as yet been heard and therefore that certain properties of even common verbs (such as whether or not they can encode causation) may as yet be unknown

to them" (p. 126). Given inconsistent information about the referent for a proper name, children may try to reconcile the inconsistency by assuming that both objects have that proper name (as in two Barbies; a "brand-name interpretation"), that the word is actually an adjective (Hall 1996), or that the proper name is actually a common name and that the researcher erred by not using an article.

3. Ignore the original information, and replace it altogether with the most recently encountered information. Indeed, one might expect that children who inferred the meaning of a new name would have a very fragile initial mapping, capable of being overwritten very easily, whereas children who received direct instruction initially would be less likely to discount that original information.

Reasoning that children who learned a new proper name indirectly might be less confident and therefore more likely to revise or discount their initial mapping, we designed a study to probe the fragility of mappings following indirect and direct instruction (Jaswal and Markman 2003). Three-year-olds learned new proper and common names, again either indirectly or directly. As before, most children in the indirect condition selected the animate object when a request was made in a proper-name frame, but had no animacy preference when the request was made in a common-name frame. Following the selection of the referent in the indirect condition or the training of the referent in the direct one, the researcher cleared the table and provided additional information in the following way: He moved an opaque box containing the original object (target), a member of like kind (generalization), and an object of the same animacy but different kind (distractor) into view, saying that he needed to "get a few things ready before going on to the next part." The target and distractor were removed from the box one at a time (in a random order), and placed on a small overturned box. As each was placed on the box, the researcher said "We're going to need this." Lastly, as the researcher removed the generalization stimulus and placed it on the overturned box, he referred to it with the same proper or common name that had earlier been associated with the target (e.g., "And we're going to need [this] Blicket"). Although the information was provided in a fairly subtle manner, there was no ambiguity about the referent for the label. It is important to point out that this information is only inconsistent in the proper-name frame, where our previous studies showed that children would expect the name to be restricted to the target. The information could be called "additional" in the common-name frame, because the researcher actually provided accurate information about the scope of the new word, namely, that it applied to another member of like kind.

Following the inconsistent or additional information, all children participated in an unrelated 1-minute distraction task designed to reduce demand characteristics, particularly following inconsistent information. As in the studies described earlier, children were then asked to perform a series of actions with an object requested by the same name used previously. A common-name (or "brand-name") interpretation would be one where the target and generalization objects were both treated as referents of the name. A proper-name interpretation would be one where a single object was treated as the only referent of the name.

Our additional/inconsistent information manipulation did indeed have an effect on the generalization results. Briefly, regardless of whether they learned the new word directly or indirectly, children were more likely than in previous studies to extend a new proper or common name to the generalization object. In fact, overall, they tended to select the generalization object more frequently than the target following both direct and indirect instruction—the opposite of what they did in the earlier studies. These results alone could simply indicate that our 1-minute delay-and-distraction task did not overcome the demand characteristic to select the last-labeled object. After all, the researcher had just called the generalization object by that very name. However, for the first time, there was also a hint of a difference between direct and indirect instruction: overall, children in the indirect condition were marginally more likely to select the generalization stimulus than children in the direct condition. There was no interaction with whether the request had been made in a proper- or common-name frame. In other words, children who learned the names indirectly may have given more weight to the inconsistent or additional information provided by the researcher, perhaps implicitly marking it in some way as learned indirectly and therefore more open to revision (see also Sabbagh and Baldwin 2001). On the other hand, an additional study failed to replicate this effect.

12.4 Conclusion

We now briefly summarize some of the conclusions we have reached about the acquisition and use of the proper-count distinction and speculate about the broader implications of these ideas for the general acquisition and use of grammatical form class. We have distinguished between the issues that need to be addressed in considering the acquisition of a grammatical form class in the first place versus its subsequent use in lexical acquisition once acquired. Obviously there is a continuum here as a distinction is becoming acquired and useful and not a simple dichotomy.

We turned first to issues in the initial acquisition of the grammatical distinction. Before the general grammatical distinction is learned, children may figure out that a given lexical item functions as a proper name—that is, a particular word, such as *Bill*, refers to a specific person while another particular word, like *chair*, refers to many different chairs. They could learn the appropriate referents and scope of *Bill* and *chair* with no knowledge at all of the grammatical form class cues that distinguish proper from common names in English. Information about these individual words could serve as data to enter into a distributional analysis that would yield the grammatical distinction. It is too glib, however, to say that children perform distributional analyses on these data without saying how the data are selected and determined to be relevant. As we argued, in the case of proper names, it is the nonoccurrence of labels that must be entered into the analysis. Because "nonoccurrence of labels" is far too undifferentiated and unspecified, no learning mechanism could register and compute all the different things that were not mentioned at any given point in time. A proposed solution to this problem is in the combined effects of the taxonomic assumption, which would lead children to expect a given word to generalize to things of like kind, and pragmatic knowledge, which allows children to notice when someone intends to refer to a given object. Given a speaker's explicit intent to refer to a given object but his or her failure to use an expected label, children would register the nonoccurrence of the label, and that could be entered into the statistical analysis they need to perform. As Gelman and Williams (1998) emphasize, all learning in any domain is selective. Although the details of the argument will differ for different grammatical categories, the general problem of selectivity must be solved. In the case of grammatical form class cues, examining the interplay between word-learning assumptions and pragmatic knowledge might be a fruitful way to consider how children work out grammatical contrasts beyond the proper-count distinction.

The second broad set of issues addressed how a grammatical distinction, once learned, facilitates the learning of new words. Knowing a word is a count noun or a proper name leads children to have different hypotheses about the appropriate referent of a word and, of course, its scope. In the case of proper names, animacy is one very salient feature that has been correlated with proper names— so much so that in an ambiguous situation where a proper name is used without the speaker making it clear which object is being referred to, children will assume a proper name refers to an animate over an inanimate object. This form of fast mapping—of quickly inferring the referent of a term in the absence of a speaker's explicit eye gaze, pointing, or other explicit cues as to their focus of attention—generates questions about the relative robustness of terms acquired through direct versus indirect means that go well beyond the example of proper names versus count nouns. In the work to date on proper names, we found no differences in the accuracy of learning—that is, children who inferred that a proper name referred to an animate object limited the scope of the name to that specific object just as much as children who were explicitly told that the proper name referred to that object. There were no differences in the robustness of the learning as measured by memory for the term after a delay of several days, with children showing excellent memory regardless of whether the term was taught directly or inferred. In one study there were at least slight differences in children's resistance to countersuggestions about the meaning of the term, suggesting that words learned indirectly may be more open to revision than those learned directly. This research is a first step in addressing issues about the stability and robustness of lexical learning, and we expect that differences will eventually emerge. Our results so far, however, point out that learning through inference can be as compelling as learning through direct ostensive instruction. In fact, we suspect there are indirect word-learning situations that may result in more elaborated meanings of new words than some direct learning ones. To take an example from Keil 1979, on hearing a phrase like "The boojum is angry," a word learner may be able to make many inferences about the *boojum* that a very straightforward ostensive labeling like "This is a boojum" might not license. Much of word learning is a protracted process requiring updating, revising, and enriching the first lexical entries established for a word. How this is accomplished is a question we need to address not just for proper versus count nouns, but for all of lexical acquisition.

References

Akhtar, N., Jipson, J., and Callanan, M. A. 2001. Learning words through overhearing. *Child Development, 72,* 416–430.

Akhtar, N., and Tomasello, M. 1996. Two-year-olds learn words for absent objects and actions. *British Journal of Developmental Psychology, 14,* 79–93.

Au, T. K., and Markman, E. M. 1987. Acquiring word meaning via linguistic contrast. *Cognitive Development, 2,* 217–236.

Baldwin, D. A. 1989. Priorities in children's expectations about object label reference: Form over color. *Child Development, 60,* 1291–1306.

Baldwin, D. A. 1991. Infants' contribution to the achievement of joint reference. *Child Development, 62,* 875–890.

Baldwin, D. A. 1993. Infants' ability to consult the speaker for clues to word reference. *Journal of Child Language, 20,* 395–418.

Baldwin, D. A., and Tomasello, M. 1998. Word learning: A window on early pragmatic understanding. In E. V. Clark, ed., *The Proceedings of the Twenty-Ninth Annual Child Language Research Forum,* vol. 8, 3–23. Stanford, CA: Center for the Study of Language and Information.

Bates, E. 1979. *The emergence of symbols: Cognition and communication in infancy.* New York: Academic Press.

Birch, S. A. J., and Bloom, P. 2002. Preschoolers are sensitive to the speaker's knowledge when learning proper names. *Child Development, 73*, 434–444.

Bloom, L. 1973. *One word at a time: The use of single word utterances before syntax.* The Hague: Mouton.

Bloom, L. 1993. *The transition from infancy to language: Acquiring the power of expression.* Cambridge: Cambridge University Press.

Bloom, P. 1994. Possible names: The role of syntax-semantics mappings in the acquisition of nominals. *Lingua, 92*, 297–329.

Bloom, P. 2000. *How children learn the meanings of words.* Cambridge, MA: MIT Press.

Bloom, L., Tinker, E., and Margulis, C. 1993. The words children learn: Evidence against a noun bias in early vocabularies. *Cognitive Development, 8*, 431–450.

Brown, R. 1957. Linguistic determinism and the part of speech. *Journal of Abnormal and Social Psychology, 55*, 1–5.

Callanan, M. A. 1989. Development of object categories and inclusion relations: Preschoolers' hypotheses about word meanings. *Developmental Psychology, 25*, 207–216.

Carey, S. 1978. The child as word learner. In M. Halle, J. Bresnan, and G. A. Miller, eds., *Linguistic theory and psychological reality*, 264–293. Cambridge, MA: MIT Press.

Carey, S., and Bartlett, E. 1978. Acquiring a single new word. *Papers and Reports on Child Language Development, 15*, 17–29.

Cartwright, T. A., and Brent, M. R. 1997. Syntactic categorization in early language acquisition: Formalizing the role of distributional analysis. *Cognition, 63*, 121–170.

Deak, G. 2000. Hunting the fox of word learning: Why "constraints" fail to capture it. *Developmental Review, 20*, 29–80.

Dockrell, J., and Campbell, R. 1986. Lexical acquisition strategies in the preschool child. In S. A. Kuczaj and M. D. Barrett, eds., *The development of word meaning*, 121–154. New York: Springer-Verlag.

Elman, J. L., Bates, E. A., Johnson, M. H., Karmiloff-Smith, A., Parisi, D., and Plunkett, K. 1996. *Rethinking innateness: A connectionist perspective on development.* Cambridge, MA: MIT Press.

Gelman, R., and Williams, E. M. 1998. Enabling constraints for cognitive development and learning: Domain specificity and epigenesis. In W. Damon, series ed., and D. K. Kuhn and R. S. Siegler, vol. eds., *Handbook of child psychology, Vol. 2: Cognition, perception, and language*, 5th ed., 575–630. New York: Wiley.

Gelman, S. A., and Markman, E. M. 1986. Categories and induction in young children. *Cognition, 23*, 183–208.

Gelman, S. A., and Taylor, M. 1984. How two-year-old children interpret proper and common names for unfamiliar objects. *Child Development, 55*, 1535–1540.

Gleitman, L. R., and Gillette, J. 1999. The role of syntax in verb learning. *Handbook of child language acquisition*, 279–295. San Diego: Academic Press.

Golinkoff, R. M., Mervis, C. B., and Hirsh-Pasek, K. 1994. Early object labels: The case for a developmental lexical principles framework. *Journal of Child Language, 21*, 125–155.

Golinkoff, R. M., Shuff-Bailey, M., Olguin, R., and Ruan, W. 1995. Young children extend novel words at the basic level: Evidence for the principle of categorical scope. *Developmental Psychology, 31*, 494–507.

Goodman, J. C., McDonough, L., and Brown, N. B. 1998. The role of semantic context and memory in the acquisition of novel nouns. *Child Development, 69*, 1330–1344.

Hall, D. G. 1991. Acquiring proper nouns for familiar and unfamiliar animate objects: Two-year-olds' word-learning biases. *Child Development, 62*, 1442–1454.

Hall, D. G. 1994. Semantic constraints on word learning: Proper names and adjectives. *Child Development, 65*, 1291–1309.

Hall, D. G. 1996. Preschoolers' default assumptions about word meaning: Proper names designate unique individuals. *Developmental Psychology, 32*, 177–186.

Hall, D. G. 1999. Semantics and the acquisition of proper names. In R. Jackendoff, P. Bloom, and K. Wynn, eds., *Language, logic, and concepts: Essays in honor of John Macnamara*. Cambridge, MA: MIT Press.

Hall, D. G., Lee, S. C., and Bélanger, J. 2001. Young children's use of syntactic cues to learn proper names and count nouns. *Developmental Psychology, 37*, 298–307.

Hall, D. G., Quantz, D. H., and Persoage, K. A. 2000. Preschoolers' use of form class cues in word learning. *Developmental Psychology, 36*, 449–462.

Heibeck, T. H., and Markman, E. M. 1987. Word learning in children: An examination of fast mapping. *Child Development, 58*, 1021–1034.

Hennon, E., Rocroi, C., Chung, H. L., Hollich, G., Arnold, K., Driscoll, K., Hirsh-Pasek, K., and Golinkoff, R. 1999, April. Testing the principle of extendibility: Are new words learned as proper nouns or category labels? Poster presented at the Biennial Meeting of the Society for Research in Child Development, Albuquerque.

Hollich, G. J., Hirsh-Pasek, K., and Golinkoff, R. M. 2000. Breaking the language barrier: An emergentist coalition model for the origins of word learning. *Monographs of the Society for Research in Child Development, 65* (3, serial no. 262).

Imai, M., and Haryu, E. 2001. Learning proper nouns and common nouns without clues from syntax. *Child Development, 72*, 787–802.

Jaswal, V. K., and Markman, E. M. 2001. Learning proper and common names in ostensive versus inferential contexts. *Child Development, 72*, 768–786.

Jaswal, V. K., and Markman, E. M. 2003. The relative strengths of indirect and direct word learning. *Developmental Psychology, 39*, 745–760.

Johnson, S., Slaughter, V., and Carey, S. 1998. Whose gaze will infants follow? The elicitation of gaze-following in 12-month-olds. *Developmental Science, 1*, 233–238.

Katz, N., Baker, E., and Macnamara, J. 1974. What's in a name? A study of how children learn common and proper names. *Child Development, 45*, 469–473.

Keil, F. 1979. *Semantic and conceptual development: An ontological perspective.* Cambridge, MA: Harvard University Press.

Kelly, M. H. 1992. Using sound to solve syntactic problems: The role of phonology in grammatical category assignment. *Psychological Review, 99*, 349–364.

Kobayashi, H. 1998. How 2-year-olds learn novel part names of unfamiliar objects. *Cognition, 68*, B41–B51.

Liittschwager, J. C. 1995. *Children's reasoning about identity across transformations.* Unpublished doctoral dissertation, Stanford University, Stanford, CA.

Liittschwager, J., and Markman, E. M. 1993, March. Young children's understanding of proper versus common nouns. Poster presented at the Biennial Meeting of the Society for Research in Child Development, New Orleans.

Liittschwager, J. C., and Markman, E. M. 1994. Sixteen- and 24-month-olds' use of mutual exclusivity as a default assumption in second-label learning. *Developmental Psychology, 30*, 955–968.

Liu, J., Golinkoff, R. M., and Sak, K. 2001. One cow does not an animal make: Young children can extend novel words at the superordinate level. *Child Development, 72*, 1674–1694.

Locke, J. [1690] 1964. *An essay concerning human understanding.* London: Collins.

Macnamara, J. 1982. *Names for things.* Cambridge, MA: MIT Press.

Maratsos, M. 1988. The acquisition of formal word classes. In Y. Levy, I. M. Schlesinger, and M. D. S. Braine, eds., *Categories and processes in language acquisition*, 31–44. Hillsdale, NJ: LEA.

Markman, E. M. 1989. *Categorization and naming in children: Problems of induction.* Cambridge, MA: MIT Press.

Markman, E. M. 1992. Constraints on word learning: Speculations about their nature, origins, and domain specificity. In M. R. Gunnar and M. Maratsos, eds., *Modularity and constraints in language and cognition*, vol. 25, 59–101. Hillsdale, NJ: LEA.

Markman, E. M. 1994. Constraints on word meaning in early language acquisition. *Lingua, 92*, 199–227.

Markman, E. M., and Hutchinson, J. E. 1984. Children's sensitivity to constraints on word meaning: Taxonomic versus thematic relations. *Cognitive Psychology, 16*, 1–27.

Markman, E. M., and Wachtel, G. F. 1988. Children's use of mutual exclusivity to constrain the meanings of words. *Cognitive Psychology, 20*, 121–157.

Merriman, W. E., Marazita, J. M., Jarvis, L. H., Evey-Burkey, J. A., and Biggins, M. 1995. What can be learned from something's not being named. *Child Development*, 66, 1890–1908.

Naigles, L. G., Gleitman, H., and Gleitman, L. R. 1992. Children acquire word meaning components from syntactic evidence. In E. Dromi, ed., *Language and cognition: A developmental perspective*, 104–140. Norwood, NJ: Ablex.

Nelson, K. 1988. Constraints on word meaning? *Cognitive Development*, 3, 221–246.

Pinker, S. 1989. *Learnability and cognition: The acquisition of argument structure.* Cambridge, MA: MIT Press.

Sabbagh, M. A., and Baldwin, D. A. 2001. Learning words from knowledgeable versus ignorant speakers: Links between preschoolers' theory of mind and semantic development. *Child Development*, 72, 1054–1070.

Saffran, J. R., Aslin, R. N., and Newport, E. L. 1996. Statistical learning by 8-month-old infants. *Science*, 274, 1926–1928.

Saffran, J. R., Johnson, E. K., Aslin, R. N., and Newport, E. L. 1999. Statistical learning of tone sequences by human infants and adults. *Cognition*, 70, 27–52.

Samuelson, L. K., and Smith, L. B. 1999. Early noun vocabularies: Do ontology, category structure and syntax correspond? *Cognition*, 73, 1–33.

Sorrentino, C. M. 1997, April. The role of mental state attribution on young children's interpretation of proper nouns. Poster presented at the Biennial Meeting of the Society for Research in Child Development, Washington, DC.

Sorrentino, C. M. 1999, April. Children and adults interpret proper names as referring to unique individuals. Poster presented at the Biennial Meeting of the Society for Research in Child Development, Albuquerque.

Tenenbaum, J. B., and Xu, F. 2000. Word learning as Bayesian inference. In L. R. Gleitman and A. Joshi, eds., *Proceedings of the Twenty-Second Annual Conference of the Cognitive Science Society*, 517–522. Mahwah, NJ: Erlbaum.

Tomasello, M. 2001. Perceiving intentions and learning words in the second year of life. In M. Bowerman and S. Levinson, eds., *Language acquisition and conceptual development*, 132–158. Cambridge: Cambridge University Press.

Waxman, S. R. 1991. Convergences between semantic and conceptual organization in the preschool years. In S. A. Gelman and J. P. Byrnes, eds., *Perspectives on language and thought: Interrelations in development*, 107–145. Cambridge: Cambridge University Press.

Waxman, S. R., and Markow, D. B. 1995. Words as invitations to form categories: Evidence from 12- to 13-month-old infants. *Cognitive Psychology*, 29, 257–302.

Wexler, K., and Culicover, P. 1980. *Formal principles of language acquisition.* Cambridge, MA: MIT Press.

Woodward, A. L. 1992. *The role of the whole object assumption in early word learning.* Unpublished doctoral dissertation, Stanford University, Stanford, CA.

Woodward, A. L. 1998. Infants selectively encode the goal object of an actor's reach. *Cognition, 69,* 1–34.

Woodward, A. L., and Markman, E. M. 1998. Early word learning. In W. Damon, series ed., and D. K. Kuhn and R. S. Siegler, vol. eds., *Handbook of child psychology, Vol. 2: Cognition, perception, and language,* 5th ed., 371–420. New York: Wiley.

Woodward, A. L., Markman, E. M., and Fitzsimmons, C. M. 1994. Rapid word learning in 13- and 18-month-olds. *Developmental Psychology, 30,* 553–566.

Wynn, K. 1992. Addition and subtraction by human infants. *Nature, 358,* 749–750.

Xu, F. 1999. Object individuation and object identity in infancy: The role of spatio-temporal information, object property information, and language. *Acta Psychologica, 102,* 113–136.

Xu, F., and Carey, S. 1996. Infants' metaphysics: The case of numerical identity. *Cognitive Psychology, 30,* 111–153.

Xu, F., and Spelke, E. S. 2000. Large number discrimination in 6-month-old infants. *Cognition, 74,* B1–B11.

13

The Nature of Word-Learning Biases and Their Roles for Lexical Development: From a Crosslinguistic Perspective

Mutsumi Imai and Etsuko Haryu

Many researchers have argued that children have a certain set of principles or biases about how words are mapped onto their meanings, and that these principles/biases enable them to map a word to its meaning even at the first exposure to the word (e.g., Markman and Hutchinson 1984; Markman 1990). Among the proposed principles or biases, the whole-object bias, taxonomic bias/noun-category bias, shape bias, mutual-exclusivity bias, and the principle of contrast have attracted much attention and generated a massive body of research (e.g., Clark 1987; Hall 1991, 1996b; Imai, Gentner, and Uchida 1994; Golinkoff, Mervis, and Hirsh-Pasek 1994; Landau, Smith, and Jones 1988; Markman and Hutchinson 1984; Markman and Wachtel 1988; Waxman and Markow 1995). Although most of the existing literature has converged into a view that these biases/ principles are used by children from a very early age, there has been much debate with respect to the specific nature of each of these biases/principles. For example, are they available prior to the onset of word learning and applied from the first word (e.g., Hollich, Hirsh-Pasek, and Golinkoff 2000; Waxman and Markow 1995)? Are they universally applied irrespective of any specific linguistic properties of the input language (e.g., Imai and Gentner 1997; Waxman, Senghas, and Benveniste 1997)?

A more serious problem that has remained unanswered, however, arises from the fact that all of these biases must be suspended or relaxed in some circumstances (Imai 1999). That is, although these word-learning biases can constrain the possible search space in mapping words onto concepts if applied in appropriate situations, they could also block the learning of a substantial portion of vocabulary if applied in inappropriate situations. For example, the whole-object bias should not be applied when a child learns a name for a substance, such as *water, sand,* and *sugar* (Soja, Carey, and Spelke 1991; Imai and Gentner 1997; Imai and Mazuka 2003). Learning names for specific individuals—that is, proper nouns—requires suspension of the taxonomic bias/noun-category bias (Hall 1991; Imai and Haryu 2001; see also Woodward and Markman 1998). The mutual-exclusivity bias must be relaxed in order for a child to learn category names at different levels of the taxonomic hierarchy as well as names for particular individuals (Gelman and Taylor 1984; Hall 1991; Imai and Haryu 2001; Taylor and Gelman 1989; Waxman and Senghas 1992). In sum, word-learning biases alone would not function properly unless their applications were appropriately controlled.

Are young children able to control word-learning biases in such a way that they would be used only in appropriate situations? The literature suggests that 2-year-olds' vocabulary includes nonobject words such as names for substances and events as well as proper names (e.g., Bloom, Tinker, and Margulis 1993; Nelson, Hampson, and Shaw 1993). This suggests that young children's word learning is not restricted to basic-level object-category terms, and in turn means that the word-learning biases are somehow suspended for the learning of those words. How, then, do children control and constrain the application of the biases? Furthermore, are the word-learning biases necessary for word learning at all on top of other types of resources that can constrain word meanings, such as semantic/ontological knowledge, social-pragmatic knowledge, and clues provided from syntax? Are the biases universally available independent of the native language or influenced by the structure of a specific language?

In this chapter, we will discuss these issues from a crosslinguistic perspective, mainly comparing word learning in English-speaking and Japanese-speaking children. Japanese has linguistic properties that provide interesting contrasts to English. In English, it so happens that there is a high correlation between semantic (ontological) classes and syntactic classes. That is, individuated entities, typically solid objects, are mapped onto count nouns, while nonindividuated entities, typically substances, are mapped onto mass nouns. Furthermore, among names for individuated entities, names for particular individuals (i.e., proper nouns) are syntactically distinguished from names for object kinds, in that count nouns, but not proper nouns, occur with determiners (e.g., Bloom 1994). Many studies have reported that English-speaking children utilize this information from syntax in inferring word meanings (e.g., Bloom and Keleman 1995; Gelman and Taylor 1984; Soja 1992; Subrahmanyam, Landau, and Gelman 1999). In fact, some researchers argue that, with this knowledge, together with other abilities children can recruit (e.g., ability to infer the speaker's intention), word-learning biases are not necessary to explain the mechanism of early word learning (e.g., Bloom 1994; see also Bloom 1993; Nelson 1988; Tomasello 1997).

In contrast to English, in Japanese different classes of nouns are not grammatically distinguished. Thus, data from Japanese children give us a way of assessing the role of the word-learning biases more directly than when studying English-speaking children. Furthermore, the comparison of how Japanese- and English-speaking children assign meanings for a novel noun in various situations should give us important insights into the issue of universality in early lexical development. In the next section, we provide a somewhat detailed description of the properties of Japanese, highlighting differences from English. We then discuss how Japanese children apply or suspend the whole-object bias, shape bias, noun-category bias (taxonomic bias), and mutual-exclusivity bias.

13.1 Linguistic Properties of Japanese

As mentioned earlier, in Japanese, there is no grammatical apparatus distinguishing between proper nouns and common nouns, nor is there any grammatical distinction between names for individuals (coded as count nouns in English) and names for nonindividuals (coded as mass nouns in English). Moreover, there is no syntactic device marking the singular-plural distinction. Thus, the following five English expressions are all translated into a single expression, "Kore (This) wa (Topic/Subject marker) *dax* desu (IS)": "This is *a dax* (single instance of an object category)," "Those are *daxes* (multiple instances of an object category)," "This is *some dax* (material name)," "This is *dax* (property)," "This is *Dax* (proper name)." In other words, when one hears "Kore wa *dax* desu" without seeing the named entity, there is no way of inferring whether *dax* refers to a single object, multiple objects, a substance, a property (such as color), or a particular individual.

One may wonder if there is absolutely no syntactic device in Japanese that flags the distinction among proper names, object-category names, or substance names. Especially those who know that Japanese is a numeral-classifier language may think that the noun's form class can be revealed or at least suggested by classifier use. However, a classifier accompanies a noun only when the noun appears with a numeral. A new word is typically introduced in the sentence frame "Kore wa X desu." Note that in this sentence, no classifier appears. In fact, unless mention of number is contextually required, the numeral + classifier construction is not ordinarily used. Furthermore, even when a noun appears with a classifier, many classifiers, including the ones most frequently used such as *hon*, *ko*, and *hai*, are not very strong identifiers of the noun's form class. For example, although *hon* is usually characterized as a classifier for long, thin *object*, what is crucial to the meaning of *hon* is the long and thin shape; class members do not need to be objects at all. For example, a typical substance such as butter can appear with *hon*. The sentence "butaa (butter) o (Acc) ni (2) *hon* totte" (Please get me two *long thin shaped* butter) is acceptable, and on hearing the sentence, the hearer usually interprets it as meaning that the speaker wants two *sticks* of butter based on contextual/pragmatic knowledge. Likewise, *hai*, a measuring classifier that is roughly translated as "a container full of" can appear both with nouns referring to substances (e.g., water, rice, and so on) and objects (e.g., olives, beans, and any other relatively small objects).

As for distinguishing proper nouns from common nouns, one may think that honorific titles such as *san* (for general courtesy) and *chan* (usually for children and people who are very close to the speaker) signal that a noun is a proper noun. However, again, many proper nouns do appear without an honorific title. Proper names for animals and places do not usually appear with such a title, and even names for people frequently appear without it. Furthermore, in child-directed speech, adults sometimes add -*san* or -*chan* to common nouns, often for animals but sometimes even for nonanimals (e.g., neko (cat)-chan, ninjin (carrot)-san) to express intimacy or affection. Thus, the use of honorific titles is not a very reliable cue for determining whether the given noun is a proper noun.

13.2 Controlling the Whole-Object Bias and the Shape Bias

In order for children to learn names for substances, the whole-object bias and the shape bias must be suspended. In the absence of direct social-pragmatic cues and syntactic cues, can Japanese children learn substance names, correctly suspending these biases in learning names of substances? Imai and Gentner (1997) asked whether Japanese children are able to generalize novel nouns in an ontologically correct fashion, extending a noun associated with an object on the basis of shape but extending a noun associated with a substance on the basis of material identity, like English-speaking children whose language does mark the ontological distinction between object kinds and substance kinds (Soja, Carey, and Spelke 1991). They found that both Japanese speakers and English speakers from 2 years of age through adulthood are able to project word meanings differently (and ontologically correctly) depending on whether a novel label referred to a complex-shaped object or a nonsolid substance. However, the crosslinguistic data also suggest that the linguistic structure of the speaker's native language influences people's construal of individuation for particular type of entities—that is, entities whose perceptual saliency is weak and ambiguous. English speakers uniformly construed such simple-shape solid entities (e.g., a kidney-shaped lump of wax) as individuated objects. In contrast, Japanese children's construal for these entities split between individuated and nonindividuated; Japanese adults in fact showed a preference for construing them as nonindividuated chunks of substances.

Imai and Gentner's (1997) results thus suggest that word learning is constrained by ontological knowledge even without explicit syntactic markers, yet there is also influence from the structure of the speaker's native language when the referred entity's perceptual saliency is low. In short, their results showed that application of the whole-object bias and shape bias is constrained by this early and universally present ontological knowledge (see also Hall 1996a; Soja, Carey, and Spelke 1991). At the same time, though, they showed that the range of application of these biases may be influenced by the structure of speakers' native language (see Imai and Mazuka 2003 for more detailed discussion of this issue).

13.3 Controlling the Taxonomic/Noun-Category Bias

It has been reported that children have a disposition to extend labels to other objects of like kinds, and this disposition has been characterized as the taxonomic bias, noun-category bias, principle of category scope, or shape bias (e.g., Golinkoff et al. 1992; Hall 1991; Imai, Gentner, and Uchida 1994; Landau, Smith, and Jones 1988; Markman and Hutchinson 1984; Waxman and Markow 1998). However, this disposition could block learning of proper names unless appropriately controlled. In the case of English, syntax provides useful information on this problem, since proper nouns and common nouns are syntactically distinguished. However, for Japanese children, this source of information is not available. We now discuss how Japanese children deal with this problem.

Earlier studies have demonstrated that English-speaking children do utilize information provided from syntax in inferring the meaning of a new word from a very early age (Katz, Baker, and Macnamara 1974; Gelman and Taylor 1984; Soja 1992; Hall, Lee, and Bélanger 2001; Waxman 1999; Waxman and Markow 1998; see also Imai 2000). Can Japanese children select the single most appropriate interpretation out of several competing alternatives without this useful clue from syntax? To examine this question, we studied how Japanese 2-year-olds and 4-year-olds interpret novel labels associated with animals and artifacts that are either familiar or unfamiliar (Imai and Haryu 2001).

13.3.1 Naming Unfamiliar Objects

We first report how Japanese children interpreted novel nouns associated with unfamiliar objects in our study (Imai and Haryu 2001).

The children were randomly assigned to the *animal* condition or to the *inanimate* condition. The structure of the stimuli and the procedure were identical across the two conditions, the only difference being that the unfamiliar objects for the one group consisted of toy animals and of the other, inanimate objects (see figure 13.1). An unfamiliar object was named in a sentence frame something like "Kore wa *neke* desu," where *neke* is the target noun. As mentioned above, it is simply impossible to infer whether the noun is a proper noun or a common noun from the structure of the sentence, although we know that, based on the results of Imai and Gentner 1997, the child would be unlikely to interpret the noun as referring to a portion of the named object or to the material of it, since the labeled objects in this study were all objects with a complex structure.

The named object was taken out of the child's view after the naming session, then it was presented again with four other objects. The four objects included a subordinate-level item, a basic-level item, a superordinate-level item, and a distractor (see figure 13.1 for a sample set). The subordinate item was identical to the original in shape, size, and material. When the original was a toy animal, the subordinate item was distinguishable from the original object by clothes and/or accessories (e.g., a hat, ribbon, or hairband). For the inanimate-object sets, the original and the subordinate item differed only in color. The basic-level item was very similar (but not identical) to the original in shape, but was different from it in material, color, and/or size. The superordinate item had a very different appearance (both in shape and color) from the original but came from the same superordinate category. A distractor item was drawn from a different ontological category (i.e., when the named object was a toy animal, then the distractor object was an inanimate object, and vice versa).

The five objects (the original and the four variations) were all presented in front of the child. The experimenter said to the child, "*neke* o sagashite," which could mean "find *a neke/nekes/Neke/some neke*." The child could select either a single object or multiple objects at one time. Since Japanese does not mark the singular-plural distinction, the instruction would not bias the child toward selecting only one or more than one object. The selected object(s) were put into a box, leaving the nonselected objects in front of the child. The

Imai and Haryu

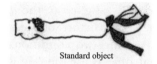

Standard object

a.   Subordinate item   Basic-level item   Superordinate item   Distractor

Standard object

b.   Subordinate item   Basic-level item   Superordinate item   Distractor

Figure 13.1
Sample stimulus sets used in Imai and Haryu's (2001) study: (a) unfamiliar animal
set; (b) unfamiliar artifact set.

experimenter then asked her whether there was any more *neke* there. This procedure was repeated until she said no to the prompt.

The following patterns were predicted: (1) if the child interpreted the noun as a proper name, she would be expected to select only the named object; (2) if she interpreted the noun as a common noun, she should select multiple objects; (3) if the child observed the shape bias and noun-category bias, she should extend the label up to the basic-level item (i.e., selecting the original, the subordinate item, and the basic-level item) but not to the superordinate item.

The child's response in each trial was classified into one of five mutually exclusive response categories: *Proper-noun* response, *Subordinate* response, *Basic-level* response, *Superordinate* response, and *Unclassifiable* response. Note that selecting a particular item (for example, a basic-level item) by itself did not lead to a credit for the particular response. Instead, to be credited as the subordinate, basic-level, or superordinate response, *a single particular combination* of the items was required out of thirty-two (2^5) possible response patterns. For example, the child received a point for the Subordinate response *only* when she selected both the standard and the subordinate item, and rejected the three remaining objects as referents. To receive a point for the Basic-level response, *all and only* the standard, subordinate, and basic-level items must be selected. To be counted as the Superordinate response, all the standard, subordinate, basic-level, and superordinate items but not the distractor must be selected. Likewise, in order for a response to be coded as a Proper-noun response, the child must select the standard object alone and must say no to the question of whether there is any more X. All twenty-eight other combinations of item selections were put in the Unclassifiable response category.

Both 2-year-old and 4-year-old Japanese children showed very clear, consistent response behavior. Furthermore, the results from the Japanese children were similar to previous results from English-speaking children (Hall 1991). The Japanese children interpreted the noun as a common name, whether it was given to a toy animal or an inanimate object. The children made common-noun interpretations (at the subordinate, basic, or superordinate level) more than 85 percent of the time for both conditions (animal: 86.4%; inanimate: 94.3%). Among the possible common-noun interpretations (i.e., Subordinate, Basic-level, Superordinate responses), the Basic-level interpretation was made most frequently (47.2%). This suggests that when Japanese children hear a novel noun associated with an unfamiliar object, either animate or inanimate, they assume by default that the noun refers to a kind of object rather than to a particular instance of the object, using shape similarity for determining the extension of the category.

13.3.2 Naming Familiar Objects

We then examined how Japanese children interpret a novel noun associated with a familiar object, whose name they already know. The structure of each stimulus set was identical to that used in the above study except that the named object was familiar to the children. Novel labels were given to instances of *bear, penguin,* and *monkey* in the animal condition. In the *inanimate-object* condition, novel labels were given to instances of *ball, cup,* and *spoon.* As in the unfamiliar-object case, Japanese 2- and 4-year-olds were examined; half of them were assigned to the *animal* condition, and the other half to the *inanimate-object* condition.

What pattern was predicted in this study? Because children already knew the basic-level names, the mutual-exclusivity bias predicted that it would be difficult for them to accept the novel labels. If this were the case, we might then expect the children to have behaved inconsistently, often showing the "unclassifiable" response or failing to show a distinct preference in response patterns. Note that the principle of contrast (Clark 1987) did not predict difficulty in learning novel names for objects that already have a name. Rather, it predicted that children should think that the extension of the novel label would not exactly overlap with that of the extension of the basic-level category they already know. However, since this principle would not tell children what other solutions are available and which should be employed, Japanese children would have three possibilities to choose from: (1) the extension of the novel noun may be restricted to the named object; (2) the extension may be broader than the basic-level category; (3) the extension may be narrower than the basic-level category, but not restricted to the named object.

It turned out that even 2-year-old Japanese children did not have much difficulty accepting novel labels given to the familiar objects. Consistent with the principle of contrast, the children rarely showed a basic-level kind interpretation in either condition. Furthermore, the children's interpretation was not equally distributed across the three possible interpretations. Rather, they converged into a single interpretation, but quite interestingly, the selected interpretation differed greatly depending on the animacy status of the named object. The children who heard a novel label in association with a familiar animal interpreted the noun as a proper name 59.1 percent of the time, whereas those who heard a novel label in association with a familiar inanimate object made a proper name response only 9 percent of the time. The children in the inanimate-object condition interpreted the new noun as a subordinate-category name (53%). (Remember that the base probability for making the proper-noun interpretation or the subordinate interpretation was 0.03125 (1/32).)

Imai and Haryu's research thus presented a fairly comprehensive picture of how Japanese children assign meanings to novel nouns. When a novel label is given to an object that does not yet have a label, children assume that the label is a name for an object category, whether the referent is an animate or inanimate object. If the named object already has an established name, and if the object is an animal, children interpret the label as a name for the particular individual rather than interpreting it as a name for a narrower or broader category. When a novel label is given to an inanimate object, they no longer interpret it as a name for a particular instance. Instead, they map the noun to a narrower category—that is, a subordinate category.

Importantly, in our study (Imai and Haryu 2001, Study 3), the Japanese 2-year-olds were able to map a novel word for a familiar animal to a subordinate category when it was presented as a compound noun (e.g., X-pengin (penguin)), consistent with results from

English-speaking children (Gelman, Wilcox, and Clark 1989). This means that Japanese children are able to utilize a linguistic cue available in their language to modify a default interpretation.

13.4 Controlling the Mutual-Exclusivity Bias

Among proposed word-learning biases, the mutual-exclusivity bias has been most controversial (e.g., Clark and Svaib 1997; Merriman and Bowman 1989; Mervis, Golinkoff, and Bertrand 1994; Waxman and Senghas 1992). The mutual-exclusivity bias is helpful if children only need to learn basic-level category labels that are mutually exclusive to one another. However, many words are not basic-level category terms, nor are they mutually exclusive to one another. Thus, the bias could potentially block learning of a substantial part of the lexicon. Nonetheless, as mentioned earlier, children's early vocabulary includes words that are not basic-level terms (Bloom, Tinker, and Margulis 1993; Nelson, Hampson, and Shaw 1993). Furthermore, there is much empirical evidence that children as young as 2-year-olds accept multiple labels referring to the same object (e.g., Clark and Svaib 1997; Gelman and Taylor 1984; Imai and Haryu 2001; Mervis, Golinkoff, and Bertrand 1994; Waxman and Senghas 1992).

On the other hand, in certain situations, the mutual-exclusivity bias may actually foster word learning. It has been observed that children have difficulty learning names of solid materials such as *wood* and *plastic*, since they (particularly English-speaking children) have a strong bias toward construing a solid, discrete entity as an individuated object rather than a substance (Dickinson 1988; Soja, Carey, and Spelke 1991; Imai and Gentner 1997; but see Prasada 1993). However, when a child hears a new word in association with an object whose first label has already been learned, because she is unwilling to accept the new word as another label for the object itself, she may turn her attention to the material kind and willingly interpret the word as a material name (Markman and Wachtel 1988; Markman 1990). Another situation in which the mutual-exclusivity bias may foster word learning is when a child has overgeneralized the word. In this case, the mutual-exclusivity bias might be beneficial for restructuring the overextended category. In this section, we consider the conditions under which children are likely to show the bias as well as the conditions under which they are likely to override it. Following that, we discuss how this bias might interact with other factors, and then what the true nature of the bias might be.

13.4.1 When Is the Mutual-Exclusivity Bias Most Likely to Be Observed?

Evidence for the mutual-exclusivity bias has been most clearly obtained by showing children a familiar object whose label has already been learned and an unfamiliar, novel object at the same time. Markman and Wachtel (1988) showed 3-year-old American children a familiar object (e.g., a cup) and another object unfamiliar to children of this age (e.g., tongs). Then the experimenter asked the children, "Show me the *dax*." To this request, the children tended to select the unfamiliar object. Markman and Wachtel further demonstrated that children tended to map a novel word to the unfamiliar object over the property of the familiar, already-named object even if the noun was given in a mass-noun syntactic frame ("Show me *pewter*"). Markman and Wachtel argued that the children selected the unfamiliar object even in the face of contradicting clue from syntax because selecting the object whose name was already known as the referent of the novel word would violate the mutual-exclusivity bias.

Further strong evidence for the mutual-exclusivity bias has been reported in a study with Japanese children. Haryu (1991; see also Haryu and Imai 1999) presented Japanese 3- and 5-year-old children with two objects, a familiar object (e.g., an apple) and an unfamiliar object (e.g., a lipstick holder). The children were assigned either to the *word-only* condition or to the *word + pragmatic context* condition. In the *word-only* condition, each child was presented with two objects, one familiar and the other unfamiliar, and was asked to identify the referent of a new word. In the *word + pragmatic context* condition, a new word was presented in a context suggesting that the experimenter intended to refer to the familiar object. For example, the experimenter introduced a puppet named Mary, and said to the child, "Mary is hungry now. I would like to give Mary (the) *heku*," where *heku* was a nonsense word. Then the experimenter placed two objects, a familiar object (e.g., an apple) and an unfamiliar object (e.g., a lipstick holder), in front of the child, and asked her to select the *heku*. In this situation, the child faced a dilemma, if they indeed had the mutual-exclusivity bias. The context suggested that the puppet wanted the familiar object, not the unfamiliar, nameless object.

There was a large interaction between *condition* and *age*. The children in the *word-only* condition, regardless of age, tended to select the unfamiliar object as the referent of the new word, replicating the finding by Markman and Wachtel (1988). However, in the *word + pragmatic context condition*, the 3-year-olds and 5-year-olds responded very differently. The 5-year-olds accepted the new word as another name for the familiar object, respecting the contextual information and overriding the mutual-exclusivity bias. In contrast, the 3-year-olds selected the unfamiliar object. That is, they gave the mutual-exclusivity bias priority over the pragmatic-contextual information. Note that this response behavior of the 3-year-olds was not due to an inability to understand the pragmatic information given. In a control study, different 3-year-old children were asked to select between the same familiar and unfamiliar objects with the same contextual cue, but without the invocation of novel words (e.g., "Mary is hungry. Which one do you think Mary wants?"). This time, the 3-year-olds selected the familiar object, incorporating the pragmatic-contextual information. These results seem to indicate that, at least for children aged 3 and under, the bias toward mapping a novel label to a novel, nameless object is very strong—in fact, strong enough to override social-pragmatic information provided in the discourse.

13.4.2 Overriding Mutual Exclusivity to Establish Lexical Hierarchies

On the other hand, the literature suggests that children as young as 2 years of age do possess different words referring to the same object in their vocabulary (Clark and Svaib 1997), and that under certain conditions, young children are able to establish lexical hierarchies (Gelman and Taylor 1984; Imai and Haryu 2001; Taylor and Gelman

1989; Waxman and Senghas 1992). Below, we consider the circumstances under which young children are able to learn that there are multiple labels sharing the same referents.

Gelman and Taylor (1984; Taylor and Gelman 1989) taught 2-year-old English-speaking children a new noun for a familiar object, and assessed their interpretation of the relationship between the new noun and the familiar name. They found that the children often interpreted the new word as referring to a category subordinate to the category denoted by the familiar name. In particular, English-speaking children utilized both clues from syntax and semantic knowledge. When a new noun was provided as a common name ("This is *a* X"), the children interpreted it as a subordinate-category name regardless of whether the named object was a toy animal or an inanimate object. When a new noun was introduced in a proper-name syntax ("This is X"), the children interpreted it as a proper name as long as the named object was a toy animal; however, when the named object was an artifact object such as a ball, their responses became random.

As reported earlier, Japanese 2- and 4-year-olds mapped a new noun associated with a familiar artifact object to a subordinate category (Imai and Haryu 2001). When a novel noun was associated with a familiar animal, they preferred the proper-name interpretation to the subordinate-category interpretation. Thus, results from studies with English-speaking and Japanese-speaking children both suggest that young children are willing to accept more than one label for one object, especially when the named object is explicitly pointed to.

13.4.3 Learning Material Names via the Mutual-Exclusivity Bias?

Imai and Haryu's study described above provides evidence that young children are able to override the mutual-exclusivity bias. However, this may have been due to the particular way the stimulus set was constructed in their study. That is, in their stimulus materials, the artifact objects that were identified as referents of the novel word were made out of the same material kind. It is possible that Japanese children preferred to interpret the label as a name of the material when they were put in a situation where two interpretations were pitted against each other. This possibility needs to be examined, especially given that Japanese does not syntactically distinguish the two interpretations. Imai and Gentner's (1997) study demonstrated that the material-name interpretation is unlikely to be made by Japanese children (or by English-speaking children) when the named entity is a solid and complex-shaped *novel* object. However, when the child knows the first label of the newly named object, the story may be different. In fact, this is exactly what Markman and her colleagues predicted (Markman and Wachtel 1988; Markman 1990). According to them, the mutual-exclusivity bias helps children override the whole-object bias and fosters learning of material names. Thus, if we set up a situation in which children can map a new word for a familiar object either to the material of the object or to a subordinate category, children should prefer the former option, especially given that the syntax does not provide any cue for either option.

In our recent research (Haryu and Imai 2002), we examined this question. Monolingual Japanese 3-year-old children were tested on five sets of stimuli. Each set consisted of a standard object and four test objects: a standard object, a subordinate item, a material item, and a distractor. The standard object was an object even 3-year-old children could easily name, but made out of a material whose name had not yet been learned by the children of this age (e.g., a plate made out of cork). The subordinate item was identical to the standard object in shape, size, and material but distinguishable from it by the color of the pattern painted on the surface. The basic-level item was very similar (but not identical) in shape to the standard, but was different from it in material and overall color (e.g., a metal plate). The material item was a portion of the material the standard object was made out of (e.g., a chunk of cork). The distractor item came from a different ontological category from the standard (e.g., a stuffed animal).

We first confirmed that the children would name the standard and the subordinate item with the familiar basic-level name. To ensure this, before test trials, the children were shown the objects in each set and asked to select all the referents of the familiar name. For example, in the plate set, the child was asked "Osara wo totte (Get me (a) plate)," and this question was repeated until she said that there were no more plates. All the children met this prerequisite, using the familiar name to refer to the standard object, the subordinate item, and the basic-level item in all the sets.

The experimenter then presented the child with a standard object and named it with a novel word, saying, for example, "Kore wa *heku* desu." As mentioned before, in the sentence "Kore (This) wa (Topic/Subject marker) *heku* (a novel word) desu(is)," it is not clear whether the novel word *heku* is a name for an object category, a name for a material, or a name for a particular individual, although the last interpretation would be very unlikely for the type of objects used in this study, as demonstrated by Imai and Haryu (2001). After learning the new word, the child was shown the four choice objects and asked to indicate which she thought was (were) the referent(s) of *heku*. As stated earlier, because Japanese does not make the singular-plural distinction, the child could select either a single object or multiple objects at one time. She was then asked whether there was/were any more *heku(s)*, and this prompt was repeated until the child said no. This procedure was repeated on each of the five sets.

The child's response in each trial was classified into one of the four mutually exclusive categories: *Synonymous* response, *Subordinate-Category* response, *Material* response, and *Other* response. A child's response was coded as a Synonymous response if the child chose both the subordinate item and the basic-level item but not the material item or the distractor item, while it was coded as a Subordinate-Category response if she selected only the subordinate item. If a child selected the subordinate item and the material item, but not the basic-level item or the distractor item, the response was coded as a Material response. Any other response patterns were put in the Other response category.

The children did not show the mutual-exclusivity bias in this situation. That is, even though they had a clear option of mapping the new word to the material of the named object to avoid allowing multiple labels for it, the Japanese children did not choose this option. Instead, they interpreted it as a subordinate-category name. This suggests that, although children have a bias toward mapping a new word to a novel object when a novel, nameless object is present, this does not mean that they have a belief that nouns denote mutually exclusive categories. When a familiar object receives a novel name, children by default assume that the noun refers to the object in its entirety rather than to a material, and look for a category that has a different boundary from the old, familiar category to map the new noun. To interpret it as a material name perhaps requires additional pragmatic-contextual clues (see Prasada 1993).

In any case, when a familiar artifact was named with a novel noun, the Japanese children did not interpret it as a proper name or a material name. Rather, they mapped it to a subordinate category. However, this solution is not the only possible one available to children under this circumstance. As mentioned earlier, when a child has overgeneralized the word, a new label may be interpreted as a cohyponym of the familiar category (i.e., as a word contrastive to the familiar word at the same level of lexical hierarchy), and this would subsequently result in restructuring the old category. Take the example of a child who has originally included sheep in the "dog" category. Hearing a new word *sheep* might narrow down the overextended "dog" category by establishing the category "sheep" (Clark 1987). In the next section, we discuss the situations in which this restructuring process may occur.

13.4.4 Narrowing Down Overextended Categories

Evidence for spontaneous restructuring of overextended categories by the introduction of a new word has been limited in diary studies (Clark 1973; Leopold 1939–1949, cited in Clark 1987). Several researchers investigated whether young children were able to modify an overextended category by the introduction of a novel word in experimental settings and failed to find clear evidence that children, especially those under 4 years of age, spontaneously modify the overextended category and establish a new category that is contrastive to the existing one (Banigan and Mervis 1988; Merriman 1986; Taylor and Gelman 1989).

Thus, the results to date seem to suggest that restructuring of overextended categories does not take place easily by simply introducing a new word to an object whose first label had already been learned. In contrast, as reviewed above, there is ample evidence that children do not have much difficulty mapping a new noun to a subordinate category. Does this mean that, when a new noun is associated with a familiar artifact object, children only consider the subordinate-category interpretation and do not spontaneously consider the possibility that the word is contrastive to (hence a *cohyponym of*) the old word at the same level of the lexical hierarchy?

We asked whether there are cases when children interpret a new noun as a cohyponym of the already-existing word and restructure the meaning of the old word, and if so, under what conditions (Haryu and Imai 2002). As stated earlier, most previous research has indicated that this process does not easily take place in young children (Banigan and Mervis 1988; Merriman 1986; Taylor and Gelman 1989). However, a finding by Waxman and Senghas (1992) suggests that young children may sometimes establish a lexical hierarchy and sometimes establish a new category that is mutually exclusive to the old one by using similarity as a clue.

Waxman and Senghas (1992) examined 2-year-olds' interpretation of two new nouns given to two unfamiliar objects both of which were members of the same superordinate category. Three pairs of objects were used for their study: (1) a horn and a flute, (2) a hook and a clip, and (3) a whisk and a pair of tongs. In each pair, they introduced each of the two words only in association with one object each. For example, they taught the word *flute* when presenting only a flute, and *horn* when presenting only a horn. They then examined whether the children would spontaneously extend one of the words (or both words) to the other object in the set. In doing this, they used two measures: children's spontaneous production of these words and their response patterns in a comprehension test.

Waxman and Senghas found intriguing patterns in children's spontaneous production. When two labels (*horn* and *flute*) were given to the horn-flute pair, the children produced one word for both the flute and horn, and the other word only for one of them, suggesting that they interpreted the two words as having an inclusion relation in the lexical hierarchy. Similar results were found with the hook-clip pair. However, importantly, this pattern was observed in only these two sets, in which the two paired objects were relatively similar to each other. When two words were introduced for the whisk-tong pair, which turned out to be less similar than the other sets in adult judgments, the children tended to restrict each word only to the object with which each word was originally associated. This latter production behavior suggests that the children interpreted the two words as mutually exclusive.

The findings from Waxman and Senghas's (1992) study thus indicate that similarity plays an important role for children in determining whether to map the new word onto a category subordinate to the familiar category or to narrow down the old, overextended category and establish a new category contrastive to the old category. Taylor and Gelman (1989) also manipulated similarity, but did not find evidence for the latter process even when the newly labeled object was "dissimilar" by their definition. However, the "dissimilar" test items in their studies were made such that color, size, and material were different from the named objects, and consequently, the shapes of the named objects and the test objects were still fairly similar. In contrast, the items in the whisk-tong pair in Waxman and Senghas's (1992) study were quite different from each other in both shape and function.

We thus conducted two studies to examine whether children are able to shift between the two solutions using similarity as a clue. Since previous research suggests shape similarity is weighed most heavily among different perceptual dimensions in label generalizations (e.g., Landau, Smith, and Jones 1988; Smith, Jones, and Landau 1992), we first manipulated shape similarity.

Two sets of stimuli were used in this study, a ball set and a spoon set. Each set consisted of a standard object and three types of object choices: a subordinate item, typical exemplars of the familiar category, and out-of-category distractors (see figure 13.2a for the contents of the spoon set used in the typical-shape condition). The standard object was an object even 3-year-old children could easily name, and that had a distinct property (e.g., a spoon with notches on the edge of its bowl-like part). The subordinate item was identical to the standard object except for color (of the dots in the ball set, and of the sticker in the spoon set). As typical member items, two other instances of the familiar category, differing in size from one another, were included. They did not have the distinct property of the stan-

(Typical-shape) standard object

Subordinate item   Typical member item   Distractors

a.

(Atypical-shape) standard object   (Atypical-shape) subordinate item

b.

Figure 13.2
Sample stimulus sets used in Haryu and Imai's (2002) study: (a) the ball set used for
the typical-shape condition; (b) the standard and the subordinate item in the ball set
used for the atypical-shape condition.

dard object, but had the same typical shape of the familiar category.
In addition, three objects were used as out-of-category distractors.
The three objects were from two types: two objects from the category
thematically related to the familiar category (that is, two pairs of
shoes for the ball set, and two cups for the spoon set), and one object
from the category used in the other set (that is, a spoon for the ball
set, and a ball for the spoon set).

   Japanese 3-year-olds were assigned to one of two conditions, the
typical-shape condition and the *atypical-shape* condition. The structure

of the stimuli was identical across both conditions. The only difference between the two conditions was in the use of different types of objects as the standard and subordinate items. (See figure 13.2b.) In the atypical-shape condition, the standard object and the subordinate item in both the ball set and the spoon set had an atypical shape for balls and spoons. However, these objects were manufactured and sold as balls (or spoons), and adults indeed recognize them as such.

Since this study examined how Japanese children mapped a new noun when there was an already-known, familiar name for the named object, it was necessary for the children to have considered the standard item and the subordinate item as referents of the familiar basic-level name prior to the introduction of the new word. To ensure this, the children were screened, and only those who called the original object by the familiar basic-level name for both sets were retained for the main test.

In the main test, the original object was labeled with a novel word (e.g., *heku*). Then it was taken out of the child's view, and again presented with the three types of object choices in the set. To examine how the child extended the novel word and the familiar name, the experimenter, pointing to each of the objects in the set, asked the child whether it was a referent of the novel word. After that, the experimenter asked the child whether each object was a referent of the familiar name (e.g., *bouru* (ball)).

The children's response patterns on each trial could be classified into one of the following four categories:

1. *Subordinate response.* A child may use the new word to refer only to the original object and the subordinate item and may use the familiar name to refer to the original object, to the subordinate item, as well as to the typical exemplars of the existing familiar category. If the child showed this behavioral pattern, we interpreted this as indicating that the child understood the new words as having a *subordinate* relation with respect to the category denoted by the familiar word—that is, the child interpreted the new word *heku* as denoting a particular subtype of the larger category of *bouru* (ball).

2. *Synonymous response.* If the child used both the new word and the familiar name in exactly the same way, selecting the original object,

the subordinate item, and the two typical exemplars as referents for both the familiar word and the novel word, she was considered to have interpreted the new word as being *synonymous* with the familiar name.

3. *Cohyponym response.* If the child applied the new word to the original and subordinate item, and excluded these objects from the extension of the familiar word, this response behavior was taken to mean that the child excluded the original object and the subordinate item from the old, familiar category and established a new category that was a *cohyponym* of the old familiar category.

4. *Others.* All other response patterns were placed in the *other* category. This response category included both uninterpretable responses (e.g., accepting the original object and the typical exemplars of the familiar category, but rejecting the subordinate item, as the referents of the novel word) and interpretable but implausible responses (e.g., restricting the novel word only to the original object and not extending it to the subordinate item, indicating a proper-name interpretation).

Japanese children's response behavior was largely different across the two similarity conditions, in a way that was consistent with Waxman and Senghas's (1992) results with English-speaking children. In the typical-shape condition, the children made the subordinate interpretation (41.7%) rather than the cohyponym interpretation (12.5%). In contrast, in the atypical-shape condition, the children made the cohyponym interpretation (68.8%) more often than the subordinate interpretation (8.3%). Thus, typicality of shape of the newly labeled object for the old familiar category greatly affected the children's interpretation of the novel word as well as the familiar word. When the shape of the named object was atypical for the old category, the children excluded the named object from the old category and established a new category that was a cohyponym of, and hence mutually exclusive to, the old category. On the other hand, if the newly labeled object had a typical shape for the familiar category, the children interpreted the word as denoting a new category subordinate to the existing category.

Haryu and Imai (2002) then conducted a follow-up study to see whether the originally preferred interpretation could be altered when a child received explicit information that the newly named atypical member of the old category shared the same function as other members of the old category. As stated earlier, the standard objects in the atypical-shape condition (the oval-shaped ball and the spoon whose bowl was square shaped) in fact were manufactured as balls and spoons, respectively. We thus wished to see whether Japanese children's tendency to exclude the named object from the old category when the named object had a shape dissimilar to other typical members of the familiar category would be altered when they were taught that the atypical-shaped object indeed had the function of the old, familiar category.

It turned out that the children were able to consider this external information to some extent, in that the children who received the common-function information made the subordinate interpretation more often than who did not (27.1% vs. 8.3%). However, the effect of the functional information was not strong enough to overturn their default preference: the cohyponym interpretation still prevailed over the subordinate interpretation (43.7% vs. 27.1%, respectively).

In summary, Haryu and Imai's research demonstrated that Japanese children who had just turned 3 years old are able to control the application/suspension of the mutual-exclusivity bias flexibly and reasonably. That is, they can determine whether to map a novel noun given to a familiar object to a subordinate category or to exclude the named object from the old category in order to establish a new category contrastive to the old one quite appropriately. It should be emphasized that the children did so by spontaneously utilizing the shape of the named object, a cue available in the situation (in fact, in *any* situation) even when the adult did not provide other explicit cues in the input. When the adult did provide explicit information about common function, the children were able to use it also, but this information was not given priority over the shape information.

13.5 Summary: How Do Japanese Children Assign Meanings to Nouns in Different Situations?

The goal of this chapter has been to provide insight into the mechanism of lexical development in light of the findings from Japanese children. To set the stage, we summarized how Japanese children assign meanings to novel nouns in different conditions, comparing similarities and differences between Japanese-speaking and English-speaking children.

First of all, Japanese children spontaneously generalized a newly learned noun to other "like" objects when it was associated with an unfamiliar object, even though the syntax of Japanese did not indicate whether a given noun is a common noun or proper noun. This, together with findings from English-speaking children (e.g., Hall 1991; Hall and Waxman 1993; Markman 1990), suggests that children universally expect that a novel noun refers to a category rather than a unique individual.

Also consistent with previous results from English-speaking children, Japanese children generalized a newly learned label associated with an unfamiliar object on the basis of shape similarity, ignoring the color, size, and material dimensions (Landau, Smith, and Jones 1988; Smith, Jones, and Landau 1992). As a result, they formed a category that approximates a basic-level category (Golinkoff, Mervis, and Hirsh-Pasek 1994; Hall and Waxman 1993).

A bias toward mapping a novel noun to a novel object, which has been characterized as the *mutual-exclusivity bias* (Markman and Wachtel 1988) or the *novel name–nameless category (N3C) principle* (Golinkoff, Mervis, and Hirsh-Pasek 1994), also seems present in Japanese children (Haryu 1991). The results from our recent studies (Haryu and Imai 2002) provide additional insights into the nature of this bias. The fact that the Japanese children interpreted a novel noun as a new name for the familiar object rather than as a material name when both options were available (and the noun's syntactic status was neutral for either interpretation) suggests that children are not unwilling to accept multiple labels for a single object, contrary to what was predicted by the mutual-exclusivity bias. Note that N3C simply predicts that children would map the new label to a category different from the old familiar category in this situation. In this sense, it may appear that the term *N3C* better characterizes the bias than *mutual exclusivity* does.

However, importantly, N3C is inconsistent with the fact that Japanese children interpreted a novel noun given to a familiar animal as a proper name, rather than a category name, although it is still consistent with the principle of contrast (Clark 1987). The principle of contrast is thus most likely to be universally shared by children speaking different languages. However, as discussed earlier, this principle can hardly narrow down the possible meaning of a new word, because it does not specify what meaning the noun should be mapped onto.

Nonetheless, Japanese children in our studies (Imai and Haryu 2001; Haryu and Imai 2002) were not unresponsive in the face of multiple competing possibilities. Although Japanese syntax does not mark the proper-noun versus common-noun distinction, Japanese children interpret a novel label given to a familiar animal as a proper name of the animal, recruiting the semantic-pragmatic knowledge that animals are good candidates for referents of proper nouns, just as English-speaking children do (Katz, Baker, and Macnamara 1974; Gelman and Taylor 1984; Hall 1996b). However, Japanese children are able to learn subordinate-category names for familiar animals, because they showed this interpretation when a novel name was given to the same familiar animal in a compound-noun form, quite similar to the behavior of English-speaking children (Gelman, Wilcox, and Clark 1989). This indicates that Japanese children are able to consider linguistic information in inferring word meaning *when it is available*.

For a novel noun associated with a familiar artifact object, Japanese children ruled out the proper-noun interpretation, again like English-speaking children (Gelman and Taylor 1984). However, the children still had to determine the single best solution out of multiple possibilities. In this situation, they had at least three options: (1) mapping it to a subordinate category; (2) mapping it to a superordinate category; (3) excluding the named object from the old familiar category to establish a new category at the same level as the old category.

Although these three solutions were all possible and plausible, the Japanese children showed a particular preference in a particular condition, and this preference was largely affected by typicality of shape of the named object for the old category. When the newly named object had a typical shape for the old familiar category, they chose option (1), while when the shape was atypical, they selected option (3). It appears that the children selected a particular solution so as to make the resulting category coherent and cohesive, with its members all having a high degree of similarity. In other words, the shape bias helps children constrain the inference about the extension of a word not only for a first label of an unfamiliar object but also for a second label of a familiar object whose first label has been learned.

13.6   Implications for a General Theory of Lexical Development

We have so far discussed how Japanese children infer meanings of novel words. We now discuss the implications we can draw from the Japanese data for a general theory of lexical development.

13.6.1   Coordination among Multiple Constraint Resources

The patterns of word learning in Japanese children summarized above suggest that children are extremely flexible word learners, able to recruit whatever useful resources are available in a given situation. However, it should also be noted that different resources must be appropriately weighed and coordinated so that children do not stop making inferences about word meanings when some of the factors are in conflict. For example, while semantic-pragmatic knowledge of animals and inanimate objects as well as syntactic cues (if available) do help children relax the noun-category bias for learning proper names, the suspension of this bias is difficult unless the labeled object is unfamiliar: when the syntactic information is in conflict with the noun object-category bias for an *unfamiliar* object (i.e., a novel label for an unfamiliar object appears in the proper-noun syntactic frame), this bias is likely to be given priority over the syntactic information (e.g., Hall 1991; Hall, Waxman, and Hurwitz 1993; Markman and Wachtel 1988).

The bias toward mapping a novel noun to a novel object also naturally interacts with other cues, most notably, social-pragmatic information. Direct pointing seems to be one of the most powerful ways to indicate that the object pointed to is the referent of the label. In such a case, even when the named object is already familiar, children seem to accept the novel word as another label for the named object and seem to look for a category containing the object as a member, but one that has a different extension boundary from that of the familiar category. Here, children are unlikely to interpret the label as a material name, presumably because they have a strong perceptual bias toward construing a solid, bounded entity with a complex structure as an individuated object rather than as a portion of a substance (see Imai and Gentner 1997; Imai and Mazuka 2003).

In contrast, when no direct pointing is provided, children's disposition toward mapping a novel word to a novel object leads them to look for a novel object in order to map the label, and this bias appears to be fairly strong. In fact, Haryu's (1991) study, as described earlier, demonstrated that this bias could sometimes override discourse pragmatics in children younger than 3 years of age, if not older. Thus, it seems that not all social-pragmatic cues are weighed equally by young children. A cue such as direct pointing is strong enough to override the bias toward mapping a new word to a novel object, whereas discourse pragmatics may be weaker as a constraint for young children.

Likewise, the bias toward generalizing nouns on the basis of shape (Baldwin 1992; Golinkoff, Mervis, and Hirsh-Pasek 1994; Imai, Gentner, and Uchida 1994; Landau, Smith, and Jones 1988) interacts with, or is constrained by, other types of cues. At one level, ontological knowledge takes precedence over this bias. For example, Japanese children do not generalize a label associated with a substance on the basis of shape, honoring the ontological principle that similarity in shape in its entirety only matters for individuated objects and not for substances, even though the syntactic cue distinguishing the two ontological classes is not available in their native language (Imai and Gentner 1997). However, at another level, shape similarity is often weighed more heavily than taxonomic relatedness or functional commonality, especially when the named object is not familiar to children and hence little prior knowledge is available (Gelman et al. 1998; Imai, Gentner, and Uchida 1994; Smith, Jones, and Landau 1996). The results of our research (Haryu and Imai 2002) provide additional support for this in that the explicit demonstration of common function did not overturn the children's default bias toward excluding a shape-dissimilar member from the old category when the member was given a different label.

13.6.2   Are Word-Learning Biases Necessary for Efficient Word Learning?

We have argued that children recruit multiple sources of information in making inferences about the meanings of new (and sometimes also familiar) words, and that word-learning biases cannot be characterized as the sole force that propels word learning. Like other theorists, we believe that word learning is most successful when multiple sources of information are redundantly available and converge to a single solution (Bloom 1993; Hollich, Hirsh-Pasek, and Golinkoff 2000; Woodward and Markman 1998). On the other hand, we disagree with the view that word-learning biases are not necessary (P. Bloom 1994; L. Bloom 1993; Nelson 1988; Tomasello 1997). For efficient word learning, it is important that children have a system that allows them to make a reasonable and plausible inference about the meaning of a newly introduced word even when little prior knowledge about the named object or few external resources to rely on are available for the inference. Word-learning biases serve this purpose, providing children with a default solution when other constraints are not immediately available in a given situation. In other words, these internal biases about word meanings make it possible for young children to make the single most plausible inference about the meaning of a given word even when other resources are sparse. This mechanism is particularly needed for Japanese children, since one very useful source of constraints—that is, the noun's form class information—is always lacking in the input.

   The studies we have reviewed above showed that word-learning biases may sometimes override other sources of constraints that are provided externally, such as discourse pragmatics (Haryu 1991), syntactic form class information (Hall 1991; Markman and Wachtel 1988), and functional information (Smith, Jones, and Landau 1996; Haryu and Imai 2002). Again, this does not mean that young children cannot spontaneously utilize these sources of information. But it is reasonable for very young children to weigh internal assumptions more heavily than externally provided information when they do not have much prior knowledge about the newly named object. In other words, it appears that word-learning biases prevail over externally provided cues when the named object is novel to the child. In contrast, when the named object is familiar, children in general are able to relax the biases by flexibly coordinating externally provided cues (e.g., Hall 1991; Imai and Haryu 2001). We speculate that children gain flexibility in the use of the biases as they mature and become more experienced word learners; eventually they are able to override the biases easily when other sources of information such as syntax or social-pragmatic cues indicate otherwise, even when a named object is novel.

13.6.3 The Nature of Word-Learning Biases

We thus conclude that children possess internal assumptions about how words should be mapped to their referents and how they should be generalized, and that these word-learning biases indeed play an important role in efficient word learning. However, let us note that such a conclusion does not lead to a commitment to view these biases as being innately endowed constraints. The studies reviewed in this chapter mainly deal with 2-year-olds or older children who were already fairly experienced word learners. We thus have little idea whether 10- to 12-month-olds who are learning their first words have the same biases as those exhibited by 2-year-old children. However, given how children flexibly and reasonably control the application of word-learning biases by other types of internal knowledge and external cues, we speculate that word-learning biases are better characterized as part of a rich, interconnected body of knowledge about the world and the lexicon children have built up in the course of linguistic as well as nonlinguistic learning experiences than as domain-specific, innate learning principles.

References

Baldwin, D. A. 1992. Clarifying the role of shape in children's taxonomic assumption. *Journal of Experimental Child Psychology, 54*, 392–416.

Banigan, R. L., and Mervis, C. B. 1988. Role of adult input in young children's category evolution: An experimental study. *Journal of Child Language, 15,* 493–504.

Bloom, L. 1993. *The transition from infancy to language: Acquiring the power of expression.* New York: Cambridge University Press.

Bloom, L., Tinker, T., and Margulis, C. 1993. The words children learn: Evidence against a noun bias in early vocabularies. *Cognitive Development, 8,* 431–450.

Bloom, P. 1994. Possible names: The role of syntax-semantics mappings in the acquisition of nominals. *Lingua, 92,* 297–329.

Bloom, P., and Kelemen, D. 1995. Syntactic cues in the acquisition of collective nouns. *Cognition, 56,* 1–30.

Clark, E. V. 1973. What's in a word? On the child's acquisition of semantics in his first language. In T. E. Moore, ed., *Cognitive development and the acquisition of language,* 65–110. New York: Academic Press.

Clark, E. V. 1987. The principle of contrast: A constraint on language acquisition. In B. MacWhinney, ed., *Mechanisms of language acquisition.* Hillsdale, NJ: Erlbaum.

Clark, E. V., and Svaib, T. A. 1997. Speaker perspective and reference in young children. *First Language, 17,* 57–74.

Dickinson, D. 1988. Learning names for materials: Factors constraining and limiting hypotheses about word meaning. *Cognitive Development, 3,* 15–35.

Gelman, S. A., Croft, W., Fu, P., Clausner, T., and Gottfried, G. 1998. Why is a pomegranate an apple? The role of shape, taxonomic relatedness, and prior lexical knowledge in children's overextensions of *apple* and *dog. Journal of Child Language, 25,* 267–291.

Gelman, S. A., and Taylor, M. 1984. How two-year-old children interpret proper and common names for unfamiliar objects. *Child Development, 55,* 1535–1540.

Gelman, S. A., Wilcox, S. A., and Clark, E. V. 1989. Conceptual and lexical hierarchies in young children. *Cognitive Development, 4,* 309–326.

Golinkoff, R. M., Hirsh-Pasek, K., Bailey, L. M., and Wenger, N. R. 1992. Young children and adults use lexical principles to learn new nouns. *Developmental Psychology, 28,* 99–108.

Golinkoff, R. M., Mervis, C. B., and Hirsh-Pasek, K. 1994. Early object labels: The case for a developmental lexical principles framework. *Journal of Child Language, 21,* 125–155.

Hall, D. G. 1991. Acquiring proper nouns for familiar and unfamiliar animate objects: Two-year-olds' word-learning biases. *Child Development, 62,* 1142–1154.

Hall, D. G. 1996a. Naming solids and nonsolids: Children's default construals. *Cognitive Development, 11,* 229–264.

Hall, D. G. 1996b. Preschoolers' default assumptions about word meaning: Proper names designate unique individuals. *Developmental Psychology, 32,* 177–186.

Hall, D. G., Lee, S. C., and Bélanger, J. 2001. Young children's use of syntactic cues to learn proper names and count nouns. *Developmental Psychology, 37,* 298–307.

Hall, D. G., and Waxman, S. 1993. Assumptions about word meaning: Individuation and basic-level kinds. *Child Development, 64,* 1550–1570.

Hall, D. G., Waxman, S. R., and Hurwitz, W. M. 1993. How 2- and 4-year-old children interpret adjectives and count nouns. *Child Development, 64,* 1651–1664.

Haryu, E. 1991. A developmental study of children's use of mutual exclusivity and context to interpret novel words. *Japanese Journal of Educational Psychology, 39,* 11–20. (In Japanese with English summary.)

Haryu, E., and Imai, M. 1999. Controlling the application of the mutual exclusivity assumption in the acquisition of lexical hierarchies. *Japanese Psychological Research, 41*(1), 21–34.

Haryu, E., and Imai, M. 2002. Reorganizing the lexicon by learning a new word: Japanese children's interpretation of the meaning of a new word for a familiar artifact. *Child Development, 73,* 1378–1391.

Hollich, G. J., Hirsh-Pasek, K., and Golinkoff, R. M. 2000. Breaking the language barrier: An emergentist coalition model for the origins of word learning. *Monographs of the Society for Research in Child Development, 65*(3) (serial no. 262).

Imai, M. 1999. Constraint on word learning constraints. *Japanese Psychological Research, 41,* 5–20.

Imai, M. 2000. Universal ontological knowledge and a bias toward language-specific categories in the construal of individuation. In S. Niemeier and R. Dirven, eds., *Evidence for linguistic relativity.* Amsterdam: Benjamins.

Imai, M., and Gentner, D. 1997. A crosslinguistic study of early word meaning: Universal ontology and linguistic influence. *Cognition, 62,* 169–200.

Imai, M., Gentner, D., and Uchida, N. 1994. Children's theories of word meaning: The role of shape similarity in early acquisition. *Cognitive Development, 9,* 45–75.

Imai, M., and Haryu, E. 2001. Learning proper nouns and common nouns without clues from syntax. *Child Development, 72,* 787–802.

Imai, M., and Mazuka, R. 2003. Re-evaluation of linguistic relativity: Language-specific categories and the role of universal ontological knowledge in the construal of individuation. In D. Gentner and S. Goldin-Meadow, eds., *Language in mind: Advances in the issues of language and thought,* 429–464. Cambridge, MA: MIT Press.

Katz, N., Baker, E., and Macnamara, J. 1974. What's in a name? A study of how children learn common names. *Child Development, 45,* 469–473.

Landau, B., Smith, L. B., and Jones, S. S. 1988. The importance of shape in early lexical learning. *Cognitive Development, 3*, 299–321.

Markman, E. M. 1990. Constraints children place on word meanings. *Cognitive Science, 14*, 57–77.

Markman, E. M., and Hutchinson, J. E. 1984. Children's sensitivity to constraints on word meaning: Taxonomic versus thematic relations. *Cognitive Psychology, 16*, 1–27.

Markman, E. M., and Wachtel, G. F. 1988. Children's use of mutual exclusivity to constrain the meanings of words. *Cognitive Psychology, 20*, 121–157.

Merriman, W. E. 1986. Some reasons for the occurrence and eventual correction of children's naming errors. *Child Development, 57*, 942–952.

Merriman, W. E., and Bowman, L. L. 1989. The mutual exclusivity bias in children's word learning. *Monographs of the Society for Research in Child Development, 54* (serial no. 220).

Mervis, C. B., Golinkoff, R. M., and Bertrand, J. 1994. Two-year-olds readily learn multiple labels for the same basic level category. *Child Development, 65*, 971–991.

Nelson, K. 1988. Constraints on word learning? *Cognitive Development, 3*, 221–246.

Nelson, K., Hampson, J., and Shaw, L. K. 1993. Nouns in early lexicons: Evidence, explanations, and implications. *Journal of Child Language, 20*, 61–84.

Prasada, S. 1993. Learning names for solid substances: Quantifying solid entities in terms of portions. *Cognitive Development, 8*, 83–104.

Smith, L. B., Jones, S., and Landau, B. 1992. Count nouns, adjectives, and perceptual properties in children's novel word interpretations. *Developmental Psychology, 28*, 273–286.

Smith, L. B., Jones, S., and Landau, B. 1996. Naming in children: A dumb attentional mechanism? *Cognition, 60*, 143–171.

Soja, N. N. 1992. Inferences about the meanings of nouns: The relationship between perception and syntax. *Cognitive Development, 7*, 29–45.

Soja, N. N., Carey, S., and Spelke, E. S. 1991. Ontological categories guide young children's inductions of word meaning: Object terms and substance terms. *Cognition, 38*, 179–211.

Subrahmanyam, K., Landau, B., and Gelman, R. 1999. Shape, material, and syntax: Interacting forces in children's learning in novel words for objects and substances. *Language and Cognitive Processes, 14*, 249–281.

Taylor, M., and Gelman, S. A. 1989. Incorporating new words into the lexicon: Preliminary evidence for language hierarchies in two-year-old children. *Child Development, 60*, 625–636.

Tomasello, M. 1997. The pragmatics of word learning. *Bulletin of the Japanese Cognitive Science Society, 4*, 59–74.

Waxman, S. R. 1999. Specifying the scope of 13-month-olds' expectations for novel words. *Cognition, 70*, 35–50.

Waxman, S. R., and Markow, D. B. 1995. Words as invitations to form categories: Evidence from 12- to 13-month-old infants. *Cognitive Psychology, 29*, 257–302.

Waxman, S. R., and Markow, D. B. 1998. Object properties and object kind: 21-month-old infants' extension of novel adjectives. *Child Development, 69*, 1313–1329.

Waxman, S. R., and Senghas, A. 1992. Relations among word meanings in early lexical development. *Developmental Psychology, 28*, 862–873.

Waxman, S. R., Senghas, A., and Benveniste, S. 1997. A cross-linguistic examination of the noun-category bias: Its existence and specificity in French- and Spanish-speaking preschool-aged children. *Cognitive Psychology, 32*, 183–218.

Woodward, A. L., and Markman, E. M. 1998. Early word learning. In W. Damon, series ed., and D. K. Kuhn and R. S. Siegler, vol. eds., *Handbook of child psychology, Vol. 2: Cognition, perception, and language*, 5th ed., 371–420. New York: Wiley.

14

Learning Words for Kinds: Generic Noun Phrases in Acquisition

Susan A. Gelman

14.1 Introduction

"Mommy sock."
—Kathryn, age 1;9; Bloom 1970

"Tigers are bad."
—Ross, age 2;9; MacWhinney 1991

Every language has the capacity to refer to kinds, with nouns such as *sock* and *tiger*. Yet how nouns are used can vary considerably, as illustrated in the two sample sentences above. Whereas Kathryn's utterance refers to a particular member of a kind (one sock), Ross's refers to a kind construed more broadly (tigers in general). This second sort of expression is the focus of the present chapter. Kind-referring expressions, such as "Tigers are bad," are also known as *generics* (Dahl 1975; Carlson and Pelletier 1995).

Generic noun phrases are expressed in English with multiple formal devices, including bare plurals (e.g., "Bats live in caves"), definite singulars (e.g., "The elephant is found in Africa and Asia"), and indefinite articles (e.g., "A male goose is called a gander"). What all these expressions have in common is a conceptual basis: they refer to a kind as a whole. Generics are interesting in the study of word learning for two primary—and seemingly contradictory—reasons: generic knowledge is vital to human reasoning, yet at the same time it presents a formidable induction problem for learners.

14.1.1 Centrality of Generic Knowledge

Kinds organize knowledge and guide inferences about the unknown. Psychological studies demonstrate that thinking about kinds leads people to make rich inferences about the world (e.g., Gelman and Markman 1986; Gopnik and Meltzoff 1997; Shipley 1993). Once one learns that something is a member of a kind (for example, that a pterodactyl is a dinosaur), one tends to infer that the entity shares properties with others of the same kind (Gelman and Coley 1990; Gelman and Markman 1986, 1987). "Category-based" reasoning is predicated of kinds (Osherson et al. 1990). More generally, "semantic" (vs. episodic) memory (e.g., Collins and Quillian 1969) tends to be generic.

Furthermore, generics refer to qualities that are relatively essential, enduring, and timeless—not accidental, transient, or tied to context (Lyons 1977). Thus, generics imply that a category is a coherent, stable entity. However, unlike utterances containing universal quantifiers such as *all, every,* or *each,* generic statements allow for exceptions. Although a generic statement applies broadly to a category, it is not considered false by the presence of individual category members for whom the property does not apply (e.g., a dog who has lost a leg in an accident). In addition, generics may not even be true for a majority of category members (McCawley 1981). For example, the generic statement "Birds lay eggs" persists, though it applies to less than half of the category of birds (excluding males and infants; Gelman et al. 1998). As a result, facts stated generically may be particularly robust against counterevidence. For instance, whereas even a single counterexample would negate the generalization "All girls are bad at math," the generic statement "Girls are bad at math" can persist in the face of numerous counterexamples.

In sum, generic knowledge is foundational in human thought, including memory representations and category-based reasoning.

14.1.2 Induction Problems Posed by Generics

Despite the importance of generic knowledge, generics pose two sorts of induction problems for learners. First, when encountering any phenomenon (e.g., a child sees a picture in a book of two horses eating hay), how can the child know if this observation generalizes to others of the same kind? For instance, do horses in general eat hay, or just the horses in this book? I refer to this as the *problem of generic knowledge* (see Prasada 2000). The child must also determine which broader kind the generalization applies to. For example, is it more appropriate to infer that horses eat hay, that farm animals eat hay, or that animals eat hay? A second, related inductive problem concerns language interpretation. When hearing an utterance, how can the child determine if the speaker has a generic interpretation in mind, or something else? For instance, a caregiver may say to a child either "The horses are eating hay" or "Horses eat hay." How is the child to figure out which utterance is kind-referring? I refer to this as the *problem of generic language*. Both induction problems must be solved for children to have a full understanding of generics.

14.1 What This Chapter Is About

This chapter concerns how generic noun phrases are acquired in early childhood. I first present in more detail the nature of the twin inductive puzzles that children face. I then review a series of studies demonstrating that, despite the challenging inductive burden, parents freely talk about generic kinds in their speech to young children, and children in turn readily acquire generic noun phrases by about $2\frac{1}{2}$ years of age. I then turn to the implications of these findings for broader theories of word learning. Specifically, I put forth two speculative proposals: First, children exploit multiple sources of information (including powerful conceptual biases, formal morpho-syntactic cues, contextual cues, and theory-based knowledge) to solve the problem of generic language. Second, generic language is itself an important source of information that guides children as they work to solve the problem of generic knowledge. I will end by arguing that generics illustrate, in a microcosm, the importance of naive theories in acquiring linguistic forms, and the importance of linguistic forms in informing naive theories.

14.2 The Inductive Problems of Generics

In this section, I lay out more explicitly the nature of the inductive problems posed by generics, focusing first on the problem of generic knowledge (which information to generalize, and to which kinds), and then on the problem of generic language (which utterances are kind-referring). This rather extensive preamble is important in order to highlight the depth of the puzzle that generics pose for a theory of acquisition.

14.2.1 Problem of Generic Knowledge

Prasada (2000, 66) concisely states the problem of generic knowledge: "How do we acquire knowledge about kinds of things if we have experience with only a limited number of examples of the kinds in question?" For example, how is it that we possess such rich and varied beliefs (horses eat hay; lima beans are detestable; Midwesterners are friendly; birds lay eggs; cars are expensive; and so on)? This knowledge cannot be reduced to knowledge of statistical regularities (Prasada 2000). Certainly we have relatively little direct experience with the full set of instances of any of these kinds. In my life, I may have eaten lima beans no more than ten times, yet I have a strong belief that lima beans—as a kind—are detestable. Indeed, in some cases people have experience with only a single instance, yet generalize that information to the broader kind. What allows us to go from a sample of ten, or even one, and to generalize to the kind as a whole (representing an untold multitude of instances)?

The problem of generic knowledge is all the more difficult in that counterexamples do not invalidate generic beliefs (McCawley 1981). Thus, if I assert that Midwesterners are friendly, and you argue that they are not, I am not going to back down if confronted with the existence of an unfriendly Midwesterner. Certainly stereotypes (which typically entail generic beliefs about human kinds) persist despite little or no direct supporting evidence.

Note that frequent experience would not solve the problem. The induction problem would persist even if we had extensive experience with members of a kind, because no amount of personal experience or direct contact can give us access to the abstract kind in its entirety. Even in the case of, say, an endangered species with only four living exemplars on earth, experience with each and every existing instance would not give us access to the kind as a whole, because the kind includes past, future, and potential instances.

Indeed, I would claim that generics can never be displayed, except symbolically. Although one can *talk* about the distinction between a kind and members of a kind, one cannot directly demonstrate or illustrate the distinction. For example, although one can show a child one (specific) dog, one cannot show a child the generic class of dogs. Likewise, one can never demonstrate, with actual exemplars, photos, or drawings, the distinction between a generic kind (rabbits) versus a plurality of instances (some rabbits). As Waxman (1999, 243) notes, "Members of object categories are distinct, and often disparate, individuals that tend to appear at different times and places.... It would be logically impossible for caretakers to assemble together all members of an object category to model explicitly the extension of the category name." Thus, generic noun phrases exemplify in especially sharp relief the well-known induction problem discussed by Quine (1960) when considering naming.

The problem of generalizing from a particular example to a kind is compounded by ambiguity regarding which kind to consider. Each object is at once a member of a varied set of categories (e.g., the same object is at once Marie, a cat, a pet, a mammal, a vertebrate, and so on), thus raising the question of how one selects the level of abstraction to which a property applies (e.g., the body temperature of your pet cat). Thus, the human capacity to generalize brings with it the question of how this capacity is constrained (Goodman 1973).

In sum, although generic knowledge is a ubiquitous feature of human thought, it requires inferential leaps that extend beyond what we can know directly from our senses.

14.2.2   Problem of Generic Language

In addition to the conceptual issues raised above, the question of how children identify an utterance as generic is exacerbated by the complexity of mapping between formal and semantic cues. Simply put, there is no one-to-one mapping between form and meaning, in the case of English generics. Command of the generic-nongeneric distinction in English requires, at the very least, morphosyntactic cues, contextual cues, and world knowledge. Thus, the use and interpretation of generics depend on a cluster of factors, all of which are important, but none of which are individually sufficient.

Morphosyntactic Cues

In English, generics can be expressed with definite singulars, bare plurals, or indefinite singulars (Lyons 1977):

a. *The bird* is a warm-blooded animal.
b. *A cat* has nine lives.
c. *Dinosaurs* are extinct.

They can be contrasted with nongeneric expressions such as the following:

d. *The bird* is flying.
e. *A cat* caught two mice.
f. There are *dinosaurs* in that museum.
g. *The bears* are huge.

Note that three of the four nongeneric examples given above match the formal properties of the noun phrases in the generic examples (the exception being (g)). Thus, generics in English are not uniquely identified with a particular form of the noun phrase, but instead are cued by a variety of additional indications, including the form of the verb. Specifically, there are at least four morphosyntactic cues that help a speaker identify an utterance as generic or nongeneric: determiners, number (i.e., singular vs. plural), tense, and aspect.

Determiners and *number* jointly operate to indicate genericity. In English, a plural noun phrase preceded by the definite determiner (*the*) cannot be generic. For example, "Bears are huge" has a generic reading, but "The bears are huge" does not. Neither determiners nor number alone indicate whether a noun phrase is generic. However, it is the interaction of the two (i.e., definiteness plus plurality) that provides information regarding genericity. Aside from this restriction, generics can use definite or indefinite articles, can be singular or plural, and can include both naming expressions ("The elephant likes peanuts") and describing expressions ("A cat that has stomach trouble eats grass") (examples from Bhat 1979, 139).

Tense is also an indication of genericity. With the exception of historic past (e.g., "*Woolly mammoths* roamed the earth many years ago"), past-tense utterances are not generic. For instance, we distinguish between "A cow says 'moo'" (generic) and "A cow said 'moo'" (nongeneric). Likewise, "The lion is ferocious" can have either a generic or a nongeneric reading, whereas "The lion was ferocious" has only a nongeneric reading. Finally, *aspect* is an important cue in English for distinguishing generic from nongeneric interpretations. For example, a statement in the simple present, such as "Cats meow," is generic, whereas a statement in the present progressive, such as "Cats are meowing," is nongeneric.

Thus, in English, some of the formal cues relevant to whether a noun phrase is generic include articles, plurality, tense, and aspect. The cues can compete (e.g., "A cat caught two mice" has a potentially generic noun phrase but a decidedly nongeneric verb), in this example with the nongeneric verb winning out in the semantic interpretation. A striking example of how the cues interact can be seen with the following set of sentences:

Do you like the mango? (specific)
Do you like mango? (generic)
Would you like mango? (indefinite ("some"))

Whether the noun phrase includes the determiner is not decisive, nor is the verb decisive. It is the combination of the determiner and the verb that is important. However, even here the formal cues are not entirely decisive, as can be seen when we consider "Would you like mango, if you were a monkey?" (in which *mango* could have a generic reading, even though the first portion is identical to the nongeneric indefinite sentence). Thus, even when we consider all formal cues simultaneously, they are insufficient to determine with any certainty whether a noun phrase is generic or not. This issue is elaborated below.

Contextual Cues
Contextual cues are also central to the identification of generics. By this, I mean the construction of the sentence, as well as extrasentential information that surrounds the utterance in discourse. Compare the two sentences that follow:

Dingoes live in Australia.
There are dingoes in Australia.

The first implies a generic reading, asserting of dingoes (as a kind) that they live in Australia. In contrast, the second implies a non-generic reading: some subset of dingoes live in Australia, others may live elsewhere. The relevant distinction here is neither the form of the noun phrase nor the tense or aspect of the verb, but rather the sentence construction.

A second sort of contextual cue involves the resolution of anaphoric references involving *they*.

"This is a tapir. They like to eat grubs."
"These are my tapirs. They like to eat grubs."

The first *they* implies a generic reading (the class of tapirs); the second *they* implies a particular reading (my tapirs). In both cases, *they* refers to a plurality, but in the first example the plurality is one that is alluded to and inferred, rather than present in the immediate context. This rather subtle implication is one that children will need to master.

A further influence concerns the semantic context, as established by prior speech and knowledge. For example, consider the two rather fanciful scenarios below:

Person 1: What color fur do blickets have?
Person 2: A blicket has purple spots.

Person 1: Something in this room has purple spots. What is it?
Person 2: A blicket has purple spots.

Intuition suggests that a generic reading is more likely in the first case than in the second (which more powerfully supports an indefinite interpretation than a generic interpretation).

World-Knowledge Cues
World knowledge can exert influences on generic interpretation, even when formal cues are kept constant. One major way is via the verb. For example, compare:

I like rice.
I want rice.

Whereas the first refers to a generic kind (rice), the second refers to an indefinite sample of the kind (equivalent to "some rice"). Indeed, note that *some* can be inserted in the second example without changing its meaning, but cannot be inserted in the first example without changing its meaning.

Likewise, the predicate can influence interpretation of the noun. Some predicates (e.g., "are extinct") require a generic reading. But the importance of semantic information is more widespread. Compare the following two sentences:

A horse is vegetarian.
A horse is sick.

Both examples have a noun phrase "a horse" that is indefinite singular; both have a predicate that is present nonprogressive. However, whereas the first example could readily be interpreted as kind-referring (meaning that horses usually or ordinarily are vegetarian), the latter is unlikely to receive a generic reading. Being sick is (typically) predicated of individuals rather than of kinds.

Yet this is complicated even further by content knowledge. For example, "A pot is dirty" is unlikely to be interpreted as generic, yet "A pig is dirty" could very well be generic. The only distinction is that we know that pigs, as a class, are reputed to be dirty by their nature. We do not wish to suggest that morphosyntactic cues are irrelevant here. For example, "Horses are sick" sounds odd, because the form pulls strongly for a generic reading whereas the content pulls strongly for a nongeneric reading, leaving it difficult to interpret.

Tense, too, though a fairly reliable marker of whether an utterance is intended to be generic, is fallible. Historic past provides an exception to the generalization that generics are present tense. For example, "Saber-toothed tigers roamed the earth many years ago" is stated in the past because the species is extinct, but the utterance is still generic. We know this, again, by means of world knowledge.

Precisely which properties are interpreted as more or less generic is itself a nontrivial cognitive question beyond the scope of this chapter. The point that is relevant here, and one to which I return in the conclusion, is that presumably the naive theories that children and adults construct are important to making this determination.

Summary
A wealth of factors—including a cluster of morphosyntactic cues (regarding determiners, plurality, tense, and aspect), discourse context, world knowledge, and perhaps prosody—appear to determine whether an utterance receives a generic or nongeneric reading by adults. In the final section we return to the question of *why* generics receive such varied expression. For now, this discussion highlights the daunting inductive task that children face in acquiring the means for producing and interpreting generics in English.

14.3 Empirical Investigations of Generic Concepts and Language

Do children have access to generic knowledge and generic language? The analysis provided above might seem to render the acquisition problem difficult or impossible. Indeed, it is at least theoretically possible that children would avoid the realm of generics until they reach an age when they can talk about all sorts of abstractions, such as "freedom" or "injustice." But no—evidence is mounting that generics are basic to children's concepts. To preview our argument, we will suggest that early language learners must have some sophisticated conceptual machinery to accomplish this.

We start with the notion of kind, which we take to be a prerequisite to generic understanding. There is some controversy concerning the age at which children first have a notion of kind (e.g., Xu and Carey 1996; Wilcox and Baillargeon 1998; Balaban and Waxman 1997; Mandler 1992). Nonetheless, most investigators grant children a notion of kind by the time of their first words (at about 1 year of age). It is widely acknowledged that kinds are foundational to the use of sortal nouns (Macnamara 1986), and that a distinction between kinds and other concepts (e.g., individuals, properties) underlies various linguistic form class distinctions (e.g., proper vs. common nouns; Hall and Waxman 1993; Markman 1989). There is also excellent evidence that by 2 years of age children use syntactic information (e.g., "This is a zav" vs. "This is zav") to distinguish names for individuals from names for object categories (Hall, Lee, and Bélanger 2001; see also Katz, Baker, and Macnamara 1974; Gelman and Taylor 1984).

How about work focusing on kinds per se—that is, generic knowledge? There is indirect evidence for early generic understanding by preschool age. Children as young as 3 or 4 years of age make kind-based inductive inferences, and even cite membership in the kind as justification for such inferences. For example, Gelman (1988) asked 4-year-old children to make novel inductive inferences concerning biologically relevant properties (e.g., eats alfalfa) from one item (e.g., a rabbit) to others either sharing kind membership (e.g., another rabbit; a dog) or not (e.g., a telephone). Children tended to justify inductions by citing the category membership of the items sharing the property (e.g., "Because it's a rabbit" or "Because it's an animal"). In contrast, they did not cite category membership when making inductions of nongeneralizable properties (e.g., is cold). (See also Prasada 2000 for discussion.) Kind-based inductions do not seem to be simply a matter of generalizing based on some other features that correlate with kind membership, because kind-based inferences are common even when the kind is posed in conflict with perceptual information (e.g., Gelman and Markman 1986; Gelman and Coley 1990). Furthermore, when pictures are unnamed, variations in the extent to which children make kind-based inferences can be linked directly to the extent to which children recognize that pictures belong to the same kind (Gelman and Markman 1987).

More direct evidence for generic understanding and use focuses on interpretation and production of generic language. There are scattered examples in the literature—some anecdotal—that preschool children produce generics. For example, Shipley (1989) mentions that, in her studies, preschool children (some as young as 3 years of age) referred to animal kinds with statements including: "Dogs go ruff-ruff and them have long tails" or "Animals can't talk"—both of which are generic. Similar examples can be found in Adams and Bullock 1986 and Callanan 1990.

We have begun to look directly at generic comprehension and production in speech directed to children and in children's own speech. We review four types of evidence below: generics in parental speech, generics in children's speech (production), children's semantic interpretation of generics, and impact of generics on children's inductive inferences. The research endeavor is ongoing and the work opens up as many questions as it answers (some of which I mention in the concluding section). Nonetheless, the point I emphasize is that preschool children readily use and understand generic language. This in turn provides clues regarding the conceptual capacities of young children—a point to which I turn in the final section of the chapter.

14.3.1 Generics in Parental Speech

First, the question of input is important to determine the frequency of generics in ordinary speech (particularly speech that children are likely to hear). Because past studies of generics have focused exclusively on linguistic and philosophical analyses, they have left wide open the question of how frequently (or conversely, how rarely) these expressions are produced. The psychological significance of generic language must rest in part on this issue. What we find (reviewed below) is that generics are surprisingly common in ordinary speech, with the vast majority of parents producing at least one generic during a brief interaction with their child.

Second, input data is critical for determining whether the sorts of inductive puzzles noted earlier still apply, in the speech that children hear. For example, if parents selectively use only one morphosyntactic form for signaling generics, if contextual cues are not needed, and so on, then this could be a means of simplifying the inductive puzzle for children. Instead, however, what we find, through a series of converging studies, is that parental input retains the complexity of mapping, thereby *not* greatly simplifying the inductive task that children face.

Third, a study of input language allows us to determine the contexts that elicit generic talk. I mean "contexts" loosely, to include domain, activity, and language. In part this is a purely logistical issue, because we wished to scout out the contexts that would most readily allow us to examine generics, in later studies focusing on children. But the contexts question is also of great theoretical interest, because it sheds light on how generic language is distinct from nongeneric language.

Frequency in Input

We first studied generics as one component of an intensive study examining how parents convey information about category structure, beyond simple labeling, during naturalistic interactions (Gelman et al. 1998). Mothers and their 20- or 35-month-old children read picture books together. Sessions were videotaped and coded extensively for a variety of explicit and implicit talk and gestures concerning categories.

One key finding concerning generics is that they were surprisingly common in maternal speech. Nearly all of the mothers made at least one statement including a generic noun phrase during the brief picture-book reading session. Mothers used generics for both relatively familiar categories (e.g., "*Kitty cats* love to unravel yarn") and relatively unfamiliar categories (e.g., "*A wok* is how people in China cook. Well, actually, *a wok* is how people in America cook like Chinese people."). They talked about the category as a whole even when all they could see on the page was a single instance ("That's a chipmunk. And *they* eat the acorns."). In a follow-up project (Pappas and Gelman 1998), mother-child pairs were videotaped while looking through a book of animal pictures. The data replicated the findings of Gelman et al. (1998), with nearly every mother (92%) producing at least one generic during the brief book-reading session.

Complexity of Form-Function Mapping

What about the mapping between form and function? This was complex even in maternal speech to these young children. One indication of complexity was that mothers used multiple forms to indicate generics, most commonly including bare plural (e.g., "Oh, how come *cars* don't, don't fly?"), plural pronoun ("'Cause *they* have a long nose"), and indefinite singular ("What's *a chicken* say?"). Thus, generics were not restricted to a single morphological type. Of the mothers who produced at least one generic, only 21 percent restricted themselves to only one or another of these three forms. Moreover, even focusing just on the singular-plural distinction, we still find extensive variability in the forms produced: 47 percent of mothers produced both singular and plural forms within a single session, 34 percent produced plural forms only, and 18 percent produced singular forms only. Mothers at times even alternated between singular and plural within a sentence ("Did you know when *a pig* gets to be big, *they*'re called hogs?"; "*Bats* are *one* of those animals that is awake all night").

A second indication of the complexity of the form-function mapping was that forms used generically were also used nongenerically in the transcripts. Thus, for example, the indefinite plural was used both generically ("A chipmunk's a little smaller than a squirrel") and nongenerically ("That's a chipmunk"). Likewise, the bare plural was used both generically ("Where do bats live?") and nongenerically ("They are bats"). We noted only one respect in which the input does simplify the mapping problem for children: the definite singular form (e.g., "The anteater has a long tongue") was apparently never used. Altogether, these results indicate that the input does not solve the mapping problem for children.

Domain Specificity

A striking feature of mothers' generics in the Gelman et al. 1998 study is that they were domain specific, appearing significantly more frequently for animals than for artifacts. The domain differences in generic usage cannot be attributed to familiarity of the category, similarity among category members, thematic relatedness among category members, or amount of maternal talk. We controlled for similarity and thematic relatedness by selecting the stimulus materials from a larger set of items that were pretested on adults, and we controlled for familiarity and amount of talk by conducting analyses that took into consideration the amount of talk and maternal ratings of child familiarity. The domain differences are also unlikely to be attributable to lack of sufficient knowledge about the artifacts. Mothers certainly knew several category-general properties true of each artifact depicted (including its parts, function, thematic associates, and appearance), and mentioned many of these properties in reference to *particular* objects and contexts. Importantly, though, mothers typically failed to mention these properties in generic form.

Why, then, did animals elicit so many more generics than artifacts did? We interpret this result as reflecting conceptual differences

Learning Words for Kinds

between animal and artifact categories. On the assumption that mothers construe animal kinds as more richly structured than artifact kinds (deeper similarities, greater coherence, and so on), they should more easily conceptualize animal categories as abstract wholes, and hence use generics.

Generics in Mandarin
Mandarin provides an interesting contrast to English, because it lacks three of the grammatical distinctions used to identify generics in English (articles, plurality, and tense). A fourth grammatical distinction (aspect) does not always appear in Mandarin, and is even ungrammatical with some verb types (Li and Bowerman 1998). As a consequence, there are sentences in Mandarin that could be translated as either generic or nongeneric in English (Krifka 1995). For example, the following sentence:

xiao3 ya1zi yao2yao2bai3bai3 de zou3 lu4
little duck waddlingly   DE walk road

could be translated in any of three different ways:

h. The duck is waddling.
i. The ducks are waddling.
j. Ducks waddle. / A duck waddles.

Only the third is generic. This does not mean that Mandarin fails to express generics. There are subtle semantic and pragmatic cues that may help clarify the status of an utterance (Krifka 1995). For example, the *absence* of specific number, time, or place markers can imply a generic interpretation. Nonetheless, the absence of particular morphosyntactic cues, such as articles, plurality, tense, and (sometimes) aspect, means that the expression of generics is less overt in Mandarin than in English. Of course, as noted earlier, English generics are also detected in part on the basis of contextual cues, such as the absence of specific time and place markers. Thus, the marking of English generics is not wholly unambiguous, and the difference between English and Mandarin is a difference of degree rather than a qualitative difference.

There is in fact a longstanding but previously untested claim that these linguistic differences lead to corresponding conceptual differences in how speakers of Mandarin versus English think about generic kinds (Bloom 1981; Moser 1996). Bloom (1981, 38) states the linguistic relativity hypothesis most starkly: "The Chinese language does not have any mechanism ... with which to signal the generic concept." He also suggests: "Perhaps the fact that English has a distinct way of marking the generic concept plays an important role in leading English speakers, by contrast to their Chinese counterparts, to develop schemas specifically designed for creating extracted theoretical entities, such as the theoretical buffalo, and hence for coming to view and use such entities as supplementary elements of their cognitive worlds" (p. 36). Thus, Bloom's suggestion has two parts: (1) that generics have no means of expression in Chinese, and (2) that this linguistic difference leads to corresponding conceptual differences. Yet Bloom's evidence for this position was insufficient, on his own admission (p. 36), resting on a task that required Mandarin speakers to render a difficult metalinguistic judgment of a single sentence, with no comparison group of English speakers.

Twila Tardif and I conducted a crosslinguistic study of generic noun phrases, comparing speakers of English and of Mandarin who were videotaped in parent-child play sessions with identical contexts across languages (Gelman and Tardif 1998). Our primary questions were whether generics could be identified in Mandarin, despite the crosslinguistic differences in how transparently they are expressed, and if so, how frequently they appear relative to English.

We gathered child-directed speech from English-speaking parents (in Ann Arbor, Michigan) and Mandarin-speaking parents (in Beijing, China) interacting with their 20-month-old children. All noun phrases (excluding pronouns, which are less frequent in Mandarin by virtue of the structure of the language) were coded in two ways: as generic or nongeneric, and for domain. Sample generics included: "*Baby birds* eat *worms*" (English) and "*da4 lao3shu3* yao3 bu4 yao3 *ren2?*" ("Do *big rats* bite *people* or not?") (Mandarin).

Despite very different formal devices for expressing generics, patterns were remarkably similar across languages. Generics were frequent in Mandarin as well as English (83% of the Mandarin-speaking mothers and 100% of the English-speaking mothers produced at least one during 30 minutes of play with their 20-month-olds). In both languages, generics were more frequently expressed for animals than for other domains. Thus, the crosslinguistic similarities argue that generic concepts are robustly expressed in the speech to small children. Interestingly, however, generics were significantly more common in English than Mandarin, suggesting that language-specific differences in how transparently generics are marked may affect frequency of use.

Importantly, the distribution of generic noun phrases differed markedly from that of nongeneric noun phrases in both languages, with generics used significantly more for animals than for artifacts, and nongenerics used significantly more for artifacts than for animals. Thus, domain differences in generic use cannot be due to differences in the salience of each domain. Moreover, there were no language differences in frequency of nongenerics.

In sum, the results suggest an interaction between cognitive universals and language-specific effects. On the one hand, we argue for cross-cultural (perhaps universal) properties of generic concepts that are expressed with linguistically different constructions. On the other hand, the frequency of expression may be modified by the manner in which generics are expressed in the language. Moreover, the ambiguity of expression may have implications for how generics are interpreted and used by children learning Mandarin.

Contexts

The frequency with which mothers produce generics is highly sensitive to interactional context. Generics are consistently produced more frequently during a book-reading activity than during free play with toys. This can be seen most clearly in the data that Tardif and I gathered in English and Mandarin, where we systematically varied the play context. Mothers and children spent 10 minutes looking through a picture book, 10 minutes playing with ordinary toys (e.g., blocks, stuffed animals), and 10 minutes playing with mechanical toys, with the three activities presented in counterbalanced order.

Book reading elicited generics at five to ten times the rate at which they were produced during toy play. Pictures are more readily construed as representations than are real objects, even toys (DeLoache 1991), and thus I speculate that they are more likely to encourage talk about the kinds that they represent. In contrast, toys are more readily construed as objects in their own right (even though in fact they are also representations), and thus are more likely to encourage talk about the ongoing activity. Interestingly, the book-reading context is also one that elicits proportionately more nouns and fewer verbs, relative to the toy-play contexts (Tardif, Gelman, and Xu 1999). Thus, contexts that encourage nouns also seem to encourage generics, whereas contexts that encourage verbs also seem to correspond to a focus on in-the-moment activities. The important point here is that factors that sway the interpretation of an entity (as representing a kind vs. as an individual object) are associated with more versus fewer generics.

Summary

Generics are highly frequent in ordinary child-directed speech. They appear early in development, being common in speech to children as young as 20 months of age—the youngest age we have studied. They are found in two languages that express generics quite differently (English and Mandarin). They also appropriately signal which kinds are more (vs. less) richly structured, as indicated by the context sensitivity of their use: used more for animals than artifacts, and more in book-reading contexts than in toy-play contexts. But are they used by children? We turn to this question next.

14.3.2   Generics Are Produced Early in Development

In this section I describe the evidence to date for children's *production* of generic noun phrases in spontaneous speech. Natural language is a valuable vehicle for examining conceptual understanding in toddlers who are not capable of handling the complex information-processing demands of many experimental tasks (Bartsch and Wellman 1995). I make two major points with these data: generics are produced as early as 2 years of age, though the frequency increases markedly between 2 and 3 years; and generics are distributed differently from nongenerics by their earliest use, suggesting a nascent semantic distinction.

Frequency of Generics in Children's Speech
Jonathan Flukes and I have analyzed data drawn from longitudinal transcripts in the CHILDES database organized by Brian MacWhinney and Catherine Snow (1990).[1] The researchers who contributed the data were Lois Bloom (1970), Roger Brown (1973), Stan Kuczaj (1976), Brian MacWhinney (1991), Jacqueline Sachs (1983), and Catherine Snow (see MacWhinney 1991). Subjects are eight children (ages 2–4 years) followed longitudinally. We included only those files in which child MLUs were at least 2.5 for three taping sessions in a row, to ensure that the children had command of the appropriate syntactic devices (e.g., singular vs. plural). We examined all utterances containing plural nouns, mass nouns, and indefinite singular nouns (totaling nearly 45,000 utterances), and coded each in two ways: (1) as generic or nongeneric, and (2) for domain (person/animal, artifact, other).

As can be seen in table 14.1, children as young as 2 years of age spontaneously produced generics in everyday conversations, although the rate of generics production increased between 2 and 4 years of age. Overall, the eight children we studied produced 3,096 generic noun phrases during the sessions recorded between ages 2 and 4 years.

Domain Specificity of Generics in Child Speech
What independent evidence do we have that children use generics to refer to kinds as opposed to individual instances? The distribution of generics across domains is suggestive in this regard. Recall that mothers produced significantly more generics for animals versus artifacts, even when we control for the frequency of talk in the two domains. Together with work suggesting that animal categories are more coherently structured than artifact categories (e.g., Gelman 1988; Keil 1989), this domain difference suggests that generics are reserved for talking about categories with particularly rich correlated structure.

Table 14.1
Relative frequency of generic noun phrases in the naturally occurring speech of children in the CHILDES database, as mean percentage of total utterances, and as mean percentage of searched utterances (mass nouns, plural nouns, and indefinite singular nouns only) within each domain

	Age 2	Age 3	Age 4
	(*N* = 6)	(*N* = 8)	(*N* = 6)
Generics as mean percent of total utterances			
Animates	0.33%	1.24%	1.82%
Artifacts	0.12	0.37	0.59
Other	0.39	0.57	0.77
TOTAL	0.83	2.17	3.18
Generics as mean percent of searched utterances within each domain			
Animates	4.52%	9.69%	13.05%
Artifacts	1.64	3.91	7.83
Other	3.20	4.56	5.01
Total number of generics	361	1,563	1,172

Importantly, we find that children at each age also provided significantly more generics for animate kinds than for artifacts (see table 14.1). Before concluding that children have an animacy bias, however, it is important to conduct an analysis of their baseline speech. In other words, we need to make sure that children's animacy bias in generics is not simply due to an abundance of animate noun phrases overall. To address this question, we computed a proportion score for each domain that was the number of generic noun phrases in that domain divided by the number of total coded noun phrases *in that domain*. Thus, each subject's data serve as his or her own control. As shown in table 14.1, even controlling for baseline frequencies of speech in each domain, there remained a strong preference for children to use generics for animates. This difference was significant even at age 2.

Generics Are Distributed Differently from Nongenerics with Respect to Number
A second piece of evidence that generics are conceptually distinct from nongenerics is found in an examination of how number (singular vs. plural) matches or mismatches nonlinguistic context. Recall

that mothers showed an occasional mismatch between the number of available category instances and the plurality of the noun phrase used (Gelman et al. 1998). Specifically, mothers at times used plural generics even when only a single instance was visible in the picture (e.g., "That's a chipmunk. And *they* eat the acorns"). Similarly, sometimes mothers shifted between singular and plural forms (e.g., "Did you know when *a pig* gets to be big, *they're* called hogs?"). This pattern is striking, because on the surface it would appear to be a blatant error: reference to a single individual with a plural pronoun. However, we suggest that the "error" is in fact not an error at all, but rather reflects the semantics of generic nouns. Specifically, *they* in the chipmunk example refers not to the chipmunk identified in the previous sentence, but rather to chipmunks as an abstract kind. If our interpretation is correct, then these mismatches suggest that generics are not tied to a particular set of instances present in the immediate context but rather refer to the category as a larger whole.

Athina Pappas and I (Pappas and Gelman 1998) designed a study to address how characteristic these mismatches are for generics, and whether they differ systematically from the use of nongeneric noun phrases. It is possible, for example, that these mismatches reflect not the semantics of generics, but rather simply slips of the tongue, or use of *they* as a gender-neutral singular pronoun. If that were the case, nongenerics should display as many number mismatches.

We asked mother-child dyads to look through picture books about animals. The books were specially created so that each page included either a single instance of a category (e.g., one crab) or multiple instances of a category (e.g., twelve to fifteen crabs), thus manipulating contexts by varying the number of items on a page. The children ranged in age from 23 to 57 months.

I focus on the child data here, though the maternal data show the same patterns. We found that there were striking differences in how generics versus nongenerics were distributed, both in the speech of parents and in the speech of preschool children. Whereas the form of *nongeneric* noun phrases was closely linked to the structure of the page (i.e., singular noun phrases were used more often when one instance was presented; plural noun phrases were used more often when multiple instances were presented), the form of *generic* noun phrases was independent of the information depicted (e.g., plural noun phrases were as frequent when only one instance was presented as when multiple instances were presented). At times this led to the sort of "mismatches" described earlier. For example, after one mother referred to an individual ostrich as "ostrich," her child replied, "They stink." In fact, subjects were no more likely to access the larger category when presented with many instances than when presented with just one. That even a single instance of the category could trigger a generic utterance suggests that subjects may be thinking about individual animals in two ways, both as individuals and as instantiations of a kind. We interpret the data as providing indirect evidence that generic noun phrases differ from nongenerics in their semantic implications, both in the input to young children and in children's own speech.

Summary

Children produce generics fairly frequently by 3 years of age. Moreover, we have two *indirect* pieces of evidence suggesting that generics differ in their semantic implications from nongenerics, for preschool children. First, whereas generics tend to be preferred for animates, there is no such preference for nongenerics. Second, whereas nongenerics tend to match the nonlinguistic context in terms of number (singulars used in the context of a single picture, plurals used in the context of multiple instances), generics tend to be independent of the nonlinguistic context (e.g., plurals used in the context of single instances as well as multiple instances) (Pappas and Gelman 1998). This is what we would predict from a semantic analysis of generics, because their meaning is not tied to any depictable or present nonlinguistic context.

14.3.3   Children Assign Appropriate Semantic Interpretations to Generics

We turn now to more direct evidence concerning children's semantic interpretation of generic noun phrases. As noted earlier, there are two important semantic features of generics. First, generics are *generally* true, and so are distinguished from indefinites (e.g., "*Bears* live in caves" is generic; "I saw some *bears* in the cave" is indefinite). The distinction between a generic reading and an indefinite reading is particularly critical because the same form of the noun phrase can be used for both (e.g., "I like rice" (generic) vs. "I want rice" (non-generic, indefinite). Second, generics need not be true of all members, and so are distinguished from universal quantifiers (e.g., *all, every, each*). In a pair of studies described below, we examine whether children appreciate these features.

Generic Scope: Yes-No Task

Michelle Hollander and I conducted a study that focused directly on what generics mean to young children, by examining their scope of application. As noted earlier, for adults, generics are distinctive in implying broad category scope (e.g., "Birds fly" is generally true of birds) yet allowing for exceptions (e.g., penguins). Thus, generics are distinct from both *all* (e.g., "All birds fly") and *some* (e.g., "Some birds fly"). We conducted an experiment to test whether preschool children appreciate this. The study was modeled after an experiment conducted by Smith (1980) that had focused on children's interpretation of *all* and *some*. In Smith's study, children aged 4 to 7 years received a series of questions regarding properties of categories. One-third of the properties were true of all members of the category in question (what we call *wide-scope properties*), one-third were true of some members of the category (*narrow-scope properties*), and one-third were true of no members of the category (*irrelevant properties*). Children were asked about each category-property pairing with either the word *all* or the word *some* (e.g., "Do all girls have curly hair?" vs. "Do some girls have curly hair?"). Smith's results indicated that by age 4, children appropriately distinguished *all* and *some*.

Hollander and I presented preschool children with three blocks of items each: generic, *all*, and *some*, in counterbalanced order. Each block included three kinds of properties: wide-scope properties (e.g., "Are fires hot?"), narrow-scope properties (e.g., "Do girls have curly hair?"), and irrelevant properties (e.g., "Do fish have branches?"). We predicted that children would treat generics as partly like *all* and partly like *some*. In particular, we predicted that children would accept both *all* properties and (to a lesser extent) *some* properties as true in generic form.

The results confirmed our predictions. With the narrow-scope properties, 4-year-olds were more likely to answer yes in response to *some* and generic questions than in response to *all* questions. Furthermore, for both generic and *all* questions considered separately, the children were more likely to affirm wide-scope properties than narrow-scope properties. In contrast, there was no significant difference between wide- and narrow-scope properties for *some* questions. These results indicate that children interpret generics as being reducible to neither *all* nor *some*. This is particularly notable given that the identical form of the noun phrase (bare plural) is used for indefinite utterances as well, but the children did not confuse generic and indefinite.

Generic Scope: Elicited Production Task

Jon Star and I conducted a study similar in logic but differing in design. Here, 4-year-old children were asked to produce their own utterances, under the guise of giving information to Zorg, an alien puppet from outer space. The prompts children heard employed one of three kinds of cues: generic (e.g., "What can you tell Zorg about dogs?"), *all* (e.g., "What can you tell Zorg about all dogs?"), or *some* (e.g., "What can you tell Zorg about some dogs?"). An analogous paper-and-pencil version of the task was developed for adults.

Transcripts of the elicitation sessions were prepared, and an independent group of adults rated the frequency with which each property was true of the category in question. Adult raters were blind to the purpose of the ratings, to the linguistic prompts provided by the experimenter, and to the linguistic format in which the property was expressed. (So, for example, "some dogs are furry," "all dogs are furry," and "dogs are furry" would all be rendered as "are furry" for the adult raters.) The adult ratings for each property were then averaged, and we thus determined for each child subject, the mean rating assigned to the properties they generated, for each category.

Results indicated that both children and adults were sensitive to the linguistic prompts provided by the experimenter. For both 4-

year-olds and adults, *all* was treated as widest in scope, *some* as narrowest in scope, and generics as intermediate, with significant differences between the three wording conditions.

14.3.4 Generics Constrain Children's Inductive Inferences

We hypothesized that generic language would provide a rich source of information for children concerning the potential scope of inductive inferences. Jon Star, Jonathan Flukes, and I conducted a study to examine whether and how children make use of information in generics as compared to other linguistic expressions to direct their inductions (Gelman, Star, and Flukes 2002).

Preschool children (mean age 4 years, 7 months) and adults participated in the study. We presented a series of animal categories, one at a time. For each page there was a target question (e.g., for the category "bears," the question page said, "Which ones like to eat ants?"). There were six pictures to choose from. Children first received a clue to help them answer the question. The clues varied in linguistic form—for example, "All bears like to eat ants," "Some bears like to eat ants," or "Bears like to eat ants" (generic). Across items, the wording was varied within subjects.

The results indicated that the induction rates for the *all*, generic, and *some* conditions were all significantly different from one another, although these differences interacted by age. Both children and adults were sensitive to the wording in the inferences they drew. For adults, generics were treated as equivalent to *all*, whereas for children, generics were treated as less powerful than *all* but more powerful than *some*. However, a follow-up study using a more sensitive measure indicated that adults (like 4-year-olds) do recognize a distinction between the inductive potential of *all* and the inductive potential of generics.

Summary
These findings argue for an early-emerging capacity to produce and interpret generics, and by extension, to readily consider and converse about abstract classes of entities. What sort of cognitive and/or linguistic capabilities could support the sustained interest in and ease

with generics found here? We turn to this issue in the following section.

14.4 Implications for Developmental Mechanisms

In this section we address two questions: How do children solve the inductive puzzle of generic language? Which is primary, generic concepts or generic language?

14.4.1 How Do Children Solve the Inductive Puzzle of Generic Language?

The expression of generic kinds in language must be learned in childhood: it is not innate (as seen by crosslinguistic variation), yet it is available within the first few years of life. What is the acquisitional process? I have already argued rather extensively that adults use multiple sorts of information to identify an utterance as generic or not. It is still an open question as to which of these cues children make use of, and at what ages. Relevant data would include information regarding: which *formal* cues children are sensitive to, including verb tense and aspect, and noun morphology (e.g., do they distinguish "What color are dogs?" (generic) from "What color are the dogs?" (nongeneric)?), which *contextual* cues children use (e.g., do they distinguish "Here's a blicket; they live in trees" (generic) from "Here are two blickets; they live in trees" (nongeneric)?), and which *knowledge* cues they use (e.g., do they distinguish "I like rice" (generic) from "I want rice" (nongeneric)?).

In the absence of such data, we can nonetheless draw inferences regarding the sorts of capacities children are likely to be using. Specifically, I will suggest that the acquisition of generics cannot be explained in terms of simple associationist theories, but instead requires that young children make use of naive theories.

Problems with DAM Models
Smith, Jones, and Landau (1996) have proposed that *dumb attentional mechanisms* (henceforth *DAMs*) can account for early word learning. Their proposal is that children keep a statistical tally of formal lin-

guistic cues as they match to real-world features. Children then come to expect certain properties to co-occur with specific linguistic frames. Smith, Jones, and Landau (1996, 145) maintain that "in learning language, children repeatedly experience specific linguistic contexts (e.g., 'This is a _____' or 'This is some _____') with attention to specific object properties and clusters of properties (e.g., shape or color plus texture). Thus, by this view, these linguistic contexts come to serve as cues that automatically control attention." This is an automatic, associative mechanism that operates independently of reflective thought. Or, to rephrase in colloquial English, the child over time "soaks in" the statistical regularities present in the input. Smith and colleagues stress the importance of concrete properties in the process of word use and interpretation. To quote again: "Young children's naming of objects is principally a matter of mapping words to selected perceptual properties" (p. 144).

This sort of theory has numerous appeals. Most notably, it proposes a very general mechanism to explain a wide range of data; it relies on well-known and well-studied cognitive principles (such as implicit learning of statistical regularities); it is a developmental account (attempting to account for developmental change, placing few demands on children, and not assuming that knowledge is built in); and it is sensitive to phenomena such as crosslinguistic variability.

However, this DAM view, I suggest, cannot account for the acquisition of the generic-nongeneric distinction.[2] Specifically, there are two major problems with proposing that children are detecting correlations between linguistic cues and concrete perceptual properties, when learning generics. First and most obviously, there are no concrete perceptual properties associated with an utterance being generic. Even if there were concrete properties that correspond to the base word (e.g., perhaps *apple* is associated with a round shape; but see Gelman and Diesendruck 1999 for counterarguments), certainly no such concrete perceptual properties signal whether the conceptual representation is generic versus nongeneric. This is an important point. To illustrate, consider the mother who solicitously asks her 2-year-old, "Do you like the mango?", as the child is tasting mango for the first time. Now consider a second mother who solicitously asks her 2-year-old, "Do you like mango?", as the child is tasting mango for the first time. The nonlinguistic contexts are identical; the conceptual implications are quite different.

The second problem with the DAM approach, in this context, is that there is no 1:1 mapping between linguistic form and meaning— even for young children. Indeed, there is nothing even approaching a 1:1 mapping. Two-year-olds in our analyses use multiple forms for generics (singular noun with determiner *a*, mass noun, bare plural noun, pronouns), and each of these forms is used for both generic and nongeneric utterances (e.g., sometimes bare plurals are generic, sometimes bare plurals are indefinite; the same is true of *a* plus singular noun).

A proponent of the DAM view might propose that children are instead attending to a multiplicity of cues "out there" in the input language and situation—not 1:1 cues, but perhaps a grid of cues that, taken together, signal genericity to the child. For example, perhaps determiners, number, tense, aspect, and prosody together form the relevant linguistic cues. The problem here is that the simplicity and on-the-face plausibility of the DAM approach decrease as the complexity of the cues increases. Is it possible for the child to track and store all of these combinations of cues over time? And how does the child know *in advance* that these are the cues to attend to? To do so, must the child consider *all* available linguistic distinctions? The combinatorial demands on processing are formidable. But even were these problems to be solved, we would still be left trying to come up with a possible set of nonlinguistic contexts that would be "associated" with these cues. In the absence of a specific proposal for how this would work (along the lines of the proposed distinction between count nouns and mass nouns supplied in Smith, Jones, and Landau 1996), it is difficult to accept—or even evaluate—such a possibility.

At the very least, the analysis of generics provided in this chapter greatly complicates the question of how one would implement an acquisitional process that depends on DAMs. I am skeptical that such an analysis is possible.

An Alternative Proposal: Multiple Cues and Naive Theories
Before sketching out my proposal, I first take a brief detour to ask *why* generics are marked in such a complex and subtle manner. Put

differently, if generics are so important, why don't they receive a single, unambiguous marker in English (or other languages)? The reason, I suggest, is that generics are marked more by their absence than by their presence. By this I mean that generic interpretations result when utterances are neither particular nor indefinite. There are many devices in language for indicating that something is particular, and it would be extraordinarily difficult (perhaps impossible) to enumerate them all. These include form of the determiner, precise number, deictics (including pointing), and tense. All of these devices serve to locate an utterance within an identifiable context (*this* place, *that* time, *those* entities). Generics contrast with specific utterances in that they cannot be pinned down to a context—they hold generally over time and situations. Thus, there is not a limited set of features or contexts that correspond to the set of generic utterances. Rather, language users assume that an utterance is generic unless that interpretation is blocked—and there are many ways to block it. Indeed, the more cues a speaker has at her command, the better. Thus, multiple sources of information—including naive theories—are *required*, given how generics work.

This view could also help explain how generics are learned in languages that do not make use of determiners, tense, and so on. Speakers in languages such as Mandarin still map a generic-nongeneric distinction onto utterances, but they are using non-morphological cues to identify specificity and resolve ambiguity. In that sense, English and Mandarin are not so different from one another. It would be interesting to know how generally this analysis applies across languages.

What are the implications of this view for acquisition? In learning generics (at least in English), the child's task is *not* to acquire a particular form, nor to map one formal set of cues onto a set of properties in the world (à la DAMs). Rather, the child's task is to filter out the specific. This can be done most successfully by considering multiple cues, given the breadth and variety of means of indicating specificity. Such cues would at the least include morphosyntactic information and theory-based inferences. Presumably the process also involves mastery of prosodic cues (e.g., stress on different words; see the earlier example), and conventions of discourse (e.g., governing the examples of anaphora given earlier). Given how readily children grasp generics early in life, and the ease with which children produce generics in multiple syntactic forms, it would appear that even young children are likewise forming a mental model of the utterance as an integrated whole, to determine if there is any indication of specificity. Any indication of specificity could be enough to block a generic interpretation.

Another prediction is that as soon as a child learns that a particular cue marks an utterance as specific, she will readily recruit that information to mark an utterance as nongeneric. For example, the determiner *the* powerfully guides adult speakers toward nongeneric interpretations (in most cases, though as noted earlier, there are exceptions, such as "The early bird catches the worm"). Tardif and I (Gelman and Tardif 1998, Study 3) found that 91 percent of an adult English-speaking sample interpreted "*The* tractor doesn't have a nose" (emphasis added) as nongeneric, whereas only 22 percent of the adult Mandarin-speaking sample did so. Interestingly, children distinguish definite from indefinite (using *the* vs. *a*) by 3 years of age (Maratsos 1974). I predict that children can likewise recruit this distinction for differentiating generic from nongeneric utterances. Specifically, if one were to conduct a microgenetic study (Siegler and Crowley 1991) examining the use of determiners to mark definiteness and to mark genericity, one would find that children immediately extend the distinction to generics as soon as the definite-indefinite distinction is mastered. Their knowledge that the determiner *the* is specific should lead children to assume that definite noun phrases *cannot* be generic. Consistent with this prediction, is that children do not at first use definite singulars ("The early bird catches the worm") as generic.

Thus, my position is that acquisition of the generic system in English requires a theory-driven assessment of when an utterance picks out specific referents, and when an utterance does not. Therefore, in addition to formal cues, conceptual analyses are highly relevant. For example, when "wanting" something, one seeks a portion or subset, whereas when "liking" something, one is (at least capable of) liking the class as a whole. As Callanan (1990, 106) notes, "Children's inferential abilities are likely to develop from a complex interaction among their theories and expectations about the properties and categories involved, the knowledge they gain through their senses, and the knowledge they gain through verbal descriptions (most notably provided by parents)." The same is true of generics. In future work it will be of interest to explore these interactions among different sources of knowledge.

In contrast, if children at first look for just a single form to mark generics (e.g., using just singular, or just plural, or using indefinite determiners either just for indefinites, or using them just for generics), this would argue against my position. However, the suggestion that children use multiple cues does not imply that children use all the information adults do. Presumably adults have access to a richer set of linguistic and pragmatic skills to mark an utterance as generic or nongeneric, and we suspect that developing this full set of skills will be a time-intensive and gradual process.

14.4.2 Which Is Primary, Generic Concepts or Generic Language?

I turn now to the question of whether generic concepts or generic language comes first. In the "concept-first" view, the conceptual notion of kind arises nonlinguistically, with generic noun phrases merely reflecting this conceptual structure. In this view, children possess an innate or early-emerging notion of kind (e.g., Gopnik and Meltzoff 1997; Macnamara 1986) as well as a rich reserve of nonlinguistic generic knowledge, and generic language merely reflects and expresses this conceptual knowledge. Alternatively, the "language-first" view proposes that generic language plays a role in the formation of kind concepts. In its strongest version, generic knowledge does not exist except for language. A. H. Bloom's (1981) analysis of generics in Mandarin versus English would fall within this position. Xu and Carey's (1996) work on kind concepts, though not focused on generics, also argues for a formative role for language.

In contrast, I strongly suspect that both directions of influence are critical. Thus, generics are indeed a reflection of children's early-developing, prelinguistic notion of kinds, but generic language also provides input to this understanding.

Prelinguistic Kind Concepts

There are several pieces of evidence that kind concepts (generically construed) emerge very early in development, and are likely not to require linguistic instantiation. First, the apparently universal capacity for generics, despite widely varying linguistic forms, at least suggests that generics are a robust form of thinking and knowing about the world (Carlson and Pelletier 1995). Second and more directly, prelinguistic infants engage in categorizing and inductive inferences that suggest they are appealing to generic kinds. Infants as young as 9 months of age are capable of extending novel words from one category instance to another (Waxman 1999). Likewise, 9-month-olds generalize novel properties from one instance of a kind to another (Baldwin, Markman, and Melartin 1993). For example, when shown a box that unexpectedly produces a sound, they attempt to elicit the same property in another box similar in appearance.

We cannot say for sure whether such generalizations are *generic* at this age—that is, they could consist of similarity-based generalizations from one instance to another instance rather than generalizations that derive from the generic class. (See also Rovee-Collier 1993 for similarity-based inferences even much earlier in infancy.) However, we do know that by $2\frac{1}{2}$ years of age such generalizations are kind-based, because the information about kinds overrides the outward appearances of the *individual* objects in consideration (Gelman and Coley 1990). For example, a 2-year-old will generalize from a brontosaurus to a pterodactyl, though only after learning that the pterodactyl is a dinosaur. Altogether, this work suggests that it is likely that there exists a prelinguistic notion of generic kind that guides children's inferences and knowledge organization (but see Xu and Carey 1996 for an alternative position).

Effects of Generic Language

Although language is not determinative of kinds, generic knowledge is not wholly independent of language, either. At the very least, language has two functions that affect children's kind concepts. First, naming serves to identify which entities belong to a kind (through use of nouns; e.g., allowing one to identify a pterodactyl as a dinosaur—this is particularly relevant in borderline or atypical cases, in which a nonlinguistic analysis might diverge from labeling). This information guides categorywide (generic) inferences, as noted earlier. Furthermore, Waxman (1999; Waxman and Markow 1995) makes the intriguing suggestion that words serve as "invitations to form categories." As Waxman (1999, 269) suggests, "Words focus infants' attention on commonalities among objects, highlighting these especially in cases where the perceptual or conceptual similarities may not be as apparent as at the basic, or folk-generic, level.... This can have dramatic consequences, inviting the child to notice deeper and more subtle commonalities than those that served as the initial basis of the grouping. In this way, naming may itself help to advance the child beyond perceptible commonalities among objects, pointing them toward a richer appreciation of the deeper, nonperceptible commonalities that characterize human concepts."

Second, generics are effective in teaching children particular categorywide generalizations, such as specific facts about the attributes of category members (Gelman, Star, and Flukes 2002). For example, by means of generic noun phrases, children learn particular facts about the physical characteristics, eating habits, behaviors, and so on of animals. When such properties are stated generically, they may become more central to children's conceptual representations than if they had been stated nongenerically. Furthermore, because these facts are stated generically (rather than as universal quantifiers), they may be particularly robust against counterevidence (e.g., "birds fly" allows for penguins, whereas "all birds fly" does not). Thus, even erroneous properties stated generically, such as stereotypes concerning gender or race, may be more difficult to counter and erase than erroneous properties stated absolutely. This possibility has yet to be tested.

I would argue that these two functions of language *cannot* be expressed without language. There is simply no unambiguous way to carry out either function, without words for things. For instance, it is difficult to imagine how a nonlinguistic species could convey that a legless lizard *really is* a lizard, even though it looks outwardly just like a snake. With language, however, such a concept is elegantly expressed (e.g., "This is a lizard"). Likewise, no process of enumerating and displaying examples can unambiguously convey that *birds* (as a kind) have hollow bones, whereas this is an uncomplicated linguistic effort. Given the relevance of these functions for induction and category-based reasoning, given the relative ease of conveying these functions via language, and given the difficulty of expressing them by nonlinguistic means, there is reason to suspect that language plays a role in the structure of people's categories.

In addition to these two demonstrated functions of language, generics may have two further implications—although this remains untested at the moment. They are briefly discussed below.

A third potential function of generics may be to imply that members of a category are alike in important ways, even beyond the particular properties mentioned in the generic statements. In other words, hearing numerous generic statements about a category may lead children to treat this category as one about which indefinitely many categorywide generalizations could be made. In short, we suggest that hearing generics may lead children to make inferences regarding the structure of the category. If this is true, then generics may serve this function even when the information is relatively superficial (e.g., "Little rabbits are called kits"), or when little or no new information is provided (e.g., with questions, such as "How do they [bats] sleep?"), because the generic form itself implies that category members are importantly alike. If so, then there should be measurable effects of introducing novel categories with generics versus nongenerics.

Shipley (1993, 270) likewise proposed that a grouping becomes a "kind" (i.e., richly structured, inference-promoting) when a person "projects a property onto individual members of a class." In other words, when a person learns a new property of a category as a whole, that category is hypothesized to cohere in novel ways. "Birds lay eggs" can be understood to mean "Birds are a kind of animal such that the mature female lays eggs" (Shipley 1993, 278). Shipley proposes that such a generic statement, "which presupposes the conceptualization of the class of birds as a single entity, should enhance the psychological coherence of the class of birds for that reason" (p. 278). For example, the child may then hypothesize that she can make numerous other novel inferences about the class of birds. This possibility has not yet been tested, and remains a question for future research.

A fourth speculation regarding the cognitive implications of generics is that the amount of generic talk overall may foster or inhibit essentialist reasoning. That is, variation in frequency of generic expression (whether it be individual, or correlated with some other factor such as language or culture) could conceivably influence essentializing more broadly. Consider a child who hears plenty of kind terms, but exclusively in reference to individuals ("Here's a soft kitty," "Baby Ben can't use that cup yet," "Those flowers could use some water"). Now consider a child who hears plenty of kind terms, but with generics mixed liberally in ("Kitties are so soft," "Baby Ben can't use cups yet," "Flowers need water").

Although we have no evidence either to confirm or disconfirm this hypothesis, I have observed striking individual variation in generic frequency, in both adults and children. In the CHILDES data, for example, the rate at which children produced generics at age 2 ranged from 0.13 percent of all utterances to nearly 3 percent, and at age 3, the rates varied from 0.30 to 6.39 percent. Individual differences are even more noticeable in the semistructured book-reading tasks. Tina Pappas and I found that, in a controlled book-reading context where each mother-child dyad was talking about the very same book, the rate of maternal generics ranged from those who produced no generics whatsoever, to one mother who produced generics on an average of 41 percent of all utterances (Pappas and Gelman 1998). Likewise, in an ongoing project examining generics concerning gender categories, the rate of maternal generics ranged from those who produced no generics, to one mother who produced generics on 67 percent of all on-task utterances (Gelman, Nguyen, and Taylor 2001). Even more remarkably, in the same study, children ranged from one who produced no generics, to another who produced generics on 92 percent of all on-task utterances!

At this point we know almost nothing about the nature and source of these massive individual differences. Are they stable over time? Are they stable over contexts? For example, does the child who produces many gender-focused generics—when looking through a book about gender—also produce many animal-focused generics, in a context that allows for such? If stable individual differences exist, do they reflect differential tendencies to focus on kinds, or to attribute immutable essences to categories? It would be intriguing to correlate individual differences in generics with scores on an essentialism scale (e.g., Haslam, Rothschild, and Ernst 2000). These questions await future research.

14.5 Conclusion

These studies describe the first systematic studies of generics in children. They are revealing about kind concepts in early childhood, beginning with children's earliest sentences. Generics illustrate, in a microcosm, the importance of naïve theories in acquiring linguistic forms, and the importance of linguistic forms in informing naïve theories.

Learning words is not like solving a jigsaw puzzle, where formal cues give you some pieces, and world knowledge and pragmatics are other pieces that can be added in earlier or later. Rather, the word-learning process is akin to the creation of a tapestry with warp and weft together constituting the textile. In this very important sense, the child "weaves" a lexicon.

Acknowledgments

Support for writing this chapter was provided by NICHD Grant R01-HD36043. I am grateful to Sandeep Prasada and Bruce Mannheim for extremely helpful comments on an earlier draft.

Notes

1. We are grateful to Thomas Rodriguez for his assistance with CHILDES.

2. More generally, I also argue that the DAM position cannot account for other aspects of word learning (Gelman and Diesendruck 1999; Gelman and Koenig 2003; see also Bloom 2000).

References

Adams, A. K., and Bullock, D. 1986. Apprenticeship in word use: Social convergence processes in learning categorically related nouns. In S. A. Kuczaj and M. D. Barrett, eds., *The development of word meaning*, 155–197. New York: Springer-Verlag.

Balaban, M. T., and Waxman, S. R. 1997. Do word labels facilitate categorization in 9-month-old infants? *Journal of Experimental Child Psychology, 64,* 3–26.

Baldwin, D. A., Markman, E. M., and Melartin, R. L. 1993. Infants' ability to draw inferences about nonobvious object properties: Evidence from exploratory play. *Child Development, 64,* 711–728.

Bartsch, K., and Wellman, H. M. 1995. *Children talk about the mind.* New York: Oxford University Press.

Bhat, D. N. S. 1979. *The referents of noun phrases.* Pune, India: Deccan College Post-graduate and Research Institute.

Bloom, A. H. 1981. *The linguistic shaping of thought.* Hillsdale, NJ: Erlbaum.

Bloom, L. 1970. *Language development: Form and function in emerging grammars.* Cambridge, MA: MIT Press.

Bloom, P. 2000. *How children learn the meanings of words.* Cambridge, MA: MIT Press.

Brown, R. W. 1973. *A first language: The early stages.* Cambridge, MA: Harvard University Press.

Callanan, M. A. 1990. Parents' descriptions of objects: Potential data for children's inferences about category principles. *Cognitive Development, 5,* 101–122.

Carlson, G. N., and Pelletier, F. J., eds. 1995. *The generic book.* Chicago: University of Chicago Press.

Collins, A. M., and Quillian, M. R. 1969. Retrieval time from semantic memory. *Journal of Verbal Learning and Verbal Behavior, 8,* 240–247.

Dahl, O. 1975. On generics. In E. L. Keenan, ed., *Formal semantics of natural language,* 99–111. Cambridge: Cambridge University Press.

DeLoache, J. S. 1991. Symbolic functioning in very young children: Understanding of pictures and models. *Child Development, 62,* 736–752.

Gelman, S. A. 1988. The development of induction within natural kind and artifact categories. *Cognitive Psychology, 20,* 65–96.

Gelman, S. A., and Coley, J. D. 1990. The importance of knowing a dodo is a bird: Categories and inferences in 2-year-old children. *Developmental Psychology, 26,* 796–804.

Gelman, S. A., Coley, J. D., Rosengren, K., Hartman, E., and Pappas, A. 1998. Beyond labeling: The role of maternal input in the acquisition of richly-structured categories. *Monographs of the Society for Research in Child Development, 63*(1) (serial no. 253).

Gelman, S. A., and Diesendruck, G. 1999. What's in a concept? Context, variability, and psychological essentialism. In I. E. Sigel, ed., *Development of mental representation: Theories and applications,* 87–111. Mahwah, NJ: Erlbaum.

Gelman, S. A., and Koenig, M. A. 2003. Theory-based categorization in early childhood. In D. Rakison and L. Oakes, eds., *Category and concept development,* 330–359. Oxford: Oxford University Press.

Gelman, S. A., and Markman, E. M. 1986. Categories and induction in young children. *Cognition, 23*, 183–209.

Gelman, S. A., and Markman, E. M. 1987. Young children's inductions from natural kinds: The role of categories and appearances. *Child Development, 58*, 1532–1541.

Gelman, S. A., Nguyen, S. P., and Taylor, M. G. 2001. *Maternal talk about gender to 2-, 4-, and 6-year-old children.* Unpublished data, University of Michigan, Ann Arbor.

Gelman, S. A., Star, J., and Flukes, J. 2002. Children's use of generics in inductive inferences. *Journal of Cognition and Development, 3*, 179–199.

Gelman, S. A., and Tardif, T. Z. 1998. Generic noun phrases in English and Mandarin: An examination of child-directed speech. *Cognition, 66*, 215–248.

Gelman, S. A., and Taylor, M. 1984. How two-year-old children interpret proper and common names for unfamiliar objects. *Child Development, 55*, 1535–1540.

Goodman, N. 1973. *Fact, fiction, and forecast.* 3rd ed. Indianapolis: Bobbs-Merrill.

Gopnik, A., and Meltzoff, A. N. 1997. *Words, thoughts, and theories.* Cambridge, MA: Bradford Books/MIT Press.

Hall, D. G., Lee, S. C., and Bélanger, J. 2001. Young children's use of syntactic cues to learn proper names and count nouns. *Developmental Psychology, 37*, 298–307.

Hall, D. G., and Waxman, S. R. 1993. Assumptions about word meaning: Individual and basic-level kinds. *Child Development, 64*, 1550–1570.

Haslam, N., Rothschild, L., and Ernst, D. 2000. Essentialist beliefs about social categories. *British Journal of Social Psychology, 39*, 113–127.

Katz, N., Baker, E., and Macnamara, J. 1974. What's in a name? A study of how children learn common and proper names. *Child Development, 45*, 469–473.

Keil, F. 1989. *Concepts, kinds, and cognitive development.* Cambridge, MA: Bradford Books/MIT Press.

Krifka, M. 1995. Common nouns: A contrastive analysis of Chinese and English. In G. N. Carlson and F. J. Pelletier, eds., *The generic book*, 398–411. Chicago: University of Chicago Press.

Kuczaj, S. 1976. *-ing, -s and -ed: A study of the acquisition of certain verb inflections.* Unpublished doctoral dissertation, University of Minnesota.

Li, P., and Bowerman, M. 1998. The acquisition of lexical and grammatical aspect in Chinese. *First Language, 18*, 311–350.

Lyons, J. 1977. *Semantics.* Vol. 1. New York: Cambridge University Press.

Macnamara, J. 1986. *A border dispute: The place of logic in psychology.* Cambridge, MA: MIT Press.

MacWhinney, B. 1991. *The CHILDES project: Tools for analyzing talk.* Hillsdale, NJ: Erlbaum.

MacWhinney, B., and Snow, C. 1990. The child language data exchange system: An update. *Journal of Child Language, 17,* 457–472.

Mandler, J. M. 1992. The foundation of conceptual thought in infancy. *Cognitive Development, 7,* 273–285.

Maratsos, M. P. 1974. Preschool children's use of definite and indefinite articles. *Child Development, 45,* 446–455.

Markman, E. M. 1989. *Categorization and naming in children: Problems in induction.* Cambridge: Bradford Books/MIT Press.

McCawley, J. D. 1981. *Everything that linguists have always wanted to know about logic.* Chicago: University of Chicago Press.

Moser, D. J. 1996. *Abstract thinking and thought in ancient Chinese and early Greek.* Unpublished doctoral dissertation, University of Michigan, Ann Arbor.

Osherson, D., Smith, E. E., Wilkie, O., Lopez, A., and Shafir, E. 1990. Category-based induction. *Psychological Review, 97,* 185–200.

Pappas, A., and Gelman, S. A. 1998. Generic noun phrases in mother-child conversations. *Journal of Child Language, 25,* 19–33.

Prasada, S. 2000. Acquiring generic knowledge. *Trends in Cognitive Sciences, 4,* 66–72.

Quine, W. V. O. 1960. *Word and object.* Cambridge, MA: MIT Press.

Rovee-Collier, C. K. 1993. The capacity for long-term memory in infancy. *Current Directions in Psychological Science, 2,* 130–135.

Sachs, J. 1983. Talking about the there and then: The emergence of displaced reference in parent-child discourse. In K. E. Nelson, ed., *Children's language,* vol. 4. Hillsdale, NJ: Erlbaum.

Shipley, E. F. 1989. Two kinds of hierarchies: Class inclusion hierarchies and kind hierarchies. *Genetic Epistemologist, 17,* 31–39.

Shipley, E. F. 1993. Categories, hierarchies, and induction. In D. Medin, ed., *The psychology of learning and motivation,* vol. 30, 265–301. New York: Academic Press.

Siegler, R. S., and Crowley, K. 1991. The microgenetic method: A direct means for studying cognitive development. *American Psychologist, 46,* 606–620.

Smith, C. L. 1980. Quantifiers and question answering in young children. *Journal of Experimental Child Psychology, 30,* 191–205.

Smith, L. B., Jones, S. S., and Landau, B. 1996. Naming in young children: A dumb attentional mechanism? *Cognition, 60,* 143–171.

Tardif, T. Z., Gelman, S. A., and Xu, F. 1999. Putting the "noun bias" in context: A comparison of Mandarin and English. *Child Development, 70,* 620–635.

Waxman, S. R. 1999. The dubbing ceremony revisited: Object naming and categorization in infancy and early childhood. In D. L. Medin and S. Atran, eds., *Folkbiology.* Cambridge, MA: MIT Press.

Waxman, S. R., and Markow, D. B. 1995. Words as invitations to form categories: Evidence from 12- to 13-month-old infants. *Cognitive Psychology, 29,* 257–302.

Wilcox, T., and Baillargeon, R. 1998. Object individuation in infancy: The use of featural information in reasoning about occlusion events. *Cognitive Psychology, 37,* 97–155.

Xu, F., and Carey, S. 1996. Infants' metaphysics: The case of numerical identity. *Cognitive Psychology, 30,* 111–153.

15

Contexts of Early Word Learning

Nameera Akhtar

Researchers in language development, particularly those who have conducted intensive naturalistic observations of children interacting with their caregivers, have long been aware of the importance of context in interpreting young children's speech (Bates 1976; Bloom 1970). For example, Bloom (1970) reports two instances in which 21-month-old Kathryn uttered "Mommy sock." In one instance she used this combination of words when picking up her mother's sock. In the other, she said "Mommy sock" to indicate that her mother was putting a sock on Kathryn's foot. In this example, the same combination of words was used to convey two entirely different meanings, and it was only through attention to context that the child's meaning or intent could be interpreted. In this chapter, I argue that context is important not only to researchers (and parents) who use it to decipher children's meanings, but also to children themselves, who use it to discover meaning in the language they hear (Bloom 1991).

There are many studies showing that toddlers actively make use of aspects of the immediate and preceding context[1] in which a novel word is uttered to determine what the speaker wants them to attend to in using that word. In brief, the view of word learning presented in this chapter is that when young children hear new content words, their objective is not to establish the abstract "meanings" of the words themselves; rather, their goal in each word-learning situation involves trying to understand to what the speaker is attending.[2] This social-pragmatic account of word learning is one that I have developed in collaboration with Michael Tomasello (Akhtar and Tomasello 1998, 2000), inspired in large part by the work of Bruner (1983) and Nelson (1985, 1986).

The studies reviewed in this chapter illustrate how young children use the discourse contexts in which words are spoken to determine to what the speaker is referring. These studies demonstrate that young children can learn new words from many different contexts beyond the ostensive "That's an X" context so often utilized in experimental studies of word learning. Indeed, the central thesis of this chapter is that paying attention to the various contexts within which words are encountered by young children can illuminate some of the processes and skills children use in acquiring those words. I begin with a brief historical overview of the growing importance of contextual approaches to cognitive development. This is followed by a review of experimental studies my colleagues and I have conducted in which we have systematically varied aspects of the context in which novel words are presented. The review is organized into sections examining different word-learning contexts. In all of these studies, the words are referential terms (specifically, object labels, action verbs, or adjectives describing visible properties). It is quite possible, indeed likely, that some of the contexts described here play less of a role in children's acquisition of different types of words (e.g., determiners, prepositions, mental-state verbs), a point to which I return at the end of the chapter.

15.1 Historical Background

Prior to the 1970s, the influence of contextual factors on cognitive performance was largely ignored in the field of cognitive development (Butterworth 1992). This is because the focus was on intellectual development within the individual child, and on establishing domain-general processes presumed to explain a given child's performance across a range of tasks and situations—that is, across contexts. Influenced in large part by the work of Piaget, cognitive skills were conceptualized as generalized (context-free) competencies possessed by individuals. Two major factors conspired to challenge this view of cognitive development in the 1970s and 1980s.

First, renewed interest in the writings of Vygotsky (1978) and other sociocultural scholars inspired many researchers to shift toward focusing on contextual factors that affect the cognitive performance of both adults and children. In addition to pointing to the importance of historical and institutional influences on children's learning, these theorists emphasized the effect of the immediate social interactional context on children's performance. Indeed, the view was that cognition is rarely (if ever) decontextualized—that is, cognitive activity is always situated in a social and physical context. Focusing on the social contexts of cognition ("everyday cognition"; Rogoff and Lave 1984) in turn led to an emphasis on making tasks assessing cognitive and linguistic development more meaningful and motivating for children (e.g., Donaldson 1978).

Second, both cross-cultural work and within-culture developmental research began to show striking situational differences in cognitive performance (Rogoff 1982). For example, cross-cultural researchers noted that adults who performed poorly on laboratory tasks assessing a given cognitive skill often appeared to use that same skill spontaneously and quite competently in their everyday activities (e.g., Gladwin 1970; Scribner 1976). Similarly, research in the United States showed that children tend to perform better in familiar environments than in laboratory settings. For example, toddlers often have difficulty with memory tests in the lab, but perform much better when required to remember the locations of objects hidden in their homes (DeLoache 1980; Wellman 1988).

The general approach of the studies I review below involves examining the real-life contexts in which children hear words and then systematically manipulating aspects of those contexts experimentally to determine whether toddlers can learn new words in those contexts. The goal is to determine what cues children might rely on when encountering words in their everyday interactions with others, without sacrificing the control that one can achieve only with an experimental design. To this end, my colleagues and I have employed "naturalistic experiments": studies that employ experimental methods of control and manipulation of variables, but, from the child's point of view, are not tests of language-learning skills but interesting games played with an adult. Thus, by introducing novel words in somewhat natural play contexts, we try to combine experimental rigor with the ecological validity of naturalistic observations.

Each of the following sections examines young children's word learning in a particular discourse context. I begin with the ostensive context in which a speaker explicitly highlights and points to an object before labeling it; in this context, the speaker is intentionally "teaching" the word to the child. I then move to other less didactic contexts in which words are encountered by young children and, where possible, compare their learning in these other contexts with learning in the ostensive context.

15.2   The Ostensive/Didactic Context

Until relatively recently, studies of early word learning have often focused exclusively on ostensive labeling utterances. Despite extensive discussion about the potential ambiguity of ostensive labels (e.g., Markman 1989), there seems to be an assumption in the literature that ostension is the simplest and most straightforward sentence type for children to interpret early in language learning. Certainly, the majority of experimental studies of word learning use this context and the labeling frame associated with it ("That's an X"). With this type of labeling the child's attention is generally on the object at the time it is being labeled; thus, joint attention and temporal contiguity of referent and label coincide, presumably making the task of forming an association between the label and referent easier (Baldwin 1995). Certainly in the ostensive context, children have the benefit of multiple sources of information as to the speaker's referential intent (pointing, gaze direction, temporal contiguity), but below I present evidence from several studies demonstrating that, by paying attention to aspects of the nonlinguistic contexts in which they hear novel words, children can learn novel words in many different nonostensive contexts.

The question of whether ostension is indeed the most effective form of labeling will be taken up in the next section. First, however, it is important to note that some researchers have observed that this type of labeling may be part of a speech style characteristic of parents in some cultural communities, but not others. Indeed, ethnographic work in other cultures and subcultures suggests that some language-learning children do not often hear these kinds of ostensive "language lessons" (see Lieven 1994 for a review). Furthermore, recent reports suggest that even in middle-class U.S. families, language researchers may have overestimated the extent to which parents use ostension in everyday activities with their children (Bloom et al. 1996). In addition to considering the extent to which ostension is actually used in various cultures, it is also important to recognize that when ostension is used it is primarily for teaching object labels. Object labels are of course only one type of word young children are expected to learn. In verb learning, it appears that ostension is relatively rarely used; verbs are most often introduced before or after (rather than during) the relevant actions in requests for action or comments on completed actions (Tomasello and Kruger 1992).

I now return to the suggestion that children learn words most readily when they are presented in an ostensive context. Current research shows that 2-year-olds can learn novel object labels in some nonostensive contexts (Tomasello and Barton 1994), but we know relatively little about whether they are *better* able to learn new labels when they are introduced in ostensive statements versus other syntactic and pragmatic contexts. For example, children sometimes hear labels embedded in requests such as "Bring me the fish," rather than an ostensive labeling statement like "This is a fish." One question is whether toddlers can learn a *novel* label from a request or directive. A second question is whether they can do so as easily as they do in the ostensive labeling context. The next section presents data addressing these two questions.

15.3 The Directive Context

To assess whether children can learn novel labels from directives, we conducted an experimental study with 18- and 24-month-olds (Callanan et al. 2001). There were thirty-two children in each age group, and they were randomly assigned to one of two conditions: an Ostensive condition in which a novel object was directly labeled ("That's a *toma*"), and a Directive condition in which the name for a novel object was introduced in the context of a directive ("Put the *toma* down here"). It is important to emphasize that the pragmatics of these two kinds of utterances were very different. In the Directive condition, the experimenter was trained to focus on directing the child's *behavior*, rather than focusing on the object and its name. The experimenter's intent in the Directive condition was "Do this with this thing," rather than to expressly label the object (as it was in the Ostensive condition).

The children were exposed to four novel objects in each of two training periods; all were treated equally, but only one served as the target of a novel word. Each child was exposed to two novel words (*toma* and *wuggie*). For any given child, both words were introduced in the directive context or both in the ostensive context. After one training period, they were given a comprehension trial ("Which one's the *toma?*") and after the other they were given a preference control trial ("Which one's your favorite one?"). The order of these two trials was counterbalanced within each age group and each condition.

The 24-month-olds performed equally well in the Ostensive and Directive conditions. The 18-month-olds, however, performed above chance only in the Ostensive condition. At both ages, children's performance on the control trials was not different from chance. Although it is possible that the ostensive labeling frame is better suited to the attentional abilities of 18-month-olds (e.g., it involves more stress on the target word), it is important to note that the position of the target word in the labeling utterance was confounded with condition: at the end of the sentence in the Ostensive condition, and in the middle of the sentence in the Directive condition. Thus, it is quite possible that sentence position of the target word (see Shady and Gerken 1999) may explain the age differences we found in children's ability to learn the novel label in the Directive condition.

To test this hypothesis, we conducted a follow-up study in which we essentially re-ran the Directive condition with another group of 18-month-olds and placed the target word at the end of the sentence. So, instead of saying "Put the *toma* down here," we asked the children to "Drop the *toma*." The experimenter was trained to place stress on the verb, not the object label, to keep the intention directive, not labeling. Performance rose dramatically in this version of the Directive condition such that children performed at above-chance levels. This finding was significantly different from both the preference control and the previous Directive condition, suggesting that part of what makes the ostensive labeling context helpful for young children's learning may be the privileged position of the target word. Ostensive statements almost always involve presenting the label at the end of the sentence and with great stress ("That's a DOGGIE"). In any case, it is noteworthy that the 24-month-old participants learned equally well in the ostensive and directive contexts, even when the target word was unstressed and was presented in the middle of the sentence in the Directive condition.

These studies demonstrate that toddlers can learn novel object labels from directives, but what of verbs? Although a directly analogous test of verb learning from directives has not been conducted, there are two relevant studies. First, Tomasello and Barton (1994) had an adult use a novel word to announce to 24-month-olds her intention to perform an action on an object: "Let's go *plunk* it." In one condition the experimenter immediately performed the target action, followed by an accidental (clumsily executed) action. In another condition she first performed the accidental action and then the intentional action. Children in both conditions learned the novel verb for the intentional action. To learn the novel verb in this study children had to discriminate the accidental from the intentional action, they had to hold the novel verb in mind until they saw the intended action produced, and they had to know that when an adult announces an intention to perform an action it is the ensuing intentional action that she intends to indicate. Thus, these findings indicate that 24-month-olds can learn verbs in nonostensive contexts, and there is some suggestion that they may do so better in the nonostensive context (when the action occurs before or after the verb is spoken) than in the ostensive context (Ambalu, Chiat, and Pring 1997; Tomasello and Kruger 1992).

A second study demonstrating verb learning in a nonostensive context was conducted by Tomasello and Akhtar (1995, Study 2). In this study, children aged 2;0 to 2;6 watched an adult perform a novel and nameless action with a novel and nameless object. The adult said

"Widget!" as she handed the child the object. The adult's behavior just before and during the use of this novel word was manipulated between groups. Children in the Action-Request group watched the adult prepare for the target action to be performed by the child (by orienting the action prop correctly) before she produced the novel word; the adult then used the novel word as if requesting that the child perform the action while alternating her gaze between the child and the action prop. Children in the Object-Labeling group saw no prior preparation of the prop, but heard the word *Widget* used as a label, while the adult alternated her gaze between the child and the object. The outcome was that children in the Action-Request condition associated the new word with the novel action, whereas children in the Object-Labeling condition associated the new word with the novel object. To learn the new verb in the Action-Request context, children had to understand from the adult's nonverbal behaviors that she was requesting an action of them (and was not labeling the nameless object). Thus, when the nonlinguistic context supported this interpretation, children took the one-word utterance "Widget" (perhaps parsed as "Widge it") to be a request for action, indicating once more the child's use of nonlinguistic context in verb learning.

In addition to learning verbs in directive contexts, children might also learn verbs through the use of prior event knowledge. After repeated interactions in a given situation, children may form a script or event representation (Nelson 1986), which allows them to anticipate or predict what is likely to happen next in a given situation. If they then hear someone ask them to perform a specific action in this same context, they may be able to associate their anticipation of the upcoming action with the new verb they hear. The studies reviewed in the next section indicate that 24-month-olds can use event knowledge to learn both novel verbs and novel object labels.

15.4 Routine (Repetitive) Contexts

Akhtar and Tomasello (1996, Study 2) examined the event knowledge hypothesis by creating a scripted situation in which 24-month-old children were able to predict which of a number of novel actions was impending. All children received the same pretraining, in which four different toy characters were each reliably associated with a different novel action, so that they would learn which character performed which action. Children were then randomly assigned to one of two experimental groups, in which they were exposed to a novel verb in one of two ways. In the Visible Referent group, the experimenter announced her intention to perform an action ("Let's *meek* Big Bird"), and then proceeded to perform the target action. In the Absent Referent group, the experimenter said the same thing but, after searching, told the child she was unable to find Big Bird. Consequently, she could not perform the target action and children in this group never saw the referent action after hearing the novel verb. Thus, there was no perceptual referent available to which the child could attach the word.

Children in both groups were able to learn the new verb, and learning was equivalent in the two groups. Thus, children in the Absent Referent group were able to determine what the adult was referring to in this scripted situation without ever seeing the referent action paired with the novel verb. To do this they used their understanding (event knowledge)—based on past experience in this context—that the adult intended to perform the target action and that the novel verb was meant to refer to that intended action (even though it was never actually performed).

In an analogous design testing children's use of event knowledge to acquire object labels, Akhtar and Tomasello (1996, Study 1) had 24-month-old children participate in a script in which an adult experimenter consistently found four nameless objects in four separate locations. One object served as the target, and the locations of all objects remained constant for a given child, enabling subjects to form expectations about which object would be found in each location. After three finding rounds, the experimenter announced her intention to find a specific object: "Now let's find the *toma!*" In the Visible Referent condition, she proceeded to find the target object. In the Absent Referent condition, she attempted to open the target location but told the child it was locked; thus, children in this group never saw the target object after hearing the novel word. Children were able to learn the object label even when they had not seen the object perceptually paired with the new word. To do so they had to rely on their knowledge of the context and to anticipate what was likely to happen next. This study was subsequently replicated with 18-month-old participants (Tomasello, Strosberg, and Akhtar 1996).

The studies of event knowledge all demonstrate that young children can actively make use of knowledge constructed from repeated events/contexts to learn novel words. They do not require the co-occurrence of the referent and word as in the ostensive context. Indeed, in these studies 2-year-olds learned object labels and verbs just as well when the referent was not perceptually available as when it was.

15.5   Relevance to the Discourse Context

The studies reviewed in the previous section illustrate that 2-year-olds were able to make use of the preceding context (i.e., their event knowledge) to determine what the experimenter was referring to, even though the referent was not visible. Although it is possible that they somewhat mindlessly (reflexively) attached the word they heard to a mental image of what was to happen next, the view presented here is that when young children hear language, they actively pay attention to what is most *relevant* in the discourse context (Bloom 1998, 2000). According to this view, children are flexible and use different sources of information in different contexts to determine what the speaker is most likely labeling. Of course what is most relevant in a given communicative context is influenced by many factors (Sperber and Wilson 1986). Because adults tend to label what is new (particularly in interactions with young children), one factor influencing relevance may be novelty in the discourse context.

Akhtar, Carpenter, and Tomasello (1996) examined the role that discourse novelty might play in the learning of object labels. Twenty-four-month-old children first played with three nameless objects with two experimenters and a parent; no language models were given. After one experimenter and the parent left the room, the child and the other experimenter played with a fourth object (the target) for an equal amount of time. The adults then returned to give the language models. On entering the room the adults looked at the group of objects (being careful not to single out any one object with eye gaze) and said: "Look, I see a *gazzer* in there! A *gazzer!*" From the child's point of view what was different about the target object was that it was new to the discourse context for the adults. The children attached the new label to the object that was new for the adults. They seemed to understand that adults tend to label things that are new to the discourse context and, moreover, that discourse novelty is determined from the speaker's point of view.

Samuelson and Smith (1998) have proposed an alternative explanation for this finding, arguing that the distinctiveness of one object (the target object) in the naming context led the children to attend to that object when it was named. That is, because the target object had been treated differently (only one adult was present when it was introduced), it later "popped out" of the naming context (where three adults were present) and captured the children's attention. This mechanistic account is argued to be more parsimonious than the social explanation favored by Akhtar et al. and was tested by replicating Akhtar et al.'s procedure with one difference: having one of the four novel objects receive special treatment (that did not involve anyone leaving the room) prior to the naming event. The children did associate the novel name with the object that had been experienced in a different context than the context in which the first three objects were experienced. Samuelson and Smith concluded that their mechanistic account involving memory and attention is all that is needed to explain Akhtar et al.'s findings. It is important to note, however, that neither Samuelson and Smith nor Akhtar et al. directly pitted the mechanistic and social accounts against one another within the same experimental paradigm (Baldwin and Moses 2001). That was the goal of a recent set of studies (Diesendruck et al., forthcoming) in which an Intentional condition almost identical to Samuelson and Smith's (1998) study was contrasted with an Accidental condition in which the change in context occurred unintentionally.

According to Samuelson and Smith's mechanistic account, the nature of the change in context is irrelevant. It is the novelty of the fourth object's context relative to the first three objects and the naming episode that matters. According to their account, there should be no difference between the two conditions. In both cases, children should pick the fourth object as the target of the novel word because, being the most novel in the context, it automatically grabs the child's attention at the time of naming. According to the social account, the nature of the change in context *does* matter, because children are sensitive to the relevance of the change in context. Indeed, when the change in context was intentional, children interpreted the name as referring to the target object. When the change in context was accidental, children interpreted the name as referring to any of the four objects, suggesting, along with other findings (e.g., Hollich et al. 2000; Moore, Angelopoulos, and Bennett 1999) that by 24 months children favor social (discourse) cues over salience when learning new words.

Two-year-olds' attention to discourse novelty may also help them determine to which ontological category a given word might belong. This was demonstrated in a study in which children heard a new word modeled as a one-word utterance ("Modi!") just as a nameless target object was undergoing a nameless target action (Tomasello and Akhtar 1995, Study 1). What differed between the two experimental groups were the behaviors leading up to the language model. In the Action-Novel condition, the experimenter and child performed multiple actions on the target object, so that when the language model was presented, the target action was the novel element in the discourse context. In the Object-Novel condition, the experimenter and child first performed the target action on multiple objects, so that when the language model was presented, the target object was the novel element in the discourse context. Children associated the word with the element that was new to the discourse context at the time of the model; most children in the Action-Novel condition associated the word with the target action and most children in the Object-Novel condition associated the word with the target object. Thus, discourse novelty can also be used by young 2-year-olds to determine a novel word's ontological status.

Another obvious candidate contributor to relevance is the topic of the discourse context. Consider, for example, that an adult is labeling the known colors of objects, and then points to another object and labels it *periwinkle*. The most relevant interpretation in this context would be that *periwinkle* was the name for the color of that object. Studies of the ability to "fast map" words to referents suggest that preschoolers are sensitive to linguistic context when interpreting novel words (Au and Markman 1987; Carey and Bartlett 1978; Heibeck and Markman 1987). That is, they can make use of contrastive information in sentences such as "Bring me the chromium one, not the blue one" to interpret chromium as a color term. There is also some evidence that 2-year-olds' interpretations of ambiguous sentences (sentences that could be interpreted as requiring an action response or a verbal response) are influenced by the preceding discourse context (Shatz 1978, Experiment 2). It is therefore quite possible that 2-year-olds' interpretations of novel ambiguous words might also be influenced by the discourse contexts in which those words are presented.

In the training phase of a recent study (Akhtar 2002), I showed 2- and 3-year-old children a target object (with a novel shape and novel texture) and told them "This is a *dacky* one." In the Shape-Relevant condition, the topic of discourse prior to this sentence was the shape of other objects—that is, two objects' shapes were described before the target object was labeled ("This is a round one; this is a square one"). In the Texture-Relevant condition, the two preceding objects' textures were described ("This is a smooth one; this is a fuzzy one"). Children were given comprehension trials on which they were shown sets of test objects and then asked "Which one is the *dacky* one?" They also received trials designed to control for preference of the relevant dimension. Children in both age groups chose objects that matched the target (relevant) dimension on the comprehension trials more frequently than on the corresponding preference trials, indicating that they were indeed paying attention to the preceding discourse topic in determining the meaning of the novel adjective. These data suggest that 2-year-olds can use implicit contrast between the target word and words used in the immediately preceding context ("This is a round one; this is a square one; this is a *dacky* one") as a cue to the referential intentions of a speaker and can thereby disambiguate the reference of a novel adjective used by that speaker.

It is possible then that being sensitive to the discourse context in which novel words are encountered may help young children reduce considerably the problem of referential indeterminacy. If they are able to determine which element of the context is most relevant to the speaker's referential intentions, they may not face the infinite number of possible interpretations that theorists have posited. It is important to note, however, that in the current study it was language itself (the descriptions of the initial objects) that provided the information as to which dimension was relevant. Thus, children had to have some understanding of the semantic domain used to set up the topic to determine the meaning of the novel adjective in this study (Klibanoff and Waxman 2000; Waxman and Markow 1998). An important question remains as to how even younger children who do not yet comprehend much language disambiguate reference (i.e., determine what is most relevant to the speaker's intentions) and acquire their earliest words. Two mechanisms have been proposed.

One relies on the observation that it is within repetitive interactions where the child has a nonverbal understanding of the context that children acquire their earliest language (Bruner 1983). Routines or scripts "create, with no need of a conventional language whatsoever, a shared referential context within which the language of the adult makes sense to the prelinguistic child" (Tomasello 1992, 70). When children develop a nonlinguistic understanding of the situations they experience regularly, they begin to anticipate the objects and actions within a given routine. Because they do not have to expend effort to understand the situation and what is going to happen next, they can focus their attentional resources on the language used by others within the routine (Nelson 1986; Akhtar and Tomasello 1996). Sharing an understanding with their social partners about the goals and sequence of the activity allows infants to focus on what their partner is focused on and thereby begin to comprehend some of the language used within the activity.

The second mechanism relies on the observation that, just as interactions between caregivers and children are repeated, so are words. Indeed, several researchers have proposed that referential indeterminacy may be significantly reduced if children can engage in cross-situational learning (Gleitman 1990; Pinker 1994; Zukow-Goldring 1997). That is, if children are able to pay attention to (and remember) the element that remains constant across different contexts in which the same word is used, the hypothesis is that they will then be able to determine the appropriate meaning of this word (see discussion of Akhtar and Montague 1999, below); thus, cross-situational learning is another mechanism by which children can disambiguate reference without knowledge of language itself.

15.6 The Overhearing Context

In the studies described thus far, as well as in the language-learning literature more generally, there seems to be an implicit assumption that children learn language only (or mainly) from speech directed to them. Studies of linguistic "input" to first-language learners invariably examine the language of mothers or other caregivers who are speaking to their children. However, in some communities, infants and young children are rarely included as direct addressees in conversational interactions with adults, at least not to the degree they are in the Western middle-class context (Crago, Allen, and Hough-Eyamie 1997; Ochs 1988; Schieffelin and Ochs 1986). Young children do, of course, pay attention to the conversations of others (Barton and Tomasello 1991; Dunn and Shatz 1989). It is therefore reasonable to hypothesize that they may be able to acquire new words in contexts in which they have only overheard those words being used by others not engaged with them. The studies described in this section demonstrate that 2-year-olds are indeed capable of learning words from others' conversations.

Studies by Oshima-Takane (1988; Oshima-Takane, Goodz, and Derevensky 1996) suggest that overhearing may play a particularly important role in the acquisition of personal pronouns. Some children make reversal errors with personal pronouns—for example, referring to themselves as "you." One possible reason for these errors is that personal pronouns, along with other deictic terms, have shifting reference—that is, the person referred to by a particular pronoun changes depending on who the speaker and addressee are. So, when a mother speaks to her child, she refers to herself as *I* or *me* and the child as *you*, but when the child speaks, she or he has to reverse the pronoun usage. As Oshima-Takane points out, models for correct usage are not available in child-directed speech alone. For example, if one only hears the word *you* in reference to oneself, one might reasonably conclude that it is a name for oneself. But (over)-hearing others addressing one another as *you* would lead to the more appropriate inference that *you* is a word used to refer to whoever is being addressed.

In this regard, it is particularly interesting that secondborn children tend to have an advantage over firstborns in learning personal pronouns (Oshima-Takane, Goodz, and Derevensky 1996). While their overall rate of language development is equivalent to that of firstborns, secondborns are more likely to use personal pronouns correctly. Moreover, an examination of maternal speech in the triadic context (mother, firstborn, and secondborn) revealed that secondborns were exposed to more pronouns in overheard conversations than in speech directed to them. Oshima-Takane, Goodz, and Derevensky (1996) interpret these findings as support for the hypothesis that secondborn children's advantage in pronoun production is linked to their opportunities to overhear pronouns being used in third-party conversations between their siblings and parents.

In a direct test of the overhearing hypothesis, Akhtar, Jipson, and Callanan (2001) examined the ability of Western middle-class 2-year-olds to learn novel object labels and novel verbs through over-hearing. In each study, children were randomly assigned to one of two conditions: Addressed or Overhearing. In the Addressed condition, the experimenter played a game with the child and introduced a novel word for one of four unfamiliar objects/actions. In the Overhearing condition, the child was positioned as an onlooker to an identical interaction between the experimenter and an adult confederate. In this condition, the experimenter introduced the novel word to the confederate instead of the child, and essentially ignored the child. The children were equally good at learning object labels when they were directly addressed as when they were over-hearers. Children aged 2;6, but not those aged 2;0, were also able to learn a new verb through overhearing (possible reasons why verbs may have been more difficult are outlined in Akhtar, Jipson, and Callanan 2001).

15.7 Learning across Contexts

Almost all experimental studies of early word learning, including
all of those described thus far in this chapter, involve presenting
children with only one naming context. It is important to note, however, that in their everyday interactions, children generally hear any
given word multiple times and often across multiple contexts; consequently, there is not just one opportunity for them to accurately
determine the referent of a given word. That is, if children are able
to pay attention to (and remember) the element that remains constant across different situations in which the same word is used, the
hypothesis is that they will then be able to determine the appropriate
meaning of this word.

Although it can be applied to any type of referential term, the
cross-situational learning hypothesis is perhaps best exemplified in
the case of adjectives. Consider, for example, a situation in which a
child hears a balloon described as *purple*. The child may not initially
comprehend this term, but after hearing the same word used to describe a variety of purple-colored objects (that have nothing in common other than their hue), the child may be more likely to conclude
that *purple* is a color term. Lisa Montague and I directly tested this
hypothesis with young children (Akhtar and Montague 1999; see also
Klibanoff and Waxman 2000, Study 2).

Three groups of children (2-, 3-, and 4-year-olds) were presented
with novel objects that differed systematically in shape and texture.
In the training phase, children were first shown one object (with a
novel shape and texture) and were told "This is a *modi* one." The
adjectival frame was used because it can be used both to describe
shapes and textures of objects—for instance, This is a round one;
This is a furry one. In the Shape condition, other objects that
matched the initial object in shape (and differed in texture) were
also labeled "*modi* ones." In the Texture condition, the subsequent
objects matched the initial object in texture (and differed in shape).
Children were given comprehension trials on which they were shown
sets of test objects and then asked "Which one is the *modi* one?"
They also received trials designed to control for preference of the
consistent dimension. If children do engage in cross-situational

learning of the sort described above, the prediction was that they would choose objects that matched the target dimension on the comprehension trials more frequently than they did on the corresponding preference trials. This was the case for all age groups tested, indicating that the children extracted what was similar across the contexts in which a novel adjective was introduced.

15.8 Summary

The studies reviewed in this chapter demonstrate that young children can learn novel words (object labels, verbs, adjectives) in a wide variety of contexts. Although there is a tendency to think of the ostensive labeling context as prototypical, it may not be for all children, even those in the Western middle class. The studies show that young children can learn words in many different contexts because they are able to tune into a wide variety of pragmatic cues to adult referential intentions (Akhtar and Tomasello 2000), even when the adults are not interacting with them (Akhtar, Jipson, and Callanan 2001). From this theoretical perspective, it is also important to recognize that even the ostensive labeling of objects may be best described in this way: children must determine the adult's referential intention by determining her focus of attention. In the ostensive context they do so with adult help in the form of gaze direction (Baldwin 1991, 1993) and pointing so that the active role the child plays in determining the speaker's referential intent tends to be overlooked.

It is important to emphasize that determining referential intent is a process that will work only for the learning of referential terms, especially terms for objects, actions, and attributes. The studies reviewed in this chapter do not have anything to say about the acquisition of other word types (e.g., prepositions, determiners). The studies also take for granted the myriad other processes involved in learning words: speech segmentation (Echols and Marti, chapter 2, this volume; Jusczyk 1997), retention of the sequences of phonemes that occur most frequently together (Fisher, Church, and Chambers, chapter 1, this volume; Jusczyk and Hohne 1997; Saffran, Aslin, and

Newport 1996), and so on. Similarly, we have examined only a subset of the discourse contexts in which young children encounter novel words. Children also make use of the linguistic (i.e., semantic and syntactic) contexts (Gleitman 1990; Goodman, McDonough, and Brown 1998; Snedeker and Gleitman, chapter 9, this volume) in which words are spoken.[3] The goal of this chapter has been primarily to highlight the active role played by young children in acquiring referential terms, and the variety of pragmatic contexts in which they can do so.

Acknowledgments

Many thanks to Maureen Callanan, Jennifer Jipson, Geoffrey Hall, and Sandra Waxman for their comments on a preliminary draft.

Notes

1. Context of course also includes linguistic context, both syntactic (Gleitman 1990) and semantic (Goodman, McDonough, and Brown 1998); in this chapter, however, I use the term primarily to refer to the discourse or pragmatic contexts in which children encounter novel words.

2. A quote from Donaldson (1978, 38) seems relevant here: "It may turn out to be a very long journey from the primary understanding of what people mean by the words they speak ... to the ultimate and separate understanding of what words mean. Perhaps the idea that words mean anything—in isolation—is a highly sophisticated notion, and a Western adult one at that."

3. Of course they can only do so after they have already learned some words and some sentence frames. Also, as Pinker (1994) has argued persuasively for the case of verb learning, use of syntactic context alone is not sufficient to gain an understanding of a verb's "root content" (as opposed to its "perspective meaning"). Some understanding of the (nonlinguistic) contexts of use of the verb is also required.

References

Akhtar, N. 2002. Relevance and early word learning. *Journal of Child Language, 29*, 677–686.

Akhtar, N., Carpenter, M., and Tomasello, M. 1996. The role of discourse novelty in early word learning. *Child Development, 67*, 635–645.

Akhtar, N., Jipson, J., and Callanan, M. 2001. Learning words through overhearing. *Child Development, 72*, 416–430.

Akhtar, N., and Montague, L. 1999. Early lexical acquisition: The role of cross-situational learning. *First Language, 19,* 347–358.

Akhtar, N., and Tomasello, M. 1996. Two-year-olds learn words for absent objects and actions. *British Journal of Developmental Psychology, 14,* 79–93.

Akhtar, N., and Tomasello, M. 1998. Intersubjectivity in early language learning and use. In S. Braten, ed., *Intersubjective communication and emotion in ontogeny,* 316–335. Cambridge: Cambridge University Press.

Akhtar, N., and Tomasello, M. 2000. The social nature of words and word learning. In R. M. Golinkoff and K. Hirsh-Pasek, eds., *Becoming a word learner: A debate on lexical acquisition,* 115–135. Oxford: Oxford University Press.

Ambalu, D., Chiat, S., and Pring, T. 1997. When is it best to use a verb? The effects of timing and focus of verb models on children's learning of verbs. *Journal of Child Language, 24,* 25–34.

Au, T. K., and Markman, E. M. 1987. Acquiring word meanings via linguistic contrast. *Cognitive Development, 2,* 217–236.

Baldwin, D. A. 1991. Infants' contribution to the achievement of joint reference. *Child Development, 62,* 875–890.

Baldwin, D. A. 1993. Infants' ability to consult the speaker for clues to word reference. *Journal of Child Language, 20,* 395–418.

Baldwin, D. A. 1995. Understanding the link between joint attention and language. In C. Moore and P. Dunham, eds., *Joint attention: Its origins and role in development,* 131–158. Hillsdale, NJ: Erlbaum.

Baldwin, D. A., and Moses, L. J. 2001. Links between social understanding and early word learning: Challenges to current accounts. *Social Development, 10,* 309–329.

Barton, M. E., and Tomasello, M. 1991. Joint attention and conversation in mother-infant-sibling triads. *Child Development, 62,* 517–529.

Bates, E. 1976. *Language and context: The acquisition of pragmatics.* New York: Academic Press.

Bloom, L. 1970. *Language development: Form and function in emerging grammars.* Cambridge, MA: MIT Press.

Bloom, L. 1991. *Language development from two to three.* New York: Cambridge University Press.

Bloom, L. 1998. Language acquisition in its developmental context. In D. Kuhn and R. S. Siegler, eds., *Handbook of child psychology, Vol. 2: Cognition, perception, and language,* 309–370. New York: Wiley.

Bloom, L. 2000. The intentionality model of word learning: How to learn a word, any word. In R. M. Golinkoff and K. Hirsh-Pasek, eds., *Becoming a word learner: A debate on lexical acquisition,* 19–50. Oxford: Oxford University Press.

Bloom, L., Margulis, C., Tinker, E., and Fujita, N. 1996. Early conversations and word learning: Contributions from child and adult. *Child Development, 67,* 3154–3175.

Bruner, J. S. 1983. *Child's talk: Learning to use language.* New York: Norton.

Butterworth, G. 1992. Context and cognition in models of cognitive growth. In P. Light and G. Butterworth, eds., *Context and cognition: Ways of learning and knowing,* 1–13. Hillsdale, NJ: Erlbaum.

Callanan, M., Akhtar, N., Sabbagh, M., and Sussman, L. 2001. *Learning words in directive and ostensive contexts.* Unpublished manuscript, University of California, Santa Cruz.

Carey, S., and Bartlett, E. 1978. Acquiring a single new word. *Papers and Reports on Child Language Development, 15,* 17–29.

Crago, M. B., Allen, S. E. M., and Hough-Eyamie, W. P. 1997. Exploring innateness through cultural and linguistic variation. In M. Gopnik, ed., *The inheritance and innateness of grammars,* 70–90. New York: Oxford University Press.

DeLoache, J. S. 1980. Naturalistic studies of memory for object location in very young children. *New Directions for Child Development, 10,* 17–32.

Diesendruck, G., Markson, L., Akhtar, N., and Reudor, A. Forthcoming. Two-year-olds' sensitivity to speakers' intent: An alternative account of Samuelson and Smith. *Developmental Science.*

Donaldson, M. 1978. *Children's minds.* London: Croom Helm.

Dunn, J., and Shatz, M. 1989. Becoming a conversationalist despite (or because of) having an older sibling. *Child Development, 60,* 399–410.

Fisher, C., Hall, D. G., Rakowitz, S., and Gleitman, L. 1994. When it is better to receive than to give: Syntactic and conceptual constraints on vocabulary growth. *Lingua, 92,* 333–375.

Gladwin, T. 1970. *East is a big bird: Navigation and logic on Puluwat atoll.* Cambridge, MA: Harvard University Press.

Gleitman, L. 1990. The structural sources of verb meanings. *Language Acquisition, 1,* 3–55.

Goodman, J. C., McDonough, L., and Brown, N. B. 1998. The role of semantic context and memory in the acquisition of novel nouns. *Child Development, 69,* 1330–1344.

Heibeck, T. H., and Markman, E. M. 1987. Word learning in children: An examination of fast mapping. *Child Development, 58,* 1021–1034.

Hollich, G. J., Hirsh-Pasek, K., and Golinkoff, R. M. 2000. Breaking the language barrier: An emergentist coalition model for the origins of word learning. *Monographs of the Society for Research in Child Development, 65* (serial no. 123).

Jusczyk, P. W. 1997. *The discovery of spoken language.* Cambridge, MA: MIT Press.

Jusczyk, P. W., and Hohne, E. A. 1997. Infants' memory for spoken words. *Science,* 277(5334), 1984–1986.

Klibanoff, R. S., and Waxman, S. R. 2000. Basic level object categories support the acquisition of novel adjectives: Evidence from preschool-aged children. *Child Development,* 71, 649–659.

Lieven, E. V. M. 1994. Crosslinguistic and crosscultural aspects of language addressed to children. In C. Gallaway and B. J. Richards, eds., *Input and interaction in language acquisition,* 56–73. Cambridge: Cambridge University Press.

Markman, E. M. 1989. *Categorization and naming in children: Problems of induction.* Cambridge, MA: MIT Press.

Moore, C., Angelopoulos, M., and Bennett, P. 1999. Word learning in the context of referential and salience cues. *Developmental Psychology,* 35, 60–68.

Nelson, K. 1985. *Making sense: The child's acquisition of shared meaning.* New York: Academic Press.

Nelson, K. 1986. *Event knowledge: Structure and function in development.* Hillsdale, NJ: Erlbaum.

Ochs, E. 1988. *Culture and language development: Language acquisition and language socialization in a Samoan village.* Cambridge: Cambridge University Press.

Oshima-Takane, Y. 1988. Children learn from speech not addressed to them: The case of personal pronouns. *Journal of Child Language,* 15, 95–108.

Oshima-Takane, Y., Goodz, E., and Derevensky, J. L. 1996. Birth order effects on early language development: Do secondborn children learn from overheard speech? *Child Development,* 67, 621–634.

Pinker, S. 1994. How could a child use verb syntax to learn verb semantics? *Lingua,* 92, 377–410.

Rogoff, B. 1982. Integrating context and cognitive development. In M. E. Lamb and A. L. Brown, eds., *Advances in developmental psychology,* vol. 2. Hillsdale, NJ: Erlbaum.

Rogoff, B., and Lave, J., eds. 1984. *Everyday cognition: Its development in social context.* Cambridge, MA: Harvard University Press.

Saffran, J. R., Aslin, R. N., and Newport, E. L. 1996. Statistical learning by 8-month-old infants. *Science,* 274(5294), 1926–1928.

Samuelson, L. K., and Smith, L. B. 1998. Memory and attention make smart word learning: An alternative account of Akhtar, Carpenter, and Tomasello. *Child Development,* 69, 94–104.

Schieffelin, B. B., and Ochs, E. 1986. *Language socialization across cultures.* Cambridge: Cambridge University Press.

Scribner, S. 1976. Situating the experiment in cross-cultural research. In K. F. Riegel and J. A. Meacham, eds., *The developing individual in a changing world*, vol. 1, 310–321. Chicago: Aldine.

Shady, M., and Gerken, L. 1999. Grammatical and caregiver cues in early sentence comprehension. *Journal of Child Language, 26*, 163–175.

Shatz, M. 1978. On the development of communicative understandings: An early strategy for interpreting and responding to messages. *Cognitive Psychology, 10*, 271–301.

Sperber, D., and Wilson, D. 1986. *Relevance: Communication and cognition*. Oxford: Blackwell.

Tomasello, M. 1992. The social bases of language acquisition. *Social Development, 1*, 67–87.

Tomasello, M., and Akhtar, N. 1995. Two-year-olds use pragmatic cues to differentiate reference to objects and actions. *Cognitive Development, 10*, 201–224.

Tomasello, M., and Barton, M. E. 1994. Learning words in nonostensive contexts. *Developmental Psychology, 30*, 639–650.

Tomasello, M., and Kruger, A. 1992. Acquiring verbs in ostensive and non-ostensive contexts. *Journal of Child Language, 19*, 311–333.

Tomasello, M., Strosberg, R., and Akhtar, N. 1996. Eighteen-month-old children learn words in non-ostensive contexts. *Journal of Child Language, 23*, 157–176.

Vygotsky, L. S. 1978. *Mind in society*. Cambridge, MA: Harvard University Press.

Waxman, S. R., and Markow, D. B. 1998. Object properties and object kind: Twenty-one-month-old infants' extension of novel adjectives. *Child Development, 69*, 1313–1329.

Wellman, H. M. 1988. The early development of memory strategies. In F. E. Weinert and M. Perlmutter, eds., *Memory development: Universal changes and individual differences*, 3–30. Hillsdale, NJ: Erlbaum.

Zukow-Goldring, P. 1997. A social ecological realist approach to the emergence of the lexicon: Educating attention to amodal invariants in gesture and speech. In C. Dent and P. Zukow-Goldring, eds., *Evolving explanations of development: Ecological approaches to organism-environment systems*, 199–250. Washington, DC: American Psychological Association.

16

Converging on Word Meaning

Megan M. Saylor, Dare A. Baldwin, and Mark A. Sabbagh

For several months, one child of our acquaintance called kitchen brooms "bathrooms," continuing to do so despite lengthy and repeated attempts to set him straight. Since he often requested that he be allowed to play with "bathrooms" (i.e., brooms), this frequently led to considerable confusion for visitors to the household and to great amusement for those in the know. Such "embarrassing" errors in word learning stand out—not just because they are entertaining, but also because they are rare. By and large, children discover appropriate meanings for new words efficiently and with a modicum of error.

Research conducted principally by contributors to this book helps to explain children's remarkable success at word learning. From infancy on, children bring a diverse set of skills to bear in deciphering word meaning, including powerful memory capabilities, categorization skills, skills for analyzing speech sounds, selective attention, default assumptions about meaning, the ability to capitalize on syntactic clues to meaning, and a facility for making appropriate inferences about others' communicative intentions. In this chapter we focus on children's sensitivity to clues regarding others' communicative intentions and on possible points of convergence between this skill and other sources of information for word learning.

Our increasing understanding of children's impressive inventory of word-learning skills is gratifying but not yet satisfying. In particular, we know almost nothing about how children's word-learning skills operate within the rich context of everyday language use. Thus, we are left with a number of specific questions, including the following: How frequently do word-learning skills conflict with one another or with the input children encounter? How often do children hear language that pits their skills against one another, as when speakers supply clues to intentions conflicting with default assumptions or syntactic clues to meaning? How do children cope with language learning in contexts complex enough to interfere with the processing needed for attention, categorization, and inferential processes?

On the flip side, there are corresponding insufficiencies in our understanding about the extent to which the language input *complements* children's word-learning skills. Quite possibly, the language children hear converges with their word-learning skills to a degree that has gone largely unrecognized (but for research addressing these issues, see Callanan 1989; Callanan and Sabbagh 2003; Hall and Waxman 1994).

We have recently carried out a series of studies designed to explore such a possible case of convergence between children's language input and their skills for word learning. This case concerns children's inferences about one small set of semantic items: words that label parts for objects, such as *handle* and *spigot*. We find children's acquisition of such part terms of only passing interest in its own right. The interest of this work lies primarily in the possibility it raises that convergence is central to children's word learning more generally.

16.1 Part-Term Learning

On hearing part terms for the first time, children are faced with a variant of the same complex inductive puzzle that they encounter for any other kind of word: how to identify "label for part" (and the appropriate part) as the meaning from among the enormous range of potential candidate meanings (Quine 1960). One tool that children might have at their disposal to ease this tricky inductive problem is recognition of a relationship between regularities in the input and speakers' labeling intentions. In other words, parental input will converge with children's skill at drawing on pragmatic information, provided the input is structured so that referential intentions are highlighted. In the case of part terms, regularities indeed emerge in parental input that could serve just this purpose of highlighting the intention to refer to a part. For one, parents tend to provide novel part terms only when children know the label for the whole object (Masur 1997). Adults also show a highly regular tendency to juxtapose novel part terms and their associated known whole-object labels within the same utterance (e.g., Masur 1997; Ninio 1980; Ninio and Bruner 1978; Shipley, Kuhn, and Madden 1983). For example, Masur (1997) found that adults introducing novel part labels to children frequently produce utterances like "It's a *bird*, ... *bird* with a big *beak!*"

We are suggesting that parents' tendency to offer novel part terms in juxtaposition with known whole-object labels complements children's sensitivity to pragmatic information. In particular, the juxtaposition between a known whole-object term and a novel term may lead children to infer something particular about speakers' communicative intentions, namely, that the speaker intends to label something other than the whole object with the second term. Otherwise, the whole-object term would have been used again to reference that aspect of the object an additional time (e.g., Clark 1987). Children may thus come to recognize that whole-part juxtaposition is a reliable surface clue to speakers' part-labeling intentions. There is good reason to believe that children possess skills for drawing on pragmatic information of this sort. After all, children are known to infer others' referential intentions from a variety of other clues, such as gestures (Kobayashi 1998), line of regard and associated head-direction and body-posture clues (Baldwin 1993a), and discourse novelty (Akhtar, Carpenter, and Tomasello 1996; Diesendruck et al. 2001).

Our goal was to test the hypothesis that parents' characteristic juxtaposition of novel part terms with known whole-object labels may converge to support children in drawing appropriate inferences about speakers' part-labeling intentions. We explored this hypothesis in two steps (Saylor, Sabbagh, and Baldwin 2002).[1] Our first study asked a general question: Does the juxtaposition of novel part and known whole-object terms that parents typically provide when intending to label novel parts help children to interpret the novel terms as referring to parts? Our second study examined whether pragmatic inferences, in particular, were facilitated by the juxtaposition clue. Taken together, then, the two studies had the potential to demonstrate convergence between regularities in parental input (e.g., whole-part juxtaposition) and children's pragmatic inferences.

In this research we faced a basic methodological challenge: how best to measure children's comprehension of part terms? Evaluating children's knowledge of labels for parts of objects is a difficult enterprise. On the one hand, children's responses to parts that are fully integrated with the whole object (e.g., a rabbit's ear) cannot easily be evaluated by noting whether they point to a part or not. In such a case, a point to the part would be ambiguous between a whole object and a part interpretation. On the other hand, children's responses to parts that have been fully disconnected from their parent whole object (e.g., a wheel from a car) are also difficult to interpret. In this case, it is not clear if a part that is removed from a whole object retains its part identity or becomes an independent whole object (Tversky and Hemenway 1984). To bypass these problems, we used a color-identification procedure to evaluate children's knowledge of labels for parts of objects. Children were presented with objects in two colors, one color for the major portion of the object, and another for a salient part (e.g., a red butterfly with a green thorax). Children were then asked to identify the part of the object by its color.

To evaluate whether children's part-term learning benefits from the juxtaposition found to occur naturally in child-directed speech, children were offered names for parts of objects in the presence and absence of such juxtaposition. In the juxtaposition condition, children were first provided with a familiar whole object label before being asked about a novel part label (e.g., See this *butterfly*? What color is the *thorax*?). The no-juxtaposition condition was identical with the exception that no whole-object label was provided (e.g., See this? What color is the *thorax*? See figure 16.1).

Twenty-four 3- to 4-year-old children participated in this first study. Children were shown twelve pictures of familiar objects. The pictures were created out of colored paper so that the major portion of the object appeared in one color, and a salient part appeared in another.

Juxtaposition:
"See this *butterfly*? What color is the thorax?"

No Juxtaposition
"See this? What color is the *thorax*?"

Figure 16.1
Labeling phrases for the juxtaposition and no-juxtaposition conditions.

Previous work suggested that the six colors used (i.e., red, green, blue, yellow, orange, purple) were within 3- to 4-year-old children's productive repertoire (Shatz et al. 1996). Half of the pictures included a salient novel part, and half a salient familiar part. The pictures were presented in the center of a standard-size sheet of white paper in one of six random orders.

After a brief warm-up session, children participated in a short pretest in which they were asked to identify the color of six color swatches that matched the colors used for the test objects. Because color-term production was our dependent measure, only children who successfully produced all six color terms in the pretest were included in the final analysis. Following the pretest, children were presented with each test object individually and asked about the color of the whole object or part in either the juxtaposition or no-juxtaposition condition (see figure 16.2).

Children were asked a total of twelve test questions: six for familiar whole objects, three for familiar parts, and three for novel parts. Across both studies, children revealed that they were highly skilled at responding to our color-identification procedure when asked for the color of familiar whole objects and parts; they systematically offered the color of the whole object when asked about familiar wholes and the color of the part when asked about familiar parts. These findings clarify that our innovative color-identification methodology provides a valid index of children's knowledge of word meanings.

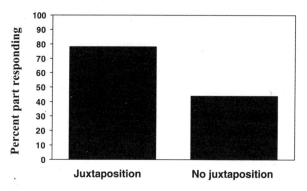

Figure 16.2
Percent part responding in the juxtaposition and no-juxtaposition conditions.

Of central interest in this first study was whether the input clue of juxtaposition would facilitate children's part-term learning. It did. First, children in the juxtaposition condition offered more part responses to test questions about novel parts than children in the no-juxtaposition condition did. For example, children viewing the red butterfly with a green thorax were significantly more likely to say *green* in response to a question about the *thorax* in the juxtaposition condition than in the no-juxtaposition condition. Furthermore, only children in the juxtaposition condition responded systematically by offering part responses at above-chance levels; children's responding did not differ from chance in the no-juxtaposition condition.

The first study clarified that juxtaposition of whole object and part labels benefited children's inferences about part-term meaning. Children indeed appear sensitive to input regularities when learning part labels. A question for the second study was whether children used the juxtaposition between familiar whole-object terms and novel terms to facilitate *pragmatic* inferences. In other words, do children rely on the juxtaposition clue to license the inference that the speaker utters the novel label with the intention to refer to the part?

Unlike other types of clues to word meaning, such as syntactic clues, pragmatic information is not bound to features of the speech stream itself. Rather, these clues should be accessible even when they

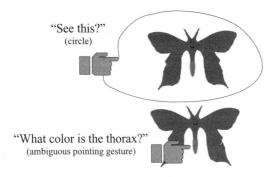

"See this?"
(circle)

"What color is the thorax?"
(ambiguous pointing gesture)

Figure 16.3
Labeling phrase for the gesture juxtaposition condition.

are not linked to linguistic channels (e.g., Tomasello and Akhtar 1995). If the juxtaposition between familiar and novel labels supports pragmatic inferences on children's part, then children should be able to infer part interpretations for novel words even when such juxtaposition is offered in a novel fashion.

To test this possibility, a new group of 3- to 4-year-old children were tested on a gesture-based version of our label-juxtaposition procedure. The procedure and materials were analogous to those in the first study. Each child participated in one of three conditions: gesture juxtaposition, gesture no-juxtaposition, and point-point control. The gestural juxtaposition was conceptually analogous to the verbal juxtaposition of the first study: a circling gesture tracing around the whole object (analogous to the presentation of the whole-object label) was juxtaposed with a referentially ambiguous point hovering two inches above the part of the object (e.g., "See this? (Circling whole object) What color is the *thorax*? (Ambiguous pointing gesture)"; see figure 16.3). The pointing gesture was ambiguous, because on its own it could be interpreted as referring to either the part or the whole object (this ambiguity was confirmed by the findings described below for the gesture no-juxtaposition and point-point control conditions).

If pragmatic inferences are behind children's sensitivity to juxtaposition, then juxtaposition in a novel, gestural format should also facilitate their learning of part terms. That is, they should treat the circling gesture indicating reference to the whole object as clarifying information for the ambiguous point, yielding the inference that the point and the attendant novel label arose from the speaker's intention to refer to the part. It is important to note here that neither circling gestures nor ambiguous pointing gestures, when taken singly, were expected to be novel to children. Rather, what was likely novel was the *juxtaposition* of the two.

Two comparison conditions were included to evaluate children's pattern of responding in the *absence* of gestural juxtaposition. First, the gesture no-juxtaposition condition included only a single ambiguous pointing gesture (e.g., "See this? What color is the *thorax*? (Ambiguous pointing gesture)"). This condition was conceptually analogous to the verbal no-juxtaposition condition of the first study, because no prior gesture was juxtaposed with the ambiguous point.

Second, in a "point-point" control condition children were presented with two gestures in sequence, just as they were in the gesture juxtaposition condition. However, the juxtaposition of the gestures was not informative, because children were presented in succession with the same ambiguous pointing gesture (e.g. "See this? (Ambiguous pointing gesture) What color is the *thorax*? (Ambiguous pointing gesture)"). This condition controlled for the possibility that children in the gesture juxtaposition condition might offer high levels of part responses simply due to the presence of two gestures, irrespective of whether the gestures were meaningfully juxtaposed or not.

The juxtaposition in this second study was provided only in the gestural modality—that is, no juxtaposition information was provided verbally. Hence, any differences observed in children's part responding would be due to gestural—not verbal—input. In all three conditions the verbal input was the same as that used in the verbal no-juxtaposition condition of the first study (e.g., "See this? What color is the *thorax*?"). Recall that the results of Study 1 revealed that this verbal information alone was not sufficient to guide children to part interpretations of novel words.

In the second study we found that gestural juxtaposition, like the verbal juxtaposition in Study 1, helped children infer part meanings for novel part terms. In particular, children in the gesture juxtaposi-

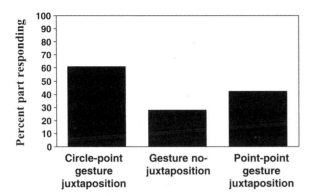

Figure 16.4
Percent part responding in the gesture juxtaposition, gesture no-juxtaposition, and point-point control conditions.

tion condition offered significantly more part responses than children in either the gesture no-juxtaposition condition or the point-point control condition. Furthermore, children's responses to test questions about novel parts did not differ between the gesture no-juxtaposition and point-point control conditions. Critically, only children in the gesture juxtaposition condition systematically gave part responses to questions about novel parts at greater-than-chance levels. In contrast, children in the point-point control and gesture no-juxtaposition conditions were largely unsystematic in their responses to questions about novel parts (see figure 16.4).

Taken together, the results from the two studies presented here provide clear evidence for one case in which input regularities converge with children's skill at inferring speakers' referential intentions. Previous research had revealed that parents reliably juxtapose whole and part labels when intending to label parts novel to children. In our studies, the presence of this reliable input clue to part meaning made all the difference to children's success at appropriately interpreting the meaning of a novel part term. In particular, children readily inferred part meaning for the novel term when juxtaposition was provided—whether in verbal or gestural modes—and remained confused about the meaning of the new term when juxtaposition was lacking.

16.2   Additional Evidence of Convergence between Input and Pragmatic Understanding

Children's ability to draw on input regularities when faced with novel part terms has also been hinted at in previous work on part-term learning. In particular, a close look at an early and elegant demonstration of the mutual-exclusivity assumption (i.e., Markman and Wachtel 1988) reveals what might be considered a first test of the role that juxtaposition plays in part-term acquisition. Mutual exclusivity is a default heuristic that has been proposed to play a role in children's part-term learning. If children adhere to the mutual-exclusivity assumption, they should avoid linking a novel label (e.g., *thorax*) to a whole object when the object involved is familiar (e.g., butterfly), and they should instead search for a different referent for the novel label, with part interpretations representing one salient alternative (e.g., Markman and Wachtel 1988; Merriman and Bowman 1989; see also Clark 1993; Mervis, Golinkoff, and Bertrand 1994).

One way to demonstrate the operation of mutual exclusivity is to compare children's inferences about word meaning when a novel label is applied to a familiar object versus a novel object. That is, if mutual exclusivity is operative, children should be more likely to interpret the novel label as referring to a part when the novel label is applied to a familiar object relative to when the novel label is applied to a novel object. To this end, Markman and Wachtel (1988) conducted a series of studies designed to explore 3- to 4-year-old children's use of the mutual-exclusivity assumption in part-term learning. However, some of their studies also may have inadvertently supplied a first test of the role that juxtaposition plays in part-term acquisition. Conveying this interpretation of their findings requires describing their methodology in some detail.

In their third study, Markman and Wachtel (1988) used the same pictures (e.g., a lung) to serve as both novel and familiar objects (for different groups of children). For example, one group of children heard the label *lung* (the name for the whole object) without any prior experience with the object, while the other group was taught *lung* before they were introduced to a novel-part term (e.g., *trachea*). During the comprehension procedure all children were asked to identify the novel part of the object (e.g., "What's a *trachea?*"). To ensure that the newly trained word (e.g., *lung*) indeed functioned as a familiar label for children in the familiar-object condition, the researcher reminded children of the just-learned whole-object label (e.g., "Remember this *lung?*") before asking the test question (e.g., "What's a *trachea?*"). In line with the predictions of the mutual-exclusivity assumption, Markman and Wachtel found that children were more likely to respond with the appropriate part of the object if they possessed prior knowledge of a name for the whole object.

In the Markman and Wachtel research, reminding children of the newly trained whole-object term in the familiar-object condition was introduced to equate the memorability of whole-object labels used in the novel and familiar conditions. However, the use of such a reminder also happened to provide the juxtaposition clue: the novel label was immediately preceded by a known label for the whole object. Thus, children's part responses in Markman and Wachtel's Study 3 may have been guided, in part, by their sensitivity to such juxtaposition. In another study examining the role of mutual exclusivity, Markman and Wachtel (1988, Study 2) did *not* provide children with immediate juxtaposition of whole-object terms and novel part terms (e.g., "What's a *boom?*"). Instead, children heard familiar whole-object labels some time prior to seeing the object being asked about and hearing the novel part terms. Under these conditions the juxtaposition clue would have been considerably weakened. While children did show some evidence of using mutual exclusivity in Study 2, their selection of parts in response to novel labels applied to familiar objects was substantially lower than in Study 1, when the whole-object term was provided immediately prior to the novel term (57% vs. 85%, respectively). Thus, in the absence of clear juxtaposition between familiar and novel labels, children had some difficulty inferring part meanings of novel words.

From the present perspective, the pattern of data across the two Markman and Wachtel studies suggests that children may have benefited from the juxtaposition clue in learning novel part terms. However, Markman and Wachtel's findings are not conducive to a direct comparison between Studies 2 and 3, because their goals for the research did not necessitate that they use the same objects in the familiar-object conditions across the two studies. Our findings provide clarifying information in this regard. In particular, in our first study, only children offered the juxtaposition between whole-object and part labels responded systematically to our test questions about novel part terms. In the absence of the relevant juxtaposition, children failed to offer part responses at above-chance levels. Clearly, juxtaposition facilitates children's inferences about part meanings.

16.3   What of Mutual Exclusivity?

Our findings might seem to bring mutual exclusivity into question. In particular, if children adhere to the mutual-exclusivity assumption, they should have avoided linking the novel label (e.g., *thorax*) to the whole object (e.g., butterfly) even in the no-juxtaposition condition. As it turned out, children reliably avoided linking the novel label to the whole object *only* when juxtaposition was present. Should we dismiss the mutual-exclusivity assumption based on this finding? In our view, the current research should *not* be taken as evidence against the operation of the mutual-exclusivity assumption (for related arguments see Hall, Quantz, and Persoage 2000). It is possible that children's recognition of the pragmatic information supplied by juxtaposition of familiar and novel terms converged with their use of mutual exclusivity to aid part-term learning. In particular, children may trigger the mutual-exclusivity assumption only in certain input contexts, and rely on pragmatic clues to define those contexts. If this is correct, the mutual-exclusivity assumption operates against a backdrop of pragmatic inferences. One way or another, then, our findings suggest that pragmatic information has some primacy in preschool-aged children's processing of novel words.

16.4   Broader Implications for Theories of Word Learning

While we have highlighted ways pragmatic skills might converge with children's input to expedite word learning, we doubt that pragmatic understanding takes children the full distance in word learning. In fact, processing challenges might necessitate augmentation of pragmatic know-how with other skills for word learning. We will discuss a few of these challenges below.

16.4.1 Processing Limitations

Our second study—involving gestural juxtaposition—showcases the flexibility inherent in preschoolers' pragmatic understanding. It is unlikely that children had seen gestures of the circle-and-point variety juxtaposed in their previous experience, yet they readily interpreted this novel, gestural version of juxtaposition as implying part reference. Clearly, children engaged in flexible, online processing of available action clues to meaning—which is the hallmark of pragmatic understanding in operation. Such flexibility seems to be one of the main benefits children derive from pragmatic bootstrapping—they can utilize clues to meaning that speakers provide even as contexts and speakers vary. At the same time, relying solely on pragmatic information imposes costs. For example, the demands of online integration of diverse clues across many modalities (e.g., intonation, gaze direction, gesture, body posture, verbal cues) spanning considerable temporal distances makes processing of pragmatic information enormously resource intensive, especially given the rapid pace at which discourse proceeds. The rate at which such processing-intensive inferences must be made may place limits on the general usefulness of sensitivity to pragmatic information for children's word learning (see Baldwin and Moses 2001 for related discussion). Future work should be geared toward addressing the impact of the processing-intensive nature of pragmatic information on children's success at word learning.

16.4.2 Input Instability

A second possible limitation of pragmatic inference as a strategy for word learning is its instability as a reliable source of information about word meaning. On some occasions speakers likely provide rich and redundant clues to their communicative intentions, making pragmatic inferences a solid base for interpreting novel words, provided, of course, that children are highly attentive to the relevant clues. On other occasions, however, clues to intentions may be relatively impoverished, because a speaker is distracted, disengaged, or uncooperative. Likewise, even when clues to intentions are rich, children's inferences about intentions may be error-ridden because they themselves are distracted or disengaged. Given such flux in the quality of the pragmatic "signal," as well as in children's processing of the signal, we should expect real variability in the quality and informativeness of pragmatic inferences vis à vis word meaning. However, it is worth pointing out that there is good reason to believe that input to children—whether in the form of language, gesture, or nonlinguistic action—typically contains exaggerated intentional clues (e.g., Brand, Baldwin, and Ashburn 2002; Bekken 1989; Fernald 1992; Iverson et al. 1999), which might improve children's "hit rate" in drawing appropriate pragmatic inferences. Nevertheless, a pragmatic bootstrapping account must come to grips with the variable quality of inferences about others' intentions and the effect of such instability on word learning.

16.4.3 Potential Underspecification of the Input

Pragmatic bootstrapping seems limited in at least one additional way: in the context of any given interaction it may not provide a direct route to the full specificity of word meaning. Melissa Bowerman first brought this limitation to our attention in connection with her groundbreaking research investigating crosslinguistic differences in the semantic systems regarding spatial relations (e.g., Bowerman 1989; Bowerman and Choi 2001; Choi et al. 1999). For example, the Korean system for labeling containment relations differs in important ways from the English system. In Korean, the verb *kkita* is used to refer to an insertion process involving objects that fit tightly or become attached (e.g., a cassette inserted into its case), whereas a contrasting verb, *nehta*, is used to refer to insertion when the objects involved bear a loose-fitting relationship (e.g., an apple inserted into a bowl). The question such crosslinguistic differences engender is how children work out the specific relations being referred to by the particular term. Imagine, for instance, a possible input scenario for one of these terms: a Korean-speaking parent produces *kkita* when directing the child to put a cassette away in its case, and ultimately performs the action herself when the child is unsuccessful. Sensitivity to pragmatic information should enable the child to appreciate quite a bit about the parent's communicative intentions, such as: "Mom is trying to get me to put the cassette away," "Mom is using the term *kkita* to refer to something about the insertion process," and the like. Could pragmatic inference take the child all the way to interpreting the parent's use of *kkita* as motivated by the intention to refer to *tight-fitting* insertion? This seems likely only if the child already comprehends the meaning of the contrasting term *nehta* and hence can utilize pragmatic inference about intended contrast on the parent's part, à la Clark's (e.g., 1993) pragmatic principle of contrast, the parent makes overt mention of the meaning difference between the two terms, or the child is capable of drawing on whatever pragmatic clues the parent might provide to highlight the difference in meaning. Of course, parents might structure their input to highlight the difference in meaning between *kkita* and *nehta*, as we have found to be the case with parents' clarification of part terms. Most of these strategies require that children already possess a fair degree of linguistic sophistication. Clearly, pragmatic inferences about meaning will become increasingly fine-tuned and specific as children gain linguistic knowledge. Pragmatic inferences in the early days of language learning will therefore often be limited in the specificity they can supply.

For all these reasons, pragmatic inference probably does not function effectively in isolation. It provides children with inferential power and flexibility, but imposes a heavy cognitive load on the learner, should vary radically in quality depending on the cooperativeness of the speaker and the alertness of the learner, and likely fails, on its own, to take the learner the full distance to meaning on many, if not most, occasions. Language learners would be better off having other, complementary, word-learning skills at their disposal (see Bloom 2000 for related points).

16.5 Propping Up Pragmatics

Children's pragmatic inferences might benefit considerably from joint action with both default assumptions about word meaning and sensitivity to syntactic regularities. In particular, complementarity among these three classes of word-learning skills may be key to word-learning success—with pragmatic inferences benefiting from the automatization introduced by default assumptions and syntactic regularities, and default assumptions relying on pragmatic clues to develop and operate effectively.

Default heuristics, like mutual exclusivity as well as the whole-object and taxonomic assumptions, complement children's sensitivity to pragmatic information nicely, in that they seem to lighten the processing load for learners. Default heuristics have typically been conceptualized as fixed assumptions that children bring to all word-learning situations; they benefit the word learner for the very reason that they are thought to apply broadly across many contexts. Learners needn't engage in laborious analysis of the multidimensional input; they can simply act on their default assumption unless there is powerful reason not to. Thus default heuristics could support sound inferences about word meaning when pragmatic inference fails by virtue of being too taxing.

This said, it is worth considering the possibility that default heuristics might actually be automatized versions of pragmatic inferences (e.g., Baldwin 1993b; Bloom 2000; Clark 1987; Diesendruck and Markson 2001). Perhaps, for example, infants initially do not possess default heuristics such as the whole-object assumption. They might be successful in learning initial labels for whole objects because they are able to infer that the speaker producing these labels intends to label the whole object. The high frequency of intentions to label whole objects in parental input might lead infants over time to assume whole-object reference as the default. Similarly, pragmatic accounts can be constructed for the other default heuristics that have been suggested. For instance, groundbreaking research by Callanan and Sabbagh (2003) along these lines hints at ways parental labeling strategies could support the emergence of the mutual-exclusivity assumption in children's development. This possibility that default heuristics are pragmatic in origin is an intriguing question for future research. In any case, however, the point remains that being able to automatize *some* inferences would be very useful to infants, and default heuristics, whatever their origin, offer that benefit.

Syntactic bootstrapping should also complement pragmatic inference. Syntactic bootstrapping involves exploiting syntactic regularities to bracket novel words as members of semantic classes (e.g., Fisher et al. 1994; Gleitman 1990; Hall, Waxman, and Hurwitz 1993; Naigles and Hoff-Ginsberg 1995). Inferences about meaning based on syntactic clues might be more stable in quality than pragmatically driven inferences, and quite possibly less processing intensive as well. To the extent that a child has accurately analyzed relevant syntactic clues, those clues should yield relatively automatic and predictable semantic inferences.

The flip side of these issues is also noteworthy: default heuristics and syntactic bootstrapping will better facilitate children's word learning if they operate against a backdrop of skill at pragmatic inference (e.g., Baldwin 1995). Default heuristics must sometimes be overridden, for example. Adults sometimes provide multiple labels for one-and-the-same whole object (e.g., couch and sofa) and children must somehow recognize that mutual exclusivity does not apply. Skill at inferring that the speaker intends to label the whole object would be one route to success at overriding the mutual-exclusivity assumption in such cases. Also, Waxman and colleagues provide evidence that default heuristics undergo developmental change, becoming increasingly refined via continuing exposure to language input (e.g., Waxman 1998, 1999; Waxman and Booth 2000; Waxman and Markow 1995; Waxman, Senghas, and Benveniste 1997). During the early phases, then, default heuristics may be somewhat ineffective guides to meaning, and other skills, such as pragmatic inference, would help to buffer against error. The same is likely true of early-phase syntactic bootstrapping: it might be error-prone, or at least yield less precise semantic inferences, than later in development. Pragmatic inference would thus provide an important source of redundancy, helping children avoid errors (e.g., broom = bathroom) that could be difficult to overcome once made.

All in all, joint action of pragmatic inference with other word-learning skills should serve children best. Sensitivity to pragmatic information enables children to flexibly take advantage of clues to speakers' intentions that are tied to the discourse context, while other skills such as default heuristics and syntactic bootstrapping make inferences about meaning more stable and tractable.

16.6 Underscoring the Importance of the Input

The research we have reported here showcases one way children's word-learning skills converge with their language input. In particular, we found that a reliable input clue to part-labeling intentions—juxtaposition of a novel word with a word referring to the whole object—was crucial in enabling 3- and 4-year-olds to interpret the novel word as referring to a part. These findings hint that children mine their language input for reliable indices of others' referential intentions, and base their inferences on the presence or absence of these indices.

We have reason to believe that the case of input regularities converging with pragmatic skills may extend beyond the part-term learning domain into others, and view this as an important direction for future investigation. Along these lines, Callanan and colleagues (e.g., Callanan 1985; Callanan and Sabbagh 2003) describe some reliable clues in parental input signaling the intention to refer to a known whole object with a novel, second label. For example, when providing a novel superordinate label for an object already known to their child at the basic level, parents typically "anchor" the new word by producing the known basic-level label as well (e.g., "It's a *mixer*. A mixer is a *machine*"; Callanan and Sabbagh 2003, 34) and often explicitly mention the "kind" relation between the known basic-level term and the novel superordinate term. Callanan (1989) found that children are better able to interpret a novel word at the superordinate level when such anchoring clues are present. Thus, children rely on input regularities to license the inference that the new word refers to the same object as the known label, and to assist in analyzing relevant differences in meaning.

Finally, convergence is not limited to a correspondence between input regularities and pragmatic inference. Convergence involves other word-learning skills as well. Default heuristics, for example, must operate in the context of convergence to be at all beneficial to children (Markman 1992, 1994). For instance, the whole-object assumption will assist children in drawing appropriate inferences about meaning only if parents are strongly inclined to label the whole object, rather than a part or a property or an action, when an object is novel to children. This kind of "input-to-heuristic" convergence has been the focus of a number of studies (e.g., Choi 2000; Choi and Gopnik 1995; Gelman et al. 1998; Hall and Waxman 1994; Mervis, Bertrand, and Pani 1995; Tardif, Gelman, and Xu 1999). This evidence points to convergence lying at the heart of semantic acquisition.

16.7   Summing Up

In this chapter we hope to have accomplished three things. One goal was to give shape to the notion of convergence as a potentially powerful force in word learning. A second goal was to test for a particular candidate case of convergence—convergence between whole- versus part-label juxtaposition in language input and children's inferences about part meaning. Children's responses revealed convergence in operation, and a subsequent study involving gestural juxtaposition clarified that pragmatic inferences in particular played a role in the convergence scenario. A final goal was to illuminate one way in which convergence—at least, the kind of convergence involving pragmatic inference—is valuable in word learning. Pragmatic inference on its own, while potentially powerful and flexible, is also potentially unreliable and overly resource intensive. Joint action of pragmatic inference with other word-learning skills, such as default heuristics and syntactic bootstrapping, should ameliorate some of these risks, in part because the latter skills lend themselves to automated inferences. Streamlining pragmatic inferences via close attention to reliable input clues—such as juxtaposition—should further facilitate appropriate inferences about word meaning.

The picture we would paint of word learning is thus even more integrative than those we have previously encountered. We suspect children not only capitalize on diverse skills for word learning, but also automatize inferences about meaning whenever possible, and mine their input for reliable indices of others' communicative intentions. These are hypotheses for which as yet there are mere morsels of evidence. We hope this soon will change.

Acknowledgments

The research reported in this chapter was supported in part by grants from the John Merck Scholars Fund and the National Science Foundation (NYI award) to Dare A. Baldwin, and by a NSF Graduate Fellowship to Mark A. Sabbagh. The chapter was prepared in part while Dare Baldwin was a fellow at the Center for Advanced Study in the Behavioral Sciences. We thank the William T. Grant Foundation for the financial support underlying this fellowship.

Note

1. Here we are only reporting two of the four studies discussed in previous publications describing this work (i.e., Saylor, Sabbagh, and Baldwin 2002); we have omitted mention of two control studies to better focus on the issues of central concern to this chapter.

References

Akhtar, N., Carpenter, M., and Tomasello, M. 1996. The role of discourse novelty in children's early word learning. *Child Development, 67,* 635–645.

Baldwin, D. A. 1993a. Infants' ability to consult the speaker for clues to word reference. *Journal of Child Language, 20,* 395–418.

Baldwin, D. A. 1993b. Interpersonal inference as a route to reducing the indeterminacy problem in word learning. *Working Papers from the Conference on "Early Cognition and the Transition to Language."* Institute for Cognitive Science, University of Texas, Austin.

Baldwin, D. A. 1995. Understanding relations between constraints and a sociopragmatic account of meaning acquisition. Paper presented at a symposium chaired by D. Baldwin and M. Callanan at the Biennial Meeting of the Society for Research in Child Development, Indianapolis.

Baldwin, D. A., and Moses, L. J. 2001. Links between early social understanding and word learning: Challenges to current accounts. In A. Imbens-Bailey, ed., special issue of *Social Development, 10,* 309–329.

Bekken, K. 1989. *Is there a motherese in gesture?* Unpublished doctoral dissertation, University of Chicago.

Bloom, P. 2000. *How children learn the meanings of words.* Cambridge, MA: MIT Press.

Bowerman, M. 1989. Learning a semantic system: What role do cognitive predispositions play? In M. L. Rice and R. L. Schiefelbusch, eds., *The teachability of language,* 133–169. Baltimore: Paul H. Brookes Publishing Co.

Bowerman, M., and Choi, S. 2001. Shaping meanings for language: Universal and language-specific in the acquisition of spatial semantic categories. In M. Bowerman and S. C. Levinson, eds., *Language acquisition and conceptual development*, 475–511. Cambridge: Cambridge University Press.

Brand, R. J., Baldwin, D. A., and Ashburn, L. A. 2002. Evidence for "motionese": Modifications in mothers' infant-directed action. *Developmental Science, 5*, 72–83.

Callanan, M. A. 1985. How parents label objects for young children: The role of input in the acquisition of category hierarchies. *Child Development, 56*, 508–523.

Callanan, M. A. 1989. Development of object categories and inclusion relations: Preschooler's hypotheses about word meaning. *Developmental Psychology, 25*, 207–216.

Callanan, M., and Sabbagh, M. 2003. *Multiple labels for objects in conversations between young children and their parents: Setting the stage for mutual exclusivity.* Unpublished manuscript, University of California, Santa Cruz.

Choi, S. 2000. Caregiver input in English and Korean: Use of nouns and verbs in book reading and toy-play contexts. *Journal of Child Language, 27*, 69–96.

Choi, S., and Gopnik, A. 1995. Early acquisition of verbs in Korean: A cross-linguistic study. *Journal of Child Language, 22*, 497–529.

Choi, S., McDonough, L., Bowerman, M., and Mandler, J. M. 1999. Early sensitivity to language-specific spatial categories in English and Korean. *Cognitive Development, 14*, 241–268.

Clark, E. V. 1987. The principle of contrast: A constraint on acquisition. In B. MacWhinney, ed., *Mechanisms of language acquisition: The 20th Annual Carnegie Mellon Symposium on Cognition*, 1–34. Hillsdale, NJ: Erlbaum.

Clark, E. V. 1993. *The lexicon in acquisition.* Cambridge: Cambridge University Press.

Diesendruck, G., and Markson, L. 2001. Children's avoidance of lexical overlap: A pragmatic account. *Developmental Psychology, 37*, 630–641.

Diesendruck, G., Markson, L., Akhtar, N., and Reudor, A. 2001. *Two-year-olds' sensitivity to speakers' intent: An alternative account of Samuelson and Smith.*

Fernald, A. 1992. Human maternal vocalizations to infants as biologically relevant signals: An evolutionary perspective. In J. Barkow and L. Cosmides, eds., *The adapted mind: Evolutionary psychology and the generation of culture*, 391–428. New York: Oxford University Press.

Fisher, G., Hall, D. G., Rakowitz, S., and Gleitman, L. 1994. When it is better to receive than to give: Syntactic and conceptual constraints on vocabulary growth. In L. Gleitman and B. Landau, eds., *The acquisition of the lexicon*, 333–376. Cambridge, MA: MIT Press/Elsevier.

Gelman, S. A., Coley, J. D., Rosengren, K. S., Hartman, E., and Pappas, A. 1998. Beyond labeling: The role of maternal input in the acquisition of richly structured categories. *Monographs of the Society for Research in Child Development, 63* (serial no. 148).

Gleitman, L. R. 1990. The structural sources of verb meanings. *Language Acquisition,* *1,* 3–55.

Golinkoff, R. M., Mervis, C. B., and Hirsh-Pasek, K. 1994. Early object labels: The case for a developmental lexical principles framework. *Journal of Child Language, 21,* 125–156.

Hall, D. G., Quantz, D. H., and Persoage, K. A. 2000. Preschoolers' use of form class cues in word learning. *Developmental Psychology, 36,* 449–462.

Hall, D. G., and Waxman, S. R. 1994. The development of a linkage between count nouns and object categories: Evidence from fifteen- to twenty-one-month-old infants. *Child Development, 63,* 1224–1241.

Hall, D. G., Waxman, S. R., and Hurwitz, W. M. 1993. How two- and four-year-old children interpret adjectives and count nouns. *Child Development, 64,* 1651–1664.

Iverson, J. M., Caprici, O., Longobardi, E., and Caselli, M. C. 1999. Gesturing in mother-child interactions. *Cognitive Development, 14,* 57–75.

Kobayashi, H. 1998. How 2-year-olds learn novel part names of unfamiliar objects. *Cognition, 68,* B41–B51.

Markman, E. M. 1992. Constraints on word learning: Speculations about their nature, origins, and domain-specificity. In M. R. Gunnar and M. Maratsos, eds., *Modularity and constraints in language and cognition: The Minnesota symposia on child psychology,* vol. 25, 59–103. Hillsdale, NJ: Erlbaum.

Markman, E. M. 1994. Constraints on word meaning in early language acquisition. In L. Gleitman and B. Landau, eds., *The acquisition of the lexicon,* 199–229. Cambridge, MA: MIT Press/Elsevier.

Markman, E. M., and Wachtel, G. A. 1988. Children's use of mutual exclusivity to constrain the meanings of words. *Cognitive Psychology, 20,* 120–157.

Masur, E. V. 1997. Maternal labeling of novel and familiar objects: Implications for children's development of lexical constraints. *Journal of Child Language, 24,* 427–439.

Merriman, W. E., and Bowman, L. L. 1989. The mutual exclusivity bias in children's word learning. *Monographs of the Society for Research in Child Development, 54* (serial no. 220).

Mervis, C. B., and Bertrand, J. 1994. Acquisition of the novel name nameless (N3C) principle. *Child Development, 65,* 1646–1663.

Mervis, C. B., Golinkoff, R. M., and Bertrand, J. 1994. Two-year-olds readily learn multiple labels from the same basic level category. *Child Development, 65,* 1163–1177.

Mervis, C. B., Bertrand, J., and Pani, J. R. 1995. Transaction of cognitive-linguistic abilities and adult input: A case study of the acquisition of colour terms and colour-based subordinate object categories. *British Journal of Developmental Psychology, 13,* 285–302.

Naigles, L., and Hoff-Ginsberg, E. 1995. Input to verb learning: Evidence for the plausibility of syntactic bootstrapping. *Developmental Psychology, 31,* 827–837.

Ninio, A. 1980. Ostensive definition in vocabulary teaching. *Journal of Child Language, 7,* 565–573.

Ninio, A., and Bruner, J. S. 1978. The achievement and antecedents of labeling. *Journal of Child Language, 5,* 1–15.

Quine, W. V. O. 1960. *Word and object.* Cambridge: Cambridge University Press.

Saylor, M. M., Sabbagh, M. A., and Baldwin, D. A. 2002. Children use whole-part juxtaposition as a pragmatic cue to word meaning. *Developmental Psychology, 38,* 993–1003.

Shatz, M., Behrend, D., Gelman, S. A., and Ebeling, K. S. 1996. Colour term knowledge in two-year-olds: Evidence for early competence. *Journal of Child Language, 23,* 177–199.

Shipley, E. F., Kuhn, I., and Madden, E. C. 1983. Mother's use of superordinate category terms. *Journal of Child Language, 10,* 571–588.

Tardif, T., Gelman, S. A., and Xu, F. 1999. Putting the "noun bias" in context: A comparison of English and Mandarin. *Child Development, 70,* 620–635.

Tomasello, M., and Akhtar, N. 1995. Two-year-olds use pragmatic clues to differentiate reference to objects and actions. *Cognitive Development, 10,* 201–224.

Tversky, B., and Hemenway, K. 1984. Objects, parts, and categories. *Journal of Experimental Psychology, 30,* 161–191.

Waxman, S. R. 1998. Linking object categorization and naming: Early expectations and the shaping role of language. In D. L. Medin, ed., *The psychology of learning and motivation,* vol. 38, 249–291. San Diego: Academic Press.

Waxman, S. R. 1999. Specifying the scope of 13-month-olds' expectations about novel words. *Cognition, 70,* B35–B50.

Waxman, S. R., and Booth, A. 2000. Principles that are invoked in the acquisition of words, but not facts. *Cognition, 77,* 33–43.

Waxman, S. R., and Markow, D. B. 1995. Words as invitations to form categories: Evidence from 12- to 13-month-old infants. *Cognitive Psychology, 29,* 257–302.

Waxman, S. R., Senghas, A., and Benveniste, S. 1997. A cross-linguistic examination of the noun-category bias: Its existence and specificity in French- and Spanish-speaking preschool-aged children. *Cognitive Psychology, 32,* 183–218.

17

The Role of Comparison in Children's Early Word Learning

Dedre Gentner and Laura L. Namy

Current theories of word learning, and of language acquisition more generally, have turned increasingly toward domain-general cognitive and social explanations of children's acquisition of language. For much of its history, a central goal of language-acquisition research has been to characterize the language-acquisition device. Recent work has begun to explore the role of general learning processes in children's language acquisition. There is increasing support for the idea that general learning mechanisms, guided by social-interactional knowledge, operate in encoding and processing both the incoming stream of language and the informational structure of the environment. These mechanisms appear to facilitate all aspects of language learning—speech segmentation, word learning, and perhaps even the acquisition of grammar. Of particular interest for this chapter is the role of domain-general mechanisms in children's lexical development.

17.1 General Processes and Word Learning

In this section, we provide an overview of some recent work that supports the notion that general cognitive and social processes support early word learning. Some of these processes account for how children identify words in the input, others speak to how children identify referents and accomplish the word-referent mapping. All are consistent with the argument that word learning is achieved on the basis of domain-general principles.

An early proposal for domain-general learning processes in language acquisition was formulated by Slobin (1973). He proposed a set of information-driven operating principles for language learning that describe how children's success at learning new forms may be predicted by aspects of the input such as regularity and salience. In particular, the acquisition of new words is influenced by their salience in the input, as determined by position in the sentence (e.g., phrase-final position) and intonational emphases. Thus, Slobin argued that word learning may be supported by general perceptual and attentional biases, and not solely by insight into linguistic structure per se.

Samuelson and Smith (1998, 2000) have argued strongly that "dumb" attentional and associative mechanisms drive early word-to-referent mappings. They demonstrate that increasing the salience and distinctiveness of a stimulus object is sufficient to heighten children's attention to it such that a subsequent ambiguous naming event will be mapped to the salient object (Samuelson and Smith 1998). These studies document how readily children can capitalize on low-level perceptual and attentional cues in the learning environment to map novel words to the correct referents. They have also made a case that children's reliance on particular properties such as shape as a basis for word extension (Baldwin 1992; Imai, Gentner, and Uchida 1994; Landau, Smith, and Jones 1998) is based on regularities in parental naming input to their young children (Samuelson and Smith 2000). Their studies suggest that children's natural sensitivity to regularities in the input can yield systematic word interpretations and extensions. Indeed, they have demonstrated experimentally precisely how readily regularities in the input facilitate word learning. Remarkably, they show that experimentally inducing a shape bias by teaching children object names that are well organized by shape results in a heightened rate of vocabulary development relative to children in control conditions who receive no training or training based on variable patterns of input (Smith et al. 2002).

Work by Namy and colleagues, Woodward, and others has provided an additional demonstration that domain-general mechanisms may drive early word acquisition. These studies have revealed that early in word learning, children are sensitive to the social-referential

cues that signal a naming event, but appear to be agnostic with respect to the form or modality that a symbol may take. That is, children appear to have no priority for acquiring words over other types
of signals as object names, early in development. For example, Namy
(2001) introduced 18-month-old children to a range of different symbolic media as names for object categories, including words, gestures,
nonverbal sounds, and pictograms, all embedded in a familiar social-
referential naming routine. Interestingly, children reliably mapped
each of these symbolic forms to the object categories, interpreting all
four symbol types as object names. However, Campbell and Namy
(2003) have found that the same-aged children fail to map either
words or nonverbal symbols to objects if they are removed from the
naming routine. This evidence implies that early in word learning,
children utilize general social communicative cues and not domain-
specific expectations about language to infer a symbolic relation between a word and its referent. These findings are bolstered by
observational studies that report children's frequent use of gestures
as names for things during the initial period of lexical acquisition
(Acredolo and Goodwyn 1985, 1988). Studies by Namy and Waxman
(1998, 2000) and by Woodward and Hoyne (1999) demonstrate that
over time, children eventually derive an expectation that names for
things should occur predominantly in the verbal modality and in
particular syntactic constructions. Thus children derive increasingly
more domain-specific expectations with experience. Importantly,
these specific expectations about the principles that govern word
learning are derived from an earlier, more general capacity to map
signals to referents on the basis of social-referential cues.

Paul Bloom (Bloom 1999, 2001; Markson and Bloom 1997; Bloom,
chapter 7, this volume) has also argued strongly against a dedicated
system for word learning. He suggests that general cognitive processes can account for the ability to map words to meaning. He
argues that some of the phenomena that have been taken as evidence that there are domain-specific word-learning capacities (such
as the naming explosion) do not accurately represent children's language development, while others generalize to other types of learning. For example, Markson and Bloom (1997) demonstrate that the
"fast-mapping" phenomenon that has been much discussed within

the context of word learning is a general phenomenon that extends to children's retention of novel general facts about objects as well as novel object names (but see also Waxman and Booth 2000 for an alternative view).

Another proposal based on the idea that domain-general mechanisms drive early word learning is Gentner's (1982) *natural partitions* hypothesis, introduced to explain the early advantage for nouns over verbs in children's lexicons (see also Gentner and Boroditsky 2001). Gentner derives the noun advantage from general cognitive and perceptual processes operating over the perceived information in the environment. In word learning, a child must not only isolate a piece of speech from the ongoing speech stream, but must also match that sound sequence with the correct piece of information from the world. In Gentner's account, certain constellations of information are reliably parsed out of the perceptual scene early in infancy more readily than others. For example, Gestalt perceptual principles such as common fate (i.e., that parts of an object move as one) and goodness of form, such as regular structure (Baillargeon 1993; Spelke 1990), lead infants to individuate animate beings and coherent objects, which tend to be crosslinguistically lexicalized as nouns (including proper nouns). Because the referents are easily picked out, the child has only to learn their names. This is not the case for verbs, however.

This brings us to the second part of Gentner's thesis, the *relational relativity* principle, which states that the meanings of even "concrete" verbs and prepositions vary more across languages than do those of concrete nominal terms (Gentner 1981; Gentner and Boroditsky 2001). Informally, this principle states that there are more ways to make verbs out of the information in the world than there are to make nouns. The range of humanly natural ways to combine semantic components into the meanings of verbs and prepositions is greater than the corresponding range for nominal terms. This means that, even when the semantic components that make up verb meanings are highly salient, children cannot be sure how to partition the relational information into word meanings. For example, Bowerman (1974, 1978) reports many causative errors in her own children's language at around 2–4 years, such as "But I can't eat her!" (meaning "I can't make her eat") and "Down your little knee" (meaning "make your knee go down"). These errors reveal semantic ambiguity in verbs and other relational terms. In learning verb meanings, children face not only the problem of discovering the correct word (as for nouns), but also the problem of partitioning the available information into word meanings. Thus, Gentner argues that the noun bias results from general cognitive encoding mechanisms that operate over the perceived information in the environment to more readily yield object names than event and relation names.

Childers and Tomasello (2002) asked whether the acquisition of nouns and verbs is influenced by a classic principle of general learning research, namely, the advantage of spaced over massed presentation. They taught 2-year-olds new nouns and verbs, or demonstrated new actions without naming, and later assessed their ability to comprehend the new terms or to reenact the actions. There were two main conclusions. First, consistent with Gentner's claims, the learning rates differed across nouns, verbs, and action imitations: imitations were learned best, followed by nouns, with verbs last. Second, all three categories were learned better when the demonstrations were spaced over several days rather than concentrated on one or a few days. This supports the claim that general learning processes hold for lexical acquisition.

Another line of theorizing, which might be termed the *social-referential* or *pragmatic* view of language acquisition, also supports the idea that domain-general knowledge and processes facilitate word learning. Baldwin, Akhtar, Tomasello, and their colleagues have demonstrated that general social-referential cues and pragmatic principles guide early word learning. For example, Baldwin and Markman (1989) have found that infants as young as 12 months employ the basic ability to follow an adult's gaze in order to infer the referent of a novel label produced by the adult. Although Baldwin finds an initial sensitivity to the referential nature of language at the very outset of word learning, children's ability to monitor and employ referential cues to naming develops gradually over time. For example, children as young as 12 months regard naming as a referential act, examining an object more when it is named than when it is presented in silence. Baldwin interprets this finding as evidence of a rudimentary appreciation that words refer to objects. However, it is not until around 18 months that children can use eye gaze to ascertain which of two possible objects an adult is labeling, independent of their own focus of interest. When children are presented with two objects and the experimenter directs her attention and labeling to the object to which the child is not attending, it is not until 18 months that children reliably employ social-referencing cues to determine the intended reference of the experimenter's label (Baldwin 1993). Furthermore, it is not until 19 to 20 months that children can infer that an adult is labeling an object that is obscured from the child's view during the labeling event (for example, when the experimenter looks into a container and labels its contents, which are hidden from the child's view). Baldwin concludes that infants' developing ability to employ referential cues in the service of language acquisition is a product of developing insights into social cognition and social interactions more generally.

Tomasello, Akhtar, and colleagues have also demonstrated an increasing appreciation of adults' cues to their intentions during labeling in children between 18 and 24 months. For example, Tomasello, Strosberg, and Akhtar (1996) found that children used socioemotional cues such as facial expression to appropriately map a novel name to a desired target object. In this study, the experimenter presented a labeling event such as "Let's go find the *wug*!" with no visible referent. The experimenter then walked with the child over to a row of buckets with lids and removed the lid from one bucket to extract a toy. The experimenter reacted to the toy with either a satisfied smile or a frown and a headshake. The experimenter then went on to extract a toy from a second bucket and provided the opposite emotional reaction from the first toy. When children were subsequently tested on their mapping of the label to the target object, they demonstrated a successful mapping of the label to the object at which the experimenter had smiled, even when the distractor was viewed (with a frown and headshake) between the naming event and the locating of the target object.

Tomasello and colleagues have also demonstrated a comparable early sensitivity to adult intentions in other tasks that do not involve language. For example, Carpenter, Akhtar, and Tomasello (1998) find that children selectively imitate intentional and not accidental actions as young as 14 months (see also Meltzoff 1995). Based on these findings, Tomasello and colleagues have argued that early word meanings are derived by establishing an intersubjective understanding of the communicative intentions of the communicator. More recently, Woodward (see, e.g., chapter 5, this volume) has argued that these social-pragmatic abilities may be grounded in early action routines. Children's developing understanding that actions on objects imply interest in and attention to the objects themselves enables them to extract the relation between a labeling event (a type of action) and the label's referent.

In sum, the possibility that general learning mechanisms can account for aspects of language learning has garnered a great deal of empirical and theoretical evidence. What is called for now are specific proposals as to the mechanisms involved, how and when these mechanisms develop, and under what circumstances these mechanisms are invoked. In this chapter we focus on one important domain-general learning mechanism, namely, comparison processing. In particular, we propose that the process of comparison—defined more precisely below as structural alignment and mapping—operates in children's early word learning and is instrumental in deriving the meanings of words. We argue that the ability to store and compare multiple similar experiences can yield insight into word meaning. In the following sections, we outline the structure-mapping mechanism and describe how it facilitates word learning. We end with some speculations concerning the role of structure mapping in other aspects of language learning, such as grammatical development.

17.2 Structure Mapping as a Domain-General Learning Mechanism

The proposal that comparison can promote deep learning is based on research in analogy and similarity (Gentner 1983, 1989; Gentner, Holyoak, and Kokinov 2001; Gick and Holyoak 1983; Markman and Gentner 1997). According to Gentner's (1983, 1989) structure-mapping theory, comparison acts to highlight commonalities, particularly relational commonalities, that may not have been noticed prior to comparison (Wolff and Gentner 2000). The process of structural alignment operates to promote common relational structure, because of its relational focus and bias toward deep common systems (for details, see Falkenhainer, Forbus, and Gentner 1989; Gentner and Markman 1997). Thus when two representations are aligned, common structure is preferentially highlighted. This can result in the extraction of common higher-order relational structure that was not readily evident within either item alone.

One implication of the claim that structural alignment heightens the salience of common structure is that comparison processes should promote performance on tasks requiring sensitivity to relational structure. In fact, there is considerable evidence that children (and adults; see, e.g., Gentner, Loewenstein, and Thompson 2003; Gick and Holyoak 1983; Kurtz, Miao, and Gentner 2001; Loewenstein, Thompson, and Gentner 1999) who are encouraged to engage in comparison subsequently succeed at more difficult or more abstract tasks than children who have not engaged in comparison. This effect of alignment in promoting abstraction is evident across a wide span of ages and cognitive tasks.

For example, Loewenstein and Gentner (2001) found benefits of comparison on preschool children's ability to perform a spatial mapping task from one model room to another. The basic task was a search task like that used by DeLoache (1989). Fido's bone was hidden in the first room (the Hiding room) and the child was told to find Rover's bone in another model room. The "Finding room" in which the child searched had the same configuration as the prior model(s), but was perceptually rather different. Prior to the task, half the children (the Comparison group) were shown the Hiding room and another room identical except for color, and were asked to explicitly point out correspondences between the two rooms; the experimenter pointed to each object in one room, and the child pointed to its corresponding object in the other. The other half of the children (the Control group) were shown these two rooms sequentially and discussed each of the objects, but were not asked to identify correspondences between the two rooms. All children then engaged in the mapping task described above between the Hiding room and the Finding room. Children who engaged in the compari-

Pretraining

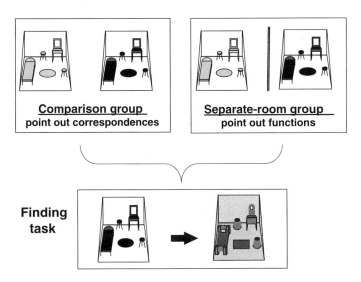

Figure 17.1
The model-room task used by Loewenstein and Gentner (2001).

son task performed better than did children who viewed the first two rooms separately. (See figure 17.1.) It appears that comparison enabled children to form a more articulated relational schema and to transfer the spatial relations in the initial model to the Finding room.

In another task, Kotovsky and Gentner (1996) demonstrated that comparison heightens children's insight into relational commonalities. In this study, 4-year-old children were given a forced-choice task in which they were shown a standard display that depicted a particular pattern (such as size symmetry, e.g., V-v-V) and were asked to determine which of two comparison figures was most similar. Both alternatives were made up of the same objects, but one had a relational configuration that matched the standard and the other did not. In one condition, the comparison figures varied along the same dimension as the standard (such as size to size)—for example, VvV (standard) with O-o-O versus O-O-o (alternatives). In the other condition, the same abstract pattern was depicted along a different dimension from the standard (such as size to color)—for instance, VvV (standard) with **X-X-X** versus **X-X**-X (alternatives). Four-year-olds could reliably choose the relational match on within-dimension trials, but were at chance on cross-dimensional matches—even those who performed extremely well on within-dimension trials. The 4-year-olds could match the higher-order relation of symmetry only when it was instantiated over the same dimension as the standard. They required substantial perceptual similarity to support the relational match.

Kotovsky and Gentner (1996) suggested that repeated within-dimension comparisons—which children are demonstrably able to align—might enable children to abstract the higher-order regularity, and thus facilitate their ability to see the more difficult cross-dimensional matches. To test this possibility, the same set of comparisons was given in a blocked fashion. A new group of 4-year-olds was given first the within-dimension trials and then the cross-dimensional trials (all without feedback, as before). Children in this condition who responded correctly to the initial within-dimension trials also performed above chance on the cross-dimension trials. This result suggests that repeated within-dimension comparisons led children to notice the common higher-order relational structure and prepared them to see that same common structure in the cross-dimensional matches.

Infants also benefit from comparison experience on object-recognition and discrimination tasks. For example, infants perform better on a facial-recognition task if they are given the opportunity to compare the target face from two different angles (Fagan 1978). Oakes (2001) has demonstrated that 4- to 6-month-old infants more readily form perceptual categories such as *dog* (and discriminate *dogs* from perceptually similar *cats*) when the infants are given the opportunity to view and compare objects in pairs than when the objects are presented one at a time.

17.3 Alignment and Word Learning

There is evidence that structural alignment facilitates lexical development. When children encounter a novel word, they must determine the meaning of the word and the range of instances to which it can be applied. That is, children must go beyond simply attaching labels to their referents. We propose that the accrual of multiple exemplars named by the same term encourages children to compare the exemplars. Gentner and Medina (1998) refer to this process as *symbolic juxtaposition*. By comparing instances that share a label, children are able to discover the common basis for the shared label, enriching their understanding of the category.

Such a process has an important role in allowing for further gains in insight *after* the initial registration of a word's meaning. In early learning, children often encounter word usages that they do not fully understand. In some of these cases they may store interpretations that are faithful to the context of learning, without fully grasping the adult meaning. The structural-alignment process provides a learning mechanism whereby children can retain specific instances and then compare across the instances to discover a word's meaning. Beyond this, we conjecture that comparison across word meanings may help children to discover the semantic regularities inherent in a particular language.

There is increasing evidence for the power of comparison to facilitate insight into word learning. Below we review and discuss our work on the role of comparison in children's acquisition of object names. We also review work by Gentner and colleagues on the acquisition of part names and relational names, as well as work by Waxman and Klibanoff on the role of comparison in adjective acquisition, and by Bowerman on the role of comparison in the acquisition of spatial terms. Taken together, this work makes a compelling case for the central role of comparison in children's word learning, across a range of grammatical form classes.

17.4 Comparison and the Acquisition of Object Names

Not surprisingly, children often depend on perceptual similarity as a basis for word extension, applying a novel word to multiple objects that share shape or other distinctive features with the exemplar on which the label was learned. For example, young children often make naive but systematic mistakes such as calling horses and cats *doggies* (Clark 1973). This pattern suggests that children have relatively shallow representations of the meaning.

This bias toward perceptual similarity as a basis for word extension might be a reasonable heuristic for young children, given their incomplete knowledge of causal and functional properties and how they enter into word meaning. The high correlation between perceptual similarity and conceptual similarity for the basic-level categories that predominate in preschoolers' lexicons means that perceptual similarity is often a good guide to a word's extension (Gentner 1978; Imai, Gentner, and Uchida 1994). However, this strategy is clearly not viable in the long term as a dominant approach to category learning. The question at hand, then, is how children come to appreciate nonobvious functional and relational commonalities among a word's referents.

We propose that structural alignment can aid children's learning of the appropriate range of referents for a novel word by elevating the salience of relational knowledge that might otherwise remain shadowy and implicit. Specifically, we claim that hearing common labels applied to multiple entities invites children to engage in comparison processes, and that the process of comparison highlights additional conceptual commonalities that are not immediately evident on surface-level inspection. If comparison renders relations more salient, and if common labels encourage comparison, this process might enable children to override compelling perceptual commonalities in favor of deeper conceptual ones.

Our work has demonstrated that this is the case. We experimentally manipulated the children's opportunity to compare objects from a given category and then tested their word extension, pitting a perceptual match against a perceptually dissimilar taxonomic match. In our initial studies (Gentner and Namy 1999), we manipulated the opportunity to compare by presenting children with either a single instance or multiple perceptually similar instances of the category before eliciting their word extensions. For example, children might have seen either one standard (e.g., an apple) or two standards (e.g., an apple and an orange) from the fruit category. After learning a novel puppet name for the standard(s) such as *blicket*, the child was asked to choose another blicket from a set including a perceptually

ONE STANDARD
"This is a *blicket*."

TWO STANDARDS
"This is a *blicket*, and
this is also a *blicket*."

"Which one of these is a *blicket*?"

PERCEPTUAL
CHOICE

TAXONOMIC
CHOICE

Figure 17.2
Sample materials used in the Gentner and Namy 1999 study. The one-standard condition was run with each of the two standards as the separate standard.

similar object from a different taxonomic category (e.g., a balloon)
or a perceptually dissimilar object from the same object category
(e.g., a banana), as shown in figure 17.2.

The standards were designed so that when either was presented
singly, the children chose the perceptually similar alternative. If
children compute similarity merely by concatenating surface commonalities, they should select the perceptual match in both conditions. Indeed, seeing two standards that are *both* more similar to the
perceptual choice than to the category choice should, if anything,

increase perceptual responding, relative to viewing a single standard. However, if comparing instances induces a structural-alignment process, children who view two standards may be led to focus on a common relational structure that they may typically not notice explicitly—such as how the objects are used and what causal activities they normally participate in. Thus, the prediction of structural-alignment theory is that comparison should lead to a shift toward category responding, despite strong perceptual similarity between the standard instances and the perceptual choice.

This is precisely what we found. When shown both standards *together*, children chose the conceptual match, despite preferring the perceptual match for *either* of the standards presented singly. This outcome provides critical evidence that comparison facilitates word extension on the basis of conceptual, and not merely perceptual, features. This remarkable finding that even when both standards individually support a perceptual choice, the two together can be aligned to reveal a common conceptual basis of responding suggests a solution to the perceptual-dependence problem discussed above. Seen in this light, children's use of perceptual features as a basis for word learning may in fact be a constructive heuristic when faced with little information about a category. Perceptual commonalities serve as the initial "hook" that encourages children to engage in comparison and extract deeper relational commonalities. Such relational commonalities may include common function (e.g., *both are edible*), mechanical causal relations (e.g., *both are strong so they can bend things*), biological causal relations (e.g., *both need water to grow*), role relations (e.g., *both grow on trees*), and progeneration (e.g., *both have babies that look like the adults but smaller*). We suggest that it is these relational systems that provide the theorylike aspects of concepts and categories. In a sense, we can think of the child as using perceptual similarity as her initial approach, moving via alignment toward something more like a theory-based common structure.

In other studies, we have demonstrated that hearing a common label encourages children to engage in comparison. We compared children's performance on the word-extension task when they were either given a novel label for the standard(s) or were simply asked to "find another one" without learning a novel label for the standards

(Gentner and Namy 1999). We found that comparison influenced performance in both the label and no-label condition. However, the effect was more pronounced and elicited greater category-based responding when common labels were used than in the no-label condition. This suggests that having a common label invites comparison processes—that words are invitations to make comparisons.

In subsequent studies, we have gone further to probe the relation between common labels and alignment processes. Namy and Gentner (2002) demonstrated more clearly that presenting two perceptually similar members of a category is not by itself sufficient to elicit taxonomic, as opposed to perceptual, responding. Rather, children must be encouraged to engage in an alignment process, and common labels prove to be a way of promoting alignment. Children were assigned to either a Unifying Label or Conflicting Label condition. In both conditions, children were shown two standard objects from the same category. As before, they were asked to select a match for the standards, choosing between a perceptually similar out-of-kind object and a perceptually similar member of the same taxonomic category. Those in the Unifying Label condition heard both standards labeled with the same novel word (e.g., "This is a *blicket*, and this is also a *blicket!*"). Those in the Conflicting Label condition heard the two standards labeled with different novel words (e.g., "This is a *blicket* and this is a *daxen!*") As in our previous studies, children who heard a Unifying label reliably selected the taxonomic match. In contrast, those who heard the Conflicting labels predominantly selected the perceptual match, as did children viewing a single standard object in the previous studies.

These results indicate that alignment is invited by hearing a common label for two exemplars. Our results also show that alignment processes are used to extend novel words to new instances. Thus, we suggest that the relation between alignment and word learning is a true bootstrapping relation. Hearing a common term invites an alignment that is then used to extend the term to new exemplars.

Now we can return to the question of how attention to perceptual similarities in word extension can (paradoxically) promote attention to deeper commonalities. Given that (as the above results demonstrate) the comparison process is such that common relational structure is preferentially highlighted, even though children's attention is often initially drawn to surface commonalities between two exemplars, the full process of comparison will result in highlighting any further relational commonalities that may be present. Given this and the fact that "dumb" surface-level commonalities are often highly correlated with deep, relational commonalities (for example, fins and gills are correlated with a different type of breathing apparatus than are legs and fur), these surface commonalities may act as initial invitations to compare, and thus point the way to deeper commonalities that become salient when the child carries out a comparison. Interestingly enough, a similar argument has been made in the area of adult problem solving. Brooks (1978, 1987), Ross (1984, 1987, 1989; Ross, Perkins, and Tenpenny 1990), and others have argued that accessing prior problems from memory based on surface similarity and then mapping the prior problems to the current problem may result in analogical abstraction processes that yield useful generalizations.

These interactions between alignment and word learning extend to category-based induction tasks as well as to word-learning tasks. For example, Davidson and Gelman (1990) taught 4-year-olds a property for a standard animal, and asked whether other target animals would also have the property. The first two studies utilized four types of target animals in an orthogonal design: they could either have the same category label as the standard or not, and could either be perceptually similar to the standard or not. The results showed that children made property inferences based on perceptual similarity but not common labels for both novel and familiar labels. In the third study, the relation between perceptual similarity and common category was made more transparent, by omitting one of the conflicting items (either the different-label/similar item or the same-label/dissimilar item). In this study, children were willing to extend inferences not only to the "natural" items (i.e., the perceptually similar items with the same category label) but also to the nonobvious items (e.g., objects with the same label that were not perceptually similar). In this way, perceptual similarity and word learning often collaborate. Perceptual commonalities facilitate the initial alignment process given a common label, which can then take the lead in extending the category to further, less transparent instances.

17.5 Beyond Nominal Categories

So far we have considered how comparison can aid in the learning of nouns denoting categories of objects or entities. We now turn to the role of comparison in learning other kinds of word meaning.

17.5.1 Learning Adjectives

The studies described above examine the role of comparison in children's acquisition of object names. However, there is evidence that comparison processes also play an important role in the acquisition of other kinds of word meanings. A series of studies by Waxman and Klibanoff (2000; Klibanoff and Waxman 2000) has demonstrated that structural alignment plays an important role in 3-year-old children's ability to map novel adjectives to the appropriate object property (such as color or texture). They designed a forced-choice adjective-learning task. The experimenter applied a novel adjective such as *blickish* to an object and then asked the child to select another *blickish* one between an object that has the same object property (e.g., bumpy) and one that has a different object property (e.g., smooth). Children were assigned to either the high-similarity "within-basic" condition, in which the set of objects were identical except for the target property, or the moderate-similarity "across-basic" condition, in which the choice objects were moderately similar but drawn from a different basic-level object category than the standard. Children in the "within-basic" condition were better able to extend the adjective than those in the "across-basic" condition. This is expected because the alignment is easier for high-similarity pairs. More interestingly, children who first successfully extended the adjective to the correct within-basic object subsequently performed well on the across-basic task. These findings suggest that children are performing an alignment on the "within-basic" sets, enabling them to identify the single property shared by the target and the correct choice and not shared by the incorrect choice. Even more impressive is that performing this alignment seems to have led children to a more portable understanding of the relation between the adjective and the object property. As in Kotovsky and Gentner's studies, making close-similarity alignments facilitated the ability to make further alignments with less perceptual support.

17.5.2 Learning Part Names

Using a similar paradigm, Gentner, Loewenstein, and Hung (2002) have demonstrated that alignment processing can facilitate the acquisition of part names. They created triads of "Martian creatures" with a standard that had a target body part and two forced-choice alternatives, one of which had the part while the other did not (see figure 17.3). They introduced children to a novel part name, saying,

"This one has a *blick*.

Which one of these has a *blick*?"

HIGH SIM

LOW SIM

Figure 17.3
Sample materials used in the part-naming task by Gentner, Loewenstein, and Hung (2002).

for example, "Look—This one [the standard] has a *wug*. Can you show me which one of those has a *wug*?" The children then selected among two forced-choice alternatives that were either perceptually similar to the standard, or perceptually distinct from the standard. As would be predicted from the ease of aligning closely similar exemplars, children more successfully applied the part term when the alternatives were highly similar to the standard.

To test whether close alignment could facilitate far alignment, in a second study children received two choice sets for each standard. Half the children received a high-similarity pair of choices, followed by a low-similarity pair. The other half received a low-similarity choice pair followed by another low-similarity pair. The prediction from structure-mapping theory is that the first group, which experienced a "foolproof" alignment on the first trial, would perform better on the second trial than the second group, even though the second group had more actual practice with low-similarity items. The results bore out this prediction. As in previous studies, children who received the high-similarity items first were subsequently more successful on the low-similarity items than children who had an equal amount of experience with only low-similarity items.

17.5.3   Learning Relational Nouns

Gentner and Klibanoff (2002) document the benefit of alignment and mapping in the acquisition of names for relational categories. *Relational categories* are categories whose membership is determined by a specific relation that category members have with another entity or category. This relation may be either temporary or enduring. Examples of relational nouns are *gift, surprise, brother, accident,* and *home.* Although such categories are common, learning their meanings might be expected to be challenging for young children, because of the early focus on object terms discussed previously (Gentner 1982; Gentner and Boroditsky 2001; Goldin-Meadow, Seligman, and Gelman 1976; Markman 1989; Waxman and Markow 1995). The difficulty of learning relational terms relative to object terms holds not only across form class—as in the advantage of nouns over verbs—but also within the nominal class (Gentner and Rattermann 1991). For example, Hall and Waxman (1993) found that 3.5-year-olds had difficulty learning novel relational nouns denoting concepts like *passenger*. Even when they were explicitly told (for example) "This one is a *blicket* BECAUSE IT IS RIDING IN A CAR," children tended to interpret the novel noun as referring to the object category.

To give children the maximal opportunity to see common relational structure across different instantiations, Gentner and Klibanoff (2002) used a combination of comparison and labeling. Three-, four-, and six-year-olds were shown picture cards and heard a novel relational noun used in two parallel contexts—for example, "The knife is the *blick* for the watermelon, and the ax is the *blick* for the tree." Then they were asked to decide on its referent in a third context, as in "What would be the *blick* for the paper?" They then chose between three picture cards: a pair of scissors (*same-relation* (correct)), a pencil (*thematic*), and another piece of paper (*taxonomic*). A control group saw the same examples without the novel relational word—for instance, "The knife goes with the watermelon, and the ax goes with the tree the same way. What would go with the paper the same way?" If common word names encouraged deeper comparison processes, and/or encouraged children to retain the results of their comparison process more firmly, children in the Word condition should outperform those in the No-Word condition. If, in contrast, the word invited attention to object properties, children in the Word condition should perform no better, and perhaps even worse, than those in the No-Word condition.

Results showed that 3-year-olds seldom selected the relational interpretation in either condition. However, both 4- and 6-year-olds hearing novel relational nouns were more likely to successfully choose the *same-relation* card than were their counterparts in the No-Word control condition. These studies suggest that by the age of 4, children can learn the meanings of novel relational nouns through comparison by abstracting common relations across situations.

17.5.4 Learning Spatial Terms

Bowerman and Choi (2001) make a case for comparison as an important mechanism of acquisition for spatial-relation terms. They note that different languages carve up the arena of spatial relations very differently, with meanings that crosscut each other in complex ways, undermining the possibility that spatial words are mapped directly to prelinguistic spatial concepts (Mandler 1992, 1996). (As noted above, this kind of crosslinguistic semantic variability is characteristic of relational meanings (Gentner 1982), so the implications extend well beyond spatial terms.) For example, the Korean verb *kkita* denotes bringing three-dimensional objects with complementary shapes into an interlocking, tight-fitting relationship. It crosscuts the English categories of *put in* and *put on*, and extends to other situations as well. (For additional examples of crosscutting spatial categories from the Tzotzil and Tzeltal Mayan languages, see also Bowerman, de León, and Choi 1995; de León 1999, 2001; Brown 2001.)

Such linguistic variability implies that children must monitor usage in order to discover which conceptual distinctions their language marks. Further, Bowerman and Choi (2003) note that children's overextension errors vary across languages in ways that reflect the semantic and statistical properties of the linguistic input. They propose that children construct the meaning of a word by carrying out comparisons across the observed referent situations. They note that "according to Structure-mapping theory, abstract relational concepts can emerge through a process of carrying out *comparisons* between exemplars. In the process of comparing, the learner tries to align structured conceptual representations with each other and to identify the ways in which they are similar and different" (Bowerman and Choi 2003, 407). This idea is consistent with R. Brown's (1958, 210) point that repetitions of a word across contexts "will orient the player toward contemporaneous stimuli and will tell him when the important nonlinguistic stimuli recur."

Evidence in support of this comparison-based construction of meaning comes from Bowerman and Choi's investigation of Dutch and English children's acquisition of the out-off distinction. Both languages distinguish between removal from containment (*uit* or *out*) —for example, Legos out of a bag, cars out of a box)—and removal from a surface (*af* or *off*), as in lid off a pot, clothing off the body. English-speaking children from the age of 2 on up systematically distinguish these; however, Dutch children in all age groups massively overgeneralize *uit* "out" to removals from surfaces (Bowerman and Choi 2001; Choi 1997). This is a striking difference, given the similarity of the languages in this area. Bowerman and Choi (2003) trace this population difference in overgeneralization to a minor (from the adult perspective) difference between the Dutch *uit* and English *out*. In Dutch, *uit* is used for the removal of clothing items, whereas English uses *off* for removing clothing (which maps to removal from an exterior surface). Although adult Dutch speakers treat the "clothing" usage of *uit* as a separate word sense, distinct from the larger meaning of removal from a container, children have no way to "wall off" this use of *uit* for clothing removal (a high-frequency and salient event in their lives). As Bowerman and Choi point out, a comparison process like the one postulated here would lead to the child's comparing the various situations named by *uit*. But when the child compares removal from surface contact (as in clothing removal) with removal from a container, the meaning arrived at is so general that the child comes to see the term *uit* as applicable to virtually any removal situation—leading to the observed overgeneralization.

17.6   Contrast, Alignment, and Word Learning

Additional evidence supporting the claim that comparison facilitates word learning comes from studies that employ the use of contrast (including contrastive labeling and contrastive information) to help children learn and refine their word meanings. The notion that alignment can facilitate awareness of critical differences as well as commonalities has been well documented. To make this more specific, work by Gentner, Markman, and their colleagues has demonstrated that during comparison, *alignable differences*—that is, those that are connected to the common structure, which typically vary along a single common dimension or differ in the same structural element—are easier to notice than *nonalignable differences*—those not connected to the common structure. When subjects are asked to list differences between two concepts, more alignable differences tend to be listed than nonalignable differences (Markman and Gentner 1993). For example, subjects asked to list the differences between a car and a motorcycle were more likely to say that cars have four wheels while motorcycles have two (an alignable difference) than to mention that cars have doors while motorcycles do not (a nonalignable difference). People also find it easier to list a difference for similar pairs (which have many alignable differences) than for dissimilar pairs (which have few alignable differences; Gentner and Gunn 2001; Gentner and Markman 1994). And finally, following a similarity comparison of a pair of pictures, an object that was alignably different serves as a better retrieval cue than does an object that was nonalignably different (Markman and Gentner 1997; Stilwell and Markman 2001).

Eve Clark (1988, 1990, 1991, 1993) has argued that contrast plays an important role in lexical development. The use of contrast involves reasoning that is not specific to language and might be inferred from general cognitive capacities (such as alignment) in conjunction with observation of human behavior. For example, if familiar words like *cat* and *dog* are used to refer to familiar objects, and a novel word *zebra* is used to refer to a novel object, this use of words may cue the child that the word *zebra* contrasts with *cat* and *dog* and is therefore likely to be a count-noun term for the same level of category as *cat* and *dog*. Note that lexical contrast will be of relatively limited utility early in development, but will increase in power as the number of words in a child's lexicon increases.

Further evidence for the use of contrast as a source of word learning comes from the fast-mapping results of Carey and Bartlett (1978). Children were shown two objects and were asked to "get the chromium one. Not the red one, the chromium one." In this study, children correctly ascertained that the "chromium" object was the nonred one, and subsequently extended the term *chromium* to other similarly colored objects. Other studies by Au and Laframboise (1990), Saylor, Baldwin, and Sabbagh (chapter 16, this volume), Gelman and Markman (1985), Heibeck and Markman (1987), Klibanoff and Waxman (2000), Landau and Shipley (2001), Waxman and Booth (2001), and Waxman et al. (1997) provide similar demonstrations that providing an alignably different contrastive entity facilitates children's mapping of a novel word to the correct aspect of meaning.

For example, Waxman et al. (1997) find that contrastive information invites differentiation into subordinate categories such as the differentiation of kinds of dogs. The experimenter introduced three subordinate kinds and told children a property of each subkind (e.g., "this one helps us herd sheep"). If the properties introduced for the three subkinds were nonalignable (e.g., one "has five babies at a time," another "has two kinds of muscles," and the third "helps us herd sheep"), the children extended the third fact throughout the basic-level category. However, if the properties were alignable—that is, they varied along a single dimension (e.g., one "helps us find birds," another "helps us pull sleds," and the third "helps us herd sheep")—then children appeared to form distinct subcategories: they restricted further inferences to the subcategories rather than extending them throughout the basic-level category. The contrastive information provided the impetus to form appropriate subkinds. Thus, structural-alignment processes not only support insight into the commonalities that link exemplars into categories, but—when alignable differences are revealed—they can also invite differentiation into subcategories.

One interesting potential use of contrast is in providing correction to children's lexical usage. Eve Clark has challenged the much-cited claim that children receive no negative evidence about key aspects of language. Clark argues that parental input may be an important source of feedback and contrast that aids children's language development (see also Huttenlocher et al. 2002). Clark suggests that parents often provide feedback after a child's utterance by modeling the correct construction. Comparing and contrasting their own (incorrect) utterance with the adult's (correct) utterance may enable children to identify the components of the sentence that are mistaken and correct them. Clark (1998) provides the following examples of parents providing implicit contrastive language that directly influences children's use of words.

Child A (2;4) wants to have an orange peeled

A: Fix it.

Mo: You want me to peel it?

A: Peel it.

Comparison in Children's Early Word Learning

Child D (2;5) (as his father swings him in his arms near top of stairs)
D: Don't fall me downstairs!
Fa: Oh, I wouldn't drop you downstairs!
D: Don't drop me downstairs!

17.7 Comparison and the Development of Grammar

Might the same comparison processes that facilitate children's lexical acquisition also contribute to children's ability to derive grammatical regularities? That is, could comparing structurally similar sentences highlight the relational commonalities that characterize grammatical constructions? Although these ideas are largely untried, there are some intriguing lines of evidence that suggest that this may be a direction worth pursuing. Two crucial aspects of grammar that must be learned are the serial transition probabilities and the regularities across sentences (Gomez and Gerken 2000). There is considerable evidence that 7- or 8-month-old infants can learn transition probabilities (Saffran et al. 1999; Saffran, Aslin, and Newport 1996). Furthermore, infants can learn relational regularities in speech stimuli through intensive serial comparison (Gomez and Gerkin 1999; Marcus 1999; Marcus et al. 1999). That is, infants can abstract a relational pattern across a set of sequences of syllables that have the same structure. For example, when 7-month-old infants are habituated to sequences with an ABA pattern—as in *pa-ti-pa, bo-fe-bo*, and so on—the infants will distinguish between new sequences of syllables in the same pattern (*de-mo-de*) versus a different pattern (*de-de-mo*). This suggests that they are deriving the common relational structure over the initial set with repeated exposure to the pattern.

Kuehne, Gentner, and Forbus (2000) have shown that this phenomenon can be modeled by a domain-general analogical learning process that utilizes progressive structural alignment. This model uses SME (the structure-mapping engine) (Falkenhainer, Forbus, and Gentner 1989) embedded in a simulation of abstraction over examples called SEQL (Skorstad, Gentner, and Medin 1988). SEQL carries out repeated comparisons across a set of items, and in so doing abstracts commonalities—in particular, common relational structure—among the items. In a simulation of the Marcus et al.

results, the model receives exactly the same set of forty-eight sequences that infants received—sixteen ABA patterns, three times each (coded in terms of twelve phonemic features per syllable). SEQL's progressive alignment across these exemplars results in "wearing away" the specific phonological features of the syllables, preserving the common structure. When SEQL is then given the same test sequences (with new syllables) that the infants received, it shows that it has abstracted the regularity in two ways: (1) it computes a lower similarity for sequences in the new (AAB) pattern than for sequences in the old (ABA) pattern, and (2) it attempts to make inferences to the new pattern (based on its stored regularity) that are false. For example, it will infer that the third syllable of *gee-do-do* should be the same as the first—an expectation that will be dashed for the new sequences, leading to a violation of expectancy. Unlike many connectionist models of this phenomenon, SEQL does not require supervised learning. Its comparison processes naturally lead to abstraction across examples. The success of this model suggests that structure-mapping processes may be able to capture important aspects of rule learning. Thus the results of the infant grammar studies could be seen as evidence for a domain-general structural-alignment process that is already present in infancy (Gentner 2003).

A second line of support for the idea that structural alignment and mapping may contribute to grammar learning is that children's early grammatical knowledge often appears highly conservative, mimicking the pattern of learning found in other cases of learning by comparison (Gentner and Medina 1998; Ross and Kennedy 1990; Medin and Ross 1989). Tomasello (2000) suggests that structural alignment may be a critical mechanism by which generative patterns and abstract linguistic constructions might be derived. He speculates that children go through several phases of alignment to move from an initially highly conservative, verb-specific understanding of constructions to an increasingly more abstract understanding of linguistic structure (Tomasello and Brooks 1999). According to Tomasello's (1992) "verb-island" hypothesis, children first learn constructions in connection with specific verbs. A child might be able to use the passive form with *push* but not with *kiss*, and the past tense with *kiss* but not with *push*. Later, children begin to align and connect these verb islands, noticing that different verbs may be used in similarly structured sentences. This process of alignment yields a more abstract and generalizable notion of a linguistic construction such as the passive.

Fisher (1996, 2000) proposes another way alignment may enter into grammar learning. Her studies suggest that structural analogies between form and meaning—for example, the parallel between the transitive sentence form and an agentive event—are a source of early understanding about verb grammar. These approaches to grammar learning suggest that general cognitive mechanisms could account for the gradual development of grammatical competence.

17.8 Future Directions

Our research program seeks to derive greater specificity about the nature of the comparison mechanism and the circumstances that elicit it. We are currently manipulating a range of factors to better understand children's use of comparison to extract relational commonalities among a word's referents. Our research program explores the range of comparisons that might facilitate lexical and conceptual development. For example, does the degree of similarity between the two standards influence the likelihood of aligning and the ease with which relational commonalities are gleaned from the alignment process? We are currently investigating whether there is an optimal level of similarity among objects that is perceptually similar enough that surface-level commonalities are present to invite comparison, but distinct enough to encourage looking beyond those surface commonalities to a relational alignment.

Based on findings from the adult literature that alignment facilitates attention to subtle differences among classes of objects as well as to commonalities (Markman and Gentner 1993; Gentner and Gunn 2001), we also plan to examine the use of alignment in revealing distinctions among categories. For example, how does alignment operate in enabling children to distinguish subordinate categories within a familiar basic-level category?

We are also exploring how the temporal and spatial proximity of the standards to be compared mediates comparison. In the tasks conducted thus far, the standards are always presented in spatial and temporal contiguity. However, in real-world learning, juxtapositions are not always so felicitous. What happens if the child encounters exemplars at different times or in different spatial contexts? We are also exploring whether children must receive explicit input encouraging comparison, or whether the process is automatically invoked when the same word is applied to a sufficient number of similar exemplars.

17.9 General Implications

The results of the studies reviewed above suggest that domain-general processes are potent in children's word learning. Our work indicates a central role for structure-mapping processes in the acquisition of the lexicon and the construction of a conceptual taxonomy, and possibly even in the development of grammar. Of course, the research reviewed above also underscores the importance of other domain-general processes such as Childers and Tomasello's (2002) finding that spaced learning is superior to massed learning of word meanings; learning of transitional probabilities (Saffran, Aslin, and Newport 1996); Samuelson and Smith's (1998, 2000) findings on general attentional mechanisms; and demonstrations of the importance of social-referential cues to word learning (Baldwin 1993; Campbell and Namy 2003; Tomasello, Strosberg, and Akhtar 1996).

It remains an open question whether domain-specific principles are also necessary to account for language learning, and if so, for which aspects. Certainly the complexity of structure evidenced in adult language seems to call for something beyond ordinary learning processes. On the other hand, the application of structure mapping and the other general mechanisms discussed here is still in its infancy. It is too soon to say how far these general processes can go, and whether and where domain-specific learning processes are necessary to explain language acquisition.

In summary, our review reveals an important role for general learning processes in the acquisition of the lexicon. Specifically, we explored the effects of structure-mapping processes. We found evidence that the process of structural alignment facilitates the discovery of commonalities and the concomitant deepening of word meanings. Structural alignment also promotes differentiation—for example, noticing alignable differences can invite the formation of subcategories. We suggest that general learning mechanisms, particularly structure-sensitive mechanisms that can reveal relational patterns, are an important force in the acquisition of meaning.

Acknowledgments

This research described here was supported by a grant from the Emory University Research Committee to Laura Namy and also by an NSF-ROLE grant 21002/REC-0087516 to Dedre Gentner. We thank Michelle Osmondson for her help in conducting the child studies, and Kathleen Braun for help with the artwork.

References

Acredolo, L. P., and Goodwyn, S. W. 1985. Symbolic gesturing in language development: A case study. *Human Development, 28*, 40–49.

Acredolo, L. P., and Goodwyn, S. W. 1988. Symbolic gesturing in normal infants. *Child Development, 59*, 450–466.

Au, T. K., and Laframboise, D. E. 1990. Acquiring color names via linguistic contrast: The influence of contrasting terms. *Child Development, 61*, 1808–1823.

Baillargeon, R. 1993. The object concept revisited: New directions in the investigation of infants' physical knowledge. In C. E. Granrud, ed., *Carnegie Mellon Symposia on Cognition, Vol. 23: Visual perception and cognition in infancy*, 265–315. Hillsdale, NJ: Erlbaum.

Baldwin, D. A. 1992. Clarifying the role of shape in children's taxonomic assumption. *Journal of Experimental Child Psychology, 54*, 392–416.

Baldwin, D. A. 1993. Early referential understanding: Infants' ability to recognize referential acts for what they are. *Development Psychology, 29*, 832–843.

Baldwin, D. A., and Markman, E. 1989. Establishing word-object relations: A first step. *Child Development, 60*, 381–398.

Bloom, P. 1999. Theories of word learning: Rationalist alternatives to associationism. In W. C. Ritchie and T. K. Bhatia, eds., *Handbook of child language acquisition*, 249–278. San Diego: Academic Press.

Bloom, P. 2001. Word learning. *Current Biology*, *11*, R5–R6.

Bowerman, M. 1974. Learning the structure of causative verbs: A study in the relationship of cognitive, semantic, and syntactic development. *Papers and Reports on Child Language Development*, *8*, 142–178. Stanford, CA.

Bowerman, M. 1978. Systematizing semantic knowledge: Changes over time in the child's organization of word meaning. *Child Development*, *49*, 977–987.

Bowerman, M., and Choi, S. 2001. Shaping meanings for language: Universal and language specific in the acquisition of spatial semantic categories. In M. Bowerman and S. Levinson, eds., *Language acquisition and conceptual development*, 475–511. Cambridge: Cambridge University Press.

Bowerman, M., and Choi, S. 2003. Space under construction: Language-specific spatial categorization in first language acquisition. In D. Gentner and S. Goldin-Meadow, eds., *Language in mind: Advances in the study of language and cognition*. Cambridge, MA: MIT Press.

Bowerman, M., de León, L., and Choi, S. 1995. Verbs, particles, and spatial semantics: Learning to talk about spatial actions in typologically different languages. In E. V. Clark, ed., *Proceedings of the Twenty-Seventh Annual Child Language Research Forum*, *27*, 101–110.

Brooks, L. R. 1978. Non analytic concept formation and memory for instances. In E. Rosch and B. B. Lloyd, eds., *Cognition and categorization*, 169–211. Hillsdale, NJ: Erlbaum.

Brooks, L. R. 1987. Decentralized control of categorization: The role of prior processing episodes. In U. Neisser, ed., *Concepts and conceptual development: Ecological and intellectual factors in categorization*, 141–174. Cambridge: Cambridge University Press.

Brown, P. 2001. Learning to talk about motion up and down in Tzeltal: Is there a language-specific bias for verb learning? In M. Bowerman and S. C. Levinson, eds., *Language acquisition and conceptual development*, 512–543. Cambridge: Cambridge University Press.

Brown, R. 1958. *Words and things: An introduction to language*. New York: Free Press.

Campbell, A. L., and Namy, L. L. 2003. *The role of social referential cues in verbal and nonverbal symbol learning*. Child Development, *74*, 1–15.

Carey, S., and Bartlett, E. 1978. Acquiring a single new word. *Papers and Reports on Child Language Development*, *15*, 17–29.

Carpenter, M., Akhtar, N., and Tomasello, M. 1998. Fourteen- through 18-month-old infants differentially imitate intentional and accidental actions. *Infant Behavior and Development*, *21*, 315–330.

Childers, J. B., and Tomasello, M. 2002. Two-year-olds learn novel nouns, verbs, and conventional actions from massed or distributed exposure. *Developmental Psychology*, *38*, 967–978.

Choi, S. 1997. Language-specific input and early semantic development: Evidence from children learning Korean. In D. I. Slobin, ed., *The crosslinguistic study of language acquisition, Vol. 5: Expanding the contexts*, 41–434. Hillsdale, NJ: Erlbaum.

Clark, E. V. 1973. What's in a word? On the child's acquisition of semantics in his first language. In T. E. Moore, ed., *Cognitive development and the acquisition of language*, 65–110. New York: Academic Press.

Clark, E. V. 1988. On the logic of contrast. *Journal of Child Language, 15,* 317–335.

Clark, E. V. 1990. The pragmatics of contrast. *Journal of Child Language, 17,* 417–431.

Clark, E. V. 1991. Acquisition principles in lexical development. In S. A. Gelman and J. P. Byrnes, eds., 31–71. *Perspectives on language and thought: Interrelations in development.* Cambridge: Cambridge University Press.

Clark, E. V. 1993. *The lexicon in acquisition.* Cambridge: Cambridge University Press.

Clark, E. V. 1998. *Lexical structure and pragmatic directions in acquisition: The status of constraints.* Chicago: Chicago Linguistic Society.

Davidson, N. S., and Gelman, S. A. 1990. Inductions from novel categories: The role of language and conceptual structure. *Cognitive Development, 5,* 151–176.

de León, L. 1999. Verbs in Tzotzil early syntactic development. *International Journal of Bilingualism, 3,* 219–240.

de León, L. 2001. Finding the richest path: Language and cognition in the acquisition of verticality in Tzotzil (Mayan). In M. Bowerman and S. C. Levinson, eds., *Language acquisition and conceptual development*, 544–565. Cambridge: Cambridge University Press.

DeLoache, J. S. 1989. Young children's understanding of the correspondence between a scale model and a larger space. *Cognitive Development, 4,* 121–139.

Fagan, J. F. III. 1978. Facilitation of infants' recognition memory. *Child Development, 49,* 1066–1075.

Falkenhainer, B., Forbus, K. D., and Gentner, D. 1989. The structure-mapping engine: Algorithm and examples. *Artificial Intelligence, 41,* 1–63.

Fisher, C. 1996. Structural limits on verb mapping: The role of analogy in children's interpretations of sentences. *Cognitive Psychology, 31,* 41–81.

Fisher, C. 2000. From form to meaning: A role for structural analogy in the acquisition of language. In H. W. Reese, ed., *Advances in child development and behavior*, 1–53. New York: Academic Press.

Gelman, S. A., and Markman, E. M. 1985. Implicit contrast in adjectives vs. nouns: Implications for word learning in preschoolers. *Journal of Child Language, 12,* 125–143.

Gentner, D. 1978. On relational meaning: The acquisition of verb meaning. *Child Development, 49*, 988–998.

Gentner, D. 1981. Some interesting differences between nouns and verbs. *Cognition and Brain Theory, 4*, 161–178.

Gentner, D. 1982. Why nouns are learned before verbs: Linguistic relativity versus natural partitioning. In S. Kuczaj, ed., *Language development, Vol. 2: Language, thought, and culture*, 301–334. Hillsdale, NJ: Erlbaum.

Gentner, D. 1983. Structure-mapping: A theoretical framework for analogy. *Cognitive Science, 7*, 155–170.

Gentner, D. 1989. The mechanisms of analogical learning. In S. Vosniadou and A. Ortony, eds., *Similarity and analogical reasoning*, 199–241. London: Cambridge University Press.

Gentner, D. 2003. Why we're so smart. In D. Gentner and S. Goldin-Meadow, eds., *Language in mind: Advances in the study of language and thought*, 195–236. Cambridge, MA: MIT Press.

Gentner, D., and Boroditsky, L. 2001. Individuation, relativity, and early word learning. In M. Bowerman and S. Levinson, eds., *Language acquisition and conceptual development*, 215–256. Cambridge: Cambridge University Press.

Gentner, D., and Gunn, V. 2001. Structural alignment facilitates the noticing of differences. *Memory and Cognition, 29*, 565–577.

Gentner, D., Holyoak, K. J., and Kokinov, B., eds. 2001. *The analogical mind: Perspectives from cognitive science*. Cambridge, MA: MIT Press.

Gentner, D., and Klibanoff, R. S. 2002. *On acquiring gifts: The development of the ability to learn relational nouns*. Unpublished manuscript, Northwestern University.

Gentner, D., Loewenstein, J., and Hung, B. T. 2002. *Comparison facilitates learning part names*. Unpublished manuscript, Northwestern University.

Gentner, D., Loewenstein, J., and Thompson, L. 2003. *Learning and transfer: A general role for analogical encoding. Journal of Educational Psychology*.

Gentner, D., and Markman, A. B. 1994. Structural alignment in comparison: No difference without similarity. *Psychological Science, 5*, 152–158.

Gentner, D., and Markman, A. B. 1997. Structure mapping in analogy and similarity. *American Psychologist, 52*, 45–56.

Gentner, D., and Medina, J. 1998. Similarity and the development of rules. *Cognition, 65*, 263–297.

Gentner, D., and Namy, L. 1999. Comparison in the development of categories. *Cognitive Development, 14*, 487–513.

Gentner, D., and Rattermann, M. J. 1991. Language and the career of similarity. In S. A. Gelman and J. P. Brynes, eds., *Perspectives on thought and language: Interrelations in development*, 225–277. London: Cambridge University Press.

Gick, M. L., and Holyoak, K. J. 1983. Schema induction and analogical transfer. *Cognitive Psychology*, 15, 1–38.

Goldin-Meadow, S., Seligman, M. E. P., and Gelman, R. 1976. Language in the two-year-old. *Cognition*, 4, 189–202.

Gomez, R. L., and Gerken, L. 1999. Artificial grammar learning by 1-year-olds lead to specific and abstract knowledge. *Cognition*, 70, 109–135.

Gomez, R. L., and Gerken, L. 2000. Infant artificial language learning and language acquisition. *Trends in Cognitive Sciences*, 4(5), 178–186.

Hall, D. G., and Waxman, S. R. 1993. Assumptions about word meaning: Individuation and basic-level kinds. *Child Development*, 64, 1550–1570.

Heibeck, T. H., and Markman, E. M. 1987. Word learning in children: An examination of fast mapping. *Child Development*, 58, 1021–1034.

Holyoak, K. J., and Thagard, P. 1989. Analogical mapping by constraint satisfaction. *Cognitive Science*, 13, 295–355.

Huttenlocher, J., Vasilyeva, M., Cymerman, E., and Levine, S. 2002. Language input and child syntax. *Cognitive Psychology*, 45(3), 337–374.

Imai, M., Gentner, D., and Uchida, N. 1994. Children's theories of word meaning: The role of shape similarity in early acquisition. *Cognitive Development*, 9, 45–75.

Klibanoff, R. S., and Waxman, S. R. 2000. Basic level object categories support the acquisition of novel adjectives: Evidence from preschool-aged children. *Child Development*, 71, 649–659.

Kotovsky, L., and Gentner, D. 1996. Comparison and categorization in the development of relational similarity. *Child Development*, 67, 2797–2822.

Kuehne, S. E., Gentner, D., and Forbus, K. D. 2000. Modeling infant learning via symbolic structural alignment. *Proceedings of the Twenty-Second Annual Conference of the Cognitive Science Society*, 286–291. Hillsdale, NJ: Erlbaum.

Kurtz, K. J., Miao, C., and Gentner, D. 2001. Learning by analogical bootstrapping. *Journal of the Learning Sciences*, 10, 417–446.

Landau, B., and Shipley, E. 2001. Labelling patterns and object naming. *Developmental Science*, 4, 109–118.

Landau, B., Smith, L., and Jones, S. 1998. Object shape, object function, and object name. *Journal of Memory and Language*, 38, 1–27.

Loewenstein, J., and Gentner, D. 2001. Spatial mapping in preschoolers: Close comparisons facilitate far mappings. *Journal of Cognition and Development*, 2, 189–219.

Loewenstein, J., Thompson, L., and Gentner, D. 1999. Analogical encoding facilitates knowledge transfer in negotiation. *Psychonomic Bulletin and Review, 6*, 586–597.

Mandler, J. 1992. How to build a baby: II. Conceptual primitives. *Psychological Review, 99*, 587–604.

Mandler, J. 1996. Preverbal representation and language. In P. Bloom, M. Peterson, L. Nadel, and M. Garrett, eds., *Language and space*, 365–384. Cambridge, MA: MIT Press.

Marcus, G. F. 1999. Do infants learn grammar with algebra or statistics? *Science, 284*, 436–437.

Marcus, G. F., Vijayan, S., Bandi, R. S., and Vishton, P. M. 1999. Rule-learning in seven-month-old infants. *Science, 283*, 77–80.

Markman, A. B., and Gentner, D. 1993. Splitting the differences: A structural alignment view of similarity. *Journal of Memory and Language, 32*, 517–535.

Markman, A. B., and Gentner, D. 1997. The effects of alignability on memory storage. *Psychological Science, 8*, 363–367.

Markman, E. M. 1989. *Categorization and naming in children: Problems of induction.* Cambridge, MA: MIT Press.

Markson, L., and Bloom, P. 1997. Evidence against a dedicated system for word learning in children. *Nature, 385*, 813–815.

Medin, D. L., and Ross, B. H. 1989. The specific character of abstract thought: Categorization, problem-solving, and induction. In R. J. Sternberg, ed., *Advances in the psychology of human intelligence*, vol. 5, 189–223. Hillsdale, NJ: Erlbaum.

Meltzoff, A. N. 1995. Understanding the intentions of others: Re-enactment of intended acts by 18-month-old children. *Developmental Psychology, 31*, 838–850.

Namy, L. L. 2001. What's in a name when it isn't a word? 17-month-olds' mapping of nonverbal symbols to object categories. *Infancy, 2*, 73–86.

Namy, L. L., and Gentner, D. 2002. Making a silk purse out of two sow's ears: Young children's use of comparison in category learning. *Journal of Experimental Psychology: General, 131*, 5–15.

Namy, L. L., and Waxman, S. R. 1998. Words and gestures: Infants' interpretations of different forms of symbolic reference. *Child Development, 69*, 295–308.

Namy, L. L., and Waxman, S. R. 2000. Naming and exclaiming: Infants' sensitivity to naming contexts. *Journal of Cognition and Development, 1*, 405–442.

Oakes, L. M. 2001, April. The role of comparison in category formation in infancy. Paper presented at the 68th Anniversary Meeting of the Society for Research in Child Development, Minneapolis.

Ross, B. H. 1984. Remindings and their effects in learning a cognitive skill. *Cognitive Psychology, 16*, 371–416.

Ross, B. H. 1987. This is like that: The use of earlier problems and the separation of similarity effects. *Journal of Experimental Psychology: Learning, Memory, and Cognition, 13*, 629–639.

Ross, B. H. 1989. Remindings in learning and instruction. In S. Vosniadou and A. Ortony, eds., *Similarity and analogical reasoning*, 438–469. New York: Cambridge University Press.

Ross, B. H., and Kennedy, P. T. 1990. Generalizing from the use of earlier examples in problem solving. *Journal of Experimental Psychology: Learning, Memory, and Cognition, 16*, 42–55.

Ross, B. H., Perkins, S. J., and Tenpenny, P. L. 1990. Reminding-based category learning. *Cognitive Psychology, 22*, 460–492.

Saffran, J. R., Aslin, R. N., and Newport, E. L. 1996. Statistical learning by 8-month-old infants. *Science, 274*, 1926–1928.

Saffran, J. R., Johnson, E. K., Aslin, R. N., and Newport, E. L. 1999. Statistical learning of tonal structure by adults and infants. *Cognition, 70*, 27–52.

Samuelson, L. K., and Smith, L. B. 1998. Memory and attention make smart word learning: An alternative account of Akhtar, Carpenter, and Tomasello. *Child Development, 69*, 94–104.

Samuelson, L. K., and Smith, L. B. 2000. Grounding development in cognitive processes. *Child Development, 71*, 98–106.

Skorstad, J., Gentner, D., and Medin, D. 1988. Abstraction processes during concept learning: A structural view. *Proceedings of the Tenth Annual Conference of the Cognitive Science Society*, 419–425.

Slobin, D. I. 1973. Cognitive prerequisites for the development of grammar. In C. Ferguson and D. Slobin, eds., *Studies of child language development*. New York: Holt, Rinehart and Winston.

Smith, L. B., Jones, S. S., Landau, B., Gershkoff-Stowe, L., and Samuelson, L. 2002. Object name learning provides on-the-job training for attention. *Psychological Science, 13*, 13–19.

Spelke, E. S. 1990. Principles of object perception. *Cognitive Science, 14*, 29–56.

Stilwell, C. H., and Markman, A. B. 2001. The fate of irrelevant information in analogical mapping. In *The Proceedings of the 23rd Annual Meeting of the Cognitive Science Society*, 988–993. Edinburgh: Erlbaum.

Tomasello, M. 1992. *First verbs*. New York: Cambridge University Press.

Tomasello, M. 2000. Do young children have adult syntactic competence? *Cognition, 74*, 209–253.

Tomasello, M., and Brooks, P. J. 1999. Early syntactic development: A Construction Grammar approach. In M. Barrett, ed., *The development of language: Studies in developmental psychology*, 161–190. Philadelphia: Psychology Press/Taylor & Francis.

Tomasello, M., Strosberg, R., and Akhtar, N. 1996. Eighteen-month-old children learn words in non-ostensive contexts. *Journal of Child Language, 23*, 157–176.

Waxman, S. R., and Booth, A. E. 2000. Principles that are invoked in the acquisition of words but not facts. *Cognition, 77*, B33–B43.

Waxman, S. R., and Booth, A. E. 2001. Seeing pink elephants: Fourteen-month-olds' interpretations of novel nouns and adjectives. *Cognitive Psychology, 43*, 217–242.

Waxman, S. R., and Klibanoff, R. S. 2000. The role of comparison in the extension of novel adjectives. *Developmental Psychology, 36*, 571–581.

Waxman, S. R., Lynch, E. B., Casey, K. L., and Baer, L. 1997. Setters and samoyeds: The emergence of subordinate level categories as a basis for inductive inference in preschool-age children. *Developmental Psychology, 33*, 1074–1090.

Waxman, S. R., and Markow, D. B. 1995. Words as invitations to form categories: Evidence from 12- to 13-month-old infants. *Cognitive Psychology, 29*, 257–302.

Wolff, P., and Gentner, D. 2000. Evidence for role-neutral initial processing of metaphors. *Journal of Experimental Psychology: Learning, Memory, and Cognition, 26*, 529–541.

Woodward, A. L., and Hoyne, K. L. 1999. Infants' learning about words and sounds in relation to objects. *Child Development, 70*, 65–77.

18

Keeping Verb Acquisition in Motion: A Comparison of English and Spanish

Jill M. Hohenstein, Letitia R. Naigles, and Ann R. Eisenberg

A: If Gertrudis had only known! The poor thing *climbed up and down* ten times, carrying buckets of water.

B: Si Gertrudis hubiera sabido! La pobre *subió y bajó (ascended and descended)* como diez veces cargando las cubetas. (Esquivel 1989/1995)

As this example illustrates, English and Spanish speakers talk differently about the same motion events. English typically describes motion events using a verb that encodes the manner of motion (e.g., *climb*) with directional information encoded in a prepositional phrase or satellite (e.g., *up and down*). In contrast, Spanish typically encodes the path (or direction) in the verb (e.g., *ascended and descended*), infrequently attaching prepositional phrases. Not surprisingly, English-learning children grow up to talk—and write—like A above, whereas Spanish-learning children grow up to talk—and write—like B above. Given that this book focuses on word learning, our focus, too, will be on how children learn these language-specific lexical-semantic patterns of motion-verb knowledge and use. However, because our argument will be that this acquisition of verb meaning is strongly tied to the syntactic system of each language, we will also discuss the language-specific syntax of motion events and its development in children.

In particular, we first provide evidence from adults that the difference between English and Spanish modes of talking about motion events is both syntactic and lexical-semantic in nature. Our subsequent review of the developmental pattern concerning when children acquire these differences highlights three relevant findings. First, the syntactic distinction is learned prior to the lexical-semantic one. Second, the first language-specific differences in motion-verb use are a result of the language-specific differences in syntax. And third, these early differences in motion-verb use by English and Spanish speakers do not yet indicate an appreciation of the deeper lexical-semantic distinctions. In other words, differences in motion-verb use in children do not yet imply different lexical-semantic generalizations about motion-verb meanings. Appreciation of these latter generalizations emerges between 4 and 7 years of age.

18.1 What Do Children Have to Learn?

The crosslinguistic difference illustrated in the example above has intrigued linguists and psychologists alike for more than 20 years, and it has figured prominently in major theories of linguistics, language acquisition, and linguistic relativity. Talmy (1975, 1985, 1991) made it the conceptual prototype of his theory of the relation between linguistic form and linguistic meaning. Gentner (1982; Gentner and Boroditsky 2001) cited it as a partial explanation for the ubiquitous finding that, in language after language, nouns are apparently learned before verbs. And Slobin's (1996) findings concerning the ways speakers of different languages narrate motion events led to his proposal of "thinking for speaking"—that is, the idea that speakers of different languages think differently as they cast their thoughts into speech. Our research questions draw on all of this previous work, but target specifically the questions of when and how the crosslinguistic difference in motion-verb use and comprehension is acquired. But first, we must capture what this difference—which has captivated so many areas of psycholinguistics—is.

Motion events are typically conceptualized as a figure moving in relation to some ground (Talmy 1975, 1985; Marr and Vaina 1982). The linguistic expression or description of a motion event can include any or all of the following components: figure (the object in motion); ground (the source, goal, or location of the motion); path (the course followed by the figure); manner (the way the figure moves); and cause (whether the motion is agentive or not). To illustrate, the sentence "The girl rolled the ball across the floor" contains all of these elements: the cause is *girl*, the manner is *rolled*, the figure is *ball*, *across* corresponds to path, and *floor* is the ground. For brevity's sake and because the different event types may correspond to specific learning patterns, we confine ourselves to discussion of internally rather than externally caused motion events—that is, those where the figure is moving more or less under its own power or volition.

These components are manifested in descriptions of motion events in several patterns across languages. We will focus on two of these, in which either the manner or the path component is conflated with, or woven into the meaning of, the main (motion) verb. Both patterns exist in some form in both English and Spanish. Manner-conflating motion verbs include *run/correr, walk/andar, jump/brincar, fly/volar,* and *crawl/gatear*; path-conflating motion verbs include *come/venir, go/ir, fall/caerse, enter/entrar,* and *descend/bajarse*. The patterns become differentiated because the choice of verb has syntactic consequences for the rest of the utterance (Talmy 1985, 1991). If the verb is manner-conflating, the path component is typically encoded in a content-rich preposition or *satellite,* and the ground component surfaces as the object of that preposition or satellite.

(1)   She's walking through the forest.

(2)   Está caminando por el bosque.

In contrast, if the verb is path-conflating, the ground component surfaces as the direct object (or object of a content-poor or "dummy" preposition; Tremblay 1996), and the manner component can be omitted entirely.

(3)   She's entering the house (running).

(4)   Está entrando a la casa (corriendo).

Thus, manner-conflating verbs are typically intransitive, whereas path-conflating verbs are typically transitive. There are two exceptions to this generalization. First, the most common path-conflating verbs, which describe general rather than specific directions, appear to follow manner-verb syntax.[1]

(5) She went through the forest.

(6) Pasó por el bosque.

Second, both manner and path verbs can appear without any ground information at all:

(7) What's she doing?
     She's walking.
     She's leaving.

(8) ¿Qué está pasando?
     Está caminando.
     Está saliendo.

(9) Let's go.

(10) Vámanos.

There have been several characterizations of how English and Spanish differ in their expression of motion events. Levin and Rappaport Hovav (1995) proposed a syntactically oriented analysis in which path verbs in the two languages are treated similarly but manner verbs are treated differently. In brief, path verbs in the two languages describe "inherently directed motion" (p. 56) and can appear with directional and ground-specifying phrases (e.g., (3) to (6) above). English manner verbs do not include directed motion as part of their core semantics but can acquire this additional meaning by rule, so that they can appear with a wide variety of directional phrases:

(11a) The children ran.

(11b) The children ran into the room.

The issue with Spanish is that it lacks the requisite rule, so that Spanish manner verbs cannot always appear with the same directional phrases:

(12a) Las niñas corrieron.

(12b) *Las niñas corrieron hacia adentro del cuarto.

Jackendoff's (1990) analysis is similar, albeit more semantically construed. He characterized path verbs as incorporating the major event GO, and manner verbs as incorporating the major event MOVE. Manner verbs become directional via a correspondence rule that incorporates a GO function into the verb; thus, when GO becomes incorporated into a manner verb such as *run*, the verb can appear with directional PPs. This correspondence rule is present in languages like English and absent in languages like Spanish.

These characterizations seem at once too narrow and too broad. They are too broad because the restrictions on Spanish manner verbs seem more subtle than simply being prohibited from appearing with directional phrases. In fact, as shown in (2), they can appear with some directional phrases; however, they certainly cannot appear as freely with them as can English manner verbs (e.g., (12b)). Aske (1989) and Slobin and Hoiting (1994) have suggested that Spanish manner verbs are only prohibited from descriptions of *telic* events (i.e., events with a definite source or end point) and/or events that include a boundary crossing (e.g., entering, exiting, crossing). Thus, (2) is permitted because the event is atelic; a direction is specified (*through*), but the ground is not the end point of the walking and no boundaries are crossed. In contrast, (12b) is not permitted because the event is telic; the end point of the running is the room, and a boundary is crossed between the outside and the inside of the room (see also Naigles et al. 1998).

Levin and Rappaport Hovav's and Jackendoff's characterizations are also too narrow because they seem to omit a larger point that Talmy (1985, 1991) and others (Gentner 1982; Slobin 1996; Berman and Slobin 1994; Naigles et al. 1998) make quite strongly—that whereas both patterns (with some restrictions) are *possible* in both languages, the manner-conflating verb pattern is more *typical* of English and the path-conflating pattern is more *typical* of Spanish. English manner verbs tend to be much more frequent than most English path verbs (Francis and Kucera 1982), whereas the opposite tends to be true of Spanish (Juilland and Chang-Rodriguez 1964). Talmy (1991) captured this as a contrast between *verb-framed* languages (e.g., Spanish) and *satellite-framed* languages (e.g., English): the frame for motion events is the path, and Spanish encodes the path in the verb whereas English encodes the path in the satellite. The importance of the satellite as a frame for English but not Spanish is shown in another syntactic contrast between the two languages. Even in the case of atelic events, there is a manner-verb construction that is permitted in English but not in Spanish:

(13) She's walking through.

(14) *Está caminando por.

That is, when the ground itself is not mentioned, English manner verbs still permit the expression of a path in the satellite or string of satellites (e.g., *She flew* back up out *of the hole*) whereas Spanish manner verbs do not. The content-rich prepositions in Spanish do not function as satellites.

In sum, the relevant contrasts for the linguistic expression of motion events are both intralanguage and interlanguage and both lexical-semantic and syntactic, as summarized in table 18.1. We will not be able to address every nuance in this chapter, but will focus on the major lexical difference, that English typically encodes manner in the verb whereas Spanish typically encodes path, and the major syntactic difference, that English allows for an elaborate system of

Table 18.1
A partial list of permitted syntactic frames by language and verb type

	Language			
	English		Spanish	
Frame	Manner	Path	Manner	Path
Intransitive				
No ground NP				
Bare V	Always	Always	Always	Always
V satellite	Always	Sometimes	Never	Never
Ground NP in PP				
V + content-rich preposition	Always	Sometimes	Sometimes	Never
V + content-poor preposition	Always	Sometimes	Sometimes	Sometimes
Transitive				
Ground NP as direct object	Rarely	Sometimes	Rarely	Sometimes

postverbal satellites and prepositional phrases (PPs) whereas Spanish PPs within the predicate are much more restricted. Before we can address children's acquisition of these motion-verb patterns, though, we must consider an issue with the adult representations. In particular, we need to know whether these two differences are distinct, or whether they are two sides of the same coin. That is, are the syntactic differences between English and Spanish descriptions of motion events an inevitable consequence of the languages' different selection of verbs, or would they appear regardless of verb type? Specifically, if a manner verb is used, the path component must be expressed in other parts of the predicate, whereas if a path verb is used, little else about the motion event need necessarily be expressed. Put another way, are the verb-lexicalization differences between English and Spanish simply a by-product of the different syntactic patterns of the two languages, or do they exist as generalizations over and above the syntactic differences? Specifically, the expression of the path component in satellites and/or PPs leaves the verb "free" to encode manner without necessarily forcing the generalization that English motion verbs typically *do* encode manner. Thus, our first discussions of the empirical literature will be summaries of findings from adult elicited-production and novel-verb interpretation studies that indicate that both the lexical-semantic and the syntactic distinctions are present in adults' linguistic knowledge.

18.2 Adult Knowledge of the Linguistic Expression of Motion Events

How do English- and Spanish-speaking adults talk about motion events? Do they differ in the types of verbs they use? Do they differ in the types of sentence structures they use? Furthermore, what can we tell about the language-specific generalizations they have made about motion verbs? In this section, we summarize the findings of Slobin and his colleagues (Berman and Slobin 1994; Sebastian and Slobin 1994; Slobin 1996) as well as those from our lab (Naigles et al. 1998; Naigles and Terrazas 1998) that address these questions.

Slobin and his colleagues asked adults (and children, as described later) to narrate a story based on a children's wordless picture book,

Frog, Where Are You? (Mayer 1969). Native speakers of English and Spanish (as well as German, Hebrew, and Turkish speakers, whose data will not be discussed) retold the story of a boy's search, including much travel through forest, meadow, and swamp, for his lost frog. Overall, the English speakers produced almost three times as many manner-conflating verb types as path-conflating verb types, whereas the Spanish speakers produced almost three times as many path verb types as manner verb types. Clearly, speakers of these different languages have different preferences in terms of motion-verb selection. Moreover, Slobin and colleagues found that English speakers used the verbs with satellites (e.g., *The dog jumps down*) and with satellites and PPs (*The owl flew out of here*), whereas Spanish speakers tended to produce their motion verbs with little or no additional information in the same clause (e.g., *Salió/He left*). To illustrate, they report that for episodes of downward motion (such as going over a cliff into some water), fully 36 percent of the descriptions in Spanish were composed of such "bare" verbs, whereas only 15 percent of the English descriptions were. Across all episodes, 82 percent of English descriptions included source or goal-of-motion specification in PPs around the verb, whereas only 60 percent of Spanish descriptions did.[2] In sum, these elicited narratives supported the earlier linguistic analyses that clear differences can be seen in both the verb types that English and Spanish speakers used, and in the types of sentences they produced.

Naigles et al. (1998, Study 2) replicated and extended these crosslinguistic differences with a task involving a different discourse context, namely, video description. We asked monolingual English-speaking high school graduates in Texas and monolingual Spanish-speaking high school graduates in Guatemala to describe in writing short videos (6 seconds long) of motion events. Overall, the English speakers produced more manner-conflating main-verb tokens (87%) than path-conflating main-verb tokens (6.4%), and the Spanish speakers produced more path-conflating main-verb tokens (65%) than manner-conflating main-verb tokens (32%). Moreover, considering only those events depicting horizontal motion (such as crossing a bridge),[3] 91 percent of the English descriptions included a PP describing the source, goal, and/or location of motion, whereas only

56 percent of the Spanish descriptions included such a PP. Another 6 percent of the Spanish descriptions included only an NP source or goal, as compared with 1.7 percent of the English descriptions. And fully 38 percent of the Spanish descriptions included no locative information at all (meaning they used a subject and a verb but no further information about the source, goal, or ground), compared with only 4 percent of the English descriptions. Finally, the Spanish speakers used a total of nine prepositions (*en, a, hasta, de, por, hacia, para, entre, sobre*), of which *a/to* and *de/from* were the most common and accounted for 45 percent of all preposition use. In contrast, the English speakers used a total of seventeen prepositions and satellites (*to, through, into, up, (away) from, across, onto, in, down, out of, over, around, back, left, toward(s)*); *to* and *(away) from* accounted for only 1.7 percent of all preposition/satellite use. Interestingly, none of the English descriptions included a satellite without an accompanying ground NP.

The findings of these two elicited-production studies are consistent with our claim that both lexical-semantic and syntactic distinctions are involved in the difference between English and Spanish expressions of motion events. That is, both the verb meanings and the sentence frames are different in corpora of English and Spanish descriptions of motion events. If these same types of utterances are produced in speech to children, as is likely, the children's input differs on both dimensions: English learners hear mostly manner verbs with directional PPs, whereas Spanish learners hear more path verbs with fewer instances of directional PPs. However, it is still possible that the two distinctions are partially if not totally interdependent. For example, perhaps English speakers use more directional PPs because they use so many manner verbs, and perhaps Spanish speakers use fewer directional PPs because of their heavy reliance on path verbs. Naigles and Terrazas (1998) attempted to disentangle the lexical-semantic and syntactic distinctions by asking English and Spanish speakers to interpret novel (i.e., nonsense) motion verbs in different sentence frames. The questions were twofold: Would speakers be sensitive to the semantic implications of the sentence frames in interpreting the novel verbs? Would speakers differ by language in their preferred interpretations of the novel verbs?

Table 18.2
Videotape layout from Naigles and Terrazas 1998

Trial	Video 1	Audio	Video 2
1	Woman skips toward tree	E: *Look, she's kradding the tree.* S: *¡Mira, ella está mecando al árbol!*	Blank
2	Blank	E: *See, she's kradding the tree!* S: *¡Ves, ella está mecando al árbol!*	Woman skips toward tree
3	Woman skips toward tree	E: *Hey, she's kradding the tree!* S: *¡Oye, ella está mecando al árbol!*	Woman skips toward tree
4	Woman marches toward tree	E: *Look, they're different now!* S: *¡Mira, ahora están diferentes!*	Woman skips away from tree
5	Woman marches toward tree	E: *Where's she kradding?* S: *¿Dónde está mecando ella?*	Woman skips away from tree
6	Woman marches toward tree	E: *Where she's kradding?* S: *¿Dónde está mecando ella?*	Woman skips away from tree

Note: E: English audio; S: Spanish audio

The participants included monolingual college-educated English speakers and college-educated native Spanish speakers whose exposure to English began at or after puberty.[4] The stimuli were triads of videos of motion events, displayed on side-by-side monitors. As shown in table 18.2, the first three presentations of the video events introduced the novel verb, which was presented in either path-verb syntax (e.g., "She's kradding the tree"/"Está mecando al árbol") or manner-verb syntax (e.g., "She's kradding toward the tree"/"Está mecando hacia el árbol"). Recall that in English and Spanish, the path frame is typically a transitive frame with the ground as the direct object or (Spanish only) an intransitive frame with a content-poor preposition (see table 18.1). The manner frame in both languages is intransitive with a content-rich preposition; because the preposition encodes the path, the verb is free to encode the manner.[5] The fourth presentation changed the video events, so that one monitor presented the old manner of motion with a new path (the manner match) and the other monitor presented the old path of motion with a new manner (the path match). The fifth and sixth presentations showed the same videos, and asked the participants to designate, by

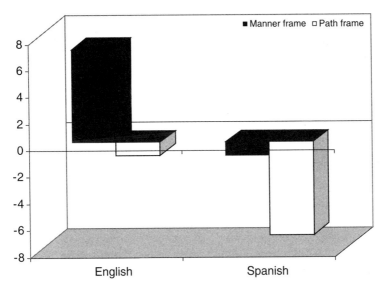

Figure 18.1
Mean manner preference (number of points to the manner screen minus number of points to the path screen) for each language group and frame condition. Adapted from Naigles and Terrazas 1998.

pointing, which of the new video events depicted the novel verb, presented in the most minimal of frames ("Where's she kradding?"/ "¿Dónde está mecando?").

There were three main findings. First, both English and Spanish speakers chose the manner match more frequently when the verb was presented in manner-verb syntax and the path match more frequently when the verb was presented in path-verb syntax. Thus, members of both language groups were sensitive to the semantic implications of the different frames and altered their interpretations accordingly. Second, across frames, the English speakers chose the manner match more frequently and the Spanish speakers chose the path match more frequently. Thus, the two groups had different overall preferences for their interpretations of the novel verb; each followed the motion-verb lexicalization pattern of their native language. Third, there was a significant interaction of language group and syntax, as shown in figure 18.1. Specifically, the speakers chose consistently when their language-specific patterns coincided with the implications of the syntax (i.e., English speakers chose the manner match in the manner-verb syntax condition and Spanish speakers chose the path match in the path-verb syntax condition) and inconsistently when the lexicalization patterns and the syntax were in conflict (i.e., English speakers in the path-verb syntax condition and Spanish speakers in the manner-verb syntax condition). These findings confirm that adult English and Spanish speakers have gone beyond the use of individual lexical items to make *generalizations* about the types of meaning that motion verbs in their respective languages encode and about the types of frames they can appear in. Moreover, the generalizations are both lexical-semantic and syntactic in nature.

In sum, research with adults implicates both a syntactic and a lexical-semantic dimension to the crosslinguistic difference between English and Spanish expressions of motion events. Specifically, the syntactic dimension involves the ubiquitous presence of path PPs and satellites in English as compared with the primarily unelaborated verb phrase in Spanish. The lexical dimension involves the strong tendency for verbs to encode the path of motion in Spanish but the manner of motion in English.

18.3   Child Acquisition of the Linguistic Expression of Motion Events

Our main questions are twofold: First, how do children acquire their lexical-semantic generalizations, that English motion verbs encode manner and Spanish motion verbs encode path? Second, what is the direction of dependence between this lexical generalization and the syntactic one? In this regard, two possibilities suggest themselves. Either the lexical-semantic distinction emerges early and perhaps facilitates the syntactic distinction, or the syntactic distinction might precede and perhaps facilitate the lexical-semantic distinction. Thus, the dependence in acquisition of the lexical-semantic and syntactic dimensions can have consequences for theories concerning the interaction of grammar and lexicon in acquisition. Below, we review the theoretical background for both possibilities. We then present three sets of studies, two involving language production and one involving novel-verb learning—studies that begin to distinguish the two possibilities just mentioned.

18.3.1 Two Views of the Interdependence of Lexicon and Grammar in Acquisition

In this section we briefly review two theoretical perspectives on how lexicon and syntax are acquired. One suggests that it is the lexicon that stimulates grammatical acquisition. The other supports the opposite view: that an understanding of syntax can drive lexical acquisitions.

Lexicon First
Current "emergentist" and "lexicalist" accounts of language acquisition (MacWhinney 1999; Bates and Goodman 1999; Tomasello 2000) have theorized that grammatical knowledge emerges from lexical knowledge. That is, children have been hypothesized to require a certain threshold number of words in their vocabularies in order to formulate grammatical categories and rules (see also Marchman and Bates 1994) and a certain threshold of verbs heard in combination with nouns in order to begin to construct sentence frames (Tomasello 1992; Goldberg 1999). Following this account, we might predict that the lexical distinction under consideration would be acquired before the grammatical one. For example, English learners would acquire many manner-conflating verbs whereas Spanish learners would acquire many path-conflating verbs, but the syntax with which these verbs were used would initially be similar across languages. These theories would predict, as well, that English and Spanish learners would show their language-specific lexical-semantic biases in a novel-verb learning task developmentally before they demonstrated an appreciation of the different distinctions conveyed by the syntactic frames. Finally, emergentist theorists might also predict that the syntactic distinctions would later be acquired via these lexical distinctions. Perhaps English learners would begin to use the path PPs so they could describe motion events more fully, whereas Spanish learners might observe that their motion verbs already adequately describe the core schema of motion events (Talmy 1991), and so

receive little impetus to incorporate locative PPs into Spanish motion-verb syntax.

Syntax First

In contrast, current grammatically oriented accounts of verb acquisition per se have proposed that children take advantage of the syntactic frames in which verbs are heard in order to narrow down or constrain the meanings of those verbs (so-called *syntactic bootstrapping*: Gleitman 1990; Landau and Gleitman 1985; Naigles 1990, 1998; Naigles and Hoff-Ginsberg 1995, 1998). Because verb syntax reflects aspects of verb meaning (i.e., causative verbs usually appear in transitive frames, motion verbs with PPs, mental-state verbs with sentence complements), the syntactic frame that co-occurs with unknown verbs can focus children's attention on specific aspects of meaning in the surrounding context (Kako 1998; Fisher et al. 1994; Naigles 1990, 1996). For example, children as young as 25 months of age have been shown to use sentence frames to distinguish novel causative verbs from novel noncausative ones (Naigles 1990; Naigles and Kako 1993). In this account, we might predict that the grammatical distinction under consideration would be acquired before the lexical one: English learners would use the V PP frame to describe motion events whereas Spanish learners would use the "bare" V frame, but the verbs used in these frames would initially be semantically similar across languages. Syntactic bootstrapping theorists might also predict that the lexical distinctions would later be acquired via these syntactic distinctions. Because the V PP frame already encodes the path of motion, English verbs acquired via this frame would typically be manner-of-motion verbs; after learning disproportionately many of these, English learners might then come to make the generalization that their motion verbs typically encode manner. In contrast, following Talmy's (1975) suggestion that the path information is most crucial to the communicative content, the "bare" V frame would facilitate the acquisition of path-of-motion verbs because the frame does not allow for path to be incorporated elsewhere. Spanish learners would thus be able to acquire disproportionately many path verbs, and the generalization that Spanish motion verbs encode path would prevail.

In sum, the theoretical debate between those who claim that grammar develops out of the lexicon and those who claim that grammar develops at least somewhat independently of the lexicon can be recast in miniature in the microcosm of children's motion-verb acquisition. We now turn to a consideration of the data on children's developing use and understanding of motion verbs in English and Spanish.

18.3.2 Elicited Production of Motion Verbs in Narratives

Sebastian and Slobin (1994; see also Berman and Slobin 1994; Slobin and Bocaz 1988; Slobin 1996) also asked English- and Spanish-learning children to narrate the frog story described earlier. The participants were 3, 4, 5, and 9 years of age. Their acquisition of the lexical distinction cannot be addressed directly, because Slobin and his colleagues did not report the number of manner-verb and path-verb types in the children's narratives. However, their analyses of the children's syntax suggest that, by the age of 3, English and Spanish learners talk differently about motion events. For example, when narrating the episodes concerning downward motion, Spanish-speaking preschoolers produced motion verbs "bare" of locative detail 56 percent of the time, whereas English-speaking preschoolers did so only 15 percent of the time.

Interestingly, the youngest English learners used the V + Satellite construction the most frequently, and then added the V + PP and V + Satellite + PP constructions at later ages. Moreover, the early satellites were mainly used with general path-of-motion verbs (i.e., *come*, *go*, and *fall*), and only later extended to use with specific manner verbs. With the Spanish learners, Sebastian and Slobin (1994) noticed an *increase* in the use of directional phrases from age 3 to ages 4 and 5 and then a decrease at age 9. The increase was due to the use of directional adverbs, such as *arriba/above* and *abajo/below*, with path verbs (e.g., *sube por arriba por el tronco/he ascends upward along the trunk*; p. 264). The presence of the path verb in Spanish renders the adverb redundant; Sebastian and Slobin suggested that these children had learned their language's prohibition of directional prepositions, but were still trying to find a way to include path information elsewhere in the predicate. Even with these adverbs, though, the Spanish learners still included less directional information than did the English learners. In summary, children aged 3 and older already use language-specific syntax in their talk about motion events. The next analyses, using spontaneous speech databases, investigate whether this language specificity exists earlier in combinatorial speech and whether it is accompanied by differences in motion-verb types.[6]

18.3.3 Spontaneous Production of Motion Verbs

How do children talk about motion events, before the age of 3? Do they seem to talk differently almost from the onset of combinatorial speech? Choi and Bowerman (1991) uncovered some very early language specificity in English- and Korean-learners' talk about motion events. Specifically, in their study, 1-year-old English learners used the same terms (the same path satellites) in reference to both caused and spontaneous motion, as is typical in English, whereas 1-year-old Korean learners used different terms (different verbs) in reference to caused-versus-spontaneous motion, as is typical in Korean. Choi and Bowerman did not report how these terms were used in combinatorial speech, however, nor did they include data from Spanish learners. In other words, there was no information about the syntactic structure of the Korean- and English-speaking children's utterances once they were forming protosentences.

We present here some analyses of 2-year-olds' spontaneous speech, drawn from a variety of English and Spanish databases. Transcripts from three Spanish learners were examined. Data from Nancy and Marisa come from Eisenberg's (1982) corpus of transcriptions. Nancy and Marisa were living in Northern California with family members who were all recent immigrants from Mexico. Spanish was spoken exclusively in their homes, so at age 2–3 years they were monolingual learners of Spanish. Our analyses come from Nancy's database at 2;1 and 2;4–2;5 and Marisa's database at 2;11 and 3;0, the points at which motion verbs first appeared in their utterances. Data on Emilio come from the Vila corpus. Emilio was a monolingual Spanish learner raised in Spain; his transcripts at 2;4 and 2;8 were downloaded from the CHILDES database (MacWhinney 2000). Transcripts from two English learners were also examined. Adam and Sarah are from the Brown 1973 corpus, also downloaded from the CHILDES database. Their transcripts were examined at 2;3 and 2;8. Adam and Nancy were the most prolific producers of motion verbs; hence, their data contributed most heavily to the analyses that follow.

In each transcript, we extracted the utterances that included internally caused verbs of motion (to be consistent across adult and child analyses) produced by the child, categorized each main verb as manner-conflating or path-conflating (see Naigles et al. 1998 for more information about our criteria), and parsed each utterance according to the grammatical categories included (e.g., NP, V, PP, Satellite, Adverb). Moreover, we noted whether each PP encoded directional (e.g., *through the hole*) or nondirectional information (e.g., *with Mommy*), and which NPs in the predicate encoded locative (e.g., *go someplace*) information. Table 18.3 presents the number of utterances that included motion verbs that were produced by each child at each age.

Table 18.3
Percent of utterances including locative/directional information (number of total motion-verb utterances)

Child	Age			
	2;1	2;3–2;5	2;8	2;11–3;0
Spanish				
Nancy	35%	31%		
N	153	100		
Marisa				18%
N				102
Emilio		6%	29%	
		16	14	
English				
Adam		34%	73%	
N		90	56	
Sarah		16%	55%	
N		6	11	

At 25 months, Nancy was our youngest and most prolific motion-verb user. She produced both specific path-conflating verbs (*salir/exit*) and manner-conflating verbs (*correr/run, bailar/dance*). However, by far her most frequent motion verbs were the general path-conflating ones *ir/go* and *venir/come*, comprising more than two-thirds of her motion-verb utterances. Approximately 35 percent of these utterances included some kind of directional or locative information, mostly in the form of PPs (*va al circo/(he) goes to the circus*) and locative adverbs (*vamos afuera/let's go outside*). She used motion verbs in single-word utterances (i.e., "bare") 59 percent of the time. At 2;4–2;5, she had added both manner verbs (e.g., *brincar/jump*) and path verbs (e.g., *llegar/arrive*); however, she still used *ir* and *venir* most frequently. She added locative and directional information only 31 percent of the time; fully 61 percent of her motion verbs were used "bare." Nancy's motion-verb utterances before 2;6 sound remarkably Spanishlike already, especially in their brevity with respect to locative and directional information. However, she was still very young, and it is possible that her brevity was due to overall grammatical/production limitations, rather than more specific knowledge about how to use motion verbs. Hence, we next turn to Adam.

Adam at 2;3 sounded very similar to Nancy at the same age. He produced both manner-conflating (*hop, walk, jump*) and path-conflating (*come, go, fall*) verbs; however, all of his path-conflating verbs encoded fairly general rather than specific directions. *Come* and *go* were also Adam's most frequently used motion verbs. Approximately 34 percent of Adam's motion-verb utterances included some kind of directional or locative information, mostly in the form of PPs (*go to the store*) and satellites (*go back, fall over, move away*). Only 33 percent of his motion verbs were used "bare," though; this included all of his utterances with manner verbs. Thus, at 2;3, Adam followed the Spanish pattern more than he did the English pattern. At 2;8, Adam had added only three new motion verbs (*jump, ride, cross*). However, his utterances containing motion verbs had expanded considerably; now, fully 73 percent included some kind of directional or locative information. Satellites provided the directional information for 63 percent of these utterances; the rest included PPs and NPs. Only 16 percent of his motion verbs were produced "bare." Thus, at 2;8, Adam already sounded like an English speaker.

We do not have transcripts for Nancy past 2;5; however, our analyses of the transcripts of Marisa and Emilio suggest that Spanish learners do not elaborate on their motion-verb utterances as they gain grammatical knowledge and produce (in general) longer utterances. Emilio at 2;4 used *ir* and *venir* most frequently, but also produced instances of *volver/turn* and *pasear/stroll.* Only one of his utterances included any directional information (*ven aquí/come here*); 75 percent were produced "bare." At 2;8, Emilio had added one more motion verb (*levantarse/rise*), and produced "bare" verbs only 43 percent of the time; however, he still included locative or directional information less than 30 percent of the time. Marisa's motion verbs included *caerse/fall, correr/run, brincar/jump, volver/turn,* and *apurarse/hurry*; however, she, like Nancy and Emilio, used *ir* and *venir* most frequently. Only 18 percent of her motion-verb utterances included directional or locative information; the majority of these were PPs (*Vamos a la banca/Let's go to the bench*). Fully 73 percent of her motion verbs were produced "bare."

The possibility exists that the brevity of motion-verb use in the Spanish learners can be attributed to the scarcity of these verbs in the transcripts we examined. Perhaps the context was inappropriate for much motion-verb use, especially in an elaborated fashion. We wondered, therefore, whether the English pattern of development that we had observed with Adam could be seen with a much smaller sample of motion verbs. Sarah provided us with the opportunity to test this, because her overall frequency of motion-verb use was closer to Emilio's than to Adam's (see table 18.3). At 2;3, Sarah produced only *go*, and only one of her utterances included any directional information (*go here*). At 2;8, her motion-verb use had expanded to include *dance, hop, come, run, fall,* and *sit,* and more than half of her motion-oriented utterances ($n = 6$) included locative or directional information. For four of these, the directional information took the form of a satellite or preposition (*fall up, sit back, come from*). In sum, Sarah's few motion-verb utterances were still sufficient to reveal the same developmental pattern as seen with Adam. Near the beginning of the third year, English learners use motion verbs with little locative elaboration; thus, these children sound more similar to the Spanish pattern than to the English one. In contrast, by the end of the third year, English learners sound like English speakers, adding directional or locative information to their motion verbs upwards of 60 to 70 percent of the time (see Slobin 1996; Naigles et al. 1998). Throughout the period we have sampled, and indeed into the later periods of development (Sebastian and Slobin 1994), Spanish learners sound like Spanish speakers, using motion verbs with brevity with regard to path-related information.[7]

The data from spontaneous speech suggests that the syntactic distinction between English and Spanish expressions of motion events emerges during the latter part of the third year. The data are less clear, though, about when the lexical distinction emerges. As mentioned above, both manner-conflating and path-conflating verbs were produced by children from both language groups (*go, come, sit, fall, stand, run, climb, lie, jump, dance, fly*). Moreover, individual children typically produced both types of verbs as well. A hint of emerging language specificity can be seen, though, in the set of verbs observed only in one of the two languages. Four of the six verbs used only by English speakers (*march, move, hop, walk, ride, cross*) were manner-conflating, whereas four of the six verbs that were only used by Spanish learners (*llegar/arrive, volver/turn, pasear/stroll, salir/exit, pasar/pass, bajarse/descend*) were path-conflating. In other words, these young English and Spanish learners may be showing the beginnings of their language-specific propensity to use manner (English) or path (Spanish) verbs.

18.3.4   The Role of Syntax in Children's Motion-Verb Acquisition

One question remains, though, concerning the developmental facts. Have the children yet made the *generalization* that motion verbs in English tend to encode manner whereas motion verbs in Spanish tend to encode path (see Naigles and Terrazas 1998)? If they have, then 3-year-old Spanish and English learners should attribute different meanings to novel motion verbs, as predicted by the lexicalist theories. However, it is also possible that the children's nascent crosslinguistic lexical-semantic differences are, at this point, simply a result of their demonstrated syntactic differences. That is, they may be producing different verb types because they are producing different sentence types; the verbs may be being learned via the syntax. If this were the case, then 3-year-olds' understanding of novel verbs would be primarily dependent on the frames these verbs appear in. That is, intransitive frames with content-rich prepositions imply manner verbs but transitive frames, or intransitive ones with content-poor prepositions, imply path verbs. Because so many of the children's verb uses included *go* and *come*, which are general path verbs that behave syntactically like manner verbs (see table 18.1), data from early spontaneous speech are indeterminate. Thus, we address this question in the novel-verb learning study that follows.

18.3.5   The Roles of Language and Syntax in Children's Novel Motion-Verb Learning

Recall that Naigles and Terrazas (1998) demonstrated that English- and Spanish-speaking adults were alike in understanding the relations between motion-verb syntax and meaning because members of both language groups interpreted novel verbs of motion differently depending on the frames they appeared in. Verbs that appeared in "manner frames," which included prepositional phrases with content-rich prepositions, were interpreted as encoding *manners* of motion, whereas verbs that appeared in "path frames," which were either transitive, or intransitive with content-poor prepositions, were interpreted as encoding *paths* of motion. However, the adults also differed by language group in that the English speakers were more likely to interpret the verbs as referring to manners of motion, and the Spanish speakers were more likely to interpret them as referring to paths of motion, over and above the effects of syntactic frame. Thus, the adult speakers had made a syntactic generalization that held across both languages and a lexical one that distinguished between language groups. Our question in the current study was, when do children make these generalizations?

This study was part of a larger research investigation into the relation between English and Spanish speakers' understanding of motion verbs and their nonlinguistic categorization of motion events (see Hohenstein 2001; Hohenstein and Naigles 1999, 2000). The participants in the study included children aged 3.5 years and 7 years, who were either monolingual speakers of English or of Spanish. The English speakers lived in Los Angeles, and the Spanish speakers lived in Mexico City. All came from middle-class families and all groups tested above average (and did not differ within ages) on both verbal and nonverbal standardized tests.

The materials in this study were almost identical to those in Naigles and Terrazas 1998; see table 18.2. Each child was presented with motion events that incorporated both a manner and a path. The events were paired with novel verbs that were presented either in manner frames (e.g., "She's kradding toward the tree") or path frames ("She's kradding the tree"). After three training trials, the events were changed so that one screen presented the same manner following a different path while the other screen presented the same path with a different manner. During these test trials, the children were asked to choose the screen that depicted the novel verb. Video sets were presented either entirely in the manner frame or entirely in the path frame. The children participating in this study viewed both sets of videos, counterbalanced for order; however, only the data from the first presentations are reported here (see Hohenstein 2001 for the within-subjects analyses).

The children viewed the stimuli in the setup of the intermodal preferential-looking paradigm (Hirsh-Pasek and Golinkoff 1996; Naigles 1998). They watched two television monitors placed side by side with a speaker in the center emitting the audio stimulus. Also in the center was a red rope light that served as a centering device. Additionally, a video camcorder placed between the monitors recorded the children's eye movements while they were watching the video stimuli. The children sat approximately 3 feet away from the video apparatus. Older children sat by themselves with their parent in the room, facing away from the videos. Younger children sat on their parent's lap while the parent was blindfolded. Children viewed the first video series and were asked to point to the monitor that showed the person engaged in the activity depicted by the novel verb. After a short break, they then watched the second video series (with the other sentence-frame audio) and were asked to perform the same task.

Keeping Verb Acquisition in Motion

Table 18.4
Screen preferences in seconds (mean (SD)) by frame condition across ages*

Group	Frame condition	
	Manner	Path
Spanish	0.43 (0.90)	−0.86 (1.78)
English	0.17 (0.95)	−0.82 (1.54)

*Positive scores indicate preferences for the manner match; negative scores indicate preferences for the path match.

Table 18.5
Screen preferences in seconds (mean (SD)) by language, age, and frame*

Language Frame	Age	
	Younger	Older
Spanish		
Manner	0.72 (0.40)	−0.17 (1.05)
Path	−0.72 (1.11)	−0.98 (2.59)
English		
Manner	0.47 (0.93)	0.38 (1.04)
Path	−0.31 (0.90)	−1.59 (0.79)

*Positive scores indicate preferences for the manner match; negative scores indicate preferences for the path match.

The eye movements of all of the children were initially coded from the videotapes by the first author (JMH). Approximately two-thirds of the children were coded for reliability purposes by raters unfamiliar with the study; there was an average of 86 percent agreement between JMH and the other coders.

The results are displayed in tables 18.4 and 18.5, and in figure 18.2. The data are presented as difference scores between the children's visual fixation on the manner-match screen during the test trials, and their fixation on the path-match screen. Thus, positive numbers indicate a preference for the manner-match screen and negative numbers indicate a preference for the path match. As table 18.4 shows, across languages and ages, children robustly preferred the manner match in the manner-frame condition and the path

Hohenstein, Naigles, and Eisenberg

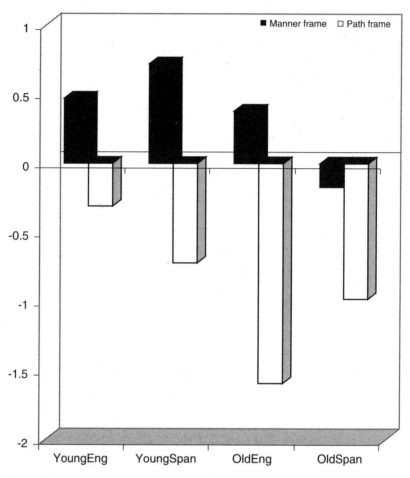

Figure 18.2
Mean manner preference (fixation on the manner screen minus fixation on the path screen) for each language and age group, by frame condition. Adapted from Hohenstein 2001.

match in the path-frame condition. Moreover, this effect held very strongly, even for the younger children in both language groups (see figure 18.2). Thus, these children show the same effect of sentence frame that had been demonstrated by the adult speakers in Naigles and Terrazas 1998. By the time they are 3.5 years of age, children have acquired the link between motion-verb syntax and meaning, such that they are able to make different conjectures about the meanings of novel motion verbs (manner-conflating or path-conflating) depending on the type of sentence frame the verbs appear in (i.e., syntactic bootstrapping). They have acquired the link between motion-verb syntax and meaning.

Table 18.5 shows the children's preferences for each language and age group for each frame condition. No difference between language groups is evident for the 3.5-year-olds, because both groups followed the interpretations suggested by the frames. In contrast, the 7-year-olds did show a significant difference between languages: the Spanish speakers preferred the path match overall, even in the manner-frame condition, while the English speakers still followed the interpretations suggested by both frames. Thus, the 7-year-old Spanish learners seemed to have made the *lexical* generalization that motion verbs in their language should encode the path of motion; they showed this path preference even when the syntactic frame in which the verbs were presented implicated a manner-verb interpretation.

In sum, when English and Spanish learners are asked to make conjectures about the meanings of novel motion verbs, they will eventually—by the time they are 7 years of age—show that they are influenced by both the frame in which the verb appears and the language they are learning. However, only the syntax effect is evident in the 3.5-year-olds; to them novel verbs in manner frames refer to manners of motion and novel verbs in path frames refer to paths of motion. These younger children do not yet show any language-specific lexical-semantic generalizations, though; the two language groups show identical effects. The 7-year-olds display this frame effect as well; however, at least one of the groups, the Spanish speakers, has also apparently acquired the lexicalization pattern of Spanish, such that they preferred the path interpretation for the novel verbs overall. Thus, the developmental pattern suggested here is that children acquire their syntactic distinctions first, exploit the syntax to acquire many of their early motion verbs, and only later realize the lexical-semantic generalization that these motion verbs manifest. Because adult English speakers showed a preference for manner interpretations, it is likely that English learners will also show this difference at some point. Without further data we cannot determine whether the 7-year-olds in this study did not perform in accordance with the adult pattern because of the small sample size or because of their young age.

18.4   Summary and Discussion

The findings from the three adult studies reviewed above implicated multiple ways in which English and Spanish speakers differ in their linguistic representations of motion events. Specifically, the production studies revealed that Spanish and English speakers typically use different verbs when they talk about motion events. Spanish speakers use verbs that encode the paths of motion, whereas English speakers use verbs that encode the manners of motion. Furthermore, speakers of these two languages also use different syntactic patterns. English speakers include directionally informative PPs almost all the time, whereas Spanish speakers do so only about half the time. English speakers also use a much wider array of directional prepositions/satellites than Spanish speakers do. The comprehension study found that, when adults are asked to interpret novel motion verbs, they show both language-general, syntactic influences and language-specific, lexical influences. That is, the English- and Spanish-speaking adults were alike in using the syntactic frame in which the verbs were placed to guide their interpretation of that verb. As predicted, the presence of a content-rich preposition in the PP facilitated a manner-verb interpretation, whereas its absence facilitated a path-verb interpretation. The adults' interpretations were not completely swayed by the syntax, though. The English speakers demonstrated an overall preference for the verbs to encode the manner of motion, while the Spanish speakers demonstrated an overall preference for the verbs to encode the path of motion. Thus, both language groups displayed a lexicalization bias that was independent of the effect of syntax.

For the purpose of our focus on motion-verb acquisition, these adult findings confirmed that children acquiring motion verbs in English and Spanish have at least two things to learn, namely, their language-specific syntax and their language-specific verb-lexicalization pattern. Learning the verb or syntactic distinctions by themselves would not be enough to manifest fully the adult patterns of speaking or understanding. Overall, the findings presented above suggest that children acquire the syntactic distinctions developmentally prior to the lexical-semantic generalizations. Moreover, they provided some suggestion that the generalization might emerge because of the syntax, because as the different syntactic patterns across languages promote the learning of different motion-verb types, the frequent use of a set of motion-verb types (e.g., *run, walk, skip, jump* versus *ascend, descend, enter, exit*) might lead to the lexical-semantic generalization. In particular, the production studies revealed that 2-year-old English and Spanish learners initially use similar verbs (*come, go, fall*) and similar frames ("bare" verbs) to talk about motion events. With development, English learners add more locative elaboration with PPs and satellites within the same clause as the motion verb; moreover, they use more specific, manner-conflating verbs such as *hop* and *march*. In contrast, Spanish learners maintain their terse descriptions of motion events and use more specific, path-conflating verbs such as *bajarse/descend* and *salir/exit*.

The findings of our small-scale, spontaneous-production study suggested that the syntactic differences in motion-verb use emerged earlier in development than the lexical-semantic differences did, and this developmental pattern was corroborated in our comprehension study. Specifically, the comprehension study found that, when asked to interpret novel motion verbs, 3.5-year-olds from both language groups were guided predominantly by the syntax in which the verb was placed. This study thus provides the first evidence for syntactic bootstrapping in children that is outside the domain of causative/transitive verbs (e.g., Naigles 1998). Moreover, these data from Spanish learners provide the first evidence for the use of syntax in novel-verb learning in a language other than English. Clearly, by the age of

3.5 years, both English and Spanish learners understand at least one aspect of the relation between motion-verb syntax and meaning and can use the former to make conjectures about the latter. The 7-year-olds in both language groups also showed that they were influenced by the syntax of the sentence; moreover, the 7-year-old Spanish speakers (but possibly not yet the English speakers) had achieved their language-specific preference for a path interpretation for the motion verbs.

Based on these data, we can sketch the developmental pattern of motion-verb acquisition in English and Spanish as follows. Children's early uses of motion verbs are similar across the two languages, and are composed primarily of general path-conflating verbs produced in "bare" intransitive sentences. By the end of the third year, though, the crucial differences in the syntactic patterns of motion verbs across the two languages are evident, even while the verbs themselves remain remarkably similar. By the middle of the fourth year (or perhaps earlier), children in both language groups understand the links between motion-verb syntax and meaning and can use the one to infer the other. Perhaps it is at this point, and because of this syntax-semantics link, that the lexicons of the two language groups will dramatically diverge; it is even possible that the hints of divergence seen late in the third year can be attributed to a beginning use of syntax in the learning of motion verbs. It apparently takes much longer, however, for children's use of predominantly manner or path verbs to lead to their language-specific motion-verb lexicalization patterns; only the 7-year-old Spanish learners showed that they had made this generalization and expected their motion verbs to encode path.

We do not yet know whether the absence of the analogous manner-verb generalization in the 7-year-old English speakers can be attributed to the relatively low power of this study or to some more extended time period needed for the manner-verb lexicalization pattern to be acquired. It is curious, though, that the Spanish learners should have acquired their verb-lexicalization pattern before the English learners because the most plausible account of how the generalizations are acquired relies on the frequency of use of categories of motion verbs (i.e., using many path verbs and few manner verbs leads to the path-verb generalization), and the adult studies discussed earlier have suggested than the manner-verb tendency in English is more pervasive that the path-verb tendency in Spanish. Because adults in Naigles and Terrazas 1998 did show a manner bias, it might be assumed that English learners will at some time in their language development also acquire this bias. Further research is clearly needed to illuminate the developmental pattern of the English learners.

This developmental pattern is more supportive of the syntactic bootstrapping account of verb acquisition than the emergentist or lexicalist accounts. That is, it was not the case that English and Spanish learners acquired their verb-lexicalization patterns first and so could have developed their language-specific syntactic patterns from these lexicalization patterns. Instead, these children acquired their language-specific syntax first and only arrived at their language-specific lexicalization patterns much later in development. It is of course possible that the children used other lexical means to learn their language-specific motion-verb syntax; however, such a proposal has yet to be advanced. The emergentist and lexicalist accounts also have little to say about how children might acquire their later-developing, verb-lexicalization patterns; in contrast, the syntactic bootstrapping account is quite straightforward. The idea would be that children's use of their language-specific syntax, from the age of 3 or so on, would lead to increasingly frequent use of manner verbs in English and path verbs in Spanish. Our data from children's spontaneous speech shows this cross-language dichotomy at its very beginnings. The prevalence of these different verb types in the two languages could then lead children, over a period of years, to the generalization that most of the motion verbs in their respective languages encoded manner (English) or path (Spanish) (see Naigles, Fowler, and Helm 1992 and Brooks et al. 1999 for discussion of the role of frequency in other generalizations made during verb acquisition). In sum, the developmental pattern suggests that the acquisition of language-specific *syntax* (at least as it pertains to motion-verb syntax) is fairly rapid in that it occurs before the age of 3, whereas the acquisition of language-specific *lexicalization patterns* (again, at least pertaining to motion verbs) takes much longer in that these may not be learned for another 4 years or so.

We end this chapter on a more speculative note. The developmental pattern highlighted here could lead to the suggestion that children across languages first map their motion terms onto the path component of motion events. Recall that the three motion verbs used most frequently by our young 2-year-olds were those that encoded general paths, *come*, *go*, and *fall*. Choi and Bowerman (1991), too, reported that the first expressions of motion used by their 1-year-old participants referred to paths; these were satellites for the English learners (e.g., *up* and *out*) and verbs for the Korean learners (e.g., *kata/go* and *ota/come*). We conjecture that this early path-oriented usage indicates a possibly universal initial preference on the part of children to talk about the path aspects of motion events. Whether this preference, if real, is social-pragmatic or lexical in nature remains to be investigated. That is, children may like to talk about paths of motion more than manners of motion, or they may find paths of motion easier to map onto lexical items than manners of motion. Casasola and Cohen (2000) have shown that barely verbal children can distinguish visual displays of paths of motion; however, no comparison has yet been made on the ease of distinguishing paths versus manners. Thus, further research is still needed to explore the developmental origins of children's talk—and thinking—about motion events.

Acknowledgments

This research was supported by a Robert Leyland Dissertation Fellowship from Yale University to Jill Hohenstein and an NIH FIRST Award to Letitia Naigles. We gratefully acknowledge the children and adults who participated in the studies reported here. We are also grateful for the contributions of and comments from Mahzahrin Banaji, Dorrit Billman, Marianella Casasola, Gonzalo Ferro, Melissa Highter, Edward Kako, Nancy McGraw, Dan I. Slobin, Paula Terrazas, and the undergraduates of the UConn Child Language Lab.

Notes

1. Notice that the construal of (5) is a bit different from that of (1). The motion event in (1) can have either a locative interpretation (she is walking within the forest)

or a directional one (she is walking from one end of the forest to the other). In contrast, the motion event in (5) is most felicitous with the directional interpretation.

2. The Spanish speakers did provide spatial information in their narratives; however, as detailed by Sebastian and Slobin (1994; see also Slobin 1996; Slobin and Bocaz 1988), this information came in the form of elaborate static locative descriptions that appeared in separate clauses from the verbs of motion. That is, their narratives set up the physical aspects of the scene first, and then only provided minimal information about the actual motion.

3. The vertical-motion events were excluded from these analyses because they generated some surprising and unconventional responses (see Naigles et al. 1998 for details).

4. It was assumed that because Spanish speakers did not start to learn English until after puberty, they would rely on their base of Spanish for linguistic knowledge more than would Spanish speakers who had learned English (or another language) at an earlier age. Moreover, any differences discovered between these Spanish speakers and speakers of English could be considered conservative because of the Spanish speakers' exposure to English.

5. Notice that the manner frames give clues to the manner meaning of the verb *both* because of the intransitive frame itself *and* because of the content-rich path prepositions. In contrast, the path-frame clues are solely syntactic because no prepositions are present at all, as in English, or because the preposition present carries little semantic content related to motion (e.g., *a, de* in Spanish).

6. We investigated combinatorial speech in particular because motion-verb use is especially rare at the one-word stage (Tomasello 1992; Vear 2001), and because we wanted to see whether the onset of combinations—with children's newfound ability to add PPs—yielded an immediate difference in motion-verb types across languages.

7. We do not, on the basis of these data, make the claim that the English and Spanish learners use the same levels of locative elaboration at the same point in grammatical development; we do not have a means of independently assessing each child's level of grammatical development. However, we can and do make the claim that, over the course of the third year, a developmental shift in grammatical elaboration of motion-event expressions is seen within one language group (English) but not within the other (Spanish). To verify that the Spanish learners do not make this shift at a later point in development—and to corroborate Sebastian and Slobin's (1994) findings with spontaneous speech data—we examined the transcripts of several Spanish learners, including Emilio, at 3;6 to 3;8. None of them used PPs with their motion verbs more than 40 percent of the time.

References

Aske, J. 1989. Path predicates in English and Spanish: A closer look. In K. Hall, ed., *Proceedings of the Fifteenth Annual Meeting of the Berkeley Linguistics Society*, 1–14.

Bates, E., and Goodman, J. 1999. On the emergence of grammar from the lexicon. In B. MacWhinney, ed., *The emergence of language*, 29–80. Hillsdale, NJ: Erlbaum.

Berman, R., and Slobin, D., eds. 1994. *Relating events in narrative: A cross-linguistic developmental study*. Hillsdale, NJ: Erlbaum.

Brooks, P., Tomasello, M., Dodson, K., and Lewis, L. 1999. Young children's overgeneralizations with fixed transitivity verbs. *Child Development, 70*, 1325–1337.

Brown, R. 1973. *A first language*. Cambridge, MA: Harvard University Press.

Casasola, M., and Cohen, L. 2000. Infants' association of linguistic labels with causal actions. *Developmental Psychology, 36*, 155–168.

Choi, S., and Bowerman, M. 1991. Learning to express motion events in English and Korean: The influence of language-specific lexicalization patterns. *Cognition, 41*, 83–122.

Eisenberg, A. R. 1982. *Language acquisition in cultural perspective: Talk in three Mexican homes*. Unpublished doctoral dissertation, University of California, Berkeley.

Esquivel, L. 1989. *Como agua para chocolate*. New York: Doubleday.

Esquivel, L. 1995. *Like water for chocolate*. Trans. Carol Christensen and Thomas Christensen. New York: Random House.

Fisher, C., Hall, G., Rakowitz, S., and Gleitman, L. 1994. When it is better to receive than to give: Syntactic and conceptual contraints on vocabulary growth. *Lingua, 92*, 333–375.

Francis, W. N., and Kucera, H. 1982. *Frequency analysis of English usage: Lexicon and grammar*. Boston: Houghton Mifflin.

Gentner, D. 1982. Why nouns are learned before verbs: Linguistic relativity versus natural partitioning. In S. Kuczaj, ed., *Language development: Language, thought, and culture*, vol. 2, 301–334. Hillsdale, NJ: Erlbaum.

Gentner, D., and Boroditsky, L. 2001. Individuation, relativity, and early word learning. In M. Bowerman and S. Levinson, eds., *Language acquisition and conceptual development*, 215–256. Cambridge: Cambridge University Press.

Gleitman, L. 1990. The structural sources of verb meanings. *Language Acquisition, 1*, 3–55.

Goldberg, A. 1999. The emergence of the semantics of argument structure constructions. In B. MacWhinney, ed., *The emergence of language*, 197–211. Mahwah, NJ: Erlbaum.

Hirsh-Pasek, K., and Golinkoff, R. 1996. *The origins of grammar: Evidence from language comprehension*. Cambridge, MA: MIT Press.

Hohenstein, J. M. 2001. *Motion event similarities in English- and Spanish-speaking children*. Unpublished doctoral dissertation, Yale University.

Hohenstein, J. M., and Naigles, L. 1999. The development of linguistically influenced thoughts. Poster presented at the Biennial Meeting of the Society for Research in Child Development, Albuquerque.

Hohenstein, J., and Naigles, L. 2000. Preferential looking reveals language-specific event similarity by Spanish- and English-speaking children. Paper presented at the Boston University Conference on Child Language Development, Boston.

Jackendoff, R. 1990. *Semantic structures.* Cambridge, MA: MIT Press.

Juilland, A., and Chang-Rodriguez, E. 1964. *Frequency dictionary of Spanish words.* The Hague: Mouton.

Kako, E. 1998. *The event semantics of syntactic structures.* Unpublished doctoral dissertation, University of Pennsylvania.

Landau, B., and Gleitman, L. R. 1985. *Language and experience.* Cambridge, MA: Harvard University Press.

Levin, B., and Rappaport Hovav, M. 1992. The lexical semantics of verbs of motion: The perspective from unaccusativity. In I. M. Roca, ed., *Thematic structure: Its role in grammar,* 247–269. Berlin: W. de Gruyter.

Levin, B., and Rappaport Hovav, M. 1995. *Unaccusativity at the syntax-lexical semantics interface.* Cambridge, MA: MIT Press.

MacWhinney, B. 2000. *The CHILDES project: Tools for analyzing talk.* 3rd ed. Mahwah, NJ: Erlbaum.

MacWhinney, B., ed. 1999. *The emergence of language.* Hillsdale, NJ: Erlbaum.

Marchman, V., and Bates, E. 1994. Continuity in lexical and morphological development: A test of the critical mass hypothesis. *Journal of Child Language, 21,* 339–366.

Marr, D., and Vaina, L. 1982. Representation and recognition of the movements of shapes. *Proceedings of the Royal Society of London, 214,* 501–524.

Mayer, M. 1969. *Frog, where are you?* New York: Dial Press.

Naigles, L. 1990. Children use syntax to learn verb meanings. *Journal of Child Language, 17,* 357–374.

Naigles, L. 1996. The use of multiple frames in verb learning via syntactic bootstrapping. *Cognition, 58,* 221–251.

Naigles, L. 1998. Developmental changes in the use of structure in verb learning. *Advances in Infancy Research, 12,* 298–317.

Naigles, L., Eisenberg, A., Kako, E., Highter, M., and McGraw, N. 1998. Speaking of motion: Verb use by English and Spanish speakers. *Language and Cognitive Processes, 13,* 521–549.

Naigles, L., Fowler, A., and Helm, A. 1992. Developmental shifts in the construction of verb meanings. *Cognitive Development, 7,* 403–428.

Naigles, L., and Hoff-Ginsberg, E. 1995. Input to verb learning: Evidence for the plausibility of syntactic bootstrapping. *Developmental Psychology, 31,* 827–837.

Naigles, L., and Hoff-Ginsberg, E. 1998. Why are some verbs learned before other verbs? Effects of input frequency and structure on children's early verb use. *Journal of Child Language, 25,* 95–120.

Naigles, L., and Kako, E. 1993. First contact: Biases in verb learning with and without syntactic information. *Child Development, 64,* 1665–1687.

Naigles, L., and Terrazas, P. 1998. Motion verb generalizations in English and Spanish: The influence of language and syntax. *Psychological Science, 9,* 363–369.

Sebastian, E., and Slobin, D. 1994. The development of linguistic forms: Spanish. In R. Berman and D. Slobin, eds., *Relating events in narrative: A cross-linguistic developmental study,* 239–284. Hillsdale, NJ: Erlbaum.

Slobin, D. I. 1996. Two ways to travel: Verbs of motion in English and Spanish. In M. Shibitani and S. Thompson, eds., *Grammatical constructions: Their form and meaning.* Oxford: Oxford University Press.

Slobin, D. I., and Bocaz, A. 1988. Learning to talk about movement through time and space: The development of narrative abilities in Spanish and English. *Lenguas Modernas, 15,* 5–24.

Slobin, D. I., and Hoiting, N. 1994. Reference to movement in spoken and signed languages: Typological considerations. *Proceedings of the Twentieth Annual Meeting of the Berkeley Linguistics Society,* 487–505. Berkeley: Berkeley Linguistics Society.

Talmy, L. 1975. The semantics and syntax of motion. In J. Kimball, ed., *Syntax and semantics,* vol. 4, 181–238. New York: Academic Press.

Talmy, L. 1985. Lexicalization patterns: Semantic structure in lexical forms. In T. Shopen, ed., *Language typology and syntactic description,* vol. 3, 57–149. New York: Cambridge University Press.

Talmy, L. 1991. Paths to realization: A typology of event conflation. *Proceedings of the Berkeley Linguistics Society,* 480–519. Berkeley: Berkeley Linguistics Society.

Tomasello, M. 1992. *First verbs: A case study of early grammatical development.* Cambridge: Cambridge University Press.

Tomasello, M. 2000. Do young children have adult syntactic competence? *Cognition, 74,* 209–253.

Tremblay, M. 1996. Lexical and non-lexical prepositions in French. In A.-M. Di Sciullo, ed., *Configurations: Essays on structure and interpretation,* 79–98. Somerville, MA: Cascadilla Press.

Vear, D. 2001. *Pragmatic, semantic, and grammatical variation in children's earliest uses of verbs: Evidence from a cross-sectional diary study.* Unpublished master's thesis, University of Connecticut.

19

Kidz in the 'Hood: Syntactic Bootstrapping and the Mental Lexicon

Jeffrey Lidz, Henry Gleitman, and Lila R. Gleitman

Recent findings and theorizing on child language acquisition suggest that the verb lexicon is built by an arm-over-arm procedure that necessarily constructs the clause-level grammar of the exposure language on the fly as it acquires individual items (Gleitman 1990; Gillette et al. 1999). This active learning process is likely to play a causal role in determining the adult linguistic representations, particularly at the interface between the lexicon and clause structure. This chapter presents two experiments designed to explore this idea. The first experiment examines an aspect of child verb learning: its sensitivity to structural information. The other examines adult representations of the same items that figured in the child experiment.

More specifically, the experimental work explores grammatical architecture in regard to relations between clause structures (or "frames") and classes of verb meanings. An apparently paradoxical fact about such verb-to-frame relations is that verbs are very choosy about the structures in which they appear, but at the same time they are "coercible"—that is, understandable in brand-new structures. For example, the sentence *Horace thought the stick to James* is both bad and good. It sounds "wrong," to be sure. Yet one easily understands it as a case of psychokinesis: Horace is causing the stick to move to James via an act of thinking. Our aim is to understand the scope and limits of such comprehensible innovation in adults, limits that apply in analogous ways to constrain the child's structure-dependent verb learning.

In the introductory remarks below, we attempt first to lay out the motivations behind recent theories of the verb-learning process that emphasize its sensitivity to linguistic-structural information. Then we introduce two well-known linguistic proposals regarding the syntax-lexicon interface that have the potential to account both for the learning facts and for adult representations at this level: the *lexical-projection hypothesis* and the *frame-semantics hypothesis*. After reporting the experimental work, we will try to adjudicate between these proposals in terms of the findings.

19.1 The Role of Syntactic Structure in Verb Learning

The extralinguistic contingencies for the utterance of a word are extraordinarily variable. Indeed, Chomsky's analysis of the relatively "stimulus-free" character of language use was a major causal factor in redirecting inquiry into the psychology of language in the present generation (Chomsky 1959). What goes for language use undoubtedly goes for language learning as well. If the adult community cannot be trusted to narrowly circumscribe the conditions under which they will utter a word, then an unaided word-to-world pairing procedure (as described in, e.g., Locke [1690] 1964; Hume [1738] 1970; Pinker 1989) cannot provide sufficient evidence for vocabulary acquisition.

Recent findings document that this problem is particularly severe for the case of verbs. Verb use even by mothers of very young children lines up poorly with ongoing events (Lederer, Gleitman, and Gleitman 1995). Relatedly, observation makes available many salient verblike descriptions of a single observed event (Landau and Gleitman 1985; Gillette et al. 1999). Consider, for example, a child walking toward her mother, bearing a doll. Suppose that the mother now says "Are you *bringing* the doll?" This event is supportive evidence for learning that /briŋ/ is English for the meaning "bring," to be sure.[1] The trouble is that the same word-world pair is just as supportive for conjecturing that "hold," "bring," "touch," "play with," "near," and so on, are the meaning of the new item. This problem reaches the limit with verbs like *give/get, lead/follow,* and the like, which describe identical events from different participant perspectives: whenever one party can be said to *give*, the recipient can be said to *get*. In these cases, cross-situational observation alone cannot redress the insufficiency of context (Gleitman 1990).

As a way to overcome the difficulties of observational learning of verb meaning, the syntactic bootstrapping hypothesis posits that one important source of additional information lies in the systematic relationships between verb meaning and syntactic structure (Landau and Gleitman 1985; Fisher, Gleitman, and Gleitman 1994; Fisher 1994; Snedeker and Gleitman, chap. 9, this volume). Because they can find a reliable mapping between syntax and lexical semantics, children make use of this mapping in learning verb meanings.

The syntactic bootstrapping hypothesis finds support in several results. First, maternal speech in several languages maps a highly overlapping verb-meaning set onto the same range of complement structures (Lederer, Gleitman, and Gleitman 1995 for English; Li 1994 for Mandarin; Geyer 1998 for Hebrew[2]). Children as young as 16 months old have been shown to be sensitive to properties of heard speech that could render aspects of these linkages useful—for example, the thematic/semantic differences between subjects and objects (Hirsh-Pasek et al. 1985). Indeed, there is some evidence that some syntax-semantics correspondences at this level are unlearned. Isolated deaf children project about the same structures for the same predicate meanings in their self-invented gestured languages (Feldman, Goldin-Meadow, and Gleitman 1978; Goldin-Meadow and Mylander 1984; Senghas et al. 1997).

There is also evidence that young children actually make use of structural evidence in their verb learning. For instance, by about 24 months they will use information from the number of noun phrases in the utterance to choose between situationally plausible interpretations that differ in argument number of the implied verb (Naigles 1990). Children this age have also been demonstrated to be sensitive to syntactic cues in learning the specially problematic verbs like *chase/flee*, which differ only in the perspective they take on the events they denote (Fisher et al. 1994; Fisher 1994). Finally, in an act-out task in which children were presented with verbs that they already knew in novel syntactic frames, young children systematically altered the meaning of the verb to fit the meaning associated with the syntactic frame (Naigles, Gleitman, and Gleitman 1993). For example, asked to act out "Noah comes the elephant to the ark," they pick up first Noah, then the elephant, and move them together to the ark. That is, ditransitive *come* must mean something like "bring." In this sense, young children are *frame compliant*, altering their construal of the verb to fit its new linguistic environment.

All of these findings go to the idea that the learning procedure in some way makes joint use of the structures and situations that co-occur with verbs so as to converge on their meanings. Neither source of evidence is strong or stable enough by itself, but taken together they significantly narrow the search space.[3]

Despite all the growing evidence for a structure-aided learning scheme for the verb vocabulary, there is at least one potentially discordant note in this literature. The tendency to reconstrue old verbs in new syntactic environments (*frame compliance* as just described, e.g., interpreting 3-argument *come* as "bring") diminishes with age (Naigles, Gleitman, and Gleitman 1993; Naigles, Fowler, and Helm 1992). Adults and even, to some extent, 5-year-olds tend to maintain the original meaning of the verb (they become *verb compliant*, acting as though the speaker must have erred in the grammar, but not in the meaning, of the sentence offered). For instance, when older subjects hear *come* in a ditransitive environment, they are inclined to construe it as they have before: they move Noah to the ark (and forget about the elephant), or they move the elephant to the ark (and forget about Noah).

Why should older children and adults seemingly lose the capacity or inclination to use semantically pertinent structural information (that is, the number of arguments) that they evidently exploited when younger to acquire the verbs in the first place? As we will try to show, the answer will not be that the younger and older populations differ either in their theory of grammar or in their lexical representations. Rather, they differ in the conditions under which they invoke the learning procedure itself (i.e., under which they "bootstrap" the interpretation from the surface syntactic evidence).

Before presenting the experiments, we want to characterize two major views of syntactic-semantic linkages that compete in the linguistics and psycholinguistics literature. These alternative architectures, in our view, hold the key to understanding the relation between structure-dependent learning procedures and adult lexical representations.

19.2 The Meanings of Verbs and Their Syntactic Representations

The *linking* problem, as framed by Carter (1976), concerns the relationship between the meanings of individual verbs and the positions their arguments take in the syntactic structure of a sentence. No one doubts that there are systematic relations between these levels of language description. Clearly, the number of noun phrases required for the grammaticality of a verb in a sentence is a function of the number of participants logically implied by the verb meaning. It takes only one to sneeze, and therefore *sneeze* is intransitive, but it takes two for a kicking act (kicker and kickee), and hence *kick* is transitive.

Of course there are quirks and provisos to these systematic form-to-meaning correspondences, even within single languages.[4] Moreover, interactions of this lexicon-syntax interface with the morphology and surface-structure architecture of particular languages add further layers of complexity in individual cases.

At the same time, *universal* linking regularities go beyond the participant–to–noun phrase regularity we have mentioned so far. A crucial instance is the relation between argument type (i.e., thematic role) and argument position in clause structure (Stowell 1981; Perlmutter and Postal 1984; Baker 1985): in the hierarchical geometry of the clause, the agent is higher than the theme, which is higher than the recipient.

Interestingly, the correlation just mentioned rises to the level of a universal absolute for the case of transitive activity verbs. In English and all languages we know of, the agent of a kicking act (and all simple acts of motion/contact) will occur in the subject position in sentences about kicking. We find no verbs (like a hypothetical verb *skick*) that could mean roughly what *kick* means but whose agent is realized in object position (see Carter 1976):

Lidz, Gleitman, and Gleitman

(1) a. John kicks Bill.
     b. *Bill skicks John.

   To return to the more general point, verbs that share certain semantic properties also share properties of their syntactic distribution
(Carter 1976; Grimshaw 1990; Gruber 1965; Jackendoff 1972, 1983,
1990; Levin 1993; for experimental evidence, Fisher, Gleitman, and
Gleitman 1991; Kako 1999). The existence of such linking regularities
in natural language suggests that speakers' grammatical knowledge
includes principles that provide a systematic mapping between semantic and syntactic structures. Of course, such knowledge constrains
both understanding and speech, including the speech of adults to
young children.
   Within this general and by now uncontroversial framework, there
is a bifurcation of theories about the architecture of the syntax-
semantics interface at this level. We mention these briefly here,
reserving further discussion until the results of the experimentation
have been presented.

19.2.1   The Lexical-Projection Hypothesis (LPH)

This kind of linking theory relies heavily on verb meanings as the
source of lexicon/syntax regularities (Chomsky 1981; Grimshaw
1990; Levin and Rappaport Hovav 1995). It holds that the meaning
of a verb determines its syntactic distribution, in accordance with a
set of (possibly universal) linking rules. The set of possible verbs is
determined by the same rules. Hence a verb like *kick*, with the meaning given in (2a), identifies two thematic roles (given in (2b)) that
map onto an argument-structure representation (2c) in accordance
with a thematic hierarchy:

(2) a. *kick:* X touches Y forcefully with X's foot   (meaning)
     b. X = agent, Y = patient   (theta roles)
     c. (X(Y))   (argument structure)

The *projection principle* (Chomsky 1981) requires that all of this lexical
information be syntactically represented. Hence, prominence in the
argument structure maps to syntactic prominence (Grimshaw 1990).

Therefore, given a structure like (3), the agent must occur in subject position and the patient in object position.

(3)

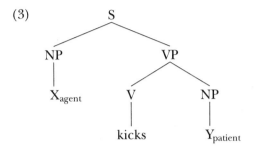

19.2.2 The Frame-Semantics Hypothesis (FSH)

This hypothesis accounts for the observed syntactic-semantic corre-spondences with quite a different apparatus (Fillmore and Kay 1993; Goldberg 1995). Though its general perspective can be identified in many different guises in the hands of different theorists, the basic idea is that syntactic structures bear meaning over and above the meanings of the lexical items in them. The interpretation of a sen-tence is dependent on unification of the verb's meaning with the structure's meaning. In this view, the lexical entry includes a mean-ing and the number of participants entailed by that meaning, as in (4).

(4) *kick:* touch forcefully with foot; 2 participants

The lexical entry for the transitive construction indicates a syntactic structure and the thematic roles assigned in the relevant positions of that structure:

(5)

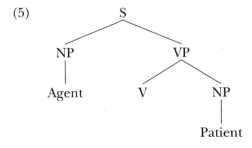

The lexical entries of the verb and the construction are then unified so that the interpretations assigned to the participants entailed by the verb are attributable to the structure, not to any inherent property of the verb:

(6)

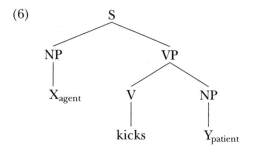

19.3 The Syntax-Lexicon Interface, and the Vocabulary-Learning Problem

The experimentation that we now report attempts a partial adjudication of these approaches, by asking how children exploit syntactic information in heard sentences. Methodologically, we build on the findings of Naigles and colleagues (Naigles, Fowler, and Helm 1992; Naigles, Gleitman, and Gleitman 1993), discussed earlier, about child responses to old verbs in new syntactic environments. Here we enlarge the types of ungrammatical structures that we ask our subjects to understand to include sentential complementation, so as to find the edges of a learning procedure that can make use of syntactic information. We believe that the boundary conditions on this procedure—the limits within which syntactic evidence influences the interpretation of co-occurring events—are informative about the character of the linking theory itself.

19.4 An Experimental Inquiry: The Limits of Frame Compliance

Our first experiment examines the limits of syntactic bootstrapping by asking children to interpret known verbs in novel syntactic environments.

Table 19.1
Pattern of grammaticality fot test items, experiment 1

	come/fall	*lift/drop*	*ask/tell*	*think/guess*
Intransitive	*Grammatical*	*	*	*Grammatical*
Transitive	*	*Grammatical*	*	*
Infinitival complement	*	*	*Grammatical*	*
TensedS complement	*	*	*	*Grammatical*

19.4.1   Design and Procedure

As in Naigles, Gleitman, and Gleitman 1993, we asked young children to act out utterances using a Noah's-ark toy, complete with animals, as the vehicle. The stimulus set consisted of thirty-two utterances containing eight verbs, two from each of four verb classes as shown in table 19.1. The full set of utterances for two sample verbs was:

(7)   a.   The giraffe falls.
     b.   *The zebra falls the giraffe.
     c.   *The zebra falls the giraffe to jump.
     d.   *The zebra falls that the giraffe jumps.

(8)   a.   *The giraffe asks.
     b.   *The giraffe asks the zebra.
     c.   The giraffe asks the zebra to jump.
     d.   *The giraffe asks that the zebra jumps.

Each child was asked to act out eight such sentences, four of them grammatical and four of them ungrammatical.[5] Within the ungrammatical items, each child's stimulus list contained sentences that we characterized as either "Far" or "Near," depending on the following properties of the verb's normal complement with respect to the complement in the frame. *Ask, tell, think,* and *guess* are "S-expecting" because they take sentential complements that denote propositions, whereas *come, fall, drop,* and *lift* are "NP-expecting," because they take NP complements that denote entities.[6] An NP-expecting verb in an ungrammatical NP-expecting frame is classified as "Near," whereas such a verb in an ungrammatical S-expecting frame is characterized as "Far." Similarly, an S-expecting verb in an ungrammatical S-expecting frame is characterized as "Near," whereas such a verb in an ungrammatical NP-expecting frame is characterized as "Far."

As can be noted from inspection of the examples in (7) and (8), sentences in the "Far" category sound noticeably more anomalous than those in the "Near" category—that is, (7c) sounds "worse" than (7b) because the former, but not the latter, violates the expectation of argument type. As the examples in (7) and (8) also show, even when the verb occurs with a frame of the type it normally expects, the utterance may still be ungrammatical. Thus (8d) exhibits *ask* in an "S-expecting" frame, but in a tensed-sentence complement of the kind more natural to such verbs as *think* (*The giraffe thinks that the zebra jumps*). In (8c), we observe *ask* in its licensed S-expecting frame, one with an infinitival sentence complement. Relatedly, the NP-expecting frames also subdivide, this time according to the number of argument positions in the clause. Thus, *come* and *fall* differ from *drop* and *lift* in that the former verbs take only one argument (as in 7a), while the latter take two arguments.

Summarizing, the materials subdivide in two crosscutting ways: first, according to the "Near" and "Far" categories, and second, into "grammatical" versus "ungrammatical" (see table 19.2).

19.4.2 Subjects

The subjects were twenty-two children between the ages of 3;1 and 3;10 (mean age = 3;7), tested individually. Subjects at this age were

Table 19.2
Categorization of grammatical and ungrammatical test items, experiment 1

		NP-expecting verbs		S-expecting verbs	
		come/fall	*drop/lift*	*ask/tell*	*think/guess*
NP frames	Intransitive	*Grammatical*	NEAR	FAR	*Grammatical*
	Transitive	NEAR	*Grammatical*	FAR	FAR
S frames	Infinitival	FAR	FAR	*Grammatical*	NEAR
	TensedS	FAR	FAR	NEAR	*Grammatical*

chosen because children at this age were most likely to be frame compliant in previous studies (Naigles, Fowler, and Helm 1992; Naigles, Gleitman, and Gleitman 1993), and we wanted to determine the extent of frame compliance that would be found with a broader range of verbs and frames than had been previously tested. Each subject was asked to act out ten sentences using toy animals from a Noah's-ark playset: two grammatical warm-up sentences containing *jump* and *hit*, followed by eight test sentences consisting of four grammatical and four ungrammatical sentences in random order. With this number of subjects performing this number of the actions, each test sentence was probed four times. Two subjects were eliminated from the study because they acted out only one grammatical sentence out of four as expected. The test items for these subjects were then given to two new subjects.

19.4.3 Coding

A coding scheme was developed during a pilot experiment in which we determined what actions were typical for grammatical sentences in the relevant frames. For ungrammatical sentences, the child's actions were coded as "Frame compliant" if they were similar to one that was typical for a grammatical verb in that frame. Actions were coded as "Verb compliant" if they ignored the frame and relied instead on the meaning of the verb.

For example, consider the sentences in (9). Example (9a) contains the verb *think* in one of its syntactically normal contexts. In response to this utterance, the subjects generally picked up a zebra and made it jump. Now if a subject confronted with (9b) did the same, we coded her response as frame compliant. If instead she acted out a scene in which the giraffe falls or one in which the giraffe jumps, the trial was coded as verb compliant.

(9) a. The giraffe thinks that the zebra jumps.
b. The giraffe falls that the zebra jumps.

To assess the reliability of the coding scheme, a second coder observed the videotaped child actions for the responses of six

Table 19.3
Percent predicted responses to grammatical sentences

Frames	Intransitive	Transitive	Infinitival	TensedS
W/grammatical verbs	70	90	80	87.5

subjects under the following conditions: this coder was not told what utterances the subject was acting out, but rather was asked to describe the subject's actions according to the coding categories. The categorizations chosen were the same as those of the original coder in 91.67 percent of cases (44 out of 48).

19.4.4   Results

Grammatical Sentences
If the coding scheme is valid, it ought to produce "frame-compliant" responses to grammatical sentences. Overall, 79.17 percent of the grammatical verb-frame pairings were acted out as predicted by the coding scheme (see table 19.3 for a breakdown of frames), a percentage that is acceptably high given the open-ended nature of the task and the tender age of our subjects. (Intercoder reliability for the grammatical sentences was 95.8% (23/24).)

Ungrammatical Sentences
Turning now to the test sentences, we found that subjects were more likely to give frame-compliant responses on "Near" verb-frame pairs than on "Far" verb-frame pairs. This was determined in the following way. For each subject we calculated a difference score, which consisted of the percentage of frame-compliant responses for "Far" verb-frame pairs subtracted from the percentage of frame-compliant responses for "Near" verb-frame pairs. If the difference score was positive, the subject was more likely to be frame compliant in "Near" trials than in "Far" trials. Fourteen out of twenty-two subjects had positive difference scores, with five having zero difference scores and three having negative difference scores (by a runs test, this tendency toward positive difference scores is significant, $p < 0.021$). We next

Table 19.4
Mean percentage of frame compliant responses by frame type

Frame	%FC (near)	%FC (far)	Difference score
Intransitive	85.71	14.29	71.42
Transitive	42.86	7.14	35.72
Infinitival	57.14	30.77	26.37
TensedS	71.43	50	21.43

pooled across subjects to derive a mean difference score of $+27.05$, which is significantly different from 0 ($t = 2.72$, $p < 0.014$).

Table 19.4 shows the percentage of frame-compliant responses given for Near verb-frame pairings and for Far verb-frame pairings for each frame, as well as the difference score for that frame. It is clear that, on a frame-by-frame basis, subjects were more likely to act out Near verb-frame pairings as grammatical than they were to act out Far verb-frame pairings as grammatical. The mean difference score for all frames was $+37.73$, which is significantly different from 0 ($t = 3.43$, $p < 0.042$).

19.4.5 Discussion

We pointed out in our introductory remarks that very young children efficiently adjust their understanding of a verb meaning in response to new information about the structures in which that verb appears, an adjustment process that we have called *frame compliance*. One of the linguistic-theoretical approaches to lexicon-syntax linking rules seems to have a ready explanation for this effect. This is the frame-semantics hypothesis (FSH), for it postulates that some meaning or interpretation is directly carried on this new structure (Goldberg 1995). If, for example, ditransitivity as represented in the geometry in (10)[7] just "means" *transfer*, it follows that *come* in *The giraffe comes the elephant to the ark* must represent the giraffe's transfer of the elephant's position.

(10)

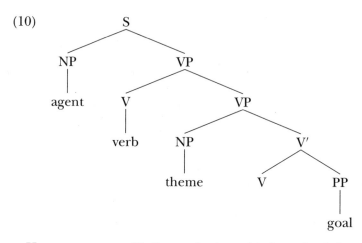

However, as we will discuss further, this hypothesis has no ready explanation for the present experimental finding: that there are differential tendencies toward frame compliance as a function of what we have called the "Near-Far" distinction. Here, the lexical-projection hypothesis (LPH) seems to offer the more telling explanation. Depending on the core lexical meaning of a verb, certain structures are projected for it. Therefore, the more semantically disparate a verb and a frame are, the more anomalous that combination will appear. Once part of a verb's meaning is known, the space of possible meaning extensions for that verb is limited by the possible linkings set up by universal restrictions on syntax-semantics correspondence. In other words, the meaning of a verb and that verb's potential for occurring in a given syntactic environment are not simply a function of the set of constructions that the verb occurs in in the input. Rather, the verb's constructional privileges are determined both by the input and by inherent restrictions on the syntax-semantics mapping.

To further solidify this position, we now turn briefly away from the learning issues—that is, from the response characteristics of toddlers—to look at how adults respond to the anomalies we have been discussing.

19.5   Experiment 2: Adult (Un)grammaticality Judgments and the Limits of Verb-Frame Integration

Naigles and colleagues (Naigles, Gleitman, and Gleitman 1993; Naigles, Fowler, and Helm 1992) found that frame compliance diminishes with age and with experience with particular verbs. Adults, and even children by age 4, for very common verbs, become verb compliant instead. In response to *The giraffe comes the elephant to the ark*, they are likely to move either the giraffe or the elephant. But unlike the younger children, they do not impute causation to the giraffe in their act outs. However, in a more metalinguistic task, subjects are able to interpret certain kinds of ungrammatical sentences consensually (Fisher 1994; Kako 1999; Nagy and Gentner 1990). In the present experiment, we used a scaled ungrammaticality-judgment task to determine whether we could find verb-frame neighborhood effects with adults.

19.5.1   Materials, Design, and Procedure

The materials for this experiment mirror those of Experiment 1. As before, we had two groups of NP-expecting verbs and two groups of S-expecting verbs. In the stimulus materials, all these verbs occurred in the following four frames: Intransitive, Transitive, Infinitival, and TensedS, as illustrated in table 19.5. And again these sentences were divided into the crosscutting Near and Far categories, as shown in table 19.6.

Table 19.5
Pattern of grammaticality for test items, experiment 2

		NP-expecting verbs		S-expecting verbs	
		come/go/ fall	*bring/lift/ drop*	*ask/tell/ teach*	*think/dream/ guess*
NP frames	*Intransitive*	Grammatical	*	*	Grammatical
	Transitive	*	Grammatical	*	*
S frames	*Infinitival*	*	*	Grammatical	*
	TensedS	*	*	*	Grammatical

618

Lidz, Gleitman, and Gleitman

Table 19.6
Categorization of grammatical and ungrammatical test items, experiment 2

		NP-expecting verbs		S-expecting verbs	
		come/go/ fall	*bring/lift/ drop*	*ask/tell/ teach*	*think/dream/ guess*
NP frames	*Intransitive*	Grammatical	Near	Far	Grammatical
	Transitive	Near	Grammatical	Far	Far
S frames	*Infinitival*	Far	Far	Grammatical	Near
	TensedS	Far	Far	Near	Grammatical

These sentences were randomized and listed on a sheet of paper with a scale next to each sentence—for example:

(11)   The zebra came the elephant to the arc   1 2 3 4 5 6 7

An instruction sheet accompanying the stimulus list asked the subjects to judge on this scale the degree of (un)grammaticality of the sentences, where 1 represented "perfectly normal" and 7 represented "extremely strange." All grammatical sentences were excluded to avoid compressing the range of responses for ungrammatical sentences. For half of the subjects, the order of the sentences on the response sheet was reversed.

19.5.2   Subjects

The subjects were sixteen undergraduates from the University of Pennsylvania, given lab credit for their participation.

19.5.3   Results

The order in which subjects received the stimulus materials had no effect, so we collapse across these order groups in presenting the results. Mean scores of verb-frame pairings are given in table 19.7. In table 19.8, we collapse these results according to the Near-Far distinction. The mean difference score for all frames is +0.44, which is significantly different from 0 ($t = 3.061$, $p < 0.0023$). This positive difference score means that for adult judgments, just as for child act-

Table 19.7
Mean grammaticality judgment scores by condition

		NP-expecting verbs		S-expecting verbs	
		come/go/ fall	*bring/lift/ drop*	*ask/tell/ teach*	*think/dream/ guess*
NP frames	*Intransitive*	Grammatical	2.29	2.85	Grammatical
	Transitive	4.83	Grammatical	2.71	4.06
S frames	*Infinitival*	5.54	4.25	Grammatical	4.61
	TensedS	5.4	5.71	3.89	Grammatical

Table 19.8
Mean grammaticality judgment scores by neighborhood

Near	Far
4.167	4.611

Table 19.9
Mean grammaticality judgment scores: verb type by frame type

	NP-expecting verbs	S-expecting verbs
NP frames	3.56 (near)	3.21 (far)
S frames	5.22 (far)	4.25 (near)

outs in Experiment 1, there is an effect of neighborhoods. "Near extensions" are less anomalous than "Far extensions."

However, a further result of the present manipulation differs from that obtained for the children: there is an interaction between frame types (S frames vs. NP frames) and the Near-Far distinction. This is because, while (as for the child subjects) there is an effect for Near versus Far among the S frames, there is no effect for Near versus Far among the NP frames for the adults (see table 19.9).

19.5.4   Discussion

One of the major features of the child act-out task was reproduced when adults were asked to provide scaled grammaticality judgments. The subjects did not simply make a yes-no decision (using only the 1 and 7 on the grammaticality scale) but gave higher anomaly scores to the "Far" instances than to the "Near" ones. So in these rankings we see a survival of the child's tendency to find some extensions of verb-frame linkages more natural than others. For adults, much as for children, there are "neighborhoods of frames."

The other finding is that adults are more accepting of extensions of frame privileges within the NP frames. We suspect that this difference is due to the flexibility associated with the English intransitive frame. The sentences used in this experiment were in the present tense. The combination of the present tense with the intransitive frame yields an elliptical reading that is acceptable almost regardless of the semantics of the individual verb item. For example, such sentences as "John hits" are rarely heard, just because this verb is strongly associated with transitive frames. Yet such a structure will occasionally be used, in case one is describing *hitting* as one of John's habitual activities, his regular business: your son's nursery school report card might say "John hits" if he is the class bully (or "John tells" if he is the class snitch, "John lifts" if he is the acrobatic expert, and so forth). More to the present point, the availability of elliptical readings for intransitive verbs means that the neighborhood effect shown both for NP frames and S frames in the child experiment was reproduced for adults only for the latter verb group.

19.6 General Discussion

The two experiments just reported add to the literature on how verb semantics can (and cannot) be extended by altering the structural environment. As in the earlier work of Naigles and associates (Naigles, Fowler, and Helm 1992; Naigles, Gleitman, and Gleitman 1993), we found that children countenanced the use of known verbs in previously unheard frames, and understood the semantic implications of such extensions. We know from Naigles et al. that adults are more reluctant to perform such extensions, but in a weaker test (judgments of grammaticality), we found a residue of the same capacity. Adults found many extensions to be, to a greater or lesser degree, well formed. The new result in the current studies was that such extensions are not treated uniformly by either population.

Adults and especially children drew a line in the sand about certain verb-to-construction pairings, beyond which they would not venture. As one of our child subjects plaintively remarked when asked to act out *Noah thinks the giraffe to jump,* "What do you want me to do?" We sympathize. That pairing is not even in the neighborhood.

We begin the discussion by describing this *neighborhood effect* as it emerges from these studies. Thereafter, we discuss what this effect may suggest about the architecture of the verb lexicon. The position we attempt to defend is that the neighborhood effects derive from constraints (partly unlearned) on how verb semantics is projected onto the syntax of the clause, just as maintained under the LPH (Chomsky 1981; Baker 1985; Levin 1993). Consensual verb-extension (or "coercion") effects derive from the heuristics of a learning procedure that deduces verb meanings by working backward from the principles of lexical projection (see Pinker 1989, 263–265).

19.6.1 Frame Neighborhoods

An important descriptive outcome of the present studies was to reveal the psychological potency of the notion of frame neighborhoods. Evidently, there is internal structure to the frame set in a language. For the sake of an analogy, consider the familiar case of phonetic segments. It is not just that there are thirty or forty sound categories in a language. Rather, the set of phones is cross-classified into a number of subgroupings, with the consonants divided from the vowels, the stops from the fricatives, and so forth. Within the set, some items are closer to each other than others, a closeness that can be understood in terms of a metric of feature overlap. The potency of the classificatory system shows up in a variety of psychological effects ranging from the perception of phonotactic regularities, to systematicities in language change and linguistic rules generally, as well as to tongue twisters, perceptual confusions, and acquisition phenomena.

Just so, evidently, for syntactic frames. In these manipulations, we could notice two crosscutting properties of frames. Verbs form one subclass that has to do with the category of complement that they license (NP-expecters vs. S-expecters). Extension across this boundary is disallowed: children cannot comprehend it, and adults hear it as grossly malformed. Within each of the two subclasses there are further subdivisions (tensed vs. infinitival sentence complementation; argument number for NP-expecters). Extension within these subdivisions is allowed: children acted out old verbs in these new environments consensually, and adults found them moderately acceptable.

In sum, in both phonological theories and in linking theories, explanation is based not on the observable elements—segments or syntactic frames—but on the system underlying them, such as feature geometries and clause-projection geometries.

We want to discuss two further issues here as they emerge from the results of this and related experimentation. The first has to do with the general usefulness of the two linking hypotheses (LPH and FSH) for describing grammatical organization, a matter we have repeatedly touched on but will expand on below. The second is the place of these hypotheses in understanding how the child constructs knowledge of the language to which he or she is exposed. In so doing, we will posit a distinction—to us it seems a critical one—between the heuristics drawn on as part of a learning algorithm and the knowledge state built up on the basis of using that algorithm.

19.6.2 Frame Semantics and Lexical Projection (Again)

At the present state of the art, neither of these general approaches has been shown sufficient to handle all of the ornate facts about the syntax-lexicon interface and its construction by language learners. But, as we next discuss, each of these hypotheses has its particular descriptive and explanatory strengths. Perhaps primary for LPH is the scope of this position in explaining cross-constructional linking properties for given verbs and sets of verbs. Symmetrically, the particular strength of FSH is in explaining the properties of coercion—that is, the environments in which a verb's meaning seems to subordinate itself to the meaning of the frame.

One Good Reason to Believe in Lexical Projection

An important virtue of LPH is that it has a principled account for why many linking regularities are cross-constructional. That is, properties of argument realization are not restricted to individual constructions, but rather are equivalent across syntactic environments. Consider, as an illustration, the linking properties of the verb *stuff*. Example (12) shows that *stuff* takes a goal argument and an optional theme argument. However, the presence of the theme depends on the presence of the goal. The theme may occur as the direct object only if the goal is also syntactically realized (Wasow 1977; Levin and Rappaport 1986).

(12)   a.   I stuffed the pillows.
        b. *I stuffed the feathers.
        c.   I stuffed the feathers into the pillows.

Importantly, this restriction on the presence of the theme argument also holds in adjectival passive constructions with the verb *stuff*, as illustrated in (13). Here the presence of the theme as subject in the adjectival passive depends on the expression of the goal ((13b) vs. (13c)).

(13)   a.   The pillows remained stuffed.
        b. *The feathers remained stuffed.
        c.   The feathers remained stuffed in pillows.

If the linking behavior of a verb is due to properties of the construction, as under FSH, then we will need to stipulate the theme restriction for the transitive construction in (12) as well as for the adjectival passive construction in (13). On the other hand, if the linking behavior of a verb is due to inherent lexical properties of the verb in conjunction with general principles of projection, as under LPH, then cross-constructional linking behavior is precisely what we expect. Thus, cross-constructional linking regularities provide evidence in favor of LPH over FSH.

One Good Reason to Believe in Frame Semantics
The meanings of certain verbs are affected by the structures in which they occur. For example, certain verbs of mental state can be interpreted as denoting motion events when they occur in the frames that motion verbs occur in. Consider (14), in which we find a mental verb in a motion frame.

(14) John thought the book to Mary.

To the extent that this sentence is understandable, it denotes an event in which John has telekinetic powers and, by thinking, causes the book to go to Mary (Fisher 1994; Gleitman 1990; Goldberg 1995; Kako 1999). That a verb's meaning can be coerced by the structure in which it occurs is surprising under LPH. If a verb's meaning determines the range of syntactic structures it can occur in, we must say that *think* is a motion verb in order to explain the consensual interpretation of sentences like (14). However, thinking events are not normally motion events. Moreover, in other syntactic frames, *think* does not denote a motion event:

(15) a. John thought about Mary.
      b. John thought that Mary was intelligent.

In sum, (14) leads us to the conclusion that *think* is a motion verb and thus can occur in the sentences licensed by motion meanings, while (15) leads us to the conclusion that *think* is not a motion verb. And so LPH requires two lexical entries for the verb *think* despite our intuitions that it is the same verb in (14) and (15). FSH, on the other hand, naturally explains the interpretation of (14). Because the motion interpretation comes from the frame and not from the meaning of the verb, the interpretive contrast between (14) and (15) falls out for free.[8]

Because the most urgent task of a language description is to account for the unlimited nature of use, the FSH seems here to have won not merely a skirmish but rather to have taken the field. This is because of its natural account of verb extension, or coercion. However, an important detail that vitiates the "explanation" just given in FSH terms is that (14) was not grammatical in the first place. To be sure, this sentence is consensually understandable, but all the same it is not quite kosher. *Think* does not "occur" in (14). Rather, it can be "coerced" to go there. In short, the right linking theory must explain two things: why verbs appear in the environments in which they do, and why other (and at the same time, not all) verbs can be made to go there.[9] As we will now describe, FSH is best seen as a learning heuristic that works just because it draws on the underlying principles of LPH.

19.6.3   Linking Linking to Learning

Findings under the heading of syntactic bootstrapping have been taken by some to support FSH (Goldberg 1995; Kako 1999), whereas the present authors have been rather more agnostic in regard to the lexical architecture that gives syntax-aided learning its ginger (e.g., Gleitman 1990; Fisher et al. 1994). After all, the FSH story goes, if learners (as well as adults) can make semantic inferences on the basis of syntactic frames, the frames must carry some semantic load. In the context *The giraffe came the zebra to the table*, the frame adds the meaning "cause" to the motion semantics ("come") that is supplied by the verb; hence, the composite meaning is equivalent to "the giraffe brought [= caused-to-come] the zebra to the table."

But there is another solution, just the one that is viable under LPH. Via two interrelated principles of lexical syntax, participants in an event will line up one to one with noun phrases in the clause (Chomsky 1981):

(16)   *Projection principle:* Lexical properties are syntactically realized.

(17)   *Theta criterion:* There is a one-to-one relation between thematic roles and argument positions.

These principles guarantee that *bring* (and not *come*) will license three-argument structures. Because *bring* denotes a two- to three-argument event, the projection principle forces there to be at least two and up to three argument positions (one for the bringer, one for the brought, and one, optionally, for the goal). The theta criterion forces these positions to be filled by independent noun phrases. Similarly, *come* will license one or two argument positions (one for the comer and one, optionally, for the goal). A third argument position for *come* (or a fourth for *bring*) will violate the theta criterion since we will have no thematic roles remaining to fill this position.

As just stated, such "principles of language design" seem at first glance too abstract to be in the heads of toddlers. But an implicit appreciation of such form-to-meaning correspondences is made more plausible by considering a variety of well-known phenomena in which these principles appear to figure.

19.6.4 Crosslinguistic Regularities in Form-to-Meaning Mappings

In every language, no matter how different these are in other respects, verbs meaning "bring" will accept three noun phrases in the clause. For instance, not all languages have different root forms for *bring* and *come*. In Kannada, a Dravidian language of southwestern India, *come* (*baru*) and *bring* (*barisu*) share a root *bar-*, the latter word including a causative suffix (*-isu*) (Sridhar 1990). But, whether the root form is the same as in Kannada or different as in English, verbs with these meanings universally will differ in their argument structure in a predictable way. The causal component of *bring/barisu* guarantees one argument position more than the noncausative *come/baru*, so that the causer can be expressed. Stated more generally, the projection principle and theta criterion map participants in an event one-to-one onto NPs in the clause.

19.6.5 The Invention of Language by Children

Another reason to suppose that principles (16) and (17) are unlearned was mentioned in the introduction to this chapter: these principles seem to be required to explain the innovations of isolated deaf children who invent their own communication systems (Goldin-Meadow and Mylander 1984; Senghas et al. 1997). For example, Feldman, Goldin-Meadow, and Gleitman (1978) showed that omission and word-ordering patterns in such a self-invented manual system could be understood by supposing that these uninstructed children assigned argument positions on the same principles, with *come* requiring one NP, *throw* two, and *bring* three.

19.6.6 Verb-Learning Effects: "Overgeneralization"

The ordinary process of verb learning in children provides further evidence that machinery formally equivalent to the projection principle is implicitly guiding the process. As Bowerman (1982) so tellingly demonstrated, we see these principles at work primarily when they have been extravagantly overused—for example, when the child says *Don't giggle me* to convey the idea "Don't make me giggle." To express externally caused giggling requires an additional argument for the ordinarily intransitive *giggle*.

In possession of such principles concerning the syntax-semantics interface, the child learner is not so helpless, as suggested by Tomasello (1992, 2000) and Goldberg (1999), as to have to learn the meaning and the syntax of each verb item separately. Bowerman's findings argue instead that the child who has culled the meaning from informative transactions with the world can project the syntax, based on general principles.

19.6.7 Verb-Learning Effects: Choosing among Situationally Plausible Interpretations

We have just discussed inferences from verb meanings to verb syntax in young children. The literature also shows us learning influences from the other direction. Often the child's observations of the scene in view will underdetermine the meaning of a new verb then said, and then the child will choose the meaning consistent with *both* the syntactic and the extralinguistic environment. A well-known case is from Naigles (1990), who showed infants at about 22–24 months a scene in which a rabbit pushed a duck into a squatting position while both rabbit and duck wheeled their free arm in a circle. A verb then heard could mean "force to squat" or "wheel arm." As shown in a preferential-looking experiment, these infants (whose spontaneous speech was limited to one or two words at a time) chose on the basis of the syntactic context in which the word was introduced. Those who heard "The duck is blicking the rabbit" later looked preponderantly at a video showing forcing to squat without arm wheeling; symmetrically, those introduced to *blicking* in the context "The duck and the rabbit are blicking" later looked predominantly at a scene predicting arm wheeling without forcing to squat. In some implicit line of thinking true of young 2-year-olds, these subjects must have reasoned "Caused motion requires NPs in two argument positions"—that is, they honored principles (16) and (17) in selecting among interpretations consistent with the extralinguistic happenings (for further evidence, see Fisher et al. 1994; Fisher 1996).

Lidz, Gleitman, and Gleitman

We have just claimed that both children's projections of syntax from knowlege of verb meaning, à la Bowerman, and their projections of verb meaning from knowledge of syntax, à la Naigles, Gleitman, and Gleitman 1993 as well as Fisher et al. 1994, derive from their underlying knowledge of lexical projection principles. For our own familiar *come/bring* example (*The zebra came the elephant to the ark*), learners apparently did the same. Faced with the ungrammatical sentence, and knowing that *come* was a motion verb, the child is able to interpret the sentence causatively. We posit that the child's deduction from the observed surface form to the meaning is based on the rules that generate the surface form—that is, on LPH—not on the surface form itself, as hypothesized by FSH. To illustrate concretely, suppose that the child with an LPH grammar has the lexical entry for *come* in (18):

(18) a. *come:* Y move toward a deictically determined location
     b. Y = theme

Now, when the child hears this verb in a transitive sentence like (19), the language-acquisition device (LAD)[10] makes the following deductions: "given that *come* is a motion verb and that some motion verbs have causative counterparts, the lexical entry for *come* must really be (20)."

(19) The zebra comes the giraffe.

(20) a. *come:* (X cause) Y move toward a deictically determined location
     b. X = agent, Y = theme

In this interpretation, the fact that young children were frame compliant is not due to the frames bearing independent semantic content. Instead, it is due to two factors: they did not have rich enough lexical representations to distinguish *come* from *bring*, and what they did know about the meaning of these verbs was compatible with the frame extensions they observed. More generally, the fact that learners can make semantic deductions on the basis of surface syntactic information does not imply that such surface information bears that semantic weight in the grammar itself.

19.6.8   Neighborhoods and the Linking Problem

We have just suggested that LPH has a principled explanation for
our findings and, more generally, for consensual verb-frame extensions by young children. But the *failures* that we obtained in frame
compliance argue the case as well as or better than its successes.
Recall that the child learners did not exhibit frame compliance in all
cases. They apparently accepted *The zebra comes the giraffe* acting out
a plausible scene with the toy animals. But in response to *The zebra
comes that the giraffe jumps,* even these youngsters who have not yet
solidified their verb representations balked. As they said, they "don't
know what to do." Under LPH, but not under FSH, we can explain
why the "Far" verb-frame pairs will not allow such extensions.

Consider what LPH predicts when the child hears a sentence like
(21). The child has the lexical representation for *fall* given in (22).

(21)   The zebra falls that the giraffe jumps.

(22)   a. *fall:* X move downward
        b. X = theme

The LAD then makes the following deduction. "In order for this to
have been uttered, *fall* must denote a relation between an agent and
a proposition. But *fall* is a motion verb and motion verbs, by their
nature, never have this character. The speaker made an error. I give
up."

A child with an FSH grammar, however, should not be so limited.
In this view, the child hears (21) and has the lexical entry for *fall* as
in (23) and the lexical entry for the Tensed S construction as in (24):

(23)   *fall:* move downward. 1 participant

(24)

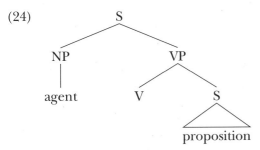

The LAD then determines a way that these two entries can be merged, such as: "The giraffe falls while thinking 'the zebra jumps,'" or "The giraffe falls and says 'the zebra jumps,'" or "The giraffe's falling causes him to realize that the zebra jumps," or something similar that merges the propositional-attitude information associated with the frame with the falling activity associated with the verb.

The choice between theories is now straightforward. The LPH predicts the limits of syntactic bootstrapping because of its very nature. Only when a given frame is plausibly projected by the child's hypothesized meaning of a given verb does that frame provide usable information to the learner. The "Far" cases in our experimentation are naturally excluded. To the extent that frames carry semantic information, they do so by virtue of the rules of lexical projection. If they carried them on their own, the learner would have no reason to reject certain verb-frame pairings and accept others, given that their experience with all of these ungrammatical pairings is equal— that is, zero. If verb meaning determines the range of possible syntactic structures that a verb occurs in (i.e., LPH), then we expect more frame compliance with "Near" verb-frame combinations than with "Far" verb-frame combinations. In short, LPH is a more psychologically useful approach as a description of the lexicon-syntax interface because it predicts the obtained neighborhood effect. Of course it is possible to doctor current FSH descriptions so as to limit the frames in which certain meaning categories of verbs can occur. But to do so is just to eradicate the crucial area in which these theories differed in the first place: LPH is a theory whose explanation of frame differences makes specific reference to the meanings of the verbs themselves. Insofar as FSH must acknowledge such verb-specific limits on clause structure, the two positions come closer together; in the limit, they may merge into the same theory.

19.6.9 Age and Lexical Innovation

Naigles and colleagues (Naigles, Gleitman, and Gleitman 1993; Naigles, Fowler, and Helm 1992) found another effect in the Noah's-ark procedure that we have so far not discussed: learners become more and more reluctant with passing developmental time to extend the meanings of old verbs when confronted with their new syntactic environments. Frame compliance diminishes and verb compliance increases with age even though, as Experiment 2 showed, a residue of frame compliance can be seen in the graded nature of adult grammaticality judgments. Why does frame compliance decrease?

As we have presented the child's use of LPH, the answer to this question is straightforward. The deduction of verb meaning based on an analysis of the surface structure is a learning heuristic. The learning device is asking itself, in effect: Assuming principles (16) and (17), what could be the meaning of a verb now heard, such that these principles projected this observed (surface) structure for it? Such a deductive procedure will be invoked only when the learner does not have secure knowledge of the verb in question. We see the procedure at work, therefore, in the child's attempt to understand the new verb *blick* under complex observational conditions (Naigles 1990). We also see it in the Noah's-ark situation for youngest learners, who plausibly have not yet closed shop on the meanings of the common verbs. They are still taking in information, guided by the principles of lexical projection, as to what partly known verbs may mean. Once learners have secure knowledge of *fall*, they consider themselves on firm ground in concluding that anyone who says "The monkey falls the giraffe" has mispoken by uttering too many NPs in the clause. This is verb compliance.

Final Thoughts

Our main purpose in the present work was to understand an apparent paradox. On the one hand, verbs are very choosy about their syntactic environments. *The soup that eats like a meal* and similar deviations from these fixed patterns make most of us wince. But on the other hand, such innovations are common and often effortlessly understood. Poets use them. So do children. Why this rigidity, and why the partial flexibility?

To explain the choosiness of verbs, we defended the position, widely accepted within linguistics, that verbs project their semantics onto clause structure in fixed ways. To explain the innovations, we pointed out that there is some lattitude in this system, which will allow children to over- and undergeneralize in certain ways in the course of learning, and will allow verbs to be understood in new environments—as long as these extensions are in the neighborhood.

Our second aim was to understand some properties of verb learning that have always been known to be connected to this interface of the verb's meaning with its licensed forms. We have suggested that the child's innovative behavior, much broader than that of adults (and often very cute), results from relative ignorance. If the verb's meaning is not fixed, then neither (within limits) is its syntactic form. But whereas novices may be ignorant of the exact meanings of certain verbs, they display a systematic understanding of the mapping rules themselves, those that generate the frame-verb correspondences. Because this is so, they are capable of going beyond their input information in at least two ways. They can pretty well deduce the subcategorization privileges of verbs whose meanings they know, without having to hear every verb in all of its licensed frames. And, as we documented in the present studies, they can deduce from newly obtained frame information new semantic properties of partly learned verbs.

Notes

1. We will represent meanings in quotation marks and forms in italics.

2. The languages in these studies were chosen on the basis of their morphosyntactic differences from English, though these differences ultimately do not figure into the mapping between verb meaning and complementation type. See also, Lidz, Gleitman, and Gleitman 2003.

3. Findings from the experimental literature (Gillette et al. 1999; Snedeker and Gleitman, chap. 9, this volume) and from corpus analysis (Mintz, Newport, and Bever 1995; Li, Burgess, and Lund 2000) suggest that co-occurrence and selectional restrictions add further probabilistic constraints to the verb-meaning discovery process.

4. For example, ditransitive verbs vary in whether they can occur in both the double-object and the prepositional-dative construction (John gave/*donated the museum his statue; John gave/donated his statue to the museum). Similarly, verbs taking clausal arguments vary in whether they allow raising or sentential subjects (it seems/ is likely/is obvious that the earth is flat; the earth seems/is likely/*is obvious to be flat; that the earth is flat *seems/is likely/is obvious).

5. Although there are many more ungrammatical cells in the table than grammatical ones, we presented each subject with an equal number of grammatical and ungram-

matical sentences to avoid losing subjects due to a large proportion of ungrammatical sentences.

6. Note that *come* and *fall* are unaccusative.

7. See Larson 1988. The proper analysis of the phrase structure of ditransitive sentences is by no means settled (see Pesetsky 1995; den Dikken 1995 and references cited therein). Nothing in our chapter hinges on the outcome of this debate.

8. Richard Kayne (personal communication) points out that not all mental-state verbs are grammatical/interpretable in the frame in (9):

(i)   *John realized the book to Mary

(ii) *John knew the book to Mary

What this illustrates is that the aspectual type of a verb must be part of its lexical entry under FSH (just as it is under LPH) and that the lexical-aspectual information must be consistent with the aspectual requirements of the frame. Thus, activity verbs like *think* are understandable in this frame, while achievement verbs like *realize* and stative verbs like *know* are not. (See van Hout 1996 for a version of FSH with aspectual information lexically represented.) Such "verb-class restrictions" on versions of FSH vitiate the claim that frames represent semantics independent of the verbs they contain, and thus make FSH and LPH harder to distinguish.

9. Coercion does not always result in perceived ungrammaticality, to be sure. In fact, one of the strongest cases adduced within FSH (Goldberg 1995; see also Kako 1999) is a sentence like *John sneezed the book off the table*. This sentence sounds perfectly grammatical, albeit slightly metaphorical (i.e., acceptable by analogy to *John threw/slid/blew the book off the table*; these are all *motion verbs*, and their prepositional phrase describes the direction or goal of that motion). The FSH has taken the normality of *sneeze* in this structural environment as an argument favoring separation between the parts of meaning that are "in the verb" and the parts of meaning that are "in the frames" themselves, independent of the verb. This argument is not really as strong as the proponents of this view sometimes claim, however. Notice that *sneezing* (also *coughing*) is the kind of physical act that under many circumstances *can* cause movement; it is one subcase of *blowing* in this regard. Therefore its naturalness in this linguistic environment follows from particulars of the verb meaning. In contrast, other inalienable acts—those that create no puff of air or other caused motion—are grotesque in this same environment (e.g., *John listened/looked the book off the table*).

10. More accurately, the language-understanding device causes the language-acquisition device to make the appropriate deduction.

References

Baker, M. 1985. *Incorporation*. Chicago: University of Chicago Press.

Bowerman, M. 1982. Evaluating competing linguistic models with language acquisition data. *Quaderni di Semantica, 3*, 5–66.

Carter, R. 1976. Some constraints on possible words. Semantikos, *1*, 27–66.

634

Lidz, Gleitman, and Gleitman

Chomsky, N. 1959. Review of B. F. Skinner's *Verbal behavior. Language, 35*, 26–58.

Chomsky, N. 1981. *Lectures on government and binding.* Dordrecht: Foris.

den Dikken, M. 1995. *Particles.* Oxford: Oxford University Press.

Feldman, H., Goldin-Meadow, S., and Gleitman, L. 1978. Beyond Herodotus: The creation of language by isolated deaf children. In J. Locke, ed., *Action, gesture, and symbol.* New York: Academic Press.

Fillmore, C. 1971. Types of lexical information. In D. D. Steinberg and L. A. Jakobovits, eds., *Semantics.* Cambridge: Cambridge University Press.

Fillmore, C., and Kay, P. 1993. *Construction grammar.* Unpublished manuscript, University of California, Berkeley.

Fisher, C. 1994. Structure and meaning in the verb lexicon: Input for a syntax-aided verb learning procedure. *Language and Cognitive Processes, 9*, 473–517.

Fisher, C. 1996. Structural limits on verb mapping: The role of analogy in children's interpretations of sentences. *Cognitive Psychology, 31*, 41–81.

Fisher, C., Gleitman, H., and Gleitman, L. 1991. On the semantic content of subcategorization frames. *Cognitive Psychology, 23*, 331–392.

Fisher, C., Hall, G., Rakowitz, S., and Gleitman, L. 1994. When it is better to receive than to give: Structural and cognitive factors in acquiring a first vocabulary. *Lingua, 92*, 333–376.

Geyer, H. 1998. Subcategorization as a predictor of verb-meaning: Evidence from Hebrew. Unpublished manuscript, University of Pennsylvania.

Gillette, J., and Gleitman, L. 1995. The role of syntax in verb learning. In W. Ritchie and T. Bhata, eds., *Encyclopedia of language acquisition.* New York: Academic Press.

Gillette, J., Gleitman, L., Gleitman, H., and Lederer, A. 1999. Human simulation of vocabulary learning. *Cognition, 73*(2), 135–176.

Gleitman, L. 1990. Structural sources of verb learning. *Language Acquisition, 1*, 1–63.

Gleitman, L., Gleitman, H., Miller, C., and Ostrin, R. 1996. 'Similar' and similar concepts. *Cognition, 55*, 321–376.

Goldberg, A. 1995. *Construction grammar.* Chicago: University of Chicago Press.

Goldberg, A. 1999. The emergence of the semantics of argument structure constructions. In B. MacWhinney, ed., *The emergence of language.* Mahwah, NJ: Erlbaum.

Goldin-Meadow, S., and Mylander, C. 1984. *Gestural communication in deaf children: The effects and non-effects of parental input on early language development.* Monographs of the Society for Research in Child Development, *49*.

Grimshaw, J. 1990. *Argument structure.* Cambridge, MA: MIT Press.

Gruber, J. 1965. *Studies in lexical relations.* Unpublished doctoral dissertation, MIT.

Hirsch-Pasek, K., Golinkoff, R., DeGaspe-Beaubien, F., Fletcher, A., and Cauley, K. 1985. In the beginning: One word speakers comprehend word order. Paper presented at the Boston University Conference on Language Development, Boston.

Hume, D. [1738] 1970. *A treatise on human nature.* Vol. 1. London: Dent.

Jackendoff, R. 1972. *Semantic interpretation in generative grammar.* Cambridge, MA: MIT Press.

Jackendoff, R. 1983. *Semantics and cognition.* Cambridge, MA: MIT Press.

Jackendoff, R. 1990. *Semantic structures.* Cambridge, MA: MIT Press.

Kako, E. 1999. *The event semantics of syntactic structure.* Unpublished doctoral dissertation, University of Pennsylvania.

Landau, B., and Gleitman, L. 1985. *Language and experience: Evidence from the blind child.* Cambridge, MA: Harvard University Press.

Larson, R. 1988. On the double object construction. *Linguistic Inquiry, 19,* 335–391.

Lederer, A., Gleitman, L., and Gleitman, H. 1995. Verbs of a feather flock together: Structural properties of maternal speech. In M. Tomasello and E. Merriam, eds., *Acquisition of the verb lexicon.* New York: Academic Press.

Levin, B. 1993. *English verb-classes and alternations.* Chicago: University of Chicago Press.

Levin, B., and Rappaport, M. 1986. The formation of adjectival passives. *Linguistic Inquiry, 17,* 623–661.

Levin, B., and Rappaport Hovav, M. 1995. *Unaccusativity.* Cambridge, MA: MIT Press.

Li, P. 1994. Maternal verb usage in Mandarin Chinese. Unpublished manuscript, University of Pennsylvania.

Li, P., Burgess, C., and Lund, K. 2000. The acquisition of word meaning through global lexical co-occurrences. *Proceedings of the Thirty-first Child Language Research Forum.* Stanford, CA: Center for the Study of Language and Information.

Lidz, J., Gleitman, H., and Gleitman, L. 2003. Understanding how input matters: Verb-learning and the footprint of universal grammar. *Cognition, 87,* 151–178.

Locke, J. [1690] 1964. *An essay concerning human understanding.* Cleveland: Meridian Books.

Mintz, T. H., Newport, E. L., and Bever, T. G. 1995. Distributional regularities of form class in speech to young children. In J. Beckman, ed., *Proceedings of the 25th Annual Meeting of the North East Linguistics Society.* Amherst, MA: Graduate Linguistics Society of Amherst.

Nagy, W., and Gentner, D. 1990. Semantic constraints on lexical categories. *Language and Cognitive Processes*, *5*, 169–201.

Naigles, L. 1990. Children use syntax to learn verb meanings. *Journal of Child Language*, *17*, 357–374.

Naigles, L., Fowler, A., and Helm, A. 1992. Developmental changes in the construction of verb meanings. *Cognitive Development*, *7*, 403–427.

Naigles, L., Gleitman, H., and Gleitman, L. 1993. Syntactic bootstrapping and verb acquisition. In E. Dromi, ed., *Language and cognition: A developmental perspective*. Stanford, CT: Ablex.

Perlmutter, D., and Postal, P. 1984. The 1-advancement exclusiveness law. In D. Perlmutter and C. Rosen, eds., *Studies in relational grammar 2*. Chicago: University of Chicago Press.

Pesetsky, D. 1995. *Zero Syntax*. Cambridge, MA: MIT Press.

Pinker, S. 1989. *Learnability and cognition*. Cambridge, MA: MIT Press.

Senghas, A., Coppola, M., Newport, E. L., and Supalla, T. 1997. Argument structure in Nicaraguan Sign Language: The emergence of grammatical devices. In E. Hughes, M. Hughes, and A. Greenhill, eds., *Proceedings of the 21st Annual Boston University Conference on Language Development*, vol. 2. Somerville, MA: Cascadilla Press.

Snedeker, J., and Gleitman, L. 2002. *Why it is hard to label our concepts*. Unpublished manuscript, University of Tilburg, The Netherlands.

Sridhar, S. N. 1990. *Kannada*. London: Routledge.

Stowell, T. 1981. *Origins of phrase structure*. Unpublished doctoral dissertation, MIT.

Tomasello, M. 1992. *First verbs: A case study in early grammatical development*. Cambridge: Cambridge University Press.

Tomasello, M. 2000. Do young children have adult syntactic competence? *Cognition*, *74*(3), 209–253.

van Hout, A. 1996. Event semantics of verb frame alternations. Unpublished doctoral dissertation, University of Tilburg, The Netherlands.

Wasow, T. 1977. Transformations and the lexicon. In P. Culicover, T. Wasow, and A. Akmajian, eds., *Formal syntax*. New York: Academic Press.

Author Index

Author Index

Subject Index